ASIAN PACIFIC AMERICAN
Experiences
PAST, PRESENT, AND FUTURE

EDITED BY
EUNAI KIM SHRAKE ■ EDITH WEN-CHU CHEN

Kendall Hunt
publishing company

Kendall Hunt
publishing company

www.kendallhunt.com
Send all inquiries to:
4050 Westmark Drive
Dubuque, IA 52004-1840

Printed in the United States of America
10 9 8 7 6 5 4 3 2

CONTENTS

Growth and Diversity: An Overview of Asian Pacific American Experiences

Eunai Shrake and Edith Wen-Chu Chen

For the past half-century, the Asian Pacific American community has experienced a phenomenal population growth and ensuing diversification. Asian Pacific Americans are one of the fastest growing racial groups in America, with its population increased from less than a million in 1960 to 16 million in 2010. The Asian Pacific American population, as many of the chapters in this anthology describe and analyze, is not a single, monolithic group. It is an extremely diverse population with respect to ethnicity, culture, religion, language, generation, socioeconomic class, multiraciality, sexual orientation, political affiliation, and other socially differentiating characteristics.

As the Asian Pacific American population grows and diversifies, Asian American Studies as an academic field has become more significant and extensive. Despite the recurring immigration backlash in general society and the current anti-Ethnic studies movement in some states such as Arizona, more Asian American Studies departments or programs have been established, more undergraduate Asian American Studies courses have been offered, and more students have been taking these courses in colleges and universities across the nation.

Having taught undergraduate introductory Asian American Studies courses over 15 years, we have become aware of the critical need for a text that is accessible to undergraduate readers that provides a broad spectrum of topics and issues covering both historical as well as contemporary Asian Pacific American experiences.

This anthology project has evolved from this need for a suitable introductory text in the field of Asian American Studies and Ethnic studies. As such, this anthology presents an overview of historical and contemporary state of Asian Pacific American experiences, featuring an array of the historical and recent research from various academic fields that are critical to understanding Asian Pacific American experiences. This anthology is arranged according to nine topics and issues that focus on the social, economic, cultural, and political roles that Asian Pacific Americans have played and continue to play in American life. Selections include both reprints of seminal articles and pioneering texts, as well as new original contributions. Reflecting the interdisciplinary nature of Asian American Studies, selections in this anthology are written from various academic disciplines.

Organization of the Book

This anthology is divided into nine parts containing a total of 29 chapters. We have selected nine themes that critically inform various aspects of Asian Pacific American historical as well as contemporary experiences.

Part I begins with the definitions of various terms used to categorize Asian Pacific Americans as a racial group, such as Asian American, Pacific Islander, and Asian Pacific American. Framing the issue in the 1960s and 1970s, the first chapter begins with a series of articles by Philip Tajitsu Nash, who reviews the evolution of Asian Pacific American identity from Oriental to Asian American to Asian Pacific American. In Chapter 2, Paul Spickard further maps out the historical and social contours of Asian American panethnicity by recognizing both mixed-race Asian Americans and ethnically mixed Pacific Islanders.

Part II presents a historical overview of Asian Pacific Americans and their adaptation and adjustment in the United States. Four chapters are included in this part. Chapter 3 by Timothy P. Fong provides an overview of Asian Pacific American immigration history from the mid-19th century to the present. In Chapter 4, Bandana Purkayastha and Ranita Ray focus on South Asian migration history, the fastest growing segment of the Asian American population according to recent Census data. As opposed to Asian Americans who largely came to the U.S. as immigrants or refugees, Native Hawaiians are indigenous people and forcibly became Americans en-masse through illegal military conquest. Told from a Native Hawaiian perspective, Chapter 5 by Haunani-Kay Trask details how Western historians have given an inaccurate portrayal of Native Hawaiian history and culture. Also included in this section is Wei Li and Emily Skop's chapter, which examines contemporary Asian Americans' settlement pattern that is reflected in new multiethnic suburban Asian enclaves as opposed to traditional urban enclaves.

Part III addresses the economic conditions of Asian Pacific Americans, which delves into how Asian Pacific Americans adjust to the American labor market. By using the most recent Census statistics, Edith Wen-Chu Chen and Dennis Arguelles in Chapter 7 present a more complex picture of Asian Pacific Americans' economic status as opposed to a popular social image of Asian Pacific Americans as a model minority. While Jennifer Lee focuses on how and why Korean Americans are heavily involved in small business and its impact on interracial relations in Chapter 8, Julie Su and Chanchanit Martorells discuss labor abuse and co-ethnic exploitation in sweatshops focusing on the El Monte Thai garment workers incident in Chapter 9. Eunai Shrake and C. Alan Shrake, on the other hand, provide new insight into Asian Pacific American entrepreneurship with their recent research on the Asian Pacific American gourmet food truck phenomenon. Based on interviews and participant observations, they examine how the food truck business challenges and revises traditional patterns of Asian Pacific American small business entrepreneurship in Chapter 10.

Part IV focuses on the historical legacy and the contemporary educational issues facing Asian Pacific Americans. The part begins with Mike Murase's pioneering study of the legacy of the Ethnic studies movement and its impact on Asian Americans in higher education in Chapter 11. Drawing from the recent Census data, Shirley Hune and Julie Park offer a rigorous analysis of the current educational status and the contemporary issues of Asian Pacific Americans in grades K–12 through higher education in Chapter 12. Chapters 13 and 14 challenge the prevalent image of Asian Pacific Americans as the model minority and discuss the adverse educational effect of this stereotype. Wayne Au and Benji Chang argue that the model minority stereotype imposes unnecessary burdens on Asian Pacific American students and serves to dispel other minorities' demand for social justice. Stanley Sue and Sumie Okazaki provide a theoretical understanding to Asian Pacific American students' high academic achievement pattern.

Part V looks into media portrayals and stereotypes. To what extend are the experiences and perspectives of Asian Pacific Americans represented in film, television, and the news? Timothy P. Fong, Valerie Soe, and Allan Aquino review the history of negative stereotypical images as well as underrepresentation of Asian Pacific Americans in film and television in Chapter 15, while Paul Niwa examines mainstream news media portrayals in Chapter 16. Niwa calls for journalists to be equipped with a greater cultural awareness and sensitivity when covering Asian Pacific Americans in the news.

Part VI explores second-generation issues including intergenerational conflict and identity formation. Stephen Murphy-Shigematsu, Karen Sein, Patricia Wakimoto, and May Wang provide a portrait of the psychosocial stress that Asian Pacific American college students experience in Chapter 17. Utilizing a participatory action approach, the authors delineate students' stress caused by intergenerational culture conflict as well as racial stereotypes imposed on them by society. In Chapter 18, Hung C. Thai highlights how second-generation Vietnamese Americans utilize the Asian cultural ideology of collectivism manifested in their family life and friendship to construct ethnic identity. On the other hand, Chapter 19 by Nazli Kibria explores the various ways that second-generation Chinese and Korean American college students approach the pan-Asian concept when they negotiate race and ethnicity.

Part VII delves into the phenomenon of intermarriage, multiracial identity, and sexuality. The late Megumi Dick Osumi chronicles the history of California's anti-miscegenation laws and their impact on early Asian Americans in Chapter 20 while C.N. Le offers a statistical analysis of the more current Asian Pacific Americans' intermarriage trend (both interracial and interethnic) by analyzing the recent Census statistics in Chapter 21. Teresa Williams-Leon focuses on multiracial and multiethnic Asians, the fastest growing segment of the Asian Pacific American population in Chapter 22. Taking President Barack Obama's racial identity as an example, she describes how this people, with multiple racial and ethnic ancestries, negotiate their personal, social, and political identities in private and public spaces. Finally, Gina Masequesmay addresses the issue of sexuality in Chapter 23. Reflecting on her participation in the Têt parade, she discusses various misconceptions about lesbian, bisexual, transgender, intersexual, queer, and questioning (LGBTIQQ) people and raises awareness about the struggles of this people in the Vietnamese American community.

Part VIII touches on several aspects of adversity confronting Asian Pacific Americans in relation to interracial conflict and anti-Asian violence. Edward T. Chang discusses the economic, cultural, and political contexts of interracial tension to explain why interminority conflict occurs, as in the Los Angeles riots, in Chapter 24. In Chapter 25, Terri Yuh-Lin Chen reviews legal cases involving anti-Asian violence, chronicling from the Chinese exclusion act to the Vincent Chin case, while Peter Chua analyzes institutional racism embedded in Department of Homeland Security policies and programs in the aftermath of September 11 in Chapter 26.

Part IX draws attention to the complexity of Asian Pacific Americans' political participation and social activism. This part begins with Eric Mar's personal reflection on his involvement in community activism that works to organize, educate, and empower the Asian Pacific American community as detailed in Chapter 27. Claire Jean Kim provides a thoughtful analysis of the precarious racial position of Asian Pacific Americans within the racial hierarchy in contemporary U.S. politics in Chapter 28. With this analysis, she proposes antiracist coalitions with other racial minority groups to engage in political actions. Finally, this part concludes with James S. Lai's chapter on the shifting terrains of Asian Pacific American politics in the 21st century in Chapter 29. He discusses the emergence of small to medium-size suburbs as the 21st-century gateway for Asian Pacific American politics, providing pipelines of local and state representatives.

The collection of articles in this anthology covers a broad range of issues that impact Asian Pacific American experiences. Despite our efforts to achieve a reasonable balance in representing the multifaceted aspects of Asian Pacific American experiences, we acknowledge that issues and themes included in this anthology are by no means exhaustive. Nevertheless, it is our hope that this anthology provides an important introduction to the study of Asian Pacific American experiences.

PART I Defining Asian American, Pacific Islander, Asian Pacific American

Inter-Change

Philip Tajitsu Nash

CHAPTER 1

Asian American Primer No. 2: Why not "Oriental"?

Has anyone ever called you an "Oriental"? Do you refer to yourself as one? For reasons of both theory and usage, this word has been in disrepute for almost two decades. It's time we all laid it to rest.

The theoretical problem with "Oriental" stems from its Latin root words "oriri" (to rise) and "oriens" (place where the sun rises). If the earth is a sphere, there is no place where the sun rises or sets ("occidental," by the way, means place where the sun sets). Rising and setting are relative to the location of the observer. Which gets to the usage problem.

The English language was invented by observers who came from tiny islands on the western end of the Euroasian landmass. Our perceptions of the world are shaped by this language and by these people. For example, we are all taught to distinguish between England, Scotland, Wales and Ireland, but are not told that the Chinese cities of Shanghai, Peking, Tianjin, Canton, Shenyang, Wuhan and Chendu each have more residents than the entire 3.5 million population of Ireland. The land areas of Europe and North America, respectively, are only 7% and 16% of the earth's surface, whereas Africa is 20% and Asia is 30%. Population-wise, Asia is 60% of the world, with North America only 8%.

The shapers of our world view and of our self-perceptions, in other words, were white European explorers, conquerors, missionaries, and others who, through historical happenstance beyond the scope of his column, have so far been able to impose their framework onto the rest of the world. Perfect examples are Greenwich Standard Time, named after a borough of London, and used to separate the world into 24 time zones, and the Mercator Projection, the 400-year-old concept of cramming a sphere onto a flat map that has artifically increased the size of Europe and North America in our minds (because of exaggerations at the poles).

"Oriental" and "occidental," then, are inherently tainted by a Eurocentric viewpoint. Even if this viewpoint was non-judgmental and value-free. I could not accept its omission of Africa and South America, as well as all Native American peoples. But it is not even value-free.

Centuries of information and misinformation about Asian peoples and countries, coupled with an exaggerated sense of self-importance for European-derived peoples, has created stereotypes about "Orientals." We are not human ("they don't value life," said a United States senator recently) and are intellectual or sexual robots. We had to be "discovered" by European explorers and "Christianized" by their missionaries. Even now our bodies don't measure up to Madison Avenue's ideals, and we must "assimilate" (stop being "Oriental") to "make it." But how can we assimilate and stop being "Oriental" when we are viewed and view ourselves as "Oriental"—something different, something from the East, something less than "white"?

In 1968, a phrase was coined which captured the essence of the dilemma and helped to solve it while creating a new consciousness. It recognized our commonalities as Asians, distinguished us from others without the negative connotations of "Oriental," and served to reassert our ethnic pride and self-importance without denigrating anyone else's heritage. We weren't inherently better or worse, we were different. We were "Asian Americans."

Next week: The rise of "Asian American."

Asian American Primer No. 3: The Rise of "Asian American"

In 1979, a well-meaning Latino television personality met with a group preparing to host New York's first Asian Pacific American Heritage Week Festival. "You'll never be able to convince the media to change its usage from 'oriental' to 'Asian American,' let alone 'Asian Pacific American,'" he said, "because 'oriental' is too thoroughly ingrained in everyone's minds."

Six years later, that arbiter of 'correctness,' the *New York Times* (which, ironically, refuses to refer to women as "Ms."), has a banner headline proclaiming. "Asian-Americans Question Ivy League's Entry Policies," and *Parade* magazine reinforces the "model minority" mythology with a cover story on Asian Americans and "The Promise of America."

As remarkable as this swift transition might seem, it is all the moreso when one considers that, until 1968, each Asian American nationality group generally referred to itself only by that nationality (as in "Chinese American" or just "Chinese"), and not by the broader continent-wide title.

Several independent factors came together to crystallize the development of an "Asian American" consciousness in early 1968. Over a decade of civil rights activism by and for Blacks had led to the development of "Black pride" movements—an assertion that one could feel good about oneself without fitting into Madison Avenue's European-American image of beauty. Both this and the notion of a separate. "Black nation," a vehicle for gaining economic as well as political freedom for Blacks, provided ideological tools for Asian' Americans trying to forge a positive identity for themselves. Commonalities based on color and perception by the white majority were found to be as important as national origin, especially for third generation Asian Americans.

On the national political scene, open rebellion and ferment were everywhere in early 1968, as Martin Luther King, Jr. was assassinated in April, Black Panther Huey Newton went on trial in May, the Poor People's Campaign came to Washington in the summer, and Kennedy was assassinated in June. The Vietnam War was raging and anti-war activities abounded.

Yet, despite these broader social movements, UCLA educator and long-time activist Yuji Ichioka recently described how the Asian American Political Alliance was formed in the San Francisco Bay area for more pragmatic than ideological reasons: "We had seen each other at anti-war and civil rights activities, but had never come together based on race. Then, because of irresponsible statements made about the Black Panthers by Oakland City Council members of Asian ancestry and a need to coalesce as Asians to protest the atrocities the U.S. was committing in Asia, some of us got the idea of finding identifiably Asian surnames on the roster of the East Bay Peace and Freedom Party. Once we had formed the Asian American Political Alliance, we worked on broader societal issues, but also focussed on specifically Asian American issues like the repeal of Title II of the Internal Security Act of 1950 [which authorized the building of concentration camps, and which was finally repealed in 1971]".

With this seemingly simple transition, groups of "Asian Americans" started showing up at rallies, and participating in demands for ethnic studies programs at San Francisco State, Berkeley, City College of New York, and elsewhere. Yet, no article or anthology I've seen specifically describes the origin of this phrase or its importance. It was, one might say, just the right phrase at the right time.

Next time: "On to Asian/Pacific American."

Asian American Primer No. 4: "Asian/Pacific American . . . And Beyond"

The reason for my long-winded review of the evolution of oriental to Asian American to Asian/Pacific American appears simple: each has seemingly represented an important phase in the development of our consciousness of ourselves and others' awareness of us.

But is that true? The answer, for "Asian/Pacific American," is "no."

The first official appearance of Asian/Pacific American (A/PA) was in the 1970 census. No one I've spoken to can figure out who coined the phrase or why it was created, except that immigration reforms in 1965 allowed enough of us in to warrant our having a category separate from "other." Yet, why were Asian and Pacific Islander peoples thrown together?

Historically, Asians and Pacific Islanders have had different experiences in this country. Asians were yellow "Asiatics" in the racist terminology of the 19th century, and were "aliens" who were excluded whenever their labor wasn't needed. Pacific Islanders were brown "Malays," granted "colonial" or "national" (still second-class) status as a result of United States control over their homelands (Philippines, Hawai'i) or were the residents of U.S. territories gained by treaties (Guam, Samoa).

Differences persist today, both culturally and politically, although the common origin from the "Far East" and the decade of governmental lumping into the "A/PA" pigeonhole have forced Asian-derived and Pacific Island-derived peoples to work together . . .

All this is not to say that the differences necessarily outweigh the anatomical or cultural similarities. We could argue for years about the relative genetic similarity of Native Hawaiians and Pilipinos or the relative cultural similarity of Tibetans and Japanese. And I'm not advocating that the term "Asian American" is inherently better than "Asian/Pacific American" (although both are clearly superior to "oriental").

The point is that we have to call ourselves something. Yet, without realizing it, we have allowed ourselves for generations to be referred to by a clearly negative term (oriental) that continues a false "east versus west" scenario, and then have happened upon terms (Asian American, Asian/Pacific American) that bring together groups that have clear differences as well as similarities.

How, then, should we define ourselves? As "minorities," when we as Asian-derived peoples are the majority worldwide? As "people of color," when we recognize the commonalities of our experiences with black as well as brown peoples at the hands of European expansionism? Or just as "Americans," when we see no parallel usage of "European American" to our Asian American?

In conclusion, as we strive for a more well-thought-out category for ourselves let us strive to accept neither a position of inherent inferiority nor a position of Asian suprematism. Let us work together for a world where each of us can be accepted as human beings and judged solely on our individual merits, not on the basis of racial, national, or other labels.

Who Is an Asian? Who Is a Pacific Islander? Monoracialism, Multiracial People, and Asian American Communities

Paul Spickard

This essay explores historically the social contours of multiraciality among people we today call collectively "Asian Americans." It further examines the relationship between multiracial Asian Americans and the monoracialist impulses of the various Asian American communities at various points in time. Beginning with the period before there was an Asian America (i.e., before the late 1960s), it then discusses the effects of new immigration and the Asian American movement on constructions of monoraciality and multiraciality among people of Asian American ancestry.

Before Asian America (1850–1960)

"Asian American" was not a term that meant anything before the late 1960s. There was rather a series of separate Asian immigrant communities—Korean, Chinese, Japanese, Filipino, and so forth. European-derived Americans tended to call them all "Orientals," but that was not an internally generated identity, nor did it organize the lives of individuals or communities in any meaningful way, except for bringing them common discrimination from Whites. Among multiracial people of Asian descent, there was a disconnected series of monoracialist discourses in the several separate communities. Most (but not all) of those communities neither accepted intermarried couples nor acknowledged multiracial people.

Chinese Americans

The experiences of multiracial people of Chinese descent in this period must be divided in two, for the situation on the U.S. mainland was very different from that in Hawai'i.

The U.S. Mainland

Before the 1960s, there was only a small Chinese population of American birth on the U.S. mainland, where Chinese men formed a mainly bachelor society. Many had wives and children back in China; others hoped to have such families one day. Only a small number of merchants brought wives over before World War II, and very, very few Chinese women came on their own. Because of the predominance of this trans-Pacific family pattern and the antimiscegenation laws of most western states, there were few interracial marriages by Chinese Americans in this period, and consequently very few racially mixed people. As noted elsewhere in this volume, some Chinese men found ways to circumvent the laws and marry non-Chinese women, and others formed less formal interracial relationships. Some of those begat children, although how many we do not know, partly because of the relentlessly monoracialist ways that both Chinese Americans and Whites have interpreted Chinese American history.

Those few mixed-race Chinese Americans who did exist generally were strangers to Chinese communities. That was even true for Edith Maude Eaton, now revered as the pioneer Chinese American writer Sui Sin Far. Eaton was the daughter of a Chinese mother and a British father who lived her adult life in Canada and the United States. She wrote sympathetic portrayals of Chinese Americans a century ago, but she had no personal place in Chinese America (Spickard & Mengel, 1997; Far, 1996).

The Chinese American family began to change in the aftermath of World War II, as several thousand Chinese American men who had served in the armed forces brought over their wives and children who had stayed behind in China (Zhao, n.d.). But although a family society would now develop in the United States, it was still a monoracial community very hostile to intermarriage, partly as a response to White oppression, but also as an expression of Chinese chauvinism. Most Chinese Americans were hostile even to marriage between different varieties of Chinese (Spickard, 1989). In addition, almost no Chinese war brides were brought back by non-Chinese servicemen. As a result, through the 1960s, Chinese American identity on the mainland was monoracial; there were few multiracial people, and there was no place for them in Chinese America.

Hawai'i

The situation was very different in Hawai'i, where almost the entire Chinese community was racially mixed (Takaki, 1983; Glick, 1980: 132–33; Char, 1975: 238–239; Linnekin, 1985: 28–34).[1] The first couple of generations of Chinese working on the plantations experienced substantial social mixing with Native Hawaiians and to a lesser extent with other ethnic groups. Many Chinese men who worked in Hawai'i married Hawaiian women even if they already had wives back home. As a result nearly everyone Chinese in Hawai'i whose ancestry goes back to the plantations has some Hawaiian forebears, and nearly everyone Hawaiian has some Chinese ancestry. Chinese churches have members who are phenotypically Hawaiian and bear Hawaiian names. The Kamehameha Schools, a private institution for Hawaiians only, admits students with names like Chan and Ing who are phenotypically Chinese. To be sure, there was some mixing between Chinese and other island groups—Japanese, Filipinos, Koreans, and some Haoles (Whites). But Chinese Hawaiians in this period had negative images of Koreans and Filipinos, and resentments against Japanese born of generations of conflict between their ancestral nations. Thus the predominant mixed-race

---

[1] There was one part of the U.S. mainland—the South after Reconstruction—where the situation approximated that in Hawai'i. There, Chinese men entered plantation labor contracts in a multiracial society that bore structural similarities to Hawai'i. A significant number of these married African American women, just as Chinese men of the same era were marrying Hawaiian women in the islands. In subsequent generations, two Chinese populations grew up in the South: a group of purely Chinese ancestry, and a segment of the Black population that acknowledged Chinese ancestry (Loewen, 1971).

group in Hawai'i in the generations before the creation of an Asian American identity was the Chinese-Hawaiians.[2]

This Chinese-Hawaiian nexus is the foundation of Local identity. It is expressed in the mixture of cuisines that is Local Food.[3] If one goes to Zippy's or Rainbow Drive-In, one can eat poi and kalua pig alongside Chinese dim sum delights (charsiu bow and siumai renamed manapua and pork hash), Japanese noodles, and Spam—the ultimate expression of island self-identity and culinary mixedness. Local identity also expresses itself in Pidgin, the polyglot language based on Hawaiian grammar that does the most to distinguish islanders from outsiders. It is this multiracial, multicultural mixing and blending to form a third cultural space that Kathleen Tyau, herself a Hawaiian-Chinese, describes so vividly in her award-winning novel, *A Little Too Much Is Enough* (1996).[4] This third-space culture comes from several generations of racial and cultural mixing on a footing of relative equality, which means that among the Chinese in Hawai'i there was widespread acknowledgment of racial mixedness and acceptance of mixed-race people into their community from a very early era.

Japanese Americans

Before the 1960s the situation for multiracial Americans of some Japanese ancestry was more like that for multiracial Chinese Americans on the mainland: there were not very many of them, and they were not welcome in the Japanese community. There were more married Japanese Americans than Chinese Americans, for the anti-immigrant movement did not succeed in banning Japanese women who came to join their husbands until after 1924. But, as with Chinese Americans on the mainland, intermarriage remained relatively infrequent—less than 5 percent in the immigrant generation (Spickard, 1989)—for much the same reasons as with the Chinese—antimiscegenation laws prohibited marriages with Whites, and Japanese Americans had strong prejudices against most other groups found in the West, including Chinese, Filipinos, and other Asians. Because of those prejudices, the Japanese American outmarriage rate in Hawai'i was even lower than on the mainland, despite Hawai'i's ideology of racial mixing. The prejudices were strong. For example, in the World War II concentration camps in the United States, Japanese American women who had been partners with Filipino men before the war were ostracized. They had to live and eat separately from other inmates, were talked about by other Japanese American women, and were sexualized by Japanese American men as fair game (Spickard, 1986).

The idea of intermarriage carried enough stigma that those multiracial people who did exist were not welcome in Japanese American families and communities. In 1940 the Japanese American Children's Home of Los Angeles was more than half-full with mixed-race children who had been abandoned by their parents (Spickard, 1986). Others roamed the streets and had to raise themselves. Very few found a place within Japanese America. As Japanese-Caucasian Kathleen Tamagawa (1932:I) described herself: "The trouble with me is my ancestry. I really should not have been born." She spent her youth trying to find a place in Japan or Japanese America before finally reconciling herself to a middle-class White identity with few Japanese connections.

---

[2] Much more has been written in White-derived social commentary about the Hapa-Haole (roughly translated, "half-White") population, because such people were important to the islands' power structure and to the maintenance of colonial domination. But such a focus overlooks the equally pervasive connection between Hawaiians and Chinese.
[3] Eric Yamamoto (1995) overemphasizes the Japanese element (see also Okamura, 1995).
[4] See also Spickard and Fong (1995).

As with Chinese Americans on the mainland, the keepers of the community's memory ignored intermarried Japanese Americans and multiracial people. The one study of Japanese American intermarriage before the 1960s (Ishikawa, 1938) looked only at Japanese Americans on the East Coast and was published in a journal so obscure that its findings have almost entirely escaped notice by historians of Japanese America. The important thing to note is that, like the Chinese community on the U.S. mainland and unlike the Chinese in Hawai'i, Japanese Americans in both places constituted themselves as a monoracial group and cast out the few people of mixed descent.

South Asian Americans

In its initial family structure, the much smaller South Asian population in the United States was a bit like the Chinese American community. Made up mainly of men who worked in California agriculture, the South Asians formed a bachelor society, although quite a few had wives and families back in the Punjab. But this was not so relentlessly a monoracial community. One group of a few hundred Punjabi men settled down in the Imperial Valley of California and married immigrant women from Mexico (Leonard, 1992). They and their mixed-race children formed almost the only Indian community in the United States in the years before there was an Asian America. They identified strongly with the Punjab, but there was little Indian content to their lives. The families spoke English and Spanish, and most were Catholic, although they did tend to eat a mixture of Mexican and South Asian dishes. Identificationally, the mixed people grew up with the label "Hindu," but as with the Hawaiian Chinese, this meant mixed—Punjabi–Mexican American.

After 1946 the immigration ban on South Asians was ended, and small but significant numbers of new arrivals came from India. This meant that there was a new generation of unmixed South Asians, including some wives of the original Punjabi men. These new migrants tended not to recognize the mixed Punjabi–Mexican Americans as South Asians. Thus early on among South Asian Americans there was a fairly high level of interracial mixing, an acknowledgment of multiraciality, and a place in the Asian Indian community for mixed-race people. With new immigration in the postwar era, however, a new monoracial discourse was asserted, and mixed people tended not to be acknowledged any longer.

Filipino Americans

The situation for mixed-race people of Filipino descent was strikingly different. In the era before a common Asian American identity was formed, Filipino communities were full of mixed couples and multiracial children. The main Filipino migration came somewhat later than for the other groups, beginning after 1920. Like the South Asians and Chinese, this was a bachelor society made up largely of farmworkers, both in Hawai'i and on the West Coast. But unlike those groups on the mainland, there was lots of intermarriage, mainly with Whites, although Filipino-White couples had to go to the same extremes as others to circumvent the antimiscegenation laws. Enough did, and had children, so that at some point nearly all second- or third-generation Filipino Americans were racially mixed (Posadas, 1989; Lasker, 1931: 92–95, 196–97; Vallangca, 1977: 36–37, 50–53; Espiritu, 1995: 53–63, 74, 127, 193–203). One of the subjects that has not been explored, but which is surely worthy of study, is the close relationships between Filipinos and Mexican Americans in agricultural districts from the Imperial Valley to Yakima. Surely more intermarriages and mixed people came from that interaction than from the South Asian–Mexican American nexus. There were also mixed families of Filipinos and Native Americans in the Pacific Northwest and Alaska.

For Filipino Americans, unlike most other Asian groups, there has long been broad acceptance of intermarriage and inclusion of multiracial people.

In summary, we may conclude three things: (1) there were more interracial marriages and multiracial people among Asian Americans than has generally been recognized, but the total numbers were still relatively small; (2) in three situations—among South Asians, Filipinos, and Chinese in Hawai'i—group identity in this period depended on the fact of mixedness; (3) two groups—Japanese Americans and Chinese Americans on the U.S. mainland—kept multiracial people on the margins or denied them group membership altogether, as those communities pursued monoracial identities.

Other Asian American Diversities and Mixednesses

The complexity presented by racially mixed people was not the only kind of multiplicity experienced by Asian Americans before the coming together of a common Asian American identity. There were in fact several other ways in which Asian Americans constituted a mixed multitude. First, there were the several nations of ancestral origin—China, India, Korea, and so forth. There also were regional differences within each of the groups. For Japanese Americans, the sharpest split was between Okinawan and Naichi Japanese (they still form almost separate communities in Hawai'i), but there were also immigrant-generation splits between people from different prefectures. The division was equally strong in the Chinese community between city Cantonese, Toisanese, Hakka, and Hong Kong Chinese, as well as between all of these groups, which were from greater Canton, and others who came from Taiwan, Fujian, Shanghai, and other parts of China. Among Filipinos, the differences among Ilocanos, Tagalog-speakers, Cebuanos, and others played a similarly divisive role.

In addition, there were significant class divisions among Asian Americans—between merchants and workers in the Chinese community; between Japanese and Punjabi farm owners and managers and their. Filipino field laborers; and so forth.

What is striking about this heterogeneity in the pre–Asian American period is the small amount of social and marital mixing among the various groups. Early on, some Filipinos and Punjabis did mix with and marry Whites and Mexicans, and their multiracial children were integrated into the Filipino and Indian communities; and some Chinese did marry Hawaiians. But beyond that there was not a lot of mixing across any of these lines, even across those subethnic lines within various national-origin groups. Although there was more mixing than the keepers of the Japanese American and Chinese American communities' monoracialist histories have recognized, there just were not many marriages between Chinese and Japanese, between Filipinos and Koreans, and so forth.

Outsiders' Views

White Americans did not see all this very clearly. They had a monoracialist discourse for Asian Americans that did not perceive the divisions within Asian America and that failed to recognize the place of multiracial Asian Americans.[5] Their perception of all Asians as a monolith amounted to lumping together the unlumpable. Non-Asian Americans' gathering of Asians together

---

[5] Nor did they perceive the diversity within the Italian and Jewish communities (Sarna, 1978).

conceptually went so far as to include Pacific Islanders; regularly, in movies, travel advertisements, and television commercials, Asians were put in the places of Hawaiians and other Polynesians, and no one seems to have noticed (Spickard, 1989).

One mechanism by which Whites lumped Asians (and Pacific Islanders) together was the Census. When Asians first emerged out of the "other" category, they were all classified as "Orientals," and later as "Asians and Pacific Islanders" (U.S. Bureau of the Census, 1963). But the White perception of commonality among Asians was more broadly cultural than just the bureaucratic labeling device that was the Census, for pulp fiction and B movies throughout the twentieth century have assumed an Asian cultural homogeneity extending from Hawai'i to Pakistan and beyond, and a sameness to people whose ancestors came from those places.

The idea of the "Orient" goes very deep in European intellectual history, dating long before the creation of Europe. Herodotus, writing in the fifth century B.C., depicted the Persian invaders of Greece as a faceless, unfeeling mass (Herodotus, 1954). From that day on, European-derived perceptions have grouped together everyone from anywhere east of the Bosporus. Edward Said (1978) has written about this as "Orientalism," although the Arab-and-Turk-focused British Orientalism he describes has a rather different content than the East-Asia-focused Orientalism that operates among White Americans.

The point is that White Americans constructed a monoracialist discourse to describe Asian Americans, and did not differentiate among the various sorts of Asian Americans, including multiracial people of Asian ancestry. As far as Whites were concerned, such people were consigned to the Asian group, even though before 1965 the largest Asian groups would not have them. This left multiracial Asian Americans with no place to be.

Pulling Apart: Monoracial Immigration Since 1965

Two countervailing forces have been at work on Asian American unity and the place of multiracial people in the last third of the twentieth century and into the twenty-first. One has been the immigration of unprecedentedly large numbers of Asian Americans as a result of the 1965 Immigration Act and various forces set in motion by the Vietnam War. The other has been the coming together of Asians of many sorts into a panethnic coalition with something like a shared identity. Both of these, however, have been mainly monoracialist discourses that have not explicitly determined what they intend to do with multiracial people of Asian ancestry.

Lots of new immigrants have come to the United States from Asia since about 1970: from China nearly three-quarters of a million; from South Asia more than four hundred thousand; from Korea more than six hundred thousand; from Vietnam more than half a million; and from the Philippines over eight hundred thousand (Ong et al., 1994:41). These immigrants have changed the demographic face of Asian America. As of the 1990 Census, there were more than a million and a half Chinese Americans; nearly as many Filipinos; about eight hundred thousand each of Japanese Americans, Asian Indians, and Koreans; six hundred thousand Vietnamese; two hundred thousand Hawaiians; and nearly a million other Asian and Pacific Islander Americans (U.S. Bureau of the Census, 1991).

Although most non–Asian Americans view all these immigrants as part of a common Asian group, most of the immigrants perceive themselves in their ethnic specificity. They may recognize that they are lumped together by White Americans, but few Vietnamese immigrants sense that they themselves have much in common with Filipinos or Koreans. Most of the new immigrants, whether they live in New York's Chinatown, Monterey Park, or Duluth, see themselves as ethnically distinct and racially fairly pure. Theirs are monoracialist world views.

Only a small minority of the immigrant generation intermarry, despite the disappearance of barriers from the White side, although the rates of intermarriage are higher than for previous generations of Asian immigrants. Their children are another matter. There is considerable evidence that, except for such tightly knit groups as the Hmong, intermarriage is a prominent fact of community life among the American-born of each of the Asian American groups. In that generation, not just Japanese, Chinese, and Filipino Americans but Koreans and Vietnamese are broadly accepting of intermarriage. And increasingly, in all the Asian communities, there are places for multiracial people.

Coming Together: Asian American Panethnicity After the 1960s

The Asian American Movement

The Asian American movement of the late 1960s and early 1970s was an emphatically monoracialist enterprise. That is, it was about the construction of a single racial identity out of ethnic specificities that were formerly disparate. In West Coast inner-city neighborhoods in the 1950s and 1960s, there grew up a generation of Chinese, Japanese, and (to a lesser extent) Filipino Americans who had known each other from childhood, who had experienced a common Orientalization from Whites, and who did not harbor their parents' antagonisms toward one another based on Asian politics. These young Asians were the first generation to attend college in large numbers, mainly West Coast public institutions, in the latter 1960s. There they encountered an environment politicized by the Civil Rights and Black Power movements and mounting opposition to the Vietnam War.

In that environment was born a movement for a common Asian American identity—what Yen Le Espiritu (1992) calls a "panethnicity"—much like the common Native American panethnicity that has emerged at various times out of individual tribal identities. William Wei (1993: 42) describes the process:

> As an ethnic-consciousness movement, the Black Power movement made Asian Americans realize that they too had been defined by European American attitudes and dominated by an Eurocentric culture. They had to rethink who they were and re-create their own cultural identity, forging distinct Asian ethnic group identities into a pan-Asian one. The foundation for this unique identity was their experience as Asians in America—a common history of oppression and resistance that would serve as the basis for a "bold culture, unashamed and true to itself."

Some varieties of Asian Americans were closer to the center of this enterprise than others. The American-born were more central than immigrants, for it was in their formers' common experiences in the United States—indeed, in their relationships to one another—that the Asian American identity was born.[6] And within this group it was really Chinese and Japanese Americans who stood at the center, with Filipinos a marginal group, and other varieties of Asian Americans, such as Koreans and South Asians, not even on the map (see Figure 2.1).

---

[6] Note that the immigrants—both the parental generation and the new immigrants—saw themselves and were seen by the American-born as more central to the various national ethnic groups.

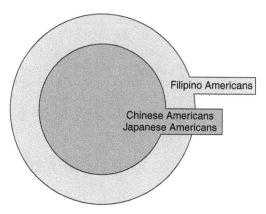

FIGURE 2.1   Centrality and marginality
of Asian American groups, 1970s.

Multiracial people of Asian ancestry were part of this map only insofar as they had earned membership in one of the constituent Asian American groups, and, in an often highly politicized atmosphere, insofar as they were willing to eschew connections to other identities.[7] Thus, in the mid-1970s, as part of a full-life commitment to the Chinese community, a Chinese-White law student in San Francisco served on his school's Asian law caucus and, after graduation, formed a small firm with three other lawyers, one Japanese and two Chinese (all monoracial). By contrast, another mixed law student, who had not grown up in Chinatown and who did not marry an Asian spouse, was not accorded a similar place in the Chinese community and did not have the same degree of acceptance in Asian American circles. However, because part-White Filipinos were seen as Filipinos by the Filipino community, they were allowed a connection to the Asian American movement on much the same basis as unmixed Filipinos.[8]

Pan-Asianism a Quarter-Century Later

At the beginning of the twenty-first century, one finds in place a similar hierarchy of Asianness, with Chinese, Japanese, and Korean Americans at the center, and the American-born slightly more central than the immigrants, but with increasing recognition of the diasporic quality of all the Asian groups. Vietnamese and Filipino Americans inhabit the second tier of Asian America, followed by other Southeast Asians and South Asian Americans (see Figure 2.2).

The places of multiracial people in this Asian American hierarchy are more fluid, and less dependent on the Asian group to which they may be attached. In the last half-dozen years,

---

[7] Mixed-race Asian Americans were often seen in the most intensely politicized period as sell-outs by definition, as more White than Asian, as White wannabes, as people whose lives and values were contiguous with people of this description: "They have rejected their physical heritages, resulting in extreme self-hatred. Yellow people share with the blacks the desire to look white. Just as blacks wish to be light-complected with thin lips and unkinky hair, 'yellows' want to be tall with long legs and large eyes" (Uyematsu, 1971).

[8] The relative acceptance of part-White Filipinos by the Filipino American community is rooted in the centuries of mixture that took place in the Philippine Islands between native Filipinos and other groups, such as the Spanish and the Chinese. The fact that the early Filipino American community was exceptionally multiracial is probably another contributing factor.

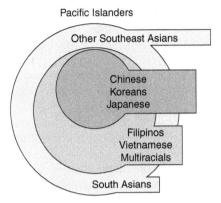

FIGURE 2.2   Centrality and marginality of Asian American groups, 1990s

mixed-race Asian Americans have been so active, and so insistent on a place in Asian America, that regardless of their specific ancestry they might be placed together as a multiracial group in the second tier along with Vietnamese and Filipinos. As the ingroup definition has been broadened to include Asians of many national origin groups, the simple, binary nature of categorizing has softened, and there has been a greater willingness to include multiracial Asian Americans in the mix. For example, in 1997 an entire issue of *Amerasia Journal* explored the theme of multiraciality (Houston & Williams, 1997); such an event would have unthinkable a dozen years earlier.[9]

It is also worth noting that the situation is now a bit different for another, growing group of mixed-descent Asian Americans: those who have more than one Asian ancestry yet no non-Asian ancestry. Informally at least, monoracial Asian Americans seem to regard such people as more Asian than people whose mixed ancestry includes non-Asian parentage. It is in some ways an affirmation of the strength of the relatively new Asian American panethnicity that for a couple of decades Japanese and Chinese Americans have been marrying each other. There is an assumption in some writings that the children of such intra-Asian intermarriages will be more Asian than people with one parent who is White, Black, or Latino (Espiritu, 1992: 167–168; Shinagawa & Pang, 1988; Kibria, 1997; Lee, 1997; Fong & Yung 1995–96). No one has yet studied this population formally to find out if such assumptions hold true.

Part of the Lump? Pacific Islanders and Asian American Ethnicity

For a long time White Americans have put Pacific Islanders in the Asian American Census category, and for about two decades some Asians have reflexively included Pacific Islanders in their formal definition of Asian Americans. Thus one reads often of the "Asian Pacific community" and finds the name "Pacific Islander" appended to many an Asian American catalogue and

---

[9] The openness to hearing the voices of multiracials also is due to the increasing consciousness in nearly every Asian community of the high rate of intermarriage and the fact that the future face of every Asian community is significantly interracial (Spickard, 1996).

institution. And the University of California, Santa Barbara, offers Asian American Studies credit for courses on Hawaiian music and Pacific Islander Americans. Most White people do not think that Hawaiians, Samoans, and Tongans are Asians, but they do not think about Pacific Islanders much, and the Asian category has seemed a convenient place to put them. It is worth nothing that in the 2000 Census, Pacific Islanders have a category of their own, although their numbers are so small that they are not likely to gain a spot on the ethnic studies map unless it is as honorary Asians (U.S. Office of Management and Budget, 1997). Even so, on the diagram of Asian America shown in Figure 2.2, Pacific Islanders occupy the tier farthest out, and while Asian Americans have not been unwelcoming to Pacific Islanders, they often do not seem to know exactly what to do with them.

For the present discussion, Pacific Islander Americans are worth contemplating because, even more than Filipinos, Pacific Islanders are conscious of themselves as a people of multiplicity. Throughout the Pacific, people have been moving around from island to island, to Aotearoa and Australia, to Hawai'i and America, for two hundred years. Almost everyone has ancestors or other relatives who have married people from other islands, Europeans, Americans, or Asians. Almost everyone is conscious of an element of mixedness in themselves, even as they embrace one or more of their binary identities. The grounds on which a person may claim membership in one group or another consist of practice (Do you act Samoan? Do you know *fa'aSamoa*?), place (Is there a Tongan place with which you identify?), and family connection (Are there Fijians who claim you as kin?) (Spickard & Fong, 1995).

But many Pacific Islanders go beyond such binary identity-claimings to acknowledge and embrace their ethnic multiplicity. This consciousness of multiplicity can constitute a third cultural (or at least identificational) space, where mixed people identify with other mixed people, not on the basis of their constituent ancestral parts, but on the basis of their very mixedness. Such a third space is the basis of the multiracial student groups that appeared on many campuses in the 1990s.

I leave you with a love story of such a third-space couple and their encounter with the binarily constructed racial environment in Japan. Akebono is one of two *yokozuna*, or grand *sumo* champions, in Japan, and a star of the opening ceremonies of the 1998 Olympic Games in Nagano. Once he was Chad Rowan, a Samoan American growing up in Hawai'i. In February 1998 he announced his engagement to Christine Reiko Kalina, a secretary at the U.S. Air Force base in Yokota, west of Tokyo. Kalina is the daughter of a Japanese woman and a White American father. There was much grumbling in the Japanese press that the match was unsuitable: she was not really Japanese (i.e., she grew up in the United States, could speak Japanese but not write it well, and had a non-Japanese father). Some of the criticism seemed to stem partly from the Japanese public's only grudging welcome to foreign *sumo* champions, even though those individuals, like Akebono, took on Japanese identities and citizenship. But consider: this is an ideally matched third-space couple, although they share no elements of ethnicity. He is a Samoan from Hawai'i taking on a high-level Japanese identity in Japan. She is a multiracial Caucasian-Japanese woman living in Japan. Both are culturally and identificationally mixed by background. Both are displaced by current location. Both are barely tolerated by the Japanese public, viewed as essentially outsiders who have usurped places that rightly belong to unmixed, Japan-born, ethnic Japanese. The press's criticism to the contrary, they are a perfect match (Efron, 1998).

PART II   History of Asian Immigration and Assimilation

The History of Asians in America

Timothy P. Fong

C H A P T E R 3

Visibility and Invisibility

In November 2004, Public Television (PBS) aired a four-part series, *They Made America*, profiling 64 influential innovators and entrepreneurs who gave birth to commercial milestones like the steamboat and important cultural symbols like the Barbie doll. This seemingly innocent documentary series touched off a raw nerve to *AsianWeek* columnist Emil Guillermo who began a personal campaign to boycott the program. The cause of Guillermo's angst was that out of all the individuals highlighted, not one was Asian American. The series is based on the book by the same name by Sir Harold Evans who is the author of the acclaimed *New York Times* bestseller *The American Century* and Editor at Large of *The Week* magazine. Evans was also the founding editor of *Condé Nast Traveler*, editorial director of *U.S. News & World Report*, and president of Random House, where he published a record number of bestsellers. "That should give you the book's perspective in a nutshell," Guillermo writes. "It's a British snob's Eastern-elitist view of American history . . . So, of course, in that context, the heroes will never be the oppressed, the workers, the slaves, the ones exploited by the boardrooms and financiers on whose labor the profits are made." Although three African Americans were highlighted in the television series, Guillermo complained, "In technology alone, the failure to include an Asian American on the list is pretty curious . . . A little perspective and balance would have been more than helpful for the show and book. It would have been accurate." Guillermo was particularly offended that the series and the book are being heavily marketed to public schools for inclusion into the core U.S. history curriculum. "An all-white history presented to schools that are majority Asian, black and Latino just makes a mockery of the diversity that's all around us."[1]

Guillermo's observations speak loudly to the fact that Asian Americans are at once visible, yet invisible. This is particularly true with regards to the history of Asians in the United States.

---

[1] Emil Guillermo, "Glaring Omissions of Masterpiece History," *AsianWeek*, November 25, 2004.

The historical experience of Asian Americans is not at all atypical of other minority groups. As a distinct racial minority group, and as immigrants, Asian Americans faced enormous individual prejudice, frequent mob violence, and extreme forms of institutional discrimination. But Asian Americans have not merely been victims of hostility and oppression; indeed, they have also shown remarkable strength and perseverance, which is a testimony to their desire to make the United States their home.

A Brief History of Asians in America

Immigration

Between 1848 and 1924, hundreds of thousands of immigrants from China, Japan, the Philippines, Korea, and India came to the United States in search of a better life and livelihood. Although this period represents the first significant wave, these immigrants were by no means the very first Asians to come to America. Recent archaeological finds off the coast of Southern California have led to speculation that the West Coast may have been visited by Buddhist missionaries from China in the fifth century. Direct evidence of this claim is still being debated, but it is known that the Spanish brought Chinese shipbuilders to Baja California as early as 1571, and later Filipino seamen were brought by Spanish galleons from Manila and settled along the coast of Louisiana. Chinese merchants and sailors were also present in the United States prior to the discovery of gold in California in 1848. Most people are unaware that Asian Indians were brought to America during the late eighteenth century as indentured servants and slaves.[2]

The California gold rush did not immediately ignite a mass rush of Chinese immigrants to America. In fact, only a few hundred Chinese arrived in California during the first years of the gold rush, and most of them were merchants. However, large-scale immigration did begin in earnest in 1852 when 52,000 Chinese arrived that year alone. Many Chinese came to the United States not only to seek their fortunes but also to escape political and economic turmoil in China. As gold ran out, thousands of Chinese were recruited in the mid-1860s to help work on the transcontinental railroad. Eventually more than 300,000 Chinese entered the United States in the nineteenth century, engaging in a variety of occupations. During this same period Chinese also immigrated to Hawaii, but in far fewer numbers than to the continental United States.[3]

Large capitalist and financial interests welcomed the Chinese as cheap labor and lobbied for the 1868 Burlingame Treaty, which recognized "free migration and emigration" of Chinese to the United States in exchange for American trade privileges in China. As early as 1870 Chinese were 9 percent of California's population and 25 percent of the state's work force.[4] The majority of these Chinese were young single men who intended to work a few years and then return to China. Those who stayed seldom married because of laws severely limiting the immigration of Chinese women and prohibiting intermarriage with white women. The result was the Chinese

---

[2] Shih-shan Henry Tsai, *The Chinese Experience in America* (Bloomington: Indiana University Press, 1986), p. 1; also see Stan Steiner, *Fusahang: The Chinese Who Built America* (New York: Harper & Row, 1979), pp. 24–35; Elena S. H. Yu, "Filipino Migration and Community Organization in the United States," *California Sociologist* 3:2 (1980): 76–102; and Joan M. Jensen, *Passage from India: Asian Indian Immigrants in North America* (New Haven: Yale University Press, 1988), pp. 12–13.

[3] Sucheng Chan, *Asian Californians* (San Francisco: MTL/Boyd & Fraser, 1991), pp. 5–6.

[4] Ronald Takaki, *Strangers from a Different Shore* (Boston: Little, Brown, 1989), pp. 79, 114.

were forced to live a harsh and lonely bachelor life that often featured vice and prostitution. In 1890, for example, there were roughly 102,620 Chinese men and only 3,868 Chinese women in the United States, a male to female ratio of 26:1.[5] Despite these conditions, Chinese workers continued to come to the United States.

Following the completion of the transcontinental railroad in 1869, large numbers of unemployed Chinese workers had to find new sources of employment. Many found work in agriculture where they cleared land, dug canals, planted orchards, harvested crops, and were the foundation for successful commercial production of many California crops. Others settled in San Francisco and other cities to manufacture shoes, cigars, and clothing. Still others started small businesses such as restaurants, laundries, and general stores. Domestic service such as house boys, cooks, and gardeners were also other areas of employment for the Chinese. In short, the Chinese were involved in many occupations that were crucial to the economic development and domestication of the western region of the United States.[6] Unfortunately, intense hostility against the Chinese reached its peak in 1882 when Congress passed the Chinese Exclusion Act intended to "suspend" the entry of Chinese laborers for ten years. Other laws were eventually passed that barred Chinese laborers and their wives permanently.[7]

The historical experience of Japanese in the United States is both different yet similar to that of the Chinese. One major difference is that the Japanese immigrated in large numbers to Hawaii, and they did not come in large numbers to the United States until the 1890s. In 1880 only 148 Japanese were living in the U.S. mainland. In 1890 this number increased to 2,000, mostly merchants and students. However, the population increased dramatically when an influx of 38,000 Japanese workers from Hawaii arrived in the U.S. mainland between 1902 and 1907.[8] The second difference was the fact the Japanese were able to fully exploit an economic niche in agriculture that the Chinese had only started. The completion of several national railroad lines and the invention of the refrigerator car were two advancements that brought tremendous expansion in the California produce industry. The early Japanese were fortunate to arrive at an opportune time, and about two thirds of them found work as agricultural laborers. Within a short time the Japanese were starting their own farms in direct competition with non-Japanese farms. By 1919 the Japanese controlled over 450,000 acres of agricultural land. Although this figure represents only 1 percent of active California agricultural land at the time, the Japanese were so efficient in their farming practices that they captured 10 percent of the dollar volume of the state's crops.[9]

The third major difference was the emergence of Japan as a international military power at the turn of the century. Japan's victory in the Russo-Japanese War (1904–1905) impressed President Theodore Roosevelt, and he believed a strategy of cooperation with the Japanese government was in the best interest of the United States. Roosevelt blocked calls for complete Japanese exclusion and instead worked a compromise with the Japanese government in 1907 known as the "Gentleman's Agreement." This agreement halted the immigration of Japanese laborers but allowed Japanese women into the United States. With this in mind, the fourth difference was the

[5] Stanford Lyman, *Chinese Americans* (New York: Random House, 1974), pp. 86–88.

[6] Chan, *Asian Californians*, pp. 27–33.

[7] Lyman, *Chinese Americans*, pp. 63–69.

[8] Yuji Ichioka, The Issei: The World of the First Generation Japanese Immigrant's, 1885–1924 (New York: Free Press, 1988), pp. 64–65.

[9] Roger Daniels, Concentration Camps: North American Japanese in the United States and Canada During World War II (Malabar, FL: Robert A. Kreiger, 1981), p. 7.

fact that the Japanese in the United States were able to actually increase in population, start families, and establish a rather stable community life.[10]

Filipino immigration began after the United States gained possession of the Philippines following the Spanish-American War in 1898. The first Filipinos to arrive were a few hundred *pensionados,* or students supported by government scholarships. Similar to the Japanese experience, a large number of Filipinos went directly to Hawaii before coming to the U.S. mainland. Between 1907 and 1919 over 28,000 Filipinos were actively recruited to work on sugar plantations in Hawaii. Filipinos began to emigrate to the United States following the passage of the 1924 Immigration Act, which prohibited all Asian immigration to this country, and there was a need for agricultural and service labor.[11]

Because Filipinos lived on American territory, they were "nationals" who were free to travel in the United States without restriction. In the 1920s over 45,000 Filipinos arrived in Pacific Coast ports, and a 1930 study found 30,000 Filipinos working in California. These Filipinos were overwhelmingly young, single males. Their ages ranged between 16 and 29, and there were 14 Filipino men for every Filipina. Sixty percent of these Filipinos worked as migratory agricultural laborers, and 25 percent worked in domestic service in Los Angeles and San Francisco. The rest found work in manufacturing and as railroad porters. Unlike the Japanese, Filipinos did not make their mark in agriculture as farmers, but as labor union organizers.[12] Both Filipino farm worker activism and Japanese farm competition created a great deal of resentment among white farmers and laborers.

Koreans and Asian Indians slightly predated the Filipinos, but arrived in much smaller numbers. Between 1903 and 1905 over 7,000 Koreans were recruited for plantation labor work in Hawaii, but after Japan established a protectorate over Korea in 1905, all emigration was halted.[13] In the next five years, Japan increased its economic and political power and formally annexed Korea in 1910. Relatively few Koreans lived in the United States between 1905 and 1940. Among those included about 1,000 workers who migrated from Hawaii, about 100 Korean "picture brides," and a small number of American-born Koreans. The Korean population in the United States during that time was also bolstered by roughly 900 students, many of whom fled their home country because of their opposition to Japanese rule. Like other Asian immigrant groups, Koreans found themselves concentrated in California agriculture working primarily as laborers, although a small number did become quite successful farmers.[14]

The first significant flow of Asian Indians occurred between 1904 and 1911, when just over 6,000 arrived in the United States. Unlike the other Asian groups, Asian Indians did not work in Hawaii prior to entering the American mainland, but they worked primarily in California agriculture. Similar to the Chinese, Filipinos, and Koreans, they had an extremely high male to female ratio. Of the Asian Indians who immigrated to the United States between 1904 and 1911, there

---

[10] Bill Ong Hing, *Making and Remaking Asian America Through Immigration Policy, 1850–1990* (Stanford, CA: Stanford University Press, 1993), pp. 28–30.

[11] Chan, *Asian Californians,* p. 7.

[12] Edwin B. Almirol, *Ethnic Identity and Social Negotiation: A Study of a Filipino Community in California* (New York: AMS Press, 1985), pp. 52–59; and H. Brett Melendy, "Filipinos in the United States," in Norris Hundley, Jr. (ed.), *The Asian American: The Historical Experience* (Santa Barbara: Cleo, 1977), pp. 101–128.

[13] Takaki, *Strangers from a Different Shore,* pp. 53–57.

[14] Chan, *Asian Californians,* pp. 7, 17–19, 37; and Warren Y. Kim, *Koreans in America* (Seoul: Po Chin Chai, 1971), pp. 22–27.

were only three or four women, all of whom were married.[15] Eighty to ninety percent of the first Asian Indian settlers in the United States were Sikhs, a distinct ethno-religious minority group in India. Despite this fact, these Sikhs were often called Hindus, which they are not. Sikhs were easily recognizable from all other Asian immigrant groups because of their huskier build, their turbans, and their beards. But like other Asians in the United States at the time, they also worked primarily in California's agricultural industry. Asian Indians worked first as farm workers, and like the Japanese, they also formed cooperatives, pooled their resources, and began independent farming.[16] Immigration restrictions, their relatively small numbers, and an exaggerated male to female ratio prevented Asian Indians from developing a lasting farm presence. One major exception can be found in the Marysville/Yuba City area of Northern California, where Asian Indian Sikhs are still quite active in producing cling peaches.[17]

Anti-Asian Laws and Sentiment

The United States is a nation that claims to welcome and assimilate all newcomers. But the history of immigration, naturalization, and equal treatment under the law for Asian Americans has been an extremely difficult one. In 1790 Congress passed the first naturalization law limiting citizenship rights to only a "free white person."[18] During the period of reconstruction in the 1870s following the end of the Civil War, Congress amended the law and allowed citizenship for "aliens of African nativity and persons of African descent."[19] For a while there was some discussion on expanding naturalization rights to Chinese immigrants, but that idea was rejected by politicians from western states.[20] This rejection is exemplary of the intense anti-Chinese sentiment at the time.

As early as 1850 California imposed the Foreign Miners Tax, which required the payment of $20 a month from all foreign miners.[21] The California Supreme Court ruled in *People v. Hall* (1854) that Chinese could not testify in court against a white person. This case threw out the testimony of three Chinese witnesses and reversed the murder conviction of George W. Hall, who was sentenced to hang for the murder of a Chinese man one year earlier.[22] In 1855 a local San Francisco ordinance levied a $50 tax on all aliens ineligible for citizenship. Because Chinese were ineligible for citizenship under the Naturalization Act of 1790, they were the primary targets for this law.[23]

The racially distinct Chinese were the primary scapegoats for the depressed economy in the 1870s, and mob violence erupted on several occasions through to the 1880s. The massacre of 21 Chinese in Los Angeles in 1871 and 28 Chinese in Rock Springs, Wyoming, in 1885 are examples

---

[15] Joan M. Jensen, *Passage from India: Asian Indian Immigrants in North America* (New Haven: Yale University Press, 1988), pp. 24–41; and Rajanki K. Das, *Hindustani Workers on the Pacific Coast* (Berlin and Leipzig: Walter De Gruyter, 1923), p. 77.

[16] Das, *Hindustani Workers*, pp. 66–67.

[17] Bruce La Brack, "Occupational Specialization Among Rural California Sikhs: The Interplay of Culture and Economics," *Amerasia Journal* 9:2 (1982): 29–56.

[18] Naturalization Act of 1790, 1 Stat. 103 (1790).

[19] Act of 14 July 1870, 16 Stat. 256.

[20] Roger Daniels, *Asian Americans: Chinese and Japanese in the United States* (Seattle: University of Washington Press, 1988), p. 43.

[21] Chan, Asian Californians, p. 42.

[22] Robert F. Heizer and Alan F. Almquist, The Other Californians: Prejudice and Discrimination Under Spain, Mexico, and the United States to 1920 (Berkeley: University of California Press, 1971), p. 129.

[23] Takaki, Strangers from a Different Shore, p. 82.

of the worst incidents. It is within this environment that Congress passed the 1882 Chinese Exclusion Act. The act suspended immigration of Chinese laborers for only ten years, but it was extended in 1892 and 1902. The act was eventually extended indefinitely in 1904.[24] The intense institutional discrimination achieved the desired result: The Chinese population declined from 105,465 in 1880 to 61,639 in 1920.[25]

Anti-Chinese sentiment easily grew into large-scale anti-Asian sentiment as immigrants from Asia continued to enter the United States. During the same period that the Chinese population declined, the Japanese population grew and became highly visible. As early as 1910 there were 72,157 Japanese Americans compared to 71,531 Chinese Americans in the United States.[26] Japanese farmers in California were particularly vulnerable targets for animosity. One of the most sweeping anti-Asian laws was aimed at the Japanese Americans but affected all other Asian American groups as well. The 1913 Alien Land Law prohibited "aliens ineligible to citizenship" from owning or leasing land for more than three years. Initially the Japanese Americans were able to bypass the law primarily because they could buy or lease land under the names of their American-born offspring (the Nisei), who were U.S. citizens by birth. The law was strengthened in 1920, however, and the purchase of land under the names of American-born offspring was prohibited.[27]

Several sweeping anti-immigration laws were passed in the first quarter of the twentieth century that served to eliminate Asian immigration to the United States. A provision in the 1917 Immigration Act banned immigration from the so-called "Asian barred zone," except for the Philippines and Japan. A more severe anti-Asian restriction was further imposed by the 1924 National Origins Act, which placed a ceiling of 150,000 new immigrants per year. The 1924 act was intended to limit eastern and southern European immigration, but a provision was added that ended any immigration by aliens ineligible for citizenship.[28]

Asian Americans did not sit back passively in the face of discriminatory laws; they hired lawyers and went to court to fight for their livelihoods, naturalization rights, and personal liberties. Sometimes they were successful, but oftentimes they were not. In the case of *Yick Wo v. Hopkins* (1886), Chinese successfully challenged an 1880 San Francisco Laundry Ordinance, which regulated commercial laundry service in a way that clearly discriminated against the Chinese. Plaintiff Yick Wo had operated a laundry service for 22 years, but when he tried to renew his business license in 1885 he was turned down because his storefront was made out of wood. Two hundred other Chinese laundries were also denied business licenses on similar grounds, although 80 non-Chinese laundries in wooden buildings were approved. The Supreme Court ruled in favor of Yick Wo, concluding there was "no reason" for the denial of the business license "except to the face and nationality" of the petitioner.[29]

The inability to gain citizenship was a defining factor throughout the early history of Asian Americans. The constitutionality of naturalization based on race was first challenged in the Supreme Court case of *Ozawa v. United States* (1922). Takao Ozawa was born in Japan but immigrated to the United States at an early age. He graduated from Berkeley High School in California

---

[24] Lyman, *Chinese Americans*, pp. 55–85.

[25] Takaki, *Strangers from a Different Shore*, pp. 111–112.

[26] Juan L. Gonzales, *Racial and Ethnic Groups in America*, 2nd ed. (Dubuque, IA: Kendall/Hunt, 1993), p. 136; and Juan L. Gonzales, *Racial and Ethnic Families in America*, 2nd ed. (Dubuque, IA: Kendall/Hunt Publishing Co., 1993), p. 3.

[27] Chan, *Asian Californians*, pp. 44–45.

[28] Hing, *Making and Remaking Asian* America, pp. 32–39.

[29] *Yick Wo v. Hopkins*, 118 U.S. 356 (1886); and Lyman, *Chinese Americans*, p. 79.

and attended the University of California for three years. Ozawa was a model immigrant who did not smoke or drink, he attended a predominantly white church, his children attended public school, and English was the language spoken at home. When Ozawa was rejected in his initial attempt for naturalization, he appealed and argued that the provisions for citizenship in the 1790 and 1870 acts did not specifically exclude Japanese. In addition, Ozawa also tried to argue that Japanese should be considered "white."

The Court unanimously ruled against Ozawa on both grounds. First, the Court decided that initial framers of the law and its amendment did not intend to *exclude* people from naturalization but, instead, only determine who would be *included*. Ozawa was denied citizenship because the existing law simply didn't include Japanese. Second, the Court also ruled against Ozawa's argument that Japanese were actually more "white" than other darker skinned "white" people such as some Italians, Spanish, and Portuguese. The Court clarified the matter by defining a "white person" to be synonymous with a "person of the Caucasian race." In short, Ozawa was not Caucasian (although he thought himself "white") and, thus, was ineligible for citizenship.[30]

Prior to the *Ozawa* case, Asian Indians already enjoyed the right of naturalization. In *United States v. Balsara* (1910), the Supreme Court determined that Asian Indians were Caucasian and approximately 70 became naturalized citizens. But the Immigration and Naturalization Service (INS) challenged this decision, and it was taken up again in the case of *United States v. Thind* (1923). This time the Supreme Court reversed its earlier decision and ruled that Bhagat Singh Thind could not be a citizen because he was not "white." Even though Asian Indians were classified as Caucasian, this was a scientific term that was inconsistent with the popular understanding. The Court's decision stated, "It may be true that the blond Scandinavian and the brown Hindu have a common ancestor in the dim reaches of antiquity, but the average man knows perfectly well that there are unmistakable differences between them today."[31] In other words, only "white" Caucasians were considered eligible for U.S. citizenship. In the wake of the *Thind* decision, the INS was able to cancel retroactively the citizenship of Asian Indians between 1923 and 1926.

Asian Americans also received disparate treatment compared to other immigrants in their most private affairs, such as marriage. In the nineteenth century, antimiscegenation laws prohibiting marriage between blacks and whites were common throughout the United States. In 1880 the California legislature extended restrictive antimiscegenation categories to prohibit any marriage between a white person and a "negro, mulatto, or Mongolian." This law, targeted at the Chinese, was not challenged until Salvador Roldan won a California Court of Appeals decision in 1933. Roldan, a Filipino American, argued that he was Malay, not Mongolian, and he should be allowed to marry his white fiancee. The Court conceded that the state's antimiscegenation law was created in an atmosphere of intense anti-Chinese sentiment, and agreed Filipinos were not in mind when the initial legislation was approved. Unfortunately, this victory was short-lived. The California state legislature amended the antimiscegenation law to include the "Malay race" shortly after the Roldan decision was announced.[32]

---

[30] *Takao Ozawa v. United States*, 260 U.S. 178 (1922); Helzer and Alquist, *The Other Californians*, pp. 192–193; and Ichioka, *The Issel*, pp. 210–226.

[31] *United States v. Bhagat Singh Thind*, 261 U.S. 204 (1923); Jensen, *Passage from India*, pp. 255–260; and Gurdial Singh, "East Indians in the United States," *Sociology and Social Research* 30:3 (1946): 208–216.

[32] Megumi Dick Osumi, "Asians and California's Anti-Miscegenation Laws," in Nobuya Tsuchida (ed.), *Asian and Pacific American Experiences: Women's Perspectives* (Minneapolis: Asian/Pacific American Learning Resource Center, University of Minnesota, 1982), pp. 1–37; and Takaki, *Strangers from a Different Shore*, pp. 330–331.

World War II and the Cold War Era

For Asian Americans, World War II was an epoch, but the profound impact was distinct for different Asian American groups. For over 110,000 Japanese Americans, World War II was an agonizing ordeal soon after Japan's attack of Pearl Harbor on December 7, 1941. The FBI arrested thousands of Japanese Americans who were considered potential security threats immediately after the Pearl Harbor bombing raid. Arrested without evidence of disloyalty were the most visible Japanese American community leaders, including businessmen, Shinto and Buddhist priests, teachers in Japanese-language schools, and editors of Japanese-language newspapers. Wartime hysteria rose to a fever pitch, and on February 19, 1942, President Franklin Roosevelt issued Executive Order 9066. This order established various military zones and authorized the removal of anyone who was a potential threat. Although a small number of German and Italian aliens were detained and relocated, this did not compare to the mass relocation of Japanese Americans on the West Coast of the United States.[33]

The order to relocate Japanese Americans because of military necessity and the threat they posed to security, was a fabrication. Even military leaders debated the genuine need for mass relocation, and the government's own intelligence reports found no evidence of Japanese American disloyalty. "For the most part the local Japanese are loyal to the United States or, at worst, hope that by remaining quiet they can avoid concentration camps or irresponsible mobs," one report stated. "We do not believe that they would be at least any more disloyal than any other racial group in the United States with whom we went to war."[34] This helps explain why 160,000 Japanese Americans living in Hawaii were not interned. More telling was the fact that Japanese Americans in the continental United States were a small but much resented minority. Despite government reports to the contrary, business leaders, local politicians, and the media fueled antagonism against the Japanese Americans and agitated for their abrupt removal.[35]

With only seven days' notice to prepare once the internment order was issued, and no way of knowing how long the war would last, many Japanese Americans were forced to sell their homes and property at a mere fraction of their genuine value. Japanese Americans suffered estimated economic losses alone of at least $400 million. By August 1942 all the Japanese on the West Coast were interned in ten camps located in rural regions of California, Arizona, Utah, Idaho, Wyoming, and Arkansas. Two thirds of the interned Japanese American men, women, and children were U.S. citizens, whose only crime was their ancestry; even those with as little as one-eighth Japanese blood were interned. The camps themselves were crude, mass facilities surrounded by barbed wire and guarded by armed sentries. People were housed in large barracks with each family living in small cramped quarters dubbed "apartments." Food was served in large mess halls, and toilet and shower facilities were communal. Many of the camps were extremely cold in the winter, hot in the summer, and dusty all year round. The camps remained open for the duration of the war.[36]

---

[33] William Petersen, *Japanese Americans* (New York: Random House, 1971), pp. 66–100; Roger Daniels, *Concentration Camps, U.S.A.* (New York: Holt, Rinehart & Winston, 1971), pp. 75, 81–82; and Jacobus tenBroek, Edward N. Barnhart and Floyd W. Matson, *Prejudice, War, and the Constitution* (Berkeley: University of California Press), pp. 118–120.

[34] Cited in Commission on Wartime Relocation and Internment of Civilians, *Personal Justice Denied* (Washington, DC: U.S. Government Printing Office, 1982), pp. 52–53.

[35] Takaki, *Strangers from a Different Shore*, pp. 379–392.

[36] Commission on Wartime Relocation and Internment of Civilians, *Personal Justice Denied*, p. 217; tenBroek, Barnhart, and Matson, *Prejudice, War, and the Constitution*, pp. 155–177, 180–181; and Daniels, *Concentration Camps: North America.*

After the first year of the camps, the government began recruiting young Japanese American men to help in the war effort. The military desperately needed Japanese Americans to serve as interpreters for Japanese prisoners of war and translators of captured documents. But to the military's incredulity, most American-born Japanese had only modest Japanese-language skills and needed intense training in the Military Intelligence Service Language School before they could perform their duties.[37] It was, however, the heroic actions of the 100th Infantry Battalion, which later merged with the 442nd Regimental Combat Team, that stand out the most among historians. The two segregated units engaged in numerous campaigns and served with distinction throughout Europe. By the end of the war in Europe, for example, the Nisei soldiers of the 442nd suffered over 9,000 casualties, and earned over 18,000 individual decorations of honor. The 442nd was the most decorated unit of its size during all of World War II.[38]

Compared to the Japanese American experience, other Asian American groups fared far better during and after World War II. Changes for Chinese Americans were particularly dramatic. Prior to the war, the image of the Chinese was clearly negative compared to the Japanese. A survey of Princeton undergraduates in 1931 thought the top three traits of the Chinese were the fact they were "superstitious, sly, and conservative," whereas Japanese were considered "intelligent, industrious, and progressive."[39] Immediately after the bombing of Pearl Harbor, Chinese store owners put up signs indicating they were not Japanese, and in some cases Chinese Americans wore buttons stating, "I am Chinese." To alleviate any further identification problems, *Time* magazine published an article on December 22, 1941, explaining how to tell the difference between Chinese and "Japs." The article compared photographs of a Chinese man and a Japanese man, highlighting the distinguishing facial features of each.[40] Just months later, a 1942 Gallup Poll characterized the Chinese as "hardworking, honest, and brave," and Japanese were seen as "treacherous, sly, and cruel."[41]

Employment opportunities outside of the segregated Chinatown community became available to Chinese Americans for the first time during the war and continued even after the war ended. Chinese Americans trained in various professions and skilled crafts were able to find work in war-related industries that had never been open to them before. In addition, the employment of Chinese American women increased threefold during the 1940s. Leading the way were clerical positions, which increased from just 750 in 1940 to 3,200 in 1950. In 1940 women represented just one in five Chinese American professionals, but by 1950 this increased to one in three. On another level, Chinese actors suddenly found they were in demand for film roles—usually playing evil Japanese characters. Shortly after the war, writers such as Jade Snow Wong and Pardee Lowe discovered the newfound interest and appreciation of Chinese Americans could be turned into commercial success through the publication of their memoirs.[42]

On the military front, Asian Americans also distinguished themselves. Over 15,000 Chinese Americans served in all branches of the military, unlike the Japanese Americans who were placed

[37] Chan, Asian Californians, p. 101.

[38] Petersen, *Japanese Americans*, p. 87.

[39] Cited in Marvin Karlins, Thomas L. Coffman, and Gary Walters, "On the Fading of Social Stereotypes: Studies of Three Generations of College Students," *Journal of Personality and Psychology* 13 (1990): 4–5.

[40] *Time*, December 22, 1941, p. 33.

[41] Cited in Harold Isaacs, *Images of Asia: American Views of China and India* (New York: Harper & Row, 1972), pp. xviii—xix.

[42] Chan, *Asian Californians*, pp. 103–104; and Lyman, *Chinese Americans*, pp. 127, 134.

only in segregated infantry units and in the Military Intelligence Service. Similarly, over 7,000 Filipino Americans volunteered for the army and formed the First and Second Filipino Infantry Regiments. About 1,000 other Filipino Americans were sent to the Philippines to perform reconnaissance and intelligence activities for Gen. Douglas MacArthur.[43] Equally significant was the War Bride's Act of 1945, which allowed war veterans to bring wives from China and the Philippines as nonquota immigrants. This resulted in a rapid and dramatic shift in the historic gender imbalance of both groups. For example, between 1945 and 1952, nine out of ten (89.9 percent) Chinese immigrants were female, and 20,000 Chinese American babies were born by the mid-1950s. Similarly, between 1951 and 1960 seven out of ten (71 percent) Filipino immigrants were female.[44]

On the broad international front, alliances with China, the Philippines, and India eventually began the process of changing the overtly discriminatory immigration laws against Asians. The Chinese Exclusion Law was repealed in 1943, and an annual quota of 105 immigrants from China was allotted. In 1946 Congress approved legislation that extended citizenship to Filipino immigrants and permitted the entry of 100 Filipino immigrants annually. Also in 1946, the Luce-Cellar Act ended the 1917 "Asian barred zone," allowed an immigration quota of 100 from India, and for the first time permitted Asian Indians to apply for citizenship since the *United States v. Thind* case of 1923. Although these changes were extremely modest, they carried important symbolic weight by helping create a favorable international opinion of the United States during and immediately after the war.[45]

Geopolitical events during the Cold War era of the 1950s and 1960s immediately following World War II continued to have important ramifications for Asian Americans. After the 1949 Communist Revolution in China, about 5,000 Chinese students and young professionals were living in the United States. These "stranded" individuals were generally from China's most elite and educated families and not necessarily anxious to return to China because their property had already been confiscated and their livelihoods threatened. They were eventually allowed to stay in the United States.[46] Several other refugee acts in the late 1950s and early 1960s allowed some 18,000 other Chinese to enter and also stay in the United States. Many of these refugees were well-trained scientists and engineers who easily found jobs in private industry and in research universities. These educated professionals were quite distinct from the vast majority of earlier Chinese immigrants because they usually were able to integrate into the American mainstream quickly, becoming the basis of an emerging Chinese American middle class.[47]

The Cold War affected immigration from Asian countries as well, but in a very different fashion. During and after the Korean War (1950–1953), American soldiers often met and married Korean women and brought them home to the United States. Between 1952 and 1960 over 1,000 Korean women a year immigrated to the United States as brides of U.S. servicemen. At the same

[43] Takaki, *Strangers from a Different Shore*, pp. 357–363, 370–378; Manuel Buaken, "Life in the Armed Forces," *New Republic* 109 (1943): 279–280; and Bienvenido Santos, "Filipinos in War," *Far Eastern Survey* 11 (1942): 249–250.

[44] Harry H. L. Kitano and Roger Daniels, *Asian Americans: Emerging Minorities,* 2nd ed. (Upper Saddle River, NJ: Prentice Hall, 1995), p. 42, Table 4–2; and Monica Boyd, "Oriental Immigration: The Experience of Chinese, Japanese, and Filipino Populations in the United States," *International Migration Review* 10 (1976): 48–60, Table 1.

[45] Chan, *Asian Californians*, pp. 105–106.

[46] Diane Mark and Ginger Chih, *A Place Called Chinese America* (San Francisco: The Organization of Chinese Americans, 1982), pp. 105–107.

[47] Chan, *Asian Californians*, pp. 108–109.

time, orphaned Korean children, especially girls, also arrived in the United States in significant numbers. Throughout the 1950s and up to the mid-1960s, some 70 percent of all Korean immigrants were either women or young girls. Korea was the site of the actual conflict, but large numbers of troops were also stationed in nearby Japan. Even higher numbers of Japanese women married American soldiers, left their home country, and started a new life in the United States. Roughly 6,000 Japanese wives of U.S. servicemen annually immigrated to the United States between 1952 and 1960, which was over 80 percent of all immigrants from Japan. These Korean and Japanese war brides and Korean orphans were spread throughout the United States and, as a result, had very little interaction with other Asian Americans already living in this country.[48] These war bride families were, however, a significant part of the biracial Asian American baby boom that is discussed in greater detail in Chapter 7.

Post-1965 Asian Immigrants and Refugees

A number of factors have clearly influenced Asian immigration and refugee policies, including public sentiment toward immigrants, demands of foreign policy, and the needs of the American economy. World War II and the Cold War years were epochal for Asian Americans, but the period since the mid-1960s has proven to be even more significant. An overview of U.S. immigration statistics shows just how important recent immigration reforms and refugee policies have affected Asian Americans.

Official records on immigrants entering the United States did not exist before 1820, but since that time it is quite obvious that the largest number of immigrants come from European countries. Between 1820 and 2010, over 39 million Europeans immigrated to the United States (see Table 3.1). In contrast, about 12 million immigrants came from Asia during the same period of time. Looking at this figure more closely, however, we find over 10.7 million immigrants from Asia arrived in the United States in the period between 1971 and 2010. Although the Chinese and Japanese have the longest histories in the United States, the largest group of Asian immigrants since 1971 has come from the Philippines. Over 2 million Filipino immigrants entered the United States between 1971 and 2010. It is also significant to note that over 90 percent of Filipino, Asian Indian, Korean, and Vietnamese have entered the United States since 1971.

This next section focuses on three broad events that have directly influenced both the numbers and diversity of Asians entering the United States since 1965: (1) the passage of the 1965 Immigration Reform Act, (2) global economic restructuring, and (3) the Vietnam War.

The 1965 Immigration Reform Act

Why did the dramatic increase in Asian immigration take place? What changes in the law or public attitudes facilitated such a rapid influx of immigrants from Asia? One important reason was the civil rights movement of the 1960s, which brought international attention to racial and economic inequality in the United States—including its biased immigration policies. This attention is the background for the passage of the 1965 Immigration Reform Act, the most important immigration reform legislation. This act, along with its amendments, significantly increased the token quotas established after World War II to allow the Eastern Hemisphere a maximum of 20,000 per country, and set a ceiling of 170,000.

---

[48] Ibid., pp. 109–110.

TABLE 3.1 Persons Obtaining Legal Permanent Resident Status by Region and Selected Country of Last Residence, 1820–2010

Region	Total	1971–2010	Percent of Immigrants Since 1971
All Countries	76,581,679	31,419,041	41.0
Europe	39,771,718	4,232,579	10.6
Asia	12,440,036	10,747,191	86.4
China*	1,950,974	1,591,398	81.5
Hong Kong†	465,656	375,108	80.5
India	1,436,353	1,395,557	97.1
Japan	614,108	248,724	40.5
Korea	1,022,980	982,116	96.0
Philippines	2,091,873	1,968,971	94.1
Vietnam	1,038,763	1,034,088	99.5
North America	22,026,410	14,556,822	66.0
Canada and Newfoundland	4,721,937	753,229	15.9
Mexico	7,809,285	6,216,693	79.6
Caribbean	4,789,491	3,699,491	77.2
Central America	1,918,562	1,701,662	88.6
South America	2,676,935	2,184,234	81.5
Africa	1,506,103	1,429,630	94.9

* Beginning in 1957, China included Taiwan.
† Data not reported separately until 1952.
Source: United States. Department of Homeland Security. *Yearbook of Immigration Statistics: 2010*. Washington, D.C.: U.S. Department of Homeland Security, Office of Immigration Statistics, 2011. Table 2, pp. 6–11.

This act created the following seven-point preference system that serves as a general guideline for immigration officials when issuing visas: (1) unmarried children of U.S. citizens who are at least 21 years of age; (2) spouses and unmarried children of permanent resident aliens; (3) members of the professions, scientists, and artists of exceptional ability; (4) married children of U.S. citizens; (5) brothers and sisters of U.S. citizens who are at least 21 years of age; (6) skilled or unskilled workers who are in short supply; and (7) nonpreference applicants.

U.S. immigration policy also allowed virtually unrestricted immigration to certain categories of people including spouses, children under 21, and parents of U.S. citizens. These provisions served to accelerate immigration from Asia to the United States. The primary goal of the

1965 Immigration Reform Act was to encourage family reunification, however, a much higher percentage of Asian immigrants initially began entering the United States under the established occupational and nonpreference investment categories. In 1969, for example, 62 percent of Asian Indians, 43 percent of Filipinos, and 34.8 percent of Koreans entered the United States under the occupational and investor categories. By the mid-1970s, however, 80 to 90 percent of all Asian immigrants entered the United States through one of the family categories.[49] Studies clearly show that most post-1965 Asian immigrants tend to be more middle-class, educated, urbanized, and they arrive in the United States in family units rather than as individuals, compared to their pre-1965 counterparts.[50]

The framers of the 1965 law did not anticipate any dramatic changes in the historical pattern of immigration, but it is clear Asian immigrants have taken advantage of almost every aspect of the 1965 Immigration Reform Act. Asians were just 6.1 percent of all immigrants to the United States between 1951 and 1960; this rose to 12.9 percent between 1961 and 1970, and increased to 35.3 percent between 1971 and 1980. The percentage of Asian immigrants peaked at 37.3 percent between 1981 and 1990 but declined to 30.7 percent between 1991 and 2000 (see Table 3.2). This decline was due to the sudden increase of mostly Mexicans who were able to apply for legal status following the passage of the Immigration Reform and Control Act of 1986 (IRCA). By the late 1990s, about 3 million aliens received permanent residence status under IRCA. The percentage of immigrants from Asia increased to 34.5 percent between 2001 and 2010.

This "amnesty" provision was only a part of IRCA, which was fully intended to control illegal immigration into the United States. IRCA also required that all employers verify the legal status of all new employees, and it imposed civil and criminal penalties against employers who knowingly hire undocumented workers.[51] While IRCA closed the "back door" of illegal immigration, another reform, the Immigration Act of 1990, was enacted to keep open the "front door" of legal immigration. Indeed, this law actually authorizes an *increase* in legal immigration to the United States. In response to uncertain economic stability at home, growing global economic competition abroad, and the dramatically changed face of immigration, the 1990 law sent a mixed message to Asian immigrants.

First of all, the law actually authorized an increase in legal immigration, but at the same time placed a yearly cap on total immigration for the first time since the 1920s. For 1992 to 1995, the limit was 700,000 and 675,000 thereafter. This appears to be an arbitrary limit, but it still allows for an unlimited number of visas for immediate relatives of U.S. citizens. This may not have a negative effect on Asian immigration because, as a group, Asians have the highest rate of naturalization compared to other immigrants.[52] Second, the law encourages immigration of more skilled workers to help meet the needs of the U.S. economy. The number of visas for skilled workers and their families increased sharply from 58,000 to 140,000. This was generally seen as a potential

---

[49] Hing, *Making and Remaking Asian America,* Appendix B, pp. 189–200, Table 9, p. 82.

[50] Hing, *Making and Remaking Asian America,* pp. 79–120; Luciano Mangiafico, Contemporary American Immigrants: Patterns of Filipino, Korean, and Chinese Settlement in the United States (New York: Praeger, 1988), pp. 1–26; James T. Fawcett and Benjamin V. Carino (eds.), *Pacific Bridges: The New Immigration from Asia and the Pacific Islands* (Staten Island, NY: Center for Migration Studies, 1987); and Herbert R. Barringer, Robert W. Gardner, and Michael J. Levine (eds.), *Asian and Pacific Islanders in the United States* (New York: Russell Sage Foundation, 1993).

[51] Roger Daniels, *Coming to America* (New York: HarperCollins, 1990), pp. 391–397.

[52] Office of Immigration Statistics, *Statistical Yearbook of the Immigration and Naturalization Service,* 2003 (Washington, DC: U.S. Government Printing Office, 2004), p. 4–5.

| | | | North | South | |
Decade/Year	Europe	Asia	America*	America	Africa
2001–2010	12.4	34.5	34.1	8.4	7.7
1991–2000	14.9	30.7	43.3	5.9	3.9
1981–1990	10.4	37.3	43.0	6.3	2.4
1971–1980	17.8	35.3	37.5	6.6	1.8
1961–1970	33.8	12.9	43.9	7.8	0.9
1951–1960	52.7	6.1	36.0	3.6	0.6
1941–1950	60.0	3.6	32.2	2.1	0.7
1931–1940	65.8	3.1	28.8	1.5	0.3
1921–1930	60.0	2.7	35.9	1.0	0.2
1911–1920	75.3	4.3	19.2	0.7	0.1
1901–1910	91.6	3.7	3.2	0.2	0.1

TABLE 3.2   Percentage of Persons Obtaining legal Permanent Resident Status by Region, Fiscal Years 1900–2010

* Includes Central America and Caribbean.

Source: United States. Department of Homeland Security. *Yearbook of Immigration Statistics: 2010.* Washington, D.C.: U.S. Department of Homeland Security, Office of Immigration Statistics, 2011. Table 2, pp. 6–11

boon for Asians who, since 1965, have been among the best educated and best trained immigrants the United States has ever seen. Third, the 1990 immigration law also sought to "diversify" the new immigrants by giving more visas to countries that have sent relatively few people to the United States in recent years. This program has been popular with lawmakers who want to assist those from Western European countries at the expense of Asians. For example, up to 40 percent of the initial visas allocated for the diversity category were for Ireland. Noted immigration attorney Bill Ong Hing found sections of the Immigration Act of 1990 "provide extra independent and transition visas that are unavailable to Asians.[53]

It is clear from the descriptions of Asian American history here that the conditions for the post-1965 Asian migrants are quite distinct from pre-1965 migrants. This seemingly obvious observation reflects the fact that international migration is not a simple, stable, or homogeneous process. Even with this in mind, the most popular frame of reference for all movement to the United States continues to be the European immigrant experience throughout the nineteenth and early twentieth centuries. The popular European immigrant analogy is highlighted in the words of welcome written on the Statue of Liberty:

Give me your tired, your poor
Your huddled masses yearning to breathe free

---

[53] Hing, *Making and Remaking Asian America*, pp. 7–8.

The wretched refuse of your teeming shore.

Send these, the homeless, tempest-tost to me,

I lift my lamp beside the golden door!

The European immigrant experience, however, is by no means universal, and it is only part of what scholars today see as a much broader picture of the international movement of people and capital. Understanding the broader dynamics of global economic restructuring is useful in comparing and contrasting post-1965 Asian immigrants with other immigrants and minority groups in the United States.

Global Economic Restructuring

What makes people want to leave their home country and migrate to another country? The most commonly accepted answer is found within what is known as the push-pull theory. This theory generally asserts that difficult economic, social, and political conditions in the home country force, or push, people away. At the same time, these people are attracted, or pulled, to another country where conditions are seen as more favorable. On closer examination, however, this theoretical viewpoint does run into some problems. Most significantly, the push-pull theory tends to see immigration flows as a natural, open, and spontaneous process, but it does not adequately take into account the structural factors and policy changes that directly affect immigration flows. This is because earlier migration studies based on European immigration limited their focus on poor countries that sent low-skilled labor to affluent countries with growing economies that put newcomers to work. The push-pull theory is not incorrect, but is considered to be incomplete and historically static. Recent studies have taken a much broader approach to international migration and insist that in order to understand post-1965 immigration from Asia, it is necessary to understand the recent restructuring of the global economy.[54]

Since the end of World War II, global restructuring has involved the gradual movement of industrial manufacturing away from developed nations such as the United States to less developed nations in Asia and Latin America where labor costs are cheaper. This process was best seen in Japan in the 1950s through 1970s, and accelerated rapidly in the 1980s to newly industrialized Asian countries, namely Taiwan, Hong Kong, Singapore, and South Korea. Other Asian countries such as India, Thailand, Indonesia, Malaysia, and the Philippines also followed the same economic course with varying degrees of success. In the 1990s mainland China increased its manufacturing and export capacity dramatically and was steering on the same economic path of other Asian nations.

Among the effects of global restructuring on the United States is the declining need to import low-skilled labor because manufacturing jobs are moving abroad. At the same time, there is an inclining need to import individuals with advanced specialized skills that are in great demand. According to research by Paul Ong and Evelyn Blumenberg (1994), this phenomenon is

---

[54] Paul Ong, Edna Bonacich, and Lucie Cheng (eds.), *The New Asian Immigration in Los Angeles and Global Restructuring* (Philadelphia: Temple University Press, 1994), pp. 3–100; and Edna Bonacich, Lucie Cheng, Norma Chinchilla, Nora Hamilton, and Paul Ong (eds.), *Global Production: The Apparel Industry in the Pacific Rim* (Philadelphia: Temple University Press, 1994), pp. 3–20.

evidenced in part by the increasing number of foreign-born students studying at U.S. colleges.[55] In the 1954–1955 academic year the United States was host to just 34,232 foreign exchange students; this number increased to 586,000 in 2003.[56] Of those 586,000 foreign students, 367,000 are from Asia. In 2002 foreign students earned 60.7 percent of the doctorates in engineering, 53.3 percent of doctorates in mathematics, and 53.4 percent of doctorates in computer science.[57] The National Science Foundation reported that between 1999 and 2009, students from the China, Taiwan, India, and South Korea made up the vast majority of Science and Engineering doctoral degrees awarded to foreign students in the United States (see Table 3.3). Many of these foreign graduate students planned to work in the United States and eventually gained permanent immigrant status. Companies in the United States have, of course, been eager to hire foreign-born scientists and engineers. Not only are highly skilled immigrants valuable to employers as workers, but many also start their own high-tech businesses. For example, Vinod Khosla is the co-founder of Sun-Microsystems, and Gururaj Deshpande is co-founder of a number of high-tech businesses worth around $6 billion.[58]

The medical profession is another broad area where Asian immigrants have made a noticeable impact. Researchers Paul Ong and Tania Azores (1994) found that Asian Americans represented 4.4 percent of the registered nurses and 10.8 percent of the physicians in the United States in 1990. Ong and Azores estimate that only a third of Asian American physicians and a quarter of Asian American nurses were educated in the United States. Graduates of overseas medical and nursing schools have been coming to the United States since the passage of the 1946 Smith-Mundt Act, which created an exchange program for specialized training. Although this exchange was intended to be temporary, many medical professionals were able to become permanent immigrants. A physician shortage in the United States during the late 1960s and early 1970s, coupled with the elimination of racial immigration quotas in 1965, brought forth a steady flow of foreign-trained medical doctors from Asian countries. A 1975 U.S. Commission on Civil Rights report found 5,000 Asian medical school graduates entered the United States annually during the early 1970s. But, under pressure from the medical industry, Congress passed the 1976 Health Professions Educational Act, which restricted the number of foreign-trained physicians who could enter the United States. Despite the passage of this law, the American Medical Association reported there were 194,600 foreign medical graduates out of 768,500 professionally active physicians in the United States in 2002.[59]

Asia is also the largest source for foreign nurses. The Philippines, in particular, is the world leader in nurse migration. A demographic profile of registered nurses in 1990 by the Center

[55] Paul Ong and Evelyn Blumenberg, "Scientists and Engineers," in Paul Ong (ed.), *The State of Asian Pacific America: Economic Diversity, Issues & Policies* (Los Angeles: LEAP Asian Pacific American Public Policy Institute and UCLA Asian American Studies Center, 1994), pp. 113–138. Note that I am distinguishing between foreign exchange students who are overseas nationals from Asian American students who happen to be foreign born.

[56] *Ibid.*, p. 173; and U.S. Department of Commerce, *Statistical Abstract of the United States, 2004–2005* (Washington, DC: U.S. Government Printing Office, 2005), p. 171, Table 265.

[57] U.S. Department of Commerce, *Statistical Abstract of the United States, 2004–2005* (Washington, DC: U.S. Government Printing Office, 2005), p. 515, Table 775.

[58] "The Golden Diaspora: Indian Immigrants to the U.S. Are One of the Newest Elements of the American Melting Pot— and the Most Spectacular Success Story," *Time Select/Global Business*, June 19, 2000, pp. B26–27.

[59] Paul Ong and Tania Azores, "Health Professionals on the Front-Line," in Paul Ong (ed.), *The State of Asian Pacific America: Economic Diversity, Issues & Policies*, pp. 139–164 and U.S. Department of Commerce. *Statistical Abstract of the United States, 2004–2005* (Washington, DC: U.S. Government Printing Office, 2005). p. 107, Table 150.

| | Science & | Non-Science & |
| | Engineering | Engineering |
Country		
China	32,973*	2,547
India	13,266	1,239
South Korea	10,824	3,227
Taiwan	5,572	2,197
Turkey	3,658	1,503
Canada	3,455	745
Thailand	2,802	484
Mexico	1,965	716
Japan	1,935	357
Germany	1,698	498

TABLE 3.3 Top 10 Countries of Foreign Citizenship for U.S. Doctorate Recipients, 1999–2009.

* China Includes Hong Kong.

Source: National Science Foundation, "Doctorate Recipients from U.S. Universities: 2009" at http://www.nsf.gov/statistics/nsf11306/theme1.cfm#3

for Immigration Studies (1998) found there were 1,896,606 registered nurses. The same study found 166,708 were foreign-born registered nurses, 49,033 of which were from the Philippines (29.4 percent). A recent survey conducted by Judith Berg and her colleagues (2004) found that Filipino nurses were generally better educated worked more full-time hours than U.S. native born nurses. The researchers also found that Filipino nurses had higher job satisfaction. Filipino nurses find work in the United States attractive because they can earn up to 20 times the salary they can make in the Philippines, and their English-speaking abilities make them highly desired by employers. The growth of the health care industry in the United States has resulted in a shortage of hospital nurses. As a result, employers see foreign-born nurses as the best solution and this has been supported by congressional legislation. Filipino nurses are attracted to the United States because of liberal policies that eventually allow them to stay permanently. Most foreign-trained nurses are brought to work initially on a temporary basis, but the passage of the Immigration Nursing Relief Act of 1989 allows nurses to adjust to permanent status after three years of service.[60]

---

[60] Paul Ong and Tania Azores, "The Migration and Incorporation of Filipino Nurses," in Ong et al. (eds.), *The New Asian Immigration in Los Angeles and Global Restructuring*, pp. 166–195; Mangiafico, *Contemporary American Immigrants*, pp. 42–43; Leon Bouvier and Rosemary Jenks, "Doctors and nurses: a demographie profile" at: http://www.cis.org/article/ 1998/ DocsandNurses.html.; and Judith A. Berg, Daisy Rodriguez Valerie Kading, and Carolina De Guzman. "Demographic Study of Filipino American Nurses," *Nursing Administration Quarterly* 29:3 (July-Sept., 2004): 199–207.

According to Christine Ceniza Choy (2004), the Filipino nurse migration to the United States is not a new phenomenon. Its roots lie in early twentieth-century U.S. colonialism and the "Americanized training hospital system" in the Philippines. Additionally, Choy argues that Filipino migration abroad cannot be reduced to an economic logic; rather, it must be understood as part of a larger transnational process "involving the flow of people, goods, services, images, and ideas across national borders."[61] This analysis further challenges the general explanations for the origins of migration found in the push-pull theory described earlier. Global economic restructuring is an important context for understanding not only why Asian immigrants have come to the United States but also how well they have adjusted and been accepted socially, economically, and politically. However, it should be noted that not all Asian immigrants are middle-class and successful professionals; a sizable number of other Asian immigrants, especially refugees, have also found their lives in America extremely difficult. The extreme diversity among Asian Americans is due in large part to the third major event affecting migration from Asia—the Vietnam War.

The Vietnam War and Southeast Asian Refugees

Since 1975 large numbers of Southeast Asian refugees have entered the United States, and today California is the home for most of them (see Table 3.4). Roughly two-thirds of all Southeast Asian refugees are from Vietnam, with the rest from Laos and Cambodia. Unlike most other post-1965 Asian immigrants who came to the United States in a rather orderly fashion seeking family reunification and economic opportunities, Southeast Asian refugees arrived as part of an international resettlement effort of people who faced genuine political persecution and bodily harm in their home countries. Southeast Asian refugees to the United States can be easily divided into three distinct waves: the first arrived in the United States in 1975 shortly after the fall of Saigon; the second arrived between 1978 and 1980; and the third entered the United States after 1980 and continues to this day. The United States has accepted these refugees not only for humanitarian reasons but also in recognition that U.S. foreign policy and military actions in Southeast Asia had a hand in creating much of the calamity that has befallen the entire region.

U.S. political interests in Southeast Asia actually began during World War II, although for years efforts were limited to foreign aid and military advisers. Direct military intervention rapidly escalated in 1965 when President Lyndon B. Johnson stepped up bombing raids in Southeast Asia and authorized the use of the first U.S. combat troops in order to contain increasing communist insurgency. The undeclared war continued until U.S. troops withdrew in 1973 at the cost of 57,000 American and 1 million Vietnamese lives. The conflict also caused great environmental destruction throughout Southeast Asia and created tremendous domestic antiwar protests in the United States.[62]

As soon as the U.S. troops left, however, communist forces in Vietnam regrouped and quickly began sweeping across the countryside. By March 1975 it was clear that the capital of South Vietnam, Saigon, would soon fall to communist forces. As a result, President Gerald Ford autho-

---

[61] Catherine Ceniza Choy, *Empire of Care: Nursing and Migration in Filipino American History* (Durham and London: Duke University Press, 2003), pp. 7, 11.

[62] Literature on the Vietnam conflict is voluminous. For an excellent and readable overview, see Stanley Karnow, *Vietnam: A History* (New York: Penguin, 1991).

Table 3.4   States with the Largest Southeast Asian Populations, 2010*

State	Vietnamese	Cambodian	Laotian	Hmong	Total
California	647,589	102,317	69,303	91,224	910,433
Texas	227,968	14,347	15,784	920	259,019
Minnesota	27,086	9,543	12,009	66,181	114,819
Washington	75,843	22,934	11,568	2,404	112,749
Massachusetts	47,636	28,424	4,530	1,080	81,670
Florida	65,772	6,267	6,152	1,208	79,399
Virginia	59,984	7,306	3,980	188	71,458
Georgia	49,264	5,423	6,638	3,623	64,948
Pennsylvania	44,605	14,118	3,280	1,021	63,024
Wisconsin	6,191	1,294	4,562	49,240	61,287

*Asian detailed group alone or in any combination.

Source: Southeast Asian Action Resource Center (SEARC), "Southeast Asians at a Glance," p. 5 at: http://www.searac.org/sites/default/files/STATISTICAL%20PROFILE%202010.Final_.20111006-1_0.pdf

rized the attorney general to admit 130,000 refugees into the United States.[63] In the last chaotic days prior to the fall of Saigon on April 30, 1975, "high-risk" individuals in Vietnam, namely high-ranking government and military personnel, were hurriedly airlifted away to safety at temporary receiving centers in Guam, Thailand, and the Philippines. This group marked the first wave of Southeast Asian refugees, who would eventually resettle in the United States. The first wave is distinct in that they were generally the educated urban elite and middle class from Vietnam. Because many of them had worked closely with the U.S. military, they tended to be more westernized (40 percent were Catholics), and a good portion of them were able to speak English (30 percent spoke English well). Another significant feature is the fact that roughly 95 percent of the first wave of Southeast Asian refugees was Vietnamese, even though the capitals of Laos and Cambodia also fell to communist forces in 1975.[64]

Once these first-wave refugees came to the United States, they were flown to one of four military base/reception centers in California, Arkansas, Pennsylvania, and Florida. From these bases they registered with a voluntary agency that would eventually help resettle them with a sponsor. About 60 percent of the sponsors were families, while the other 40 percent were usually churches and individuals. Sponsors were responsible for day-to-day needs of the refugees until they were able to find jobs and become independent. The resettlement of the first wave of refugees was

---

[63] The quota for refugees under the 1965 Immigration Reform Act was only 17,400, so President Gerald Ford instructed the attorney general to use his "parole" power to admit the 130,000 refugees. The use of parole power was also used to bring European refugees to the United States during the 1950s. For more detail, see Hing, *Making and Remaking Asian America*, pp. 123–128; and Paul J. Strand and Woodrow Jones, Jr., *Indochinese Refugees in America: Problems of Adaptation and Assimilation* (Durham, NC: Duke University Press, 1985).

[64] Chan, *Asian Californians*, p. 128; and Chor-Swan Ngin, "The Acculturation Pattern of Orange County's Southeast Asian Refugees," *Journal of Orange County Studies* 3:4 (Fall 1989—Spring 1990): 46–53.

funded by the 1975 Indochinese Resettlement Assistance Act and was seen as a quick and temporary process. Indeed, all the reception centers closed by the end of 1975, and the Resettlement Act expired in 1977.

The second wave of Southeast Asian refugees was larger, more heterogeneous, and many believe even more devastated by their relocation experience than the first wave. The second wave of refugees were generally less educated, urbanized, and westernized (only 7 percent spoke English and only about 7 percent were Catholic) compared to their predecessors; at the same time they were much more ethnically diverse than the first wave. According to statistics, between 1978 and 1980, about 55.5 percent of Southeast Asian refugees were from Vietnam (including many ethnic Chinese), 36.6 percent from Laos, and 7.8 percent from Cambodia. The second wave consisted of people who suffered under the communist regimes and were unable to leave their countries immediately before or after the new governments took power.[65]

In Vietnam, the ethnic Chinese merchant class was very much the target of resentment by the new communist government. Many of the Chinese businesses in Vietnam were nationalized, Chinese language schools and newspapers were closed, education and employment rights were denied, and food rations were reduced. Under these conditions, about 250,000 escaped North Vietnam, seeking refuge in China. Roughly 70 percent of the estimated 500,000 boat people who tried to escape Vietnam by sea were ethnic Chinese. The treacherous journey usually took place on ill-equipped crowded boats that were unable to withstand the rigors of the ocean or outrun marauding Thai pirates. The U.S. Committee for Refugees estimates at least 100,000 people lost their lives trying to escape Vietnam by boat.[66] Along with the Chinese, others in Vietnam, particularly those who had supported the U.S.-backed South Vietnamese government and their families, were also subject to especially harsh treatment by the new communist leadership. Many were sent to "reeducation camps" and banished to work in rural regions clearing land devastated by 30 years of war.

The holocaust in Cambodia began immediately after the Khmer Rouge (Red Khmer) marched into the capital city of Phnom Penh on April 17, 1975. That same day the entire population of the capital was ordered to the countryside. After three years it has been broadly estimated between 1 and 3 million Cambodians died from starvation, disease, and execution out of a population of less than 7 million. In 1978 Vietnam (with support from the Soviet Union) invaded Cambodia, drove the Khmer Rouge out of power, and established a new government under its own control. Famine and warfare continued under Vietnamese occupation, and by 1979 over 600,000 refugees from Cambodia fled the country, mostly to neighboring Thailand. In Laos, the transition from one government to another was initially rather smooth compared to Vietnam following the fall of Saigon. After over a decade of civil war, a coalition government was formed in April 1974 that included Laotian communists, the Pathet Lao. But shortly after communists took power in Vietnam and Cambodia, the Pathet Lao moved to solidify its full control of the country. It was at this time that troops from both Laos and Vietnam began a military campaign against the Hmong

---

[65] Ngin, "The Acculturation Pattern of Orange County's Southeast Asian Refugees," p. 49; and Ngoan Le, "The Case of the Southeast Asian Refugees: Policy for a Community 'At-Risk,'" in *The State of Asian Pacific America: Policy Issues to the Year 2020* (Los Angeles: LEAP Asian Pacific American Public Policy Institute and UCLA Asian American Studies Center, 1993), pp. 167–188.

[66] For more details, see Strand and Jones, *Indochinese Refugees in America*; Barry L. Wain, *The Refused: The Agony of Indochina Refugees* (New York: Simon & Schuster, 1981); and U.S. Committee for Refugees, *Uncertain Harbors: The Plight of Vietnamese Boat People* (Washington, DC: U.S. Government Printing Office, 1987).

hill people, an ethnic minority group that lived in the mountains of Laos who were recruited by the U.S. government to fight against communist forces in the region. The Hmong were seen as traitors to the communist revolution, and massive bombing raids were ordered against them that included the dropping of napalm and poisonous chemicals. Thousands of Hmong were killed in these fierce assaults, and those who remained had little choice but to seek refuge in neighboring Thailand. The Hmong were not the only people in Laos who were persecuted. By 1979 roughly 3,000 Hmong were entering Thailand every month, and as late as 1983 an estimated 75 percent of the 76,000 Laotians in Thai refugee camps were Hmong people.[67]

The world could not ignore this massive outpouring of refugees from Southeast Asia, and in 1979 President Jimmy Carter allowed 14,000 refugees a month to enter the United States. In addition, Congress passed the Refugee Act of 1980, which set an annual quota of 50,000 refugees per year, funded resettlement programs, and allowed refugees to become eligible for the same welfare benefits as U.S. citizens after 36 months of refugee assistance (this was changed to 18 months in 1982).

Many of the Southeast Asians who came in the third wave are technically not considered refugees, but are in actuality immigrants. This has been facilitated by the 1980 Orderly Departure Program (ODP), an agreement with Vietnam that allows individuals and families to enter the United States. ODP was a benefit for three groups: relatives of permanently settled refugees in the United States, Amerasians, and former reeducation camp internees. By the end of 1992, over 300,000 Vietnamese immigrated to the United States, including 80,000 Amerasians and their relatives, as well as 60,000 former camp internees and their families.[68]

Although most Southeast Asian Americans live in California, many are surprised to see how widely dispersed this population is. For example, the population of Hmong Americans living in Minnesota (66,181) and Wisconsin (49,204) together is larger than the number of Hmong Americans in California (91,224). Next to California, the largest number of Cambodians can be found in Massachusetts. Over 30,000 Vietnamese American lived in Louisiana, 7,700 lived in Mississippi, and 8,400 lived in Alabama after the devastation wrought from Hurricane Katrina in 2005. Many former refugee Vietnamese Americans were forced to become refugees once again as they were displaced and relocated following the massive storm and flood damage to their homes and businesses. The media coverage focused overwhelmingly on the black and white victims of the hurricane, and so Vietnamese American communities throughout the U.S. took it upon themselves to raised money, to send supplies, and to offer homes to other Vietnamese Americans in the Deep South. Many Vietnamese Americans have resettled in places like Houston, Texas, as well as San Jose and Orange County in California that already had large Vietnamese American communities.[69]

---

[67] Chan, *Asian Californians*, pp. 121–138; Kitano and Daniels, *Asian Americans: Emerging Minorities,* pp. 170–191; U.S. Committee for Refugees, *Cambodians in Thailand: People on the Edge* (Washington, DC: U.S. Government Printing Office, 1985); and U.S. Committee for Refugees, *Refugees from Laos: In Harm's Way* (Washington, DC: U.S. Government Printing Office, 1986).

[68] U.S. Committee for Refugees, *Uncertain Harbors*, pp. 19–20; and Ruben Rumbaut, "Vietnamese, Laotian, and Cambodian Americans," in Pyong Gap Min (ed.), *Asian Americans: Contemporary Trends and Issues* (Thousand Oaks, CA: Sage, 1995), · p. 240.

[69] Zen T.C. Zheng, "Mall First Stop for Evacuees; Many Finding Food, Clothing, Guidance, and Care," *Houston Chronicle,* September 8, 2005; Mai Tran and Claire Luna, "Katrina's Aftermath: Vietnamese in O.C. Fear for Gulf Relatives," *Los Angeles Times,* September 3, 2003; and Vanessa Hua, "Coats Being Collected for Hurricane Victims," *San Francisco Chronicle,* October 8, 2005.

Conclusion

This chapter briefly describes the history and recent growth of the Asian population in the United States. Historians as well as legal scholars such as Bill Ong Hing (1993 and 2004), Angelo N. Ancheta (1998), and John S.W. Park (2005) have also examined Asian American experience and have shown the tremendous legal barriers faced by Asian Americans in the United States.[70] The notion of Asian Americans as the "perpetual foreigner" has had a distinctive impact on their experiences with discrimination and violation of civil rights at the hands of the legal system. At the same time, this chapter also highlights the significance of the 1965 Immigration Reform Act, global economic restructuring, and the Vietnam War as three broad events that profoundly impacted both the number and type of migrants who have come to the United States from Asian countries. In order to examine post-1965 Asian Americans comprehensively, it is particularly important to look at the rapid growth of the population, personal history, nativity, length of time in the United States, pre-migration experiences and traumas, education, socioeconomic class background, and gender. Chapter 2 details the social and economic diversity of immigrant and American-born Asians, as well as their settlement patterns and impact on various communities across the United States.

---

[70] Bill Ong Hing, *Making and Remaking Asian America Through Immigration Policy, 1850–1990* (Stanford, CA: Stanford University Press, 1993), Bill Ong Hing, *Defining America Through Immigration Policy* (Philadelphia: Temple University Press, 2004), Angelo N. Ancheta, *Race, Rights, and the Asian American Experience* (New Brunswick: Rutgers University Press, 1998), and John S. W. Park. *Elusive Citizenship: Immigration. Asian Americans and the Paradox of Civil Rights* (New York: NYU Press, 2004).

South Asian Americans

Bandana Purkayastha and Ranita Ray

C
H
A
P
T
E
R

4

South Asian Americans are primarily people whose roots are in five "main" countries: India, Pakistan, Bangladesh, Sri Lanka, and Nepal. Nepalese and the other two South Asian ethnic groups, Bhutanese and Maldivians, together number less than 10,000,[1] and so data on these groups is often difficult to obtain. Asian Indians are by far the largest South Asian group, ranking third in size of all the Asian American groups after Chinese and Filipinos. Asian Indians are also the fastest growing Asian ethnic group, which may partly explain why the general perception of South Asians is usually dominated by the characteristics and cultural symbols of Asian Indians.

The category "South Asian," which indicates a very diverse group of people from five countries, is a U.S. invention. The South Asian American ethnic category has been created by a combination of U.S. government classification policies, formal political classifications, and ideological representations to "lump" people together. The term "Asian American" itself is an umbrella category, initially proposed by activists in the 1960s who sought an alternative to the more commonly used term Oriental. Today, Asian American is the accepted term, especially in government and academic research.[2] As people of South Asian origin lobbied to be included in the Asian American census category in the late 1970s, and subsequently joined Asian American organizations, they found that they did not easily fit the Asian American category for political and cultural reasons and because people equated Asian Americans with East Asian phenotypes. Even today, not all South Asian Americans agree with the label because they see themselves differing along religious affiliations, customs, practices, languages, and class locations. Some South Asians have come together, however, to form all kinds of organizations. For instance, since the 1980s, domestic violence organizations such as Sakhi and Manavi have been organizing as South Asian American organizations, bringing together people of different nationalities to recognize some of their commonalties. Second-generation South Asians may be more likely to embrace the label; they come together as they create a common ethnic lifestyle—by consuming fashions, music, arts, movies—in the U.S. They also form groups and organizations that are based on multinational, multiethnic ties.

---

[1] South Asian American Policy and Research Institute, "Making Data Count: South Asian Americans in the 2000 Census with Focus on Illinois," http://saapri.org/pdfs/Web-Document5.pdf.

[2] K. Connie Kang, "Yuji Ichioka, 66; Led Way in Studying Lives of Asian Americans," *Los Angeles Times*, Sept. 7, 2002. http://articles.latimes.com/2002/sep/07/local/me-yuji7.

Immigration Policies

In the late 1800s, the first major South Asian group in the U.S. were Indians, mostly Sikh farmers and laborers from the Punjab region of British-controlled India. This primarily male population was recruited to fulfill the cheap labor needs of the rail, agricultural, and lumber industries in California, Oregon, and Washington. Their presence was tied to the continual need for cheap labor after the Chinese exclusion law that was passed in 1882. Fears about the "tide of turbans" on the West Coast led to a backlash against these Indian immigrants, similar to that faced by their Chinese and Japanese predecessors.[3] A series of laws curbed their chances of engaging in a variety of occupations. By 1917 an Asian migration ban was passed to stop all Asians, from any part of the world, from migrating to the United States, and Indians were included in the Asian category. In addition, the restrictions on citizenship and associated rights, such as being able to own property, eroded the opportunities of these early groups. The race-based ban on migration and the restrictions on female—especially Asian female—migration, coupled with the strict antimiscegenation laws in place locally, meant that there was little opportunity to form normal families or communities in the United States. Thus, the population of Indian migrants dwindled away; a few men were able to marry Mexican women and forged new ethnic communities such as the Punjabi-Mexicans.[4]

These restrictions lasted till 1965. After the Civil Rights movement, most overtly race-based laws were scrutinized and the immigration laws were rewritten. The ban on Asian migration was rescinded, and the new immigration laws gave preferences to highly skilled professionals—doctors, scientists, engineers. Secondly, the "family reunification immigration quota" allowed these migrants to sponsor the migration of their families to the United States over several years. The immigrant visas led to the arrival of a highly educated group of mostly male migrants from India, and a smaller number from Pakistan—which included the contemporary Bangladesh till 1971—between 1965 and the mid-1980s. South Asian women and their children arrived primarily because of the family reunification category. The quotas set for each country determine how many migrants and family members can come each year.

In the beginning, after the amendment of the Immigration Act of 1990, Nepalis, and Bangladeshis benefited from diversity visas, which were offered to countries that were underrepresented or had a low rate of immigration to the United States. Along with these routes for economic migrants (and family reunification), some Sri Lankans have been able to migrate as refugees, after the prolonged civil conflict in their country since 1983. Like other refugees, their numbers are controlled by the U.S. classification of who is a refugee.

Since the mid-1980s, new sets of immigration restrictions have begun to control legal migration. The full incorporation of spouses has been delayed because of the long delays to get spousal visas and the need for the married partners to prove to the Citizenship and Immigration Service (CIS), two years after migration, that they are still married in order to get the full legal right to stay in the United States. In addition, the rapid growth of guest-worker status for highly skilled professionals—visas that allow economic opportunities to work for short periods of time but do not allow social benefits or political rights—has begun to negatively affect migration from South Asia. Although the numbers of South Asians grew from 36,100 between 1960 and 1970, to more

---

[3] The ways in which people of South Asian origin have been organizing to become "a group" is discussed in detail in Bandana Purkayastha. *Negotiating Ethnicity* (New Brunswick, NJ: Rutgers University Press, 2005).

[4] Until 1947, Indians refers to the contemporary Indians, Pakistanis, and Bangladeshis.

than 2 million by 2000 according to the Census Bureau, as we describe later, the picture varies by nationality and gender.

While migration trends are mostly described in "gender-neutral" terms, the experience of female South Asian American migration to the United States encapsulates how immigration laws favors men. Even though females may be highly educated and dominate the fields of management, professional, sales and office-related occupations. Their credentials are rarely classified as "highly skilled," a term reserved for the hard sciences, medicine, and technology skills, which have been male-dominated fields. Thus highly educated males have greater opportunity to migrate as highly skilled workers, while females have to come as spouses and prove their marriages after two years in order to get legal permission to work.[5]

While migration from all five countries has steadily increased, in terms of absolute numbers, India holds the dominant position. For instance, according to the Statistical Abstract of the United States, in 2004, 70,100 Indians, 12,100 Pakistani and 8,100 Bangladeshi arrived in the United States. Sri Lanka and Nepal were not listed separately; however, the immigration statistics yearbook shows that in 2006, 2,192 refugees arrived from Sri Lanka.

Current Status of South Asian Americans

Indian Americans

Asian Indians recorded a growth rate of 106 percent between 1990 and 2000, highest among all of the Asian American ethnic groups. Currently, most Indian American migrants are economic or family-reunification migrants, most arriving after the Civil Rights movement that opened up many opportunities for work and residence for nonwhites. A significant portion of Indian Americans settled in the suburbs and about 80 percent of those in the labor force are in white-collar professions. There are few "ethnic ghettos" for Indians, though Jackson Heights in Queens, New York, and New Jersey have concentration of ethnic businesses that point to commercial ethnic enclaves.[6] There is a distinct group of less affluent Indians—for instance, the Indian taxi drivers or the Indian gas station attendants in New York City.[7] They also have a high prevalence in the motel industry. Overall, Indians have consistently ranked among the top ethnic groups in terms of education and earnings since the 1960s. According to the latest census. Indian median household income stands at $80,759 compared with $53,000 for the white American population, and the average education of Indian women and men is consistently higher than that of whites, who are generally considered to be the standard for such comparisons.[8] (Table 4.1)

Indians are multilingual, and they follow multiple cultures and religions. Most are Hindus; Muslims and Sikhs, along with Christians and Jains, are among the other religious groups represented among Indians.

---

[5] Vijay Prashad, *The Karma of Brown Folk* (Minneapolis: University of Minnesota Press, 2000).

[6] Bandana Purkayastha. "Skilled Migration and Cumulative Disadvantage: The Case of Highly Qualified Asian Indian Immigrant Women in the U.S.," *Geoforum*, 36 (2004): 181–196.

[7] Madhulika Khandelwal, *Becoming Indian, Becoming American: An Immigrant Community in New York City* (Ithaca, NY: Cornell University Press, 2002).

[8] Diditi Mitra, "Driving Taxis in New York City: Who Wants to Do It?" *Working USA* 7, no. 2 (2003): 76–99.

TABLE 4.1 Indian Americans at a Glance	
Population	2,449,173
Median age	32.1
Education:	
Less than high school	9.8
College and above	67.9
Average household size	3.05
In labor force	68.5%
Median household income	$80,759
Per capita income	$35,385
Poverty:	
Overall	8.3%
Child	7.2%
Senior	8.5%
Foreign-born	1,803,617
Speaks English less than "very well"	22.8%

Source: 2005–2007 American Community Survey 3-Year Estimates,
U.S. Census Bureau.

Pakistani Americans

Migration from Pakistan follows a pattern similar to India, though the numbers have been substantially smaller. By 2007, the Census Bureau indicated that there were about 193,893 Pakistani Americans in the United States. Like the Indians, with fewer language barriers—English is widely spoken among professionals—and high educational credentials, Pakistani Americans are well-represented in the fields of medicine, engineering, finance, and information technology. Like Indian Americans, most live in suburbs and are, consequently, geographically dispersed. Most Pakistani Americans are Sunni Muslims, although Shias are represented, too (Table 4.2).

Bangladeshi, Sri Lankan, and Nepali Americans

Migrants from Bangladesh, Nepal, and Sri Lanka show a slightly different trajectory of migration because more people from these countries arrived after 1980. Bangladesh was officially a part of Pakistan until 1971, so Bangladeshi migration, as we understand the term now, could not begin until the 1970s. The first wave of immigrants was generally composed of professionals, well-educated and affluent. In 1973, 154 Bangladeshi immigrants arrived in the United States, and in 2007, there were 62,057 Bangladeshis Americans. Bangladeshis, like Nepalese, have also benefited from "diversity" visas. They are concentrated in metropolitan New York area; other large

TABLE 4.2 Pakistani Americans at a Glance	
Population	193,893
Median age	29.6
Education:	
Less than high school	13.9%
College and above	54.6%
Average household size	3.73
In the labor force	62.1%
Median household income	$57,502
Per capita income	$23,387
Poverty:	
Overall	15.9%
Child	19.2%
Senior	8.5%
Foreign-born	137,146
Speaks English less than "very well"	29.0%

Source: 2005–2007 American Community Survey 3-Year Estimates,
U.S. Census Bureau.

enclaves of Bangladeshis can be found in Los Angeles, Miami, Washington, DC, and Atlanta. Bangladeshi Americans formed Bengali civic organizations and clubs in the locales where they settled. Bangladeshis are overwhelmingly Muslim, though their strong affiliations with the culture and language have led them to form ethnic and religious communities that are distinctive from other groups. Bangladeshis have often rejuvenated older Indian commercial enclaves, their stores and restaurants marked distinctively with Bengali signs.[9] Almost 50 percent of Bangladeshis speak English less than well, markedly different from their Indian, Pakistani, and Sri Lankan counterparts in which the great majority speak English well.

Unlike India, Pakistan, Bangladesh, and Sri Lanka, the official policies of Nepal discouraged migration until the 1970s. Between 1970 and 1989, there were 1,229 Nepalis admitted to the United States.[10] The CIS Yearbook shows a gradual increase in the number of Nepalis admitted per year, ranging from 212 in 1992 to 1,138 in 2002.[11] Like the other four groups, some Nepali students who

---

[9] U.S. Bureau of Census, http://factfinder.census.gov.

[10] Nazli Kibria, *Muslims in Diaspora: Bangladeshis at Home and Abroad* (New Brunswick, NJ: Rutgers University Press, forthcoming); Nazli Kibria. "South Asian Americans" in *Asian Americans: Contemporary Trends and Issues*, ed. Pyong Gap Min (Beverly Hills, CA: SAGE Publications, 2005), 206–227.

[11] P. Upadhyay. "The social assimilation of Nepali immigrants in the United States and the role of English language training in the Process" (Unpublished PhD dissertation, University of Connecticut, Storrs, CT, 1991).

TABLE 4.3 Bangladeshi Americans at a Glance	
Population	62,057
Median age	31.8
Education:	
Less than high school	16.2%
College degree or higher	47.0%
Average household size	3.67
In the labor force	65.5%
Median household income	$41,897
Per capita income	$16,250
Poverty:	
Overall	24.0%
Child	31.0%
Senior	18.2%
Foreign-born	47,169
Speaks English less than "very well"	46.4%

Source: 2005–2007 American Community Survey 3-Year Estimates,
U.S. Census Bureau.

came to the United States for higher education were able to change their student status to work-related visas. Nepalis are scattered in larger cities around the United States, and local informal and a formal national organization of Nepali Americans keep group networks alive.[12] Nepali Americans are primarily Hindu.

The earliest Sri Lankans to enter the United States were classified as "other Asian." In 1975, 432 Sri Lankans immigrated to the United States. The ongoing civil war between the Sri Lankan government and armed Tamil separatists, which began in the early 1980s, has led to several hundred thousand Tamil civilians fleeing Sri Lanka. Many sought political asylum in the West. According to 2007 U.S. Census data, there were 30.323 Americans with Sri Lankan ancestry. Many Sri Lankans have settled in large metropolitan areas such as Chicago, Los Angeles, New York, Newark, and Miami, which already have Sri Lankan and Indian communities. Sri Lankan Americans practice mostly Hinduism and Buddhism. Their levels of education—92 percent Sri Lankans have high school or higher vs. 86.5 percent whites, while 29.8 percent Sri Lankans have graduate or professional degrees compared to 10.5 percent whites—and median household incomes—$61,793 compared to $53,000—are higher than that of whites.

---

[12] CIS Yearbook, Table 3 (2003).

TABLE 4.4 Sri Lankan Americans at a Glance	
Population	30,323
Median age	36.7
Education:	
Less than high school	8.1%
College degree or higher	56.5%
Average household size	2.80
In the labor force	68.4%
Median household income	$61,793
Per capita income	$33,621
Poverty:	
Overall	11.0%
Child	10.4%
Senior	4.7%
Foreign-born	25,297
Speaks English less than "very well"	21.3%

Source: 2005–2007 American Community Survey 3-Year Estimates, U.S. Census Bureau.

Key Issues

Religion and Culture

While most non-South Asians are unable to tell South Asian Americans of different origins and cultures apart, the "South Asian-American" label is an amalgam of groups with diverse histories. At the same time, because of the relatively large proportion of Indian migrants (relative to other South Asian Americans), the public face of "South Asian American" often reflects Indian characteristics. Thus, certain religions and cultural rites and rituals are more recognized than others. Shared cultural festivals such as the worship of the Goddess Durga is recognized as an Indian event, while the Nepali celebration, Dashain, which also focuses on the same Hindu goddess, is rarely recognized by other South Asian Americans.[13] Shared "home-country" cultural icons—for instance, Rabindranath Tagore—is more identified with Indians in the United States, even though he is revered by Bengali Indians and Bangladeshi Bengalis and is the author of the national anthems of India *and* Bangladesh. Pakistani Americans, who often share the sociodemographic characteristics of Indian Americans, are only seen as a separate entity in matters of religion. Their highly educated character is less recognized than that of Indian Americans.

---

[13] Bidya Ranjeet and Bandana Purkayastha, "A Minority Within a Minority," in *Body Evidence: Intimate Violence Against South Asian Women in America*, ed. Shamita Das Dasgupta (New Brunswick, NJ: Rutgers University Press, 2007).

All South Asians have to contend with finding a religious space in multicultural, but Christian-dominant, America. Since Hinduism and Islam are not Congregationalist religions, significant transformations of these religions and religious communities are taking place in order to fit in with U.S. laws, most of which were based on the Christian experience. For instance, Hindu temples have to identify members in order to meet the legal designation of not-for-profit entities. Sikh men's ability to carry the five symbols of their faith—which includes a symbolic ceremonial dagger and keeping long hair covered with turbans—has been a very contentious issue in schools and travel sites. Muslim Americans have to increasingly contend with a post-9/11 climate where many people fear Muslims. Post–immigrant–generation Hindus, Muslims, and Sikhs find themselves marginalized as schools recognize Christian holidays but little else.[14]

Like the different linguistic groups, a great deal of religious diversity exists within South Asian America.[15] Hinduism itself is extremely diverse, and while a huge number of temples have been, and are being, built across the United States, none of these temples are ever able to accommodate the cultural practices of more than a few major groups. Nonetheless, there is a move to try and homogenize some central practices of Hinduism, through these temples, so that temples become de facto community centers as well.

Muslim South Asian Americans face a different challenge of finding or creating a niche for themselves in mosques.[16] Because the cultures of Arab American, non-Arab American Muslims, and South Asian American Muslims are very diverse, Pakistani, Bangladeshi, Indian, and other South Asian American Muslims have to work out cultural similarities in order to come together as South Asian American Muslims.

Sikh Americans, who have been present in the United States since the 19th century, have, over time, developed separate identities, that are often based on their religion rather than their ancestral roots.[17] A large number of gurudwaras, which work as community gathering places as well, testify to Sikh presence in America, and also depict the diversity within Sikhism. In the aftermath of 9/11, when Sikhs were attacked because they appeared to resemble the turban-wearing terrorists featured constantly on the media, Sikh Americans have been very active in educating Americans about their religion and challenging the erosion of their civil liberties, separately from Indian Americans. The Sikh American experience clearly depicts how groups might need to keep religion as their main identity marker, especially if they are discriminated against on the basis of their religious symbolism.

Second-generation South Asians struggle to create their place on college campuses through student organizations, in which notions of religion and ethnicity sometimes are conflated. On college campuses, the presence of "Indian student associations" and "Pakistani student associations" leads to a bifurcation of interests, all Muslim issues are assumed to be the purview of

---

[14] Anjana Narayan and Bandana Purkayastha, *Living Our Religions: Hindu and Muslim South Asian American Women Narrate Their Experiences* (Sterling, VA: Kumarian Books, 2008).

[15] Khyati Joshi, *New Roots in America's Sacred Ground: Religion, Race and Ethnicity in Indian America* (New Brunswick, NJ: Rutgers University Press, 2006); Prema Kurien, "Multiculturalism and 'American' Religion: The Case of Hindu Indian Americans," *Social Forces* 85, no. 2 (2006): 723–741; Anjana Narayan and Bandana Purkayastha, *Living Our Religions: Hindu and Muslim South Asian American Women Narrate Their Experiences*, (Sterling, VA: Kumarian Books, 2008).

[16] Anjana Narayan and Bandana Purkayastha, *Living Our Religions: Hindu and Muslim South Asian American Women Narrate their Experiences* (Sterling, MD: Kumarian Press. 2008).

[17] Nazli Kibria, *Muslims in Diaspora: Bangladeshis at Home and Abroad* (New Brunswick, NJ: Rutgers University Press, forthcoming).

[18] Darshan Singh Tatla. *The Sikh Diaspora: The Search for Statehood* (Seattle: University of Washington Press, 1999).

PSAs, while ISAs become increasingly Hindu-culture focused. Bangladeshi, Sri Lankan, Nepali Americans are particularly affected, as are other South Asians, who are not Hindu or Muslim, or those who do not believe in the type of Hinduism projected in these groups find themselves marginalized. Since the late 1990s and 2000s, more *South Asian* student organizations are cropping up in colleges: however, given the very great diversity of cultures among each of the five groups—based on language, religion, histories, practices—there is ongoing dissent about whose culture counts as South Asian. A new "desi culture" has been growing, as members of the post—immigrant—generation try to find commonalties among themselves.[19]

Discrimination and Racial Profiling

Since 9/11, South Asians have often been confused with Middle Easterners and subject to stereotyping, discrimination, and racial profiling. They face discrimination in terms of airport security policies and often have to go through "random" security checks. With the increasing blurring of "national security" and policing services, there are newfound fears about "foreigners," especially those who look Muslim. In 2006 at a campaign event, Senator Conrad Burns of Montana discussed the threat of terrorism, declaring that the United States confronted a "faceless enemy" of terrorists who "drive cabs in the daytime and kill at night." Pakistani and Bangladeshi Americans, who, according to country-of-origin histories, do not belong to one group, now find their master status as Muslims forces them and their children to contend with the common forms of discrimination directed toward them as they work and/or travel. In addition, South Asian Americans of all cultural backgrounds encounter a renewed marking of their appearance. In 2006, Senator George Allen of Virginia referred to a young Indian American, who was working for his opponent's campaign, as macaca (which is a pejorative epithet used by francophone colonialists in Central Africa's Belgian Congo for the native population). The press picked up on this comment, and there were many discussions about whether it was racist. Less noticed was the other part of Allen's comment. Addressing Sidarth, Allen said, "Welcome to America," thus casting the American-born campaign worker, solely on the basis of his appearance, as a foreigner.[20] There is a long history of various groups of Asian Americans being dubbed as foreigners in the United States, and this incident was a reminder to the larger group of yet another incidence of racism. New groups are being formed and South Asian Americans are working together with organizations such as ACLU to combat racism.

Creating a South Asian American Identity

The number of Indian Americans and their financial influence drives statistics about the aggregated category South Asian American. In fact, it is often difficult to find detailed data on Bangladeshi, Nepali, and Sri Lankan migrants from official sources such as the census. When popular magazines such as *Newsweek* feature the power and influence of South Asian Americans, the overwhelming majority are South Asian Americans of Indian origin.[21]

---

[19] Bandana Purkayastha, *Negotiating Ethnicity: Second-Generation South Asian Americans Traverse a Transnational World* (New Brunswick, NJ: Rutgers University Press, 2005).

[20] Purkayastha, *Negotiating Ethnicity: Second-Generation South Asian Americans Traverse a Transnational World*: Sunaina Maira *Desis in the House: Indian American Youth Culture in New York City* (Philadelphia: Temple University Press, 2002).

[21] Tim Craig and Michael Shear, "Allen Quip Provokes Outrage, Apology," *Washington Post*, Aug. 15, 2006; Page A01.

Notable South Asian Americans

Amar Bose—Indian American billionaire, founder of Bose Corporation, revolutionized the technology of speakers and acoustics.

Gayatri Chakravorty Spivak—Indian American university professor at Columbia University; a foundational theorist of post-colonial studies.

Sanjay Gupta—Indian American physician (neurosurgeon) and media commentator on health issues at CNN, CBS, and *Time* magazine.

Fred Hassan—Pakistani-American, CEO at Schering Plough.

DeLon Jayasinghe—Sinhalese (Sri Lankan) American hip-hop artist.

Jawed Karim—Bangladeshi American co-founder of YouTube and lead technical architect of PayPal.

Neal Katyal—Indian American professor of law at Georgetown University Law School and lead counsel in the landmark Supreme Court case *Hamdan v. Rumsfeld*.

Jhumpa Lahiri—Indian American author whose books include *The Namesake*, and the Pulitzer Prize-winning short stories collection, *Interpreter of Maladies*.

Mira Nair—Indian American filmmaker, her recent films include *The Namesake* and *Mississippi Masala*.

Indra Nooyi—Indian American CEO of Pepsi, one of eleven women in the world to hold a CEO position in a Fortune 500 company.

Bidya Ranjeet—Nepali American academic administrator; founding member and past president of Nepali Women's Global Network and member of the Nepali American Council.

Asif Saleh—Bangladeshi American Wall Street executive, who is better known for launching Dristipath, the blog that has become a leading tool of transnational human rights activism.

Amartya Sen—Indian American, with roots in Bangladesh, who is a Nobel laureate in economics, currently at Harvard University; noted for his work on wide-ranging social justice issues.

Shaziya Sikandar—Pakistani American artist and 2006 recipient of the MacArthur Fellow genius award.

Sunita Williams—Indian American NASA astronaut; second woman of Indian descent to head into space after astronaut Kalpana Chawla was killed in the Challenger disaster.

Fareed Zakaria—Indian American, editor of *Newsweek* and host of Fareed Zakaria GPS on CNN.

Politics has, on occasion, brought some South Asian Americans together. South Asian Americans mostly vote Democrat,[22] though some prominent South Asian Americans—Governor Bobby Jindal of Louisiana and the conservative pundit Dinesh D'Souza—are Republicans. Many South Asian Americans—women and men—run for local office and intern with senators and congressmen, according to reports in ethnic papers such as *News India Times*, *India Today*, and *Times of India*. The multiple Asian American coalitions that are being built, especially as Asian Americans lobby for commissions on par with other racial-ethnic groups in the states, also create some avenues for South Asian Americans to act in unison. Equally important, at the civil society level, are a range of organizations from women working on domestic violence issues,[23] to groups working on transnational

---

[22] Pramit Palchaudhuri "South Asians Living in USA Favour Democrats," *Hindustan Times*, May 5, 2007. http://www.hindustantimes.com/StoryPage/StoryPage.aspx?section-Name=NLetter&id=520e5d4b-316f-4281-8a78-7939e1d79cfe&Headline=South+Asians+living+in+USA+favour+Democrats.

[23] Pei-Te Lein, Margaret Conway, and Janelle Wong, *The Politics of Asian Americans* (New York: Routledge, 2004).

citizenship and labor rights. They testify to the depth and breadth of political participation among this group.[24] This political participation also opens up opportunities for deepening pan-ethnic ties.

Perhaps most important is the creation of South Asian America through academic and popular writing. For instance, the writing of South Asian American scholars such as Vijay Prashad's *The Karma of Brown Folk* (or the authors referenced here), literary writings on and by South Asian Americans, such as *Our Feet Walk the Sky* or *Patchwork Shawl*, gather the collective histories and create the imaginaries of South Asian America. More recently, the launch of the flagship journal for South Asian American writing—*Catamaran*—brings together a range of literary and artistic productions that are creating new ways of imagining and living South Asian America.[25] *Catamaran* has featured South Asian American authors, poets, artists, playwrights, filmmakers, and academics, ranging from Tibetans, who have come to the United States from their exiled home in India, to first- and second-generation Pakistani, Indian, Bangladeshi Americans, who may have originated from Asia, Africa, or Europe.

Lastly, the coalitions being built to create a presence of South Asian Americans among Asian Americans—blurring phenotypic boundaries, and those of culture, ethnic history, and religion—also point to the new pan-ethnic group-building work that is under way. Social gatherings, informal and formal organizations, memberships in civic and political organizations, lobbying for resources, and challenging discrimination are all steps in the process of establishing the presence of South Asian Americans as Americans.

Further Reading

Abraham, Margaret. *Speaking the Unspeakable: Marital Violence among South Asian Immigrants in the United States.* (New Brunswick, NJ: Rutgers University Press, 2000).

Das Dasgupta, Shamita, ed. *Body Evidence: Intimate Violence Against South Asian Women in America* (New Brunswick, NJ: Rutgers University Press, 2007).

Das Gupta, Monisha. *Unruly Immigrants: Rights Activism, and Transnational South Asian Politics in the United States* (Durham, NC: Duke University Press, 2006).

Kibria, Nazli. *Muslims in Diaspora: Bangladeshis at Home and Abroad.* (New Brunswick, NJ: Rutgers University Press, forthcoming).

Narayan, Anjana and Purkayastha, Bandana. *Living Our Religions: Hindu and Muslim South Asian American Women Narrate Their Experiences.* (Sterling, VA: Kumarian Books, 2008).

Prashad, Vijay. *The Karma of Brown Folk.* (Minneapolis: University of Minnesota Press, 2000).

Purkayastha, Bandana. *Negotiating Ethnicity: Second-Generation South Asian Americans Traverse a Transnational World.* (New Brunswick, NJ: Rutgers University Press, 2005).

Shankar, Lavina and Srikanth, Rajini, *A Part, Yet Apart: South Asians in Asian America* (Philadelphia: Temple University Press, 1998).

---

[24] Margaret Abraham, *Speaking the Unspeakable: Marital Violence among South Asian Immigrants in the United States* (New Brunswick, NJ: Rutgers University Press, 2000).

[25] Monisha Das Gupta, *Unruly Immigrants: Rights Activism, and Transnational South Asian Politics in the United States* (Durham, NC: Duke University Press, 2006).

[26] See for instance, Vijay Prashad, *The Karma of Brown Folk* (Minneapolis: University of Minnesota Press. 2000); Lavinia Shankar and Rajini Srikanth, *A Part Yet Apart: South Asians in Asian America* (Philadelphia: Temple University Press, 1998); Women of South Asian Descent Collective. *Our Feet Walk the Sky: Women of the South Asian Diaspora* (Berkeley: University of California 1994); Shamita Das Gupta, ed., *Patchwork Shawl: Chronicles of South Asian Women in America* (New Brunswick, NJ; Rutgers University Press, 1998); *Catamaran* edited by Shona Ramaya and Rajini Srikanth (Storrs: Asian American Studies Institute and Asian American Cultural Center, University of Connecticut).

From a Native Daughter

Haunani-Kay Trask

This article was originally a speech, delivered in 1982, that caused several complaints from haole historians at the University of Hawai'i to the American Studies Department where I was teaching. They felt it was biased and anti-white. Of course, Hawaiians in the audience loved it.

> E noi'i wale mai nō ka haole, a,
> 'a'ole e pau nāhana a Hawai'i 'imi loa
> Let the *haole* freely research us in detail
> But the doings of deep delving *Hawai'i*
> will not be exhausted.
>
> —KEPELINO
> 19th-century Hawaiian historian

When I was young the story of my people was told twice: once by my parents, then again by my school teachers. From my *'ohana* (family), I learned about the life of the old ones: how they fished and planted by the moon; shared all the fruits of their labors, especially their children; danced in great numbers for long hours; and honored the unity of their world in intricate genealogical chants. My mother said Hawaiians had sailed over thousands of miles to make their home in these sacred islands. And they had flourished, until the coming of the *haole* (whites).

At school, I learned that the "pagan Hawaiians" did not read or write, were lustful cannibals, traded in slaves, and could not sing. Captain Cook had "discovered" Hawai'i and the ungrateful Hawaiians had killed him. In revenge, the Christian god had cursed the Hawaiians with disease and death.

I learned the first of these stories from speaking with my mother and father. I learned the second from books. By the time I left for college, the books had won out over my parents, especially since I spent four long years in a missionary boarding school for Hawaiian children.

When I went away I understood the world as a place and a feeling divided in two: one *haole* (white), and the other *kānaka* (Native). When I returned ten years later with a Ph.D., the division was sharper, the lack of connection more painful. There was the world that we lived in— my ancestors, my family, and my people—and then there was the world historians described. This world, they had written, was the truth. A primitive group, Hawaiians had been ruled by bloodthirsty priests and despotic kings who owned all the land and kept our people in feudal subjugation. The chiefs were cruel, the people poor.

But this was not the story my mother told me. No one had owned the land before the *haole* came; everyone could fish and plant, except during sacred periods. And the chiefs were good and loved their people.

Was my mother confused? What did our *kūpuna* (elders) say? They replied: Did these historians (all *haole*) know the language? Did they understand the chants? How long had they lived among our people? Whose stories had they heard?

None of the historians had ever learned our mother tongue. They had all been content to read what Europeans and Americans had written. But why did scholars, presumably well-trained and thoughtful, neglect our language? Not merely a passageway to knowledge, language is a form of knowing by itself; a people's way of thinking and feeling is revealed through its music.

I sensed the answer without needing to answer. From years of living in a divided world, I knew the historian's judgment: *There is no value in things Hawaiian; all value comes from things haole.*

Historians, I realized, were very like missionaries. They were a part of the colonizing horde. One group colonized the spirit; the other, the mind. Frantz Fanon had been right, but not just about Africans. He had been right about the bondage of my own people: "By a kind of perverted logic, [colonialism] turns to the past of the oppressed people, and distorts, disfigures, and destroys it" (1963:210). The first step in the colonizing process, Fanon had written, was the deculturation of a people. What better way to take our culture than to remake our image? A rich historical past became small and ignorant in the hands of Westerners. And we suffered a damaged sense of people and culture because of this distortion.

Burdened by a linear, progressive conception of history and by an assumption that Euro-American culture flourishes at the upper end of that progression, Westerners have told the history of Hawai'i as an inevitable if occasionally bitter-sweet triumph of Western ways over "primitive" Hawaiian ways. A few authors—the most sympathetic—have recorded with deep-felt sorrow the passing of our people. But in the end, we are repeatedly told, such an eclipse was for the best.

Obviously it was best for Westerners, not for our dying multitudes. This is why the historian's mission has been to justify our passing by celebrating Western dominance. Fanon would have called this missionizing, intellectual colonization. And it is clearest in the historian's insistence that *pre-haole* Hawaiian land tenure was "feudal"—a term that is now applied, without question, in every monograph, in every schoolbook, and in every tour guide description of my people's history.

From the earliest days of Western contact my people told their guests that *no one* owned the land. The land—like the air and the sea—was for all to use and share as their birthright. Our chiefs were *stewards* of the land; they could not own or privately possess the land any more than they could sell it.

But the *haole* insisted on characterizing our chiefs as feudal landlords and our people as serfs. Thus, a European term which described a European practice founded on the European concept of private property—feudalism—was imposed upon a people halfway around the world from Europe and vastly different from her in every conceivable way. More than betraying an ignorance of Hawaiian culture and history, however, this misrepresentation was malevolent in design.

By inventing feudalism in ancient Hawai'i, Western scholars quickly transformed a spiritually based, self-sufficient economic system of land use and occupancy into an oppressive, medieval European practice of divine right ownership, with the common people tied like serfs to the land. By claiming that a Pacific people lived under a European system—that the Hawaiians lived under feudalism—Westerners could then degrade a successful system of shared land use with a pejorative and inaccurate Western term. Land tenure changes instituted by Americans and in line with current Western notions of private property were then made to appear beneficial to the Hawaiians. But in practice, such changes benefited the *haole*, who alienated the people from the land, taking it for themselves.

The prelude to this land alienation was the great dying of the people. Barely half a century after contact with the West our people had declined in number by eighty percent. Disease and death were rampant. The sandalwood forests had been stripped bare for international commerce between England and China. The missionaries had insinuated themselves everywhere. And a debt-ridden Hawaiian king (there had been no king before Western contact) succumbed to enormous pressure from the Americans and followed their schemes for dividing the land.

This is how private property land tenure entered Hawai'i. The common people, driven from their birthright, received less than one percent of the land. They starved while huge *haole*-owned sugar plantations thrived.

And what had the historians said? They had said that the Americans "liberated" the Hawaiians from an oppressive "feudal" system. By inventing a false feudal past, the historians justify—and become complicitous in—massive American theft.

Is there "evidence"—as historians call it—for traditional Hawaiian concepts of land use? The evidence is in the sayings of my people and in the words they wrote more than a century ago, much of which has been translated. However, historians have chosen to ignore any references here to shared land use. But there *is* incontrovertible evidence in the very structure of the Hawaiian language. If the historians had bothered to learn our language (as any American historian of France would learn French) they would have discovered that we show possession in two ways: through the use of an "a" possessive, which reveals acquired status, and through the use of an "o" possessive, which denotes inherent status. My body (*ko'u kino*) and my parents (*ko'u mākua*), for example, take the "o" form; most material objects, such as food (*ka'u mea'ai*) take the "a" form. But land, like one's body and one's parents, takes the "o" possessive (*ko'u 'āina*). Thus, in our way of speaking, land is inherent to the people; it is like our bodies and our parents. The people cannot exist without the land, and the land cannot exist without the people.

Every major historian of Hawai'i has been mistaken about Hawaiian land tenure. The chiefs did not own the land: they *could not* own the land. My mother was right and the *haole* historians were wrong. If they had studied our language they would have known that no one owned the land. But was their failing merely ignorance, or simple ethnocentric bias?

No, I did not believe them to be so benign. As I read on, a pattern emerged in their writing. Our ways were inferior to those of the West, to those of the historians' own culture. We were "less developed," or "immature," or "authoritarian." In some tellings we were much worse. Thus, Gavan Daws (1968), the most famed modern historian of Hawai'i, had continued a tradition established earlier by missionaries Hiram Bingham (1848) and Sheldon Dibble (1909), by referring to the old ones as "thieves" and "savages" who regularly practiced infanticide and who, in contrast to "civilized" whites, preferred "lewd dancing" to work. Ralph Kuykendall (1938), long considered the most thorough if also the most boring of historians of Hawai'i, sustained another fiction—that my ancestors owned slaves, the outcast *kauwā*. This opinion, as well as the description of Hawaiian land tenure as feudal, had been supported by respected sociologist Andrew Lind (1938). Finally, nearly all historians had refused to accept our genealogical dating of A.D. 400 or earlier for our arrival from the South Pacific. They had, instead, claimed that our earliest appearance in Hawai'i could only be traced to A.D. 1100. Thus at least seven hundred years of our history were repudiated by "superior" Western scholarship. Only recently have archaeological data confirmed what Hawaiians had said these many centuries (Tuggle 1979).[1]

Suddenly the entire sweep of our written history was clear to me. I was reading the West's view of itself through the degradation of my own past. When historians wrote that the king owned the land and the common people were bound to it, they were saying that ownership was the only way human beings in their world could relate to the land, and in that relationship, some one person had to control both the land and the interaction between humans.

And when they said that our chiefs were despotic, they were telling of their own society, where hierarchy always results in domination. Thus any authority or elder is automatically suspected of tyranny.

And when they wrote that Hawaiians were lazy, they meant that work must be continuous and ever a burden.

And when they wrote that we were promiscuous, they meant that love-making in the Christian West is a sin.

And when they wrote that we were racist because we preferred our own ways to theirs, they meant that their culture needed to dominate other cultures.

And when they wrote that we were superstitious, believing in the *mana* of nature and people, they meant that the West has long since lost a deep spiritual and cultural relationship to the earth.

And when they wrote that Hawaiians were "primitive" in their grief over the passing of loved ones, they meant that the West grieves for the living who do not walk among their ancestors.

For so long, more than half my life, I had misunderstood this written record, thinking it described my own people. But my history was nowhere present. For we had not written. We had chanted and sailed and fished and built and prayed. And we had told stories through the great blood lines of memory: genealogy.

To know my history, I had to put away my books and return to the land. I had to plant *taro* in the earth before I could understand the inseparable bond between people and *'āina*. I had to

---

[1] See also Fornander (1878–85). Lest one think these sources antiquated, it should be noted that there exist only a handful of modern scholarly works on the history of Hawai'i. The most respected are those by Kuykendall (1938) and Daws (1968), and a social history of the 20th century by Lawrence Fuchs (1961). Of these, only Kuykendall and Daws claim any knowledge of pre-*haole* history, while concentrating on the 19th century. However, countless popular works have relied on these two studies which, in turn, are themselves based on primary sources written in English by extremely biased, anti-Hawaiian Westerners such as explorers, traders, missionaries (e.g., Bingham [1848] and Dibble [1909]), and sugar planters. Indeed, a favorite technique of Daws's—whose *Shoal of Time* was once the most acclaimed and recent general history—is the lengthy quotation without comment of the most racist remarks by missionaries and planters. Thus, at one point, half a page is consumed with a "white man's burden" quotation from an 1886 *Planters Monthly article* ("It is better here that the white man should rule...," etc., p. 213). Daws's only comment is, "The conclusion was inescapable." To get a sense of such characteristic contempt for Hawaiians, one has but to read the first few pages, where Daws refers several times to the Hawaiians as "savages" and "thieves" and where he approvingly has Captain Cook thinking, "It was a sensible primitive who bowed before a superior civilization" (p. 2). See also—among examples too numerous to cite—his glib description of sacred *hula* as a "frivolous diversion," which, instead of work, the Hawaiians "would practice energetically in the hot sun for days on end...their bare brown flesh glistening with sweat" (pp. 65–66). Daws, who repeatedly displays an affection for descriptions of Hawaiian skin color, taught Hawaiian history for some years at the University of Hawai'i. He once held the Chair of Pacific History at the Australian National University's Institute of Advanced Studies.

Postscript: Since this article was written, the first scholarly history by a Native Hawaiian was published in English: *Native Land and Foreign Desires* by Lilikalā Kame'eleihiwa (Honolulu: Bishop Museum Press, 1992).

feel again the spirits of nature and take gifts of plants and fish to the ancient altars. I had to begin to speak my language with our elders and leave long silences for wisdom to grow. But before anything else, I needed to learn the language like a lover so that I could rock within her and lie at night in her dreaming arms.

There was nothing in my schooling that had told me of this, or hinted that somewhere there was a longer, older story of origins, of the flowing of songs out to a great but distant sea. Only my parents' voices, over and over, spoke to me of a Hawaiian world. While the books spoke from a different world, a Western world.

And yet, Hawaiians are not of the West. We are of *Hawai'i Nei*, this world where I live, this place, this culture, this *'āina*.

What can I say, then, to Western historians of my place and people? Let me answer with a story.

A while ago I was asked to appear on a panel on the American overthrow of our government in 1893. The other panelists were all *haole*. But one was a *haole* historian from the American continent who had just published a book on what he called the American anti-imperialists. He and I met briefly in preparation for the panel. I asked him if he knew the language. He said no. I asked him if he knew the record of opposition to our annexation to America. He said there was no real evidence for it, just comments here and there. I told him that he didn't understand and that at the panel I would share the evidence. When we met in public and spoke, I said this:

There is a song much loved by our people. It was written after Hawai'i had been invaded and occupied by American marines. Addressed to our dethroned Queen, it was written in 1893, and tells of Hawaiian feelings for our land and against annexation to the United States. Listen to our lament:

Kaulana nā pua a'o Hawai'i	Famous are the children of Hawai'i
Kūpa'a ma hope o ka 'āina	Who cling steadfastly to the land
Hiki mai ka 'elele o ka loko 'ino	Comes the evil-hearted with
Palapala 'ānunu me ka pākaha	A document greedy for plunder
Pane mai Hawai'i moku o Keawe	Hawai'i, island of Keawe, answers
Kokua nā hono a'o Pi'ilani	The bays of Pi'ilani [of Maui,
	Moloka'i, and Lana'i] help
Kāko'o mai Kaua'i o Mano	Kaua'i of Mano assists
Pau pu me ke one o Kakuhihewa	Firmly together with the sands of Kakuhihewa
'A'ole a'e kau i ka pūlima	Do not put the signature
Maluna o ka pepa o ka 'enemi	On the paper of the enemy
Ho'ohui 'āina kū'ai hewa	Annexation is wicked sale
I ka pono sivila a'o ke kānaka	Of the civil rights of the Hawaiian people
Mahope mākou o Lili`ūlani	We support Lili'uokalani
A loa'a 'e ka pono o ka 'āina	Who has earned the right to the land
Ha'ina 'ia mai ana ka puana	The story is told
'O ka po'e i aloha i ka 'āina	Of the people who love the land

This song, I said, continues to be sung with great dignity at Hawaiian political gatherings, for our people still share the feelings of anger and protest that it conveys.

But our guest, the *haole* historian, answered that this song, although beautiful, was not evidence of either opposition or of imperialism from the Hawaiian perspective.

Many Hawaiians in the audience were shocked at his remarks, but, in hindsight, I think they were predictable. They are the standard response of the historian who does not know the language and has no respect for its memory.

Finally, I proceeded to relate a personal story, thinking that surely such a tale could not want for authenticity since I myself was relating it. My *tūtū* (grandmother) had told my mother who had told me that at the time of the overthrow a great wailing went up throughout the islands, a wailing of weeks, a wailing of impenetrable grief, a wailing of death. But he remarked again, this too is not evidence.

And so, history goes on, written in long volumes by foreign people. Whole libraries begin to form, book upon book, shelf upon shelf. At the same time, the stories go on, generation to generation, family to family.

Which history do Western historians desire to know? Is it to be a tale of writings by their own countrymen, individuals convinced of their "unique" capacity for analysis, looking at us with Western eyes, thinking about us within Western philosophical contexts, categorizing us by Western indices, judging us by Judeo-Christian morals, exhorting us to capitalist achievements, and finally, leaving us an authoritative-because-Western record of their complete misunderstanding?

All this has been done already. Not merely a few times, but many times. And still, every year, there appear new and eager faces to take up the same telling, as if the West must continue, implacably, with the din of its own disbelief. But there is, as there has been always, another possibility. If it is truly our history Western historians desire to know, they must put down their books, and take up our practices. First, of course, the language. But later, the people, the *'āina*, the stories. Above all, in the end, the stories. Historians must listen, they must hear the generational connections, the reservoir of sounds and meanings.

They must come, as American Indians suggested long ago, to understand the land. Not in the Western way, but in the indigenous way, the way of living within and protecting the bond between people and *'āina*. This bond is cultural, and it can be understood only culturally. But because the West has lost any cultural understanding of the bond between people and land, it is not possible to know this connection through Western culture. This means that the history of indigenous people cannot be written from within Western culture. Such a story is merely the West's story of itself.

Our story remains unwritten. It rests within the culture, which is inseparable from the land. To know this is to know our history. To write this is to write of the land and the people who are born from her.

Sources

Bingham, Hiram. 1981. *A Residence of Twenty-one Years in the Sandwich Islands*. Tokyo: Charles E. Tuttle.

Daws, Gavan. 1968. *Shoal of Time: A History of the Hawaiian Islands*. Honolulu: University of Hawai'i Press.

Dibble, Sheldon. 1909. *A History of the Sandwich Islands*. Honolulu: Thrum Publishing.

Fanon, Frantz. 1963. *The Wretched of the Earth*. New York: Grove Press.

Fornander, Abraham. 1980. *An Account of the Polynesian Race, Its Origins, and Migrations and the Ancient History of the Hawaiian People to the Times of Kamehameha I*. Routledge, Vermont: Charles E. Tuttle.

Fuchs, Lawrence H. 1961. *Hawaii Pono: A Social History*. New York: Harcourt Brace & World.

Kuykendall, Ralph. 1978. *The Hawaiian Kingdom, 1778–1854: Foundation and Transformation*. Honolulu: University of Hawai'i Press.

Tuggle, H. David. 1979. "Hawai'i," in *The Prehistory of Polynesia*, ed. Jessie D. Jennings. Cambridge: Harvard University Press.

Enclaves, Ethnoburbs, and New Patterns of Settlement among Asian Immigrants

Wei Li and Emily Skop

Since the late 1960s, the combination of global economic restructuring, changing geopolitical contexts, and shifting American immigration policies has set in motion significant flows of Asian immigrants and refugees to the United States. Even as refugee admissions wax and wane, family-sponsored immigration continues to grow, and record numbers of highly skilled, professional immigrants and wealthy investors have also joined the flow. At the same time, patterns of Asian immigrant settlement have changed. Traditional central city enclaves such as "Chinatown," "Little Tokyo," or "Manila Town" no longer absorb the majority of newcomers from various countries of origin and with diverse socioeconomic backgrounds. Instead, many Asian immigrants (especially upper- and middle-class newcomers) tend to avoid central city enclaves since they have the financial resources to settle directly in suburbs that offer decent housing, high-performing schools, and superior living conditions and public amenities. As a result, more and more suburban neighborhoods in the nation are becoming increasingly multiracial, multiethnic, multilingual, multicultural, and multinational. This new pattern of Asian American settlement challenges the widely accepted characterization of the suburbs as the citadel of non-Hispanic white, middle-class America.

This chapter discusses the issues surrounding the changing settlement patterns among Asian American groups in the United States. It will first provide a brief demographic overview of contemporary Asian America, followed by a description of shifting geographic distributions of the Asian American population at the state and metropolitan levels. The chapter then focuses on different settlement types among Asian American groups within metropolitan areas, from traditional central city enclaves to multiethnic suburbs (known as "ethnoburbs"), and demonstrates the similarities and differences between these settlement types. The chapter concludes with a discussion of the implications of divergent settlement forms for the economic, cultural, and political incorporation of contemporary Asian Americans as well as of the way these patterns reinforce transnational processes in globalizing world.

Demographic Overview of Asian Americans

Since the mid-nineteenth century, Asian Americans have been present in the United States, traditionally working as laborers in agriculture, fishing, mining, manufacturing, and construction, and as service workers and small business owners. Historically, however, their numbers and growth rates have been low, primarily because of exclusionary national immigration and naturalization laws (like the 1882 Chinese Exclusion Act, the 1917 Asiatic Barred Zone, and the 1923 *U.S. v. Bhagat Singh Thind* Supreme Court case) and restrictive state legislation on marriage, landholding, and voting (including antimiscegenation laws and anti-alien land laws). These discriminatory regulations, along with other prohibitive social practices, resulted in declining Asian immigration, extreme sex ratio imbalances, limited occupation choices, and forced spatial segregation in isolated communities. Imbalanced natural growth rates among different Asian American groups and the lack of significant and self-sustaining communities of Asian Americans existed well into the twentieth century.

In the 1960s the situation began to change. Since then, the number of Asian Americans has dramatically increased, primarily because of shifting U.S. immigration policies, rapid economic development in Asia, as well as sometimes unstable geopolitical situations in home countries, as in Vietnam during and after the Vietnam War. Thus, the local, lived experiences of Asian Americans in the United States are set within the shifting landscape of globalization.

Because international economic restructuring promotes the flows of capital, information, services, and people across national borders, there has been a growing demand for a highly skilled workforce and capital investors to engage in an advanced economy. When such needs cannot be fulfilled domestically, the United States, along with other developed countries, looks overseas for an alternative source of labor and investors. Many immigrants from Asia are well prepared for, and fit into, the employment needs of the globalizing U.S. economy: this fact is partially the result of the economic take-off of the four Asian Little Dragons (Hong Kong, Singapore, South Korea, and Taiwan) beginning in the 1960s, followed by mainland China, India, and some ASEAN countries (e.g., Indonesia, Malaysia, and Thailand) in more recent decades. As these economies have become increasingly incorporated into the global economy, a highly educated and highly skilled middle- and upper-class population, some with entrepreneur experiences, has emerged. Many of these individuals are primed to immigrate to the United States because they have high levels of education, professional training, entrepreneurial skills, and/or financial resources needed in the burgeoning knowledge-based economy.

At the same time, a large number of lower-skilled and less-educated individuals, lured by family sponsorship and American job opportunities, join the immigrant waves from Asia. In fact, family reunification is the most important avenue through which many individuals qualify for admission and "lawful permanent residence" in the United States. Family reunification is particularly important for immigrants from places like the Philippines, Vietnam, and China. Moreover, the end of the Vietnam War in 1975 yielded large refugee flows from Southeast Asia. Many Vietnamese, Cambodian, Laotian, and Hmong refugees arrived penniless and mentally distressed after surviving war and trauma when their lives were constantly threatened. But as refugees, they were able to access a variety of social service programs that distinguishes their experiences from those of other types of newcomers to the United States.

The unprecedented growth of the Asian population in the United States since the 1960s could not have taken place without the key role of the state in initiating flows. The first of many U.S. immigration policies to prompt this growth was the 1965 Immigration Act, which opened the door to new flows of immigration from all parts of the world, including Asia, since the national-origin quota system was abolished and a preference system was introduced based on two general categories of admission: family sponsored and employment based. More recently, the 1980 Refugee Act facilitated the migration and settlement of many Southeast Asian refugees in the United States. Then, the Immigration and Nationality Act of 1990 prompted the growth of highly skilled immigration from Asia, especially from India and China, to the United States. The 1990 legislation tripled the ceiling on employment-based visas and created the H-1B nonimmigrant visa program to allow for the admission of temporary workers employed in "specialty occupations" that require highly specialized knowledge and at least a bachelor's degree or its equivalent; INS data reveals that Asia is the leading contributor of both employment-based immigrants and H-1B temporary workers. At the same time, the legislation allowed H-1B visa holders to bring their immediate families with them (under the H-4 visa program) and also made H-1B visa holders eligible to adjust their legal status to that of permanent residence during their six-year maximum visa period, thus allowing Asian immigrants further opportunities for settling in the United States. Additionally more recent immigration legislation created L-1 visas (which allow companies operating both in the United States and abroad to transfer certain classes of employee from its foreign operations to the U.S. operations for up to seven years) and EB-5 visas (for investor immigrants who bring $1 million and create at least ten jobs).

The result of all of these shifting immigration policies is the rapid and continued growth of the Asian immigrant population in the United States. Even though Asian Americans remain a relatively small part of the total population—currently less than 5 percent—they are among the fastest growing minority groups in the United States today (with a growth rate of 18.1 percent in the first four years into the twenty-first century alone). According to the U.S. Census, from 1990 to 2004, the increase in the Asian American population was upwards of 80 percent, from 6.9 million in 1990 to 12.1 million in 2004.[1] In comparison, the total U.S. population grew by 21 percent, from 248.7 million in 1990 to 285 million in 2004.[2]

Contemporary Asian America is not only growing but also more diverse than it has ever been. The population includes first-generation immigrants as well as increasing percentages of second- and third-generation American-born natives. At the same time, among all subgroups, the Chinese remain the largest subgroup with a total of 2.9 million in 2004, a 76 percent increase from 1990. Other Asian American subgroups include the rapidly increasing Asian Indian population, which reached 2.2 million in 2004 (a 175 percent increase from 1990), the fast-growing Vietnamese population, which grew to almost 1.3 million in 2004 (a 106 percent increase from 1990), the more moderately growing Filipino (2.1 million) and Korean (1.3 million) populations, whose populations grew approximately 50 percent since 1990, and the slowly declining Japanese population, which numbered 847,562 in 1990 and 832,039 in 2004. The majority of this increase in contemporary Asian America stems from immigration, but clearly, natural increase has begun to stimulate the growth of a burgeoning, native-born Asian American population.

Geographic Distribution of Asian Americans

The geographic distribution of Asian Americans in the United States has always been uneven, but fairly stable, with the same ten states appearing on the list year in and year out. California, New York, and Hawaii, as historical destination states, have traditionally had the largest numbers of Asian Americans. These three states remained as the top three concentrations for the Asian

---

[1] All 2000 and 2004 data used here includes only Asian Americans who chose the "Asian alone" racial category.

[2] The Census 2004 data should be viewed with caution. It is based on sample data from the American Community Survey, which was not fully implemented across the nation until July 2005. This means that the data is subject to sampling error, especially among minority populations.

population until 1990, when new patterns began to emerge. Most importantly, Hawaii was surpassed by Texas in 2000 and by both Texas and New Jersey in 2004; by 2004, it was ranked number five among the top ten states for Asian Americans. At the same time, Illinois, Washington, Florida, Virginia, and Massachusetts have been on the list of top ten states for the Asian American population since 1990, with little change between years.

These top ten states still dominate Asian Americans' presence in the United States, with more than three-quarters of the national total. However there is a slight trend towards deconcentration, largely due to the rapid increase of some nontraditional destination states for Asian Americans. As shown in Table 6.1, the share of top ten states combined has slightly decreased in recent years, from 79 percent in 1990 to less than 76 percent in 2004. California shows the most marked (though minor) decline among these states; only 35 percent of Asian Americans, compared with nearly 40 percent in 1990, call this traditional destination "home" in 2004.

The most dramatic changes in the geographic distributions of Asian Americans have occurred among states that historically have had very limited numbers of Asian Americans. These new destination states include Nevada and Georgia; both states ranked highest in terms of the overall growth of Asian Americans; Nevada experienced a 271 percent increase from 1990 to 2004 (45 percent of which occurred in the 2000–2004 period alone), and Georgia's Asian American population grew by 223 percent between 1990 and 2004 (38 percent of which occurred in the 2000–2004 period alone). In fact, by 2004, the number of Asian Americans in Georgia reached 238,281, which means that this state is now ranked thirteenth in terms of its Asian American population, whereas in 1990 it ranked much lower. Arizona, Delaware, and New Hampshire also experienced at least 100 percent growth between 1990 and 2000, and more than 30 percent increase from 2000 to 2004.

TABLE 6.1   Asian Americans in the U.S. and Top Ten States, 1990–2004

	1990—% National Total	2000—% National Total	2004—% National Total
National total	*6,908,638*	*10,242,998*	*12,097,281*
1	California—39.6	California—36.1	California—35.2
2	New York—10.0	New York—10.2	New York—10.0
3	Hawaii—7.6	Texas—5.5	Texas—5.8
4	Texas—4.5	Hawaii—4.9	New Jersey—5.0
5	Illinois—4.1	New Jersey—4.7	Hawaii—4.3
6	New Jersey—3.9	Illinois—4.1	Illinois—4.2
7	Washington—2.8	Washington—3.1	Washington—3.2
8	Virginia—2.3	Florida—2.6	Florida—2.9
9	Florida—2.2	Virginia—2.5	Virginia—2.7
10	Massachusetts—2.1	Massachusetts—2.3	Massachusetts—2.3
% top ten total	*79.0%*	*76.2%*	*75.6%*

Source: Calculations based on U.S. Census—1990 STF1; 2000 SF2; 2004 ACS.

Asian Americans are largely urban bound, and this population continues to cluster in traditional immigrant gateways, which have built upon a rich history of immigration from Asia (and elsewhere), and which have been continually reshaped as a result. In fact, the ten metropolitan areas with the largest Asian populations are the same in 2004 as in 1990, as Table 6.2 illustrates. Los Angeles, New York, and San Francisco continue to be the highest-ranking metropolitan areas. Silicon Valley now ranks as the fourth largest Asian American population concentration and has become increasingly important as a destination since 1990. Meanwhile, Honolulu, which used to have one of the largest Asian populations, continues to sustain population losses, primarily because (1) fewer and fewer Asian Americans are moving to this metropolitan area; and (2) the Asian Americans already living there are rapidly aging, so natural increase no longer plays as important a role in the growth of the population.[3]

Interestingly, even though traditional immigrant gateways are still the most significant centers for Asian Americans, these metropolitan areas' share of recent Asian population gains dropped noticeably in recent years. From 2000 to 2004, fewer than half (47 percent) of Asian American

TABLE 6.2 Metropolitan Areas with Largest Asian American Populations, 2004

2004	Rank 2000	1990	Metro Area	Population 2004	Share of Metro Area Population (%)
1	1	1	Los Angeles–Long Beach–Santa Ana, CA	1,712,127	13.2
2	2	2	New York–Northern New Jersey–Long Island, NY-NJ-PA	1,616,489	8.6
3	3	3	San Francisco–Oakland–Fremont, CA	879,495	21.2
4	4	5	San Jose–Sunnyvale–Santa Clara, CA	491,876	28.2
5	6	6	Chicago–Naperville–Joliet, IL-IN-WI	454,300	4.8
6	5	4	Honolulu, HI	413,015	45.9
7	7	7	Washington–Arlington–Alexandria, DC-VA-MD-WV	405,859	7.9
8	8	9	Scattle–Tacoma–Bellevue, WA	308,600	9.7
9	9	8	San Diego–Carlsbad–San Marcos, CA	283,037	9.7
10	10	10	Houston–Baytown–Sugarland, TX	281,894	5.4

Source: Calculations based on Frey's (2006) analysis of U.S. Census—1990 STFI; 2000 SF2; 2004 ACS.

---

[3] Another possible contributing factor is the way that changing self-identification racial categories provided by the U.S. Census skew the results. Some individuals are selecting the multiple-race category, rather than the "alone" racial category. We only analyze Asian Americans who chose the "Asian alone" racial category in 2000 and 2004 (see note 1).

population increase occurred in these metropolitan areas, compared to the majority (53 percent) in the 1990s. As a result, some important emerging and expanding metropolitan areas that may not commonly be thought of as Asian American population centers have become important destinations, especially since 1990. Table 6.3 outlines the metropolitan areas exhibiting the highest growth rates for Asian Americans, and provides a measure of where the newest gains in population are taking place. Most of this increase occurs because of significant in-migration, as Asian Americans move to newly emerging immigrant gateways. These metropolitan areas may not commonly be thought of as Asian American destinations, nor do they have significant concentrations of the group; in other words, less than 3 percent of the total population is Asian American,

TABLE 6.3   Metropolitan Areas with the Highest Asian American Growth Rates, 2000–2004 and 1990–2000

Rank 2004	Metro Area	Population Change 2000–2004 (%)	Rank 2000	Metro Area	Population Change 1990–2000 (%)
1	Las Vegas–Paradise, NV	38.5	1	Las Vegas–Paradise, NV	191.2
2	Riverside–San Bernardino–Ontario, CA	31.1	2	Atlanta–Sandy Springs–Marietta, GA	169.4
3	Orlando, FL	30.2	3	Austin–Round Rock, TX	140.8
4	Atlanta–Sandy Springs–Marietta, GA	28.5	4	Orlando, FL	125.3
5	Stockton, CA	28.4	5	Dallas–Fort Worth–Arlington, TX	108.7
6	Tampa–St. Petersburg–Clearwater, FL	28.4	6	Tampa–St. Petersburg–Clearwater, FL	103.2
7	Austin–Round Rock, TX	28.2	7	Phoenix–Mesa–Scottsdale, AZ	93.4
8	Phoenix–Mesa–Scottsdale, AZ	27.0	8	Minneapolis–St. Paul–Bloomington, MN-WI	92.3
9	Sacramento–Arden–Arcade–Roseville, CA	25.6	9	Detroit–Warren–Livonia, MI	87.3
10	Dallas–Fort Worth–Arlington, TX	24.8	10	Houston–Baytown–Sugar Land, TX	81.9

Source: Calculations based on Frey's (2006) analysis of U.S. Census—1990 STF1; 2000 SF2; 2004 ACS.

and most have fewer than sixty thousand Asian American residents. Even so, ten years ago, Las Vegas, Riverside, Orlando, Atlanta, Stockton, Tampa, Austin, and Phoenix were not metropolitan areas known in terms of their Asian American populations. But today, each of these newly emerging immigrant gateways is experiencing tremendous population change, sometimes as much as a 200 percent increase in their Asian American population from 1990 to 2004.

Of course, the geographic distributions of Asian Americans vary by subgroup. The traditional immigrant gateway states and metropolitan areas account for the lion's share of most individual Asian American groups. Even so, nearly half of all U.S. states (twenty-four) witnessed a 100 percent or more increase in their Chinese population, topped by Georgia (233 percent) and Kentucky (208 percent). Similarly twenty-nine states witnessed at least a 100 percent increase in their Vietnamese population growth, led by Alabama (476 percent), whereas sixteen states saw their Filipino population more than double, led by Nevada (387 percent). The growth rates of Asian Indians are likewise remarkable during the same period, with many of the highest growth states known for their high-tech economic development, e.g., Utah (538 percent), Arizona (480 percent), Washington (401 percent), Colorado (290 percent), and North Carolina (266 percent). On the other hand, while the population of Japanese grew steadily in some states, about two dozen states experienced absolute decrease among this group.

In terms of metropolitan-level distributions, the New York metropolitan area has the largest number of Chinese and Asian Indians, and the second largest share of Koreans. The greatest percentages of Koreans, as well as Filipinos, live in the Los Angeles metropolitan area. This metropolitan area is the second most important concentration for Chinese and Japanese, while adjacent suburban Orange County has the most Vietnamese. Honolulu has the most Japanese and second most Filipinos. Washington, DC, is the third most important center of Asian Indian and Korean settlement, while Chicago and San Diego act as the second-most and third-most concentrations for Asian Indians and Filipinos, respectively. Finally, Houston and Dallas, both locations that are not typically thought of as Asian American population centers, are home to more than 6 percent of the nation's Vietnamese and nearly 8 percent of its Asian Indians. So, there is considerable regional variation among Asian American subgroups. Though there are clearly some significant concentrations of each group in particular states and particular metropolitan areas, the overall trend is towards deconcentration, and the expansion of the Asian American population to new destinations.

Changing Asian American Settlement Forms

Metropolitan areas in the United States have traditionally been magnets for Asian American immigration, but in the modern metropolis, more complex residential geographies materialize. This is the case primarily because metropolitan areas have undergone major restructuring since the earliest immigrants arrived in U.S. cities. Indeed, the central city has lost its former preeminence as the staging ground for the integration of immigrant newcomers. This shift away from the central city takes place as economic activity moves to exurbia, diverse housing types and housing qualities appear throughout metropolitan areas, and automobiles transform the urban landscape. The changing geography of immigrant settlement is also directly related to a shifting global political and social context, and the diversifying socioeconomic and ethnic origins of immigrants as a result of amended U.S. immigration policy.

Urban ecology describes the process of immigrant spatial succession and assimilation, and its role in the development of the metropolis. The enduring Chicago School model suggests that, upon entry, new arrivals settle in central city ethnic enclaves to save transportation costs, locate near employment opportunities, access the cheapest housing, and gain support from coethnic networks. When the immigrants (and/or their children) move up the economic ladder, they move away from ethnic-specific, central city enclaves to suburbs where they are spatially dispersed among, and racially mixed with, the majority white community. Inherent in the model is the idea that the residential location of immigrants (and subsequent generations) reflects (and affects) the degree of sociocultural and economic incorporation of that ethnic group.

This scenario traditionally fits many Asian immigrants' settlement patterns. For instance, San Francisco's "Chinatown" (known among Chinese immigrants as "the fist big city") has been a historical gateway for Chinese immigrants since the nineteenth century. The 1882 Chinese Exclusion Act further solidified this process, as large numbers of Chinese Americans, immigrants as well as native born, sought refuge and sanctuary in the central city ethnic enclave. Filipinos, also hoping to take advantage of coethnic social networks and to avoid discrimination and violence, settled in "Manila Town," which was adjacent to San Francisco's "Chinatown." Other Chinese enclaves existed in Sacramento (known among Chinese immigrants as "the second city") and Stockton (known among Chinese immigrants as "the third city"). Similarly, the Japanese established "Japan Town" in San Francisco and "Little Tokyo" in Los Angeles. During the late-nineteenth and early-twentieth centuries, "Chinatowns" and other Asian central city enclaves were established across the country in many major metropolitan areas, almost exclusively in inner-city neighborhoods where low rents and run-down conditions predominated.

Some better-off Asian Americans moved out of Asian American—specific enclaves once they achieved socioeconomic success, but others were stuck in these central city neighborhoods regardless of their socioeconomic status as the result of restrictive covenants or discriminatory practices by realtors, lenders, or neighbors. In fact, large-scale suburbanization of Asian Americans did not begin until World War II and after, when mainstream jobs were finally opened up to Asian Americans, racial discrimination in the housing market became outlawed, and the American urban landscape became a predominantly suburban landscape. Even then, however, the suburbanization trend included mostly well-to-do Asian Americans. This process became known as the "uptown vs. downtown" phenomenon: assimilated immigrants or native-born Asian Americans with the economic means moved to suburbs and left the elderly, recently arrived, and poorer immigrants behind in downtown "Chinatowns" or other Asian central city enclaves.

Today, some central city Asian enclaves have survived and endured. Indeed, some of these communities continue to serve as immigrant gate-ways, especially the "Chinatowns" of New York City and San Francisco, as well as the smaller ethnic enclaves in other major cities like Chicago and Los Angeles. New immigrants land in these traditional ethnic neighborhoods with job opportunities and housing options, kinship ties and/or social support networks, regardless of their immigration status and English proficiency or lack thereof.

Whether these central city enclaves will persist is a topic that is constantly subject to debate. While "Chinatowns" may remain significant areas of concentration, given the fact that emigration from China continues at unprecedented rates and the fact that this subgroup is already the largest and longest established of all Asian American subgroups, other predominant Asian American subgroups, like Japanese and Filipinos, face different situations. The former subgroup does not have large new immigrant inflows to sustain central city enclaves, while the latter groups do not have long-lasting ethnic enclaves in most cities to which to turn. Moreover, contemporary globalization trends include a variety of divergent and competing processes that make these central city enclaves a nexus for change. Foreign investment, in the form of financial inflows crossing the Pacific Ocean, as well as the emergence of gentrification in most major downtowns, means that these sites are ripe for urban restructuring. The situation becomes even more complex as these ethnic enclaves become increasingly heterogeneous due to the influx of a variety of newcomers from a multiplicity of sending communities, with heterogeneous legal, demographic, and socioeconomic profiles ranging from undocumented migrants to prominent politicians; from poor immigrants to wealthy second- and later-generation Americans who made their fortunes either in the United States or overseas.

So, the traditional notion of spatial assimilation that the Chicago School characterizes no longer encompasses the spectrum of sociospatial experiences of Asian Americans. While some Asian Americans disproportionately stay in centralized ethnic enclaves, other newcomers are more diverse in their residential behavior. The changing social geography of cities, combined with the recent influx of heterogeneous immigrants, as well as the fact that second-generation (and later) offspring are reaching adulthood, results in both dispersed and concentrated forms.

Perhaps the most intriguing pattern exhibited by Asian Americans is their rapid rate of suburbanization in the United States. Indeed, empirical studies have documented the remarkable suburban-bound trend of contemporary Asian Americans. Data from the 2004 American Community Survey indicates that Asian Americans are more likely to reside in the suburbs than in the central cities of the 102 largest metropolitan areas in the United States. Indeed, over half (54.6 percent) of Asian Americans in these metropolitan areas live in the suburbs. A majority or near majority of every Asian American group lives in suburbia—nearly 60 percent of Asian Indians and Koreans, and about 50 percent of Chinese and Vietnamese.

These results illustrate that newly arrived immigrants do not consider the often crowded and run-down neighborhoods in central cities as their ideal places to live. Most tend to have the financial resources to afford the newer houses, nicer neighborhoods, and better schools that suburbs typically offer. But poorer Asian Americans are also making their way to the suburbs; many are locating in predominantly renter-occupied and/or older inner-ring housing in less affluent suburbs. Consequently, increasing numbers of Asian Americans settle directly in the suburbs without ever having experienced living in a central city ethnic enclave.

Many Asian Americans live in scattered suburbs across metropolitan areas in what are known as dispersed, "heterolocal" communities. In these suburban communities, recent immigrants arrive in a metropolitan area and quickly adopt a dispersed pattern of residential location, all the while managing to maintain and re-create a cohesive community through a variety of means, at a variety of scales, from the local to the transnational. At the same time, immigrants in these suburban communities remain largely invisible because there are few significant, conspicuous concentrations in any particular neighborhoods. The sprinkling of job opportunities near major employers (particularly among highly skilled immigrants working in knowledge-based industries) and the location of well-ranked school districts are oftentimes the only clues to more dense clusters in particular suburban neighborhoods. Though some immigrant institutions and businesses also tend to be located near knowledge-based companies, they are not spatially concentrated either. The newcomers typically occupy what have been habitually thought of as "white" suburban neighborhoods, schools, workplaces, strip malls, movie theaters, and parks. Consequently, the quintessential ethnic enclave (i.e., "Little India" or "Manila Town") does not develop. As a result of living, working, and socializing in the spaces and places associated with "whiteness," the immigrants reinforce their invisible status within the larger sociopolitical community, though many newcomers preserve their ethnic identities through social and religious gatherings. Interestingly, the inconspicuousness of these "heterolocal" cultural landscapes means that immigrants and natives alike interact within both public and private spaces of the community. The scattered patterns of Asian Americans in particular suburban communities is quite common, as in the case of the "saffron suburbs" in metropolitan Phoenix, or the "melting pot suburbs" of the Dallas—Ft. Worth and Washington, DC, metropolitan areas.

With the mushrooming of the Asian American population, particularly in the past decade, it is likely that previously dispersed groups will become increasingly more concentrated in the suburbs. In some places, chain migration has already begun to play an important role in the further agglomeration of Asian Americans. In some cases, Asian American realtors, along with overseas developers who are promoting particular neighborhoods, also direct customers to certain communities. Thus, sizeable concentrations emerge where once there were just a few families. Research on the Chinese in San Gabriel Valley in Los Angeles demonstrates this process. When the Asian American population reached a critical mass here in the mid-1990s, and as immigrants became increasingly heterogeneous, suburban residential concentrations materialized. In time, a wider range of ethnic-specific businesses and professional services proliferated, including travel agencies and language schools, realtors, ethnic supermarkets, and immigration, financial, and legal services. A more complete ethnic institutional structure emerged, as did a more collective political voice. The outcome was an "ethnoburb" (i.e., an ethnic suburb), where visible, nonwhite ethnic clusters of residential areas and business districts materialize in the suburbs; and where both established and newer immigrants increasingly seek political representation. Unlike traditionally segregated ethnic enclaves, "ethnoburbs" are open communities where daily interactions occur among multiethnic and multilingual neighbors.

The San Gabriel Valley case is not unique. Filipinos have created their own "ethnoburb" in Daly City, California, as a result of suburbanization and immigration; and Vietnamese congregate in suburban Orange County, California, as result of refugee secondary migration. Koreans have become increasingly concentrated both residentially and commercially in places like Bergen County, in northern New Jersey. Similarly, Asian Indians have a large presence in Edison, New Jersey, which, along with the surrounding communities of Middlesex County, is commonly known throughout the state and the New York metropolitan area as being a main center of Asian American cultural diversity. Moreover, comparable dynamics at the global, national, and local levels have made the transformation of predominantly white suburbs to multiethnic suburbs possible in other large metropolitan areas across the Pacific Rim.

In some cases, Asian Americans have established suburban enclaves in places where a particular group has a large concentration in a smaller geographic area. For instance, Vietnamese Americans, including first-generation refugees and their offspring, have lived in the easternmost suburbs of New Orleans since the late 1970s, making the area probably the densest Vietnamese settlement in the nation. In an area known as "Village d l'est and Versailles" Vietnamese Americans counted for 41.7 percent of total population in 2000. Sadly, as a victim of Hurricane Katrina in 2005, this suburban ethnic enclave's future was unclear. But a few months later, many have already returned and rebuilt their houses and businesses. And a community redevelopment plan carved by local Vietnamese Americans and architects from Vietnam envisions this neighborhood becoming a future "Asian Quarter" of New Orleans, a parallel to the famous French Quarter in downtown.

Most suburban communities are multiethnic communities; newcomers establish a significant concentration within particular neighborhoods but do not necessarily constitute a majority of the population. The ever-increasing heterogeneity within the immigrant community (stemming from a diversity of primary languages, provincialisms, religious affiliations, class statuses, and family types) results in more complex community structures. And with continued growth of the knowledge economy and flexible U.S. immigration policy, spatially clustered and socioeconomically heterogeneous multiethnic communities are likely to continually develop and increase. Unfortunately, this pattern could potentially lead to inter- and intragroup tensions. With increasing concentration and a large influx of immigrants with various backgrounds in American suburbs, there is an imperative need to examine the dynamics under which these communities evolve. The worry is that tensions among newcomers and longtime residents of various backgrounds may arise due to rapid changes of local demographic composition, residential and business landscapes, and community and political dynamics.

Suburban Communities: Implications for Economic, Cultural, and Political Incorporation

Immigrants are often perceived as those who arrive poor and uneducated, who achieve the "American dream" after many years of hard work as manual laborers or through the success of their American-born children. In contrast, many Asian immigrants arrive armed with academic degrees, proficiency in English, professional training, and/or financial resources. They have the advantages and the means to integrate into U.S. society at a much faster pace.[4] Asian Americans also possess the capabilities and know-how to rapidly transform local residential, business, and community landscapes in the suburbs that they call "home."

The new suburban Asian American communities have important implications in terms of Asian American cultural, economic, and political incorporation. Asian Americans have integrated into various aspects of the local fabric by owning/operating businesses, presenting their cultural heritage, and participating in both grassroots and electoral politics. And, as more immigrants become American citizens, many actively participate in local economic, cultural, and political affairs.

Cupertino, California, offers a rich case of transformation from a predominantly non-Hispanic white American suburb to a multiethnic community. Known as the "high-tech heart of Silicon Valley," Cupertino's residential landscapes have been altered with the influx of Asian Americans. Commercial infrastructures display prominent Asian signatures, and multicultural activities abound in community centers. Asian Americans have become an integrated part of daily life, and participate in community affairs and electoral politics. But the transformation has not been without controversies, and sometimes has involved racially connoted incidents. Both Cupertino's city government and its residents are aware of these potential forces dividing their community, and have carried out both top-town and bottom-up initiatives to address such concerns. They are committed to becoming a "model multicultural community in the twenty-first century." How this process happens in other rapidly changing suburban communities remains to be seen, though there is evidence that the metamorphosis of traditionally "white" suburban neighborhoods prompts a variety of reactions, including collectivity, cooperation, and/or conflict.

As Asian Americans settle in the suburbs, suburban Asian American businesses flourish, including those serving the mainstream market's increasing taste for Asian food, fashion, or other

---

[4] This is not to say that there isn't any disparity in the integration experiences of Asian Americans. There are a growing number of Asian Americans with less education and lower occupational status, and the "glass ceiling" effect is often encountered by higher-status individuals. We in no way want to add to the myth of the "model minority" that already circles around this minority group by suggesting that all Asian Americans are successful.

culture, as well as those primarily serving coethnics. The latter is especially true in "ethnoburbs." Moreover, contemporary Asian American businesses range from traditional mom-and-pop small retail stores, gift shops, and restaurants to professional services, such as those provided by health, finance, insurance, real estate, and high-tech firms. At the same time, many of these businesses are no longer solely family owned and operated: often firms take on paid employees. Given that central city Asian American enclaves occupy smaller geographic areas with limited capability for further spatial expansion, the suburban Asian American ethnic economy will become an increasingly important and integrated part of the general U.S. economy. As this process unfolds, and to ensure the overall success of Asian American—owned businesses, many hope that new immigrants will be provided more opportunities not only to learn about American business practices and government regulations but also to receive small business loans, in order to assist in their economic incorporation.

At the same time, with the increasing and rapid exchange of immigrants from all parts of Asia to the United States, the influence of Asian arts and culture has great consequences in this new setting. Asian immigrants and American-born natives blend both contemporary and traditional elements of Asian culture with American culture to create a hybridized Asian American culture, which includes literature, music, and the visual arts. In celebration of this transnational culture, Asian American festivals proliferate in both central city enclaves as well as in suburban settings. These festivals are popular in both traditional Asian American immigrant gateways such as New York City and San Francisco and in smaller Asian American communities such as in Phoenix, Arizona, or Austin, Texas. Chinese Lunar New Year celebrations, the Japanese American Masturi festival, the Vietnamese Tet, and more pan-Asian festivals aim at incorporating both historical and contemporary cultural traditions as well as educating other Americans about their cultures. Asian-language schools are also flourishing, often with the hopes of providing native-born Asian Americans with new cultural encounters and language skills beyond those experienced as a consequence of growing up in the United States. Concomitantly, Asian-language media, including print and audiovisual, has rapidly expanded across the country. These activities and institutions not only serve to preserve Asian American culture but also facilitate the overall integration process. Asian languages and cultures have increasingly become part of the "mainstream," evident in Mandarin, Cantonese, Korean, and other Asian-language immersion programs in public schools and the "Asian-inspired fashion" in designing world.

Cultural activities and festivals contribute to the appreciation and mutual understanding of different groups in various communities, but political participation, both in grassroots and electoral politics, is more complicated. Still it is a key step for the overall incorporation of Asian Americans. Many new immigrants, due to their lack of understanding of American politics and/or their noncitizen status, typically stay away from overt forms of political activism. They often use their participation in community organizations as a way to become involved in local politics. For instance, because these neighborhoods are usually located in superior school districts, they guarantee a better-quality education for the immigrant second generation. Many immigrant parents become involved in local school activities and some run for offices of local school boards.

In addition, sometime business organizations, trade unions, and professional organizations also serve political functions. Thus active participation in community-centered activities and political activism are not necessarily mutually exclusive. Indeed, active participation in community organizations and volunteering in local events probably serves as a pre-step for further political integration and activism. Still, it is important to note, especially for many Asian immigrants, particularly those of voting age, that it will take time to acquire English proficiency, to become naturalized, to get used to the American political system, and, for those interested in serving as political candidates, to build up their political resumes.

Among those areas with a strong Asian American presence, especially among later-generation Asian Americans, participating in grassroots and/or electoral politics is more common, as well as more imperative. Oftentimes, participation is a direct response to outlandish cries from some long-time, native-born, non-Hispanic white suburban residents that immigrants are either "unassimilated" or "taking over our city." Thus, in ethnoburbs, where there are more educated and middle-class Asian American residents and voters, the potential political impacts on local, state, and eventually national political scenes are increasingly becoming more apparent and more important. Many actively participate in the political process as fundraisers, campaigners, and/or volunteers. Meanwhile, increasing numbers of Asian Americans are being elected or appointed to political positions.

Summary

By outlining the changing demographics and geographic distributions of Asian Americans, along with the differences among various contemporary community forms within metropolitan areas, from traditional central city enclaves to multiethnic suburbs (known as "ethnoburbs"), this chapter begins the process of understanding the varied characteristics, outlooks, and concerns of Asian American communities in the United States. This kind of analysis is critical in creating a successful future, since Asian Americans are rapidly transforming what were previously known as the citadels of non-Hispanic white America to increasingly multiracial, multiethnic, multicultural, and multilingual communities.

Notes

We are grateful for the invaluable research assistance of Yun Zhou at Arizona State University. All possible errors that remain, however, are entirely ours. Inquiries can be sent to us at wei.li@asu.edu or eskop@prc.utexas.edu.

Bibliography

Asian American Justice Center and Asian American Legal Center. 2006 *A Community of Contrasts: Asian Americans and Pacific Islanders in the United States*. Washington, DC: Asian American Justice Center.

Frey, William H. 2006. *Diversity Spreads Out: Metropolitan Shifts in Hispanic, Asian, and Black Populations since 2000*. Washington, DC: Brookings Institute.

Lai, Eric and Dennis Arguelles, eds. 2003. *The New Face of Asian Pacific America: Numbers, Diversity, and Changes in the Twenty-First Century*. San Francisco, CA: Asian Week.

Li, Wei, ed. 2006. *From Urban Enclave to Ethnic Suburb: New Asian Communities in Pacific Rim Countries*. Honolulu: University of Hawaii Press.

Logan, John R. 2001. *From Many Shores: Asians in Census 2000*. Albany, NY: Lewis Mumford Center for Comparative Urban and Regional Research.

Skop, Emily. Forthcoming. *Saffron Suburbs: The Social and Spatial Construction of an Asian Indian Community*. Chicago: University of Chicago Press.

Zelinsky, Wilbur and Barrett A. Lee. 1998. Heterolocalism: An Alternative Model of the Sociospatial Behaviour of Immigrant Ethnic Communities. *International Journal of Population Geography* 4: 1–18.

Study Questions

1. In the article "Southeast Asian Women in Lowell," Pho and Mulvey describe the experiences of Lowell's Southeast Asian women as a series of "losses and gains" that are complex in their origins and even more complex in their solutions. How has economic necessity changed the structure of the traditional patriarchy? How have expanded opportunities for women in these families changed the transmission of traditional values within these families? What unique economic, social, and cultural challenges do these women face from the communities in which they live and from their own families? How do these challenges differ by generation (mothers vs. daughters)? How have women empowered themselves in the face of these challenges? What kinds of coping mechanisms do these women employ?

2. One of the consequences of changing gender roles within Southeast Asian families in Lowell has been an upsurge of domestic violence directed toward women. What are some of the risk factors that expose these women to domestic violence? Which risk factors were identified as the most important? How do these factors figure into counseling and education programs?

3. How does transnationalism truly affect what we consider to be an Asian American identity? To what extent would a transnational household promote or retard adaptation to an American or Asian American cultural identity? Will Asian Americans whose families have been in the United States for several generations distance themselves from these newcomers, from individuals with stronger ties to the homeland countries? How different may contemporary transnational households shared by Filipino, Chinese, Koreans, Japanese, and Asian Indians differ from those sustained by the first wave of pre—World War II immigrants from these countries?

4. To which regions of the country have Asian immigrants historically settled and why? Why have Asian immigrants historically settled in urban locales? What advantages did they derive from these enclaves?

5. At what point, according to the authors, did Asian immigrants begin to settle in "ethnoburbs"? How do the authors define this term? How do "ethnoburbs" differ from ethnic enclaves? What are some of the cultural, economic, and political implications of living in the suburbs?

Suggested Readings

Abraham, Margaret. 2002. Addressing Domestic Violence and the South Asian Community in the United States. pp. 191–202 in Linda Vo and Rick Bonus (eds.), *Contemporary Asian American Communities: Intersections and Divergences*. Philadelphia: Temple University Press.

Bao, Jiemen. 2005. Merit-Making Capitalism: Reterritorializing Thai Buddhism in Silicon Valley, California. *Journal of Asian American Studies* 8(2): 115–42.

Cimmarusti, R. A. 1996. Exploring Aspects of Filipino-American Families. *Journal of Marital and Family Therapy* 22(2):205–17.

Espiritu, Yen. 1995. *Filipino American Lives*. Philadelphia: Temple University Press.

Espiritu, Yen Le. 2003. *Home Bound: Filipino American Lives across Cultures, Communities, and Countries*. Berkeley: University of California Press.

Fong, Timothy. 1994. *The First Suburban Chinatown: The Remaking of Monterey Park, California*. Philadelphia: Temple University Press.

Gill, Dhara S. and Bennett Matthews. 1995. Changes in the Breadwinner Role: Punjabi Families in Transition. *Journal of Comparative Family Studies* 26(2): 255–64.

Glenn, Evelyn Nakano and Rhacel Salazar Parreñas. 1996. The Other Issei: Japanese Immigrant Women in the Pre—World War II Period. Pp. 124–40 in Silvia Pedraza and Rubén G. Rumbaut (eds.), *Origins and Destinies: Immigration, Race, and Ethnicity in America*. Belmont, CA: Wadsworth.

Kang, K. Connie. 1995. *Home Was the Land of the Morning Calm*. New York: Addison-Wesley.

Kibria, Nazli. 1993. *Family Tightrope: The Changing Lives of Vietnamese Americans*. Princeton, NJ: Princeton University Press.

Kallivayalil, Diya. 2004. Gender and Cultural Socialization in Indian Immigrant Families in the United States. *Feminism & Psychology* 14(4): 535–59.

Lessinger, Johanna. 1995. *From the Ganges to the Hudson: Indian Immigrants in New York City*. Boston: Allyn and Bacon.

Li, Wei. 1999. Building Ethnoburbia: The Emergence and Manifestation of the Chinese Ethnoburb in Los Angeles' San Gabriel Valley. *Journal of Asian American Studies* 2(1): 1–28.

Liu, Haiming. 2005. *The Transnational History of a Chinese Family: Immigrant Letters, Family Business, and Reverse Migration*. New Brunswick, NJ: Rutgers University Press.

Matsumoto, Valerie. 1993. *Farming the Homeplace: A Japanese American Community in California, 1919–1982*. Ithaca, NY: Cornell University Press.

Pyke, Karen. 2000. "The Normal American Family" as an Interpretive Structure of Family Life among Grown Children of Korean and Vietnamese Immigrants. *Journal of Marriage and the Family* 62(1): 240–55.

Smith-Hefner, Nancy J. 1998. *Khmer American: Identity and Moral Education in a Diasporic Community*. Berkeley: University of California Press.

Toji, Dean S. and Karen Umemoto. 2003. The Paradox of Dispersal: Ethnic Continuity and Community Development among Japanese Americans in Little Tokyo. *AAPI Nexus* 1(1): 21–46.

Vo, Linda and Mary Y. Danico. 2004. The Formation of Post-Suburban Communities: Koreatown and Little Saigon, Orange County. *International Journal of Sociology and Social Policy* 24(7/8): 15–45.

Ying, Yu-Wen and Chua Chiem Chao. 1996. Intergenerational Relationship in Iu Mien American Families. *Amerasia Journal* 22(3): 47–64.

Yoshioka, M. R., J. DiNoia, and K. Ullah. 2001. Attitudes toward Marital Violence: An Examination of Four Asian Communities. *Violence against Women* 7(8): 900–926.

Zhao, Xiaojian. 2002. *Remaking Chinese America: Immigration, Family, and Community, 1940–1965*. New Brunswick, NJ: Rutgers University Press.

Zhou, Min and Carl L. Bankston III. 1998. *Growing Up American: How Vietnamese Children Adapt to Life in the United States*. New York: Russell Sage Foundation.

Zhou, Min and Susan S. Kim. 2006. Community Forces, Social Capital, and Educational Achievement: The Case of Supplementary Education in the Chinese and Korean Immigrant Communities. *Harvard Educational Review* 76(1): 1–29.

Films

Flanary, Lisette Marie and Evann Siebens (codirectors/coproducers). 2003. *American Aloha: Hula beyond Hawai'i* (documentary).

Friedman, Daniel and Sharon Grimberg (directors/producers). 1997. *Miss India Georgia* (56-minute documentary).

Ishizuka, Karen L. (producer). 1993. *Moving Memories* (31-minute documentary).

Koster, Henry (director). 1961. *Flower Drum Song* (comedy).

Krishnan, Indu (director). 1990. *Knowing Her Place* (40-minute documentary).

Mallozzi, Julie (director). 2004. *Monkey Dance* (65-minute documentary).

Mishran, Ahrin and Nick Rothenberg (coproducers). 1994. *Bui Doi: Life Like Dust* (29-minute documentary).

Moyers, Bill (producer). 2003. *Becoming American: The Chinese Experience* (87-minute documentary).

Nakasako, Spencer (producer/director). 1998. *Kelly Loves Tony* (57-minute documentary).

Uno, Michael T. (producer/director). 1988. *The Wash* (94-minute drama).

Yasui, Lise (producer/director/writer). 1988. *A Family Gathering* (60- or 30-minute documentary).

PART III   Work, Labor, and Economic Adaptation

Bamboo Ceilings, the Working Poor, and the Unemployed: The Mixed Economic Realities of Asian Americans and Pacific Islanders

CHAPTER 7

Edith Wen-Chu Chen and Dennis Arguelles

Much attention has been given to the success and achievements of Asian Americans. Their image as the successful or model minority is not a new one. This term originally referred to Japanese and Chinese Americans and became popular in the 1960s with magazine headlines such as "Success Story of One Minority Group in the U.S." and "Success Story: Japanese American Style" (*New York Times Magazine*, January 1966; *U.S. News and World Report*, December 26, 1966). Accused of "Outwhiting the Whites," Asian Americans are often regarded as a problem- free minority (*Newsweek*, June 21, 1971).

The household incomes of Asian Americans are often used as evidence of their success (Highley, 2010), which exceeds that of all other racial ethnic groups, including Whites. According to the U.S. Census data, Asian Americans have the highest median household income ($69,143) compared to all racial and ethnic groups (U.S. Census 2007–2009, see Figure 7.1). In other words, their median household income was not only higher than Latinos' and African Americans', but also exceeded that of Whites' ($54,412). This pattern of Asian Americans outpacing Whites has helped support the popularly held image that Asian Americans are a successful minority group facing little discrimination and racial barriers.

Edith Wen-Chu Chen, PhD, is Professor in the Asian American Studies Department at California State University, Northridge.

Dennis Arguelles is the Director of Community Economic Development for Search to Involve Pilipino Americans and former president of the Asian Pacific Policy and Planning Council. He received his BA in Political Science and MA in Urban Planning from UCLA.

The policy implication is that Asian Americans do not need special poverty or job training programs, and that economic struggle is not an issue for them as for many African Americans and Latinos.

This kind of data has led scholars, journalists, and the general public to believe that racism is not significant in the lives of Asian Americans, and that they are relatively free of economic

Article by Edith Wen-Chu Chen, PhD, a Professor in the Asian American Studies Department at California State University, Northridge, and Dennis Arguelles, Director of Community Economic Development for Search to Involve Pilipino Americans and former president of the Asian Pacific Policy and Planning Council. He received his BA in Political Science and MA in Urban Planning from UCLA.

69

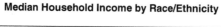

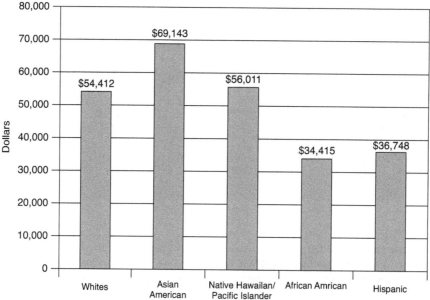

FIGURE 7.1

Source: U.S. Census Bureau, American Community Survey 2007–2009.

problems. It is a commonly held belief that Asian Americans do not experience discrimination, and some may even believe that being Asian may come with special advantages. Some scholars have even gone so far as to suggest that Asian Americans will soon merge into the White category, suggesting that race is not a disadvantage in their lives (Hacker, 1992; Zhou, 2007).

Other scholars and researchers have vigorously challenged the idea of Asian American success on several grounds. With respect to income data, they argue that the use of national median household income data is a poor indicator of the economic well-being of Asian Americans and racial progress (Suzuki, 1989; Asian American Center for Advancing Justice, 2011). The data masks the reality that Asian American households are generally larger and have more people working and contributing to the household income compared to Whites. Asian Americans are more likely than Whites and African Americans to have three or more workers in a household, which helps explain their larger household income (Asian American Center for Advancing Justice, 2011). Also, Asian Americans tend to live in large metropolitan areas (Los Angeles, New York, San Francisco, etc.) where the salaries are higher to account for the higher cost of living (see Figure 7.2).

Are Asian Americans Really That Successful?: A Closer Look

A more accurate measure of racial equality would compare individual income data and control for regional differences, educational level, type of jobs, skills, experience, age, and so on. A number of studies point out that when these factors are taken into consideration, Asian Americans earn less than Whites, which suggests that they face discrimination in the workplace.

Top Ten Metropolitan Areas where Asian Americans Live

1. Los Angeles-Long Beach-Santa Ana, CA
2. New York-Northern New Jersey-Long Island, NY, NJ, PA
3. San Francisco-Oakland-Fremont, CA
4. San Jose-Sunnyvale-Santa Clara, CA
5. Honolulu, HI
6. Chicago-Naperville-Joliet, IL-IN-WI
7. Washington-Arlington-Aexandria, DC-VA-MD-WV
8. Seattle-Tacoma-Bellevue, WA
9. Houston-Sugarland-Baytown, TX
10. Dallas-Ft. Worth-Arlington, TX

FIGURE 7.2
Source: U.S. Census American Community Survey, 2005–2007.

Asian Americans are known to be well represented at top universities—18% of Harvard University enrollment; 24%, Stanford University; and 46%, University of California–Berkeley—yet they make up only a paltry 2% of the top executive positions in Fortune 500 companies, according to a Center for Work–Life Policy report (Stafford, 2011). Asian American professionals may face a *glass ceiling* or *bamboo ceiling*—informal workplace norms and barriers that prevent them from being promoted to upper management and executive positions (Woo, 2000; Stafford, 2011).

While it is often perceived that Asian Americans excel in the fields of engineering and sciences, Asian American engineers and scientists are grossly underrepresented in management positions and are underpaid compared to Whites (*Los Angeles Times*, July 15, 1988; Wong & Nagasawa, 1991; Woo, 2000). For instance, at the National Institutes of Health (NIH), Asian Americans made up 13.49% of the workforce but less than 3.3% of the executive force in 2006 (Ruttimann, 2009). A 2005 U.S. Equal Employment Opportunity Commission Gallup Poll revealed that Asian Americans had the highest reports of discrimination (31%) of all the minority groups (Ruttimann, 2009). Similarly, on college campuses and universities, Asian American faculty have reported struggles advancing through the academic pipeline (Chen & Hune 2011). They make up more than 10% of full-time faculty, but less than .4% of college and university presidents (Ryu, 2010).

Aside from examining how they are advancing by occupation, a look at per capita income at the same regional area can also provide clues to how Asian Americans are faring economically relative to other racial and ethnic groups. The Los Angeles–Long Beach–Santa Ana metropolitan area has the largest number of Asian Americans in the country (U.S. Census Bureau, 2005–2007). When comparing the per capita income of Asian Americans to the other major racial groups, the idea of Asian American success begins to dim. Per capita income refers to the household income divided by the number of people living in the household. This is a better measure of economic well-being since it adjusts for the fact that Asian Americans tend to have more people working and living in the household than Whites and the general U.S. population. When comparing the per capita income of Asian Americans in the Los Angeles–Long Beach–Santa Ana metropolitan area, their income figure is significantly less than Whites ($30,025 vs. $35,103), although these figures are higher than the per capita income figures for African Americans and Latinos (Figure 7.3).

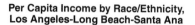

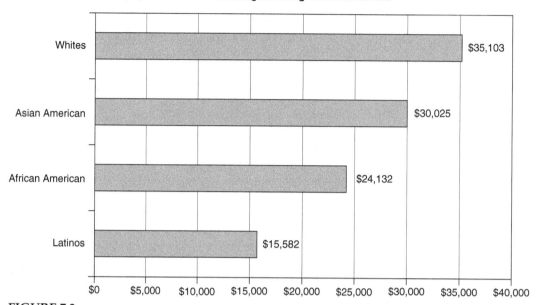

FIGURE 7.3
Source: U.S. Census Bureau, American Community Survey 2007–2009, 3-year estimates.

An even more precise understanding of Asian American economic well-being would consider the ethnic diversity that makes up the umbrella term "Asian American." Asian Americans are not a monolithic group, but rather a group composed of over thirty ethnic groups with different pre-migration and settlement experiences that impact their economic adjustment. For example, Japanese Americans have been in the United States for several generations and are doing better ($41,265) than later-arriving groups such as Vietnamese, Cambodian, Laotian, and Hmong (Figure 7.4). In addition, these Southeast Asian groups have unique circumstances associated with being refugees, involuntarily forced out from their homelands—many of whom arrived with very few material resources, little English-speaking abilities, and the necessary skills to adjust to their new urban environments. Looking at ethnic-specific data reveals that Native Hawaiians/Pacific Islanders, Thai, and Vietnamese have per capita income figures similar or worse off than African Americans. Cambodian American per capita income figures are the lowest of all the selected Asian American Pacific Islander groups, doing far worse than African Americans and more similar to that of Latinos in the Los Angeles–Long Beach–Santa Ana area. Comparison data for Hmong at the same regional data could not be calculated due to their smaller numbers, but at the national level, their per capita income ($10,949) is the lowest of all racial and ethnic groups nationwide, even lower than that of Latinos (Asian American Center for Advancing Justice, 2011).

Occasionally the terms "Asian American," "Asian Pacific American," or "Asian American Pacific Islander" are used interchangeably. These latter two terms refer to both Asian American and Pacific Islanders, and their data has previously been reported together, although there are greater steps at the federal and local levels to report separate "Asian American" and "Native Hawaiian and Pacific Islander" categories. The two separate categories reflect an acknowledgment that

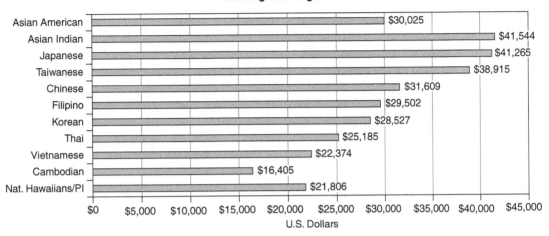

Per Capita Income of Selected AAPI Groups, Los Angeles-Long Beach-Santa Ana

- Asian American: $30,025
- Asian Indian: $41,544
- Japanese: $41,265
- Taiwanese: $38,915
- Chinese: $31,609
- Filipino: $29,502
- Korean: $28,527
- Thai: $25,185
- Vietnamese: $22,374
- Cambodian: $16,405
- Nat. Hawaiians/PI: $21,806

U.S. Dollars

FIGURE 7.4
Source: U.S. Census Bureau, American Community Survey 2007–2009.

Asian Americans Hit Hard by the Economic Crisis

By Dennis Arguelles, Director of Community Economic Development at Search to Involve Pilipino Americans

Married in 1998, the Aquinos purchased their first home in 2002. Mr. Aquino, a licensed vocational nurse (LVN) and Ms. Aquino, a registered nurse, had dreamed about starting their own business and operating an assisted-living facility for disabled adults. Mr. Aquino had managed a similar facility in the Philippines and because of his growing back problems, had hoped to eventually get away from the physically taxing work of being an LVN. By 2006, their home had increased in value substantially and they decided to leverage the new equity to purchase a second home that would serve as the assisted-living facility. They also took a substantial amount of cash out of their home for start-up capital. In addition to continuing in their existing jobs, throughout most of 2007 Mr. and Ms. Aquino worked diligently to launch their business, including making needed renovations, getting required permits and licenses, recruiting qualified personnel, and marketing their facility to eligible clients. The burdens of two mortgages and supporting their two young children were difficult, but the future of their new business looked promising.

Then, in 2008, circumstances changed drastically. Several families who had expressed interest in placing relatives at the facility pulled out, citing financial hardships and other factors. Despite continued recruitment efforts, they lacked enough clients to make the facility viable.

By late 2008 the cost of operating the facility had exhausted the family's savings and they started falling behind on the facility's mortgage payments, partly because they had unwittingly agreed to overly burdensome loan terms. In 2009, the Aquinos decided to close down the new business and sell the second home, but not before its value had plunged almost 25%. Additionally, to comply with various licensing requirements, the Aquinos had made numerous modifications to the home. Unfortunately, these changes made it very difficult to sell the home to prospective buyers. Throughout most of 2009, the Aquinos sought relief from their bank by way of a short sale or loan modification. The bank was generally unresponsive, continuing to assess late fees and eventually initiated foreclosure. By mid-2010 the foreclosure process was complete and the property had lost 40% of its value.

Unfortunately, this was not the end of trouble for the Aquino family. The stress from losing both their business and property had taken a toll on their health and Mr. Aquino's back problems became so acute that in 2010 he was unable to continue his work as an LVN. This made meeting the mortgage on their original home, which was fully leveraged to help start the business, increasingly difficult. Other personal debts, medical expenses, and educational costs also piled up. Disability insurance helped somewhat, but Ms. Aquino had to work over 60 hours per week at various nursing facilities to help make ends meet. In 2011, Ms. Aquino began experiencing her own health problems and missed extended periods of work, resulting in their falling behind on their remaining mortgage.

In less than four years the Aquinos had gone from having a positive net worth, healthy assets, and cash savings to being saddled with debts that threaten to haunt them for several years and even decades. They worry about their ability to pay for their children's college education, much less save enough for their own retirement. Their story may sound like the perfect storm of misfortune, despair, and bad timing, but it actually represents the all-too-common experiences of numerous Asian Pacific Islander families pursuing the American dream at the height of the worst economic recession in decades.

Native Hawaiians and Pacific Islanders may share a distinct history from Asian Americans who largely came to the U.S. as immigrants or refugees. Some argue that Native Hawaiians share more in common with Native Americans than Asian Americans. Native Hawaiians, for example, are not immigrants but are indigenous people and forcibly became Americans through illegal military conquest. Native Hawaiian struggles include land rights, self-sufficiency, and cultural reclamation, and many hope to achieve sovereignty similar to the status accorded to Native Americans. As with other Pacific Islanders, a large number of Native Hawaiians have reluctantly left for the "continent" in search of better economic opportunities.

Many Asian Americans are Struggling

The use of national median household income as a proxy for economic success hides the reality that many Asian Americans are struggling financially. The Asian American population is one with mixed economic realities. Past studies have suggested that in metropolitan areas, for every Asian American household that makes $75,000 or more, there is almost another household living in poverty (Ong & Hee, 1994; Shinagawa & Kim, 2008). In other words, while Asian Americans are well represented in the professions, a sizeable portion of Asian Americans are part of the working poor, even with families that have two parents working (Asian American Federation, 2008). While the Asian American population includes engineers, scientists, doctors, and nurses, they are also small business owners, restaurant workers, and seamstresses.

About two million Asian Americans live in poverty, or about 12.5% of the population (Asian American Federation, 2008). Poor and low-income Asian Americans are especially prevalent in large metropolitan areas where the cost of living is higher. In New York City, for example, almost one in five Asian Americans are poor, and nearly 41% are low-income (Asian American Federation, 2008). Many of these Asian Americans form part of America's working poor. What is distinctive about poor Asian American families is they are more likely to include those in which both parents work, normally a family structure that is a protective factor against poverty in White households (Asian American Federation, 2008). During the economic crisis of 2008, Asian Americans had the lowest unemployment rate. However, for those that did suffer from unemployment, they remained unemployed the longest compared to any other major minority group, including African Americans and Latinos (Noguchi, 2010). Many rely on work in their ethnic enclaves and have a harder time finding a job when unemployed due to language barriers and lacking networks beyond their enclaves. "If you have a Vietnamese employee working for a Vietnamese employer in Little Saigon in Orange County, that does not transfer to an ability to get a job in Koreatown in Los Angeles," according to Kent Wong, who teaches at UCLA's Center for Labor Research and Education (Noguchi, 2010). They include underpaid garment workers, restaurant workers, and domestics.

It should be noted that during the economic crisis of 2008, when the bubble burst, Asian Americans were disproportionately affected. Many Asian Americans had just prior invested in real estate and other assets that plummeted in value. Asian Americans were disproportionately distressed by foreclosures. Some, like a lot of Korean merchants, were really hit hard because they used the equity in their homes to finance their business ventures. When the economy collapsed, they not only lost their businesses, but their homes as well. The sad thing is a lot of predatory lending also took place during this time, including unscrupulous agents exploiting their own ethnic groups.

The number of Asian American women working and their working hours are likely underestimated by the U.S. Census. This is especially true for those who are working in small family businesses or in sectors that rely heavily on cheap immigrant labor. Industries such as garment manufacturing and electronics assembly often do not fully document the number of hours their employees work, especially since workers are often paid by the piece (Foo, 2002). Besides working in low-wage sectors, immigrants who lack language abilities but have a small amount of capital may open small family businesses as a source of livelihood. However, in order for these family businesses, such as liquor stores and restaurants, to survive, they depend on the free or cheap labor of women and children. Even though the business may be registered under the husband's name, the wife and/or children are often working at the store, although not as registered employees (Park, 1989).

In conclusion, when a closer examination of the data is taken into account, the success of Asian Americans is overestimated. While it is true that growing numbers are middle-class professionals, they are less likely to be in decision-making positions compared to Whites with similar levels of education and skills and more likely to receive lower pay. Even more damaging is that the model minority image hides the fact that a significant portion of the Asian American and Pacific Islander population is poor, with Samoans, Cambodian, Laotian, and Hmong refugees especially in need of immediate attention.

Some community-based Asian American and Pacific Islander organizations believe that they have been overlooked and underfunded precisely due to the widely held model minority image. The realities are that many Asian American and Pacific Islander organizations are underserved and in need of special services (Asian American Center for Advancing Justice, 2011). (See Sidebar, "Surviving on Hope: Long Beach's Cambodian Community.")

Surviving on Hope: Long Beach's Cambodian Community

By Dennis Arguelles, Director of Community Economic Development at Search to Involve Pilipino Americans

Sara Pol-Lim, the Executive Director of the United Cambodian Community (UCC), shares a large corner office with several other staff members on the second floor of a two-story building in the heart of Long Beach's Cambodia Town. It is a modest headquarters for UCC, one of the oldest and largest nonprofit community service organizations in Southern California's Cambodian community. But considering that, just a few years earlier, UCC faced insolvency, the facility and the services it provides are a testament to Pol-Lim's leadership and the work of the organization's savvy Board of Directors. "We were saved by the community" says Pol-Lim, "hundreds of people gave small donations, $5, $10, whatever they could afford. When we put the word out we raised $5,000 in just one week."

UCC's resurgence could not have come at a more critical time. Just as the agency was getting back on its feet, the national and local economy took a nose dive. Services in the community were needed more than ever. Pol-Lim credits the economic recession with exacerbating hardships the community had already faced for decades, especially after welfare reform policies in the 1990s led to what she describes as the "sacrificing" of so many first-generation Cambodians: "They simply learned to deal with less, but the cost was tremendous hardship and disparity."

Still, she has hope for future generations of Cambodian Americans. Looking to increase its effectiveness, UCC recently shifted its mission to a greater focus on advocacy and policy development. It diversified its Board of Directors, which now has the involvement of numerous other ethnic groups and communities. Justifiably, the community still suffers from the trauma of the "Killing Fields," but UCC is working to expand a range of preventative, rather than social service, programs. "Our goal is to help community members become their own advocates," says Pol-Lim. She is also calling for efforts to establish a Cambodian genocide memorial in the United States. "It's part of the healing process our community needs."

References

Asian American Center for Advancing Justice. (2011). *A Community of Contrasts: Asian Americans in the United States: 2011*. Retrieved January 15, 2012, from www.apalc.org/pdffiles/Community_of_Contrast.pdf.

Asian American Federation. (2008). *Working but Poor: Asian American poverty in New York*. New York: Author.

Chen, E. W. C., & Hune, S. (2011). "Asian American Women Faculty in the Pipeline," in *Women of Color in Higher Education: Changing Directions and New Perspectives*, eds. Gaetane Jean-Marie Brenda Lloyd-Jones. Bingley, UK: Emerald Group Publishing.

Foo, L. (2002). *Asian American Women: Issues, Concerns, and Responsive Human and Civil Rights Advocacy*. New York: Ford Foundation.

Hacker, A. (1992). *Two Nations: Black and White, Separate, Hostile, Unequal*. New York: Charles Scribner's Sons.

Highley, S. (2010). "Asian-Americans Flock to America's Wealthy Suburbs," in *Racial Integration of the Wealthiest 1000 Places in America*. Retrieved February 5, 2011, from http://higley1000.com/archives/201.

Los Angeles Times (July 15, 1988). "Asian American Finding Cracks in Glass Ceiling."

New York Times Magazine (January 1966). "Success Story of One Minority Group in the U.S."

Newsweek (June 21, 1971). "Success Story: Outwhiting the Whites."

Noguchi, Y. (October 8, 2010). "Asians Out of Work Longest Among U.S. Minorities," National Public Radio. Retrieved January 15, 2011, from http://www.npr.org/templates/story/story.php?storyId=130408243.

Ong, P., & Hee, S. (1994). "Economic Diversity," in *The State of Asian Pacific America: Economic Diversity, Issues & Policies*, ed. Paul Ong. Los Angeles: LEAP Asian Pacific American Public Policy Institute and UCLA Asian American Studies Center.

Park, K. (1989). "Impact of New Productive Activities on the Organization of Domestic Life: A Case Study of the Korean Community," in *Frontiers of Asian American Studies*, eds. Gail Nomura, Russell Endo, Stephen H. Sumida, and Russell C. Leong. Pullman: Washington State University Press.

Ruttimann, J. (May 29, 2009). "Breaking Through 'Bamboo Ceiling' for Asian

American Scientists," Retrieved January 10, 2010, from http://sciencecareers.sciencemag.org/career_magazine/previous_issues/articles/2009_05_29/science.opms.r0900072.

Ryu, M. (2010). *Minorities in Higher Education 2010*. Washington, DC: American Council on Education.

Shinagawa, L. H., & Kim, D. Y. (2008). *A Portrait of Chinese Americans: A National Demographic and Social Profile of Chinese Americans*. College Park: OCA and the Asian American Studies Program, University of Maryland.

Stafford, D. (August 21, 2011). Despite Academic Achievements, Asian Americans hit bamboo ceiling. *McClatchy-Tribune News Service*.

Suzuki, B. (1989). Asian Americans as the "model minority." *Change, 21*(6), 13–19.

U.S. Census Bureau, American Community Survey 2007–2009, Detailed Tables; generated by Edith Wen-Chu Chen; using American FactFinder.

U.S. Census Bureau, American Community Survey 2005–2007.

U.S. News and World Report (December 26, 1966). "Success Story: Japanese American Style."

Wong, P., & Nagasawa, R. (1991). "Asian American Scientists and Engineers: Is There a Glass Ceiling for Career Advancement?" *Chinese American Forum, 6*(3), 3–6.

Woo, D. (2000). "The Glass Ceiling at 'XYZ Aerospace,'" in *Glass Ceilings and Asian Americans: The New Face of Workplace Barriers*. Walnut Creek, CA: AltaMira Press.

Zhou, M. (2007). "Are Asian Americans Becoming White?" *Contexts, 3*.

Striving for the American Dream

Struggle, Success, and Intergroup Conflict among Korean Immigrant Entrepreneurs

Jennifer Lee

CHAPTER 8

It takes intellectual sophistication to resist blaming the economic ills of the ghetto on the immediate agents of exploitation, whether Jewish or not, and to see these ills as products of impersonal social and economic forces that transcend the responsibility of particular individuals.[1]

Introduction

The highest self-employed immigrant ethnic group in the United States, Koreans have changed the commercial landscape of today's cities. Fresh fruit and vegetable markets, nail salons, dry cleaners, and fresh fish stores have become ubiquitous symbols of Korean immigrant entrepreneurship. Koreans offer their services not only to fellow ethnics but also to the white and minority populations alike. Studies estimate that approximately one-third of Korean immigrant families are engaged in small business, figures that parallel the staggering self-employment rate of Jewish immigrants, in the early twentieth century. Following in the footsteps of Jewish immigrants, Korean immigrants are experiencing rapid economic mobility through self-employment. Second- and third-generation Jewish Americans have largely moved into the primary labor market (with substantial portions in professional and white-collar occupations), and today's second-generation Koreans are quickly following suit.

Korean immigrant entrepreneurs seem to have "made it" in their new host country. Touted as "model minorities," Koreans have become symbols that the American dream is alive—if an individual works hard enough, delays gratification, makes sacrifices, and most of all perseveres, he or she can make it too. The opportunity structure is equal, and the path open to anyone who wants to follow it.

However, their relatively rapid economic success has come with social costs. Black nationalists have charged Korean merchants with disrespectful treatment toward their customers, prejudice, and exploitation of the black community. They have also accused Korean merchants of buying all of the stores in their neighborhoods, draining the communities of their resources, and failing to "give back" by hiring local residents (Lee 1993; Min 1996). Labeled as "absentee owners," Korean storeowners are accused of owning businesses in poor black neighborhoods yet not living in these neighborhoods, thereby removing the profits from the communities in which they serve (Min 1996).

---

[1] Quoted from Selznick and Steinberg 1969, 130.

The tension between Korean merchants and black customers crystallized in 1990 with an eighteen-month-long boycott of a fruit and vegetable market in the Flatbush section of Brooklyn, New York (Lee 1993).[2] Much of the media coverage focused on individual-level differences between Korean merchants and black customers, pointing to the cultural and linguistic misunderstandings between two minority groups while ignoring the structural conditions under which intergroup conflict can emerge. The friction mounted on March 16, 1991, when Korean storeowner Soon Ja Du shot and killed African American teenager Latasha Harlins in South Central Los Angeles. Finally, the tension climaxed on April 29, 1992, after four white police officers were acquitted of beating 25-year-old African American motorist Rodney King. The nation remained paralyzed as it watched buildings in South Central and Koreatown burning while inner-city residents looted stores, taking everything from televisions and VCRs to food and diapers. The worst domestic uprising in the twentieth century ended with a toll count of 16,291 arrested, 2,383 injured, 500 fires, and 52 dead (Njeri 1996). Korean merchants suffered almost half of the property damage, amounting to more than $400 million, affecting more than 2,300 Korean-owned businesses in Los Angeles (Ong and Hee 1993). The nation was left stunned.

I address four main research questions in this article. First, I investigate why Korean immigrants enter self-employment at such high rates, especially compared to native-born Americans. Second, I examine the resources that these immigrants utilize in starting and maintaining their businesses. Third, I explore the "retail niches" that Korean immigrants dominate, and also study the reasons why they choose to locate in inner-city neighborhoods. Finally, I investigate the interactions between Koreans and blacks and examine the structural conditions under which tension between merchants and customers becomes racially coded and turns into conflict.

The study is based on thirty face-to-face, in-depth interviews of Korean merchants in five predominantly black neighborhoods in New York City and Philadelphia.[3] Each of these neighborhoods has bustling commercial strips lined with small businesses that offer a variety of merchandise, some of which is geared specifically for a black clientele, including wigs, ethnic beauty supplies, inner-city sportswear, and beauty salons and barber shops that service black customers. The data also includes seventy-five indepth interviews of black customers from each of these research sites. African American research assistants conducted face-to-face, open-ended interviews of local residents from these communities who were asked about their shopping experiences in Korean-owned stores and about their opinions of Korean merchants more generally.[4] Unlike previous studies of black-Korean relations that include interviews of only the Korean merchants, my study, by including interviews of black customers, enables me to examine these relations from both perspectives.

Choosing Self-Employment as a Means to Upward Mobility

Post-1965 Korean immigrants come to the United States with relatively high levels of "human capital," measured by educational attainment and occupational skills. Thirty percent of Korean immigrants ages twenty-five and over have completed four years of college—about twice the rate

---

[2] "Black" refers to a generic category that includes African Americans, West Indians, and Africans.

[3] The research sites include three low-income and two middle-income black communities. The three low-income neighborhoods are West Harlem, NY, East Harlem, NY, and West Philadelphia, and the two middle-income communities include Jamaica, Queens, and East Mount Airy, Philadelphia.

[4] The customers were paid $10 to thank them for taking their time to participate in the study. The funds were provided by a Dissertation Improvement Grant from the National Science Foundation, SBR-9633345.

for the U.S. native-born population—and a large proportion held white-collar and professional jobs in Korea (Yoon 1997). Yet because the supply of college graduates in South Korea exceeds the demand for such a highly educated workforce, the average rate of unemployment in Korea for male college graduates is 30 percent. Hence, Koreans view immigration to the United States as a more viable route to mobility, not only for themselves but also for their children. Yet after their arrival to the United States, Korean immigrants often find that they are unable to transfer their "human capital" into commensurate professional occupations, and consequently, turn to self-employment.

Social scientists note that certain ethnic groups, particularly when they are immigrants, enter self-employment to overcome disadvantages in the American labor market (Light 1972; Light and Bonacich 1988; Min 1984; Yoon 1997). A language barrier, unfamiliarity with American customs and culture, and the inability to transfer educational and occupational capital leave immigrants severely disadvantaged to compete with the native-born in the primary labor market. For example, U.S. companies often have little understanding of educational and work credentials obtained outside of the country. Whereas a degree from Seoul National, Yonsei, or Ewha Universities immediately connotes academic rigor and high status in Korea, companies in the United States have difficulty translating and measuring these credentials. Furthermore, like many first-generation immigrants, Koreans have difficulty mastering a new language, thereby making their transition into an English-speaking workforce extremely difficult.

Compared to the native-born, immigrants have fewer "high-priced salable skills" (Light 1972) and therefore turn to self-employment as an alternative to entering the secondary labor market where they would receive relatively low wages in unskilled or low-skilled occupations. Hence, Korean immigrants opt to open small businesses not because self-employment is their primary occupational choice but instead because their alternatives in the U.S. labor market are less promising and less lucrative. In short, self-employment becomes a means of achieving upward mobility in the face of severe handicaps in the primary labor market.

However, disadvantages in the labor market alone cannot explain why Korean immigrants enter self-employment at such high rates since ethnic groups who find themselves similarly disadvantaged in the labor market such as Laotians and Malaysians have self-employment rates of less than 3 percent (Yoon 1997). To explain the variance in the rates of self-employment, social scientists have focused on the importance of class and ethnic resources and social capital in the development and success of small business among immigrant groups such as Cubans, Israelis, and Koreans.

Resources Used in Business

Class and Ethnic Resources

Class resources are characterized as human capital, economic capital, and wealth, and ethnic resources are defined as "forms of aid preferentially available from one's own ethnic group."[5] Social capital, in the form of rotating credit associations, has also contributed to the survival of Korean-owned businesses. These resources are invaluable to business success and are used not only at the initial stages of capitalization but also throughout business ownership. Access to class and ethnic resources and the utilization of social capital are crucial to understanding how Korean immigrants are able to open small businesses at such high rates.

---

[5] Pyong Gap Min and Charles Jaret, "Ethnic Business Success: The Case of Korean Small Business in Atlanta," *Sociology and Social Research* 69 (1984): 432.

Korean business owners use a variety of class and ethnic resources such as personal savings, loans from family and coethnic friends, and advertising in Korean-language newspapers to purchase their businesses. But unlike previous literature that stresses the significance of rotating credit associations (*gae*) in the formation of businesses (Light 1972; Light and Bonacich 1988), I find that the majority of Korean immigrant merchants do not use this resource at the start-up phase. Table 8.1 indicates that only 7 percent acquired capital to open their business through funds from a rotating credit association. By contrast, 76 percent bought their businesses using a combination of other resources: personal savings, loans from family and coethnic friends, and credit from the previous coethnic storeowner. The remaining 17 percent bought their business from a family owner—usually a brother, sister, or in-laws who immigrated several years before they did.

When coethnics purchase businesses from one another, rather than going through a third financial party like a bank, the new Korean owner will normally pay the previous owner one-third of the business's value as a down payment and the remaining two-thirds in monthly installments over a period of a few years. Bates (1994) notes that Koreans use this debt source more frequently than other groups since Korean are more likely to purchase retail firms that are already in business.

Social Capital—The Rotating Credit Association

Although the use of rotating credit associations may not be as prevalent at the start-up phase, this resource is highly utilized at the later stages of business. Rotating credit associations range in both membership size and value, with participation extending from only a few people to over thirty, and the value ranging anywhere from $100 to over $100,000. Korean merchants report that the average *gae* ranges from ten to twenty people, with each member contributing between $1,000 and $2,000 into a pot totaling $10,000 to $40,000. Each member contributes to the fund, and every member takes turns in receiving the lump sum of money. For example, a Korean merchant explained that she belonged to a rotating credit association with twenty members. Each member contributed $2,700 per month, and the first member who received the pot received $51,300 ($2,700 × 19). The pot rotated according to a predetermined schedule until each member received his or her share. After receiving the pool of money, each individual must contribute $3,100 until the rotation is complete. Therefore, the member who received the money first got only $51,300 while the one who received the pot last was rewarded with $58,900—the surplus accounting for interest and appreciation for those at the tail end of the rotation. Implicit in such a system is a high degree of mutual trust, obligation, and expectation among its members.

Rotating credit associations are less important when Korean merchants purchase their first business but become very significant after they have already established their businesses for various purposes such as buying new merchandise or equipment, remodeling, or purchasing their second business. *Gae* also serve as a crucial economic resource when merchants have little cash flow or in case of unforeseen emergencies, such as break-ins or fires, that are not uncommon in low-income neighborhoods. Even though the use of *gae* varies among Korean merchants, all have admitted that the rotating credit association is a resource they *could* draw upon if they needed to quickly accumulate capital. The facility with which Korean immigrants can draw upon such ethnic resources attests to their easy access to social and economic capital.

Sociologist James Coleman explains (1988, 98),

Social capital is defined by its function. It is not a single entity but a variety of different entities, with two elements in common: they all consist of some aspect of social structures, and they facilitate certain actions of actors—whether persons or corporate actors—within the structure. Like

TABLE 8.1 Resources Korean Merchants Used in Starting Their Business		
Means of Establishing Business Ownership	**Number of Businesses**	**Percent**
Savings + loans from family/ friends + credit from previous coethnic storeowner	23	76
Bought from a family member	5	17
Rotating credit association (*gae*)	2	7
TOTAL	30	100

other forms of capital, social capital is productive, making possible the achievement of certain ends that in its absence would not be possible. Like physical and human capital, social capital is not completely fungible but may be specific to certain activities. A given form of social capital that is valuable in facilitating certain actions may be useless or even harmful to others.

Central to Coleman's concept of social capital is the role of closure in the social structure; closure facilitates the trust needed to allow actions such as exchange, lending, and borrowing from members within the social structure. Also essential is the degree to which these relations are indispensable, or the extent to which members within the social structure depend on one another. Coleman offers the rotating credit association as a prime example by which social capital is manifested among its members as a form of obligation, trust, and expectation, the absence of which would prevent such a system from functioning.

Social capital differs from economic or human capital in that it is not a tangible resource but is instead the capacity of individuals to command and mobilize resources by virtue of membership in networks (Portes 1995). But without a group's economic capital, a high degree of social capital is not nearly as beneficial. For example, Stack (1974) and Liebow (1967) illustrate that informal networks of exchange exist among poor African Americans in urban communities, but they "swap" resources that are significantly smaller in scale such as food stamps, a few dollars, food, or child care. The high degree of social capital among Korean immigrant entrepreneurs, coupled with their wealth of economic resources, gives them a distinct advantage in business over other ethnic groups.

Koreans are not the only ethnic group to benefit from social capital. In fact, first-generation immigrants of many ethnic backgrounds draw upon their versions of rotating credit associations. However, as these groups acculturate into the American social structure, they utilize this resource far less frequently. For example, whereas first-generation Jewish immigrant entrepreneurs used mutual loan associations, later generations have long abandoned this tradition. Second-generation Koreans, like the sons and daughters of Jewish immigrants, have also abandoned this practice.

As instrumental as *gae* may be, some Korean merchants have become wary of using rotating credit associations since they realize the inordinate amount of trust involved for such a system to operate. Many have heard of *gae* failures where one person will take the lump sum of money and leave the country. For instance, a Korean merchant who has used *gae* a few times illustrates the risks involved and the difficulty in holding someone legally responsible for defaulting:

Some people, they don't do *gae* because no matter what they don't trust because it could happen too. When a guy gets $40,000, after a couple of months, you don't see him anymore. Then where are you going to go get him? You cannot tell anybody what happened. It's no protection. . . . So let's say you owe a big company, you don't pay enough on your credit card. They're going to send you a thousand letters. They going to send you [to a] collection [agency], but those big companies can afford it, but a lot of people, you want to get $10,000 from that guy who run away. You want to hire a lawyer, you want to go to court, this and that, time and money, headache. Forget about it. They know what is the risk, so they don't even want to involved.

Although Korean merchants explain that there are no legal ramifications to defaulting since none of these agreements is written, the social sanctions—such as loss of standing in the immigrant community and exclusion from it—are strong enough to prevent losses on a regular basis.

Korean merchants not only complain of the risks; they also mention the costly interest payments, which can be as high as 30 percent, surpassing the legal limit in New York state, for instance, which must be less than 25 percent. Although rotating credit associations may be helpful to those who need cash very quickly, they also function as financial investments for more affluent coethnics who benefit from accruing high interest payments.

Although not all Korean merchants have participated in *gae*, all have admitted to borrowing funds from their family or coethnic friends at one point, either at the start-up phase or while in business. Koreans often borrow tens of thousands of dollars from other family members or coethnic friends. The high degree of social and economic capital remains the most valuable resource for these immigrant entrepreneurs that should be underscored, since the availability of cash resources can determine whether small businesses will be able to withstand emergencies such as break-ins or slow periods when cash flow is extremely tight (Lee 2002).

Ethnic Succession and Vacant Niches

By the last quarter of the twentieth century, the once ubiquitous Jewish shopkeeper had faded from the scene: the storekeepers' sons and daughters had better things to do than mind a shop; and their parents, old, tired, and scared of crime, were eager to sell out to new groups of immigrant entrepreneurs. . . the Jewish withdrawal from New York's traditional small business sectors provided a chance for a legion of immigrants, and not just Koreans.

(Waldinger 1996, 100–101)

The Jewish exodus from the inner cities left a vacant niche for Korean immigrants to ethnically succeed them in small business.

Entering the Inner City

Immigrant entrepreneurs such as Koreans open businesses in black neighborhoods largely because there is little competition from larger, chain corporations that predominate in white, middle-class neighborhoods and suburban malls. Considered high-risk and high-crime neighborhoods, poor black communities are largely ignored by larger corporations, consequently leaving a vacant niche for Koreans to set up shop. And because the market is less saturated in low-income neighborhoods, rent is relatively cheaper. Korean immigrants also claim that running a business in a middle-class, white neighborhood is more difficult because they do not have the language fluency and middle-class mannerisms to deal with a more educated and sophisticated clientele. For example, when asked why she opened a business in a low-income, black neighborhood as opposed to a middle-income, white neighborhood, a Korean store-owner in Harlem replies,

> Because easier. First of all, you don't have to have that much money to open up the store. And second of all, easier because you don't need to that much complicate. White people is very classy and choosy, and especially white people location is not like this, mostly they go to mall. Here they don't have many car, so easier, cheaper rent. When you go to white location, Second Avenue, Third Avenue, rent is already cost $20,000, you know, and they don't have any room for us. But black people area, other people hesitate to come in because they worry about crime and something like that, so they got a lot of room for Koreans.

After gathering experience and accumulating capital running businesses in low-income neighborhoods, some Korean storeowners often leave the inner city and open stores in safer, middle-income white neighborhoods.

Immigrant entrepreneurs also cluster in particular "retail niches" (Lee 1999). The newest immigrant storeowners find themselves in the most physically exhausting, labor-intensive businesses that require relatively little capital and have low profit margins, such as green groceries, take-out restaurants, and fresh fish stores (Light and Bonacich 1988). The extremely long hours and physically demanding labor often insures that first-generation immigrants will be the ones to occupy these lines of business. Accordingly, Korean immigrants presently dominate these niches, but they are merely the successors in a line of immigrant ethnic groups who occupied these business lines before them. Immigrant entrepreneurs will continue to succeed one another and flourish in low-income black neighborhoods because they bring products and services to an underserviced population by taking advantage of previously unfilled niches. As long the second and third generation find better opportunities in the mainstream labor market, retail businesses (particularly those catering to a low-income clientele) will remain a protected niche among immigrant groups who will continue to ethnically succeed one another.

"Mass Marketing" a Once-Exclusive Product

Immigrant entrepreneurs concentrate mostly in retail trade and manufacturing, and their success often depends on their ability to "mass market" a once-exclusive product. In other words, they take a luxury product and make it cheaper, thereby making it more accessible for a wider population. For instance, before Korean-owned manicure salons opened on virtually every block in New York City, manicures used to be only available in full-service beauty salons. In upscale salons, manicures would cost about $20, making them accessible to an elite group of people, namely, upper- and upper-middle-class white women. Koreans took this luxury service out of the beauty salon and mass marketed the manicure. They made it cheaper by charging women only $7, consequently making manicures more widely available to a greater population (Kang 1997). Koreans have used the same strategy in selling fresh flowers, once only available at florist shops, now readily available at corner delis.

These business owners have successfully adapted to the changing demands of the service economy by bringing small, full-service retail shops close to both high- and low-income consumers (Sassen 1991). Korean-owned manicures and delis have become a ubiquitous symbol of New York City, as evidenced by a recent article in the *New York Times* by a woman who moved out of the city and complains, "There are no Koreans. Which explains why you can never find flowers and why manicures cost $15."[6] This strategy of "mass marketing" transcends industries and also explains immigrants' success in marketing ethnic beauty supplies (including both hair and skin care for an ethnic clientele) and ethnic urban sportswear. Since low-income blacks cannot afford to purchase designer clothing, Korean-owned businesses that sell designer knock-offs for the urban teenage market prosper in this market.

Interethnic Conflict: Korean Merchants and Black Customers

The relationship between black customers and Korean merchants has been popularized and exploited by the media with splashy newspaper headings that read, "Will Black Merchants Drive Koreans from Harlem?" (Noel 1981), "Blacks, Koreans Struggle to Grasp Thread of Unity" (Jones 1986), "Cultural Conflict" (Njeri 1996), and "Scape-goating New York's Koreans."[7] "Black-Korean conflict"—as it quickly became framed and labeled by both journalists and scholars—was featured in mainstream and ethnic presses alike, spilling over into other forms of popular culture. Spike Lee's poignant film *Do the Right Thing* and Ice Cube's controversial lyrics in the rap song "Black Korea" brought black-Korean tension and conflict to the fore in both communities. The shooting of African American teenager Latasha Harlins by Korean storeowner Soon Ja Du on March 16, 1991, in South Central Los Angeles intensified tensions between these minority communities. And finally, the "not guilty" verdict rendered by a Simi Valley jury in the Rodney King case on April 29, 1992, sparked the Los Angeles riots—the first multiethnic riot in U.S. history. Although many ethnic groups were involved, the riots were framed as the culmination of black-Korean conflict—an oversimplified and misleading framework that failed to capture the depth and complexity of the issues at hand. In this section of the article, I describe the daily interactions between Korean merchants and black customers and also shed light on the larger structural processes under which simple economic arguments transform into racialized anger.

Dispelling the Myths: The Intersection of Race, Class, and Experience

To be a Korean merchant in an inner-city neighborhood such as New York's Harlem or South Central Los Angeles is a mixture of prosaic routine and explosive tension, of affectionate customers and racial anger. Yet despite the violent media image of Korean merchants armed with 9-millimeter handguns and black customers looting stores during the Los Angeles riots, most striking is the sheer ordinariness of most merchant-customer relationships. In fact, for most merchants and customers, their everyday shopping experiences boil down to a simple formula: "business as usual" (Lee 1996). However, there is a considerable amount of variation within the merchant-customer relationship, and there are two important factors that shape the daily interactions between Korean business owners and their black clientele: (1) the merchants' experience and (2) the class composition of the customer population.

Korean merchants who are veterans on the street have far better relations with their black customers than newer merchants who have little experience dealing with a minority clientele.

---

[6] Laura Zigman, "Living Off-Center on Purpose," *New York Times*, December 12, 1996, C6.

[7] "Scapegoating New York's Koreans," *New York Post*, January 25, 1990.

With time, merchants come to realize that contrary to the dominant stereotypes, inner-city residents are not all welfare queens, drug addicts, or criminals; experience teaches Korean storeowners that even the poorest neighborhoods are economically and culturally diverse. For example, merchants who have been in business for ten or fifteen years know and recognize their customers, speak with them more frequently than newer merchants, and generally feel more comfortable doing business in low-income black neighborhoods. They see their customers as a diverse population, recognizing differences in ethnicity, class, and character. Years of experience have taught veteran business owners that negative experiences—no matter how traumatic—come few and far between.

Class differences also matter. Running a small business in a low-income, urban neighborhood is not easy, especially for new immigrants who come from an ethnically homogeneous country, and therefore have little understanding of the nuances of America's pluralistic society. Without prior business experience and with only a loose command of the English language, they set up shop in inner cities where they are exposed to persistent poverty and its resultant consequences— welfare dependency, teenage pregnancy, single motherhood, unemployment, and drugs (Wilson 1987). From the black customers' perspective, Korean merchants not only appear successful, but they also seem to take away business opportunities for blacks. While immigrant merchants may not directly compete with black merchants or black residents for jobs, low-income residents are more likely to *perceive* immigrant newcomers as outside competitors who take away opportunities from them.

Frustrated by the infusion of immigrant newcomers who barely speak English, yet seem to easily set up shop in their communities, black customers often direct their resentment toward immigrant merchants (Rieder 1990). Poor black customers often question what U.S. government agency helped them out and also wonder why aid has not come their way. It is a common misperception among low-income black customers that immigrants, especially Korean immigrants, receive special loans from the government to help them open businesses. Although this is untrue, low-income residents are quick to embrace the misconception because they cannot otherwise explain how these "foreigners" are able to accumulate the mass amounts of capital and "take over" the businesses in their communities.

However, the scenario is far different in middle-class black communities. When Korean merchants serve middle-class black customers, the tension between these groups virtually disappears. Middle-class customers do not perceive Korean merchants in their communities as economic competitors who take away opportunities from them since most middle-class blacks have jobs, are economically stable, and therefore do not express feelings of economic and ethnic antagonism. Instead, they view merchants as businessmen and women who provide services for the community and have the right to open a business wherever they choose. Economic security affords this opinion. The stark differences in low- and middle-income black neighborhoods reveals that class—rather than race or ethnicity—is more salient in determining the level of tension or conflict between blacks and Koreans.

Racially Coding Economic Arguments

Writing about the black-Jewish relationship of the 1960s, Herbert Gans (1969, 10) noted, "When Negroes express their anger in anti-Semitic terms, it is only because many of the whites who affect their lives are Jewish; if the ghetto storeowners, land-lords and teachers were Chinese, Negro hostility would surely be anti-Chinese." Although most merchant-customer encounters in black neighborhoods may be quite ordinary, when tensions arise, both merchants and customers can lose cognitive control, and even those who do not normally engage in stereotypes may do so under strained conditions. Seemingly trivial economic arguments between black customers and out-group merchants such as Koreans can quickly become racially coded. In this tricky area of merchant-customer conflict, Robert K. Merton's concept of "in-group virtues" and "out-group vices" is particularly useful. Merton (1968) demonstrates that similar patterns of behavior by in-group and out-group members are differently perceived and evaluated. Yet because the most apparent distinction between Korean merchants and their black customers is race, the economic relationship is often over-looked by customers as a source of tension in favor of racial or ethnic explanations.

All of the Korean merchants have admitted that at some point while they have been doing business, particularly at the beginning, economic arguments have become racially or ethnically coded. For example, a furniture storeowner in West Philadelphia explains when customers become very angry over economic disputes, "the argument always comes down to race." Accusations such as, "You damn Orientals are coming into our neighborhoods taking over every fucking store!" are not uncommon when merchants and customers come to a halt over exchanges or refunds.

For instance, when the Korean storeowner refused to take back the floor display furniture model that he recently sold to a female customer at a discount, she immediately uttered to her mother, "He's just a chink and a gook." Incensed by the racial insult, the Korean merchant retorted, "Now wait a minute, what would happen if I called you a nigger? What would happen then? You're sitting here calling me these names, what if I did that to you?" Infuriated by the hint of a racial epithet, the woman threatened to start picketing outside of his store. Quickly realizing the potential problems that could ensue from this incident, the Korean merchant immediately called the Philadelphia Commission on Human Relations to intervene, which later proved to be unnecessary since the woman did not follow through on her threat. The Korean furniture storeowner comments about the situation:

> I called up City Hall because I thought it was going to be a problem, but it wasn't. The next day they were gone, but it just shows that it's totally backwards. It's reverse racism is what it is. And anytime there's an argument about anything, it always comes down to, "You damn Orientals are taking over all the businesses in the neighborhood!" or "You Koreans are doing it!"
>
> This isn't all the time, but every once in a while you get a customer who's totally unreasonable, and if things don't go their way, they pull that old card out of their pocket, the race card, and throw it down. And it's a shame that they got to stoop to that level just to get what they want. I mean if they were to talk to me reasonable, without yelling and ranting and raving, we probably would have got things worked out more to their liking. But you can't come in here and yell at somebody and expect to get what you want.

Even Korean merchants who are veterans of the black communities they serve—who know most of their customers—fully recognize that their nonblack status can easily make them targets for hostile customers and boycotters. For example, a Korean carry-out restaurant owner who has been in the Harlem community for thirteen years explains that racial tension is a fact of life in Harlem. As a mainstay in West Harlem's community, she has many customers who frequent her eating establishment on a daily basis. Yet even she understands that as a nonblack merchant on 125th Street in New York's Harlem, she is always at risk of potential conflict such as a boycott, regardless of how many people in the community support her,

We always feel like a boycott could happen no matter how you famous on 125th Street, no matter how much they like you, no matter how you good in this community. Always one bum or one knucklehead hates you. He can bring you a ton of problem. So far, people support me but some people against me too.

When asked whether this insecurity stems from the simple fact that she is not black, she immediately confirms,

That's right. And they can put me as Korean merchant coming here to make money out of this community. So I got a thousand of them full of respect, it don't mean anything. Something happen, a thousand people I don't know them, they can against me, coming here for protesting, hollering, shut down business. It could happen, you know. Some person get mad at me, so I argue, and he could start picket outside. Maybe some other people say, "You crazy, why you do that to this store?" But few people going to do that.

And a lot of those protesters, they don't know me, they could stay there shouting and give me a lot of trouble because it always could happen no matter how much you are good to this community or something like that. And that kind of crazy thing can happen, and nobody can stop it. . . . Nobody can move those protesters out in front of my door. They got a right to stand there and shouting. And the ones who shouting, I don't know them, and they don't know me. They just want to be here. They angry because I'm Korean. But they not get mad at me, they get mad some place else.

When customers engage in stereotypes, they may not necessarily react to the objective features of the situation, but rather to the symbolism that the situation represents. For instance, when merchants refuse a customer's request for a refund or an exchange, their refusal becomes symbolic of stingy, cheap commercial outsiders who exploit the community in which they serve. And similarly, when black customers become angry and yell at merchants, storeowners may quickly engage in stereotypes about blacks—that they are ignorant, uneducated, and irresponsible. In each scenario, merchants and customers alike may interpret and racially code what are essentially economic arguments. Race can polarize the simplest interactions and become mobilized in conflict-ridden ways.

In order to defuse tensions in poor black communities, Korean merchants hire black employees and managers to act as "cultural brokers" between them and their predominantly black clientele (Lee 1998). Black employees serve as bridges who link the linguistic and cultural differences; they also serve as visible symbols that merchants are "giving back" to the low-income communities in which they serve. Most critically, black employees act as conflict-resolvers who can quickly deracialize rising tensions between merchants and customers.

Placing Black-Korean Conflict in the Context of Urban Poverty

In the context of urban poverty, small arguments can explode into racial conflict. This heightened tension can result from the daily strains and frustrations of inner-city life—joblessness, crime, and persistent poverty—leading customers to racially code economic arguments. An African American customer in Philadelphia explains the complexities of the merchant-customer relationship and offers insights about the tension and frustration resulting from life in the inner city:

Well there is a certain amount of sensitivity here because black folks, living the way we do, we have a certain amount of cynicism, so when we go into these stores, we're like angry, cursing them out and everything, and they're like, "You come in my store and you're cursing at me! You get out my store!" And a lot of people around here, they're stealing, they're strung out on something, don't know no better, trying to be cool. It's a whole myriad of things. That's why when I walk into a store, they're watching me. I haven't stole a thing in my life, too scared. I'm not going to say I never had a thought, but I'm just too scared, and I'm not going to do it. And there's a certain amount of despair, which is why they don't care if they get caught.

The media often depicts merchant-customer interactions in poor, inner-city neighborhoods as the principle sources of black-Korean tensions. However, the source of this tension lies in the nature of the economics of poverty and its resultant pattern of dominant-subordinate contact between merchants and customers. These tensions are symptoms of larger circumstances in which both the merchants and the customers are victims. As David Caplovitz (1967, 192) stated in his classic work, *The Poor Pay More*, "the consumer problems of low-income families cannot be divorced from the other problems facing them. Until society can find ways of raising their educational level, improving their occupational opportunities, increasing their income, and reducing the discrimination against them—only limited solutions to their problems as consumers can be found." This was true in the 1960s when Jewish merchants predominated in poor black neighborhoods and still holds true today as a new legion of immigrants has entered these communities.

Conclusion

Immigrant entrepreneurs have made distinct inroads in many large U.S. cities. Approximately one-third of Korean families are engaged in small business, representing the highest rate of self-employment among all U.S. ethnic groups. Their access to class and ethnic resources, coupled with their utilization of social capital, contributes to the extraordinary rate of entrepreneurship. And once a nucleus of entrepreneurs becomes established, ethnic networks have a "fateful effect," paving the path for other family members and coethnic friends to follow suit.

Running a small business in an inner-city neighborhood is not what Korean immigrants had in mind when they came to the United States. Because they have been educated and trained as white-collar professionals, self-employment is a symbol of downward mobility for many Korean immigrants who find themselves extremely underemployed. Korean immigrant entrepreneurs work twelve to sixteen hours a day, six to seven days a week in physically demanding and routine work. To succeed in a competitive market, they exploit themselves, their family members, and fellow ethnics. However, given the obstacles they face in the primary labor market and their inability to transfer their education and pre-immigrant skills, Koreans turn to self-employment as an alternative to working in relatively low-wage salaried jobs. Entrepreneurship becomes the ladder to reaching the American dream of upward mobility.

This dream was shattered on April 29, 1992—the first day of the Los Angeles riots—when they suffered devastating losses totaling $400 million in property damage. Koreans now refer to this unforgettable turning point as *Sai-I-Gu* (April 29 in Korean). The worst domestic uprising of the century placed black-Korean conflict in the fore. However, this dyadic relationship fails to capture the depth and complexities facing the nation's inner-city communities. Placing black-Korean conflict at the core of the Los Angeles riots also distorts the nature of most merchant-customer interactions. Most day-to-day encounters are not fraught with racial animosity but rather are characterized by civility (Lee 2002).

Against the backdrop of inner-city poverty, heightened tension can transform small economic arguments into racialised conflict. A Korean merchant's refusal to give a cash refund for a defective beeper or an already-worn dress may become symbolic of cheap, exploitative "out-group" business owners who make money from the community and drain it of its resources. The irate customer who is not given the refund may not necessarily react to the objective features of the situation but rather to the symbolism that the situation represents, leading the customer to racially code economic arguments. Even though civility may characterize the daily lives for both merchants and customers, the normalcy of everyday encounters does not preclude the possibility of interethnic conflict such as boycotts or urban riots.

In speaking of black-Jewish relations, Gans (1969, 3) explains that

> it is more useful to look at the Negro-Jewish relationship from a longer sociological perspective. From that perspective, the recent incidents are only more visible instances in a long series of primarily economic conflicts between blacks, Jews, [and other ethnic groups] which are endemic to New York and to several other large American cities, and which can only be dealt with through economic solutions.

Korean merchants are not the first group to experience conflict with the black customers in poor neighborhoods and they will undoubtedly not be the last until we address the structural problems that plague inner-city communities.

Notes

The author wishes to thank Herbert Gans, Kathryn Neckerman, Katherine Newman, John Skrentny, Rob Smith, Roger Waldinger, and Rhacel Parreñas for helpful comments on an earlier version of this paper. The author gratefully thanks the International Migration Program of the Social Science Research Council, the Andrew W. Mellon Foundation, and the National Science Foundation SBR-9633345 for research support on which this paper is based. The University of California President's Office provided research support during the writing of this paper. This article is based on the author's book, *Civility in the City: Blacks, Jews, and Koreans in Urban America* (Cambridge, MA: Harvard University Press, 2002).

References

Abelmann, Nancy and John Lie. 1995. *Blue Dreams*. Cambridge, MA: Harvard University Press.

Bates, Timothy. 1994. An Analysis of Korean-Immigrant-Owned Small-Business Start-Ups with Comparisons to African-American and Non-Minority-Owned Firms. *Urban Affairs Quarterly* 30: 227–48.

Bonacich, Edna. 1987. "Making It" in America: A Sociological Evaluation of the Ethics of Immigrant Entrepreneurship. *Sociological Perspectives* 30: 446–66.

Caplovitz, David. 1967. *The Poor Pay More*. New York: Free Press.

Coleman, James S. 1988. Social Capital in the Creation of Human Capital. *American Journal of Sociology* 94: S95–S121.

Gans, Herbert J. 1969. Negro-Jewish Conflict in New York City. *Midstream* 15: 3–15.

Jo, Moon H. 1992. Korean Merchants in the Black Community. *Ethnic and Racial Studies*. 15: 395–410.

Jones, Jon. 1986. Black, Koreans Struggle to Grasp Thread of Unity. *Los Angeles Times*, May 1.

Kang, Miliann. 1997. Manicuring Race, Gender, and Class. *Race, Gender, and Class* 4: 143–64.

Kim, Illsoo, 1981. *The New Urban Immigrants*. Princeton, NJ: Princeton University Press.

Lee, Heon Cheol. 1993. *Black-Korean Conflict in New York City*. Ph.D. Dissertation, Columbia University.

Lee, Jennifer. 1996. Business as Usual. *Common Quest: The Magazine of Black-Jewish Relations* 1: 35–38.

Lee, Jennifer. 1998. Cultural Brokers. *American Behavioral Scientist* 41: 927–37.

Lee, Jennifer. 1999. Retail Niche Domination among African American, Jewish, and Korean Entrepreneurs. *American Behavioral Scientist* 42: 1398–1416.

Lee, Jennifer. 2002. *Civility in the City*. Cambridge, MA: Harvard University Press.

Liebow, Elliot. 1967. *Tally's Corner*. Boston: Little, Brown.

Light, Ivan H. 1972. *Ethnic Enterprise in America*. Berkeley: University of California Press.

Light Ivan and Edna Bonacich. 1988. *Immigrant Entrepreneurs*. Berkeley: University of California Press.

Light, Ivan and Angel A. Sanchez. 1987. Immigrant Entrepreneurs in 272. SMSA's. *Sociological Perspectives* 30: 373–99.

Merton, Robert K. 1968. Self-fulfilling Prophecy. *Social Theory and Social Structure*. New York: Free Press.

Min, Pyong Gap. 1984. From White-Collar Occupations to Small Business. *Sociological Quarterly* 25: 333–52.

Min, Pyong Gap. 1996. *Caught in the Middle*, Berkeley: University of California Press.

Njeri, Itabari. 1996. Kimchee and Grits. *CommonQuest: The Magazine for Black-Jewish Relations* 1: 39–45.

Noel, Peter. 1981. Koreans Vie for Harlem Dollars. *NY Amsterdam News*, July 4.

Ong, Paul and Suzanne Hee. 1993. *Losses in Los Angeles Civil Unrest April 29–May 1, 1992*: Los Angeles: Center for Pacific Rim Studies, University of California.

Park, Kyeyoung. 1997. *The Korean American Dream*. Ithaca, NY: Cornell University Press.

Portes, Alejandro. 1995. *The Economic Sociology of Immigration: Essays on Networks, Ethnicity, and Entrepreneurship*. New York: Russell Sage Foundation.

Rieder, Jonathan. 1990. Trouble in Store. *New Republic* 203: 16–22.

Sassen, Saskia. 1991. The Informed Economy. In John Mollenkopf and Manuel Castells (eds.), *Dual City: Restructuring New York*. New York: Russell Sage Foundation, pp. 79–101.

Selznick Gertrude J. and Stephen Steinberg. 1969. *The Tenacity of Prejudice*. New York: Harper & Row.

Stack, Carol B. 1974. *All Our Kin*. New York: Harper & Row.

Waldinger, Roger. 1996. *Still the Promised City?* Cambridge, MA: Harvard University Press.

Wilson, William Julius. 1987. *The Truly Disadvantaged*. Chicago: University of Chicago Press.

Yoon, In-Jin. 1997. *On My Own*. Chicago: University of Chicago Press.

Exploitation and Abuse in the Garment Industry

The Case of the Thai Slave-Labor Compound in El Monte

Julie A. Su and Chanchanit Martorell

On August 2, 1995, the public was horrified by the discovery of an apartment complex in El Monte, California, where seventy-one Thai garment workers had been held in slavery for up to seven years, sewing clothes for some of the nation's major garment manufacturers and retailers (Adelson 1996). From their homes in impoverished rural Thailand, these Thai women and men dared to imagine a better life for themselves, a life of hard work with just pay, decency, and opportunity. What they found instead was an industry—the garment industry—that mercilessly reaped exorbitant profit from their hard labor and then closed its corporate eyes, believing that if it refused to acknowledge these practices, the industry could collectively claim not to be responsible.

The Thai women and men were forced to work between seventeen and twenty-two hours a day in a barbed-wire enclosed compound (Feldman, McDonnell, and White 1995; White 1995b). They were crowded eight or ten to a bedroom that was designed for two. Rats often crawled over them during their few precious hours of sleep. Armed guards kept constant surveillance of their every movement and censored and monitored their actions, phone calls, and letters home, while threats, fear, and intimidation imposed strict discipline and obedience to the captors' unceasing demands and cruel authority (White 1995b).

The fact that these crimes occurred in the garment industry is no accident. The major manufacturers and retailers who control the industry have constructed a notoriously abusive production process in which poverty wages, long hours, and illegal working conditions are standard business practices (McDonnell and Feldman 1995a; Nifong 1995; Stepick 1989). This is a story about how the workers suffered, endured, and eventually galvanized to change their lives and to advocate for reforms in a major global industry.

The Thai workers were industrial home workers, forced to eat, sleep, live, and work producing garments in the place they called "home." The slave-labor compound in which the Thai workers were confined was a two-story apartment complex consisting of seven units, surrounded by a ring of razor wire and iron guardrails with sharp ends pointing inward. Their captors, emulating slave-labor practices of the past who supervised garment production and enforced manufacturer specifications and deadlines, ruled with fear and intimidation (White 1995b). Restricted from leaving the compound, the workers depended on their captors for food and basic necessities, for which they were forced to pay exorbitant prices.

These workers labored over sewing machines in dark garages and dimly lit rooms, making clothes for major brand-name manufacturers and nationwide retailers destined for some of the largest department stores in America. Garments bearing the labels Anchor Blue, Tomato, Clio, B.U.M., High Sierra, Nothing But Blue, Axle, Cheetah, and Airtime defined life behind barbed wire. Many of these labels were privately owned by well-known retailers, such as Mervyn's, Miller's Outpost, and Montgomery Ward. Others were sold on the racks of May Department Stores, Nordstrom, Sears, and Target (McDonnell and Feldman 1995b; Swoboda and Pressler 1995).

The story of the Thai garment workers—and indeed of the approximately one million immigrant workers who labor over sewing machines each day in the United States and many millions more in other countries—cannot be told without the story of this systemic corporate exploitation. This chapter ties the human suffering epitomized in the experience of the enslaved Thai workers to the corporate giants in the garment industry who created the conditions for their enslavement.

Global Perspective: International Trade of Low-Income Labor

How could these workers be so misled and deceived into traveling to a distant country, the United States, and be forced into slavery? To answer that question, an examination of the harsh conditions and realities of their lives in rural Thailand offers some insight into how many immigrant workers fall prey to human traffickers and smugglers who make false promises of decent wages abroad, luring desperate men and women into a life of suffering, hopelessness, and misery in a foreign country (Wijers and Lap-Chew 1997). An analysis of the global economy also illuminates how an El Monte slave sweatshop could exist. Conventional analysis has focused in part on an ethnically situated relationship with the global mobility of capital. In the case of the United States, industries that are closely linked to local production centers, such as the garment industry, require structural explanations of the global movement of labor due to the specific attraction of this country to workers from developing countries (Sassen 1988). National, regional, and international migration patterns also reflect increasing numbers of migrants responding to the international demand for domestic workers and sweatshop workers (Global Alliance Against Traffic in Women [hereafter GAATW] 1997).

For some industries in the United States, the global movement of exploitable labor represents the latest competitive advantage. These industries generate substantial profits from the movement of undocumented labor without bearing the cost of relocation, as they engage in the exploitation of the most vulnerable workforce, primarily disenfranchised, rural, uneducated men and women from developing countries (Matthew 1996).

Inequitable global structures and economic relations divide the world and designate certain economically disadvantaged countries as "sending" countries and those nations of the privileged, industrialized world as "recipient" countries (GAATW 1997).

Lured by the opportunity to work and achieve economic security in the United States, unskilled workers from developing countries attempt to escape abject poverty in their country of origin only to find exploitation and abuse in their new country (Matthew 1996). Their undocumented status undermines their ability to voice their grievances for fear of deportation and retaliation. The vulnerability of the undocumented and their ignorance of their legal rights make it easy for employers to abuse immigrant workers, denying them such rights as legal minimum wage, benefits, compensation for overtime, and safe working conditions (Cho 1994).

Unfortunately, existing labor laws fail to protect workers from such abuses and unfair labor practices. Lax enforcement and the sometimes hypocritical positions taken by labor officials—the very labor officials charged with enforcing these laws—make legal protections all but illusory. For example, the U.S. Department of Labor, whose responsibility is to ensure compliance with federal labor laws, entered into an agreement with the Immigration and Naturalization Service (INS) that all but ensured that exploited workers would be reported to and then deported by the INS. This agreement created a disincentive to workers from ever approaching the Department of Labor to report violations. Despite some modifications to the INS—Department of Labor agreement in recent years, these labor officials do not provide adequate protection for the victims of labor infractions and violations.

Labor law enforcement alone would hardly end the abuse of low-wage workers. Similarly, the California Labor Commission, the agency with primary labor law enforcement duties, has never recovered from the massive budget cuts it faced during Governor Pete Wilson's administration. Within the context of globalization, conditions are worsening for women as a result of the following: structural adjustment programs, International Monetary Fund and World Bank policies, free-trade agreements, export processing and free enterprise zones, the operations of multinational corporations, and the political-economic mechanisms and social impacts of privatization and deregulation (GAATW 1997). Exploitative working conditions are particularly acute for women from economically underprivileged countries. Against a background of shrinking options for earning a livelihood and burdened by the responsibility of maintaining and sustaining their families, women are having to migrate in large numbers to seek viable means of employment (ibid.).

Immigrants from Thailand, particularly Thai women, are especially vulnerable to exploitation. The rigid and well-defined hierarchy of Thai society ranks people according to their status and authority (Fleg 1980). Traditional Thai values confer on Thai women a social position that is inferior to that of males and thus predisposes many women to enter exploitative forms of labor (Meyer 1995). For uneducated women from poor rural areas, both educational and economic opportunities are also virtually nonexistent. Because women are structurally denied equal access to the formal and regulated labor markets, they are generally relegated to the ever expanding service sector. Much of women's work in the service sector is informal, undervalued, underpaid, unprotected, stigmatized, and in some cases criminalized. The result is a continuing marginalization of women in the workforce and the feminization of poverty, migration, and cheap labor. Globalization has serious consequences for women, particularly those who belong to cultural communities already marginalized by poverty, ethnicity, and regional factors (GAATW 1997).

National, regional, and international migration patterns reflect this labor division with increasing numbers of migrant women responding to the national and international demand for domestic workers, marriage partners, sex and entertainment workers, and sweatshop workers. However, at the same time, many countries have enacted restrictive immigration policies that adversely affect migrant women by rendering them more vulnerable to abuse, poverty, and violence and less able to negotiate fair wages (Wijers and Lap-Chew 1997).

Compounding their poverty is the obligation imposed by dominant Thai culture on them to take responsibility for the welfare and well-being of their family members. A daughter is expected to repay her debts accumulated during childhood, to which the debts for the care of her own children are added (Meyer 1995). Feeling trapped by their social class and forced to assume overwhelming financial responsibilities, women often seek opportunities abroad as unskilled workers, leaving their families behind (Fernandez-Kelly and Garcia 1989). Moreover, the norm in such a situation is for the woman to seek out opportunities for repaying her obligations and to maintain as much as possible her own relative independence (Meyer 1995). This self-sacrifice is exactly what led the Thai women unsuspectingly to the El Monte slave compound in an attempt to fulfill their filial obligations and create a better life for their families back home.

"Trafficking" in women and labor migration of women must be understood in the context of, on the one hand, traditional female roles, structural disadvantages suffered by women in the gendered labor market, and the world-wide feminization of labor migration and, on the other, the increasingly restrictive immigration policies of recipient countries like the United States (GAATW 1997).

In the face of stark poverty at home, it is questionable whether immigration is a matter of choice. Often evaluated in the context of a combination of "push" and "pull" factors that compel individuals to immigrate, immigration must be understood as a matter of economic necessity owing to the economic and social changes in developing countries that virtually preclude continuing their traditional, rural way of life. Migration should be viewed as a selective phenomenon, and an individual's motivations to immigrate are known to be associated with certain demographic, economic, social, and even psychological attributes (Desbarats 1979).

Knowledge of the demographic and occupational characteristics of Thai immigrants can allow, to a certain extent, some inferences to be made about individual motivation to immigrate. Studies have shown a gradual change in the occupational composition of Thai immigrants from one characterized by a handful of educated, middle-class Thais thirty years ago to one characterized more recently by an increase in the proportion of unskilled workers and women as well as by a decline in the average level of English proficiency at the time of arrival (ibid.).

Case Study: The El Monte Compound

What They Left Behind

Among the seventy-one workers from the infamous El Monte garment slave shop, only four are men. Every one of the sixty-seven women left families behind in small and impoverished rural villages of the northeast provinces of Thailand. Most families farmed for subsistence and lacked any formal schooling beyond the equivalent of a fourth-grade education in the United States. Without education or employment, these women initially migrated to Bangkok and other urban areas to find work in garment factories. In their twenties and thirties, the majority left behind spouses and often small children in their villages.

It was in these urban garment factories that recruiters associated with the El Monte slave sweatshop found them. The recruiters promised a better income in the United States that would support and improve the livelihood of their families. The recruiters told tales of earning between $1,200 and $2,400 per month, fifty times more than what the workers earned in Thailand. The recruiters painted a picture of decent living accommodations, vacations, and visits to places that capture the beauty of America. As one worker put it, "We understood we were going to the City of Angels." The recruiters offered to handle all the travel arrangements and visa requirements and travel with the workers to their destination.

Believing themselves to be in the United States legally and having no understanding of the visa or documentation requirements, the workers each incurred a $5,000 debt to the El Monte slave sweatshop operators for the passage fees, which they were expected to pay back through work (White 1995a). At the wages they were promised, the workers believed they could do so in a matter of months. The conditions in which they were expected to work, and their perpetual inability to ever be free of their captors, however, were beyond imagination.

What They Found in the United States

The workers' hopes and dreams of a better life were dashed as soon as they stepped into the El Monte apartment complex that served as the garment factory. On arriving at Los Angeles International Airport, generally in groups of four to ten, the workers were taken in the back of a truck to the apartment complex. Once there, they were no longer free to come and go at their will. Each group of newly arrived workers was introduced to their new lives in the United States with an ominous warning: "You have been brought here to work, do not dare try and escape." The workers heard, for the first time, that their home and place of work were one and that they were not permitted to leave it (White 1995a).

Having lured them with false promises, the captors confined the workers behind barbed wire and guarded them with armed personnel, forcing them to live in cramped rat- and roach-infested quarters and to sleep on thin mats on the floor. Stripped of all human dignity, the workers were locked up like caged animals.

The workers were indentured laborers to the slave sweatshop operators, a seven-member Thai-Chinese family who demanded that they toil endlessly. Any breaks in the tedium were short and strictly for a brief meal or a quick nap. The operators did not permit them to socialize or interact with one another. Groups of three or more workers conversing together were strictly prohibited. Workers were reprimanded if they smiled or paused to rest.

Any means of free entry or exit in the apartment units, such as the balconies and windows, were boarded up, leaving only small openings for light (White 1995a). Some workers sewed in the living rooms of each apartment unit, while others sewed in the garages. A short string tied to the outside of each garage door indicated how far the garage door could be opened—just a crack to let in light and air but enough to ensure human confinement.

Their food, personal supplies, and tools had to be purchased from the slave sweatshop operators, who established a commissary in one of the garages. For all items and goods, the operators charged five to ten times the normal retail price (White 1995a). A stick of deodorant cost $12 compared to $2 in most stores outside the El Monte compound. The vegetables the workers planted, nurtured, and picked themselves in the small patches of dirt outside the apartment building had to be purchased from the operators. The operators themselves also lived on the premises to ensure constant vigil over the workers. The workers' mail and phone calls to and from Thailand were censored. Any mention of the terrible conditions in El Monte would result in severe punishment. While laboring for seventeen to twenty-two hours a day, seven days a week, for as little as sixty cents an hour, these workers lived and worked under the constant threat of harm to themselves and to their families in Thailand (Schoenberger 1995). They were warned that if they resisted or tried to escape, they would be beaten—and to prove it, the slave sweatshop operators showed the pictures of one worker who was caught and beaten for trying to escape.

The Raid and Work of Sweatshop Watch

Before the August 1995 raid, the Thai workers suffered in conditions of involuntary servitude, some for as long as seven years. On the day of the raid, a multiagency team that included the California Labor Commission and the U.S. Department of Labor, as well as the California Employment Development Department, the California Occupational Safety and Health Administration, state marshals, and El Monte police stormed the apartment complex at five o'clock in the morning. However, the raid did not mean freedom for the workers from their miserable and agonizing ordeal. Rather, the INS was brought in to immediately place these workers, victims of some of the most heinous crimes imaginable, on a government bus that brought them straight to a new detention center. The workers were regarded as criminals.

Immediately, a coalition of nonprofit, community-based, and civil rights organizations, attorneys, and community members, working together as Sweatshop Watch, mobilized to support and offer social and legal services to the Thai workers. Sweatshop Watch was formally established in 1995 as a statewide network dedicated to eliminating the exploitation and illegal and inhumane conditions that characterize garment industry sweatshops. Southern California members include the Asian Pacific American Labor Alliance, the Asian Pacific American Legal Center, the Coalition for Humane Immigrant Rights of Los Angeles, the Korean Immigrant Workers' Advocates, the Thai Community Development Center, and the Union of Needletrades, Industrial and Textile Employees (UNITE).[1] These groups reacted immediately to secure the release of the Thai workers from continued detention. This time, their incarceration was in the hands not of their original captors but of the U.S. government.

Working around the clock and battling tremendous INS resistance, members of Sweatshop Watch demanded to meet with the Thai workers in INS detention to advise them of their legal rights and to advocate for their immediate release (Schoenberger and Hubler 1995). In detention, the workers were frightened and bewildered. Forced to wear prison uniforms, they were shackled by the INS each time they were transported from the federal detention facilities at Terminal Island in San Pedro to the downtown Los Angeles holding facility. Sweatshop Watch members set up a makeshift office using the pay phones in the INS basement waiting room. The advocates insisted not only that the continued imprisonment of the Thai workers was inhumane but also that it sent the wrong message about justice in the United States, that if workers are used as exploited labor in this country and report the abuses, they will be sent to the INS and imprisoned a second time (Hubler and White 1995; R. Scheer 1995). Such unfair treatment of workers forces operations like the El Monte slaveshop even farther underground.

By broadcasting the workers' plight through the news media to maintain public scrutiny on federal government agencies, Sweatshop Watch members continually kept the INS office open into the early hours of the morning. The activists and lawyers steadfastly refused to accept "paperwork" or "closing time" as an excuse for denying the workers their long-awaited freedom. After meeting with federal prosecutors and public defenders to obtain reduction of the bail for each worker from $5,000 to $500, Sweatshop Watch publicly announced to the community that bonds were needed. Sweatshop Watch members themselves posted over fifty bonds.[2] After nine long days and nights, the workers were finally freed from government confinement.

The workers' hard-won release ended neither their struggles nor those of Sweatshop Watch. Led by the Thai Community Development Center, Sweatshop Watch members mobilized to find transitional housing, emergency food and clothing, medical care, and jobs (Schoenberger, McDonnell, and Trinidad 1995). Churches, shelters, supermarkets, and hospitals donated places to stay,

---

[1] Northern California members of Sweatshop Watch include the Asian Immigrant Women Advocates, Asian Law Caucus, and Equal Rights Advocates.

[2] "Attorneys from Sweatshop Watch's Southern California member organizations, Asian Pacific American Legal Center, UNITE and Korean Immigrant Workers Advocates immediately stepped in to help and sought the release of the workers from custody, convincing the court to reduce bail from $5,000 to $500 per person" (*Sweatshop Watch* 1995).

food, and much-needed medical attention for everything from tuberculosis, skin ailments, and gastrointestinal diseases to untreated tumors and near blindness. One worker whose teeth had rotted from long neglect and who was forced to extract eight of his own teeth while confined in El Monte received a new set of teeth from a generous dentist (C. Scheer 1995).

The greatest obstacle was finding jobs in the garment industry that paid minimum wage and overtime and complied with health and safety laws. As a testament to the Herculean efforts of community groups, most of the Thai workers were reemployed within a few months after their freedom (Chang 1996; Lu 1995). The role of Sweatshop Watch members in the case of these Thai workers is only one example of the value of ethnic- and language-specific community groups in the efforts to eliminate the horrors that characterize this industry. In most instances, low-wage immigrant workers depend on support from community organizations to advocate for their labor rights (*Sweatshop Watch* 1995; Welch 1996). It is also a lesson in the value of broad cooperation among community-based organizations, civil rights groups, legal advocates, and organized labor in the struggle for garment workers' rights.

Sweatshop Watch continues to bring attention to these issues and to pressure retailers and manufacturers to take responsibility for the working conditions of workers who sew their products.[3]

The Garment Industry and the Workers' Civil Lawsuit

After the August 2 raid, eight of the workers' captors, the on-site operators of the slave sweatshop, were taken directly into federal custody, facing charges of involuntary servitude, kidnapping, conspiracy, smuggling, and harboring of the Thai workers (Feldman and Ingram 1995; McDonnell and Feldman 1995c). In February 1996, they pled guilty to, among other charges, criminal counts of involuntary servitude and conspiracy (McDonnell and Becker 1996). It was the courageous testimony of the Thai workers that made the criminal case possible (Krikorian 1996). The conclusion to the criminal case, however, did not signal that the workers' legal struggles were over.

Lawless Industry

The El Monte slaveshop is only a symptom of a larger problem that is inherent to the present structure of the garment industry. The manufacturers and retailers are at the very top of a production pyramid whose base consists of innumerable small contractors and individual workers. From their position of power, they dictate the production prices for garment work to the contractors and subcontractors who, in turn, are forced to make their profits by cutting into the wages of their workers. The result is an insidious system of wealth accumulation built on labor exploitation (Bonacich and Waller 1994).

The industry structure is a profit-making system in which corporations, specifically garment manufacturers and retailers, compete to see who can create the most efficient exploitation of garment workers. El Monte was only the most extreme example in recent memory of subcontractors who realized the profit potential of holding workers captive to maximize their productivity and to minimize their resistance.

---

[3] The Coalition "is a statewide network or organizations, attorneys, community leaders, organizers, and advocates committed to eliminating the exploitation that occurs in and the illegal and inhuman conditions that characterize sweatshops" (Mission statement, Coalition to Eliminate Sweatshop Conditions).

As heinous as the conduct of the slave sweatshop operators was, it represents only the outward continuum of abuse in the garment industry, where gross violations of labor laws are a matter of routine business and corporate practice (Silverstein and White 1996; White 1996). These corporations, as much as the workers' direct captors, were the target of the workers' long fight for justice.

The El Monte compound was just one facility of a slave sweatshop operation that began as early as 1988. This slave sweatshop operation used a "front" factory in downtown Los Angeles, where Latina and Latino workers labored long hours, seven days a week, for subminimum wages in unhealthful and degrading conditions. The front factory performed a different stage of the garment manufacturing process. The Latino workers sewed buttons and button holes and performed ironing, finishing, checking, and packaging. The El Monte slave site, where the Thai workers lived and sewed, was an integral part of the production process for each of the manufacturers and retailers, where the actual sewing occurred. Together, the El Monte apartment complex and the downtown front factory constituted one business operation sharing common ownership, control, coordination, and assets and performing work for the same companies (White 1995b, 1996). The manufacturers and retailers arranged for the Thai and Latino workers' services through the sweatshop operators, who did business as "SK Fashions," "S&P Fashions," and "D&R Fashions" (ibid.).

The manufacturers and retailers sent quality-control inspectors to the downtown sweatshop facility to ensure that workers were following manufacturers' and retailers' orders. The downtown facility had fewer than ten sewing machines, clearly not enough to have produced the volume of garments at the quality and speed demanded by the manufacturers and retailers. In fact, if the manufacturers' and retailers' professed ignorance of the Thai workers is real, then from their vantage point, the cut cloth was "magically" transformed into clothing, sometimes practically overnight. Manufacturers' quality-control inspectors either knew or should have known that the orders they were constantly submitting to the sweatshop operators could not possibly have been filled at the downtown front shops they visited. In 1995, another downtown facility was opened, employing approximately fifty Latino workers, although this facility was never registered as required by law. Had manufacturers properly assumed their legal responsibilities to ensure that workers who make their garments are paid legally and are not sewing in their homes, the El Monte slave site could have been discovered and the workers' suffering ended earlier or avoided altogether.

The existence of the El Monte compound demonstrates that the illegal conditions in the garment industry have deteriorated from sweatshops to slaveshops under the tacit control of manufacturers and retailers. Ironically, the industry's reaction to the discovery of garment workers forced to labor behind barbed wire and in involuntary servitude—an industry enriched by the Thai and Latino workers—was to restate emphatically that their practices should continue with impunity. The feigned shock and surprise of manufacturers and retailers, particularly those whose garments were sewn by the Thai workers, was followed by blanket denials of responsibility. Their insistence that they were protected from legal liability displayed a callous disregard not only for the lives of workers but also for all applicable laws (Editorial 1996b). The industry exhibits a historical amnesia about its own role in creating a structure designed to enable corporations to employ unfair labor practices and illegal production processes and then claim ignorance of their existence (White 1995b, 1996).

Asian and Latino Immigrants in the Garment Industry

Asian and Latino garment workers often labor side by side (Sassen 1988). However, they too seldom organize together to change the conditions they share. Asian and Latino immigrant workers come from different countries, cultures, and backgrounds and do not speak a common language. Asian workers themselves are a diverse and multiethnic group. Moreover, differences between them are exacerbated by a situation common in the garment industry: Their immediate supervisors are also Asian. Thus, Latino workers often associate Asians with their exploiters.

In the case of the struggle of the El Monte slave sweatshop workers, Asians and Latinos defied those barriers and united to fight back. Once the Thai workers were liberated and began experiencing life outside the walls of their garment slave sweatshop, they came into contact with other garment workers and began a new process of discovery that expanded their sense of community to include all working people. They began to understand that life outside the walls of their forced labor camp was not free of hardship and sorrow for those who labored to produce garments in more "legitimate" businesses. First, they discovered that their Latino counterparts in the front factories owned by the captors may have been free to come and go, but they were still subjected to the same degradation and exploitation. Now, having experienced for themselves the challenges of everyday working conditions in common, everyday sweatshops, they, like the Latino workers who served in the front shops, learned that injustice is still the norm in the garment industry and that little of the vast wealth they produce ever trickles down into their own hands.

Workers Unite and File Suit against Manufacturers and Retailers

The Thai and Latino workers, represented by lead counsel, the Asian Pacific American Legal Center, filed a landmark federal civil rights lawsuit in federal district court in Los Angeles (James 1995). The system of peonage and involuntary servitude to which the Thai workers were subjected violated the U.S. Constitution and the Racketeering Influenced and Corrupt Organizations Act (RICO). Operation of the El Monte slave site further violated the minimum-wage and overtime compensation requirements of the Fair Labor Standards Act and the California Labor Code, federal and state prohibitions on industrial home work, false imprisonment, extortion, and unfair business practices. The lawsuit held responsible the individual operators of the slave sweatshop and the manufacturers and retailers whose profits were derived on the backs of slave labor. In addition to their immediate captors, the Thai and Latino workers named Mervyn's, Miller's Outpost, B.U.M. International, Montgomery Ward, Tomato, L.F. Sportswear, New Boys, Bigin, and others in their lawsuit (Kang 1995).

The lawsuit exposed the dirty laundry that characterizes the multi-billion-dollar garment industry. Clothing manufacturers dictate not only styles, materials, cut, cloth, volume, and patterns but also the prices they are willing to pay to have their garments produced. In short, manufacturers, and increasingly retailers, exercise virtual total control over the entire garment production process (McDonnell 1995). In addition, they sell the clothes made in sweatshops and slaveshops for profit. Sweatshop operators act, in effect, as manufacturers' supervisors and managers over others. Under the law, these and other facts make them employers of garment workers, bound by all the provisions of the federal and state labor laws.

Manufacturers argue that the sweatshop workers who make their clothes are not their own employees but, rather, work for independent contractors (Arevalo 1995).[4] However, nominal contracting relationships are routinely ignored under both federal and state law, and employer-employee

---

[4] Answer of Defendant Montgomery Ward & Co. to SAC, at 24 (asserting the affirmative defense that the Thai plaintiffs were not employees but independent contractors).

relationships are found where an analysis of the factors underlying the relationship belies the independent contractor status.

Manufacturers routinely underpay their contractors, which, in turn, ensures that garment workers will not be paid minimum wage or overtime. The workers' lawsuit alleged that the manufacturers and retailers named in this suit employed the slave sweatshop and its front factory to produce garments at prices too low to permit payment of minimum wage and overtime. Manufacturers responded to these allegations by claiming that they paid the "industry standard" or "fair market value" (Arevalo 1995). Even if this were the case in the garment industry, it provided no defense since the industry price itself is substandard and artificially depressed by rampant abuses. Manufacturers cannot evade liability with the hollow claim "But everyone else is doing it!" This lawsuit charged that these types of unfair business practices were not only unfair but illegal. In fact, the manufacturers' self-serving reaction only highlights the workers' point that manufacturers create and perpetuate an industry that profits from its insistence on operating outside the law.

In addition, the lawsuit alleged, the manufacturers' negligence in hiring industrial home workers and in failing to supervise the activities of the slave sweatshop made them liable under the law. The manufacturers knew or reasonably should have known that these workers were employed in violation of the prohibitions on home work and without regard to the wage, hour, safety, and registration requirements set by law. The lawsuit further claimed that the manufacturers' violations of the California Industrial Homework Act and Garment Manufacturing Registration Act constituted negligence per se.

The workers also claimed that retailers' violation of the "hot goods provision" of the Fair Labor Standards Act, prohibiting the shipping or sale of goods made in violation of minimum-wage and overtime laws, constituted negligence. When the district court upheld this claim, it gave workers a powerful tool against those who insist that they are "merely" retailers and therefore are completely removed from the manufacturing process. The court recognized that those who sell garments for profit have a responsibility to prevent those goods from being made in sweatshop conditions. If a retailer ignores this responsibility, workers can legally hold them accountable.

The workers won several victories in this lawsuit, which concluded in June 1999. Their settlements with all the manufacturers and retailers were critical in helping the workers rebuild their lives. In March 1996, the manufacturers and retailers sought to have the lawsuit dismissed, claiming that the workers had no basis for bringing them to court. The court refused to grant the manufacturers' and retailers' motions to dismiss. In denying these motions, the district court rejected manufacturers' argument that they cannot be deemed joint employers and that their willful ignorance absolves them of responsibility. This decision clearly indicates that manufacturers cannot both profit from labor law abuses and then claim those laws do not apply to them in an industry infamous for its egregious abuses of workers.

By filing this lawsuit, the workers sued not only to win back wages but also to place the entire garment industry on notice that this kind of exploitation must end. Manufacturers and retailers can no longer resort to false claims of ignorance or hide behind disingenuous cries of surprise. They have created, perpetuated, and profited from an industry designed to give them the greatest monetary benefit with the least legal liability, regardless of the terrible human cost (Bonacich and Waller 1994; Holstein 1996).

The addition of the Latino workers in this suit sends a broader warning to manufacturers and retailers in the entire industry: They will be held accountable not only to workers who labor in involuntary servitude behind barbed wire but also to the hundreds of thousands of garment workers, mostly Latinas (Fernandez-Kelly and Garcia 1989), who are paid poverty wages and forced to work seven days a week in economic servitude in sweatshops throughout the country. These workers teach all communities a lesson on the possibility—indeed necessity—of racial unity in the face of exploitations.

The Role of Government Agencies

Politics Over People

Were it not for the coalition of community groups, the workers would not enjoy the freedom and life as they know it today. They would not have accessed the legal system, allowing them to pursue justice through their own civil lawsuit.

Federal and state labor agencies are grossly underfunded. With only a handful of investigators to cover hundreds of thousands of low-wage workers in multiple industries, enforcement of existing labor laws is all but nonexistent.

Exacerbating this problem, the competition between immigration enforcement against workers and labor law enforcement in favor of workers places workers in the crossfire. The INS operates as an arm of lawless employers, exacerbating the vulnerability of low-wage workers and making situations like those in El Monte possible. Rather than the workers, the lawless employers themselves, including garment manufacturers and retailers, should be targeted by the government. It is these employers who benefit from the immigration of workers to the United States and then benefit further from government complicity in their exploitative business practices.

Recommendations for Change

The experience with the El Monte incident is a case study of how law enforcement agencies, labor officials, and other government agencies must significantly improve their performance to ensure that the rights of low-wage individuals are protected. Rather than being viewed merely as "illegal aliens," low-wage immigrant workers must be recognized as human beings whose basic human rights have been violated. They thus deserve an opportunity to assert their rights and to seek legal protection, not summary deportation. Their legal rights should be thoroughly explained to them in the event that the federal government places them in custody, and supportive services should be offered by contacting community groups that can provide assistance. Workers with the courage to come forward to eliminate the abuses rampant in the low-wage workforce should remain free of INS retaliation. The INS should not be involved where labor laws have been violated.

In comprehensively addressing the tide of trafficking in women from undeveloped countries like Thailand into the United States for forced labor, as occurred in El Monte, it is necessary for governments to understand the dynamics of the marketplace—the sheer desperation and economic necessity driving the victims to seek opportunities abroad. Indeed, this dynamic drives workers to cross borders in the face of tremendous risks for their very survival. The international trade of unskilled, exploitable labor taking place must also be recognized as the latest competitive advantage for global capitalism. Corporations that profit from cheap labor gain the most from the desperation of workers. However, they simultaneously undermine worker protections established in many countries, including the United States. Workers who come forward to help enforce these protections should be protected and encouraged. As in the El Monte cases, the workers should be permitted to remain in the United States legally. This should be considered not merely a gesture of goodwill but also what the workers deserve for their cooperation with the government to enforce U.S. laws.

As a principle, workers should have the right to paid work, to migrate, to safe working conditions, to just compensation, and to human dignity. Laws and policies should clearly address the abusive conditions that workers and women from developing countries are frequently subjected to in the process of recruitment and transport as well as exploitative and abusive working conditions such as denial of freedom of movement, withholding of papers, deceit about the nature of conditions of work, and physical as well as psychological abuse (GAATW 1997).

Laws prohibiting trafficking, forced labor, and slavery-like practices are rarely enforced, especially in the context of women's labor. Abuse of immigrants through forced labor and slavery-like practices, whether during recruitment and travel or on the work site, are violations of basic human rights. Human rights strategies should be based on the recognition of the interrelatedness of all rights—economic, social, racial, cultural, civil, and political. Both collective and individual rights need to be recognized within the human rights framework regardless of citizenship or legal status (GAATW 1997).

Governments have the obligation to enact laws and organize structures of government, including criminal, immigration, asylum, labor, and family laws, to ensure that victims of forced labor, as well as abusive labor conditions—forced or not—can use such laws and legal structures to vindicate their rights. This access to justice must effectively redress violations committed by the state as well as abuses by nonstate actors. In order to hold the state accountable, workers must have the information and power to become active participants in open and genuinely democratic decision making (GAATW 1997).

As the El Monte case demonstrated, taking advantage of the gap created by hypocritical official policies and nonenforcement of protections for the poor, organized crime steps in. The unregulated character of sweatshop work creates the conditions for abusive recruitment practices and exploitative conditions of work, extending from humiliating treatment to outright forced labor and slavery-like practices (GAATW 1997).

In prosecuting groups or individuals holding others in a form of debt peonage or indentured servitude, the definition of slavery must be expanded beyond physical restrictions to include psychological and emotional torture and the more subtle forms of control owing to the fulfillment of dominant culturally imposed obligations. The GAATW, representing aboriginal women, domestic workers, sex workers, migrant workers, and activists, as well as human rights and labor advocates, scholars, and activist-writers, defines forced labor and slavery-like practices as "the extraction of work or services from any woman or the appropriation of the legal identity and/or physical person of any woman by means of violence or threat of violence, abuse of authority or dominant position, debt-bondage, deception or other forms of coercion." The GAATW's definition of trafficking can also be adopted. This definition is consistent with the understanding that trafficking refers to "all acts of violence in the recruitment and/or transportation of women within and across national borders for work or services, including physical/psychological violence or threat of physical/psychological violence, abuse of authority or dominant position, debt-bondage, deception or other forms of coercion."

In part because of confusion about the definition of trafficking, the GAATW reconceptualized the definitions of trafficking, forced labor, and slavery-like practices to more accurately expose the abusive elements and to place women's rights, agency, and integrity at the center of the definition and therefore also at the center of the legislation, policies, and conventions. These definitions are a tool for raising public consciousness and for insisting on government accountability. Since most governments define trafficking simply by recruitment and transport for the purposes of prostitution, regardless of conditions of force, any enforcement of current legislation implies the criminalization of migrant and nonmigrant workers. The definitions of trafficking and slavery-like practices adopted by the GAATW incorporates both recruitment and transportation practices as well as conditions of work. By doing so, the actual conditions of work—not merely the act of migrating—become relevant.

Hypocritical and discriminatory attitudes and actions of governments, consulates, and embassies toward trafficked persons should be exposed. The U.S. government must stop using illegal immigration status as justification for failure to prosecute abuses against trafficked persons such as rape, violence, debt-bondage, and abusive employment practices. Destination countries should be held accountable for violations of human rights within their national boundaries.

Taken from the GAATW's North American Regional Consultative Forum on Trafficking in Women held in Canada in 1997, the following recommendations can be made to governments when cases similar to El Monte occur. In addition, a greater focus on the structural demand for trafficked labor—that is, industry-based demand to which traffickers respond—must be embraced by national and international policy. Although the recommendations specifically address the rights of women, they can also be applied toward the rights of anyone who is a victim of trafficking, forced labor, or slavery-like practices:

1. Ratify the Slavery Convention of 1926; the 1956 Supplementary Convention on the Abolition of Slavery, the Slave Trade, and Institutions and Practices Similar to Slavery, the ILO Convention on Forced Labor (No. 29); Abolition of Forced Labor Convention (No. 105); On Freedom of Association (No. 87); Protection of Wages (No. 95); Convention on the Protection of the Rights of All Migrant Workers and Members of Their Families; the Convention on the Elimination of All Forms of Discrimination Against Women; the International Covenant on Civil and Political Rights; the International Covenant on Economic, Social, and Cultural Rights; and the Universal Declaration of Human Rights.

2. Ensure the civil, political, economic, social and cultural rights of trafficked persons as persons and as workers. These rights include:
   - Safe, just and equitable living and working conditions;
   - Internationally recognized health and safety standards;
   - Freedom to control working and living conditions as domestic workers;
   - Right to due compensation in cases of violation of human rights.

In order to ensure rights which are not identified above, the government needs to set up a commission focusing specifically on the various sectors of labor and with the mandate of reviewing and revising policy and legislation in order to extend the following rights:
   - Full independent legal status, regardless of marital status, migrant status or occupation;
   - Legal recognition of trafficked persons' economic activity in all sectors of the economy (including the informal) in accordance with non-discriminatory labor standards which may have to be reviewed, revised or developed.
   - The ability to make claims against all entities who share responsibility for the exploitation of labor, including direct and indirect employers, such as corporations who create the conditions for exploited labor.

3. Guarantee the right of all workers to organize, form unions and bargain collectively.
4. Repeal repressive and discriminatory immigration laws and policies and other laws and policies *vis-à-vis* housing, welfare, health and education.
5. Take measures to end abuse by police and immigration officials of trafficked persons, such as taking bribes, blackmail, sexual and physical abuse and harassment, forcible STD and HIV testing and involuntary sterilization.
6. Adopt a Code of Conduct which guarantees basic legal protection and possibilities of redress to victims of trafficking, forced labor and slavery-like practices.

   This Code of Conduct should be consistent with the Standard Minimum Rules (proposed by GAATW) for the treatment of victims of trafficking. These rules include:

   - The right to freedom from persecution or harassment by those in positions of authority.
   - Access to adequate, confidential and affordable health, social and psychological care.
   - Access to competent translators during all interactions with the government.
   - Access to free legal assistance and legal representation during criminal or other proceedings.
   - Access to legal possibilities for compensation and redress.
   - Provisions to enable victims to press criminal charges and/or take civil action against their violators, such as a permit to remain legally in a country during criminal and/or civil proceedings and adequate witness protection.
   - Assistance to return to their home country if they wish to do so.
   - Legal rights to stay, regardless of formal witness status, if victims do not want or cannot return to their home country.
   - Protection against reprisals both in countries of origin and destination, from their violators or oppressive and/or discriminatory measures of the authorities.
   - Abolition of summary deportation.
   - Encouragement, adequate financial resources and legal protection for organizations of the victims affected, as well as for community organizations who work in solidarity with them.
   - Establishment of a system to monitor and regulate abusive employers, domestic worker recruitment and placement agencies.
   - Development and enforcement of occupational and safety regulations and labor codes to regulate work sites that are not currently covered by such regulations. Enforcement of laws against sexual assault when such abuse occurs with the provision that trafficked persons who report such abuse are not threatened with loss of residency, immigration, or citizenship rights.

7. Ensure that comprehensive protections and remedies are available to all trafficked persons, whether or not they are victims of abusive recruitment and/or transportation practices, and/or forced labor or slavery-like practices.

   - Work together with grassroots and community organizations to develop a comprehensive national program to assist victims of abuse in the context of labor and migration with legal assistance, health care, job training, shelter and financial assistance if required. Adequate resources should be allocated to implement this program.
   - Sponsor human rights education in relevant languages and in accessibly written language.
   - Recognize the contribution of immigrant workers' labor to the economies of the United States and ensure commensurate remuneration.

- Diplomatic arms of governments should respond to the needs of individuals in their countries who flee abusive situations, and provide resources and information to protect their rights.
- Provide information and resources about rights, employment situations, and avenues of recourse in cases of abuse to prospective immigrants (in Consulates and Embassies of destination countries).
- Allocate adequate funds to grassroots and community organizations to advocate for and serve the needs of migrant persons in countries of origin and destination. Governments should provide these organizations with relevant statistics and data at no cost.

Rebuilding Their Lives

One of the most impressive examples of the strength of the human spirit is the workers' resilience and ability to adjust to life outside of El Monte. Having had virtually no contact with the outside world, the majority knew very little about life in a major U.S. metropolis such as Los Angeles. While in El Monte, their captors fed them lies about life on the outside. They were told only of fear and violence in a society dominated by wicked people. This psychological torture helped the captors keep the workers enslaved.

The long neglect of their health also resulted in serious physical problems. The workers suffered from a variety of ailments, including ulcers, tooth decay, gum disease, numbness to their extremities, cysts, and lymph node disorders (White 1995a).[5] Despite their struggles, pain, and afflictions, they found strength in one another and in their inner reserve of hope to endure and overcome what they once thought was their permanent fate. Remarkably, the workers harbor no feelings of vengeance toward their captors.

In an effort to rebuild their lives, and through the assistance of community groups like the Thai Community Development Center, the Asian Pacific American Legal Center, and the Korean Immigrant Workers Advocates, they were able to obtain work permits, social security cards, and California IDs and to study English and basic life skills, find decent jobs and housing, learn to drive, and obtain medical care (Schoenberger, McDonnell, and Trinidad 1995).

Today, the Thai and Latino workers are living and struggling to try and fulfill their dreams of supporting themselves and their families. They have greater control over their own future and have been empowered with independent decision-making skills. Although the Thai workers are no longer under a patronage relationship, they have entered the world of the low-wage workforce in Los Angeles. Being skilled only in garment work and speaking very little English, they are unable to access other economic opportunities or other skilled and higher-paying jobs. In a fiercely competitive industry dominated by sweatshops, it is hard for any garment worker to find a shop free of labor violations and hazardous working conditions.

The Thai and Latino workers have come a long way since they first came together to demand changes in the garment industry in 1995. They have been studying English, taking the bus to work, paying their bills, and buying their own groceries. However, they also remain in the unenviable world of immigrant workers in the garment industry; that is, they have joined the pool

---

[5] "Many continue to suffer from physical and mental ailments. They have been tested for tuberculosis, blurred vision, headaches, back pains and ulcers" (Lu 1995).

of hundreds of thousands of garment workers in Southern California who toil long hours and struggle to survive on poverty wages (Holstein 1996; Sassen 1988).[6] For the Thai workers, their freedom from enslavement has not meant freedom from poverty or from a host of other problems stemming from the long years of neglected health, physical exhaustion, and psychological abuse. It is difficult to evaluate the emotional costs of their ordeal and nearly impossible to place a monetary value on each day of freedom of which they were deprived.

The suffering endured by these Thai and Latino workers should sound a warning. As long as politicians rely on scapegoating low-wage immigrant workers for the social and economic ills that plague our society rather than trying to solve these very real problems, sweatshops and slaveshops will continue to flourish. As long as workers face retaliation, intimidation, or deportation for standing up for their rights and pursuing their legal claims, major corporations in the garment industry will continue their exploitation with impunity while slave-shops and sweatshops are driven farther underground (Sterngold 1995). Yet the state and federal agencies charged with enforcing labor laws have been subjected to over a decade of massive budget cuts, which result in continual government neglect, thereby leaving workers unprotected (Headden 1993; Lee 1997; Rofe 1995).[7] Exacerbating the problem, organized labor has been unable to successfully unionize workers in an industry that poses numerous challenges. The legal system further creates barriers to workers' ability to stand up for themselves. When manufacturers and retailers of the clothes made in sweatshops and slaveshops generate substantial profits on a yearly basis and can deny all accountability to the workers who toil for them, working conditions that society pretends no longer exist in our country will thrive. It is no accident that the El Monte slave shop existed in the garment industry; in fact, the structure of the industry all but invites such abuse.

The horror of the Thai workers' servitude brought to the public's attention conditions that garment workers live with—and that garment manufacturers create and profit from—every day. With their lawsuit, the Thai and Latino workers stated clearly and courageously, "No more!" The way to end abusive and regressive practices is to hold sweatshop operators and manufacturers and retailers jointly responsible, under the existing laws, for their treatment of workers. Isolated victories by workers and one-time handouts by corporations expressing "sympathy" for exploited laborers will not change the structure of an industry designed to protect profit and privilege by depressing wages and working conditions. Government forums (McKay 1996) and calls for good corporate practices are not enough (Holstein 1996; Ramey 1996). Manufacturers and retailers need to ensure that the basic dignity of workers who produce their clothes is protected. If corporations can invest in massive amounts of creative advertising and marketing techniques, the industry has ample resources to protect garment workers.

The industry has proven that it could easily survive—indeed thrive—by providing decent wages and working conditions to its workers. However, it has become addicted to superprofits that are achieved only by taking freedom from workers.

---

[6] Industrial Welfare Commission minimum wage order, MW-96 (revised) (as adopted by the Living Wage Act of 1996). MW-96 (revised) raised the minimum wage per hour to $5.00, effective on March 1, 1997. The minimum wage at the time El Monte occurred was $4.25.

[7] "Under Jimmy Carter, the [U.S. Labor Department] had 1,600 wage and hour inspectors to police 90 million workers. Under President Reagan, that number was slashed to 700. . . . Today, the Labor Department claims just 800 wage and hour inspectors, and the number is not expected to grow anytime soon" Headden (1993). "Because of budget cutbacks in the 1980's, the state and federal agencies entrusted with ensuring safe working conditions 'can't enforce laws that are on the books'" (Rofe 1995).

Exploited immigrant workers are being blamed for a whole host of the social and economic ills that plague our society. It needs to be underscored that immigrant workers' work yields considerable financial gains for all parties but the workers themselves. Not only do "trafficking" networks and corporations make huge profits, but remittances of workers form an important source of foreign exchange for their home countries as well. It should also be emphasized that the labor of immigrant workers contributes significantly to the economies of the destination or recipient countries. In fact, the labor of immigrants such as Asian and Latino garment workers in the United States is crucial to sustain economies of the economically privileged countries and maintain standards of living at the current level.

The Thai and Latino workers fought to place the responsibility for their exploitation where it properly belongs. Together, these Thai and Latino workers—who share neither a common language nor a common culture—defied attempts to divide them by ethnic barriers (Ochoa 1995). What they do share is a common hope that, by holding the manufacturers and retailers in the industry liable, inhumane and illegal working conditions in the garment industry will one day be eliminated and that the horrors endured by the Thai workers will never, ever, be repeated.

Bibliography

Adelson, Andrea. 1996. "Officials Link 2 Retailers to Sweatshop-Made Goods." *New York Times*, May 20.

Arevalo, Penny. 1995. "After the Raids." *California Law Business*, September 25.

Bonacich, Edna, and David V. Waller. 1994. "Mapping a Global Industry: Apparel Production in the Pacific Rim Triangle." In Edna Bonacich et al., eds., *Global Production: The Apparel Industry in the Pacific Rim*. Philadelphia: Temple University Press.

Chang, Kenneth. 1996. "Not Home Free: Thais Freed from Sweatshop Are Adjusting to Life in U.S. but the Future Is Uncertain." *Los Angeles Times*, June 19.

Cho, Mil Young. 1994. "Overcoming Our Legacy as Cheap Labor, Scabs, and Model Minorities." In Karen Aguilar-San Juan, ed., *The State of Asian American: Activism and Resistance in the 1990s*. Boston: South End Press.

Desbarats, Jacqueline. 1979. "Thai Migration to Los Angeles." *The Geographical Review* 69 (3), 302–318.

Editorial. 1996a. "Garment Industry Abuses Live On." *Los Angeles Times*, February 20.

———. 1996b. "The Still-Tattered Fabric of the Apparel Industry: Firms, Government and Public Must Ensure Job Safety." *Los Angeles Times*, August 22.

Feldman, Paul, and Carl Ingram. 1995. "8 Suspects in Sweatshop Ring Plead Not Guilty." *Los Angeles Times*, August 22, A1.

Feldman, Paul, Patrick McDonnell, and George White. 1995. "Thai Worker Sweatshop Probe Grown." *Los Angeles Times*, August 9.

Fernandez-Kelly, Patricia M., and Anna M. Garcia. 1989. "Informalization at the Core: Hispanic Women, Homework, and the Advanced Capitalist State." In Alejandro Portes, Manual Castells, and Lauren A. Benton, eds., *The Informal Economy: Studies in Advanced and Less Developed Countries*, pp. 247–264. Baltimore: The Johns Hopkins University Press.

Fleg, John-Paul, 1980. *Thais and North America*. Yaumouth, Maine: Intercultural Press. Global Alliance Against Traffic in Women (GAATW). 1997. "Plan of Action from the North American Regional Consultative Forum on Trafficking in Women." Conference Report. Victoria, British Columbia, Canada, April 30–May 3.

Gonzalez, Hector. 1991. "Thais Get on with Lives: Ex-Sweatshop Slaves United in Legal Suits." *San Gabriel Valley Tribune.*

Headden, Susan. 1993. "Made in the USA." *U.S. News and World Report*, November 22.

Holstein, William J. 1996. "Santa's Sweatshop." *U.S. News and World Report*, December 16.

Hubler, Shawn, and George White 1995. "INS Accused of Blocking Probe of Sweatshops." *Los Angeles Times*, August 10, B1.

James, Ian. 1995. "Freed Thai Workers File Lawsuit." *Los Angeles Times*, September 6, B3.

Kang, Connie K. 1995. "Thai Workers Sue Top Clothing Businesses Over El Monte Plant." *Los Angeles Times*, October 25, B1.

Krikorian, Michael. 1996. "Woman, 66, Gets 7-year Sentence for Running Sweatshop." *Los Angeles Times*, April 30.

Lee, Don. 1997. "Many Find Labor Officer Slow to Act." *Los Angeles Times*, January 13.

Lee, Patrick, and George White. 1995. "INS Got Tip on Sweatshop 3 Years Ago." *Los Angeles Times*, August 4, A1.

Lu, Elizabeth. 1995. "Nightmare Continues for Thai Workers." *Los Angeles Times*, October 26, B1.

Matthew, Linda Miller. 1996. "Gender and International Labor Migration: A Networks Approach." *Social Justice: A Journal of Crime, Conflict and World Order* 23 (3).

McDonnell, Patrick J. 1995. "Sweatshop Items Were for Big Firms U.S. Says." *Los Angeles Times*, August 26, B1.

McDonnell, Patrick J., and Macki Becker. 1996. "7 Plead Guilty in Sweatshop Slavery Case." *Los Angeles Times*, February 10.

McDonnell, Patrick J., and Paul Feldman. 1995a. "Labor: Top Retailers May Have Bought Goods Made in Sweatshop." *Los Angeles Times*, August 12.

_____. 1995b. "New Approaches to Sweatshop Problem Urged." *Los Angeles Times*, August 16.

_____. 1995c. "9 Indicted in Alleged Operation of Thai Case." *Los Angeles Times*, August 18, B1.

McKay, Peter. 1996. "Cooperation Urged to Fight Sweatshops." *Washington Post*, July 17.

Meyer, Walter. 1995. "Thai Women, Prostitution and Tourism." In Amima Mama, ed., *Beyond the Mask*. London: Routledge.

Nifong, Christina. 1995. "Raid Reveals Seamy Side of US Garment Making." *Christian Science Monitor*, August 16.

Ochoa, Alberto M. 1995. "Language Policy and Social Implications for Addressing the Bicultural Immigrant Experience in the United States." In Antonia Darder, ed., *Culture and Difference*. Westport, Conn.: Bergin and Garvey.

Ramey, Joanna. 1996. "Apparel's Ethics Dilemma: Coping with Charges of Abuse." *Women's Wear Daily*, March 18.

Rofe, John. 1995. "Officials Close in on Sweatshops Latest L.A. Discoveries Stir State, Federal Action." *The San Diego Union-Tribune*, August 26.

Sassen, Saskia. 1988. *The Mobility of Labor and Capital*. London: Cambridge University Press.

Scheer, Christopher. 1995. "Savoring Freedom: Thai Sweatshop Workers Recall Their Pasts and Contemplate Their Futures as They Celebrate with Supporters and Tour the Site of Possible New Jobs." *Los Angeles Times*, August 14.

Scheer, Robert. 1995. "The Slave Shop and the INS Indifference." *Los Angeles Times*, August 8.

Schoenberger, Karl. 1995. "Escapee Sparked Sweatshop Raid." *Los Angeles Times*, August 11.

Schoenberger, Karl, and Shawn Hubler. 1995. "Asian Leaders Call for Release of Thai Workers." *Los Angeles Times*, August 10, B12.

Schoenberger, Karl, Patrick J. McDonnell, and Elson Trinidad. 1995. "Feasting on Kindness: Thais Freed from Sweatshop Discover Good Side of Life in America." *Los Angeles Times*, August 20.

Silverstein, Stuart, and George White. 1996. "Hazards Found in Nearly 75% of Garment Shops." *Los Angeles Times*, May 8.

Stepick, Alex. 1989. "Miami's Two Informal Sectors." In Alejandro Portes, Manuel Castells, and Lauren A. Benton, eds., *The Informal Economy: Studies in Advanced and Less Developed Countries*, pp. 111–131. Baltimore: The Johns Hopkins University Press.

Sterngold, James. 1995. "Agency Missteps Put Illegal Aliens at Mercy of Sweatshop." *New York Times*, September 20.

Sweatshop Watch. 1995. "Slave Conditions in Southern California Garment Shop." *Sweatshop Watch* 1 (1, fall).

Swoboda, Frank, and Margaret Webb Pressler. 1995. "U.S. Targets 'Slave Labor' Sweatshop Back Wages Sought from Clothing Makers." *Washington Post*, August 16.

Welch, Michael. 1996. "The Immigration Crisis: Detention as an Emerging Mechanism of Social Control." *Social Justice: A Journal of Crime, Conflict and World Order* 23 (3).

White, George. 1995a. "Garment 'Slaves' Tell of Hardship They Describe 17—Hour Days, Broken Promises." *Los Angeles Times*, August 4, D1.

———. 1995b. "Workers Held in Near-Slavery, Officials Say." *Los Angeles Times*, August 3.

———. 1996. "El Monte Case Sparked Efforts to Monitor, Root Out Sweatshops," *Los Angeles Times*, August 2.

Wijers, Marjan, and Lin Lap-Chew. 1997. *Trafficking in Women, Forced Labor and Slavery-Like Practices in Marriage, Domestic Labor and Prostitution.* Amsterdam: Foundation Against Trafficking in Women.

Emergence of a New Entrepreneurship: The Asian American Food Truck Phenomenon

Eunai Shrake and C. Alan Shrake

CHAPTER 10

Since the first Kogi Taco truck rolled out onto the streets of Los Angeles in 2008, serving Asian and Mexican fusion food while utilizing Twitter to allow its clientele to track them down, a number of Asian American gourmet food trucks have popped up in America's metropolitan cities. Combining food with social media, the emerging Asian American food truck industry has brought a whole new focus on Asian American entrepreneurship as well as on the American culinary culture.

Today, there are more than fifty Asian-owned or Asian-themed food trucks traversing the Los Angeles area.[1] Offering multiethnic fusion dishes such as kogi (marinated beef) taco, kung pao chicken taco, peking duck taco, adobo burrito, bibim burrito, kimchi quesadilla, kogi sliders, and bulgogi burger, as well as ethnic dishes such as sushi, wonton, banh mi, adobo, dosa, and pad thai, Asian American food trucks have spread out to other metropolitan cities, including New York, San Francisco, Seattle, Philadelphia, Miami, Chicago, and Austin.

This chapter explores the emerging Asian American food truck phenomenon and its contribution to the legacy of Asian immigrant entrepreneurship and to sociocultural trends in Los Angeles. More specifically, this chapter examines how this new business trend has changed the Asian American small business world and poses to be a dynamic sociocultural space. The chapter intends to provide a preliminary exploratory investigation based on ethnographic observations of Asian American food trucks at various food truck

Contributed by Eunai Shrake, PhD, a Professor in the Asian American Studies Department at California State University, Northridge, and *C. Alan Shrake*, a Lecturer in the Geography Department at California State University, Northridge, and G.I.S. Instructor at College of the Canyons. He received his MA in Geography from the University of California Los Angeles and GIS training from the University of California, Riverside.

---

[1] Foodtruckmaps.com as of January 6, 2012, lists 218 food trucks in the Los Angeles area, out of which fifty-five are Asian-owned or Asian-themed food trucks. This number doesn't include Hawaiian-themed food trucks. Authors also found approximately five more Asian American food trucks that are not included in this list. Food truck vendors estimated that there are actually more than seventy Asian American food trucks traversing the Los Angeles area, the collective estimation of which would constitute about one-third of all food trucks in the larger Los Angeles area.

Variable	N	Percent
TABLE 10.1 Demographic Characteristics of the Truck Vendor Sample		
Gender (N = 19)		
Male	14	74%
Female	5	26%
Age group (N = 19)		
20's	8	42%
30's	10	53%
40's	1	5%
Generation (N = 19)		
1st	1	5%
1.5	2	10%
2nd	14	75%
3rd	1	5%
4th	1	5%
Educational background		
High school	2	10%
College and beyond	15	79%
Culinary school	2	10%

Note: Interviewed trucks include two Chinese American (Dim Sum, Don Chow Tacos), two Japanese American (Lomo Arigato, Aloha Fridays), two Korean American (KogiBBQ, The Bun), one Vietnamese American (Nom Nom), two Filipino American (WhiteRabbit, Pogi Boys), one Thai American (Streets of Thailand), one Indian American (Bollywood Bites), and one Malaysian American (Mama's Food Truck). There were 19 people involved in these 12 trucks either as sole proprietors or business partners.

lots[2] throughout Los Angeles, and formal and informal interviews with Asian American food truck vendors and their patrons.

As shown in Table 10.1, Asian American food truck vendors we interviewed tend to be young, more advanced in generation, and highly educated. Out of nineteen vendors who are involved in twelve Asian American food trucks we interviewed, fourteen (74%) are male and five (26%) are female, and except for one vendor who just hit forty, most of the vendors are in their twenties (42%) and thirties (53%). Parallel to this young age profile, the majority of the vendors (85%) belong to second and higher generations. In addition, the majority of them (89%) have some sort of college degree. We refer throughout this chapter to members of various generations as "Asian American" but are aware that the term itself may carry varying nuances in identity.

[2] According to Foodtruckmaps.com, the food truck stops are proliferating in almost every neighborhood in the Los Angeles area: from Central to East to South to Westside to NorthEast and NorthWest.

The Changing Nature of Asian American Entrepreneurship

The history of economic participation by first-generation Asian Americans has been characterized by a high rate of self-employment (Le, 2007).[3] The phenomenon of the extraordinary rate of Asian American entrepreneurship has been attributed to the intricate interaction between proscriptive factors, such as language and cultural barriers that restrict new immigrants from full participation in the primary labor market, and nurturing factors, such as class and ethnic resources many Asian Americans have brought with them (Lee, 2007; Light & Bonacich, 1988; Greene & Owen, 2004). Class resources refer to socioeconomic and educational backgrounds of the individual immigrant while ethnic resources point to cultural features of an ethnic group such as family solidarity and ethnic network that provide members of the group with various forms of aid for capital formation and labor utilization (Hurh, 1998). Overcoming labor market disadvantages with effective utilization of class and ethnic resources, many Asian Americans turn to self-employment, typically engaging in ethnic business that serves other members of their ethnic community. As such, Asian American small business tends to be family oriented (e.g., mom-and-pop stores), catering to co-ethnic clientele by providing specific ethnic goods and services. The proliferation of this ethnic business is directly tied to the growth of Asian American ethnic enclaves.

Asian American food truck vendors, however, are decidedly different from their parental counterparts. The majority of Asian American food truck vendors are raised and educated in the United States, many with college degrees. Unlike first-generation Asian American small business entrepreneurs who often suffer from acculturation barriers, these food truck vendors have capitalized upon their U.S. education and its resultant acculturation to American society, which appears to have influenced their motivations and business strategies in embarking on this particular breed of small business enterprise. In fact, the Asian American food truck trend has created a new business model by bringing changes to the traditional style of first-generation small business in various aspects of entrepreneurship such as business motivation, marketing strategies, business format, resource utilization, the goods they serve, clientele, and business locations.

Business Motivation

In contrast to first-generation small business owners, who are often forced into self-employment for sheer economic survival, the food truck vendors express a personal interest and aptitude in self-employment, a desire for vocational autonomy, and disinterest in the corporate workplace as the salient motivating factors. Ross, a fourth-generation Japanese American vendor of the "Aloha Fridays" truck, expresses his desire for vocational autonomy and his disinterest in the corporate workplace:

> I was an accountant in MySpace for three years. Then I wasn't moving up. I got sick of it. I quit my job and bought this [truck] and started my own business. . . . I was sick of working for someone else. Working at my corporate job, I was capped off at a certain amount. I want to be able to make whatever I could. Just put the potential to be endless, basically.

---

[3] 2000 Census 5% PUMS data shows that about 20% of first-generation Asian Americans in general, and 28% of Korean Americans in particular, are engaged in small business enterprise.

Similarly, a second-generation Taiwanese American vendor, who just graduated from a prestigious university, also states that though he doesn't have any problems to compete in professional job market, he is more interested in having his own business rather than a corporate job.

While both of them address their indifference to corporate jobs and personal aptitude in business to be their main motivation, Brian, a second-generation Korean American vendor of "The Bun" truck, emphasizes the freedom of choice and open opportunities in various vocational fields that he can enjoy as a second generation as opposed to his parents' generation:

> I worked for an investment firm as an accountant. But I always wanted to open up a restaurant. It fits my personality. . . . This is absolutely a free choice. My parents' generation is more restricted in what they can do. Obviously, they are rallied around the Korean community. There are very limited things that they can do. They are typecast in certain things. But our generation has more avenues to be successful. We are getting into different industries now, whether it is acting, art, or the food truck business. Whatever you want to do, whatever you are passionate about, there's an opportunity now.

Alice, a second-generation Korean American spokesperson of the "Kogi" truck, also focuses on vocational autonomy and freedom of choice as important business motivations that differentiate second-generation from first-generation counterparts:

> We want to do what interests us and is fun doing. We are Americans. . . . We branch out for anything. We are not going to be stuck in a pigeonhole. We don't want to be limited. . . . We want to go beyond economic capital. We want to build cultural capital.

While all these vendors address their disinterest in corporate workplace and personal aptitude in self-employment as the important motivating factors, Brian and Alice highlight the first- and second-generation difference in business motivation by focusing on the second generation's advantages in vocational choice. Alice specifically emphasizes her motivation to go beyond the first generation's goal of economic survival by referring to her business goal to build cultural capital. Her comment demonstrates that, in addition to economic motivation, these advanced generation Asian American food truck vendors may have added concern for marketing Asian American culture to the mainstream.

Marketing Strategies: Use of Social Media

Before the food truck, most Asian American small businesses relied on ethnic networking such as ethnic media (radio, TV, newspapers) and ethnic business directories for marketing their business. Food trucks revolutionized this traditional marketing strategy by connecting their business with their customers through social media (Twitter, Facebook, website). Food trucks, with their mobile nature, update their frequently changing locations via instantaneous Twitter feed to allow their customers to track them down. They also utilize other social media such as Internet and Facebook to advertise the truck's menu and schedule as well as to provide sites for their customers to communicate with each other. Being mobile and utilizing social media, these food trucks introduce Asian American food and culture to various demographics by bridging geographic distance. In so doing, they create a community of wired customers that transcends a fixed locality.

Dominic, a second-generation Chinese American vendor of "Don Chow Tacos," talks about how he utilizes social media to advertise and promote his food truck business:

> Twitter is my eyes and ears on the street. . . .We don't want to be one directional. We want to be conversational. We want to open up the line [with social media] to eliminate disconnection between consumers and business owners. If you have questions, by all means, talk to us. If you have complaints, we want to hear about it. . . . I want to hear the community at large speak. . . . As a social media, Web 2.0 definitely contributes to two-way conversation. You know, not just Twitter, not just Facebook, we are talking Web also. People post their reviews on urban spoon, blogs. . . . We want to reward these people on Twitter who follow us.

Misa, a second-generation Chinese American vendor of "Nom Nom," also addresses the technical operation of her business by using social media:

> We do Twitter, we do Facebook, and we just ensure that we're always keeping our customers, our "Nomsters," up to date as to where the truck is. For example, yesterday the generator broke down and we weren't able to serve, and they need to know, minute by minute, what is going on. If we're not able to serve them, we want to let them know immediately, so that's a great way that those things and Twitter allow us to keep in touch with them. We also have our website and blog. . . . So, really all these tools have allowed us essentially to stay in business. Without these tools, we may not be able to reach these people.

Patty, a 1.5-generation Thai American vendor of "Streets of Thailand," relates her use of social media to the first- and second-generation difference in business marketing:

> The difference I see would be marketing. . .social networking. Things have changed now. It's not just prep the food and go sell. It is more like. . .you have to do marketing when you have high competition. You kind of have to fight for the parking space and fight for customers, and in order to do that you need a lot of e-commerce, a lot of network marketing, basically a lot of social media. . .Twitter and Internet stuff. It needs communication skills and also cultural and technological knowledge.

As in the above quotes, most food truck vendors ascribe their knowledge of social media and the familiarity of the mainstream culture as the important difference between first-generation entrepreneurs and themselves. The social media use alone embodies a generational and cultural difference (i.e., technological use and cultural inclination toward mass appeal) in marketing strategies that extend beyond traditional ethnic media and business directories.

Business Clientele

Another important change that the food truck business has brought to the traditional Asian American small business world is diversification of business clientele. Utilizing social media and offering fusion food, Asian American food trucks attract diverse and multiethnic customers. The food truck vendors express a clear interest in reaching "youthful, urban, multiethnic, wired and communal" (Romano, 2009) customers. Their efforts toward reaching this diverse audience seemed substantiated by our observations of customers at various truck stops. Although the racial and age demographics of food truck customers reflect the population composition of the serving areas and serving time, our observation of food truck customers has revealed the great racial and age diversity. Specifically, the cultural combination of fusion cuisine presents the possibility of universal appeal across not only racial distinctions, but also broader familial, generational, and geographic boundaries. Alice surveys the "Kogi" clientele:

> There's no pattern. You get all kinds of people. It just reflects the area. When we go to Eagle Rock, we get families, babies in strollers, Filipino and Latino "lolas." It's a family event. In Hollywood, we get cool White hipsters. In Venice, we see crunch beach hipsters, bar hoppers. In Rowland Heights, we get teenage Chinese boys ditching SAT prep classes. In Santa Monica, in front of the Yahoo Center, we get white-collar workers in suits.

Similarly, Eric, a third-generation Japanese American vendor of "Lomo Arigato," also describes the race and age diversity in his clientele:

> My business seems to do better in Asian areas. However, there is a great diversity in race and age among customers. I see high school students to families who bring their own chairs. They are from all racial backgrounds. They are mostly fun-loving, outgoing people who are wanting to do new stuff, trendy stuff.

Kim, a second-generation Filipino American vendor of "Pogi Boys," also adds,

> They are young, 18 and up, very diverse. Especially in Southern California, I see a lot of professional individuals, I see families, I see college students, high school students. . . . I see every facet of, every backgrounds of people here.

Complimenting the vendors' description of their customers, we, too, observed that food truck crowds at different times and locations comprised a well-blended clientele. During our visits to various truck lots in high-tech office parks, college campuses, and other popular truck stops in downtown and Westside of Los Angeles during lunch hours, we observed mostly young Caucasian and Asian American customers in their late twenties and thirties. When we visited these food trucks in community festivals and residential areas, we saw many young parents with babies in strollers and families with grandparents.

This increased diversity in business clientele implies that Asian American food trucks have brought a shift from the traditional Asian American small business model focused on co-ethnic clientele, to a mainstreaming of Asian American small business.

The food truck vendors also discuss generational differences regarding approaches to financing, business format, and customer service. Most of the interviewed vendors operate as sole proprietorships or partnerships rather than family businesses, and have relied on their own personal savings, rather than on bank loans or "rotating credit associations" (Light & Bonacich, 1988) that financed many first-generation business ventures. This may reflect the comparatively less capital required for launching a food truck as opposed to a full-service or sit-down restaurant.

Taken together, it seems that the Asian American food truck business deviates from conventional understanding of immigrant entrepreneurship in many ways. For example, the food truck business has brought changes in its customer base, business format, marketing strategies, and resource utilization. In addition, Asian American food truck vendors tend to show different business motivations than their first-generation counterparts. As such, Asian American food trucks challenge and revise the traditional Asian American small business world and, as a result, they created a new business model in the Asian American business community.

Culinary and Cultural Fusion

The significance of the Asian American food truck phenomenon goes beyond its influence to Asian American entrepreneurship. It also has brought a cultural shift in American culinary, as well as mainstream, culture. The popularity of Asian American food trucks can be understood as part of the trend toward multiculturalism in America. Specifically, Asian American food trucks tap into a demand for multicultural consumption. Cleverly combining traditional Asian dishes with familiar ingredients to appeal to the mainstream palate, Asian American food truck vendors are experimenting with fusion cooking by "marrying the exotic with the familiar" (Johnston & Baumann, 2010). In the process, they have turned Asian dishes, which were previously considered "exotic" to the mainstream palate, into widely accepted and popular high-end American food (Mannur, 2006). Indeed, Asian American food trucks, forged from the transnational exchanges of cuisine and culture, exemplify culinary multiculturalism and transnational cultural mixing.

One can discern the hybrid nature of the food truck simply by perusing the litany of menu items offered by these trucks: kung pao chicken taco, kogi sliders, kimchi quesadilla, peking duck taco, adobo burrito, bulgogi burger, kogi gyro, and baprito, to name a few. In a city with a large ethnic diversity like Los Angeles, the fusion appeal of Asian American food trucks carries particular significance. Alice of "Kogi" speaks to the business's multicultural appeal as its originating philosophy:

> For us, Kogi [food truck] is about L.A. It is an expression of our own experience growing up as the second generation in multicultural L.A. In Koreatown, Latinos and Koreans have lived side by side for generations. Taco and tortilla were ingredients always there with us. Nothing is forced or contrived. Our main chef, Roy, wants to make sure he does the justice to taco, paying homage and respect to loncheras who've been doing this since the 1970s. . . . What our food truck is pushing or appealing to people is . . . an L.A. flavor so that when they have kimchi quesadilla or the [kogi] taco, they feel nothing foreign, nothing to dissect, nothing exotic about it. . . . When they see kogi taco or kimchi quesadilla ten years from now, hopefully people will think, "Oh, that's so L.A."

In a similar note, Dominic of "Don Chow Tacos" also addresses the multicultural aspect of his food truck, aptly summing up the concept of his truck as "Chino Meets Latino":

> My father had owned two restaurants in the past. So, I kinda grew up in the restaurant industry. . . . We needed to modify what we consider traditional Chinese food to fit a more Americanized palate. And we took Mexican food. Why we chose Mexican? One, I grew up in L.A. You can't avoid having great Mexican food. . . . I took the best of what I knew of both ways. Same with Lawrence [business Partner]. We mixed them together. . .taco and tortilla—they are a blank canvas. You can paint it however you want.

As Alice and Dominic describe, Asian American food trucks, by melding two cultures, contribute to culinary multiculturalism and thus enrich Angeleno/Californian culture and identity.[4]

---

[4] Patric Kuh (2011), a food critic for *Los Angeles Magazine*, wrote, "The Kogi truck melded two cultures in one Kimchi quesadilla" and "the amalgam seemed completely of Los Angeles."

Not surprisingly, many customers also attribute the major part of the food truck contribution to its influence on mainstream culinary culture. A Chinese American second-generation male in his thirties comments, "The Asian American food truck symbolizes cultural fusion of Asian culture and mainstream culture. It navigates between different identities in America, building a new identity, a hybrid identity." An African American male in his twenties also offers, "This is a cultural innovation. Take the food you love and Americanize it. Through the conglomeration of styles, you multiculturalize America."

In addition to culinary multiculturalism, Asian American food trucks also contribute to creating a transnational culture. Strolling around food truck lots, one can witness how transnational culture is deeply ingrained in the food truck culture. Alongside the fusion atmosphere that characterizes Asian American food trucks, we saw trucks such as "Happy Cup Ramen," "Boba Truck," and "Dumpling Station," highlighting more traditional or "homier" fare by incorporating cultural influences from Asian countries. Those trucks serve more simple Asian dishes such as sushi, adobo, dumpling, dosa, ramen, and boba drinks, adding more transnational flavors to the food truck trend.

To enhance the native cultural tone, some trucks also include Asian pop music in their playlists. In many food truck lots, Asian music flows from the truck's sound system and people from all ethnicities and nationalities congregate, implicating the Asian American food truck as a part of our transnational and hybridized culture.

Michael, a second-generation Filipino American vendor of "WhiteRabbit," attributes his business motivation to this transnational aspect of food truck when he states,

> We just recognized the need for Filipino food in the community but hasn't got any exposure. You don't see much Filipino food out in the masses, so our primary goal is to get it out there. This is just a great way to get it out to people so that everybody knows about our culture.

Misa, the Nom Nom truck owner, also addresses enhancing visibility of Asian cuisine as a part of her truck's cultural contribution;

> There's two different parts to that [contribution]. . . . We are offering jobs. . . . That's one aspect of it. Another aspect of it as you look at it, Nom Nom is a way of promoting the Vietnamese cuisine and bringing [to people] the opportunity to try it. . . . It's so great to help people open their eyes to this great sandwich [bahn mi] that people have never tried before.

In short, the Asian American food truck vendors aspire to serve their customers dishes that manifest Asian or Asian American culture. Indeed, the Asian American food truck scene is a multicultural as well as transnational space, where people with diverse ethnic and age backgrounds wait in line, enjoying together transnational and hybridized food and culture. This cultural experience could help people from diverse backgrounds to understand and appreciate each other. The Asian American food truck, with its food and its diverse customers, presents diverse qualities that make multicultural America, where Asian American culture is indeed Asian and American.

The Street as Social Space

In addition to economic and cultural remapping, the new wave of food trucks is changing the street culture in Los Angeles by creating a communally constructive social space. Several local-area observers have written on the food truck's contribution to urban street life. Kuh (2010) describes how food trucks contribute to "spawning street life," and a *Good Magazine* article (2010) remarks, "for a city with notoriously sparse street life, [food trucks bring] new life to the street of L.A., transforming otherwise empty, unused, and essentially dead spaces into lively, popular, and profitable hubs." Along with other food trucks popping up to profit from the Kogi truck's popularity, Asian American food trucks play a vital role in creating this vibrant street life that brings people together throughout Los Angeles.

In our visits to truck stops in mid-Wilshire during lunch hours, in Granada Hills during dinner time, and in Venice beach around midnight, we witnessed how Asian American food trucks have influenced street life in Los Angeles. A fleet of brightly colored food trucks—collectively surrounded by long lines of customers who are talking, laughing, and mingling with complete strangers, creating a buzz that fills the sidewalk—seem to prove that Asian American food trucks have brought many streets to life.

Dominic, the vendor of "Don Chow Tacos," reinforces this observation of street renewal in relation to his participation in the Chinatown revitalization movement:

> We have done a couple of Chinatown [fundraising] events. What we did there was . . . they tried to raise awareness over last summer. . . . They tried to do Chinatown Arts Night. So we did participate. We gave a percentage of sales for the night. And we also alerted our Twitter followers. "Hey come, check out Chinatown. They have new exhibits going on. They have DJs and fun night. Just come out. There's lots of food and fun.". . . I want to help rebuild Chinatown. When I grew up there, nobody went out at nighttime. It was desolate. It was a ghost town. Now there are lots of galleries. There is lots of nightlife going on. You know, now communities are kinda coming together.

While Dominic discusses the revitalized street life in L.A.'s urban area, Chatsworth Street in Granada Hills, located northwest of the Los Angeles metropolis in the San Fernando Valley, provides an example of the revitalized street life that mobile ethnic fare can bring to a small suburban community. Prior to the appearance of food trucks, this main thoroughfare of mom-and-pop stores was settled into a nightly routine of quiet darkness indicative of the typical suburban streets of America at night—deserted from people locked in their homes. Now on every Wednesday and Friday, from early evening to late night, the street is filled with people from all racial and age groups, strolling the street or standing in order lines or sitting on a curb to eat their ordered food. Taking advantages of this enlivened street life, many stores remain open until 10:00 P.M., despite "official" hours running only until 6:00 P.M. Two of the customers we interviewed describe the scene as "a street renaissance" and "a street fair every day."

Food trucks also offer diverse people a space to hang out and establish social relations while forging a sense of community. Gelt's (2009) description of the food truck scene is "a sort of roving party, bringing people to neighborhoods they might not normally go to, and allowing for interactions with strangers they might not otherwise talk to"; it is not uncommon to see people waiting in long order lines in a party mood, lively chatting and interacting with each other. During our visits to various food truck stops, we overheard many customers making new acquaintances on the spot and sharing personal interests including music, hobbies, and current social issues. As such, for the food truck customers, the Asian American food truck and its surroundings function as a social space where they can freely socialize.

The customers also speak to the invitational atmosphere around the food trucks. A customer in his twenties states, "If you go to a restaurant, you rarely speak to people at the next table. But when you come to the food truck, you often socialize with total strangers while waiting in line." Another customer in her thirties, who identified herself as biracial, affirms that, "Standing and waiting in a long line together, it's natural you interact with others. It gives a lot more opportunity to bond with people." Still another customer adds a very informal and lighthearted remark, "It's hip. It's a lot of fun to meet people."

Echoing the customers' comments, Wang (2009), in his opinion piece, describes his socializing experience at a food truck site when he writes, "I couldn't remember ever spending even 15 minutes on an L.A. sidewalk talking and mingling with complete strangers, let alone downtown at 10:00 P.M."

Further highlighting this point, Alice of "Kogi" truck describes her observation of convergence among people in the "Kogi line," which she affectionately refers to her customers:

> At a stop next to the Japanese American National Museum [in downtown L.A.], I saw someone who looked like a hardcore thug and another who looked like a mild-mannered office mouse. They are from totally different ethnic backgrounds, but they were talking to each other while waiting in line. It was the biggest thing that impacted me. Looking at the line . . . people talking with strangers. L.A. is not that kind of city. If you go to a restaurant, you only sit with people you know. If you are sitting at a bus stop, you sit the opposite side the stranger is sitting. You don't talk to strangers. There's something very special about the Kogi line. It is an open social space.

All in all, our observation and interview data suggest that Asian American food trucks, through their journey crossing many cities and streets, have become a part of the unique street culture in Los Angeles and function as a new urban social space, where people of diverse cultural, racial, and economic backgrounds can be conjoined together through affordable gourmet food. The substance of what we observed around the food trucks is that the trucks created an opportunity for residents to converse and interact—an opportunity engendered by the duration of the lines, the choice of experimenting with different and fusion cuisine, and the anticipation of satiating their hunger. It represents an opportunity made possible further by the unbounded space of the streets.

Crossing Class Lines

Returning to the inherent features of a food truck, we cannot help but point out that it involves street food. Another distinct feature often observable in Asian American food trucks, however, involves fusion cuisine or specialized food, which is often rendered as gourmet food. A *Time* magazine article (Stein, 2010) aptly summarizes this Asian American food truck's unique feature of being both gourmet and street food when it depicts the Kogi truck as "Gourmet on the Go." Similarly, many magazine articles, food reviews, and restaurant directors repeatedly render Asian American truck food as inexpensive, gourmet fusion, street food. As a result, Asian American food trucks are heralded as melding two conflicting food concepts: gourmet and street food.

This interesting combination brings us to ponder how race and class issues are implicated in the food truck business. By connecting gourmet food, previously a source of status and distinction for economic and cultural elites, with street food, previously dominated by the working-class immigrants, do Asian American food trucks contribute to a democratization of class and culture?

In the realm of gourmet food, despite its broadening consumer base in recent years, a persistent race and class division still remains (Mannur, 2005). In other words, gourmet food continues to remain in the domain of economic and cultural elites, namely White and relatively affluent, indirectly maintaining social inequality based on class and race (Johnston & Baumann, 2010). In this context, by making highly exclusive gourmet food accessible for a wider population, the Asian American food truck appears to have helped fuel what is called the "democratization of luxury," similar to what Vietnamese American nail salons have done by mass marketing the manicure, which was once accessible only to upper-middle-class White women.

In fact, a few customers addressed this democratizing effect as one of the significant contributions that Asian American food trucks have made. Although most of the customers attributed the popularity of Asian American food trucks to convenience, proximity, choice of food, and a fun and hip experience, more than half of them expressed their excitement with the "gourmet food at a fast-food price." When asked about contributions Asian American food trucks made to society, a few customers suggested that the juxtaposition of gourmet food with moderate pricing helped to transcend class lines. For example, a Caucasian female customer in her fifties says, "Asian American food trucks serve a high-quality product. By bringing it to the street, they definitely contribute to narrowing down the gap between ethnic and class groups." Another Caucasian male customer in his twenties states, "I think these food trucks mix economic class. Look around. Look at people and their faces. They are from all racial and economic backgrounds. Food trucks bring us together." Even one Korean American male customer in his twenties declares, "The Korean [Asian] American food truck provides accessibility of gourmet food to a majority of people. . . . It is a class equalizer."

As enthusiastic as his customers, Brian of "The Bun" truck also claims that food trucks contribute to help reduce class disparity. He states,

> That's true, we are not going to slums. But you know, when you're in a place like downtown L.A., there's all sorts of people out there. You know, whether you are from low class or upper class. . . . That's so great about DTLA. There's everybody, all sorts of different people there. When you serve gourmet fusion food as we do, for seven bucks or eight bucks, it's every type of people who try the food. The doctor, the plumber, or whoever. It definitely cuts disparity in that way.

However, a careful examination of the geographic areas these food trucks traverse and the customers they serve indicates that the claim that food trucks help reduce class and race disparity may be an overstatement. Rather, the food trucks appear to be more like a "middle of the road" phenomenon. Most of the key truck stops for these Asian American food trucks are located in more privileged mid-city and outlying suburbs, segregated from the urban core where low-income, working-class minorities reside. As Wong (2009) points out, by drawing people in more "gentrified zones and up-and-coming neighborhood," these Asian American food trucks serve "mostly upwardly mobile customers who are more urbane, tech-savvy, and with disposable income." In other words, the Asian American food truck is not for people on a limited budget, but for people who have the resources, both temporal and financial, to dine out searching for quality food.

In a word, the Asian American food truck phenomenon appears to present two sides of a coin: democratization of luxury and class division reflected in their locations and clientele. On one hand, Asian American trucks play a role in narrowing the class gap by bringing affordable quality food to people of middle- and low-middle-class backgrounds. On the other hand, they may simply perpetuate the class and racial division inherent in the city of Los Angeles and in American society (Wang, 2009).

Conclusion

The emergence of Asian American food trucks exemplifies a dynamic sociocultural and economic space where elements of entrepreneurialism, ethnicity, and food intersect. Specifically, the success and popularity of these Asian American food trucks as examined in this limited research seem to have brought a possibility of change in the socioeconomic and cultural landscape of Southern California in general and Asian American communities in particular.

On one hand, Asian American food trucks have changed the traditional Asian American ways of doing small business. As a daring economic space for mostly second-generation entrepreneurs who attempt to market ethnicity and culture to the mainstream, these food trucks not only enhanced visibility of Asian American culture but also set off a new business model in the Asian American business community.

In addition, the booming food truck business is a concrete example to show how multiculturalism is embedded in American social, cultural, and economic life. Functioning as a creative social space, the Asian American food truck brings people with diverse backgrounds together, generating a sense of community and tolerance toward "the other." In other words, it shows how American culture is a place of new immigrants bringing in new styles and flavors, "adding and enriching it rather than a melting pot tale of different ethnic groups assimilating into one dominant culture" (Liu & Lin, 2009).

On the other hand, the Asian American food truck phenomenon may simply reflect the existing class and racial division rather than closing the race and class gap in our society. Though the Asian American food truck has made a valuable contribution to narrowing the class gap by making highly selective gourmet food accessible to a wider population, it cannot be claimed that these food trucks contribute to closing the existing class and race divisions. These food trucks traverse more gentrified and middle-class areas in Los Angeles, not crossing the urban core where working-class minorities reside. In this sense, the Asian American food truck mirrors class and race divisions, which parallel geographic locations in Los Angeles.

Whether this relatively new Asian American food truck phenomenon is merely a fad or it will outlive the hype remains to be seen. However, the aspect of the recent wave of food trucks clearly lends itself to future discussion, when we have the opportunity for proper perspective and reflection upon these food trucks as an established business model. This pilot study has identified several important issues to be further investigated, such as labor and compensation issues between the vendors and their employees and the environmental issues involving carbon emissions, disposal of water and trash, and city zoning. For now, however, we simply note that the recent Asian American food truck phenomenon evinces a possible shift in the connotation of street food, social class, and racial dynamics, but we call for further explorations from scholars of different training to develop more concrete, comprehensive, and persuasive accounts of the trend and its social impact.

References

Gelt, Jessica. "Kogi Korean BBQ, A Taco Truck Brought to You by Twitter." *Los Angeles Times*. February 11, 2009.

Greene, Patricia and Margaret Owen. "Race and Ethnicity," in *Handbook of Entrepreneurial Dynamics: The Process of Business Creation*. eds. William B. Gartner, Kelly G. Shaver, Nancy M. Carter, and Paul D. Reynolds. Thousand Oaks, CA: Sage, 2004. pp. 26–38.

Hurh, Won Moo. *The Korean Americans*. Westport, CT: Greenwood Press, 1998.

Johnston, Josée, and Shyon Baumann. *Foodies: Democracy and Distinction in the Gourmet Foodscape*. New York: Routledge, 2010.

Kuh, Patric. "The Year Our Food Went Mobile: The Food Truck Fad Has Revolutionized How We Engage with Our Cuisine and Our City, But Does It Live Up to The Hype?" *Los Angeles Magazine* 55, no. 6 (2010): 106.

Kuh, Patric. "Off-Roading: Roy Choi, The Guy Behind the Kogi Truck Fleet, Expands His Repertoire But Stays True to His Vision at A-Frame." *Los Angeles Magazine* 56, no. 3 (2011): 122.

Le, C. N. *Asian American Assimilation: Ethnicity, Immigration, and Socioeconomic Attainment,* New York: LFB Scholarly Publishing, 2007.

Lee, Jennifer. "Striving for the American Dream: Struggle, Success, and Intergroup Conflict among Korean Immigrant Entrepreneurs," in *Contemporary Asian America: Multidisciplinary Reader.* eds. Min Zhou and J. V. Gatewood. New York: New York University Press, 2007. pp. 243–258.

Light, Ivan, and Edna Bonacich. *Immigrant Entrepreneurs: Koreans in Los Angeles 1965-1982.* Berkeley: University of California Press, 1988.

Liu, Haiming, and Lianlian Lin. "Food, Culinary Culture, and Transnational Culture: Chinese Restaurant Business in Southern California." *Journal of Asian American Studies* 12, no. 2 (2009): 135–162.

"Los Angeles's Food Truck Revolution." *Good Magazine.* March 3, 2010.

Mannur, Anita. "Model Minorities Can Cook: Fusion Cuisine in Asian America." In *East Main Street: Asian American Popular Culture.* eds. Shilpa Davé, Leilani Nishime, and Tasha G. Oren. New York: New York University Press, 2005. pp. 72–94.

Mannur, Anita. "Asian American Food Scapes," *Amerasia Journal.* 32. no. 2. (2006): 1–5.

Romano, Andrew. "Thanks to Twitter and the Web, L.A. is Obsessed with the Korean Tacos of America's First Viral Restaurant." *Newsweek,* March 9, 2009: 55.

Stein, Joel. "Gourmet on the Go." *Time.* March 29, 2010.

Wang, Oliver. "To Live and Dine in Kogi L.A." *Contexts* 8, no. 4 (2009): 69–71.

PART IV   Education and the Model Minority Myth

Ethnic Studies and Higher Education for Asian Americans

Mike Murase

One approach to understanding the experience of Asians in America is a study of the history of ethnic studies and the context of the system of higher education in which it arose. It is a good point of departure for several reasons. First, the history of development of ethnic studies is in itself a significant part of Asian American history. It marks the first organized effort within the context of the formal educational system to reinterpret the history of Third World peoples in this country to accurately reflect our perspectives: as an ideal it represents an honest attempt—through rigorous research and investigation, through critical analysis of ourselves and of the social institutions in our society, through dynamic and innovative approaches in instruction and sharing, and through bold new attempts to actively *apply* what is learned to reshape our society—to disseminate the life stories of millions of non-white people in America.

Secondly, a study of ethnic studies raises the question of why ethnic studies was necessary and why its maintenance and growth seem so tenuous. It presents an opportunity to delve into deeper questions of why the resistance to ethnic studies is so strong The examination leads to the conclusion that the priority within the system of higher education in the United States has been and will continue to be the maintenance and transmission of class privileges.

Thirdly, such a study leads to an examination of the process by which ethnic studies came about—the struggles that were necessary to overcome serious and determined resistance on the part of powerful institutions. It is an account of a historic event that was created by a peculiar mix of objective social conditions and the subjective will and determination of many people working together to make knowledge more relevant to themselves and more useful to society in general.

The first Asian American studies courses were initiated seven years ago in 1969. Programs were established at San Francisco State College (now California State University at San Francisco) and at the University of California at Berkeley only after the most prolonged and violent campus struggles in this country's history.

The immediate origins of the struggle may be traced to the fall of 1966. In the wake of the civil rights movement that had grown for a century after the Civil War and had flared in the late 1950s and early 1960s, Black and other Third World students presented a proposal to the administration of San Francisco State College for the admission of more Third World and other economically and culturally disadvantaged students, and for a Black-controlled Black Studies Department.

Students had been taught that all groups who had serious grievances got a fair hearing and that in order to make changes, they must make use of the "proper channels." So the students exhausted every possible avenue in the bureaucratic maze. They wrote proposal after proposal to deans and presidents. They wrote letters and appeals to campus and community newspapers. They met for endless hours and days with various administrators. They negotiated with the authorities at the school. For *sixteen months*, they negotiated and waited patiently:

> Although Black and other Third World peoples have been waiting hundreds of years for justice in America, still they were patient . . . But how could they "negotiate," after all, when the administrators had all the power? But the students had power, too, if they had the courage to use it together. They had the power to stop the school from operating. And that's what they did. They were through with brainwashing.[1]

By fall of 1968, the students had tried every "reasonable" way to raise the issues of ethnic studies, lack of student control, and easier access to higher education for minority peoples. Yet they received no indication that there would be recognition and rectification of injustices deeply rooted in the system of education. On November 6, 1968, a general student strike was called by the Third World Liberation Front (TWLF), "a coalition based on the operative and substantive principle of self-determination for each of its constituent organizations as representatives of their *communities* within the context of the academic setting."[2]

The students who spearheaded the strike were Blacks, Chicanos, Native Americans and Asian Americans. As minority group members in a system of higher education that had systematically excluded them, they had a special awareness of the depth of American racism. They were keenly aware of the way public schools had robbed them of their true heritage. They were among children of all races who went through school learning and relearning "American" history. . . . three, four and even five times—at least once each in elementary, junior high and high schools, and for those who were admitted to college, yet another course in "American" history. At each level of schooling, students were taught the same one-sided and distorted history of "our (European) forefathers" who settled along the Atlantic seaboard, and of the "pioneers in their covered wagons" who journeyed westward "to tame the wilderness."

The long and rich history of several million native Americans who lived for centuries in North America before the first white ever set foot on this land was ignored or distorted. American "Indians" were presented most often as troublesome savages who impeded the fulfillment of the European settlers' "divine right" of Manifest Destiny.

Black children were taught that their ancestors were slaves who were "emancipated" through the benevolence of white men in the North. Blacks were also portrayed most often as primitive savages who had to be "domesticated." But no mention was made of the fact that white men hunted down 100 million Blacks in the interior of Africa to sell them as slaves, and that during a 400-year period, five Africans were killed for every one that made it to the "New" World.[3]

---

[1] Research Organizing Cooperative of San Francisco, "Strike At Frisco State: The Story Behind It," pamphlet, n.d., pp. 21–22.

[2] Penny Nakatsu, keynote address at the National Asian American Studies Conference II, held at California State University at San Jose, July 6–8, 1973.

[3] Shih Chun, "Why It Is Necessary to Study World History," *Peking Review*, No. 21, May 26, 1972, p. 3.

Chicano children were taught—in English—stories about "illegal" immigration of wetbacks despite the fact that parts of California and all of the Southwest once belonged to Mexico, and that Spanish was widely spoken. The massive influx of white settlers into Mexican territory was inspired by (1) the discovery of gold in California and other rich minerals in the Southwest, (2) the completion of the transcontinental railroad by Chinese and other immigrant workers, and (3) the development of large cattle and sheep ranches, all of which took place only in the last half of the nineteenth century.

It was during this period in which the first Asians arrived in significant numbers. Yet, for the most part, the Asian American experience was omitted from the educational curriculum or has received only token mention. A sentence or two on Pearl Harbor and a line about Chinese "coolies" was the sum total of our history. Asians were depicted as oxen-like creatures who performed menial tasks, as the following example from Mark Twain's writing illustrates:

> They are a harmless race when white men either let them alone or treat them no worse than dogs; in fact, they are almost entirely harmless anyhow, for they seldom think of resenting the vilest insults or the cruelest injuries. They are quiet, tractable, free from drunkenness, and they are as industrious as the day is long. A disorderly Chinaman is rare, and a lazy one does not exist . . . He always manages to find something to do.[4]

In each of these cases, Third World people have been portrayed as faceless, dumb creatures upon which some external actor (white man) had done something to them, rather than actors and doers in and of themselves who have played vital roles in shaping the course of American history. Asian Americans had no sense of our roles, contributions and struggles in this country because we were not taught about ourselves.

So then, it was not surprising that Third World students played the leading role in the struggles for ethnic studies and for a more flexible admissions policy which would better meet their educational needs. But the San Francisco State strike involved not only the students from that campus, but it also mobilized thousands of other students, people from Third World communities all over the state, rank-and-file members of unions, an overwhelming majority of the faculty, and ultimately, the whole political apparatus of the state of California.

A comprehensive account of the five-month-long strike would be too lengthy to be repeated here. Yet a brief recapitulation of the progression and scope of activities during the strike is necessary to approximate the sense of commitment and deepening frustration felt by Third World students.

The Strike

In the fall of 1968, despite the fact that 70% of all public school students in San Francisco were Third World,[5] they represented only 16% of the entire student body at San Francisco State College.[6] At the same time, the administration announced that 47 full-time teaching positions were unfilled, but Black Studies courses were to receive only 1.2 teaching positions of the 47 available.[7] Yet, the

---

[4] Samuel Clemens (Mark Twain), *Roughing It* (Hartford: American Publishing, 1880), p. 391.

[5] Loren Baritz, *The American Left: Radical Political Thought in the Twentieth Century* (New York: Basic Books, Inc., 1971), p. 453.

[6] Nakatsu, loc. cit.

[7] Black Students Union, "Black Students Union Demands and Explanations," mimeograph, n.d.

authorities at the college continued to insist that they were doing everything possible to facilitate the demands of the Black Students Union (BSU) and other Third World organizations.

Finally, after two years of "negotiations," the Trustees moved to have a Black instructor, George Murray, fired; and the BSU called for a student strike to begin on November 6, 1968. The Third World Liberation Front quickly came into being and was composed of Latin American Student Organization, Intercollegiate Chinese for Action, Pilipino American Collegiate Endeavor, and Asian American Political Alliance. By the first day of the strike, the Third World Liberation Front was well organized; the Students for a Democratic Society (SDS) and other unaffiliated white students began to mobilize for the strike. The strike leaders picketed buildings on campus and took up the chant which was to be echoed on campuses across the country, "On strike, shut it down! On strike, shut it down!" A set of demands was formulated. The demands revolved around the establishment of a School of Ethnic Studies, student control, faculty for the program, minority admissions and the specific case of George Murray.

They held a rally culminating in a march to the office of President Smith. The strikers also marched around the campus, closing down classes one by one. Smith responded by calling the San Francisco Police Tactical Squad, a special unit within the police department trained for smashing campus unrest and urban ghetto rebellions.

The student strike picked up momentum and spread. By the third day of the strike, most departments reported attendance below 50%. "On strike, shut it down!" The rhythmic chanting of a thousand voices reverberated throughout the campus. The first arrests came the following week when two students discovered the Tactical Squad occupying the boiler room and tried to alert other students. The presence of armed police on campus created an atmosphere of uneasiness and tension. With uniformed men marching around the plaza and walkways, students began to understand the extent to which the administration was threatened by their demands and their ultimate power.

> They discovered that brainwashing in the classroom wasn't the only weapon in the establishment's arsenal. When brainwashing failed, the authorities turned to headbusting. American education is a system of social control . . . but education is not the only means. When everyday mechanisms of control break down, then the Trustees and administrators resort to extraordinary means.[8]

On November 13, during the noon hour, the Tactical Squad appeared in front of the BSU office, standing in formation and intimidating students. The presence of police attracted more students. Some began shouting, "Pigs off campus! Pigs off campus!" Others hailed them with dirt clods and food. Then, in an instant, the police broke formation and began chasing and clubbing students indiscriminately. Students became outraged. The Tactical Squad, with their guns drawn, was forced off campus by some 2000 strikers who fought back. "Pigs off campus! Pigs off campus!" President Smith was forced to close down the campus indefinitely.

Throughout the month of November, students formed discussion groups to talk about the issues involved. At the suggestion of a faculty, a "crisis" convocation was called to "resolve the issues." BSU-TWLF agreed to participate in the convocation as an educational tactic, but when President Smith tried to resume classes, the striking students walked out of the convocation. All the while, 200 plainclothes police occupied the college. In the signal word of the day, the campus was definitely "polarized."

---

[8] Research Organizing Cooperative of San Francisco, p. 22.

Meanwhile, the faculty played a mediating role by first suggesting department meetings and suspension of classes, and later, the resumption of classes and withdrawal of police from campus. The Student Strike Committee responded in a leaflet issued on November 25 entitled, "Rely on the People—Build the Strike:"

. . .

The faculty has played a dual role in this strike. On one hand, many members took a positive step by going out on strike and trying to win other faculty members to join them. But, on the other hand, the faculty has seen itself as a buffer zone between the administration, its cops, and striking students. We see this as an untenable position. In this stike one must clearly take either the administration side or the side of Third World liberation . . .

By supporting Smith's plan to resume classes on December 2, whether or not the demands are met, the faculty is taking a strike-breaking position.

The BSU-TWLF made their position clear with respect to division of labor and on the question of leadership within the strike:

Certain segments of the faculty have tried to impress on students that the faculty will resolve the issues of the strike. This says that the faculty has the power to resolve the conflict, and they see themselves in the leadership position. Both of these hypotheses are wrong.

They explained further:

Students should realize that their power flows from the strength of the people involved in the struggle. It is this attitude, relying on ourselves, that will win. Winning will not come from relying on the faculty or the administration. The faculty must be won to the idea that they must unite with white students supporting the Third World demands. Also, the idea that some faculty members believe they are in a position to lead students in this fight must be defeated. *The BSU-TWLF are in the leadership of this struggle.* The position for the faculty and other white students is to support the demands. They, along with white students, must take the offensive in fighting racism among other white faculty, white students and in the white community.[9]

On Tuesday, November 26, the BSU-TWLF called an end to the convocation when the administration acted in breach of good faith by singling out some striking students for suspension. Unable to pacify students and restore order to the San Francisco campus, President Smith submitted his resignation at a meeting of the Trustees in Los Angeles that afternoon. A half hour later, the Trustees appointed linguistics expert S.I. Hayakawa as president.

Hayakawa, who was in agreement with the political philosophy dominant among the Trustees and Governor Reagan, served well as the middle-man minority with his hardline "state of emergency" tactics and 650 policemen. On the Monday after Thanksgiving, Hayakawa reopened the campus and called for the resumption of regular classes. When he saw that students were not responding to his call, he marched off campus to a sound-truck rented by the Strike Committee, climbed on it and tore loose the speaker wires from the sound system. When he was reminded that he was violating the students' right of free speech, he retorted, "Don't touch me, I'm the president of the college."[10]

---

[9] San Francisco State Strike Committee, "On Strike—Shut It Down," 1969, p. 4.

[10] Baritz, p. 461.

The next morning, on December 3, a picket line formed by thirty students at a classroom building was routed by forty club-swinging Tactical Squad men. The picketers were chased into the student Commons where all students were indiscriminately hassled and clubbed. Following a noon rally where Third World community leaders spoke in support of the strike, a march on classroom buildings was met with 650 police. A bloody two-hour battle ensued between thousands of students and police. Hayakawa summed up the day by saying that it was his "most exciting day since I rode a roller coaster on my tenth birthday."[11]

In the days and weeks that followed, support for the demands of the Third World Liberation Front and the strike continued to mount. Community people picketed the San Francisco City Hall and the Hall of Justice to protest the presence of armed police on campus. They marched through downtown to the San Francisco *Chronicle* and *Examiner* buildings to protest racist, one-sided media coverage of the strike.

On campus, confrontations between students and police became a daily occurence. By the third month of the strike, 300 professors (members of AFT Local 1352) and the Teaching Assistants' Union (AFT Local 1928) struck in support of TWLF demands, and classroom count showed the strike to be 85% effective.[12] The entire campus was paralyzed for the remainder of that semester as clerical and library staff workers joined the strike. Other union workers chose to honor the picket lines and stopped deliveries to the college and dormitories. Supplies were cut off and garbage began to pile up all over the campus. Police on horseback chased students, using mace and billy-clubs on them. Strikers retaliated by throwing stink bombs in order to clear the classrooms. They clogged up toilets all over the campus. Striking teachers refused to give final exams, refused to turn in grades. The campus was immobilized.

During the period between December 2, 1968 and January 30, 1969, 600 striking students and bystanders were arrested. According to statistics gathered by doctors on injuries to those arrested, 56 suffered head injuries including two fractured skulls and one fractured eye orbit.[13] Other arrestees sustained a variety of injuries from police clubbing and macing: ruptured spleens, fractured ribs, broken hands, arms and legs, and welts and burns to stomach and groin areas.[14]

Rather than break the strike as the administration had hoped for, the mass arrests gave the students increased determination to fight against and defeat those who would go to any lengths to maintain a system based on racism and class biases. In its fourth month, the TWLF-called strike continued to build and grow.

The San Francisco State strike engulfed the whole state and captured the attention of the entire country. Students at other colleges began organizing and made similar demands for an equitable admissions policy and for relevant, truthful education.

Across the Bay, at the University of California at Berkeley, students followed the events of San Francisco State attentively. Students from the Afro-American Students Union, Mexican American Student Confederation and the Asian American Political Alliance, which made up the Third World Liberation Front, had gone through similar experiences in "negotiating" with Chancellor Roger Heyns during the academic year 1967-68. On January 21, 1969, the Third World Liberation

---

[11] San Francisco *Chronicle*, December 4, 1968.

[12] Baritz, p. 463.

[13] These statistics do not include injuries sustained before December 2, injuries not reported, and injuries to people who were not arrested. In many police sweeps, no arrests took place but demonstrators were beaten.

[14] Research Organizing Cooperative of San Francisco, p. 31.

Front called for a general strike "for the betterment of conditions of Third World students."[15] Principal among the demands was the establishment of a free and independent Third World College. They explained the global context from which their aspiration flowed; their protests were not limited to institutions of higher learning:

> Rather, they were part of a larger Third World movement representing the growing awareness of Third World people throughout the world of their common experiences under colonial domination, within and without the continent of the United States. The Third World movement was and continues to be a demand of colonized peoples for freedom and self-determination—for the right to control and develop their own economic, political, and social institutions.[16]

The strike at Berkeley involved thousands of students and community people, and lasted for more than forty days. One hundred and fourteen students were arrested. 155 students faced university disciplinary measures, and countless others were beaten and and harassed by the police. During the strike, a number of meetings took place where issues of ethnic studies and open admissions were discussed. At one meeting of the Berkeley Division of the Academic Senate on March 4, 1969, the faculty voted in support of ethnic studies by a margin of 550 to 4:

> It is the sense of the Berkeley Division of the Academic Senate that it favors the establishment of an Ethnic Studies Department. . . . Its structure should be of sufficient flexibility to permit evolution into a College.[17]

The Third World Liberation Front strike came to a close on April 7, 1969 when Chancellor Heyns announced that President Hitch had authorized the establishment of an independent Department of Ethnic Studies.

Relative calm was restored to the two campuses, but it was clear that the issues raised by the strikes—ethnic studies, student control, and access to education by children of Third World and working people—were dramatized, but not solved, by the strikes.

At UCLA, the emergence of ethnic studies took a different course which reflected the differing conditions on that campus. In the fall of 1968, a new team of administrators headed by Chancellor Charles Young took over for the retired Chancellor Franklin Murphy. Chancellor Young was well aware of the "basic inequities in our social system which have mitigated against full and equal participation in that system by members of certain ethnic groups."[18] The administration was also aware that many Third World students had begun to organize and had attempted to initiate meetings with the administration to discuss the possibility of establishing ethnic studies and increasing minority student enrollment.

The school year began after a summer of social upheaval which included the Democratic Convention in Chicago and ghetto rebellions, but because UCLA had a reputation for being a school with relatively few instances of student "unrest" and social protest, Chancellor Young was anxious to maintain the image of UCLA as a peaceful campus.

---

[15] University of California, Berkeley, Ethnic Studies Committee of the Department of Ethnic Studies, "A Proposal for the Establishment of the College of Third World Studies," unpublished manuscript, dated September 18, 1974, p. 3.

[16] Ibid., p. 2.

[17] Ibid., p. 1.

[18] *Daily Bruin*, November 14, 1968, p. 1.

Young explained his perception of his role as an administrator in an interview with the campus newspaper:

> I am going to have to devote a part of my time to what is really a basic public relations—political kind of effort. . . . I'm going to try to prevent having any (demonstrations.)[19]

In his letter to the Academic Senate, Young reiterated that tension will exist between those who seek change and those who oppose it, and that "our task is to keep that tension at an absolute minimum."[20]

By January, the administration had designed a conciliatory measure dictated by fear: the "American Cultures Project." Under this plan, the Black, Chicano, Asian American and Native American components were organized as research units called Centers which were to take into account "the uniqueness of each individual group,"[21] and "determine a need, mount data through research, perceive goals and directions, and *solve problems through direct action*." (Emphasis added.)[22] These ethnic studies centers did not have the authority to offer courses.[23] Initial courses in ethnic studies were offered through the much less "permanent" Council on Educational Development, another new program whose charge was to encourage innovative and experimental courses. Thus, the mechanisms for a modified version of ethnic studies were set up according to the administration's plan. Although the program was born in the absence of a campus-wide strike, the struggle for ethnic studies was not without its violence. On January 17, 1969, Black Panthers John Huggins and Alprentice "Bunchy" Carter were shot to death immediately following a meeting of the Black Students Union in Campbell Hall on the UCLA campus. It was reported at the time that disagreements about prospective candidates for the directorship of the Afro-American Studies Center led to the shootings of the Black Panthers by an opposing faction of "Black militants."[24] Reports of the Senate Intelligence Committee in 1976 recently revealed that the FBI undertook a two-year (1969–1971), nation-wide program to discredit the Black Panther Party by such illegal means as provoking hostilities between the Panthers and rival groups. The FBI's covert involvement in activities of various colleges and universities has also been recently disclosed.

In the succeeding years, many Asian American studies courses have been introduced into the curricula of colleges and universities throughout the country, often in response to pressures from Asian American student organizations. In every case, these campus struggles represent long hours spent by many dedicated students to establish these programs. Many of the ethnic studies programs began as experimental courses taught by existing faculty members or by specially appointed instructors. A few of the campuses were able to develop reasonably autonomous and permanent programs. Numerous state-wide and national conferences on ethnic studies were held, and a number of journals, periodicals and bibliographies were produced to supplement curriculum materials.

---

[19] *Daily Bruin*, September 30, 1968, p. 15.

[20] *Daily Bruin*, November 14, 1968, p. 1.

[21] Quote by Vice-Chancellor Paul Proehl (University Relations), January 20, 1969.

[22] Quote by Joaquin Acosta, who was the assistant to Vice-Chancellor Proehl and administration's liaison with Third World student organizations. *Daily Bruin*, January 20, 1969, p. 1.

[23] Technical requirements in the university permit only "departments" to offer courses, but "centers" cannot offer courses.

[24] For details on Black Panther shooting and FBI involvement, see various issues of *Daily Bruin*, January, 1969.

Programs, however, continued to be limited by the small number of courses offered, and the temporary and experimental nature of the courses. There were also "internal" problems that arose in some of the budding programs:

> Faculty and students, sometimes, did not agree on program objectives, courses, and means of implementation, leading to major conflicts or disillusionment by one or both parties. The early absence of qualified instructors on many campuses and the dearth of curriculum materials also created difficulties.[25]

In the brief period of seven years or so, the Asian American programs have made great contributions in an effort to grasp concrete knowledge of the history of Third World peoples and to redirect that knowledge to the practice of changing social conditions in our society, but they have also continued to suffer from growing pains. Some of the difficulties can be attributed to . . .

> . . . a decline in student interest. Part of this can be traced to the graduation of the initial group of student participants who helped to establish these programs, and the absence of committed replacements. Part is due to discouragement because of intraprogram conflicts, the constant struggle for recognition and funding, or the development of highly conventional academic programs with little concern for contemporary community problems . . . [S]ome of the decline in interest might be related to the general slackening of student concern with activism and social problems, including those in the area of race and ethnic relations.[26]

But in the final analysis, it has been the lack of commitment to ethnic studies on the part of the governing bodies of the schools, and the subsequent lack of resources, that have placed severe limitations on the programs.

With the general economic crisis beginning in 1973, there has been a persistent effort by school authorities to chip away at the concessions that were made during the height of campus struggles. Budget cuts in higher education and social services began with ethnic studies courses, minority admissions and scholarship programs for Third World students, as administrators became increasingly reluctant to "expand or even continue what they see as basically innovative and experimental 'fringe' programs."[27] Thus, Third World students were hardest hit by recent cutbacks.

> The most striking example of a pattern of racism in cutbacks is the drop in the number of minority students enrolled in college. . . . Minority enrollments had been steadily rising since 1968, due to a mass upsurge of Third World students and their allies in the 1960's. . . . But in the last two years, those hard-won gains have come under sharp attack. A University of Michigan official summed up the general policy of college administrators on the cutbacks, asserting that "nonessential programs," which included third world studies programs, would be the first to be cut.[28]

When the actual attempts at financial cutbacks and diminution of autonomy were made by school authorities, they were met by a new "generation" of students who rallied to the defense of programs from which they had benefited.

---

[25] Russell Endo, "White Ethnic Studies: A Reexamination of Some Issues," *Asian Americans: Psychological Perspectives* (Palo Alto, Calif.: Science and Behavior Books, Inc., 1973), edited by Stanley Sue and Nathaniel N. Wagner, p. 282.

[26] Ibid.

[27] Ibid., p. 283.

[28] *Guardian*, May 7, 1975, p. 6.

Student dissatisfaction surfaced again on the campus of the University of California at Berkeley when, in 1974, the administration moved to integrate the independent Ethnic Studies Department into the larger College of Letters and Science.[29] An Ethnic Studies Defense Committee was formed to oppose the integration of ethnic studies into a larger curriculum and to demand the establishment of the College of Third World Studies as originally contemplated. The student resistance to the erosion of hard-fought gains has not been entirely successful. Some financial aid admissions programs have been cut back or eliminated. Student groups acknowledged and reasserted their role in bringing about progressive change.

A similar group called the Student Support Committee for Ethnic Studies was organized at UCLA in 1974 when a faculty committee denied proposals for several ethnic studies courses. The student group continued to meet with administration representatives until early 1975, when the administration released a Five Year Review of the ethnic studies centers, in which the administration-appointed review committee recommended the implementation of an umbrella-type structure over the centers to exercise more authority over them. Students organized a series of rallies and demonstrations to communicate their grievances and mistrust of the university.[30]

At still another University of California campus, at Santa Barbara, a week of protest and marches against minority cutbacks culminated in "a tense three-hour occupation of the North Hall Computer Center by seventeen members of the Students for Collective Action" on May 4, 1975.[31]

As the cutbacks were announced on campuses through the country, there was also a nationwide response from Third World student activists. On the West Coast, campus mobilization took place on virtually every campus of the University of California system as well as California State University at Los Angeles, Loyola, Claremont and Pepperdine. On the East Coast, forty members of the Third World Coalition staged a take-over of the administration building. At Brandeis University, students occupied the sociology building from April 29 to May 5, 1975 to protest a cutback totalling $2.2 million in their educational budget.

In New York City, several hundred Hunter College students occupied the dean's office and about 1500 students and faculty of the City University of New York demonstrated outside the Board of Higher Education to protest Mayor Beame's $69.7 million cut from the university's budget that would have effectively dissolved the SEEK (Search for Education, Elevation and Knowledge) program whose constituency was mainly Third World.[32]

Institutional responses to the need for ethnic studies, and for overall *quality* and *equality* in the educational process, mirror the racial discrimination of an entire society. Asian Americans and other Third World peoples have been confronted with the stubborn remnants of over a century of racism.

The history of Third World peoples in this country has been one of resistance and struggle in a hostile environment. Oppressed and exploited, Asian immigrants were forced to accept verbal and physical abuse at times, but they also waged an unyielding struggle against the unjust treatment they faced in every sphere of their lives: employment discrimination and exclusion, prohibition against land ownership, antimiscegenation laws, disproportionate taxes, disenfranchisement and lack of citizenship rights, and social discrimination.

---

[29] *The Asian Student*, newsletter of Asian Students Union of UC Berkeley, Vol. 3, no. 1 (November 1974), p. 10.

[30] *Rafu Shimpo*, May 17, 1975. p. 1.

[31] *Daily Nexus*, University of California at Santa Barbara, Vol. 55, no. 123, May 5, 1975, p. 1.

[32] *Guardian*, May 14, 1975, p. 5.

In the field of education, as in other areas, efforts were made to win basic democratic rights. Sometimes, the courts were used to seek judicial remedies; most often, various ethnic groups struggled in isolation from one another and tried to win concessions only for themselves. Recently, Asian American students have united with other ethnic groups and progressive people to change the educational system.

Viewed in this light, the struggles of Asian American students for a just system of higher education is a significant chapter in Asian American and American history—one that is certain to continue as Asian American students continue their efforts to gain for themselves and others, equal education that is both high in quality and relevant. In this sense, their search for their past leads Third World students to participate in the very process of making history.

The Historical Development of Higher Education in the U.S.

In the preceding section, an attempt was made to provide a description of what took place in the struggles for ethnic studies and for the admission of more minority students. But what of the causes? The history of ethnic studies and admission policies reveals the defects in our educational system. But what of the whole society? It is not enough to describe the events, but we must also analyze and place them in their historical context. The brief seven-year history recaptures, in many ways, the effects of long-standing inequities in the colleges and universities. In order to put a *part* into its proper context, we must also understand the *whole*.

In the United States today, about three out of ten persons are direct participants in the educational process. Out of a population of nearly 214 million, over 58.9 million students go to public and private schools at all levels, from kindergarten through graduate school. About 3.1 million persons are employed as classroom teachers, and an additional 300,000 are working as principals, supervisors, counselors and instructional staff members.[33]

Most of us are required by law to attend schools from ages five to sixteen; many of us spend twelve to sixteen or more years as students. No one can deny the enormous influence that the system of education has on all of us in shaping our patterns of behavior, morality, aspirations, political outlook . . . and the very way in which we think. We become adept at following instructions, learning by rote and memorizing data. We learn that there are no rewards for raising questions about the prevailing assumptions of the society in which we live.

The issues highlighted during the struggles of the late 60s raised a fundamental question about the very nature of the system of higher education: What are the implicit goals of the universities, and whom do they serve? Questions relevant to this inquiry are: What purposes do colleges and universities, and the educational system as a whole serve in America? What are the means by which control is accomplished? How have minority peoples in general, and Asian Americans in particular, been affected by this sytem?

Historically, colleges and universities in America did not always have the prominence that they are accorded in modern society. They neither existed in great numbers nor had a direct effect on the lives of most. The development and proliferation of institutions of higher learning paralleled the growth and expansion of Industrial America. The structure and goals of universities were adapted to suit the changing needs of the captains of industry.

Before the middle of the nineteenth century, most colleges were controlled by the religious denominations which founded them. Harvard College was founded 1637 to avoid "an illiterate

---

[33] Statistics are from U.S. Department of Health, Education and Welfare, *HEW News*, bulletin no. HEW-F67, 1975.

ministry . . ."[34] The state of Massachusetts provided for the establishment of reading schools because illiteracy was "one chief project of that old deluder, Satan, to keep men from knowledge of the Scriptures."[35] Students were invariably the children of wealthy landowners and merchants who were preparing themselves for positions of power and prestige in the young and developing country. The curriculum included the arts, the classics and theology.

For the overwhelming majority of the people, formal education was limited to basic reading skills. The average worker required little technical expertise. Skills were learned at home or as apprentices. Thus, institutions of higher learning played a well-defined role, educating only a handful of ministers, doctors, lawyers and children of the elite.

This pattern continued until the industrial revolution. With the development of a northern based textile industry in the 1840s, and the end of the Civil War, America entered a new era in which northern capitalists won complete hegemony in the economic and political spheres of American life. Robber barons like John D. Rockefeller, Andrew Carnegie, and Commodore Vanderbilt amassed large fortunes and consolidated their power; they built their empires in the steel, oil, and railroad industries, often at the expense of the native Americans whose lands they seized, Chinese and other immigrant workers whose labor they exploited, and weaker competitors whose aspirations they crushed.

Sweeping changes took place in the industrial and political life of the country. The tempo of technological development accelerated and business organization became increasingly complex. The capitalists began to reinvest some of their huge stockpiles of profits into higher education to insure a supply of skilled labor necessary for their industry.

> At the same time that colleges and universities were springing up at practically every crossroads, a reorientation of their purpose gradually took place under the impact of demands for a more practical education. . . . With the force of big money behind them, scientific, technological, and commercial instruction chipped substantial niches in the standard course of study.[36]

Colleges shifted their focus from an intellectual, "impractical" education to an education designed to meet the practical needs of industry.

The impact of business on the educational system was swift and massive. The need to train technicians and workers can best be seen by the size of the investment made by the robber barons.[37] From 1902 to 1938, the leading foundations, Carnegie and Rockefeller, spent a total of $680 million on colleges and universities to ensure the training of technical, scientific and administrative workers for their companies.[38] The classical colleges that were superfluous to business and industry became obsolete, or even permanently transformed into institutions for the training of workers in business and industry. This shift affected not only the class backgrounds of the

---

[34] Walter Lunden, *The Dynamics of Higher Education* (Pittsburg: Pittsburg Printing Company, 1939), p. 188. Also cited in David N. Smith, *Who Rules the Universities?* (New York: Monthly Review Press, 1974).

[35] Edmund Morgan, *The Puritan Family* (New York: Harper and Row, 1966), p. 26.

[36] Merle Curti and Roderick Nash, *Philanthropy in the Shaping of American Higher Education* (New Brunswick: Rutgers University Press, 1965), p. 60.

[37] Lunden, p. 177. Between 1878 and 1898 alone, $140 million was poured into the system of higher education. According to Curti and Nash, pp. 78–79, many of the technical and scientific schools designed solely for industrial research purposes profited the most. Illinois Institute of Technology, for example, received a $20 million contribution from photography magnate George Eastman.

[38] Ernest V. Hollis, *Philanthropic Foundations and Higher Education* (New York: Columbia University Press, 1938), p. 283.

student population, but also its numbers. In 1850, only 120 colleges existed;[39] but in the fifty years following the Civil War, 453 colleges were founded.[40] In 1870, only 67,350 students were enrolled in colleges; by 1890 this figure had reached a total of 156,756 students, and by 1910, it had surpassed 355,000.[41] Not only the magnitude but the character of higher education was influenced. To better suit specialization and departmentalization of the labor force, colleges developed a structural device to fragment the curriculum which came to be known as the elective system.

Post-graduate education was also expanded to accommodate further stratification and to train students for new "problems of internal personnel management, marketing, salesmanship, research, efficiency engineering, and public relations" as well as problems created by "the emergence of a stable and effective trade union movement."[42]

A necessary consequence of the rapid expansion of colleges and universities was the corresponding emergence and growth of the public high school. As a response to the needs of mushrooming business enterprises, the high school became the screening mechanism for universities as well as the institution for the effective socialization and pacification of the emerging working class movement, and one of the justifications for a stratified workforce based on class distinctions. Those in power reasoned that

> . . . the extension of the high school (to the children of working people) would provide the more intelligent son of the worker with an education that would enable him to find an honorable and profitable place within the existing industrial system, and prevent him from becoming an agitator.[43]

Secondary education thus became the primary institution through which *skilled* and *passive* workers could be created.

With more high schools than ever before, the need for qualified teachers to socialize the students became acute; teacher-training programs quickly and for the first time integrated large numbers of women into the system of higher education.[44]

At the turn of the century, most of the endowments were concentrated in a few colleges that were most responsive to the needs of the corporations. Rockefeller invested over $128 million in the General Education Board which he set up in 1902 to coordinate his philanthropy.[45] The trustees of the Board had within their power the ability . . .

---

[39] John S. Brubacher and Willis Rudy, *Higher Education in Transition: An American History* (New York: Harper, 1958), pp. 62–63.

[40] Lunden, p. 175.

[41] Richard Hofstadter and C. Dewitt Hardy, *The Development and Scope of Higher Education in the United States* (New York: Columbia University Press, 1952), p. 31.

[42] Ibid., p. 93. In 1850, there were only eight graduate schools in the country, but the numbers soared rapidly to 198 within eleven years, and to 2,382 by 1890, and finally rose to 5,668 by the beginning of the twentieth century. According to Elbert Vaugh Wills, *The Growth of American Higher Education* (Philadelphia: Dorrance & Company, 1936), p. 99, also cited in David N. Smith, p. 183, schools of business administration were established between 1881, when Wharton School of Finance and Commerce opened, and 1925.

[43] Merle Curti, *The Social Ideas of American Educators* (Patterson, N.J.: Pageant Books, 1935), p. 220.

[44] The 11,000 women enrolled in colleges in 1870 comprised only one-fifth of all college students. Mabel Newcomer, *A Century of Higher Education for American Women* (New York: Harper, 1959), p. 19. By 1900, women had become forty percent of the college population, according to Laurence R. Veysey, *The Emergence of the American University, 1865–1910* (Chicago: University of Chicago Press, 1965), p. 1. Moreover, according to Newcomer, p. 91, 43,000 of the 61,000 women enrolled in coeducational colleges in 1900 were in teacher training courses.

[45] From 1902 to 1934, only 20 institutions received more than 73 percent of the funds disbursed. See Hollis, p. 285. According to Curti and Nash, p. 222, between 1923 and 1929, over $88.5 million out of a total of $103 million donated by the largest foundations went to 36 colleges and universities out of the more than a thousand institutions in the country at the time.

. . . to determine whether or not an institution would continue to exist. Coercion may not have been overt, but in making grants the board naturally selected those institutions whose policies and programs they approved. As a result these practices became unofficial standards for many other colleges.[46]

The recipients of the huge sums of money from companies like Standard Oil, DuPont, General Electric and Shell Petroleum were colleges that could adapt themselves best to the needs of the emerging chemical and electrical industries, as well as to the increasingly sophisticated needs of the steel and oil industries.

As the dependency of corporations on universities increased, so did their control of them. Grateful college administrators "drafted men of money into the service of collegiate direction until at the end of the (nineteenth) century the roster of American trustees of higher learning read like a corporation directory."[47] Leading capitalists had become firmly entrenched in positions of power with the university structure through appointments on various boards of trustees. By 1917, the rich and powerful had a firm grip on the reigns of the educational system.

[C]ollege and university boards are almost completely dominated by merchants, manufacturers, capitalists, corporation officers, bankers, doctors, lawyers, educators and ministers. The nine occupations contain nearly four-fifths of the total number of trustees.[48]

According to a survey conducted in 1924, the average annual income for 734 trustees included in the survey was $35,000, during a time when the average worker was paid $1,563.[49] Furthermore, during the Great Depression of the Thirties, the average income of the trustees was over $61,000, a full sixty times the income of the average worker.[50]

Corporate control of the educational system has continued uninterrupted to the present. Rosters of most boards of trustees and regents still read like corporation directories. A cursory examination of the Board of Regents for the University of California shows California to be no exception.[51]

With the advent of World War II, state and federal governments have played key roles in supporting the military-industrial complex's educational objectives. Universities were a vital source of military personnel. The Reserve Officers Training Corp (ROTC) usually supplied 45% of all

---

[46] Curti and Nash, pp. 216–17.

[47] Charles and Mary Beard, *The Rise of American Civilization* (New York: MacMillan, 1936), Vol. 2, p. 470.

[48] A survey of Scott Nearing, cited in David N. Smith, p. 38.

[49] A survey by Hubart Park Beck, cited in David N. Smith, p. 40.

[50] Troy Duster, "The Aims of Higher Learning and the Control of Universities" (University of California at Berkeley, n.d.), cited in David N. Smith, p. 40.

[51] For examples, listed below are four of the Regents and their "affiliations" past and present:
Edward W. Carter—President of Broadway-Hale Stores; director of AT&T; Southern California Edison; director of Del Monte Corporation; Irvine Ranch; director of Pacific Mutual Life Insurance Company; United California Bank; director of Northrop Corporation; Pacific Telephone and Telegraph Company; Western Bancorporation.
Frederick G. Dutton—Former Assistant U.S. Secretary of State; director of Irvine Foundation; Southern Counties Gas Company; attorney.
William Matson Roth—Director of Pacific Intermountain Express Company; Atheneum Publishers; Mandell Industries; U.S. Leasing Corporation; Matson Navigation Company; Crocker Citizens National Bank; Crown-Zellerbach Corporation.
William French Smith—Attorney for Ronald Reagan; director of Pacific Lighting Corporation; director of Pacific Telephone and Telegraph Company; director of Mutual Life Insurance Company; director of Crocker Bank.

Army officers on active duty; 65% of all first lieutenants and 85% of all second lieutenants are graduates of the ROTC program.[52]

In the years following World War II, as America and the world entered the period of the Cold War, the federal government poured more money and resources into weapon development and space exploration programs. The Korean War and the conflict in Indochina led to the augmentation of budgets in every sphere of military spending. In this effort, every Presidential administration took an active part in beefing up war-oriented educational programs. Truman appointed a Commission on Higher Education in 1946 for the purpose of conducting an intensive reexamination of the university system and its function in national defense. The National Science Foundation was founded in 1950 to promote engineering and scientific research for the armed forces. In 1956, President Eisenhower appointed the second Commission on Higher Education, and two years later, the National Defense Education Act (NDEA) was passed as a governmental response to the technological advances made by the Soviet Union as evidenced by the launching of the Sputnik satellite. The United States became panic-stricken: tens of billions of dollars were allocated for the massive NDEA scholarship and assistance programs with the rationale that,

> . . . the present educational emergency requires additional effort at all levels of government. It is therefore the purpose of this Act to provide substantial assistance in various forms to individuals, and to states and their subdivisions, in order to insure trained manpower of sufficient quality and quantity to meet the national defense needs of the United States.[53]

The Kennedy Administration forcefully backed state investment in educational matters. The Manpower Development and Training Act of 1962 and subsequent bills helped to keep the rising unemployment level in check and swelled the ranks of highly skilled workers.

An additional $1.2 billion was allocated for the Higher Education Facilities Act, which was signed into law by President Johnson the following year. A number of other bills and laws, including the Higher Education Act of 1965 and the Elementary and Secondary Education Act of 1965 were passed throughout the 1960s. Undergraduate students—especially Third World students and economically disadvantaged students—benefited very little from the government spending since most of the funds were ear-marked for various weapon-development centers within the university-military-industrial complex.

The University of California system and a number of other prestigious institutions around the country are involved in numerous other research endeavors financed by the U.S. government. In the academic year 1967-68, UCLA had no less than 79 research projects that were financed by the Department of Defense.[54] Additionally, names of some courses offered by the UCLA Extension Program suggest further complicity of the university with the military: "The Guidance and Control of Tactical Missiles," "Integrated Logistic Support," and "Advanced Missile Flight

---

[52] UCLA Strike Committee, "The Three Wars," pamphlet, n.d., n.p.

[53] Homer Babbidge and Robert Rosenzweig, *The Federal Interest in Higher Education* (New York: McGraw Hill, 1962), pp. 50–51.

[54] UCLA Strike Committee pamphlet. The UCLA Medical School, Baylor University, the University of Texas, Stanford Research Institute and Cornell Aeronautical Laboratory all collaborated with the Army Chemical Center in testing and developing various chemical and biological weapons. See Sidney Lens, *The Military-Industrial Complex*. Between 1960 and 1969, $2.5 billion were spent on deadly gases and germs; some 5,000 technicians and scientists were engaged in developing "poison chemicals ranging from the 'mild' CS (gas) used in Vietnam to GA, GB and V nerve agents that are odorless, tasteless, invisible, and can kill a human being in a matter of seconds." Chicago *Daily News*, August 12, 1969.

Dynamics," to name a few.[55] And perhaps not as striking, but nevertheless concrete evidence of the role of the university in the military-industrial complex is a project officially known as the Academic Advisory Council on Thailand (AACT, popular name of Thailand Project), which is funded by the State Department and its Agency for International Development (AID). The role of the Thailand Project is to "organize, coordinate and conduct investigations, seminars or conferences, under AACT auspices dealing with development and counterinsurgency problems, issues, and activities, including research, relating to AID operations in Thailand."[56] Professors from various departments, including Political Science and Anthropology, were employed in this project.

Finally, the link between the university and the military is made through mutual cooperation in recruitment efforts. At UCLA, the Placement Center participates in the recruitment of Central Intelligence Agency (CIA) personnel. The National Security Agency (NSA) sends recruiters to various departments and ethnic studies programs to recruit individuals to study foreign countries in depth and gather intelligence data on customs, lifestyles, and social and political institutions. Certain "trouble spots" like the Middle East, Chile, the Philippines, and Africa have been its recent focus.

As corporate and federal involvement in higher education increased, the goals of the universities were reevaluated by the authorities to attract more corporate investment and federal "assistance." In a survey conducted by sociologist Edward Gross in 1964, 7,000 administrators and faculty members from 68 major universities were questioned. The respondents were asked to place in rank-order a list of 47 goals of the university. Out of the top 12 goals, only the sixth mentioned "students," and even that was in connection with scientific research. Ranking first was the goal of protecting the faculty's right to academic freedom. Goals No. 2 through No. 12 were all related to research and/or to the maintenance of a good image of the university. In contrast, the bottom 12 goals were predominantly concerned with the welfare of students.[57]

So the system of education, which has become largely state-supported (taxpayer-supported), continued to maintain the illusion that it was indeed responsive to the aspirations of people and that it created maximal opportunities for everyone. Yet in reality, the mass education system has had quite different goals and has had quite the opposite result—that of fulfilling the needs of war-oriented capitalist economy.

---

[55] UCLA Strike Committee.

[56] Amendment III, paragraph B-6 of *Contract*, cited in UCLA Strike Committee.

[57] The top twelve goals of university officials are: (1) Protect the faculty's right to academic freedom; (2) Increase or maintain the *prestige* of the university; (3) Maintain top quality in important programs; (4) Ensure the *confidence of contributors;* (5) Keep up to date; (6) Train students for *scientific research;* (7) Carry on *pure research;* (8) Maintain quality in all programs; (9) Ensure the *favorable appraisal* of validating bodies (government agencies, foundations, etc.); (10) Ensure efficient goal attainment; (11) Disseminate new ideas; and (12) Carry on *applied research.* In contrast, the bottom twelve goals (out of forty-seven) dealt more directly with students: (47) Elevate the *student* culturally and make a person who is able to think for himself; (46) Preserve the character of the school; (45) Involve *students* in the administration of the school; (44) Emphasize *undergraduate instruction;* (43) Keep interdepartment harmony; (42) Develop faculty interest in university rather than to their own jobs or professional concerns; (41) Protect and facilitate the *students' right* to advocate direct action on social and political concerns; (40) Accommodate *students* of high potential; (39) Educate *every high school graduate* to his utmost capacities; (38) Develop the inner character of *students* so that they can make sound, correct moral choices; (37) Provide special training to part-time and adult *students,* and (36) Make sure that the faculty is heard on all important issues. Compiled from Edward Gross and Paul V. Grambsch, *University Goals and Academic Power* (Washington, D.C.: American Council on Education, 1968).

The Impact on Asian Americans

Throughout the period of industrial growth and stratification of the workforce, Third World peoples were systematically excluded from even the lowest rungs of the educational ladder. Native Americans were forced onto reservations where they received little or no formal education as a colonized people. In many states in the South, it was illegal to conduct classes for Black children. The non-English speaking Chicanos and Asian immigrants were effectively left out of the developing educational system.

In September of 1859, a segregated day school for Chinese was opened in the basement of the Chinese Chapel in San Francisco, but it was closed within ten months because of the lack of interest on the part of the Chinese (government perspective), and of the lack of meaningful and relevant curriculum (Chinese American perspective). In an 1859 report concerning this school, Superintendent Denman of the San Francisco Board of Education stated:

> The teacher has been faithful and energetic in the discharge of his difficult duty but the prejudices of caste and religious idolatry are so indelibly stamped upon their [Chinese] character and existence that his task of education seems almost hopeless. According to our laws, the Mongolians can never be elevated to an equality with the Anglo-Saxons and receive the title and immunities of American citizens. They, therefore, take but little interest in adopting our habits or learning our language and institutions.[58]

In many cases, instruction in any language other than English was forbidden. For example, in one state, a law was passed in 1919 which provided that:

> [No] person shall in any private, public, denominational, or parochial school teach any subject to any person in the first eight grades in any language other than the English language.[59]

It was argued that the purpose of the act was "to protect the child's health by limiting his mental activities," and that the enforcement of this law will "promote civic development by inhibiting training of the immature in foreign tongues before they could learn English."[60]

In 1925, the legislature of Hawaii and the department of public instruction adopted regulations which provided as follows:

> No foreign language (meaning any school but a Sabbath school conducted in any language other than the English or Hawaiian languages) shall be conducted without a written permit from the department and unless a fee of one dollar per pupil will have been paid. . . . No pupil was to attend a foreign-language school for more than one hour each day nor for more than six hours per week. . . . The department had the power to appoint inspectors for these schools. Violation of a provision was a misdemeanor.[61]

Over 200,000 pupils and 300 teachers of various Asian ancestries were affected by this legislation. Had it not been struck down by the courts a year later, this would have meant that $200,000

---

[58] Cited in "Education of Children in Chinatown," *Gidra*, Vol. III, No. 12 (December 1971).

[59] Milton R. Konvitz, *The Alien and the Asiatic in American Law* (Ithaca, N.Y.: Cornell University Press, 1946), p. 220.

[60] Ibid., p. 221.

[61] Ibid., p. 222. See also *Farrington v. Tokushige*, 273 U.S. 284 (1926).

(a dollar per pupil) would have been paid although none of the foreign-language schools received any public funds, and all of the children also attended public schools taught in English.

While foreign-language schools were prohibited or discouraged, at the same time, most of the public and private schools taught in English were limited to white children only. The segregation of Asian children continued in California into the twentieth century, and followed the general patterns of segregation found in other parts of the country with respect to Blacks. The segregation led to an international crisis in the early 1900s.

In 1905, the San Francisco School Board relied on an 1870 California law and ordered Asian children to attend a separate, all-Asian school. This law, which remained on the books formally until 1946, read in part as follows:

> . . . trustees shall have the power to exclude children of filthy and vicious habits, or children suffer-
> ing from contagious or infectious diseases, and also to establish separate schools for Indian children
> and for children of Mongolian or Chinese descent.[62]

The following autumn, the Board passed a second resolution which was implemented immediately:

> . . . principals are hereby directed to send all Chinese, Japanese or Korean children to the Oriental public
> school [located near the earthquake-devastated Chinatown] on and after Monday, October 15, 1906.[63]

Agitation against Japanese became blatant and intense in labor-dominated San Francisco as many called for the complete exclusion of Japanese as they had done to Chinese in 1882. Candidates of all major parties stood on platforms to exclude Asians.[64] The San Francisco School Board made clear their intentions for setting up separate schools:

> . . . not only for the purpose of relieving the congestion at present prevailing in our schools, but
> also for the higher end that our children should not be placed in any position where their youthful
> impressions may be affected by association with pupils of the Mongolian race.[65]

Newspapers also got embroiled in the anti-Asian campaign and employed various scare tactics. The San Francisco *Chronicle* disseminated hatred of Asians, explaining that:

> . . . whatever the status of the Japanese children while still young and uncontaminated, as they
> grow older they acquire the distinctive character, habits and moral standards of their race, which
> are abhorrent to our people. We object to them in the familiar intercourse of common school life as
> we would object to any other moral poison.[66]

---

[62] Quoted and discussed in William Thomas, "San Francisco and the Japanese," *World Today*, Vol. II (December, 1906), p. 1310. Cited in David Brudnoy, "Race and the San Francisco School Board Incident: Contemporary Evaluations," *California Historical Quarterly*, Vol. 50 (1971), p. 76.

[63] Quoted in the Metcalf Report, "Final Report on the Situation Affecting the Japanese in the City of San Francisco, California," message from the President of the United States to Congress (December 18, 1907), p. 3.

[64] Brudnoy, p. 79.

[65] John P. Young, "The Support of the Anti-Oriental Movement," *Annals of the American Academy of Political and Social Science*, Vol. 34 (September, 1909), p. 236.

[66] San Francisco *Chronicle*, November 6, 1906.

Other stories contended that many Japanese adults had infiltrated the classrooms:

> It is difficult to tell the age of a Japanese boy or man, and we have learned from experience that we could not take their word for it. The parents of white children—especially of girls in the adolescent period—began to feel that these men should be excluded from the public schools altogether. . . .[67]

The racism against Japanese and other Asians did not end with words as attacks on Japanese grew more frequent: people were stoned by ruffians, businesses were wrecked and children were bullied.

News of the mistreatment of Japanese citizens in California soon travelled to Japan. The San Francisco School Board incident became an international concern as Japanese authorities reminded the American government of a treaty which was in effect at the time, which read in part as follows:

> Article I: . . . The citizens or subjects of each High Contracting Power (Japan and the United States) shall . . . in all . . . matters connected with the administration of justice . . . enjoy all the rights and privileges enjoyed by native citizens or subjects. . . .[68]

Other appeals were made by concerned Japanese educators, expressing indignation and hope. The Dean of the University of Tokyo wrote to President Jordan of Stanford University in California:

> . . . to pass a law condemning the Japanese wholesale, for no other reason than that they are Japanese, would be striking Japan in her most sensitive point. An open declaration of war would not be resented so much. The reason is not far to seek. Japan has had a long struggle in recovering her rights as an independent state. . . . If . . . her old friend . . . should turn her back on her and she would no longer associate with her on even terms, the resentment must necessarily be very bitter.[69]

President Theodore Roosevelt's private response was that he was "more concerned over the Japanese situation than almost any other. Thank Heaven we have the navy in good shape."[70] Still, uncertain about the military strength of Japan, Roosevelt played the mediating role between racist Californians on the one hand and Japan and the Japanese community in San Francisco on the other.

Attacks against the Japanese in California continued, and they were accused of "imperiousness impudence, of taking honors away from white children."[71] White citizens argued that California was making a gift to the Japanese by setting up separate schools, and that therefore the Japanese should be grateful with the privilege, and not demand equal treatment.

> It is the height of Oriental conceit to demand more. It is the climax of Japanese swell-headedness to persist in their demands. This insistence in demanding that they be allowed to attend white schools proves their unfitness to enjoy such a privilege. The sons of Nippon should be made to understand that . . . they cannot compel the Young Giant of the West to abrogate her laws or destroy, her customs simply to meet the Japanese caprice or tickle Japanese fancy.[72]

---

[67] Cited in Brudnoy, p. 302.

[68] Discussed in part in *The Japanese School Segregation Case, No. 4754, in the Supreme Court of the State of California, Keikichi Aoki v. M. A. Deane* (March, 1907). Cited in Brudnoy, p. 76.

[69] Quoted in *World Today*, Vol. II (December, 1906), pp. 1312–13.

[70] H. F. Pringle, *Theodore Roosevelt: A Biography* (New York, 1931), p. 407.

[71] Brudnoy, p. 85.

[72] Quoted in Brudnoy, p. 305.

President Roosevelt wanted to avoid war with Japan if it were at all possible, because the Japanese military was at full force following a victory over Russia. Californians, on the other hand, insisted on separate educational facilities for white and Third World children, and eventual exclusion altogether of the Japanese, "whether the putting out of the way involves the U.S. in war (or not.)"[73] A delegation of civic leaders and government officials from California went to Washington, D.C. to negotiate with the federal government. In 1907, a compromise was reached wherein

> . . . the Californians got what they most wanted—assurances that the influx of coolies would be stopped; the federal administration got what it most wanted—a promised repeal of the school order. The San Francisco delegation, fully aware that a surrender on the school issue would cause a storm of protest in their city, were [sic] reluctantly brought around to Roosevelt's point of view. . . .

The Yellow Peril scare was created more in the minds of men than in reality as there were only 93 Japanese children, one-third of them American-born, in the San Francisco school system at the time. Additionally, the census of 1910 listed a total of 41,346 Japanese in the whole state, of which 4,518 lived in San Francisco, less than two percent of the population of that city.[74]

The school order as it applied to Japanese was rescinded, and the "Gentlemen's Agreement" limiting Japanese immigration to the United States was concluded. The children of Chinese immigrants were still excluded from regular schools, as were the relatively few Korean children living in San Francisco. The San Francisco School Board incident was officially closed, but Roosevelt spent the next two years building up the navy, and in San Francisco, mobs renewed their attacks on the Japanese community.

American (white) courts had consistently upheld segregationist legislation passed by various (white) legislatures that separated Black and white children into different, unequal schools. The laws were made by white persons to . . .

> . . . protect themselves against the infusion of blood of other races, on the assumption that if the children of different races associate daily in school rooms, the races will at last intermarry, and so the purity of each race is jeopardized by the mingling of children in school rooms.[75]

In the case of *Gong Lum v. Rice*,[76] decided in 1927, the state court and the Supreme Court held unanimously that it was not a denial of equal protection to classify a Chinese as "colored." Martha Lum, an American-born Chinese, applied for admission to a school that was open to white children only. There were no "Negro" schools in her district. Martha's father was a taxpayer in the school district and the county. Yet the trustees of the high school district and the State Superintendent of Education denied her admission to the school. The state court held that the law required a separation of pupils into a *white group*, on the one hand, and a *group consisting of all other races*, on the other. The Supreme Court upheld, in this case and in dozens of others like it, the racist rule of "separate but equal" facilities for white and for Third World children.[77]

---

[73] Ibid.

[74] Thomas Bailey, *Theodore Roosevelt and the Japanese American Crises* (Palo Alto, Calif.: Stanford University Press, 1934), p. 134.

[75] Brudnoy, p. 83.

[76] Konvitz, p. 228.

[77] 275 U.S. 78 (1927). Cf. 163 U.S. 537; 211 U.S. 45; 332 U.S. 631.

Objective conditions in schools throughout the country showed that the doctrine of "separate but equal" was nothing more than legal fiction. Yet it was not until 1954 that this rule was overturned by the Supreme Court in the case of *Brown v. Board of Education of Topeka*.[78] In spite of the court ruling, practices have proved to be less than ideal. In the twenty years following the *Brown* decision, the inner-city schools remained virtually unaffected as they continued to be segregated and of low quality.

The educational system has become the major mechanism through which a neatly stratified workforce is created. Schools at all levels have become the training ground for workers who are socialized to be obedient in whatever roles they are assigned.

> The key thing about work under capitalism is that the vast majority of jobs are oppressive, dehumanizing, unsatisfying and require Ideally (for the boss) a high degree of obedience to supervisors. Schools work to provide workers who are suitable for this kind of work.[79]

Much as we like to believe that schools teach children important cognitive skills and standards of morality, the one thing that schools do best is teach obedience in school and later in work. Students are taught to do and accept repetitive and meaningless work, day after day, year after year. Thus the schools serve as the prototype of the work experience. Students learn to do repetitive and meaningless tasks, to take orders and to compete. In the end they are essentially taught to conform.

Moreover, schools indoctrinate students that non-conformity to societal norms is an individual problem of a particular student. They teach that in society, there must necessarily be important, powerful and prestigious positions, and that those who fill those positions have earned them by virtue of some special talent, intelligence, or through diligent work. Thus class differences are legitimized. What is disguised ever so subtly is that the standards for measuring qualities like intelligence and behavior by the schools are designed to replicate or reveal the socio-economic status of parents or the cultural and racial background of children. Put another way, a child who has visited Valley Forge on his family vacation is more likely to know that George Washington slept there, and a child who received a set of ABC blocks for Christmas is more likely to remember configurations of the alphabet.

Questions that are most familiar to the middle-class, white, suburban child with a Christian background are most often included in the IQ tests, while questions more familiar to poor and Third World children are systematically omitted. Consider, for example, the Wechsler Test. Some questions are:

1. Who wrote *Hamlet*?
2. Who wrote the *Iliad*?
3. Where was Christ born?
4. What does *audacious* mean?
5. What does *plagiarize* mean?[80]

---

[78] 347 U.S. 483; 74 S. Ct. 686; 98 L. Ed. 873 (1954).

[79] David Finkelhor, "Education Under Capitalism," *Up Against the American Myth*, edited by Tom Christoffel, David Finkelhor and Dan Gilbarg (New York: Holt-Rinehart-Winston, 1970), p. 321.

[80] Jerome Kagan, "The I.Q. Puzzle: What Are we Measuring?" *Inequality in Education* (Center for Law and Education, Harvard University, July 1973. How would middle-class white children fare against urban Black youths if the questions asked were, for example: Who is the leader of the "Miracles?" What does "greez" mean? What are "chitterlings?" And what if Asian Americans were asked: What is "Manzanar?" What is a "wok?" Consider also, the children of blue-collar workers or welfare mothers: What are "the projects?" What is a food stamp? What is "chump change?"

If the Wechsler Scales were translated into Spanish, Swahili and Chinese and given to every ten-year-old in Latin America, East Africa or China, the majority would obtain IQ scores in the mentally retarded range because *they have not been exposed to the information requested*. It seems intuitively incorrect (and absurd) to conclude that all the children of the world except middle-class America and possibly Europe are retarded.[81]

Other tests have been developed in the twentieth century beginning with the College Entrance Examination Board in 1900 and the Scholastic Aptitude Test in 1920. Today, the tests that by far affect students at all levels are administered by the Educational Testing Service (ETS). In the fall of 1974, 2.5 million Americans took one of these ETS-administered tests:

16,000 in order to qualify for prestigious "pre-secondary" schools;

20,000 in order to qualify for exclusive secondary schools;

1,800,000 high school juniors and seniors and graduates who want to go to college;

100,000 more who want a head start in college by getting advanced placement or by becoming National Merit Scholars;

300,000 college seniors and graduates who want to go on to graduate schools;

74,000 college students who want to go to business schools; and

120,000 aspiring law students.[82]

All of the tests that decided or played a significant role in shaping the lives of 2.5 million students in one year are

. . . written by 58 people who work for a private untaxed, unregulated corporation called the Educational Testing Service. They are backed by a staff of 3,000, most of whom work at the headquarters located on the secluded 400-acre Princeton "campus" that has its own hotel, lake, and flock of ducks, golf course, tennis courts and swimming pool.[83]

Since 1948, ETS has doubled its size and profits every five years. Their gross annual receipts were reported at a staggering $53 million tax-free. ETS has a near-monopoly status, and test questions reflect the same cultural, racial and class biases as those of the IQ tests discussed above. Additionally, even if we assume the negligibility of those biases, the reliability in determining the lives of so many must be put in question:

Even ETS admits that aptitude and achievement cannot be measured in terms nearly as specific as the score that is recorded. If, for example, among possible scores ranging from 200 to 800 you get a 600 on your SAT, this only means that there is a two-in-three chance that your "true" score—the score you would receive if all external factors, like luck in guessing, could be eliminated—would fall somewhere between 570 and 630. There is also a one-in-three chance that your true score will fall somewhere below 570 or above 630.[84]

---

[81] Ibid.

[82] Steven Brill, "College Entrance Exams: How Valid?" Los Angeles *Times*, October 13, 1974.

[83] Ibid.

[84] Ibid.

This one-dimensional way of testing does not test for creativity, stamina, motivation or ethics. But it doesn't much matter to ETS or to the university system which *individuals* are hampered or aided by this testing method, as long as the general pattern of social stratification according to class and race and its legitimization is maintained.

> An ETS study reveals that there is a direct, continuous correlation between family income and SAT scores; the correlations is, in fact, consistent for seven different categories of income. Other ETS data show that males do better than females. Probably the most significant difference is associated with skin color: non-whites have much lower median scores than whites.[85]

The tests are designed so that those test-*takers* who are made in the image of the test-*writers*—that is, white, middle and upper class males—have the greatest chance of success.

For poor and Third World students who "pass" the first hurdle, there are more stumbling blocks in the educational obstacle course. Equally frustrating are the preconceived, stereotypic notions of school personnel, and the demeaning depictions of themselves which minority students find in a racist curriculum. Counselors and advisors perform the task of assigning students to particular courses of study and majors. In this process, students are again confronted with a situation in which their values and aspirations are often placed at odds with the values and assumptions of the counselor. For Asian American students, cultural patterns of interaction with authority figures, adopted through a century of oppression, come into play. Even with such a vast difference in the frame of reference and perspective, counselors often direct students to classes that *the counselors* feel are best suited for students despite contrary views or reluctance expressed by students. The Black student who aspires to become a lawyer is encouraged to take wood shop; the Asian student who has hopes of becoming a novelist is exhorted to take chemistry; the woman who wishes to become a doctor is told to major in elementary education.

When students enter the classroom, they are faced with racist textbooks and teachers who know nothing about what students do with their lives outside the classroom. They are taught to take orders and to compete. Grades are substituted for test scores as the single one-dimensional measure of students. In this system, some are supposed to succeed and others are supposed to fail. It can be no other way as long as the function of schools is to stratify the workforce.

The competitive system affects all children, but there were other biases that have had particular effects on generations of Asian American and Third World children. There is no question that the frame of reference affects perspective. In a course inappropriately titled "World History," students were taught that significant developments in human history occurred in Europe and later in the United States. Such courses are invariably textbook-centered and followed a chronological arrangement. The emphasis was on political history—dates and men, wars and governments. Little attention was given to other considerations, such as how people lived, what they created, how they viewed themselves and others.

> The study of areas beyond Europe entered this version of world history only peripherally, mainly when these areas were "discovered" by Europeans and later by Americans during periods of overseas exploration and colonization. In one major textbook published in the 1940's, fifty important

---

[85] An additional note on ETS is that, in conformity with university and government functions, the ETS does much more than merely test and classify students. Potential CIA agents are sorted out by the ETS as are would-be medical specialists, finance managers, stock-brokers, foreign service officers and law enforcement officers. Students who need financial assistance must have their "need" verified by ETS. Ibid.

dates in world history were listed and the only one which referred to Asia was the notation of Japan having been "opened" by Commodore Perry.[86]

Consider the way in which students study countries in Asia. Because the major motivation for studying other cultures is related to current events and narrowly conceived national self-interests, the treatment reflects this narrow concern. Of the eleven study-guide questions used in this course, eight mention the United States by name: "Why is Southeast Asia important to the U.S.? What is the nature of Chinese Communist threat to the U.S.? What are the 'trouble spots' in Asia, and how do they affect the U.S.? . . ." The connotation of words such as "threat" or "trouble spots" is clear.

> Consider, too, the invidious words which are used consistently to characterize the peoples and cultures of "non-Western" countries—words such as "backward," "underdeveloped," or "emerging." To refer to contemporary India as "emerging" is especially ironic when we recall that it was India and the "Far East" which Columbus was eagerly seeking when he discovered the "New World" (which, of course, was "new" only from the European viewpoint). This designation, however, encouraged the explorers to claim lands as if they were uninhabited and *really* new.[87]

The distorted perceptions and American biases found in international studies can also be found in textbooks and courses about Asian *Americans*. In a study of 300 social studies textbooks currently available for elementary and secondary schools, there was a consistent pattern of neglect and stereotyping with regard to China and Chinese Americans.

> About 75% of the 300 texts made no mention of Chinese at all. Of the remaining seventy-six, fifty-three (17% overall) gave a token representation with a picture of an Asian, often in an interracial group of Americans, and/or one or two lines mentioning the existence of urban Chinatowns (e.g. "San Francisco's Chinatown is a must stop for visitors to the lovely city of the Golden Gates."), several lines about Chinese railroad workers, the laundry and culinary skills of Chinese people, or their relation to China where their ancestors first developed silk.[88]

In a similar study of textbooks with regard to Japanese Americans, researchers rated the books for accuracy of content. Not surprisingly, nine out of ten books examined were evaluated at an *average* rating of "zero" on a scale of zero to five.[89] Omissions and distortions are more blatant with respect to Pilipinos, Koreans, Southeast Asians and Pacific Islanders. The general neglect of the Asian American is not a phenomenon limited to school teachers, but manifests itself at the highest levels of American society. On May 10, 1969, 20,000 people, many of them Chinese Americans,

---

[86] Seymour H. Fersh, "Studying Other Cultures: Looking Outward Is 'In,'" reprinted by The Asia Society from National Council for Social Studies, Washington, D.C., 1968 Yearbook, Chapter 8, p. 1.

[87] Ibid., p. 7.

[88] Albert H. Yee, "Myopic Perceptions and Textbooks: Chinese Americans' Search for Identity," *Journal of Social Issues*, Vol. 29, number 2 (1973), p. 107.

[89] The textbooks were rated according to the following criteria:
- Does content reflect true history and contributions of Japanese Americans?
- Are ethnocentric views worked against, while encouraging a positive self-image?
- Are serious "sins of omission" successfully avoided?
- Are social group differences presented in ways that will cause students to look at the multi-racial character of our country?
- Does the text seek to motivate students to examine their own attitudes and behaviors and to comprehend their duties and responsibilities?

From Carol Hatanaka and Naomi Katayama, "The Treatment of Japanese Americans in Elementary Social Studies Textbooks in Los Angeles City Schools" (Unpublished thesis, 1974).

gathered at Promontory Point, Utah, for the centennial celebration of the completion of the trans-continental railroad. The main speaker was Transportation Secretary John Volpe, who extolled those who labored on the railroad with a series of rhetorical questions:

> Who else but *Americans* could drill ten tunnels in mountains thirty feet deep in snow? Who else but *Americans* could chisel through miles of solid granite? Who else but *Americans* could have laid ten miles of tracks in twelve hours?[90]

The Chinese delegation sat silent, stunned by the total omission of their ancestors who played *the* key role in building the Central Pacific line over the Sierra Nevadas. No mention at all of 12,000 Chinese "coolies." More often than not, the initial reaction to such slights was to dismiss them as individual "identity" problems. But as people came together to confront the ever-present racism and lack of respect for Third World peoples, a demand to have themselves depicted accurately and from their perspective developed. These attempts to challenge even seemingly harmless omissions and distortions have sometime led them into courtrooms.

In March, 1972, Raquel Gutierrez, Ron Hirano, Kay Gurule and Rudy Salinas sued the California Board of Education to prevent the latter from using certain textbooks in the California schools *(Gutierrez v. State Board of Education)*. Their contentions were based on a newly adopted California law, which reads in part:

> The [School] Board shall, when adopting textbooks and teacher's manuals for use in elementary schools for the teaching of courses in civics and history of the United States and the State of California, include only such textbooks which correctly portray the role and contribution of the American Negro and members of other ethnic groups and the role and contributions of the entrepreneur and labor in the total development of the United States and of the State of California.[91]

Franklin Odo, an instructor in Asian American Studies at California State University at Long Beach and a member of the Ethnic Studies Task Force appointed by the State Board of Education, characterized the portrayal of Asian Americans and Asians in twelve basic social science textbooks adopted by the Board as "grossly inadequate and manifestly demeaning."[92]

In a written statement to the court, Odo provided some examples of omissions and distortions found in textbooks:

Social Sciences: Concepts and Values (Harcourt, Brace, Jovanovich, 1970). Chinese Americans were mentioned superficially on one page out of 366 pages, this textbook entirely omitted mention of Japanese, Pilipinos, Koreans and Samoans.

Social Studies and Our Country: Concepts in Social Sciences (Laidlaw Brothers, 1970). There were only two pictures of Asians out of a total of 136, both of them in a "passive" pose.

The Human Adventure (Field Educational Publications, 1970). The following passage illustrates the biases found in this book: "The East (Asia) was tied to the past in ways that prevented change and future growth. The West (America), though primitive and barbaric, would be able to grow without being held back by past traditions." This passage implicitly states that Asians are

---

[90] Yee, loc. cit.

[91] California Education Code, section 9305.

[92] Franklin Odo, a Declaration submitted to the court in the case of *Gutierrez v. State Board of Education*.

incapable of change and progress, and that Native Americans are "primitive and barbaric" people who would not hold back Westerners from expansion.[93]

These are examples of the treatment Asian Americans have received in textbooks used in classrooms throughout the state of California. Omissions and distortions of the histories of other nationalities are no less pervasive and are in many ways more offensive.

In addition to class and race biased testing mechanisms, ignorant and indifferent counselors and advisors, and ethnocentric textbooks, Third World students also suffer from patterns of racial and economic segregation in schools reflecting the segregated character of neighborhoods and the unequal distribution of wealth. These factors continue to manifest themselves in unequal educational facilities between Third World and low-income area schools, on the one hand, and suburban white middle-class schools on the other. The net effect of such a system is that it necessarily reproduces the hierarchical division of labor. Both the quantity and quality of one's education correlate with the social position and wealth of parents and family. Among those who graduate from high school, children of families earning over $15,000 are over six times more likely to attend college as are the children of families earning less than $3,000 per year.[94] Further stratification takes place among junior colleges, state colleges and the Universities as figures for 1964 illustrate below:[95]

Annual Family Income and Access to Higher Education in California, 1964

Annual Family Income	All Families	Families w/o Children in California Public Higher Education	Families with Children in California Public Higher Education		
			Junior College	State College	University of California
Less than $6,000	30.9%	31.9%	24.0%	14.3%	12.5%
$6,000–$9,999	37.0%	37.3%	36.5%	34.2%	24.2%
$10,000–$13,999	19.8%	19.4%	21.6%	30.7%	24.6%
$14,000 and over	12.3%	11.4%	17.9%	20.8%	38.7%
Median Income	$8,000	$7,900	$8,800	$10,000	$12,000

A more recent survey conducted in 1975 among Los Angeles city high school graduates indicated that of those from low-income areas eligible to enroll at the University of California or other similar institutions, only 60% did. By contrast, 80% of the UC-eligible graduates from high-income areas entered four-year colleges.[96] According to a report issued by the Assembly Permanent Subcommittee on Post-secondary Education, lack of money remained a major reason why scholastically eligible low-income students—who are usually Third World students—failed to go

---

[93] Ibid.

[94] For recent evidence of these points, see U.S. Bureau of Census, *Current Population Reports*.

[95] Bowles, p. 223.

[96] Jack McCurdy, "Many of Poor Eligible for UC Fail to Enroll," Los Angeles *Times*, November 12, 1975.

to college.[97] Many Third World students are denied admission to universities because the lack of prerequisites which sometimes results from unavailability of the required courses in their high school curriculum or from lack of adequate counseling.

Unequal schooling manifests itself in more than differences in years of schooling attained by students from different social classes and nationalities. Differences in dress codes, rules of conduct, opportunities for choices and the overall campus atmosphere are all reflections of social class positions of the various student bodies. In the inner-city schools attended by mostly Third World and working class children, authoritarian methods of disciplining students are favored by administrators, teachers and parents alike. That the working class parents often seem to prefer more authoritarian educational methods is perhaps a reflection of their own experiences, which have demonstrated that submission to authority is an essential ingredient in one's ability to get and hold a steady job.[98]

The inequalities in the educational system that affect Third World children are not accidental. They have been long recognized and discussed in numerous volumes. No one can deny that the effects have been devastating on Black and Chicano children. But what of the Asian American?

Many questions have been raised recently—especially in the context of special minority admissions programs for professional and graduate schools—about the status of Asian Americans as economically and culturally disadvantaged: Have they been able to achieve "successes" in the educational system? Have they been able to escape the deteriorated conditions of ghetto schools? Should they really be considered "minorities"?

An examination of Asian Americans in public schools provide some clues. Public schools that service recognized Asian American neighborhoods such as Chinatowns, Little Tokyos, and Manilatowns are in need of upgrading. Most Asian American students living outside those areas also attend secondary schools where they are likely to be stifled in their educational development—schools that have all the earmarks of sub-standard inner-city schools. Most Asian Americans in Los Angeles schools attend working-class schools with other Third World and working class children. In 1975, 63.3% of Asian students attended high schools where more than half of the student body was comprised of Third World students. In contrast, only 20.4% of the Asian students in Los Angeles high schools attended schools with two-thirds white student population. To further illustrate the difficulty of entering colleges faced by Third World students, 81.6% of Black students in Los Angeles schools attend high schools where the average drop-out rate is 33.2%, and 85.7% of Asian Americans attend schools with an average drop-out rate of 25.5%. These figures contrast unfavorably with 78% of white students who attend schools with a drop-out rate of 17.9%.[99]

Even within the schools themselves, students from different classes and nationalities are given different educations. "Tracking" (the practice of placing students in either college pre-patory or vocational curriculum) was systematized by the California Master Plan for Higher Education which was passed into law by the state legislature in 1960. The effect of the Master Plan was to systematize and legitimize all the preexisting inequalities in the school system by standardized testing and tracking of students according to so-called "objective" standards. Not

---

[97] Ibid.

[98] Bowles, p. 224.

[99] Figures computed from abstracts published by the Los Angeles City Schools District, 1974–75.

only did this Plan coordinate the stratification and facilitate the inequalities in primary and secondary schools, it also served to create a class stratification within higher education by creating and expanding the junior college system to "cool out" working class children who aspired to go to four-year colleges. The Master Plan outlined the official policy of class and race discrimination that determined who attended college. Drastic changes took place in California higher education: In 1960, for example, 12 percent of the students at San Francisco State College were Black; in less than a decade, by 1968, Black student population at that school dropped to three percent.[100]

The handful of Third World students who were able to make it through the maze of obstacles before them, and enroll in colleges found themselves isolated from their families and communities. Many of them struggled all of their lives for a chance to get a "decent" education they needed for a "good job." Yet many were faced with the most blatant contradictions in the system of higher education. On the brink of "success" they discovered that "making it" in American education really meant only individual success which required that they divest themselves of all remnants of their cultural backgrounds.

The "successful" Asian American student might become a scholar in one of our universities—and learn to speak a Chinese dialect that 90 percent of the Chinese in this country do not understand—while Chinatown ghettos continue to exist in San Francisco, New York, Los Angeles and elsewhere with the country's highest tuberculosis and suicide rates, sweatshops and overcrowding.

The "successful" Asian American might become an engineer or an agency bureaucrat who plays an active part in the destruction of Little Tokyos, Manilatowns and Chinatowns under the guise of urban renewal, leaving residents and small businesses in those communities with no place to go, as high-rise tourist hotels, banks and corporations take over.

The "successful" Black college student can "make it" by becoming a public school teacher—and watch his Black students become numbed to an environment that is totally unsuitable for learning. Or he can become a social worker and hand out subsistence monies and false promises to fellow human beings.

A "successful" Chicano can make it by joining a big corporation—perhaps the Safeway Stores which will pay him $12,000 a year to be their public relations man while Safeway sells inferior food to Chicanos in the barrios at exorbitant prices, and sells Gallo wines and grapes to undermine unionizing efforts of Chicano and Pilipino farmworkers.

For the Third World student to be a "success" meant that he or she faces the very real possibility of turning his/her back on the community from which he/she came and become oblivious to its problems.[101] Many Third World students at colleges across the country decided in the 60s that they could not live that kind of life. They rejected the individual, competitive values of American education, and its definition of success, and they demanded instead an education that is relevant to their lives in their communities.

Those students who participated in the struggles for more relevant education and open admissions understood well the obstacles they faced. They came to learn through their struggles,

---

[100] Research Organizing Cooperative, p. 2.

[101] It should be noted here that most University of California campuses are located in "prime" areas of the state, far removed from and least accessible to Third World and working class communities. The Berkeley campus is set on a sprawling hillside overlooking the San Francisco Bay; UCLA is in suburban Westwood, adjacent to exclusive Bel Air residences; and Santa Cruz, San Diego, Irvine and Santa Barbara campuses are in secluded areas overlooking the Pacific.

. . . the fundamentally conservative functions of the institutions, namely, the reproduction of the social class system from generation to generation, and the legitimization of the resulting inequalities in higher education. Acquiescence to class stratification is encouraged by maintaining the illusion that social mobility and personal betterment are possible through open access to higher education.[102]

The struggles that led to ethnic studies and minority admissions challenged "the hierarchy of credibility associated with academic work and the nature of biases existing in knowledge, [and provided] an alternative approach to gaining new explanations" for the problems currently faced by Third World people in America, albeit within the framework of the existing system of higher education.[103]

In the 1960s, Third World students recognized the ever-increasing need to challenge and reshape higher education to meet the needs of their communities, and engaged in prolonged struggles to win those demands. In the era of the 1970s, with the economic crisis facing American society, government and school officials are making renewed efforts to cut back and phase out ethnic studies and other progressive programs. These conditions call for demands to be raised again to maintain the hard-fought gains made in progressive, relevant educational programs. Students of ethnic studies need to reexamine the goals of the university and our social system as a whole, and reassess our personal and individual educational and occupational goals. Then we must *understand* the needs of our communities, and of the whole society. But the educational process cannot stop there:

. . . the most important problem does not lie in understanding the laws of the objective world and thus being able to explain it, but in *applying* the knowledge of these laws actively to change the world.[104]

Theory—the intellectual understanding of how social systems function, and for what ends— is important precisely and only because it can be a guide to our actions and behavior. What we learn must be put to practical use for the good of society. Finally, because the resistance to change—ethnic studies, and other programs that emphasize equality, quality and relevance—is so great, the task of making these changes calls for scientific collective action in which people come together to do practical work in a coordinated way.

---

[102] Bowles, "Contradictions in U.S. Higher Education," *Political Economy: Radical versus Orthodox Approaches*, edited by James Weaver, 1971, p. 494.

[103] George Kagiwada and Isao Fujimoto, "Asian American Studies: Implications for Education," *Personnel and Guidance Journal*, Vol. 51, No. 6 (February 1973), p. 402.

[104] Mao Tse-tung, "On Practice," July 1937.

Educational Trends and Issues

Shirley Hune and Julie J. Park

One of the more enduring images of Asian Americans is their reputation in the area of education as being intelligent overachievers who are good at math and science. From the joke that UCLA stands for "University of Caucasians Lost among Asians" to the high percentages of Asian Americans enrolled in Ivy League institutions, the public perception persists that Asian Americans do not face major barriers or challenges in the educational realm. A result of this assumption is that Asian Americans are a relatively understudied group in education. At times, Asian Americans have been left out of policy discussions or reports because their experiences are thought to be almost identical to those of whites. For instance, a CNN.com feature published in 2003, "Back to School: The American Student," went so far as to omit Asian Americans in its demographic breakdown of American college students, naming the overall college racial/ethnic population as being 81.4 percent white, 13 percent black, and 9.1 percent Hispanic, with some overlap because of multiracial students.[1]

This section includes entries on the educational issues that affect this growing population. Some of the entries provide a sociohistorical context for common stereotypes around Asian American students, such as Hyeyoung Kwon and Wayne Au's entry on the model minority myth and Eunai Shrake and Hyeyoung Kwon's entry on parental pressures and expectations. Others such as Tracy Buenavista and Tam Tran's piece on undocumented students draw attention to an issue that few have associated with Asian Americans. This overview includes information on the diverse experiences of Asian Americans in education, selected historical aspects of their education, pertiuent issues in K–12 education, and key issues in higher education.

A Diverse Community

One of the problems in understanding Asian American educational experiences is the common practice of not examining the vast differences that exist within this diverse population. The umbrella term "Asian American" encompasses a population that includes more than twenty-four

---

[1] CNN.com. "Back to School: The American Student." CNN.com, 2003. http://www.cnn.com/SPECIALS/2003/back.to.school/college/social.html.

different ethnic groups.[2] Socioeconomic background, immigrant status, gender, and English-language ability among other variables contribute to different educational opportunities and experiences for individuals and groups of Asian Americans. Additionally, in data collection and reporting, Pacific Islanders, an umbrella term for another twenty-four highly diverse ethnic groups, are also often lumped together with Asian Americans.

The use of data that does not separate by ethnic subgroup helps contribute to the notion that Asian Americans are a "model minority" and educationally successful. As a group. 49 percent of Asian Americans have a bachelor's degree compared to 28 percent of the total U.S. population for those 25 years and older in 2007; however, this rate of attainment varies widely by ethnic subgroup, from 11 percent for Laotian Americans to 71 percent for Taiwanese Americans. Public and policy discussions on achievement, diversity, and education tend to focus on the experiences of Asian Americans of Chinese and Japanese descent, and increasingly Korean and Asian Indian Americans. For instance, an article published on January 7, 2007, in *The New York Times*, entitled "Little Asia on the Hill," addressed how the Asian American enrollment at the University of California—Berkeley exceeded 40 percent.[3] The article focused on the high enrollment of Chinese American students and the strong emphasis that their families placed on academics.

Such news coverage reflects a popular public perception that Asian Americans are "overrepresented" in higher education, considering that some Asian American groups have higher college attainment rates than the general population; however, because of the misperception that all Asian Americans excel academically, the educational experiences and lower educational attainment rates of Southeast Asian Americans, such as Vietnamese, Cambodian, Hmong, and Laotian Americans, are seriously neglected. Also, socioeconomic differences within Asian American subgroups that affect educational opportunities are often ignored. As a result, policies meant to promote access and equity to high-quality education for traditionally disadvantaged students often overlook Asian Americans. One example of this oversight occurred when The College Board released a report on minority students in 1999 entitled "Reaching the Top." The report grouped Asian Americans together with whites and did not include mention of the unique challenges that many Asian Americans encounter in the educational system.[4]

Still, contrary to popular belief, wide disparities exist between and within Asian American ethnic groups. Some Asian American groups have much lower Americans over the age of twenty-five have a bachelor's degree, in contrast to 28 percent of the U.S. general population.

One explanation for the wide disparities of educational attainment among Asian American groups, as well as differences between all U.S. and all Asians, can be found in the foreign-born data of the U.S. census. In 2000, 69 percent of Asian Americans reported being born outside of the United States compared with 11 percent of the general U.S. population.[5] Hence, much of the high educational attainment among certain Asian American subgroups is a result of selective immigration to the United States. In other words, the immigration of highly educated Asians who

---

[2] Robert Teranishi, *Asian Americans and Pacific Islanders, Facts, Not Fiction: Setting the Record Straight*, (New York: National Commission on Asian American and Pacific Islander Research in Education and The College Board, 2008).

[3] Timothy Egan, "Little Asia on the Hill," *The New York Times*, Jan. 7, 2007. http://www.nytimes.com/2007/01/07/education/edlife/07asian.html.

[4] The College Board, *Reaching the Top: A Report of the National Task Force on Minority High Achievement* (New York: College Board Publications, 1999).

[5] Terrance J. Reeves and Claudette E. Bennett, *We the People: Asians in the United States* (Washington, DC: U.S. Census Bureau, 2004).

obtained a bachelor's degree or more elsewhere are a form of brain gain for America, but a brain drain for their homelands. The overall lower educational attainment of Southeast Asian groups is also related to the impact of the U.S. wars in their countries of origin and the legacy of their refugee exodus requiring them to start over in America. These students may attend high schools that are unresponsive to students' unique needs as English language learners or bicultural students.[6] Consequently, the differences in educational attainment within the Asian American community are largely related to structural forces, such as the way that different Asian American subgroups immigrated to the United States. In particular, the Immigration and Nationality Act of 1965 and various military conflicts resulted in drastically different sets of educational opportunities and socioeconomic circumstances for different Asian American subgroups.

One way to help remedy the vast misconceptions regarding the educational experiences of Asian Americans is for institutions and organizations to collect and make available both aggregate and disaggregated data on Asian Americans by ethnic group (e.g. Filipino, Cambodian, Korean) and by social and economic status. Such data would contribute to more complete analyses of the diversity and complexity of the Asian American population. At a minimum, educational data for Asian Americans and Pacific Islanders must be presented separately. In addition, qualitative studies of individual ethnic communities that draw attention to the dynamics of social class and gender provide rich detail that is missed when relying only on quantitative data. Multiple data sources better serve all groups and sectors of the Asian American population in assessing their education in the United States.

Struggle for Access To and Equity in Education

The predominant arena of educational participation for Asian Americans is in U.S. public schools and higher educations institutions. Asian Americans have experienced discrimination and forced segregation in the U.S. educational system. They have used multiple strategies, such as petitions to local authorities and challenging the legal system up to the Supreme Court, as well as contemporary civil rights activism to fight for equity in education.

The early history of Asian American education, as for other minority groups in the United States deemed inferior and incapable of being first-class citizens, is one of denied access to public education followed by segregated schooling. While the 1954 *Brown v. Board of Education* Supreme Court decision is the landmark case for black/white school desegregation. Asian Americans also have a long history of contesting segregated schools. For instance, in the mid-nineteenth century, Chinese American students in San Francisco had to attend separate schools from the general population. In 1905, ninety-three Japanese and Korean immigrants created an international incident when the Japanese government protested the San Francisco school board's decision to assign them to the separate "Oriental School." It took the intervention of President Theodore Roosevelt in order for the school board to allow Japanese students to attend public schools with whites.[7] Segregated schooling for Asian Americans continued in some parts of California into the 1930s and in Mississippi until 1950.[8]

The rounding up and incarceration into barbed wire camps with military guards during World War II of some 110,000 Japanese Americans, including 30,000 children, disrupted the education of Japanese American youth. Japanese American parents worked to ensure the continuity of

---

[6] Stacey J. Lee, *Up Against Whiteness: Race, School and Immigrant Youth* (New York: Teachers College Press, 2005).

[7] Victor Low, *The Unimpressible Race* (San Francisco: East/West Publishing Co., 1982).

[8] Sucheng Chan, *Asian Americans: An Interpretive History* (Boston: Twayne, 1991).

schooling, and even created schools themselves when, on occasion, none were available. They also sought to provide opportunities for school-age children to sustain their cultural heritage.[9] More than 5,000 Japanese American college students also persisted in their educational goals. Many Japanese American college students were successful in completing their degrees elsewhere, but others had their earlier hopes and dreams derailed, some for a lifetime.[10]

In the 1974 *Lau v. Nichols* decision, Asian Americans had an historic role in expanding the educational rights of language minority groups, as explained in Hyeyoung Kwon and Eunai Shrake's entry on bilingual education. As a result of the lawsuit, filed by Chinese Americans who argued that schools were ill-equipped to educate limited English proficient (LEP) students, the U.S. Supreme Court redefined educational access and equity and called for new remedies that included bilingual programs, teachers, and teacher assistants.

During the late 1960s and early 1970s, as part of the social movements of the period, Asian Americans demonstrated and sat in with other student groups of color and supportive whites to challenge institutional inequities in higher education. Their primary demands focused on increased college access for minority, female, and low-income students, more minority faculty, and the establishment of ethnic studies programs. To this day, students continue to challenge institutions with petitions, sit-ins, and occasional hunger strikes to secure or expand Asian American Studies programs.[11] Sophia Lai's entry on Asian American Studies traces the development of this movement. Glenn Omatsu also discusses how the development of Asian American Studies was influenced by the pedagogy of the Freedom Schools movement of the Civil Rights era.

In the 1980s, Asian Americans opposed discriminatory practices adopted by both Ivy League and elite public institutions that sought to restrict the enrollment of Asian American students.[12] More recently, they have challenged anti-affirmative action initiatives and decisions by policy makers and institutions to exclude Asian Americans from programs serving minority students. As Julie Park's entry on affirmative action explains, Asian Americans have come out as both supporters and opponents of the policy. Many Asian Americans maintain they are a minority group that faces barriers to accessing and succeeding in higher education.[13]

Asian American faculty women and men have also taken action when they have been unjustly denied tenure, merit, or promotion. Here again the Asian American struggle for equity has benefited others. For example, Rosalie Tung's tenure case led to a 1990 U.S. Supreme Court decision that called for universities to adopt a more open, impartial, and consistent review process for all faculty. Tung had been denied tenure by the University of Pennsylvania's Wharton School of Business, but argued that she had been unfairly treated during the tenure process because of her gender and national origin. The resilience of many Asian American faculty members to seek justice is part of a long and ongoing historic resistance against inequities in the U.S. educational system.[14]

---

[9] Thomas James, *Exile Within: The Schooling of Japanese Americans 1942–1945* (Cambridge, MA: Harvard University Press, 1987).

[10] Allan W. Austin, *From Concentration Camp to Campus* (Urbana: University of Illinois, 2004).

[11] Shirley Hune and Kenyon S. Chan, "Special Focus: Asian Pacific American Demographic and Education Trends," in *Minorities in Higher Education, 15th Annual Status Report*, eds. Deborah Carter and Reginald Wilson (Washington, DC: American Council on Education, 1997), 39–67 and 103–107.

[12] Dana Takagi, *Retreat from Race: Asian American Admissions and Racial Politics* (New Brunswick, NJ: Rutgers University Press, 1992)

[13] Sharon S. Lee, "Over-Represented and De-Minoritized: The Racialization of Asian Americans in Higher Education," *Interactions: UCLA Journal of Education and Information Studies* 2, no. 2 (2006).

[14] Sumi Cho, "Converging Stereotypes in Racialized Sexual Harassment: Where the Model Minority Meets Suzie Wong," in *Critical Race Feminism*, ed. Adrien Wing (New York: New York University Press, 1997), 203–220.

The struggle for access and equity in Asian American education continues today, as certain states have passed laws restricting or even banning bilingual education, and Asian American college students often face unsupportive campus climates.

Issues in K–12 Education

Role of Socioeconomic Status

In recent years, a series of studies have emerged that highlight the role of income and socioeconomic status within certain Asian American subgroups. One example of this work is Jamie Lew's research on Korean American high school students.[15] Her work draws attention to a category of Asian American students who are all but invisible in the existing research: high school dropouts. She found marked differences in the high school experiences between working class students and students from families with greater financial resources. For instance, Lew found Korean American parents from wealthier backgrounds could send their children to private tutoring and supplementary educational institutions, while parents who had to work longer hours and had limited finances were unable to provide such resources.

Standardized Testing

Since the passage of No Child Left Behind, there has been a greater focus on testing students in America's schools. Wayne Au's entry on standardized testing provides information about the different ways that standardized tests are used in schools, as well as the impact of such tests on Asian American students. While statistics suggest that Asian American students tend to perform well on such tests, breaking the data out by socioeconomic status and ethnic subgroup shows that not all Asian American students are excelling in this area.

Supplementary Education

For many Asian American students, education goes beyond what they experience in public or private schools; they may attend supplementary educational institutions such as language schools or cram schools. From New York City to Los Angeles, such institutions sponsor a wide curriculum of language, arts, music, dance, and athletics. In addition, ethnic entrepreneurs have created private, for-profit schools in Chinese and Korean communities to prepare youth for the rigors of getting into a prestigious college. The Chinese-run "buxiban" or "kumon" program and the Korean-run "hagwons" are noted for their SAT, PSAT, and AP preparation. Nonprofit and for-profit community-supported schools are a form of social capital that help explain, along with immigration policies that favor the entry of highly motivated, skilled, and professional classes from Asia to the United States, why certain Asian American communities have demonstrated academic success in U.S. schooling.[16]

---

[15] Jamie Lew, *Asian Americans in Class: Charting the Achievement Gap among Korean American Youth* (New York: Teachers College Press, 2006).

[16] Min Zhou and Susan Kim, "Community Forces, Social Capital, and Educational Achievement: The Case of Supplementary Education in the Chinese and Korean Immigrant Communities," *Harvard Educational Review* 76 (2006): 1–29.

Racism in Schools

The model minority myth assumes that all Asian American students are excelling in school, which in turn would suggest that Asian American students face few barriers to succeeding in schools; however, researchers have found that some school environments are unsupportive of Asian American students. Stacey J. Lee studied a well-resourced high school that did little to facilitate the well-being of the first- and second-generation Hmong American students that attended the school. She argues that the school perpetuated a dominant culture that privileged white students and marginalized Hmong students. Furthermore, the school did little to meet the distinct needs of the Hmong student population. In the twenty-first century, blatant discrimination against Asian Americans and other students of color still occurs in school settings. This discrimination may be especially prevalent for South Asian American and Arab American children following the events of September 11, 2001.[17]

Diversity in the Curriculum

One major concern in K–12 education is the lack of multicultural perspectives reflected in the curriculum. Depending on the region of the country, the history and experiences of Asian Americans and other communities of color may or may not be included in social studies, history, and language arts curriculum. Asian Americans have acted to remedy this problem by working to include Asian American stories and perspectives in the curriculum. One notable initiative is Pin@y Educational Partnerships (PEP), a collaboration between San Francisco public schools, a community center, and the San Francisco State University Asian American Studies Department. PEP developed innovative curricula on Filipino American issues that have been taught by undergraduates, graduate students, and teachers in middle and high schools.[18] One little-known fact is that when President Barack Obama was an Illinois state senator, he introduced SB890, which mandated that the role of contributions of different American ethnic groups, including Asian Americans, be taught in public schools.[19]

Asian American Teachers and Administrators

Related to the issue of underrepresented Asian American voices in existing curriculum are the relatively low numbers of Asian Americans teaching in K–12 schools. Researchers have identified the need to recruit greater numbers of Asian American students to the teaching profession.[20] They have also noted that Asian American student teachers often encounter subtle forms of racism or questions about their identities, particularly when teaching in areas with lower concentrations of Asian Americans.[21] Additionally, there are few Asian Americans who serve on school boards

---

[17] Khyati Joshi, "The Racialization of Hinduism, Islam, and Sikhism in the United States. *Equity & Excellence* 39 (2006): 211–26.

[18] Pin@y Educational Partnerships, Allyson Tintiangco-Cubales, "Pin@y Educational Partnerships," http://pepsf.org/.

[19] Yvonne M. Lau, "President-elect Barack Obama's Chinese Connection: One 'Jia,'" U.S.-China Media Brief. http://www.aasc.ucla.edu/uschina/cac_chicago.shtml.

[20] Xue Lan Rong and J. Preissle, "The Continuing Decline in Asian American Teachers," *American Educational Research Journal* 34 (1997): 267–93.

[21] Roberta M. Newton, "Racialized Experiences of Asian American Student Teachers," in *Asian American Identities, Families, And Schooling*, eds. Park Clara, A. Goodwin Lin, and Stacey J. Lee (Greenwich, CT: Information Age Publishing, 2003), 77–104.

or in top administrative positions. One high-profile Asian American superintendent of a major metropolitan area is Michelle Rhee, who was appointed chancellor of the District of Columbia Public Schools system in 2007.

Trends in Higher Education

Student Growth

The most notable trend is the increased presence of Asian American and Pacific Islander students, especially Asian Americans, in higher education institutions at all levels. Their undergraduate enrollment grew 40.5 percent from 1993 to 2003. In this same period, Asian American graduate enrollment grew 64.5 percent while their professional degree participation increased 59.6 percent.[22] Overall, Asian Americans alone comprised 6.6 percent of all undergraduate enrollees and 6.6 percent of all college enrollees (undergraduate, graduate, and professional) in fall 2006.[23] As Tracy Buenavista and Dimpal Jain note, Asian American student groups and organizations reflect their population growth on college campuses.

Community College Presence

Another trend is that the proportion of Asian American students who attend community colleges compared with four-year institutions has remained relatively constant throughout the years, being about 56 percent and 44 percent at four-year and two-year colleges, respectively.[24] This trend challenges the notion that Asian Americans are largely in four-year elite institutions. Why do so many Asian American students choose community colleges? As Jonathan Lew and Winnie Wang explain in their entry on community colleges, cost and location close to home are key reasons. Tuition costs are lower at community colleges than at four-year institutions, an important consideration for low-income house-holds. The vast majority of Asian Americans also reside in the Western states, which have a large number of community colleges.

Increased Participation of Asian American Women

One of the most significant trends is the increased enrollment of Asian American women in college. Their college enrollment parallels a general U.S. trend of a gender shift in education for all racial/ethnic groups. It was not until the mid 1990s, however, that the numbers of undergraduate Asian American women began to exceed their male counterparts, a situation held by women in other racial and ethnic groups a decade or more earlier. By 2003–04, Asian American women were earning more associate, bachelor, master's, professional, and doctoral degrees than their male counterparts.[25] While rates of participation have increased for Asian American women, the rate of participation for Asian American men at the undergraduate level has not increased at the same level.

---

[22] Bryan J. Cook and Diana I. Córdova, *Minorities in Higher Education, Twenty-Second Annual Status Report* (Washington, DC: American Council on Education, 2006).

[23] The Chronicle of Higher Education. "The 2008–9 Almanac, College Enrollment by Racial and Ethnic group, Selected Years." http://chronicle.com/weekly/almanac/2008/nation/0101403.htm.

[24] Ibid.

[25] Cook and Córdova, *Minorities in Higher Education, Twenty-Second Annual Status Report*.

Marginalization of Asian American Issues and Concerns

A fourth trend is the continued lack of attention given to Asian American issues and concerns by educational institutions and their personnel at all levels. In higher education, whether as students, faculty, staff, or administrators, Asian Americans have long identified the many ways in which they and their interests are ignored to their detriment. Asian American student concerns have received little attention by many student affairs offices across the country.[26] Tracy Buenavista highlights the often overlooked issue of student retention for Asian American students in higher education, along with the challenges that some students face staying in college.

Outlook

In response to failures to include the Asian American population and their perspectives in educational matters, national educational groups and Asian American scholars and community organizations have collaborated in producing a number of public policy reports with research findings of economic and educational disparities in the Asian American community all along the pipeline beginning with elementary schools. In contrast to the dominant group's public discourse of Asian American communities as a model minority, community-based public policy reports identify them as a community in "crisis."[27]

Some developments point to a greater awareness of the educational needs of Asian Americans. For instance, history was made when a federal designation for Asian American Pacific Islander (AAPI) Serving Institutions was passed as part of the College Cost Reduction and Access Act of 2007, making AAPIs the newest population group to be eligible for Minority Serving Institution status. This program makes higher education institutions with at least a 10 percent AAPI student enrollment and a certain threshold of low-income students eligible to apply for certain federal grants.[28] Still, numerous challenges exist to ensure that all Asian Americans can have a high quality educational experience. In the coming years, many policy decisions will be made around issues such as high stakes testing; teacher quality, pay and accountability; and access to higher education, including affordability, and the extent to which they will affect the lives of Asian American students and educators alike. Asian American ethnic groups need to be included in efforts to close the achievement gap being addressed by school systems nationwide and to be part of a seamless pre-K through higher education and beyond pipeline.[29] In addition, more attention needs to be given by the larger U.S. society, the educational community in general, and Asian American communities to the widening educational gap across Asian American ethnic groups and within ethnic groups.

---

[26] Marylu K. McEwen, Corinne Maekawa Kodama, Alvin N. Alvarez, Sunny Lee, and Christopher T. H. Liang, eds., *Working with Asian American College Students* (San Francisco: Jossey-Bass, 2002).

[27] Asian American Justice Center, *A Community of Contrasts: Asian Americans and Pacific Islanders in the United States* (Washington DC: Asian American Justice Center, 2006).

[28] Julie J. Park and Robert Teranishi, "Asian American Pacific Islander Serving Institutions: Historical Perspectives and Future Prospects," in *Understanding Minority Serving Institutions*, eds. Marybeth Gasman, Benjamin Baez, and Caroline Turner (Albany: SUNY Press, 2008), 111–26.

[29] Shirley Hune and David Takeuchi, *Asian Americans in Washington State: Closing Their Hidden Achievement Gaps. A report submitted to The Washington State Commission on Asian Pacific American Affairs* (Seattle, WA: University of Washington, 2008).

You're Asian, How Could You Fail Math?

Unmasking the Myth of the Model Minority

Wayne Au and Benji Chang

> Have you ever sat next to an Asian student in class and wondered how she managed to consistently get straight A's while you struggled to maintain a B-minus average?
> —*from* Top of the Class: How Asian Parents Raise High Achievers-and How You Can Too

In January 1966, William Petersen penned an article for The New York Times Magazine entitled, "Success Story: Japanese American Style." In it, he praised the Japanese-American community for its apparent ability to successfully assimilate into mainstream American culture, and literally dubbed Japanese Americans a "model minority" the first popular usage of the term.

By the 1980s, Newsweek, The New Republic, Fortune, Parade, U.S. News and World Report, and Time all had run articles on the subject of Asian-American success in schools and society, and the Myth of the Model Minority was born. The Myth of the Model Minority asserts that, due to their adherence to traditional, Asian cultural values, Asian-American students are supposed to be devoted, obedient to authority, respectful of teachers, smart, good at math and science, diligent, hard workers, cooperative, well-behaved, docile, college-bound, quiet, and opportunistic.

Top of the Class (quoted above) is a perfect modern example. Published in 2005, the authors claim to offer readers 17 "secrets" that Asian parents supposedly use to develop high school graduates who earn A-pluses and head to Ivy League colleges. It's a marketing concept built purely on the popular belief in the Myth of the Model Minority.

However, in both of our experiences as public school teachers and education activists, we've seen our share of Asian-American students do poorly in school, get actively involved in gangs, drop out, or exhibit any number of other indicators of school failure not usually associated with "model minorities."

A critical unmasking of this racist myth is needed because it both negatively affects the classroom lives of Asian American students and contributes to the justification of race and class inequality in schools and society.

Masking Diversity

On the most basic level, the Myth of the Model Minority masks the diversity that exists within the Asian-American community. The racial category of "Asian" is itself emblematic of the problem. Asia contains nearly four billion people and over 50 countries, including those as diverse as Turkey, Japan, India, the Philippines, and Indonesia.

From *RethinkingSchools, Vol. 22, No. 2 (Winter 2007–2008)* www.rethinkingschools.org by Wayne Au and Benji Chang.

The racial category of "Asian" is also historically problematic. Similar to those categories used to name peoples from Africa and the Americas, the definition of Asia as a continent (and race) and division of Asians into various nations was developed to serve the needs of European and U.S. colonialism and imperialism.

The category of Asian gets even fuzzier in the context of the United States, since there are over 50 ways to officially qualify as an Asian American according to government standards. Pacific Islanders and "mixed race" Asians are also regularly squished together under the banner of Asian or Asian Pacific islander (which, out of respect for the sovereignty of Pacific peoples, we refuse to do here).

Masking the Class Divide

The Myth of the Model Minority, however, masks another form of diversity-that of economic class division. As Jamie Lew explains in her 2007 book, Asian Americans in Class, there are increasing numbers of working-class Korean-American students in New York City performing more poorly in schools than their middle-class counterparts.

Similarly, Vivian Louie found class-based differences in her study of Chinese-American students. Her research indicated that middle-class Chinese-American mothers tended to have more time, resources, and educational experience to help their children through school and into college than mothers from working-class Chinese-American families, who had longer work hours, lower-paying jobs, and lower levels of education.

These class differences are sometimes rooted in specific immigrant histories and are connected to the 1965 Immigration Act. The Act not only opened up the United States to large numbers of Asian immigrants, but, among a handful of other criteria, it granted preference to educated professionals and those committing to invest at least $40,000 in a business once they arrived.

As a consequence, some Asian immigrants, even those within the same ethnic community, enter the United States with high levels of education and/or with economic capital attained in their countries of origin. Others enter the United States with little or no education or money at all. These educational and financial heritages make an important difference in how well children gain access to educational resources in the United States.

In other words, whether we are talking about African-American, white, Latina/o, indigenous, or "model minority" Asian-American students, the first rule of educational inequality still applies: Class matters.

Masking Ethnic Inequity

To add to the complexity of Asian-American diversity, many of the class differences amongst Asian Americans also correlate with ethnic differences. According to the 2000 census, 53.3 percent of Cambodians, 59.6 percent of Hmong, 49.6 percent of Laotians, and 38.1 percent of Vietnamese over 25 years of age have less than a high school education. In contrast, 13.3 percent of Asian Indians, 12.7 percent of Filipinos, 8.9 percent of Japanese, and 13.7 percent of Koreans over 25 years of age have less than a high school education.

These educational disparities are particularly striking considering that, for instance, 37.8 percent of Hmong, almost 30 percent of Cambodians, and 18.5 percent of Laotians have incomes below the poverty line (compared to 12.4 percent of the total U.S. population). Indeed, the 2000 census reveals relatively consistent high education rates and income amongst South Asian, Korean, and Chinese Americans, and relatively low education rates and low income amongst Cambodian, Lao, and Hmong Americans. Hence, the Myth of the Model Minority serves to obscure the struggles of poor or "under-educated" families working to gain a decent education for their children.

Masking Economic Circumstance

One of the most cited statistics proving the Myth of the Model minority is that Asian Americans even out earn whites in Income. What is obscured in this "fact" is that it is only true when we compare Asian American household income to white household income, and the reality is that Asian-Americans make less per person compared to whites. Statistically, the average household size for Asian Americans is 3.3 people, while for whites it is 2.5 people.

Consequently, Asian-American households are more likely than white households to have more than one income earner, and almost twice as likely to have three income earners. When we take these issues into account, Asian-American individuals earn $2,000 on average less than white individuals.

The statistics on Asian-American income are further skewed upward when we look at the economies of the states where the majority live. The three states with the highest proportion of Asian Americans, Hawai'i, California and New York, all have median income levels in the top third of states. This means that, regardless of statistically higher household incomes, the high cost of living in states with large Asian-American populations guarantees that Asian Americans, on average, are more likely to have less disposable income and lower living standards than whites.

Masking Racism

While the above statistics may be remarkable in the face of the Myth of the Model Minority, they also point to another serious problem: The myth is regularly used as a social and political wedge against blacks, Latina/os, and other racial groups in the United States.

The racist logic of the model minority wedge is simple. If, according to the myth, Asian Americans are academically and socially successful due to particular cultural or racial strengths, then lower test scores, lower GPAs, and lower graduation rates of other groups like African Americans and Latina/os can be attributed to their cultural or racial weaknesses.

Or, as one high school guidance counselor in Stacey J. Lee's book, *Unraveling the Model Minority Stereotype*, puts it, "Asians like . . . M.I.T., Princeton. They tend to go to good schools . . . I wish our blacks would take advantage of things instead of sticking to sports and entertainment."

The Myth of the Model Minority also causes Asian-American students to struggle with the racist expectations the myth imposes upon them. An Asian-American high school student in Lee's book explains. "When you get bad grades, people look at you really strangely because you are sort of distorting the way they see an Asian."

Unfortunately, some East and South Asian Americans uphold the myth because it allows them to justify their own relative educational and social success in terms of individual or cultural drive, while simultaneously allowing them to distance themselves from what they see as African-American, Latina/o, indigenous, and Southeast-Asian-American educational failure.

As Jamie Lew observes, the Myth of the Model Minority ". . . attributes academic success and failure to individual merit and cultural orientation, while underestimating important structural and institutional resources that all children need in order to achieve academically." In doing so, the Myth of the Model Minority upholds notions of racial and cultural inferiority of other lower achieving groups, as it masks the existence of racism and class exploitation in this country.

The Challenge of Educating Asian America

One of the difficulties of unmasking the Myth of the Model Minority is that the diversity of the Asian American experience poses substantial challenges, particularly in relation to how race, culture, and ethnicity are typically considered by educators.

For instance, Asian-American students challenge the categories commonly associated with the black-brown-white spectrum of race. Many Asian American students follow educational pathways usually attributed to white, middle-class, suburban students, while many others follow pathways usually attributed to black and Latina/o, working-class, urban students.

Other Asian-American groups challenge typical racial categories in their own identities. Pilipinos,[1] for instance, don't quite fit into the typical categories of South, East, or Southeast Asian, nor do they quite fit the category of Pacific Islander. Further, some argue that Pilipinos have a lineage that is more closely related to Latina/os because they were in fact colonized by Spain. Consequently, because of their particular circumstances, many Pilipinos more strongly identify with being brown than anything else. As another example, many high-achieving, middle-class South Asians consider themselves "brown," especially after the discrimination endured after 9/11.

Asian-American students also challenges typical notions of immigration and language by blurring the typical dichotomies of native language vs. English and immigrant vs. American-born. Some Southeast Asian refugees, like those from Laos, may develop fluency in multiple languages and attend universities, even as their parents are low-income and do not speak English. On the other hand, there are groups of Pilipinos who grow up highly Americanized, who have been taught English their whole lives, but who have some of the highest dropout and suicide rates.

Asian-American students also challenge popularly accepted multicultural teaching strategies because they are often a numerical minority in classrooms, and multicultural teaching strategies designed to meet the needs of classroom majorities can leave out the culturally specific needs of Asian-American students. These can include the language acquisition needs of students who come from character-based languages (e.g., Chinese, Japanese), social and ideological differences of students from majority Muslim nations (e.g., Pakistan, Indonesia), and psychological issues that emerge from student families traumatized by U.S. intervention/war policies (e.g., Korea, Vietnam, Thailand).

From the Fukienese-Chinese student in an urban Philadelphia classroom with mostly Black or Latino/a students, to the Hmong student who sits with two or three peers in a mostly white school in rural Wisconsin, to the Pilipino student in a San Diego suburb with predominantly Pilipino classmates and some white peers, Asian-American youth do not fit neatly into the typical boxes of our educational system.

Unmasking the Myth in Our Classrooms

Despite the diversity and complexity inherent in working with Asian-American populations, there are many things that educators can do to challenge the Myth of the Model Minority. Similar to other communities of color, effective steps include recruiting more educators from

---

[1] Pilipino is a term used by some activists in the Pilipino-American community as means of challenging the way that Spanish and U.S. colonization of the Islands also colonized the language by renaming them the Phillippines after King Phillip, and introducing the anglicized "f" sound which did not exist in the indigenous languages there.

The authors would like to thank Anjela Wong and Mira Shimabukuro for their assistance with this article and recognize that some data used here came from a National Education Association report on the status of Asian and Pacific Islanders in education authored by Stacey J. Lee and Kevin Kumashiro. Benji Chang (chang_benji@hotmail.com) is a former teacher in the Los Angeles Unified School District and is currently a doctoral student in the Graduate School of Education at the University of California, Los Angeles. Wayne Au (wayne.wk.au@gmail.com), a former Seattle Public Schools and Berkeley Unified School District teacher, is currently an assistant professor in the Department of Secondary Education at California State University, Fullerton. Au is also an editorial board member for Rethinking Schools.

Asian-American backgrounds, promoting multilingual communication in instruction and parent involvement, and developing relationships between parents, community groups, and schools.

Within the classroom, teachers can make use of several strategies to counter the Myth of the Model Minority in their own classrooms. The following list offers a starting point to address the realities of Asian-American students' lives.

Don't Automatically Assume That Your Asian-American Students Are "Good" Students (or "Bad," for That Matter), and Get to Know Them

Personally get to know students and their family's practices, which widely vary from home to home, despite their "membership" in specific ethnic or linguistic groups. Start by researching the specific histories and cultures of the students in your classroom to better understand the historical and political contexts of their communities. Also, bring the lives of all of your students, Asian Americans included, into your classroom. Have them consider, reflect, and write about how their home lives and experiences intersect with their school lives and experiences.

Develop strategies to personally engage with students and their communities, whether through lunchtime interactions or visits to their homes, community centers, and cultural or political events. While we recognize the limited resources of all teachers, learning about your Asian-American students and their communities takes the same energy and commitment as learning to work with any specific group of students.

Rethink How You Interpret and Act Upon the Silence of Asian-American Students in Your Classroom

Asian-American student silence can mean many things, from resistance to teachers, to disengagement from work, to a lack of understanding of concepts, to thoughtful engagement and consideration, to insecurity speaking English, to insecurity in their grasp of classroom content. Rather than assume that Asian-American student silence means any one thing, assess the meaning of silence by personally checking in with the student individually.

Teach about Unsung Asian-American Heroes

Teachers might include the stories of real-life woman warriors Yurl Kochlyama and Grace Lee Boggs, for instance. Kochlyama has been involved in a range of efforts, from working closely with Malcolm X in Harlem, to Puerto Rican sovereignty, to freeing political prisoners like Mumia Abu Jamal. Boggs' efforts have included work with famed Marxist Humanist Raya Dunayevskaya, organized labor, and the Detroit Freedom Summer schools.

Or perhaps teach about Ehren Watada, the first commissioned officer to publicly refuse to go to war in Iraq because he believes the war is illegal and would make him a party to war crimes. Learning about heroes like these can help students broaden the range of what it means to be Asian American.

Highlight Ways in Which Asian Americans Challenge Racism and Stereotypes

Schools should challenge racist caricatures of Asians and Asian Americans, including viewing them as penny-pinching convenience store owners, religious terrorists, kung fu fighting mobsters, academic super-nerds, and exotic, submissive women.

One way to do this is to introduce students to stereotype-defying examples, such as Kochiyama, Boggs, and Watada. There are also many youth and multi-generational organizations of Asian Americans lighting for social justice in the U.S. These include Khmer Girls in Action (KGA, Long Beach), and the Committee Against Anti-Asian Violence/Organizing Asian Communities (CAAAV, New York).

These organizations are extremely important examples of how youth can be proactive in challenging some of the issues that affect our communities, and their work challenges the stereotypes of Asian Americans as silent and obedient.

Illustrate Historical, Political, and Cultural Intersections Between Asian Americans and Other Groups

There are historical and current examples of shared experiences between Asian Americans and other communities. For instance, teachers could highlight the key role of Asian Americans in collective struggles for social justice in the United States. Possible examples include: Philip Veracruz and other Pilipino farm workers who were the backbone and catalyst for the labor campaigns of Cesar Chavez and the United Farm Workers in the late 1960s and early 1970s; Chinese students and families who challenged the racism of public schools in the *Lau v. Nichols* case of the 1970s that provided the legal basis for guaranteeing the rights of English language learners and bilingual education; Asian-American college students who in 1967–1969 organized with Black, Latina/o, and Native Americans at San Francisco State University in a multiethnic struggle to establish the first ethnic studies program in the nation, united under the banner of "Third World Liberation."

Weave the Historical Struggles, Culture, and Art of Asian-American Communities into Your Classroom

As part of a curriculum that is grounded in the lives of all of our students, teachers can highlight Asian-American history, culture, and art in their classroom practices to help Asian-American students develop not only positive self-identity, but also empathy between Asian Americans and other racial, cultural, or ethnic groups. Teachers might use novels by Carlos Bulosan, John Okada, Nora Okja Keller, Lê Thi Diem Thúy, Jessica Hagedorn, Jhumpa Lahiri, or Shawn Wong; poetry by Lawson Inada, Li-Young Li, Marilyn Chin, Nick Carbón, or Sesshu Foster; spoken word by Reggie Cablco, Ishle Park, Beau Sia, or I Was Born With Two Tongues; hip-hop music by Blues Scholars, Skim, Native Guns, Himalayan Project, or Kuttin Kandl; and history texts by Ron Takaki, Sucheng Chan, Peter Kwong, or Gary Okihiro.

When it comes to dealing with Asian Americans in education, it is all too common for people to ask, "What's wrong with the Myth of the Model Minority? isn't it a positive stereotype?" What many miss is that there are no "positive" stereotypes, because by believing in a "positive" stereotype, as, admittedly, even many Asian Americans do, we ultimately give credence to an entire way of thinking about race and culture, one that upholds the stereotypic racial and cultural inferiority of African Americans and Latina/os and maintains white supremacy.

The Myth of the Model Minority not only does a disservice to Asian-American diversity and identity, it serves to justify an entire system of race and class Inequality. It is perhaps for this reason, above all else, that the Myth of the Model Minority needs to be unmasked in our classrooms and used to challenge the legacies of racism and other forms of inequality that exist in our schools and society today.

Asian American Educational Achievements: A Phenomenon in Search of an Explanation

Stanley Sue and Sumie Okazaki

Great concern has been expressed over the educational achievements of American students in general and of ethnic minority students in particular. In 1984, Skinner wrote an article entitled "The Shame of American Education." Skinner's article lamented the educational mediocrity of American schools in terms of student achievements, motivational levels, and learning. Spence (1985), in her American Psychological Association Presidential Address, also noted the lack of excellence in schools, especially in fostering the learning of math and science. Indeed, there has been growing concern that Americans are falling behind students from other countries in educational achievements. The problems are particularly apparent in the schooling of ethnic minority students, such as Blacks, Hispanics, and American Indians, who show lower levels of educational attainments, grades, graduation rates, and school persistence (see California State Department of Education, 1986).

In ethnic minority research, one of the most remarkable phenomena has been the high educational achievements demonstrated by some Asian American groups over the last four decades. Although Asian Americans have been subjected to similar prejudice and discriminatory practices encountered by other ethnic minority groups, their educational attainments have been increasing. In this article we examine the achievements and two of the major explanations that have been proposed for the achievements of Asian Americans, involving possible hereditary or cultural advantages. The topic, of course, is highly controversial. Genetic explanations for racial or ethnic group differences in intelligence and achievements have generated intense debates. Even attributing Asian American achievements to cultural factors can result in disputes involving cultural "superiority" or deficits.

From the very outset, let us make four points. First, as a group, Asian Americans do demonstrate exceptional achievement patterns. However, Asian Americans represent a heterogeneous group with marked within- and between-group variations in a number of characteristics (Barringer, Takeuchi, & Xenos, 1990; Sue & Abe, 1988). We also know that the high achievement levels must be tempered. Asian Americans show not only high educational attainments but relatively higher proportions of individuals with no education what-soever compared with Whites and ethnic minority groups (Sue & Padilla, 1986). Second, although there is growing interest in Asian American achievements, research findings have not been able to shed much light on the factors that account for the achievement levels. This fact is caused in part by the lack of research on the phenomenon and by the failure to clearly devise adequate or critical tests. Third, in the search for factors that influence achievement levels, single explanations cannot adequately account for the observed performance patterns. Thus, research on heredity, culture, child-rearing practices, educational experiences, and personality, among other topics, has yielded interesting but inconclusive results. Fourth, explanations for Asian American achievements must incorporate what we call *relative functionalism*. Although cultural explanations propose that achievement is a result of Asian cultural values that extol the virtues of education, or of cultural practices that maximize skills in gaining education, the concept of relative functionalism also considers the problems of achieving in noneducational types of endeavors—those that are not a clear and direct outcome of educational performance. Perceived limitations in mobility in these endeavors increase the relative value or function of education as a means of achieving success.

Achievement Levels

In recent years, a number of popular magazines have portrayed Asian Americans as extraordinary achievers: *U.S. News and World Report* (Asian Americans: Are They, 1984); *Newsweek* (A Formula for Success, 1984): *New York Times* (Why Asians Are Going, 1986); *Chronicle of Higher Education* (Asian Students Fear, 1986); *Los Angeles Times Magazine* (When Being Best, 1987); *Time* (The New Whiz Kids, 1987); *National Education Association Today* ("Whiz Kid" Image, 1988); and *Asian Week* (Probing Into, 1990). These periodicals have pointed to the high levels of educational attainments shown by Asian Americans and supported by empirical evidence.

As indicated in Table 14.1, Asians and Pacific-Islander Americans exceed the national average for high school and college graduates. The rate of graduation from colleges and universities are higher, whether men or women are considered or whether Asians are compared solely with

TABLE 14.1 Schooling Completed by Sex and Race/Ethnicity for Persons 25 Years or Older, 1980

Race/ethnicity	High School Graduates (%)		4 + Years College Completed (%)	
	Men	Women	Men	Women
White	69.6	68.1	21.3	13.3
Black	50.8	51.5	8.4	8.3
Hispanic	45.4	42.7	9.4	6.0
AI/Alaskan	57.0	54.1	9.2	6.3
Asian/PI	78.8	71.4	39.8	27.0
Chinese	75.2	67.4	43.8	29.5
Filipino	73.1	67.4	32.2	29.5
Japanese	84.2	79.5	35.2	19.7
Korean	90.0	70.6	52.4	22.0
Asian Indian	88.8	71.5	68.5	35.5
Vietnamese	71.3	53.6	18.2	7.9

Note: AI/Alaskan = American Indian/Alaskan Native; Asian/PI = Asian/Pacific Islander. Bureau of the Census (1983, 1984).

Whites (Bureau of Census, 1983, 1984). Other indicators such as measures of pursuit of higher education and persistence also reveal a strong involvement in education. For example, 86% of Asian Americans versus 64% of Whites are found in some kind of higher education program, two years after high school graduation; and for those who entered a four-year university, 86% of Asian Americans stayed the following year, compared with 75% for Whites, 71% for Blacks, and 66% for Hispanics (Peng, 1988). Within the University of California system, which enrolls the largest number of Asians in the United States, fully 26% of Asian American high school students (not including foreign students) in 1985 qualified for entry, whereas only 13% of non-Asian students did. Asians also had the highest proportion of students graduating within five years of entry: 63% compared with 61% for Whites, 43% for Blacks, 50% for Hispanics, and 46% for American Indians. These figures do not include foreign students. The high levels of educational achievements can also be seen in reports from the College Board. College-bound Asian American seniors (about 10% of them were foreign students) receive superior high school grades and consistently demonstrate higher Scholastic Aptitude Test scores on the mathematics (SAT-M) subscores, but lower English verbal (SAT-V) subscores than do White or all non-Asian students. For example, in 1989, Asian Americans achieved average scores of 409 on the SAT-V and 525 on the SAT-M compared with scores of 427 on the SAT-V and 476 on the SAT-M for all other students. The high school grade point average of Asian American students was also higher than those of all other students, 3.25 versus 3.08 (College Board, 1989). (For all students, women had slightly lower SAT scores than did men, but they had superior high school grades.) Hsia (1988) noted high achievements not only in these scores but also among the finalists and winners in the National Merit Scholarship Program, Presidential Scholars, and Westinghouse Science Talent Search Program. The evidence for high educational attainments is quite convergent.

Explanations for the Achievement Patterns

Is it possible to find a simple or parsimonious explanation for the achievement levels of Asian Americans? For example, we know that educational achievements of individuals are directly related to the social class of parents (Jencks, Crouse, & Mueser, 1983). Perhaps Asian Americans are "advantaged" in terms of socioeconomic standing and provide their children with special resources and opportunities. There is no strong evidence that this can explain the racial or ethnic differences. In a report by Arbeiter (1984) on college-bound seniors, the median parental income of Asian Americans was lower than that of Whites, $25,400 and $32,900, respectively; the educational attainments of the parents were comparable. Yet, Asian Americans were found to have higher high school grades and SAT-M scores than did Whites.

Perhaps some of the educational achievements can be accounted for by the inclusion of foreign students among the Asian Americans or by the inclusion of Asian immigrants who already have high levels of education and subsequently become naturalized American citizens or permanent residents. The available evidence does not support this possibility. Using data from the 1980 U.S. Census, Kan and Liu (1986) compared the percentage of native- and foreign-born individuals who had completed four years of college. Although there was a tendency for foreign-born individuals to have higher educational levels, perhaps because of immigration policies favoring the educated, American-born Asians exceeded American-born Whites in the proportion of those with four years of college education. Whites, 18%; Chinese, 42%; Japanese, 27%; and Koreans, 27%. Filipinos (15%) and Asian Indians (13%) born in the United States had somewhat lower percentages than did Whites.

Heredity

Is it possible that Asians are innately superior to Whites in intelligence? Consensus exists that the heritability of intelligence is high (Vernon, 1982). However, to fully address this question, it is necessary to demonstrate that Asian Americans are higher not only in educational attainments but also in intelligence and cognitive functioning. Unfortunately, few studies have compared these groups on intelligence measures. After examining studies on IQ test performances, Sowell (1978) concluded that Chinese and Japanese Americans equal or exceed the national average. In a review of intellectual test results for Chinese and Japanese Americans, Vernon also argued that these two groups were superior. However, sample sizes for the reviewed studies were small, and estimates were based on performance rather than on verbal tests, inasmuch as English is not the first language for many Asian Americans—a major limitation in making ethnic comparisons.

Because only small samples of Asian Americans are available, investigators have examined the question of racial differences in intelligence by studying overseas, or foreign, Asians. In 1977, Lynn calculated the mean IQ of Japanese in Japan from standardization studies of the Wechsler (1949, 1955) tests in Japan. Using only the performance subtests, he found that at every age level the Japanese children outperformed the Americans. He discounted other explanations such as test bias and environmental advantage. Lynn (1977) reasoned that because the tests were developed in the United States, it is unlikely that they would be biased in favor of the Japanese. Furthermore, at the time Japanese had lower per capita income than did Americans Lynn concluded that heredity plays an important role in explaining the group differences. The conclusion was refuted by other investigators, especially Flynn (1982), who reanalyzed Lynn's data. He criticized Lynn for a variety of reasons, but particularly for not taking into account the yearly average gains in IQ that have occurred; the American norms used to compare with Japanese performances were established several years earlier. In addition, Flynn noted that Lynn vacillated between using Whites and all Americans (Whites and other ethnic minority Americans) as the standard by which to compare Japanese performances. By correcting for these factors, Flynn found little differences in IQ performance between Americans and Japanese. The debate between the two investigators has continued (see Flynn, 1987; Lynn, 1987). It has highlighted the methodological and conceptual problems in cross-national studies of intelligence and has revived the controversies regarding the meaning of intelligence, methods to estimate intelligence, and validity of instruments. In view of the problems, the hereditary perspective has received little empirical support.

The most extensive work on cross-national comparisons in intelligence has been conducted by Harold Stevenson and his colleagues (Stevenson & Azuma, 1983; Stevenson, Lee, & Stigler, 1986; Stevenson et al., 1985; Uttal, Lummis, & Stevenson, 1988). Stevenson et al. believe that Lynn failed to take into account the fact that the Japanese samples tended to have higher socioeconomic standing and a higher representation of urban than rural children than did the American samples from which the norms were constructed. Stevenson wanted to use a direct approach to comparing cognitive abilities. First- and fifth-graders in Japan, Taiwan, and United States were carefully selected and matched on demographic variables. Cognitive measures—verbal and performance tests—were devised with considerable attention to task equivalence and appropriateness for the different cultures and languages. Achievement tests for mathematics and reading were also constructed. Reliability for the measures was found to be generally good. Results on the cognitive measures revealed a few group differences on subtests, but no overall difference in intelligence. Distribution and variability of scores were similar for each sample. On mathematics achievement tests, Chinese performed well, whereas Americans had relatively low scores.

Cognitive performance was a fairly good predictor of mathematics achievement scores but not of verbal scores. There were no general differences in cognitive functioning between the samples, and superiority of Asians in math was not attributable to higher levels of cognitive functioning among the Asian samples. Obviously, group differences in complex characteristics or behaviors such as intelligence may be attributed to the interaction of innate characteristics, cultural roots, and other environmental conditions (Greenfield & Childs, in press), but the hypothesis that Asians are genetically superior in intelligence would appear to be refuted by empirical data.

Culture

The other major explanation for the achievements of Asian Americans is cultural in nature. Cultural institutions, such as schools, may affect learning and performance. For example, in their extensive observations in the three societies, Stevenson, Lee, and Stigler (1986) found that U.S. schools spent less time on academic activities, U.S. teachers imparted less information, and there was less emphasis on homework in U.S. than in Chinese or Japanese schools. However, in explaining the achievements of Asian Americans, differences in school experiences cannot fully account for the high achievement levels of Asian Americans, especially those born and educated in this country.

The most popular cultural view is that Asian family values and socialization experiences emphasize the need to succeed educationally. Largely on the basis of anecdotal and observational evidence rather than on empirical findings, investigators have identified the following values or practices in Asian families that may promote educational achievements: demands and expectations for achievement and upward mobility, induction of guilt about parental sacrifices and the need to fulfill obligations, respect for education, social comparisons with other Asian-American families in terms of educational success, and obedience to elders such as teachers. From structured interviews with Asian American students, Mordkowitz and Ginsburg (1987) provided anecdotal support for a cultural interpretation involving family socialization for high achievements. The students reported that their families emphasized educational accomplishments, held high expectations for achievements, controlled the behaviors of the students, and considered schooling very important. Such anecdotal evidence about Asian culture and socialization practices must be tempered. Culture is a concept that has been used to explain all phenomena, but one that is difficult to define and to test.

A cultural interpretation proposes that socialization patterns and institutional practices within a culture can aid, be irrelevant to, or hinder educational pursuits. Hard work, respect for education, and the motivation to become educated, among other traits, foster academic success. In the cultural model, the research task is to identify relevant cultural values and practices and correlate them with educational attainments. Three implications are generated by the model, as shown in Table 14.2. First, cultural factors (e.g., child-rearing practices, and socialization experiences characteristic of the cultural group) should correlate strongly with achievement levels. Second, with increased acculturation to mainstream American values (and extinction of Asian cultural values), achievement levels should diminish. Third, to improve educational attainments for all groups, Americans should selectively adopt certain Asian cultural values. Certainly, the American business community has explored alternative corporate practices, often modeling after the Japanese, who are perceived as being successful economic and business entrepreneurs.

Despite much anecdotal speculation, few rigorous studies have tested the cultural thesis, and available research provides little support. In examining possible cultural factors in achievements,

TABLE 14.2 Contrasting the Cultural and Relative Functionalism Perspectives	
Culture	**Relative Functionalism**
Assumptions and predictions	
Cultural values can aid, be irrelevant to, or hinder educational pursuits. Asian American values foster educational achievements. Asian cultural values are directly related to educational achievements. With increased acculturation, educational achievements decline.	Asian Americans experience and receive limited mobility in noneducational areas of success. The greater the limitations in noneducational areas the more salient education becomes as a means for mobility.
Research tasks	
Identify relevant cultural values and correlate with educational achievement over time.	Examine perceptions of mobility in noneducational areas; correlate perceptions with educational pursuits and priorities.
Societal implications	
Inculcate in others those Asian American values that facilitate educational achievements.	In addition to cultural values, the status and situation of Asians in American society must be studied

Note: The relative functionalism perspective does not disagree with the assumptions, tasks, and implications of the cultural thesis. It simply adds another dimension to explain the achievements of Asian Americans.

Dornbusch and colleagues (Dornbusch, Prescott, & Ritter, 1987; Dornbusch, Ritter, Leiderman, Roberts, & Fraleigh, 1987; Ritter & Dornbusch, 1989) have recently reported on their ongoing investigations of thousands of high school students in California, including one of the largest population of Asian Americans ever surveyed. The project investigated the relation between family variables and academic achievement for various ethnic minority groups. Several interesting findings that have relevance for our discussion emerged from the rich data collected. First, Asian American students exhibited the highest grade point average among all groups, including Blacks, Latinos, Whites, and others. Second, on the basis of the responses to the questionnaires, students from the ethnic groups were compared on the type of family in which they had been reared: Parental communication patterns that foster unquestioning obedience to parents (authoritarian style), freedom for the child to choose what to do with minimal parental involvement (permissive), and expectations for mature behavior and encouragement of open two-way communications between parents and children (authoritative). Asian American students came from families high on authoritarian and permissive and low on authoritative characteristics, the opposite of White students. Their parents also had the lowest level of parental involvement among the groups studied. Third, for all groups and irrespective of social class, authoritarianism and permissiveness were inversely related, whereas parental involvement was directly related to academic achievements. (Parenting style, however, was a weaker predictor of grades for Asians than for Whites.) Thus, the very characteristics associated with the Asian American group predicted low academic achievements for all groups; yet, Asian American students had higher levels of academic achievements. The results suggest that although parenting styles may account for within-group achievement levels for Asian Americans, they fail to explain between-group differences (i.e., between Asian Americans and the other groups). The findings do not support the cultural hypothesis that Asian Americans differ from other groups in achievements because of differences in upbringing. Although ethnic differences in parenting styles do exist, they fail to account for the observed ethnic differences in achievements.

Other variables examined by the investigators did not reveal group differences. Asian American responses were not significantly different from the other groups on reasons cited for working hard, parental pressures for achievement, need for making parents proud, not embarrassing family, and sacrifices made by the family for educational pursuits, variables that have often been used and supported by anecdotal examples to explain Asian achievements. Only on one response was there a significant group difference: Asian Americans were more likely to believe that success in life has to do with the things studied in school. This belief was directly related to high school grades. The inability to find variables that could explain the success of Asian American students led the investigators to conclude that "Something associated with being Asian is having a positive impact on school performance independent of the family process variables that may work so well in predicting performance among Whites" (Ritter & Dornbusch, 1989, p. 7).

The findings, of course, do not invalidate a cultural explanation. Perhaps other family or socialization variables are important, singly or in combination, and more studies should be conducted. However, the difficulty in finding cultural factors that strongly correlate with Asian American achievements and that can serve as an explanation for differential achievement patterns is troublesome for such a widely held thesis. It is not that "culture" is unimportant. If one excludes genetic factors as a significant determinant of the higher levels of achievement attained by Asian Americans, then some features of the culture are likely to play an important role. Because not all cultural differences will be germane, the challenge is to determine those features that are relevant to educational achievement for that culture. The evidence suggests that proximal values such as the importance of study and working hard, rather than distal values and behaviors such as socialization practices, may be important predictors of achievement. Moreover, cultural values do not operate in a vacuum. By focusing on Asian cultural as well as hereditary explanations, important contextual factors in the larger society are ignored. We propose that cultural values are weakly related to achievement, inasmuch as cultural values are often too global, or distal to achievements. A better model would posit that cultural values or socialization patterns affect a mediator (a more proximal variable such as effort or motivation), which is likely to show a stronger correlation with achievements. The mediator is also influenced by other variables, besides culture, such as opportunities for advancement in other areas of life.

Relative Functionalism

The academic achievements of Asian Americans cannot be solely attributed to Asian cultural values. Rather, as for other ethnic minority groups, their behavioral patterns, including achievements, are a product of cultural values (i.e., ethnicity) and status in society (minority group standing). Using the notion of relative functionalism, we believe that the educational attainments of Asian Americans are highly influenced by the opportunities present for upward mobility, not only in educational endeavors but also in noneducational areas. Noneducational areas include career activities such as leadership, entertainment, sports, politics, and so forth, in which education does not directly lead to the position. To the extent that mobility is limited in noneducational avenues, education becomes increasingly salient as a means of mobility. That is, education is increasingly functional as a means for mobility when other avenues are blocked. Several propositions are apparent. First, similar to the cultural explanation, relative functionalism assumes that there is in any particular group a drive for upward mobility and that cultural values and practices can affect educational attainments. Second, when opportunities for upward mobility are limited or are perceived to be limited in other areas, educational achievements should increase. This is particularly true with groups that are culturally oriented toward education and have experienced academic success. Third, trying to change American educational values and practices in the direction of Asian values may result in only small increments in educational attainments, inasmuch as mainstream Americans have other avenues of mobility.

Table 14.2 contrasts the assumptions made by the cultural and relative functionalism perspectives. In the cultural interpretation, investigators traditionally assume that some ethnic groups have cultural values that match or fit the society in which they live. For example, in the classic book *Assimilation in American Life*, Milton Gordon (1964) argued that the extraordinary achievements of Jews in this country can primarily be explained by cultural, middle-class values such as thrift, sobriety, ambition, and ability to delay immediate gratification for long-range goals. Sue and Kitano (1973) have also found that many social scientists attribute the educational success of Chinese and Japanese Americans to cultural values that promote upward mobility in this country—values that emphasize hard work, family cohesion, patience, and thrift. However, many Asian values such as emphasis on the collective rather than on the individual, hierarchical role structures rather than egalitarian relationships, and respect for authority are not fully consistent with White, middle-class values (Hirschman & Wong, 1986). Another problem with the cultural explanation is that cultural values are not necessarily predictive of educational attainments. As noted by Ogbu and Matute-Bianchi (1986), the Chinese in China, presently and in the past, have not shown relatively high rates of educational attainments and literacy. This has led investigators to question why children of Chinese peasants do so well in American schools in contrast to their peers in China. Indeed, in mainland China, where intellectuals are under increased scrutiny, receive inadequate salaries, and find other jobs more financially rewarding, we see a decline in the proportion of students applying for admission into graduate programs in that country.

As argued by Steinberg (1981), cultural values interact with conditions in any particular society. In the case of Jews, he noted that

> In terms of their European background, Jews were especially well equipped to take advantage of the opportunities they found in America. Had Jews immigrated to an industrial society without industrial skills, as did most other immigrants, their rich cultural heritage would have counted for little. Indeed, a parallel situation exists today in Israel, where Jews immigrating from underdeveloped countries in North Africa typically lack the occupational and educational advantages of the earlier settlers, and despite the fact that all share the same basic religion, the recent immigrants find themselves concentrated at the bottom of Israeli society. Thus, in large measure Jewish success in America was a matter of historical timing. That is to say, there was a fortuitous match between the experience and skills of Jewish immigrants, on the one hand, and the manpower needs and opportunity structures, on the other. It is this remarkable convergence of factors that resulted in an unusual record of success. (p. 103)

In the case of Chinese and Japanese Americans, Suzuki (1977) has also taken issue with a cultural interpretation of their success. Although acknowledging that respect for education is a cultural value among these two groups, he also advanced the proposition that Asian Americans came to pursue education because of their status as a minority group. Many labor unions discriminated against Asians, refusing them union membership during the 1940s. In addition, technological advancements and an expanding economy after World War II required educated professionals and white-collar employees. Thus, one development limited occupational opportunities for manual laborers and the other placed a premium on professional-technical skills requiring advanced education. In such a situation, mobility through education took increased significance, above and beyond the contributions of Asian cultural values. Using a similar argument, Connor (1975) attributed the high educational attainments of Japanese Americans to the denial of opportunities to participate in social and other extracurricular school activities in the pre-World War II period. This also set the stage for emphasizing educational achievements.

For relative functionalism to be a viable explanation, at least three issues must be addressed. First, relative functionalism and the cultural thesis would predict decreasing educational achievements with acculturation of Asian Americans. However, each differs in the factors that account for decrements in performance. One proposes that increased opportunities for mobility make education a less preferred avenue for mobility, whereas the other assumes that a loss of cultural values is responsible for decreased achievement levels. Is there evidence that opportunities for mobility influence achievements? Second, relative functionalism assumes that limitations in mobility in noneducational endeavors influences educational levels. Is it possible that educational values and attainments affect interest or performance in noneducational means of mobility? Third, is there evidence that Asian Americans perceive or experience limitations in non-educational avenues for mobility?

Unfortunately, critical tests comparing the cultural and relative functionalism models have not been conducted. Dornbusch et al. (1987) and Ritter and Dornbusch (1989) have found that Asian American achievement levels tend to be inversely related to the number of generations in the United States, apparently supporting a cultural interpretation (i.e., decreased maintenance of Asian cultural values results in lower academic grades). With increased acculturation, it has been assumed that Asian values of hard work, discipline, and respect for education have eroded. However, an inverse relation between acculturation to American values and academic achievements is not incompatible with relative functionalism. Increased acculturation also results in more avenues for mobility. For example, Sue and Zane (1985) found that recent Chinese immigrants were significantly more likely than were acculturated Chinese to agree with the statement that their choices of academic majors were influenced by their English skills. These students had low English proficiency, averaging in the 18th percentile on the verbal portion of the Scholastic Aptitude Test. They confined their selection of majors to fields requiring quantitative skills (e.g., mathematics and computer sciences) rather those requiring more sophisticated English proficiency (e.g., social sciences and humanities). Increased English proficiency is likely to be related to knowledge of American society and ways of getting ahead, which may ultimately decrease the relative value of education as a means of mobility. In addition, it is highly likely that the recent immigrants perceive career limitations and, therefore, avoid those fields such as the social sciences and humanities, in which English facility and interpersonal skills specific to American society are needed. Mathematics and sciences are more likely to emphasize technical competence. Here we have an example of directing educational pursuits because of perceived limitations in certain career areas.

With respect to the other questions involving cause-effect (Do educational achievements limit interest or pursuit of noneducational endeavors, or do limitations in these endeavors influence educational pursuits?) and perceptions of limitations in noneducational avenues, no studies have directly examined the issues. Obviously, if Asian Americans perform well in education and consequently assume professional and technical positions, they may be more motivated to continue this pattern of mobility. They may even deemphasize activities in such areas as sports, the entertainment industry, and political positions because they have been successful in securing education-based careers. However, there is evidence from various sources that many Asian Americans perceive limitations in their career choices or upward mobility because of English language skills or social discrimination (Sue, Sue, Zane, & Wong, 1985). In a survey of Asian American students at the University of California, Berkeley, Ong (1976) found that respondents cited as reasons for obtaining an education (a) ability to make money, increasing the chances for a better job, and (b) the difficulty in finding other avenues for advancement because of discrimination. Hirschman and Wong (1986) have argued that "Education was a channel for the social mobility of Asians, partly because they were frozen out of some sectors of the economy" (p. 23). Hearings sponsored by the U.S. Commission on Civil Rights (1980) resulted in testimonies that documented restrictions in occupational mobility, especially for those without much education (Pian, 1980; Wang, 1980). The point is that education is perceived as a viable means for mobility, in view of limitations for success in other areas. Thus Asian Americans expend great efforts in attaining an education because they have been successful and also because without a strong educational background, their mobility is limited. Research strategies that focus on the relation between cultural values and education provide an incomplete picture.

If Asian Americans encounter and perceive restrictions in noneducational areas of mobility, as do other ethnic minority groups such as Blacks and Latinos, why do these other ethnic groups fail to adopt education as a means of mobility? Addressing this question—and that poses a real challenge—is beyond the scope of this article. It is worth nothing that ethnic minority groups have different cultural backgrounds and different historical and contemporary experiences in the United States. Precisely because of the importance of the interaction between culture and minority group status, we maintain that cultural interpretations of the success of Asian Americans are inadequate.

More specifically, Ogbu and Matute-Bianchi (1986) have proposed that individuals develop folk theories of success (e.g., "If I get a good education, I will succeed in getting a good job and maintain a high standard of living" or "Even if I get a good education, people will discriminate against me"). Factors such as cultural values, discrimination, past success, beliefs in self-efficacy, availability of successful role models, and so on, influence the folk theories. Mickelson (1990) has found that although Blacks hold favorable *abstract* attitudes concerning the value of education, they are less likely than Whites to believe in the value of education in their own lives. As mentioned previously, Ritter and Dornbusch (1987) found that Asian Americans tended to believe that success in life has to do with the things studied in school. The folk theory for Asian Americans may be, "If I study hard, I can succeed, *and* education is the best way to succeed."

Conclusions

In trying to explain the educational success of Asian Americans, the tendency has been to compare and contrast genetic and cultural explanations. Because the evidence does not support a genetic interpretation, many have simply assumed that Asian cultural values, beliefs, and practices are responsible for their academic achievements. In contrast, we have suggested that the effects of culture have been confounded with the consequences of our society. Although culture is certainly an important factor in achievements, education has been functional for upward mobility, especially when participation in other arenas, such as sports, entertainment, and politics, has been difficult. One could argue that educational success, increased numbers of educated Asian role models, and limitations in mobility in other areas contribute to performance, above and beyond that which can be predicted from Asian cultural values.

Several implications can be drawn from our analysis. First, studies that examine the relation between cultural values and achievements may yield low correlations, inasmuch as achievement patterns are influenced by many factors. These factors may influence mediators of achievement such as motivation and effort. Second, attention should be paid to individual differences within the Asian populations. Although cross-national studies may provide significant insights for studies of Asian Americans, it should be recognized that the social context of overseas Asian and Asian Americans differs quite dramatically, particularly in majority-minority group status and in societal values and practices. Differences among Asian Americans are also important to consider. For example, Sue and Abe (1988) examined predictors of educational performance among thousands of Asian American and White students. Regression equations significantly differed not only between Asian Americans and Whites but between some of the different Asian groups (Chinese, Japanese, Koreans, Filipinos, and East Indians/Pakistanis). Dornbusch et al. (1987) have also found important differences in school acculturation and achievement patterns among various Asian American groups. Third, in predicting educational achievements, investigations into perceptions, expectancies, and beliefs over opportunities for other areas of mobility may be important. Perhaps the greatest problem in the research is the failure to study the phenomenon of mobility in general, because educational attainments may be strongly influenced by these other avenues for mobility. Finally, some have objected to the notion that Asian Americans are a "minority" group, precisely because they have become well educated. From our perspective, Asian Americans are indeed a minority group and their achievements can be fully understood only if attention is paid to their experiences in society.

References

Arbeiter, S. (1984). *Profiles. college-bound seniors, 1984.* New York: College Entrance Examination Board.

Asian Americans: Are they making the grade? (1984, April 2). *U.S. News and World Report*, pp. 41–47.

Asian students fear top colleges use quota systems. (1986, November 19). *Chronicle of Higher Education*, pp. 1, 34–36.

Barringer, H.R., Takeuchi, D. T., & Xenos, P.C. (1990). Education, occupational prestige and income of Asian Americans: Evidence from the 1980 Census. *Sociology of Education, 63*, 27–43.

Bureau of the Census. (1983). *Asian and Pacific Islander population by state: 1980 Census of population* (Supplementary report PC80-1-C). Washington, DC: U.S. Department of Commerce.

Bureau of the Census. (1984). *Detailed population characteristics: 1980 Census of population* (PC80-1-D1-A). Washington, DC: U.S. Department of Commerce.

California State Department of Education. (Ed.). (1986). *Beyond language: Social and cultural factors in schooling language minority students*. Los Angeles: California State Department of Education, Evaluation, Dissemination, and Assessment Center.

College Board. (1989). *College-bound seniors: 1989 SAT profile*. New York: College Entrance Examination Board.

Connor, J.W. (1975). Changing trends in Japanese American academic achievement. *Journal of Ethnic Studies, 2*, 95–98.

Dornbusch, S. M., Prescott, B. L., & Ritter, P. L. (1987, April). *The relation of high school academic performance and student effort to language use and recency of migration among Asian-and Pacific-Americans*. Paper presented at the meeting of the American Educational Research Association, Washington, DC.

Dornbusch, S. M., Ritter, P. L., Leiderman, P. H., Roberts, D. F., & Fraleigh, M. J. (1987). The relation of parenting style to adolescent school performance. *Child Development, 55*, 1244–1257.

Flynn, J. R. (1982). Lynn, the Japanese, and environmentalism. *Bulletin of the British Psychological Society, 35*, 409–413.

Flynn, J. R. (1987). The rise and fall of Japanese IQ. *Bulletin of the British Psychological Society, 40,* 459–464.

A formula for success. (1984, April 23). *Newsweek,* pp. 77–78.

Gordon, M. (1964). *Assimilation in American life.* New York: Oxford University Press.

Greenfield, P., & Childs, C. P. (1991). Developmental continuity in bio-cultural context. In R. Cohen & A. Siegel (Eds.), *Context and development.* Hillsdale, NJ: Erlbaum.

Hirschman, C., & Wong, M.G. (1986). The extraordinary educational attainment of Asian Americans: A search for historical evidence and explanations. *Social Forces, 65,* 1–27.

Hsia, J. (1988). Limits on affirmative action: Asian American access to higher education. *Educational Policy, 2,* 117–136.

Jencks, C., Crouse, J., & Mueser, P. (1983). The Wisconsin model of status attainment: A national replication with improved measures of ability and aspirations. *Sociology of Education, 56,* 3–19.

Kan, S. H., & Liu, W. T. (1986). The educational status of Asian Americans: An update from the 1980 Census. *P/AAMHRC Research Review, 5 (3/4),* 21–24.

Lynn, R. (1977). The intelligence of the Japanese. *Bulletin of the British Psychological Society, 30,* 69–72.

Lynn, R. (1987). Japan: Land of the rising IQ. A reply to Flynn. *Bulletin of the British Psychological Society, 40,* 464–468.

Mickelson, R. A. (1990). The attitude-achievement paradox among Black adolescents. *Sociology of Education, 63,* 44–61.

Mordkowitz, E. R., & Ginsberg, H. P. (1987). Early academic socialization of successful Asian American college students. *Quarterly Newsletter of the Laboratory of Comparative Human Cognition, 9,* 85–91.

The new whiz kids. (1987, August 31). *Time* pp. 42–51.

Ogbu, J. U., & Matute-Bianchi, M. E. (1986). Understanding sociocultural factors: Knowledge, identity, and school adjustment. In California State Department of Education (Ed.), *Beyond language: Social and cultural factors in schooling language minority students* (pp. 73–142). Los Angeles: California State Department of Education, Evaluation. Dissemination, and Assessment Center.

Ong, C. (1976). *The educational attainment of the Chinese in America.* Unpublished manuscript, University of California, Berkeley, Department of Anthropology.

Peng, S. (1988, April). Attainment status of Asian Americans in higher education. Paper presented at the National Association for Asian and Pacific American Education (NAAPE) Conference, Denver, CO.

Pian, C. (1980). Identification of issues. In U.S. Commission on Civil Rights (Ed.), *Civil rights issues of Asian and Pacific Americans: Myths and realities* (pp. 7–20). Washington DC: U.S. Government Printing Office.

Probing into the success of Asian American students. (1990, January 26). *Asian Week,* p. 7.

Ritter, P. L., & Dornbusch, S. M. (1989, March). *Ethnic variation in family influences on academic achievement.* Paper presented at the American Educational Research Association Meeting, San Francisco.

Skinner, B. F. (1984). The shame of American education. *American Psychologist, 39,* 947–955.

Sowell, T. (1978). (Ed.) *Essay and data on American ethnic groups.* Washington, DC: Urban Institute.

Spence, J. T. (1985). Achievement American style: The rewards and costs of individualism. *American Psychologist, 40,* 1285–1295.

Steinberg, A. (1981). *The ethnic myth: Race, ethnicity, and class in America.* Boston: Beacon Press.

Stevenson, H. W., & Azuma, H. (1983). IQ in Japan and the United States: Methodological problems in Lynn's analysis. *Nature, 306,* 291–292.

Stevenson, H. W., Lee, S., & Stigler, J. W. (1986). Mathematics achievement of Chinese, Japanese, and American children. *Science, 231,* 693–699.

Stevenson, H. W., Stigler, J. W., Lee, S., Lucker, G. W., Kitamura, S., & Hsu, C. (1985). Cognitive performance and academic achievement of Japanese, Chinese, and American children. *Child Development, 56,* 718–734.

Sue, S., & Abe, J. (1988). *Predictors of academic achievement among Asian American and White students* (Report No. 88–11). New York: College Entrance Examination Board.

Sue, S., & Kitano, H. H. L. (1973). Stereotypes as a measure of success. *Journal of Social Issues, 29*, 83–98.

Sue, S., & Padilla, A. (1986). Ethnic minority issues in the United States: Challenges for the educational system. In California State Department of Education (Ed.), *Beyond language: Social and cultural factors in schooling language minority students* (pp. 34–72). Los Angeles: California State Department of Education, Evaluation, Dissemination, and Assessment Center.

Sue, S., Sue, D. W., Zane, N., & Wong, H. Z. (1985). Where are the Asian American leaders and top executives? *P/AAMHRC Review, 4*, 13–15.

Sue, S., & Zane, N. (1985). Academic achievement and socioemotional adjustment among Chinese university students. *Journal of Counseling Psychology, 32*, 570–579.

Suzuki, R. H. (1977). Education and the socialization of Asian Americans: A revisionist analysis of the "model minority" thesis. *Amerasia Journal, 4*, 23–52.

U.S. Commission on Civil Rights. (Ed.). (1980). *Civil rights issues of Asian and Pacific Americans: Myths and realities*. Washington, DC: U.S. Government Printing Office.

Uttal, D. H., Lummis, M., & Stevenson, H. W. (1988). Low and high mathematics achievement in Japanese, Chinese, and American elementary-school children. *Developmental Psychology, 24*, 335–342.

Vernon, P. E. (1982). *The abilities and achievements of Orientals in North America*. New York: Academic Press.

Wang, L. C. (1980). Federal exclusionary policy. In U.S. Commission on Civil Rights (Ed.), *Civil rights issues of Asian and Pacific Americans: Myths and realities* (pp. 21–24). Washington, DC: U.S. Government Printing Office.

Wechsler, D. (1949). *Wechsler Intelligence Scale for Children*. New York: Psychological Corporation.

Wechsler, D. (1955). *Manual, Wechsler Adult Intelligence Scale*. New York: Psychological Corporation.

When being best isn't good enough. (1987, July 19). *Los Angeles Times Magazine*, pp. 22–28.

"Whiz kid" image masks problems of Asian Americans. (1988, March). *National Education Association Today*. pp. 14–15.

Why Asians are going to the head of the class. (1986, August 3). *New York Times*, pp. 18–32.

PART V   Media Portrayals and Stereotypes

Portrayals in Film and Television

Timothy P. Fong, Valerie Soe, and Allan Aquino

CHAPTER 15

Today's images of Asian Americans in popular culture have improved and provide more breadth than in the past. In earlier days popular images of Asians and Asian Americans were predominantly mediated by non-Asian studio executives and writers—as a consequence, Hollywood's earlier characterizations of Asians and Asian Americans were often quite negative and demeaning. Some of these images are still perpetuated today, and Asian American media watchers and critics continue to complain about racist stereotypes that emerge in popular culture. Many film scholars argue that Hollywood films and television programs are not merely harmless entertainment, but are reflective of race, class, and gender ideologies and pressing social and political concerns.[1]

Historical Images

Images of Asians in mainstream Hollywood motion pictures can be traced back to the mid-to-late 1800s when Asian migrants first arrived in large numbers to the United States.

Popular comic strips such as "The Yellow Kid" and "The Ting-Ling Kids" emerged in the 1890s and depicted racial caricatures of Chinese Americans for mass audiences. Throughout the ensuing decades, Asians were commonly portrayed in the press as the "Yellow Peril," an invasion of faceless and destructive Asiatics who would eventually overtake the nation and wreak social and economic havoc. The dominant ideology of Western superiority versus Eastern inferiority eventually led to the passage of the 1882 Chinese Exclusion Law, as well as a multitude of other anti-Asian legislation.

Silent films included early moving images of Asian Americans such as *Tsing Fu, the Yellow Devil* (1910), where the sinister Chinese wizard plots revenge against a white woman who rejects his lecherous intentions. The rise of Japan as a military and industrial power following the 1905 Russo-Japanese War was the inspiration for *The Japanese Investigation* (1909), which prominently featured the threat of U.S. involvement in an Asiatic war. For decades Hollywood films have consistently played on the theme of "Orientals" as the "other."

Encyclopedia of Asian American Issues Today, Vol. 2 (Editors Edith Wen-Chu Chen and Grace J. Yoo). "Portrayals in Film and Television" by Timothy Fong, Valerie Soe, and Allan Azuino. Copyright © 2010 by ABC-CLIO, LLC. Reproduced with permission of ABC-CLIO, LLC.

---

[1] Darrell Y. Hamamoto, *Monitored Peril: Asian Americans and the Politics of TV Representation* (Minneapolis: University of Minnesota Press, 1994), 3.

Yellowface

Popular Asian characters such as Charlie Chan and Fu Manchu were created by white writers and producers and usually portrayed by white actors grotesquely made up to look Asian. All of the Asian characters in Fu Manchu movies were played by non-Asian actors. The first two Charlie Chan movies hired Japanese American actors for the lead role, but as the films gained popularity, they were quickly replaced by white actors who colored their hair jet black and used scotch tape to alter the shape of their eyes.

This practice, commonly known as yellowface, entails non-Asian performers playing Asian characters. Yellowface is a variation on the term "blackface," the practice popular in the late nineteenth and early twentieth centuries of white performers darkening their faces in order to impersonate African Americans. As with blackface performers, actors in yellowface take on the most exaggerated and stereotypical attributes of the race they are imitating. In the case of Asians, this includes buck teeth, slanted eyes and accented English. Yellowface has a long tradition in Hollywood films. Its popularity is partly because of several factors, including overt racism and discrimination against Asian American performers. One of the main institutionalized causes of the use of yellowface was the United States Motion Picture Production Code of 1930, or the "Hays Code," Hollywood's self-censoring doctrine that forbade, among many other things, portrayals of miscegenation, or intimate relationships between performers of different races. Because of this, non-Asian actors could not be depicted in romantic relationships with Asian actors—when the plot of the film called for this aspect, non-Asian performers were cast as Asian characters in yellowface, with their eyes cosmetically masked, their skin darkened and their teeth made prominent with prosthetics.

In classic yellowface performances, Paul Muni and Louise Rainer, both Austrian Jews, played the lead roles in the epic *The Good Earth* (1937), the film adaptation of Pearl Buck's classic novel about heroic Chinese peasants. Other well-known actors played roles in yellowface that were simply not available to Asian Americans. For example, Katharine Hepburn played a feisty Chinese peasant woman in *Dragon Seed* (1941), and Marlon Brando played a Japanese interpreter in *Teahouse of the August Moon* (1956). Another famous yellowface character was Charlie Chan, depicted by non-Asians including Warner Oland, Sidney Toler, and Roland Winter in the *Charlie Chan* film series (1931–44). In *Breakfast at Tiffany's* (1961), Mickey Rooney plays perhaps the most infamous example of a yellowface role, as a Japanese photographer with thick glasses, squinty eyes, and buck teeth. *The Year of Living Dangerously* (1983), starring Mel Gibson and Sigourney Weaver also holds another notable yellowface performance, in which actress Linda Hunt plays Billy Kwan, a male Chinese-Australian photographer. Other well-respected actors who have performed in yellowface include Shirley MacLaine, Peter Sellers, Nicolas Cage, and Eddie Murphy, among others.

Television also has a famous example of yellowface in the series, *Kung Fu* (1972–1975). The program was originally conceived by Bruce Lee, who desperately wanted to play the lead role of a Shaolin priest who escapes China in the late nineteenth century after avenging the death of his mentor, and finds adventure wandering around the American West. It would have been the perfect vehicle for Lee to fully demonstrate his potent martial arts prowess in front of a national audience that wanted more after his debut in *The Green Hornet*. When *Kung Fu* eventually premiered on television, the starring role was given to actor David Carradine. In addition, the character was changed from Chinese to half-Chinese, half-white. Lee was terribly embittered by this rejection, and it was at this point he left the United States to make his mark in Hong Kong martial arts films.

Yellowface fell out of general practice by the 1990s, although recent films including *Grind-house* (2007), *Balls of Fury* (2007), and *I Now Pronounce You Chuck And Larry*, (2007) continue this unfortunate tradition. However, a more subtle form of yellowface, known as whitewashing, in which characters that are originally Asian are changed to white characters, took place with the casting of the film *21* (2008). Based on the best-selling book *Bringing Down the House*, the story focused on the MIT Blackjack Team that used sophisticated card-counting techniques to win thousands of dollars at casinos across the country. Most of the team members featured in the book were Asian American, but producers of *21* changed the ethnicity of these characters, including main character Jeff Ma, to white. Asian Americans protested the whitewashing of the characters but the producers were unapologetic, stating, "most of the film's actors would be white, with perhaps an Asian female." Similarly, the live-action version of the popular animated series *Avatar: The Last Airbender* (2010), which is set in Asia, was cast entirely with white leading actors, further prompting protest from the Asian American community. In response to the complaints, actor Jackson Rathbone stated, "I think it's one of those things where I pull my hair up, shave the sides, and I definitely need a tan. It's one of those things where, hopefully, the audience will suspend disbelief a little bit."[2] Though not as flagrantly offensive as classic yellowface performances, whitewashing continues decades-old practices of excluding and erasing Asian American roles from Hollywood screens.

Portrayals of Asian Men

Evil Villains

Asian American men have often been portrayed as evil villains, bad guys and enemy combatants. Typical representations include despotic, cruel villains such as Ming the Merciless, from the popular *Buck Rogers* film series (1939); Fu Manchu (*The Mask of Fu Manchu*, 1932), first popularized in Sax Rohmer's pulp fictions of the early 20th century; and the buck-toothed, fanatical Japanese kamikazes and enemy soldiers found in World War II films propaganda films from the United States. Popular media images of Asian males have historically been depicted as either uncontrollably lustful or completely asexual. Fu Manchu's lasciviousness toward white women was, of course, never directly acted upon on screen, but the threat was always there, which only served to enhance the most negative images of Asians and the Yellow Peril. On one hand, Fu Manchu possessed superhuman intellect and ambition, and on the other, he was subhuman in his immorality and ruthlessness.

These portrayals have continued in the last couple of decades. Chow Yun-Fat appeared in *Pirates of the Caribbean 3: At World's End* (2007) as Sao Feng, a Singaporean pirate described as "an unscrupulous and honour-less coward who will do anything to join with the winning, even if it means betraying his best friends." He wears a queue, a Fu-Manchu style mustache, and long, "mandarin" fingernails and meets his violent demise while attempting to rape the film's heroine, Elizabeth. When the film was released in China, ten minutes of footage of Sao Feng were cut from the film, presumably because its stereotypical nature was offensive to the Chinese people.[3]

---

[2] Larry Carroll, "'Twilight' Star Jackson Rathbone Hopes To 'Show His Range' In 'Last Airbender'," *MTV*, Jan. 15, 2009.

[3] "China Gives Bald Pirate the Chop," Associated Press, June 15, 2007, http://www.cnn.com/2007/SHOWBIZ/Movies/06/15/china.pirates.ap/index.html.

Jet Li also portrayed an evil villain character, in *The Mummy: Tomb of the Dragon Emperor* (2008), in which the martial arts superstar played Emperor Han, a malevolent resurrected mummy who "threatens to plunge the world into his merciless, unending service."

These characterizations perpetuate the stereotype of Asian men as inhuman killers bent on fanatical destruction, with an unnatural lust for white women and, in many cases, desiring world domination and the destruction of Western civilization. Such portrayals depict Asians as subhuman, perhaps as a justification for World War II atrocities such as Hiroshima and Nagasaki, and later conflicts such as the Korean and Vietnam wars.

Emasculated Males

In another recurring Hollywood stereotype, Asian American men are emasculated, sexless males who are clumsy rather than threatening in their attraction to white women. Charlie Chan, the cherubic and inscrutable Chinese American detective from Honolulu, originated in a series of novels by Earl Derr Biggers and quickly made it into the movie houses, with almost fifty Charlie Chan movies released between 1926 and 1949. Chan exemplified the completely asexual Asian male character. Although he was married and had a large family, the films only introduced two of his sons. Audiences never saw his wife and Chan was never enticed by other women nor were any women enticed by him.

This stereotype came to full fruition in the character of Long Duk Dong in John Hughes's teen comedy *Sixteen Candles* (1984). In this popular film, Gedde Watanabe portrayed a nerdy, socially inept, and decidedly unsexy Japanese exchange student nicknamed "The Donger," who uttered comical phrases such as "What's happenin', hot stuff?" and "No more yanky my wanky!" As Eric Nakamura, editor of *Giant Robot*, notes, "It's like every bad stereotype possible, loaded into one character."[4] Even virile Bruce Lee in his megahit *Enter the Dragon* (1972) was precluded from having any interest in women, unlike his white and black costars. Lee may have been one of the very few sexually chaste action heroes in Hollywood. A similar example can be found in Chow Yun-Fat's first Hollywood feature film, *The Replacement Killers* (1998), where at the end he says goodbye to his female costar, Mira Sorvino. In the theater version of the film, Chow touches Sorvino's face, and they both walk away in opposite directions, assuring no sexual tension or contact. In the alternative ending that is included in the DVD release of the film, Chow passionately kisses Sorvino before the two separate. As they walk away in opposite directions they both turn around and look longingly at each other, creating at least an image of sexual attraction, albeit unrequited.

Further enforcing this stereotype, *Fargo* (1996) included a scene where a nerdy Japanese American male made inappropriate romantic overtures to the main female character. Other iterations of the emasculated, sexless Asian American male appeared in *Anna and the King* (2000), in which the romance between the lead characters played by Jodie Foster and Chow Yun-Fat culminated in a chaste dance, and in *Romeo Must Die*, (2000), which concluded with leads Jet Li and Aaliyah, as the modern-day Romeo and Juliet, sharing not a kiss but a platonic embrace. In *Deuce Bigalow: European Gigolo* (2005), an Asian male prostitute further perpetuates the stereotype of the emasculated, poorly endowed Asian male, stating, "I take my three inches elsewhere!"

---

[4] Alison MacAdam, "Long Duk Dong: Last of the Hollywood Stereotypes?" *All Things Considered*, National Public Radio, March 24, 2008.

Even the most famous Asian American male on television, Lt. Sulu (George Takei), in the original *Star Trek* series (1966–1969), was an obvious sexless character. While all the primary male members on the starship *Enterprise* had intergalactic encounters with women—human and alien—Lt. Sulu was almost always left alone.

However, the Jackie Chan film, *The Medallion* (2003), does end with Chan and his female costar, Claire Forlani, running off together as a couple ready for the next fight. This was a genuine rarity for an Asian man in Hollywood.

Who is Harlemm Lee?

In the summer of 2003, Harlemm Lee (born Gerry Woo) won the national television talent show *FAME*. Aired on the NBC-TV network, *FAME*'s contestants gave live vocal performances on a weekly basis. Audience viewers telephoned their votes for who among the featured singers performed best; singers with the most votes would return to compete in the following week's broadcast. Lee, 35 at the time, had struggled for years in the recording industry, yet bested a number of his younger fellow competitors. Week after week, primetimes viewers voted for Lee and, as a result, he won a management deal from a top music manager, a year of training at the Debbie Allen Dance Academy, and free accommodations at the W Hotel in Los Angeles to help him launch his career. Soon after this victory, Lee would fall into obscurity.

By November 2003, Lee released his album, *Introducing Harlemm Lee*, which, despite positive reviews, moved only five hundred copies and was pulled from shelves because of low sales. In June 2004, Lee posted a message on his Web site thanking fans for his support, admitting his disappointment at the state of his post-*FAME* career. "I have been completely invisible since winning *FAME* and unable to capitalize from all my hard work and national exposure," he wrote. "If it weren't for my unemployment checks and my year-long stay at the W Hotel, I would be completely penniless and homeless." Lee stated that he was denied the most basic promotion and marketing resources, with justification given to him by industry executives was that his story was not "compelling enough." In his Web site message, Lee added "without [the industry's] machinery behind you, you will definitely not be seen or heard."

By contrast, Lee's story could not be more different (or as well known) as singer William Hung's. In January of 2004, Hung, then a 21-year-old engineering student from University of California–Berkeley, gained instant notoriety with his performance of the Ricky Martin song "She Bangs" for the enormously popular *American Idol* talent show. Accompanying his off-key vocals with an odd jig, Hung completed only the first chorus when judge Simon Cowell stopped him. After Hung questioned Cowell's intensely adamant disapproval, Cowell replied, "You can't sing, you can't dance, so what do you want me to say?"

With complete sincerity, Hung declared that he had no professional vocal training and had "no regrets at all." Perhaps it was in his grace in the face of his rejection that captured attention, but Hung became an instant comic pop star. He was featured in numerous television talk shows, news programs, commercials, music videos, and print articles; he has his own fan Web site, has given concerts across the U.S. and Asia, and has released three CDs.

Unlike Harlemm Lee, William Hung's first CD, *Inspiration*, sold more than 3,000 units on the day of its release. He has since sold tens of thousands more. According to Chi-hui Yang, director of the San Francisco International Asian American Film Festival, Hung's popularity was based upon his image: "What informs that kind of humor is something that is deeply rooted in the American depiction of Asian men as ineffective, effeminate, or wimpy, and I think William Hung fits right into it." Hung's popularity has persisted, much to the chagrin of many who view him as a racial caricature reflecting previous decades of stereotypes. Primary among these is the image of the asexual and buffoonish foreigner often exploited as a comic device—in Hung's case, a clumsy "oriental" with a discordant accent. "On the other hand," Yang continues, "someone like Harlemm Lee," who is enormously talented, has not gone very far [Hung] feeds back into the people with the marketing dollars and knowing what the American public wants to see or what is familiar."

—Timothy P. Fong and Allan Aquino

Servants and Sidekicks

One of the most common roles for Asian American males in Hollywood was as domestic servants to whites. Easily the most famous Chinese domestic servant was Victor Sen Yung, who was the character Hop Sing in the *Bonanza* series that ran for fourteen years (1959–1973). Even Bruce Lee got his start on television as the faithful houseboy Kato in the show *The Green Hornet* (1966–1967).

Drawing from the Charlie Chan stereotype, police detectives are another common role for Asian American males on television. A recent example is seen in the San Francisco—based show, *Nash Bridges* (1996–2001) starring Don Johnson, where Cary-Hiroyuki Tagawa had a reoccurring role as Lt. A. J. Shimamura. Except for Sammo Hung in *Martial Law* (1998–2000) and Pat Morita starring in his own short-lived series, *Ohara* (1987–1988), all Asian American detectives have played sidekick roles to white males. For example, Jack Soo as Sergeant Nick Yemana had a secondary role in the program *Barney Miller* (1975–1982). In the popular television show *Hawaii Five-0* (1968–1980), actors Jack Lord and James MacArthur led a group of Asian American detectives to solve crimes in the aloha state. Asian American actors Kam Fong and Zulu, among others, played silent background roles, rushing off when orders were given. In the series *Midnight Caller* (1988–1991), actor Dennis Dun played Billy Po, the assistant to the show's lead star, Jack Killian (Gary Cole), a radio talk show host who worked to solve crimes in his spare time. Although Dun's character was much more developed than the standard Asian detective sidekick, his role was clearly the helper to the hero.

Asian Actors in Hollywood

The best-known Asian actors in Hollywood all came to the United States following phenomenal success in Asia and nearly all are limited to martial arts/action hero roles. Of these, the most well-known are Jackie Chan, Chow Yun-Fat, and Jet Li. Chan was born in Hong Kong and was formally trained at the China Drama Academy, where he learned martial arts, acrobatics, singing, and acting. His breakthrough Hong Kong martial arts movie was *The New Fist of Fury* (1976), which was a remake of the original Bruce Lee classic of the same name. For the next two decades Chan made numerous action/comedy films in Asia, where he became widely popular; however, it wasn't until the Hong Kong–made *Rumble in the Bronx* (1996) that Chan caught the eye of Hollywood producers. Chan's first major U.S.-made movie was *Rush Hour* (1998), which was unique in the sense that it combined Chan's martial arts/comedy skills together with a culture clash with his partner, an African American cop (Chris Tucker). The film was a smash hit, and Chan went on to star in a string of other comedies of the same general formula that feature his marital arts prowess, including *Shanghai Noon* (2000), *Rush Hour 2* (2001), *The Tuxedo* (2002), *Shanghai Knights* (2003), *The Medallion* (2003), and *Around the*

World in 80 Days (2004). Although his movies are popular and make lots of money, Chan yearns to move on beyond his typecast roles. "It's all the same, cop from Hong Kong, cop from China," Chan admits. "Jet Li, Chow Yun-Fat and I all face the same problem. Our roles are limited."[5]

Chow Yun-Fat made more than seventy films and was Asia's biggest star before making his film debut in the United States. His first two Hollywood films, *The Replacement Killers* (1998) and the *Corruptor* (1999), were both full of action but empty in plot. His third film, *Anna and the King* (2000), was a big-budget extravaganza that also starred Jodie Foster. This film provided him the opportunity to temporarily break out of the action film mold, but he returned to the action-film genre in *Crouching Tiger, Hidden Dragon* (2000) and again in *Bulletproof Monk* (2003). His recent roles have been more varied, and he has appeared in both action-adventure films, such as *Curse of the Golden Flower* (2006), *Pirates of the Caribbean: At World's End* (2007), and *Dragonball Evolution* (2010), and dramatic films, including *The Children of Huang-Chi* (2007) and *Shanghai* (2009). Chow, however, has still not replicated his enormous popularity in Asia in the many years since his move to Hollywood.

As a child, Jet Li was a national martial arts champion in China before beginning his film career. After becoming one of the most popular movies stars in Asia in films such as *Once Upon A Time In China* (1991) and *Fist Of Legend* (1994), Li made his Hollywood debut in the first villainous role of his career, in *Lethal Weapon 4* (1999). He has since had martial arts–related starring roles in several Hollywood films, such as *Romeo Must Die* (2000), *Kiss of the Dragon* (2001), *Unleashed* (2005), and *War* (2007). In 2007 Li returned to Asia to star in the historical epic *The Warlords* (2008) and teamed up for the first time with his main martial-arts movie star rival, Jackie Chan, for a Hollywood version of the legend of the Monkey King, *The Forbidden Kingdom* (2008).

Because of the visibility of these three Hong Kong imports who work primarily in action films, as well as the success of Bruce Lee in the 1970s, martial art roles still predominate for Asian men in Hollywood. Recent examples include *Batman Begins* (2005), which includes martial arts training sessions by a mysterious Asian master and the animated film *Kung Fu Panda* (2008). Asian martial artists also frequently appear as antagonists in films by white action stars such as Jean Claude Van Damme (*Kickboxer*, 1989), Chuck Norris, (*Missing In Action*, 1984) and Stephen Seagal (*Out For A Kill*, 2003; *Into The Sun*, 2005). These roles also update the evil villain stereotype, portraying Asians as inhuman killing machines who are therefore expendable.

Asian American Actors in Hollywood

Asian American men with talent but without accents have had a much more difficult time in Hollywood than their compatriots from Hong Kong. In *La Bamba* (1987), Lou Diamond Phillips portrayed rock star Ritchie Valens, a romantic lead, and soon after gained fame playing Mexican American or Native American characters in popular films like *Stand and Deliver* (1988) and the *Young Guns* series (1988–1990). Though Phillips is Filipino American, his film career has been largely based upon non-Asian roles. Phillips notably wrote and starred in the 1991 thriller *Ambition*, which cast Dr. Haing S. Ngor as a character called "Tatay" (Tagalog for father). In 2008 he played Bolivian Socialist Mario Monje in *Che: Part Two—Guerilla*, whose character dialogue was entirely in Spanish. Likewise, Enrique Iglesias, known primarily as an international "Latin Pop" recording artist, has played non-Asian characters in films like *Once Upon a Time in Mexico* (2003)

---

[5] "Chan Complains of Limited Roles," *AsianWeek*, Oct. 7, 2004, http://www.committee100.org/publications/outsourcing/jackychan.htm (accessed on August 3, 2009).

and television shows such as *Two and a Half Men* (2007). Unbeknownst to the public at large, Enrique and his brother, Julio Iglesias Jr., are of Filipino *mestizo* descent.

In the early 1990s Jason Scott Lee emerged as another Asian American actor cast as a romantic lead with broad major market appeal, paralleling the career of Japanese American actor Sessue Hayakawa in the early silent screen era. Hayakawa was a short-lived and extremely rare exception to the more typical evil Asian male stereotype in films made in the past. Lee starred in *Map of the Human Heart* (1992), *Dragon: The Bruce Lee Story* (1993), and *Jungle Book* (1994). He also provided his voice to animated cartoons *Lilo & Stich* (2002) and *Lilo & Stich* 2 (2005). Paolo Montelban, the handsome Filipino American singer and actor best known for his role as Prince Charming in the Disney movie, *Cinderella* (1997), has also learned the limits of casting for Asian American men. Following his critically acclaimed film debut in *Cinderella*, he was immediately cast as the lead in the short-lived television martial arts show *Mortal Kombat* (1998–1999). He was not seen on the big screen again until he appeared in the Filipino American independent film, *American Adobo* (2001) and in a small role in *The Great Raid* (2005).

Dwayne "The Rock" Johnson, a multiracial Samoan American, emerged as a popular World Wrestling Federation personality in the late 1990s. He soon built a significant film-resumé, starring in big-budget action vehicles, such as *The Scorpion King* (2001), and comedies, such as *Get Smart* (2008). His characters are typically of nondescript racial or ethnic backgrounds, and his roles depend upon his large, muscular phenotype for physical spectacle.

Korean American actor John Cho made his film debut in the independent Asian American film *Shopping for Fangs* (1997). Cho later appeared in other Asian American films, including *Yellow* (1998) and *Better Luck Tomorrow* (2002), while also taking small roles in Hollywood productions including *American Pie* (1999) and *American Beauty* (1999). His breakout Hollywood role was in the stoner comedy *Harold and Kumar Go to White Castle* (2004). He was then cast as Mr. Sulu, one of the lead characters in the 2009 big-screen installment of *Star Trek* (2009), and was also named one of People Magazine's 2006 Sexiest Men Alive, which belies the stereotype of the emasculated Asian male. It remains to be seen whether Cho will continue on to dramatic or romantic leading-man roles in Hollywood.

Portrayals of Asian American Women

Asian American women have two dominant stereotypes in mainstream American film and television. The dragon lady stereotype originated in the early twentieth century and was codified in several roles by Chinese American actress Anna May Wong (*Thief of Bagdad*, 1924: *Shanghai Express*, 1932; *Daughter of the Dragon*, 1931). The dragon lady stereotype typically portrays an Asian woman who is sneaky, untrustworthy, and devious, and who uses her sexuality as a weapon to deceive and ensnare unfortunate men. More recent variations on the dragon lady stereotype include several portrayed by Lucy Liu in films such as *Payback* (1999), *Kill Bill: Vol. 1* (2003), and the television series *Ally McBeal*, in which Liu plays the scheming lawyer Ling Woo, whose theme music was from the Wizard of Oz's Wicked Witch of the West. Liu's role in the animated film *Afro Samurai: Resurrection* (2009) has the actress voicing Sio, "a seductive and sadistic mastermind out to destroy (the) samurai."

The other prevalent stereotype of Asian American women is known variously as the lotus blossom, geisha girl, china doll, or Suzie Wong (for the seminal title character in the 1957 Richard Quine film *The World of Suzie Wong*). This characterization presents Asian women as passive, sexually compliant and easy to seduce, often as willing partners to European American men. A continuation of long-held stereotypes of Asian women as prostitutes (see the Page Act, 1875), the popularity of these roles grew exponentially after World War II, during which many U.S. servicemen in the

Pacific Theater first encountered Asian populations. Films such as *Love Is a Many Splendored Thing* (1955), *Teahouse of the August Moon* (1956), *Sayonara* (1957), *The World of Suzie Wong, A Girl Named Tamiko* (1962), and *You Only Live Twice* (1967) engraved the image of sexy, submissive Asian woman into the American consciousness. Later films such as *Full Metal Jacket* (1987), *Braddock: Missing in Action 3* (1988), and *Balls of Fury* (2007) continued to perpetuate this stereotype. In *I Now Pronounce You Chuck and Larry* (2007), several Asian women (including Tila Tequila) are seen as scantily clad "Hooters" girls, who sexually perform for the white male protagonists.

The Asian Girlfriend

Another common representation of Asian American women portrays characters who are romantically involved with white men. Asian American film scholars suggest that this practice reflects white male privilege, in which white men enjoy the license to sexually, politically, and socially dominate women of color.[6] The last year of the hit program *M*A*S*H* (1972–1983) featured a female Asian character, Soon-Lee (Rosalind Chao), who eventually married the cross-dressing corporal Max Klinger (Jamie Farr). Their marriage continued into a post-*M*A*S*H* spinoff, *AfterMASH* (1983–1984). Chao also regularly appeared in the show *Star Trek: The Next Generation* (1987–1994) and its spin-off *Star Trek: Deep Space Nine* (1993–1999) as botanist Keiko Ishikawa, wife of Transporter Chief Miles O'Brian (Colm Meaney). In the hit comedy series, *Friends* (1994–2004) Lauren Tom had a recurring role from 1995 through 1996 as Julie, the girlfriend of one of the show's main characters, while Ming-Na played a sharp-talking gallery owner, social butterfly, and love interest in the show *The Single Guy* (1995–1997).

Other Stereotypes
Perpetual Foreigner

Asian Americans have often been portrayed as "perpetual foreigners," non-native interlopers into American culture. Characteristics of this stereotype include camera-wielding Japanese tourists (*Armageddon*, 1998), hostile Korean merchants and shopkeepers speaking strongly accented English (*Falling Down*, 1993; *Menace II Society*, 1993; *Do The Right Thing*, 1989), unethical bad drivers (*Crash*, 2006), and other depictions that emphasize the "foreign-ness" of Asians in the United States. The hit independent film *Juno* (2007) further reinforced the perpetual foreigner stereotype—its only Asian character is a girl found protesting outside of a family-planning clinic. The character proclaims that "babies want to be borned," in broken yet unaccented English, suggesting that even American-born Asians are unable to speak English correctly. By inference, Asians can never fully belong in this country, are not fully American, and are undermining American culture with their barbaric, backward customs and manners. The perceived inability of Asians to acculturate in the United States thus prevents their full acceptance into mainstream American life.

Model Minority

Asian Americans are perceived as the model minority: successful, well-behaved, assimilated members of mainstream American society who have overcome prejudice and racism. In mainstream media this manifests itself in guises such as Asian Americans in high-paying professions—doctors,

---

[6] Darryl Hamamoto, *Monitored Peril* (Minneapolis: University of Minnesota Press, 1994), 46.

lawyers, and accountants. These roles are often supporting characters with little depth or development. These portrayals also contradict the reality that many Asian Americans, notably Southeast Asians and Pacific Islanders, live near or below the poverty line and often struggle to survive in the United States.

Another version of the model minority is the Asian geck, often a computer nerd, who is a straight-A student who brings up the bell curve. A recent characterization of this type is Hiro Nakamura of the television series *Heroes* (2006-present, NBC-TV), a nerdy, bespectacled Japanese office worker who loves science fiction and "manga," or Japanese comic books. However, because Hiro is a featured character on the show, his character has been much more layered and developed than previous, more one-dimensional representations such as those mentioned above. Another film that both exploits and deconstructs the model minority stereotype is *Harold and Kumar Go to White Castle* (2004). The title characters at first appear to be typical model minorities—Harold, a Korean American, is an investment banker, and Kumar, of Indian descent, is applying for medical school. Most of the film, however, centers on their getting stoned, pursuing women, and searching for White Castle hamburgers, activities that counter the model minority myth.

Progress in Representations

Canadian born Sandra Oh began her career acting in independent Asian Canadian and Asian American films, winning two Best Actress Genies (the Canadian equivalent of the Academy Awards) for her roles in those films. Her breakout role in the award-winning film *Sideways* (2004) led to a recurring role in the television drama *Grey's Anatomy*, for which she has won a Golden Globe award as well as several Emmy nominations. Oh's character, Cristina Yang, is multilayered and complex and evades the simplistic characterizations and stereotyping too often found in roles for Asian women in Hollywood.

In the fall of 1994, Korean American comedian Margaret Cho was the first Asian American woman to star in her own situation comedy, *All-American Girl*. The show floundered creatively, however, and was canceled after one season. It was also somewhat controversial in the Asian American community, as some Asian Americans thought that the program perpetuated stereotypes, notably of Asian American men.

Following the cancellation of the series, Cho concentrated on her stand-up comedy career and her one-woman stage shows, including *I'm The One That I Want* (in which she chronicled her misadventures with *All-American Girl*), *Notorious C.H.O.* (2002), and *Assassin* (2005), which became popular and critical successes. In 2008 Cho launched a new television series, a reality show on cable channel VH1 titled *The Cho Show*, over which, as writer and producer, she maintained creative control. A combination of unscripted elements and setup situations, the series followed Cho in her daily life as a comedian in Los Angeles. The show was a success and presented a much more realistic and interesting view of Cho than her earlier sitcom, in part because of the program's focus on her strong, unconventional personality.

In 2008, Clint Eastwood directed and co-starred in *Gran Torino*, the first mainstream film to feature a Hmong American cast. In the film, Eastwood portrays Walt Kowalski, a Korean War veteran and former Detroit autoworker who is compelled to resolve his guilt and racial prejudice after being welcomed into his Hmong neighbors' social circle. The film pushes beyond the typical stereotypes of other Hollywood portrayals of Southeast Asians as "chinks" or "commie gooks" and provides cursory insights about this otherwise invisible Asian American group. Casualties of the CIA's secret, illegal war in Laos, the Hmong characters are depicted with complexity and humanity as they struggle with their new lives in the United States.[7]

Lack of Presence in Television

Despite these gains, Asian Americans still lack a solid presence in the television mainstream. A 2007 analysis of Asian Americans on television from the National Asian Pacific American Legal Consortium (NAPALC) shows 2.5 percent Asian Pacific Islander American (APIA) representation on television, which is only slightly more than the representation a decade ago. In total, there were eighteen APIA actors on prime-time television. Out of 113 prime time programs, only thirteen featured at least one reoccurring Asian American, Pacific Islander, or multiracial Asian American/Pacific Islander character. Only three programs on television in fall 2004 had more than one APIA character (*ER*, *Hawaii*, and *Lost*).

Other findings were as follows:

- Of the thirteen television programs, APIA actors were featured far less than non-APIA actors. White actors took up 83.3 percent of the screen time on these thirteen specific programs, while APIA characters consistently had the lowest screen time. The multiracial APIA actors, some of whom played white characters, received significantly more screen time than nonmultiracial APIA actors. In this study, male APIA actors (11) outnumbered female APIA actors (7).
- A number of television programs were located in cities such as Honolulu, San Francisco, Queens (New York), Seattle, and New York City that have large APIA populations, but had no regular APIA cast member. For example, the programs *Half and Half* on UPN and *Charmed* on WB were set in San Francisco but neither had an APIA cast member. There were seven television programs set in Los Angeles that had no regular APIA cast member. Two shows set in Honolulu, *Hawaii* on NBC and *North Shore* on FOX, had relatively high APIA representation on the cast (27 percent), although APIAs represent 63 percent of the city's population.

The characterizations of APIAs on television are not as stereotypical and limited as in the past. Of the eighteen APIA characters on television, five were in the medical field (two doctors, one medical examiner, one forensic psychologist, and one paramedic), three were in law enforcement (one captain and two officers). There was one linguistic specialist, one bartender/nightclub owner, one "brainy student," and two whose occupation is unknown because they are survivors of a plane crash forced to live on a remote island (*Lost*).

Organizing for Change

Because their representation in Hollywood has often been negligible or distorted, Asian Americans have organized in various ways to speak out against and take action in support of more realistic images. Founded in 1992, the Media Action Network for Asian Americans (MANAA) monitors television, motion pictures, print, advertising, and radio, advocating for balanced, sensitive, and positive portrayals of Asian Americans.

---

[7] Kurashige, Scott. "Living for Change: An American Icon Looks in the Mirror". *Michigan Citizen*. January 11–17, 2009, http://www.boggscenter.org/fi-scott_kurashige-01-17-09_grand_torino.html.

Since 1999 NAPALC has led the Asian Pacific American Media Coalition, a group of nineteen organizations, in a campaign against the lack of diversity in television programming. More recently, Web sites such as Angry AsianMan.com have been effective loci for Asian Americans organizing to protest inaccuracies and stereotypes in representations of Asians in Hollywood. These include campaigns against the whitewashing of the film versions of *Avatar: The Last Airbender* and *21*.

Outlook

In recent years, the medium of cyberspace has played an influential role, especially in terms of mass audience access for Asian American artists. Internet-only performers Happy Slip (Filipina American Christine-Gambito), KevJumba, and David Choi have thousands of subscribers on their You Tube channels, bypassing traditional means of distribution to directly reach their target audiences. Because they maintain complete creative control over their output, these performers are not subject to the stereotyping that is prevalent in conventional mainstream media.

Asian Americans have also found success in television's reality and talent shows, where unscripted programming allows them to represent themselves on their own terms. In 2003, Dat Phan was the winner of *Last Comic Standing*, the popular NBC stand-up comedy competition reality show. Much of his material is based upon his experience growing up as a Vietnamese American and pokes fun at Asian stereotypes. Filipino American comedian Jo Koy (Joseph Glenn Herbert) also has gained notoriety with his edgy observational humor and original insights. Recent appearances include *BET's Comic View, Showtime at the Apollo*, and *The Tonight Show with Jay Leno*.

In 2006, Korean American Yul Kwon became the first Asian American to win *Survivor*, the popular CBS-TV reality show. On the show Kwon was a strong, intelligent, and empathetic leader, whose negotiating skills led to his victory. Because of his famously toned physique and good looks, he also became an object of desire and was named one of *People* Magazine's Sexiest Men in 2006, countering the stereotype of the emasculated Asian male. In 2009, Filipino American Lou Diamond Phillips was the winner on ABC-TV's *Survivor*-like series *I'm a Celebrity . . . Get Me Out of Here!*

In 2007, the dance crew JabbaWockeeZ, with several Asian American members, won MTV's *America's Best Dance Crew* competition. (Kaba Modern, another Asian American crew, also competed on the show). Jabbawokeez has achieved mainstream success and recognition, and its widespread appeal offers hope for the further dissolution of barriers for Asian Americans in mass media. Crew members notably danced with Shaquille O'Neal in an exhibition performance during the 2009 NBA All-Star Game. As one admirer notes, "I'm an African American woman who has always had an eye on hip-hop internationally, so when my friends act shocked about Asians in hip-hop, I just tell them the Asian community has been bringin' it for years."[8]

Outside of the Hollywood mainstream, Asian American independent film-makers are also making their mark on the screen, as discussed further in the Independent Film entry.

---

[8] "Letters to the Editor: Chol Soo Lee, AZN TV, R.I.P., JabbaWockeeZ Love" *AsianWeek*. April 9, 2008.

Taking Control of the News

Paul Niwa

Less than a month before Lunar New Year 2011, The Wall Street Journal splashed the cover of its Personal Journal section with the headline "Why Chinese Mothers are Superior."[1] In the cold type that followed, America's largest newspaper printed the most outrageous snippets of Yale Law Professor Amy Chua's memoir of parenthood, *Battle Hymn of the Tiger Mother*,[2] ensuring the book would be a bestseller.

In the excerpt, Chua wrote that she called her daughter "stupid" to motivate her. She recalled an episode where she threatened to give her child's toys to the Salvation Army for failing to practice the piano. And Chua bragged that "Chinese parents can order their kids to get straight As. Western parents can only ask their kids to do their best."

Within a week, the media flooded both newsprint and the airwaves with the Tiger Mother. NPR's Fresh Air called Chua "nuts."[3] The New York Times columnist David Brooks wrote that Chua was a "wimp" for "coddling" her daughters and "protecting them from the most intellectually demanding activities."[4] ABC News hired Asian American actors to play a scene in a restaurant where a Tiger Mother scolded her daughter for getting an A- to see if customers would intervene.[5] A New York Post columnist coaxed his city's school district chancellor to toughen the curriculum by writing, "It's time to channel your inner Tiger Mom."[6]

Readers of the book were treated to something very different from the newspaper excerpt. In her memoir, Chua second guesses her child rearing methods even though it appears her daughters grew up to be well-adjusted, high achieving young women. Reviewers ignored or struggled to reconcile the complex, loving relationship between Chua and her daughters with the storyline that they wanted to use of the "crazy," "abusive" immigrant mother. Months after the book was

---

Contributed by Paul Niwa, an Associate Professor of Journalism at Emerson College in Boston. As a television producer, he helped NBC and Gannett launch six newscasts, two television channels and one of the world's first online newscasts. He is also an editorial board member of the Pacific Citizen newspaper.

---

[1] Amy Chua, "Why Chinese Mothers Are Superior," *The Wall Street Journal*, January 8, 2011, Eastern edition, sec. C.

[2] Amy Chua, *Battle Hymn of the Tiger Mother*, First Edition. (Penguin Press, 2011).

[3] "Tiger Mothers: Raising Children The Chinese Way : NPR," *NPR.org*, n.d., http://www.npr.org/2011/01/11/132833376/tiger-mothers-raising-children-the-chinese-way.

[4] David Brooks, "Amy Chua is a Wimp," *The New York Times*, January 18, 2011, Late edition, sec. A.

[5] "'Tiger Mother' Attacks Kid for A-, Bystanders Pounce", n.d., http://abcnews.go.com/WhatWouldYouDo/tiger-mother-rips-kid-minus/story?id=13578536#.TyrSkeNSS6Q.

[6] Michael Goodwin, "Where are New York's Tiger Kids?," *New York Post*, January 19, 2011, All Editions edition.

published on January 11, 2011, Wesley Yang wrote in New York magazine that "Western readers rode roughshod . . . and made of Chua a kind of Asian minstrel figure,"[7] a caricature of what non-Asians envisioned of Asian Americans.

Whether she had realized it, Chua successfully captured the attention of the news media not because she was extraordinary, but because she fit a popular narrative of Asian Americans being unusual and foreign. It is extremely difficult for Asian Americans to be recognized by the press for their individual achievements outside of a set storyline of what mass media envisions the racial group to be. This causes Asian Americans to take media matters into their own hands by pioneering new forms of communication and creating their own messages for their own audience.

The News That's Fit to Print

Although journalists like to cite Finley Peter Dunne's quote "comfort the afflicted, and afflict the comfortable," journalism scholars have described the "Fourth Estate" as unconscious agents of the powerful. Tight budgets and deadlines cause journalists to use convenient storylines and sources of information that serve society's elite. When Asian Americans don't fit these storylines, they are often left out of the news, even when they have a direct stake in the story.

One example of the community's invisibility in the news is the issue of bullying by teenagers. Bullying has been a persistent national story, creating a public perception that harassment is becoming more frequent and severe. But, a joint study by the US Departments of Education and Justice in 2011 found that incidents of bullying have declined overall since 1995, while bullying continues at high rates among Asian Americans.[8]

US Secretary of Education Arne Duncan told the liberal think tank Center for American Progress in November 2011 that "Asians are more likely than other groups to be bullied in the classroom and are a staggering three times more likely to be cyber-bullied once or twice a month."[9] Other studies confirm this finding, showing that Asian American teens are the group most likely to be harassed by other students.[10] Yet, journalists rarely present Asian Americans and their stories of how they have been bullied.

It takes extraordinary efforts by Asian Americans to get noticed by members of the press. Students at South Philadelphia High School complained for years about being bullied by African American students. The school staff responded by closing English as a second language classes and by sometimes using racial insults against the students.[11]

In December 2009, at least 30 Asian American South Philadelphia High School students were beaten by a large group of African American students during a lunch break. Thirteen of them

---

[7] Wesley Yang, "Paper Tigers; What happens to all the Asian-American overachievers when the test-taking ends?," *New York* (May 16, 2011).

[8] Zhang J. Robers and J. Truman, *Indicators of School Crime and Safety: 2010* (Washington, DC: National Center for Education Statistics, U.S. Department of Education, and Bureau of Justice Statistics, Office of Justice Programs, U.S. Department of Justice, October 2011), http://nces.ed.gov/pubs2011/2011002.pdf.

[9] "How to Better Serve Growing U.S. Asian American Communities", n.d., http://www.americanprogress.org/issues/2011/11/aapi_event.html.

[10] Michele Mouttapa et al., "Social network predictors of bullying and victimization," *Adolescence* 39, no. 154 (Summer 2004): 315–335.

[11] Kristen Graham, "Asian students describe violence at South Philadelphia High," *McClatchy—Tribune Business News*, December 10, 2009, http://search.proquest.com/docview/455807286?accountid=10735.

were taken to the hospital. When Asian American students refused to go to school the next day, journalists finally came to ask why. Stories about the indifference of "Southern High" administrators were published internationally throughout the two week school boycott.[12]

Asian American advocacy groups accused the school district of not taking the brawl seriously. Some victims of the attack were not interviewed a week after the incident, and the district's report months later tried to blame an unnamed Cambodian American student for encouraging African American students to beat up Asian Americans on-and-off campus.[13]

Press coverage of the attack sparked Asian American protests in cities across the United States. A US Justice Department inquiry was called and federal investigators accused the school district of "deliberate indifference" to the harassment of Asian American students and "intentional disregard" for their safety.[14] But when newsroom cameras left Southern High, the district quietly laid off security guards and a community liaison officer who put herself in harm's way to protect Asian American students during the melee.[15]

When news breaks, Asian Americans are rarely seen, even when they are relevant to the story. The most important news event of 2010 was the Deepwater Horizon Oil Spill. The BP owned rig spilled 4.9 million barrels of oil into the Gulf of Mexico, spreading over 3,800 square miles and creating the worst environmental disaster in American history.

The fishing industry in the Gulf States was severely affected with a shortened season and at least $2.5 billion in lost revenue in 2010. The Louisiana State Department of Wildlife and Fisheries estimates that one-third of its 14,000 boat fishing fleet was owned by Southeast Asian Americans.[16] In ports where Asian Americans moored, ethnic Vietnamese fishermen were known for taking in half of the catch. After the oil spill, a third of the Gulf of Mexico fishing grounds were closed, depriving these fishermen of their livelihood.[17]

Many Vietnamese Americans were also excluded from aid programs designed to help supplement income until compensation checks from BP arrived.[18] Only 10% of Vietnamese American fishermen who applied to help in the cleanup were asked by BP to show up for work. The claims forms from BP were initially only available in English. When the company eventually provided translators, fishermen said the translators' skills were so poor they didn't even know basic words like "seafood."[19]

---

[12] Kristen Graham, "Many Asian students fear return to S. Phila. classes," *McClatchy - Tribune Business News*, December 5, 2009, http://search.proquest.com/docview/455858842?accountid=10735.

[13] Dafney Tales, "Asian group hits report on school fights," *Tribune Business News*, February 24, 2010.

[14] Jeff Gammage and Kristen Graham, "Feds find merit in Asian students' claims against Philly school," *McClatchy - Tribune Business News*, August 28, 2010, http://search.proquest.com/docview/747822934?accountid=10735.

[15] Karen Heller, "School hero not taking job loss quietly," *McClatchy - Tribune Information Services*, July 4, 2010, http://search.proquest.com/docview/578159702?accountid=10735.

[16] Monique Johnson, "Oil Spill Threatens Livelihood of Vietnamese Community", May 26, 2010, http://nola10.nytimes-institute.com/2010/05/26/oil-spill-threatens-livelihood-of-vietnamese-community/.

[17] Bill Sasser, "Vietnamese, Cambodian fishermen among hardest hit by BP oil spill; Many Vietnamese and Cambodia fishermen are without work now because of the BP oil spill, and some still feel the effects of Hurricane Katrina. BP is trying to help, but there's a language barrier.," *The Christian Science Monitor* (Ipswich, MA, May 8, 2010).

[18] Nancy Mock et al., *Resilience Framework: Deepwater Horizon Oil Spill Impact Assessment* (Tulane University Disaster Resilience Leadership Academy, April 15, 2011), http://www.drlatulane.org/groups/community-resiliency-deep-water-horizon-oil-spill/DRLA_DWH_Oil_Spill_Assessment_Complete_Report.pdf.

[19] Sasser, "Vietnamese, Cambodian fishermen among hardest hit by BP oil spill; Many Vietnamese and Cambodia fishermen are without work now because of the BP oil spill, and some still feel the effects of Hurricane Katrina. BP is trying to help, but there's a language barrier."

Despite thousands of articles and non-stop television coverage, the plight of the Southeast Asian American community is largely unknown to most Americans. The major press only published five articles about Vietnamese American fishermen in 2010. This coverage is inadequate compared to the Asian American proportion of the fishing fleet.

Asian Americans are often invisible in the news media despite being at the center of the story. A study of Asian American neighborhood coverage by metropolitan daily newspapers found that the community's neighborhoods were mentioned in less than 1% of articles even though they were all centrally located and newsworthy.[20] Studies of journalistic sourcing have often found that Asian Americans are cited so infrequently that they are often statistically insignificant.[21]

The news media also ignored Asian Americans after the September 11 Attacks, the biggest news event so far this century. Manhattan's Chinatown is only ten blocks from Ground Zero and was inside the exclusion zone in the days after the attacks. The Asian American Federation of New York with the backing of the Federal Reserve Bank of New York reported that more than 40 garment factories closed in Chinatown and revenue declined as much as 70% at restaurants in the three months after September 11. Out of 37,000 workers employed in Chinatown, 24,000 were temporarily out of work. At least 24% of working residents lost their jobs.[22]

Even though Chinatown is a five minute walk from Ground Zero, only the New York Times sent journalists to cover the neighborhood's economic catastrophe in the year following the attacks. An Asian American reporter wrote all but one of the ten articles.

The representation of Asian Americans in newsrooms can improve coverage of the community. But, very few newsrooms employ an Asian American journalist. Out of the newsrooms that responded to a 2011 American Society of Newspaper Editors (ASNE) survey, 88% of them had not hired a single Asian American. The proportion of minority journalists in the survey has shrunk three years-in-a-row.[23]

The picture is not better at broadcast stations. The 2011 RTNDA/Hofstra survey found that Asian American journalists comprise 3.5% of television newsroom employees and 0% of radio journalists.[24]

Asian Americans rarely ascend to newsroom manager positions that control who is hired, which stories are assigned, and how stories are framed. Only 2.2% of television news directors were Asian American in the 2011 RTNDA/Hofstra survey.[25] In a 2004 Medill AAJA study, no newspaper in the country had an Asian American in one of the top three positions in the newsroom.[26]

---

[20] Paul Niwa, "Source Diversity within a Reporter's In-Group: Metropolitan Daily Newspapers and Sourcing within Asian Pacific American Communities." (presented at the AEJMC Annual Meeting, Washington, DC, 2007).

[21] Paula M. Poindexter, Laura Smith, and Don Heider, "Race and Ethnicity in Local Television News: Framing, Story Assignments, and Source Selections.," *Journal of Broadcasting & Electronic Media* 47, no. 4 (December 2003): 524–536.

[22] Shao-Chee Sim, *Chinatown One Year After September 11th: An Economic Impact Study* (New York: Asian American Federation of New York, November 2002), http://911chinatown.mocanyc.org/report/Asian%20American%20Federation%20of%20New%20York/AAFNY%20Study%202.swf.

[23] *ASNE Newsroom Census* (American Society of Newspaper Editors, 2011), http://asne.org/key_initiatives/diversity/newsroom_census.aspx.

[24] Bob Papper, *RTDNA/Hofstra Women and Minorities Survey* (RTDNA/Hofstra University, 2011), http://www.rtdna.org/pages/research/women-and-minorities.php.

[25] Ibid.

[26] "Cultural Stereotypes a Factor in Low Numbers of Asian Americans in Newsroom Management Positions," *PR Newswire*, August 5, 2004.

Since Asian American journalists are unlikely to be hired or promoted to management, they often serve in "the field" as reporters. This makes them more noticeable, and it may give the Asian American community a false impression of the diversity and inclusiveness of newsrooms.

Even in these more public roles, some Asian American broadcast journalists have questioned whether they are being "ghettoized" to the least desirable work hours or the least prestigious beats.[27] Journalism studies researchers write that minority journalists may feel pressured to "fit in" to newsroom culture or face being pigeonholed into obscure assignments, making them less effective at being advocates for their communities.[28]

Lack of access to newsrooms leaves Asian Americans with little control over how their community is covered by journalists. Since newsrooms have little time to reflect and shape their story-lines, reporters usually head into the field with a preset "focus" for the story they are assigned to pursue. Inadvertently, Asian Americans are ignored when they don't fit expectations. In the rare cases where an Asian American is the story, reporters often accentuate the person's foreignness in a way that separates the community from the rest of American society.

In 2007, A Korean American student named Seung-Hui Cho opened fire on his classmates and professors at Virginia Tech, killing 32 people and wounding 25 others. He shot himself as police officers approached him.

Cho had been diagnosed with a severe form of a depressive disorder as early as middle school, and instructors noticed his declining mental stability in college. A videotape he mailed to NBC News just before the shooting showed signs of paranoia and grandiose delusions that are indicative of schizophrenia.[29]

Instead of treating this mass murder as the lone act of a mentally ill individual, the press tried to find explanations in Cho's heritage. Journalists around the country flocked to Korean American restaurants and churches for reaction from the community. CNN showed Koreans in Seoul apologizing for the shooting, as if their ethnicity was responsible.

This kind of framing of atrocities is unusual. White Americans perpetrate most mass murders in the United States. But, it would be considered absurd in a newsroom to run to a smorgasbord, an Episcopalian church or to interview passersby in Berlin to get community reaction every time a white American commits a similar crime.

Framing the community in ridiculous, unusual or outrageous ways places Asian Americans outside the norms of society. In the Tiger Mother example, the academic excellence of Asian Americans is attributed to inhumane, un-American parenting.

Another way newsrooms exoticize Asian Americans is by hypersexualizing them. In the summer of 2011, News Corporation Chairman Rupert Murdoch was summoned to a British parliamentary hearing to answer questions about an alleged cover up of voice mail hacking practices at one of his newspapers. But, his Asian American wife Wendi Deng Murdoch stole the headlines.

Wendi Deng Murdoch caught and slapped a protestor who tried to throw a cream pie in her husband's face during the hearing. Dozens of profiles were written about her figure and fashion the next day, including one by The Guardian. The UK newspaper, which has more American

---

[27] Sheree R. Curry, "AAJA Asks: Are We Being Ghettoized?," *Television Week* 24, no. 33 (2005): 19–20.

[28] C. A Steele, "Newspapers' representations of tolerance and intolerance," *Mass Comm Review* 21, no. 3 (1994): 173–186.

[29] *Report of the Virginia Tech Review Panel: Presented to Timothy M. Kaine, Governor; Commonwealth of Virginia* (TriData Division, System Planning Corporation, December 2009), http://www.governor.virginia.gov/tempcontent/techPanelReport-docs/8%20CHAPTER%20IV%20LIFE%20AND%20MENTAL%20HEALTH%20HISTORY%20OF%20CHOpdf.pdf.

readers than the Washington Post, described how as a California college student, Deng Murdoch seduced a married 53-year-old factory manager, convinced him to pay her tuition and then dumped him upon graduation.

After calling attention to the Murdoch couple's May-December marriage, The Guardian wrote that Wendi Deng Murdoch was "said to regularly admonish him [the News Corporation Chairman] for not taking enough care of his health – scoldings [sic] Murdoch seems to enjoy,"[30] inferring some type of dragon-lady sexual relationship.

Asian American men are also hypersexualized, but in an emasculated manner that portrays them as incapable, undesirable and morally unfit to be leaders in American society. A study of three political elections found that journalists often framed the Asian American male candidates as "submissive," "shy" or "indecisive" and frequently mentioned the Asian American candidates as "cunning," "calculated" and "prone to corruption" to emphasize foreignness. The study also observed that the race of the Asian American male candidate was frequently used while the white candidates' ethnic backgrounds were rarely mentioned.[31]

The "permanent foreigner" storyline has been used so prevalently that editors and the public find it is easy to accept even when there is no supporting evidence. In 1999, journalists descended on the Los Almos National Laboratory in the middle of the New Mexico desert when a rumor surfaced that a Chinese American scientist was being investigated for stealing nuclear secrets for China.

The federal government was suspicious that American secret technology was used to help design China's latest nuclear weapon. Federal officials illegally leaked Wen Ho Lee's name to journalists, and the scientist's name appeared in print and broadcast before charges were filed in court. The US Department of Energy later accused Lee of stealing the "crown jewels" of nuclear weapons science for China. Lee was held in solitary confinement in a federal jail for nine months while he awaited trial.

When it came time for prosecutors to present evidence in court, it became obvious to the judge that the government had no evidence of espionage. The US Department of Energy later admitted to Congress that the documents that it claimed Lee stole were not "top secret" and that "99 percent of it was unclassified in the open literature."[32]

In August 2000, fewer journalists attended court when a judge freed Lee than were present when Lee was accused. The scientist pleaded guilty to one count of mishandling documents so that he could be released from jail earlier. At Lee's sentencing, a federal judge apologized to the scientist for denying bail and dressed down the federal prosecutor for misconduct and misrepresenting evidence to the court.[33]

---

[30] Caroline Davies, "Phone-hacking scandal: Deng leapt to husband's defence as assailant took aim and struck: Wife whispered encouragement - and then quickly hit back at pie-thrower," *The Guardian* (London, July 20, 2011), Regional News edition, sec. Front.

[31] H. Wu and Tien-Tsung Lee, "The submissive, the calculated, and the American dream.," in *Conference Papers—International Communication Association* (presented at the Conference Papers—International Communication Association, International Communication Association, 2003), 1–23.

[32] Matthew Purdy With James Sterngold, "The Prosecution Unravels: The Case of Wen Ho Lee," *The New York Times*, February 5, 2001, sec. U.S., http://www.nytimes.com/2001/02/05/us/the-prosecution-unravels-the-case-of-wen-ho-lee.html?ref=wenholee.

[33] Wen Ho Lee and Helen Zia, *My Country Versus Me: The First-Hand Account by the Los Alamos Scientist Who Was Falsely Accused of Being a Spy*, Abridged. (CD, 2002).

The press was quick to judge Lee, violating its own standard of ethics by revealing the name of a private citizen before it is read in open court. In 2006, Lee received a $1.6 million settlement from the federal government and five media companies for violating his privacy.[34]

Wen Ho Lee and The New York Times have indicated that elected officials and federal appointees pursued prosecution to deflect attention from political problems of the Clinton Administration.[35] Studies have found that other stories that frame Asian Americans as foreigners have been often used to the advantage of society's elite. One study noticed that California journalists wrote about the "wave" of Asian immigrants and Asian language signage in neighborhoods during the English-only referendum during the 1980s.[36] Other researchers have found that stories of Asian American achievement have been used by the press to wedge apart a coalition of minority racial groups.[37]

The Asian American community may also be complicit in exoticizing itself in the lens of the media. Organizations frequently invite journalists to cultural festivals, and newsrooms are often eager to document such colorful events. But, celebrations of heritage can easily be interpreted as spectacles of foreignness on American soil.[38]

As permanent foreigners in the eyes of the media, Asian Americans can be easily swept up by the foreign affairs topics of the day. US interaction with Asia repeatedly affects Asian American communities.[39] Tensions over the 1937 Japanese occupation of Shanghai inspired newspaper editorials that paved a path toward the unconstitutional incarceration of Japanese Americans after the Pearl Harbor attack. During the Vietnam War, Asian Americans became victims of discrimination as the media reported about the sneakiness of the Viet Cong militia.

In the 1980s, economic competition with Japan led to union protests and a "Buy America" campaign. Video of autoworkers destroying a Japanese car with sledgehammers was shown repeatedly on the news, building support for protectionist trade policies. Asian Americans often became victims of the growing resentment. In 1982, a Chinese American named Vincent Chin was beaten to death in Detroit by a laid off autoworker and his stepfather. In a climate of Japan-bashing encouraged by the news media, Chin's assailants were able to plea bargain manslaughter charges and avoid time in prison.[40]

---

[34] Adam Liptak, "News Media Pay in Scientist Suit," *The New York Times*, June 3, 2006, sec. Washington, http://www.nytimes.com/2006/06/03/washington/03settle.html?ref=wenholee.

[35] Sterngold, "The Prosecution Unravels"; Zia, *My Country Versus Me*.

[36] Kathy H. Rim, "Model, Victim, or Problem Minority? Examining the Socially Constructed Identities of Asian-Origin Ethnic Groups in California's Media," *Asian American Policy Review* 16 (January 2007): 37–60.

[37] Ibid.; Francis Dalisay and Alexis Tan, "Assimilation and contrast effects in the priming of Asian American and African American Stereotypes through TV Exposure," *Journalism & Mass Communication Quarterly* 86, no. 1 (Spring2009): 7–22; Sherri Grasmuck, Jason Martin, and Shanyang Zhao, "Ethno-Racial Identity Displays on Facebook.," *Journal of Computer-Mediated Communication* 15, no. 1 (October 2009): 158–188.

[38] David C. Oh and Madeleine Katz, "Covering Asian America: A Content Analysis Examining Asian American Community Size and Its Relationship to Major Newspapers' Coverage.," *Howard Journal of Communications* 20, no. 3 (Jul–Sep2009): 222–241.

[39] Dorothy B. Fujita-Rony, "1898, U.S. Militarism, and the Formation of Asian America.," *Asian American Policy Review* 19 (January 2010): 67–71.

[40] Christine Choy and Renee Tajima-Pena, *Who Killed Vincent Chin?* (Filmakers Library, 1987), http://filmakers.com/index.php?a=filmDetail&filmID=220.

South Asian Americans faced similar discrimination after the September 11 Attacks. Bold headlines like "Bastards!" from the San Francisco Examiner or "Reign of Terror" from the Boston Globe magnified and legitimized the anger of Americans.[41] South Asian Americans were targeted in the years following the attacks even though their heritage is different from the terrorists.

Diminutive Mass Media

Despite decades of inadequate coverage, the era of Asian American invisibility and foreignness in the major media is coming to a close. The influence of mass media, whether it be in the hands of a corporation or a community organization is waning.

Newsrooms have faced steady and steep audience declines for more than two decades. Americans tell survey takers that television is their most prevalent source of news. But in 2011, the network evening news programs were only watched by 4–6% of television households on a given night. Only one-out-of-five of those households had a viewer between the ages of 18–49, indicating that the television news audience is already too old to be of interest to most advertisers.

A century ago, virtually every household subscribed to a newspaper. Today, national newspapers like The Wall Street Journal or The New York Times are delivered to less than 1% of American households. Metropolitan dailies like San Francisco Chronicle, The Philadelphia Inquirer or The Seattle Times are read by less than 15% of households in their regions. Although journalists perceive themselves to be serving the overall population, their niche has become so small it could be argued that mainstream media is now ethnic media for white elites.

Asian Americans have already created their own ethnic media. Today, more than 100 newspapers and more than a dozen broadcasters provide entertainment and news to the racial group.

Since the target audience is narrower than other newsrooms, ethnic media can frame stories with angles that are more relevant to Asian Americans. For example, ethnic newspapers during the 1990s reported on how welfare reforms would affect Asian Americans while other metropolitan daily newspapers often focused on welfare fraud.[42]

Chinese and Vietnamese radio stations continue this tradition in major coastal cities. They play an important role in helping immigrants acclimate to the US by helping them become familiar with US news topics. Their lively call-in shows also teach immigrants how to question governmental authorities.[43]

Most Asian American media outlets are in-language publications and broadcasters that primarily serve immigrants. While three-out-of-four Asian Americans are foreign born, Asian American newsrooms face serious challenges as this group settles in the country.

Census figures show that Asian Americans overwhelmingly speak English competently.[44] Surveys have found that Asian Americans are so fluent that they prefer to get their news in English.[45] A 2005 New California Media (now known as New American Media) study found that only

---

[41] "Today's Front Pages," *Newseum.org*, September 12, 2001, http://www.newseum.org/todaysfrontpages/default_archive.asp?fpArchive=091201.

[42] William Wong, "Asian-Americans and Welfare Reform.," *Nieman Reports* 53, no. 2 (Summer 1999): 47.

[43] Ching-Ching Ni, "Out There: Chinese find community on radio dial," *Los Angeles Times*, November 24, 2009, sec. A.

[44] Hyon Shin and Robert A. Kominski, *Language use in the United States 2007*, American Community Survey Reports (US Census Bureau, April 2010), http://www.census.gov/hhes/socdemo/language/data/acs/ACS-12.pdf.

[45] Kathy H. Rim, "Latino and Asian American Mobilization in the 2006 Immigration Protests.," *Social Science Quarterly (Blackwell Publishing Limited)* 90, no. 3 (2009): 703–721.

13% of Asian Americans prefer an Asian-language radio station to an English language station.[46] A 2008 poll by the National Asian American Survey found that only 20% of Asian Americans went to Asian language media for political information.[47] Researchers are starting to see indications that younger immigrants have such weak heritage language proficiency that they cannot understand in-language ethnic media.[48] These surveys show that ethnic media are in danger of losing their audience if they do not shift to English.

The financial ability for Asian American media to move to English-language content is complicated. Ethnic newspapers receive advertising placed by Asian American public relations and advertising firms. These consultancies have protected their businesses from national advertising agencies by insisting that their clients use in-language ads to reach Asian Americans.[49]

The financial fragility of Asian American newsrooms was exposed in the Great Recession of 2008 that claimed four publications alone in San Francisco - AsianWeek, Ming Pao Daily, Pinoy Today and Nichi Bei Times.[50] Comcast closed its AZN channel and the ImaginAsian channel drastically scaled back its operations. The publications that survived reportedly had to cut staff, beat down vendor prices, and translate content from other newspapers instead of reporting their own stories. At some media outlets, reporters volunteered to work for free, community members pitched in to write and publishers solicited donations from readers.[51]

The biggest challenge for Asian American ethnic newspapers is coming from the Internet. The US Census Bureau reported in 2010 that 77% of Asian American households have broadband Internet service—a vastly higher subscription rate compared to all other racial groups.[52]

One of the most important roles of Asian American media is to help immigrants stay connected with their ethnic homelands. In the past, ethnic media were the gatekeeper to this information. But today, the Internet provides quick and cheap access to media companies in Asia with more resources to create websites and stream video. Many of these overseas newsrooms have created sites in English to be more accommodating to a foreign audience.

Asian America's News Media

Asian Americans may not have access to major newsrooms and their ethnic media may be in financial peril, but that does not mean that the community is muffled. Asian Americans have never been well served by traditional media. They have historically used emerging media to spread information and discuss ideas.

In the 1970s, Asian Americans quickly adopted small, cheap 16 millimeter cameras to place themselves at the forefront of a community film movement. One of the first of these films was "Wong Sinsang" (1971), a depiction of Asian American isolation told through the story of Director

---

[46] *The Ethnic Media in America: the Giant Hidden in Plain Sight* (New California Media, 2005), http://www.npr.org/documents/2005/jul/ncmfreport.pdf.

[47] Jane Junn et al., *Asian Americans and the 2008 Election.* (National Asian American Survey (NAAS), 2008).

[48] Carrie La Ferle and Mariko Morimoto, "The Impact of Life-Stage on Asian American Females' Ethnic Media Use, Ethnic Identification, and Attitudes Toward Ads.," *Howard Journal of Communications* 20, no. 2 (June 2009): 147–166.

[49] Randi Schmelzer, "The Asian Answer," *PR Newswire* (New York, March 13, 2006), 9 edition, sec. 11.

[50] Benny Evangelista, "Ethnic Newspapers Gaining," *San Francisco Chronicle*, September 20, 2009.

[51] "Local Ethnic Editors Share How They Adapt to Changing Times," *Examiner*, August 3, 2011.

[52] "Race a factor in high-speed Internet use, report finds," *Chicago Tribune*, November 9, 2010.

Eddie Wong's father.[53] Wong's group, Visual Communication produced films in a way that encouraged community participation. The audience was asked to help find shooting locations, suggest sources to interview and critique editing choices. Today, this method of collaborative storytelling in journalism is called "crowdsourcing."

The community film movement was influential in Asian American neighborhoods throughout the 1970s and 1980s. In San Francisco, Curtis Choy's "Fall of the I-Hotel" (1983) depicted the lives of retired Filipino "old timers," many of whom worked as migrant workers in the fields of California's Central Valley. In the film, a broad coalition of activists blockaded themselves at the I-Hotel to try to stop the redevelopment of the Manilatown neighborhood.[54]

Asian Americans have learned to use their own media to amplify and preserve the voice of their relatively small racial group. The "Fall of the I-Hotel" has kept the memory of Manilatown alive for more than a generation. In 1987, "Who Killed Vincent Chin?" by Christine Choy and Renee Tajima-Pena helped Asian Americans recognize that Japan-bashing led to the lynching of the 27-year-old Chinese American.[55] Vincent Chin's death started a nationwide Asian American movement. Decades later, Choy and Tajima-Pena's film continues to play in community theaters and college lecture halls, reminding the racial group of the importance of civil rights. "Who Killed Vincent Chin?" was awarded the Alfred I. DuPont-Columbia University Award, broadcast journalism's most prestigious honor. It remains one of the finest examples of Asian American journalism.

Asian Americans also experimented with the alternative press. In 1969, a group of UCLA students started the Gidra newspaper to encourage Asian Americans to vocalize their opinions. The Gidra was influential in the Yellow Power protests of the 1970s, building interest in Japanese American Redress and organizing support for former Los Angeles Coroner Thomas Noguchi as he waged a political battle to keep his job.[56] Although the Gidra is the best known newspaper of the Asian American alternative press, similar publications sprouted in other cities.

Today, Asian Americans are continuing to lead in emerging media by being trendsetters on the Internet. They are continuously experimenting with new ways to spread news and ideas with a mix of entertainment, viral marketing and two-way communication.

Numerous studies have found that Asian Americans are the most wired racial group. A 2007 Intertrend survey showed that Asian American men spend 50% more time online than other American adults.[57] A 2011 study found that 8–18 year old Asian Americans spend more than three hours a day accessing the Internet on a mobile device – twice as much time as white youth.[58] The Pew Internet and American Life Project wrote that Asian American adults are the most active

---

[53] Jun Okada, "'Noble and Uplifting and Boring as Hell' Asian American Film and Video, 1971–1982.," *Cinema Journal* 49, no. 1 (Fall 2009): 20–40.

[54] Chonk Moonhunter (Firm);CrossCurrent Media.;National Asian American Telecommunications Association and Curtis Choy, *Fall of the I Hotel* (San Francisco : Distributed by NAATA/CrossCurrent Media, 1993).

[55] Filmakers Library, inc.;WTVS-TV (Television station : Detroit, Mich.);Film News Now Foundation and Christine Choy, *Who Killed Vincent Chin?* (New York : Filmakers Library, 1988).

[56] Lori Lopez, "The Yellow Press: Asian American Radicalism and Conflict in Gidra - ERIC Top Paper.," *Conference Papers— International Communication Association* (Annual Meeting 2009): 1–28.

[57] "Selling to the community.," *Advertising Age* 78, no. 42 (October 22, 2007): 6.

[58] Nadra Kareem Nittle, "Minority youth media consumption may be hampering academic achievement," *Chicago Defender*, July 13, 2011, 106 edition.

and most experienced news website users.[59] A study of Facebook found that Asian Americans were early adopters of the social media site and continue to be the most likely racial group to use the site.[60]

Asian Americans are deeply embedded in the development of the Internet. Asian American entrepreneurs like Jerry Yang of Yahoo!, Naveen Selvadurai of Foursquare and Bill Nguyen of La La Media have introduced disruptive and transformative technologies that have changed the way people use the web. Jen Hsun Huang of NVIDIA, Vic Gundotra of Google, and Shantanu Narayen of Adobe are leading companies that provide the tools that are defining how journalism is practiced in the 21st century.

Asian Americans have quickly learned how to apply and customize these technologies. The website AsianAvenue.com launched in 1997 and was one of the first blogs on the web. In its pages, Asian Americans figured out viral marketing before the term existed. AsianAvenue users used the Internet in 1998 to organize a national campaign to find a bone marrow donor for a leukemia patient. In 1999, a discussion erupted about a Skyy Vodka magazine advertisement that depicted a kimono-clad Asian woman pouring a drink for a white woman.[61] A member of the website's audience wrote that the ad promoted the stereotype that Asian women are "spies and hookers."[62] Skyy Vodka pulled the ad after hearing about the online complaints.

The AsianAvenue website was sold in 2008. But, 8asians.com and mymomisafob.com have taken its place as the online coffee houses where Asian Americans gather to discuss the news. The blogs AngryAsianMan and Disgrasian often spark that discussion by aggregating information about the Asian American community and posting commentaries on how Asian Americans are covered by the major media.[63] Asian Americans have also created their own TV guide. ChannelAPA makes it easy for them to watch their actors and support their shows.

In the age of traditional media, small, geographically dispersed clusters of Asian Americans were drowned out by the mainstream. But, Asian Americans have figured out how to use the Internet to find and unite each other into a global audience with critical mass. For example, Pakistani Americans started an online Taqwacore culture in the shadow of the September 11 Attacks to express their frustration over the unfairness of anti-Muslim discrimination. In decades earlier, these Pakistani American youth would have been culturally isolated. But online, Taqwacore punks invite audience members from the US, the UK and South Asia to remix their music, essays and poetry on YouTube and Facebook.[64]

YouTube has emerged as one of the most important platforms of Asian American media. Asian Americans headline three of the top 20 most subscribed channels on YouTube. The top woman on YouTube is Michelle Phan, whose vlog of beauty tips garnered an endorsement deal

---

[59] Ronald Roach, "Survey: Asian Americans Are the Most Wired Ethnic Group.," *Black Issues in Higher Education* 18, no. 24 (January 17, 2002): 44.

[60] Akito Yoshikane, "The Yellow Brick Avenue," *Hyphen Magazine*, Fall 2010.

[61] Ibid.

[62] Kim Girard, "Vodka maker clips ad after community criticism", August 31, 1999, http://news.cnet.com/Vodka-maker-clips-ad-after-community-criticism/2100-1017_3-230488.html.

[63] Yoshikane, "The Yellow Brick Avenue."

[64] Dhiraj Murthy, "Muslim punks online: A diasporic Pakistani music subculture on the Internet.," *South Asian Popular Culture* 8, no. 2 (July 2010): 181–194.

with Lancôme.[65] The second most popular man on YouTube is Ryan "NigaHiga" Higa. His social commentaries on subjects like bullying, Asian American discrimination and the NBA lockout frequently have a larger audience than any network newscast.

Asian Americans have become adept at producing viral videos to magnify their influence. Slam Poet Beau Sia used YouTube in 2007 to convince comedienne Rosie O'Donnell to apologize for mocking Asian Americans on the ABC television talk show "The View." Actor George Takei uploaded an appeal for donations after Japan's 2011 earthquake. And filmmaker Eric Byler persuaded actor Daniel Dae Kim in 2006 to denounce US Senator George Allen of Virginia on YouTube after the politician used a racial slur against an Indian American journalist. [66] The video received more than 400,000 views and was credited by the Democratic Party for helping to defeat the incumbent senator.

The speed of the Internet allows Asian Americans to quickly confront racist attacks. In March 2011, a UCLA political science student posted a webcam rant on YouTube about the problem of "these hoards of Asian people that UCLA accepts into our school every year." In her three-minute video, she also complained that Asian students talked on their cell phones in the library sounding like "Ching Chong Ling Long Ting Tong."[67] Asian Americans quickly drowned the student out by sharing the video clip with each other, creating a fan page on Facebook, and posting their own counterattacks on YouTube. Several of their songs, webcam rants and parodies were seen on YouTube more than 4 million times. The online activity was so big that major American newspapers and broadcasters could not ignore the story. A week later, the student apologized in the UCLA student newspaper and withdrew from school.[68]

Asian Americans also used the Internet to defuse the Tiger Mother memoir. To show the absurdity of the caricature, Asian Americans distributed a series of Tiger Mother memes. One of the photo memes showed Amy Chua with the text, "All I care about is that you're happy . . . and a doctor." During Halloween, Asian American parents emailed each other pictures of their kids in tiger cub costumes.

Asian Americans are well positioned to control and share their own information and messages as technology democratizes the gathering and distribution of news. By mixing humor and political statements, the community inspires civic engagement, which is the reason why a free press is protected in a healthy democracy.

---

[65] Austin Considine, "Asian-Americans find an outlet on YouTube," *International Herald Tribune*, August 1, 2011.

[66] Sharon Chae, "Art, Media, and Social Responsibility for Asian Americans: Profile of Eric Byler, Filmmaker.," *Asian American Policy Review* 16 (January 2007): 25–27.

[67] "alexandra's anti-asian video about 'manners' | angry asian man", n.d., http://blog.angryasianman.com/2011/03/alexandras-anti-asian-video-about.html.

[68] "Creator of video gone from UCLA", n.d., http://140.234.16.9:8080/EPSessionID=104dc4274bb14c2762b18bb3bb4904d/EPHost=search.proquest.com/EPPath/docview/857681984/abstract?source=fedsrch&accountid=10735.

PART VI Second Generation, Culture Conflict, and Ethnic Identity

Asian American Student Stress: The Other Side of Achievement

Stephen Murphy-Shigematsu, Karen Sein, Patricia Wakimoto, May Wang

"It's an insane amount [of pressure] . . . Parental expectations get ingrained into your expectations. Then you see your peers, and you just want to do as good as them."

As the young woman spoke, others nodded, and empathized with her predicament. She was a 1.5 generation female Chinese American university student participating in a focus group to discover the kinds of stress Asian American students were experiencing. Her narrative, along with those of other Asian American student participants, challenges the stereotype that Asian Americans are "problem-free." "Model minority" stereotypes have created images of highly successful, well adjusted students, and low utilization of mental health services among Asian American college students has been cited as evidence of their lack of problems (McEwen, et al., 2002; Meyer, et al., 2009). However, these images are being shattered by evidence that the population is facing what some observers describe as a mental health "crisis." (Eisenberg, et al., 2007, Shea, et al., 2008). This study examines whether Asian American college students have unmet mental health needs and provides a portrait of the particular stresses they may face. Understanding their specific mental health needs is crucial if universities want to better address the mental health issues of Asian American college students, the fastest growing ethnic group in the U.S. (U.S. Census, 2010).

Contributed by Stephen Murphy-Shigematsu, Consulting Professor, Department of Anesthesia, Stanford University School of Medicine and Lecturer in Asian American Studies. He is the author of *When Half is Whole* and *Multicultural Encounters; Karen Sein,* MBA, a professional in health care management. She holds a MBA from Harvard Business School and an undergraduate degree in public health from UC Berkeley, where she worked on this research project as part of her honors thesis; *Patricia Wakimoto,* DrPH, Associate Researcher, UC Berkeley School of Public Health and Assistant Scientist with Children's Hospital & Research Centers in Oakland; *May C. Wang,* DrPH, Associate Professor, Department of Community Health Sciences, UCLA School of Public Health.

Is There a Problem?

In recent years, mental health problems among college students have increased dramatically both in frequency and type. The types of problem include anxiety, depression and suicidal thoughts related to social relationships, parental expectations, and sexual assault (Benton, et al., 2003; Lee, et al., 2009). Amidst the heightened attention being given to mental health on campuses, the plight of Asian American students has come to light, partly from nationally publicized suicides and violent acts that shattered their image as model minorities. The fiery suicide of Elizabeth Shin at MIT in 2000 led to a landmark legal suit against the university (Haas, et al., 2003). The Virginia Tech massacre in 2007 by Seung-Hui Cho in 2007 was another shocking and tragic case (Shuchman, 2003) that destroyed the stereotype of the problem-free Asian American student. In response, some schools have hired counselors specifically to work with Asian American students and one university has created a task force to study their particular needs (Ramanjuan, 2006).

Family pressure to fulfill a particular role as a child is often identified as related to mental health issues (Lowe, 2009). Problems with cultural adaptation, language barriers, and racism and discrimination also contribute to mental health issues (Meyer, et al., 2009). Young Asian Americans experience stress trying to live up to many standards and expectations, such as doing well in school, helping support the family, and taking care of elderly family members (Okazaki, 1997; McKewen et al., 2002; Qin, 2009).

These recent developments may be surprising to those who know that Asian Americans in general have very low utilization rates of mental health services compared to other racial and ethnic groups, regardless of gender, age, and location (Zhang et al., 1998; USDHHS, 1999; Appel et al, 2011). While this may appear to be an indication of good mental health, those who do utilize services tend to have more severe cases suggesting that Asian Americans may either avoid using mental health services or delay help-seeking until problems become serious (USDHHS, 2001; McKinney, 2005).

Asian American youth are at particular risk. Asian American females, aged 15 to 24 years old, have the highest rate of depressive symptoms of all gender and racial groups and the highest suicide mortality rates of all young women (Schoen, et al., 1997; National Center for Health Statistics, 2000). In the geographic area where we did our study, Asian American youth show the greatest increases of all ethnic groups in juvenile crime and substance abuse (Arifuku, 2004). These data depict a stark contrast to the "model minority" image of Asian American students as well behaving high achievers.

Considerable media coverage and scholarly attention have been given to the "overrepresentation" of Asian Americans in colleges, especially at highly selected ones. We therefore deliberately chose a sample from a highly competitive university to see if there is a particular kind of stress stemming from being stereotyped as model minority and expected to achieve. We are concerned that the perception of Asian Americans as "whiz kids" and "model minority" coupled with the underutilization of mental health services have masked their mental health needs, and misled university policy makers to believe that Asian Americans are "problem free" with minimal needs for mental health resources (Museus and Chang, 2009; Suzuki 2002).

Our concern is supported by research on Asian American college students in which they report commonly experiencing isolation, segregation, and being stereotyped (Suyemoto, 2009). Asian American college students have also reported higher levels of depressive symptoms (Liu, et al., 1990; Young et al, 2010), greater social anxiety, and interpersonal difficulties than their white counterparts (Okazaki, 1997). A recent study confirms that Asian American students have lower levels of mental health and higher levels of psychological distress and depression than other students (McKinney, 2005). Other studies reveal greater anxiety over making mistakes, more self-doubt (Castro & Rice, 2003), and greater psychological insecurities, such as low self esteem, anxiety and emotional disturbance (Bankston & Zhou, 2002). We conducted this study to gain a better understanding of the kinds of stress Asian American students experience, and bring more light to the other side of achievement.

Methodology: A Participatory Action Approach

We used a participatory action research model to empower students to study and develop interventions in their own community. In participatory action research, a group of people identify a problem and do something to resolve it, aiming to contribute both to the practical concerns of the community, and to further the goals of social science. There is a dual commitment in participatory action research; 1) to study a system, and, 2) concurrently collaborate with members of the system in changing it in what is together regarded as a desirable direction. In our study, academic researchers became consultants and guides for the student researchers.

Students interested in studying the mental health health of Asian American students were recruited and trained to assume an active role in formulating, designing, and carrying out research. Specifically, they engaged in problem definition and study implementation, and actively participated in the development of the study design, and in data gathering, analysis, and interpretation. Nine undergraduate students were recruited through a campus-wide research program that provides students with research experience. All nine student researchers were second or third generation Asian Americans—Chinese, South Asian, or Vietnamese—and there were seven females and two males. We conducted eight training sessions during which the student researchers received instruction from the consulting researchers on topics such as research ethics, recruitment strategies, and qualitative research methodology. The student researchers prepared a Human Subjects protocol, which was approved by their university's institutional review board, received intensive training to conduct focus groups by one of the consulting researchers, and developed the recruitment and data collection protocols including the focus group guide. Focus group participants were recruited from a highly competitive public university in the United States. A convenience sample was recruited from Asian American interest clubs and classes through email and verbal announcements, and campus flyers as well as word of mouth. To be eligible, participants had to be aged 18 years or older, and self-identify as Asian American.

We chose a highly selective college for our study because the media attention given to this group of students suggests that they are a model minority, while there are many indicators that this is a distorted image (Lee, et al., 2009). We do not know if there are differences between these students and those at less selective colleges. The students who chose to participate may also be different in some ways to other Asian American students.

A focus group guide was developed by the student researchers. It included the questions designed to capture participants' college and pre-college experiences that are relevant to their perceived sources of stress and methods of coping with stress. The final list of questions was reviewed by the consulting researchers and pre-tested by the student researchers among their friends. Most of the student researchers gained experience in conducting a focus group. Eight of the nine student researchers conducted one focus group each, and the ninth coordinated the data collection effort. To ensure some control over the conduct of the focus group sessions by eight different student researchers, all of the focus group sessions were attended by one of the consulting researchers.

Forty-seven Asian American students participated in the eight focus groups. Participants ranged in age from 18 to 22 years and about 70 percent were female. They represented 20 different academic majors that covered the Biological Sciences (36.2%), the Social Sciences (21.3%), and Engineering (8.5%). Nineteen percent of the students chose to double major. The majority of the participants were second-generation (51.1%), followed by 1.5-generation (31.9%) and first-generation (17.0%). Only 17.4 percent of participants spoke only English at home. Half of the participants (50.0%) reported primarily speaking a language other than English at home; these languages were Chinese (78.3%), Korean (8.7%), Vietnamese (8.7%), and Tamil (4.4%). Another 32.6 percent of participants were from bilingual households, speaking English and Chinese, Korean, or Tagalog. The largest ethnic group represented was Chinese (59.6%), followed by Taiwanese (14.9%), Korean (10.6%), and Vietnamese (6.4%). Most participants came from two-parent households (87.2%) and had parents with high levels of education. A majority of parents had attained a graduate school degree (67.4% of fathers and 42.6% of mothers) or a college-level education (13.0% of fathers and 29.8% of mothers).

The two-hour focus group sessions were audio-taped and a fellow student researcher also took notes and later transcribed the tapes. After the eight focus groups were completed, the student student researchers were further trained to examine the transcripts for themes by one of the consulting researchers. All nine student researchers independently read each transcript, and together, they discussed their analyses of the transcripts. At least one consulting researcher was present to guide these discussions and assist with the consolidation of themes that were used to structure the stories of individual focus group participants. The transcripts were analyzed using the steps of narrative structuring, in which individuals relate the information about their experiences that is most relevant to them and organize this information in a way that is representative of how they see themselves (Kvale, 1996). In particular, they were analyzed in relation to contextual factors that locate identities within social and cultural context. Eventually, three types of narratives emerged as described below, focusing on participants' reports of the stress in their lives, reasons for the stress, and how they achieved their current identity: 1) Honoring Parents; 2) Finding Individual Self; and, 3) Developing Asian American Identity.

Findings: Stress Narratives

Narrative of Honoring Parents

"I feel that kids are their retirement plan. Basically, when you grow up, the faster you become something, the faster you can make money, the better. Your parents are going to take care of you when you are small, and once you get a job, then you take care of them. Both of my parents work really, really, really hard . . . They earn money and give it to me. They don't buy a sports car. My dad always wanted to buy a Mercedes Benz and drive around in it, but he spends that money on me. He could have bought it, so I kind of have to do well and show him that I am as good an investment as the Mercedes and make them happy." (first-generation male)

One common narrative was of the need and desire to fulfill filial piety by honoring the wishes and actions of parents. In all focus groups, students described the traditional Asian cultural values that they thought their families adhered to. These included having respect for elders, upholding family honor, and a sense of collectivity. Many identified with these values and said that they desired to pass them on to their own children in the future. In five of the focus groups, students felt that there were cultural gender differences that distinguished the experiences of male from those of female Asian American college students. Asian American women were perceived as having an easier time acculturating and being accepted by mainstream society, but at the same time facing more rigid expectations and restrictions growing up in a traditional Asian household.

There was awareness expressed of the great sacrifice made by parents and the psychological burden this placed on the students. This sacrifice was described with both gratitude and as incurring obligation. In two focus groups, students framed this obligation as needing to "pay off" the investment that their parents had made in them. Some students explained that they were expected to support their families after they graduated from college. This expectation was coupled with pressure to major in a discipline that would yield a financially rewarding career. For some, living up to their parents' expectations was seen as a way of expressing gratitude.

Many of the stresses that the students and their families faced reflected issues of the immigrant experience. The need to be successful, as defined by educational attainment and financial return in a career, was commonly mentioned by students. Students from several of the focus groups described their parents' tenacity in pursuing a living in America. The students perceived their own educational and career accomplishments as an extension of that work ethic. For example, a second-generation female shared,

> My parents always tell me, "We came here a few years before when there were no generations of people who had settled here . . . We came here for you. We got out of poverty." There is pressure to maintain [standards of achievement] and to exceed that level, to work hard and forego other things. Yes, there is definitely a different kind of stress . . . taking into consideration [my parents'] situation, they did the best they could with what they knew. They show me they cared—maybe not the way I would like it—but primarily and mostly for my welfare . . . It's a culture clash, but I really believe deep down they want me to be happy, even though their definition of 'happy' is different than mine.

This student clearly articulates the stress associated with honoring parents. She feels pressure to achieve and honor their sacrifice by her own sacrifice. The situation is further complicated by an awareness of a cultural clash in how one shows concern and how happiness is defined. Another student, a 1.5-generation female, explained her perception of the relation between the parents' sacrifice and the students' stress, and different concepts of happiness,

> It seems like the parents work so hard to give the kids a better life that they're ruining their kids. They're stressed out all the time and they look at their kids and are like, "Why aren't you working harder? I've worked so hard and sacrificed so much to get you here. You're not making my sacrifice worth it." And then the kids are like, "Well that doesn't make me happy," and the parents are like, "Well happiness doesn't mean anything because we gave up our happiness."

A majority of the participants described their parents as being major sources of influence in their lives, whether it was in choosing an academic major and future career, or in shaping their personal set of values. They acknowledged the sacrifices their parents had made for them and expressed gratitude. Students' sense of filial piety created a deep obligation to fulfill family expectations that permeated their lives, even after leaving home for college. The burden of being continually bound to their family responsibilities was an issue perceived as being distinctive to the Asian American college student experience. One second-generation male articulated the direct connection he feels between his family and his stress,

I think what distinguishes my stress from my non-Asian friends is that with every decision I make, I'm making it by taking my family into consideration. I think everything from "What's my major going to be?" to "I can't study abroad because who's going to take care of my grandma?" or "What am I going to do, who's taking care of my parents?" I make plans around my family responsibilities.

Honoring parents was expressed as an obligation but also related to a need to allow parents to control their lives. So it was not only stress from trying to fulfill their parents' academic pressure and expectations and the burden of needing to repay the sacrifice, but being burdened by what some experienced as excessive control by their parents. The students expressed these sentiments in stories of discipline, punishment, curfews, and parental control of social activities. A second-generation female described how her upbringing instilled a sense of desperation in needing to succeed, a kind of psychological control,

[My mom] tried to instill a fear in me of being on the street and starving, "In China, people eat one bowl of rice. If you don't do your homework, I'll beat you with a whip. If you don't work hard, you're not going to live that long. People don't have that much to eat. If you don't work hard, you don't maintain that level." I can see that fear wash on me all day.

However, nearly all of the students expressed a sense of appreciation for the way they were raised by their family and described their parents as having "done the best that they could." This sentiment was shared even if they disagreed with their strict upbringing. Some did mention the effects of harsh methods of discipline, as this second-generation female put it, "*I do appreciate the way my parents raised me, but their ways made me harbor a lot of resentment . . .*"

The use of physical punishment as a form of discipline was mentioned in three focus groups, specifically "being beaten" and "being hit." Two 1.5 generation females shared the extent of the physical discipline,

My mom would hit me when I was little [for lying]. I would be angry for days after because it hurt so bad. I remember I couldn't sit down for 3 days . . . When I grew older, she started throwing punches at me.

My mom still hits me. My mom slapped me for getting a B in history in sixth grade. After that point she [would] freak out and throw things at me.

The narratives of honoring parents revealed both the appreciation for sacrifice and the burden it imposes. Obligation is both imposed by parents and accepted by students. In either case it brings stress to the young Asian American.

Narrative of Finding Self

A second stress narrative was related to finding a sense of self. This theme was expressed in various ways, such as in narratives of separating oneself from the need to fulfill the expectations of parents and finding one's own desires and interests. Other expressions were the internalization of social and cultural values and norms and how these create stress for the developing adolescent. Another style of this narrative was how individuals cope with conflict between their desires and those of their parents.

Students expressed appreciation for their parents' role in achieving academic success, some even attributing their success to parental pressure. However, there was conflict between the parents' and students' perspectives on the purpose of a college education. Students expressed sentiments that parents did not understand that their college and educational experiences should reflect more than a means of professional attainment. This conflict was often reflected in the difference between what students defined as a "rewarding" and "successful" experience in college. One second-generation female explained,

> Maybe my parents see "rewarding" related to "success." A lot of the things that we do in college like volunteering or tutoring that may not be considered success but are rewarding [to me].

Students also felt that following the cultural value of obedience hindered their ability to communicate and interact socially with others. Being "non-confrontational" and acquiescing to others also meant that they had to suppress their emotions. One student described being taught to "give in, pretend [that a problem] doesn't affect you" and "let the other person have their way" (1.5-generation female). Students felt a conflict between their cultural values and the social expectation to assert themselves as independent adults in American society; they perceived these Asian values to be stifling to their own aspirations and their innate wishes to articulate themselves. A 1.5-generation male shared how he felt like he was affected psychologically and socially in terms of his ability to individuate, often described as a major challenge of adolescence,

> [You're] not supposed to be emotional . . . You can't talk bad, can't have your own mind, can't express what you want to do, who you want to date, who you want to be . . . [My] parents were taught to always obey and not to have their own say, [so] they teach us the same thing. It hurts [our] leadership skills.

Trying to live up to the high expectations of parents and others also meant difficulty in discovering one's own vocation, a major challenge of identity development. Many students also noted their parents' preference for majors and careers in the sciences and felt pressured to become physicians, lawyers or other professionals. Even the students who felt their parents did not expect them to major in certain fields of study perceived the pressure to conform to these "parentally approved" areas of studies.

While some students resisted their parents, those who chose to defy their parents' expectations felt selfish and guilty for pursuing their own aspirations. Out of fear of disapproval, some students in two focus groups still hadn't told their parents that they had picked "unacceptable" majors. One second-generation female described the disapproval she would receive from her family for failing to fulfill family expectations,

> [In Chinese culture,] the family is the central unit of existence. And to take care of your parents, you sometimes have to sacrifice your own wishes. You can't have a job somewhere else because your parents are old and you have to support them. You can't put them in a nursing home . . . [It's] family versus your own independence.

The perception of unspoken or implicit expectations was another significant theme when students talked about their families and parents. Students' stress also derived from having to define these tacit expectations. No one expressed it as starkly as one 1.5-generation female student, *"Ninety percent of my stress comes from my parents. It's not as much what they say, but what's unsaid."*

Students whose academic and professional interests did not align with their parents' expectations were often conflicted about which path to pursue. Some students would mitigate the conflict by rationalizing that the major or career they picked was purely out of their own choice. A 1.5-generation male shared,

> My parents always had implicit expectations on what I was supposed to be. I wanted to be a bioengineer . . . I knew they wanted me to be one so I chose it . . . What they wanted me to be or do they don't say outright, but they comment on my decisions, so it makes you change your mind.

Students described growing up with high family expectations for academic achievement as "stressful" and "full of pressure." This drive for achievement becomes internalized over time. One second-generation male compared the ingraining of values from his upbringing to the beating of a drum,

> When you first hear it, when you grow up with your parents, they're beating and it's just around you. But after that's gone, you still hear it within yourself. It first got there by your parents—that outside source—and then the beating, "I have to do this. I have to do this."

Other sources of stress come from peers and immediate social environment. For instance, one 1.5-generation female described how seeing the high achievement among her Asian American peers reinforced the pressure to meet her parents' expectations. Although they knew that other college students also felt high pressure to succeed, students in half of the focus groups felt that the type of pressure they faced as Asian Americans was something their non-Asian peers could not fathom.

The chasm between personal and parental desires is often dealt with in a stoic rather than an assertive attitude in terms of problem solving. The students generally expressed unfamiliarity with the counseling services offered on campus or perceived these services to be impersonal and not relevant to their lives. They shared that their attitudes about mental health and the use of psychological counseling were largely influenced by beliefs espoused by their family and culture. Depression and other mental health problems were described as being a "weakness," "selfish," and "what white people do when they get bored." Because mental health problems were not considered true diseases, counseling services were perceived as unnecessary. While some students had utilized career counseling services, most perceived counselors as uncaring strangers who would not be able to help. Other students said that only in grave situations, if their everyday functioning was severely debilitated for example, could they overcome the stigma to use psychological counseling services.

Students' most common resources for stress relief included talking to friends, parents and family members, while others felt that talking to their parents would only exacerbate their stress. In two focus groups, a significant theme was the need for self-reliance. Students were often told by parents to "just get over it" if they were feeling sad or depressed. Some students felt they had to suppress their emotions and deal with their problems on their own.

Only two students reported having used the campus counseling services. Unfortunately, these students had ambivalent or negative perceptions of the counselors. One second-generation, female student said, *"I've gone to [counseling] services and they don't care about you, but at the same time they do let you know things that apply to your situations."* Another second-generation, female student shared, *"I have an indirect experience. I was dating this guy, and I made him go to [the counseling center], and they didn't do anything, they just gave him addresses, and they didn't follow up at all.*

Some people go on a whim and if they don't follow up, they won't go back." Some students suggested that having counselors of the same ethnic background might be helpful. One second-generation male opined,

> I think that I'd want to see diversification of the counselors that we already have. I really felt that maybe if I'd spoken to an Asian counselor, they'd be more sympathetic about what I spoke because of the shared experiences.

Narrative of Asian American Identity Development

A third stress narrative was the Asian American identity development, which involved dealing with internal and external stereotypes. Some students felt stereotyped by others in ways that limited their freedom. For example, when peers at school assumed that they were smart or did well in particular subjects just because they were Asian American, some students felt they had to live up to this stereotype. A second-generation male noted, *"I feel that there is a lot of pressure to be smart because the Asian stereotype is a nerd studying at home . . . I guess I'm trying to fulfill the stereotype and that pressures me."* Others felt respect by their peers, while at the same time troubled when confronted with stereotypes. A second-generation female explained,

> I feel annoyed by the stereotypes [of Asian Americans] and I'm annoyed because I tend to fall into them . . . I'm [a biology major], play piano, and am pre-med. I'm interested in these things, but I still feel pressure to change things because people expect that if I have any personality whatsoever I'd be different from the stereotype, but I'm not. I don't want to change anything just to prove that I'm unique, but people think I'm an unthinking robot and it bothers me a little bit.

A heightened awareness of cultural differences between Asians and other groups was another common theme among students. Some students perceived the Asian community to be insular and described their families as only socializing and interacting with people from their own ethnic group. For some, college life also reflected a limited social circle; although they acknowledged the need to mix with different kinds of people, it was difficult for them to change. A second-generation female shared,

> It's more like I can identify with Asian Americans and second-generation ones especially. It's weird because I'm American and I grew up here, but when I talk to people I sometimes feel like a foreigner . . . I still feel different among them . . . I think it's really difficult to form long-lasting relations with non-Asians.

The expectations of Asian American college students from their peers and social environment represented a microcosm of expectations that were perceived to stem from society at large. Students in three of the focus groups pointed to images of Asian Americans in the media as sources of social expectations of them to be perpetual foreigners who are nerdy and passive: *"A lot has to do with media stereotypes, such as being short and not speaking good English, no leadership skills . . . preconceptions and stereotypes play big roles."* (second-generation male). Some students believed in these limited representations of Asian Americans until they came to college. A 1.5-generation male who was raised in a predominantly white community remembered, *"I grew up thinking that Asians wear thick glasses, are good at math, do not do sports, and were not good at sports. When I moved to California, I was more exposed to more Asians and saw many different types that don't fit the stereotypes."*

The internalization of these societal expectations also made students feel negative towards themselves as Asian Americans. Males in the focus groups, in particular, expressed how they were affected by portrayals of Asian American males as undesirable and emasculated. For example, a second-generation male noted, *"I always saw images of Asians in the media as being dorky, being nerds with no lives, [wearing] thick glasses . . . and at one point I was actually ashamed of being Asian, because of that stereotype and the fear of fulfilling it."* In addition, students also felt affected by the lack of visible Asian American role models in society. One 1.5-generation male explained, *"When I was a young child growing up, I think maybe [the media creates an] inferiority complex between Asian Americans and people of other ethnicities . . . [the images on TV are] a representation of what you'll be like in the future."*

In three of the focus groups, students shared how they struggled with their ethnic identities. Students expressed not knowing what it meant to be "Asian American" in relation to their bicultural backgrounds; they also described a yearning to connect with others going through the same identity search. Some students established a sense of belonging through Asian American student organizations. For example, a 1.5-generation male described his experiences joining a Vietnamese American student association,

> For me, I think my experiences in [the club] made it easier to belong . . . . my freshman year, I had a diverse group of friends but for some reason I couldn't identify with them. I mean, you try to be friends but they couldn't understand me. Like when I'm talking on the phone in Vietnamese and they feel weird . . . I mean mostly it's just little things but they all add up to them not really understanding what you're going through, so it's hard to get close to them. So as I joined [the club] I met more people who had the same problems and were going through the same things . . . it made my college experience better in that I feel like I belong more.

However, among the Asian American peer community, students acknowledged tensions related to generational status. The second-generation students referred to the first-generation Asian Americans as "FOBs" (an acronym for "Fresh Off the Boat" in reference to recent immigration status). The first-generation students were also perceived to be more studious and socially isolated, which made them the subject of ridicule with second-generation Asian Americans. One second-generation female shared her attitudes toward first-generation Asian Americans,

> From my point of view, the FOBs that we make fun of are the ones that just hang out with themselves and speak their own language to each other. And we're like, "Why are they doing that? They live in America now, they should try to assimilate."

On the other hand, first-generation students felt their social isolation was forced upon them because the second-generation students did not accept them. A first-generation male described his understanding of the generational dichotomy,

> Most likely, FOBs are going to be smarter than ABCs [American-born Chinese]. ABCs tend to be more socialized and have a more diverse group of friends, while FOBs will stick with themselves. But that's kind of like [something] you can't do anything [about] because other people don't like them. If ABCs don't accept them, and if your 'own kind' doesn't accept you, how can you expect other diverse races to accept you?

The first-generation students resented these stereotypes. For instance, one first-generation female shared how she thought antagonism towards first-generation students was a reflection of second-generation Asian Americans' struggle with their ethnic identity,

> It really frustrates me when [second-generation Asian Americans] talk about themselves as being 'Asians' [and] say they have Asian pride; but I don't think they can really say they identify themselves as being 'Chinese' or 'Korean'. . . I think they always say they're 'Chinese-American', or 'Korean-American.' It just shows it's a higher standard to grow up; it's a social status. It's better, more prestigious to be 'American.'

Adolescent identity development alone is complicated. Factored with generational and ethnic differences, these statements uncover the tremendous struggle one experiences in Asian American identity development, making it difficult for youth to find a nurturing place to grow.

Discussion: "The Stress of Achievement"

The three stress narratives expressed by these Asian American college students provided an important view into their perceived sources of social and emotional stress and mental health needs. As previous research has shown, high-achieving Asian American students are stressed by academic demands and unclear career direction (Ying, et al., 2004), and their high academic achievement may come with significant social and psychological costs (Lew, et al., 1998). Maintaining the high academic standards placed upon them may lead to greater socioemotional difficulties, anxiety, and social isolation (Sue & Zane, 1985). Asian American students have significantly fewer cross-racial social interactions and a lower sense of coherence, which may put them at risk of meeting social and interpersonal challenges outside the academic arena (Ying, et al., 2001). They may be subjected to microaggressions, harassments, peer discrimination and other subtle racism that adversely affects their health (Sue, et al. 2007).

Certainly, these sources of stress are not unique to Asian American students. However, the students in this study clearly see their stress as related to their immigrant status, Asian culture, and being Asian in American society. Furthermore, the traditional cultural value of honoring parents (Hwang, 1999; Park, 2007) was perceived as a major source of stress. Parental sacrifice was both appreciated and viewed as a burden. Students felt that the cultural norm of obeying parents was an issue that particularly distinguished them from their non-Asian peers. They viewed their academic performance as a measure of personal achievement as well as of upholding their family's honor. None of the focus group participants was past the second generation and the "immigrant mentality" of working hard to survive was still a major theme that was reflected in the students' family experiences. Studying hard and achieving academically were seen as ways of honoring parents.

The narrative of honoring parents directly related to the second stress narrative of individuation and finding a sense of self (Kroger, 2007). Parental relationships created a web of interdependency in which the need to honor parents influenced the students' emerging developmental needs for individuation and identity in adolescence and early adulthood. Students expressed appreciation for their parents' role in achieving academic success, but they also expressed the difficulty of separating oneself from the need to fulfill parental expectations. Some expressed recognition of how parental norms and expectations were internalized, creating little room for the developing self, and a struggle with the sense of obligation that left no room for personal desire. In college, some students developed new self understanding, new interests, and new vocational desires. However, their parents' wishes continued to influence majors and career fields deemed acceptable. The academic expectations from their parents were not only to do well, but to do well in certain restricted fields determined by parents, sometimes from childhood.

Some stress experienced by Asian American college students certainly comes from the normal developmental challenges of adolescence and young adulthood. In addition, Asian American students may face further stresses specific to their ethnic minority status and cultural heritage (Smedley, et al., 1993; Liu and Goto, 2007). These challenges could partially pertain to their need for establishing their ethnic identities within a larger society (Yoo & Lee, 2005; Kiang et al, 2010). On a personal level, they may experience this as a struggle between being "good" and being "popular" (Qin, 2009). Asian American college students may internalize the model minority myth by selecting inapt majors. Consequently, the incongruence among their interests, strengths, and chosen field of study may create barriers to competence in college (Toupin and Son, 1991) and later in life.

Students also attributed a source of stress to having to negotiate their bicultural identities among various environments (e.g. family, school, and peer relations). Many felt they were in a double-bind, being compelled culturally to stay integrated with their families while they were expected to be independent young adults by Western norms. The difficulty in finding self also related to the narrative of Asian American identity development. The results showed that students found it problematic to define themselves as Asian American because whether they met their peers' social expectations or not, they felt that stereotypes limited their ability to be recognized for their own individuality. Many first-generation students experienced prejudice from their Asian American peers, reinforcing the findings of a previous study showing inter-generational conflict (Kim, et al., 2003). This intra-group hostility may be representative of second-generation students' projection of their insecurities with their Asian American identity. Perhaps, ridiculing the first-generation students allowed the second-generation students to create an "us versus them" dichotomy and to assert themselves as being different from the stereotypes.

Asian American students may struggle to straddle two competing and often conflicting value systems. American society dictates that they must demonstrate independence, assertiveness, and individuality, but these values conflict with traditional Asian cultural values of filial piety, interdependency, modesty, and collectivism (Wu, 1992). Studies show a high degree of alienation between parents and children as adolescents struggle with their identity development (Qin, 2006). The importance of a strong sense of ethnic identity is indicated in studies correlating it with high self-esteem, social connectedness, and sense of community (Lee, 2003; Lee & Yoo, 2004; Tsai, Ying & Lee, 2001, Yoo & Lee, 2005).

Policy Implications and Future Directions

Our study raised the question of why Asian Americans do not seek help to the same degree as others. Shame and stigma regarding mental illness; internalization of the 'trouble-free and academically successful' stereotype; and the paucity of culturally competent university counseling staff may be some reasons (Uba, 1994; Yang et al., 2002; McKinney, 2005). Most studies trying to answer this question have focused on understanding students' use of mental health or psychological counseling services (Ting, 2009), while there are few published reports of efforts to develop preventive programs that aim to promote mental health and well-being.

Our findings, together with those of other studies (e.g. Lee, 2009; Suyemoto, 2009), indicate a need for understanding the mental health of Asian American college students from a multidimensional framework. Low utilization rates of mental health services on college campuses by Asian American students should not be viewed as an indication of wellness. In our study, few students had utilized mental health services and those who did, perceived the services as inadequate and insensitive to their needs as Asian Americans. In contrast, career counseling services were perceived as useful and accessible. The general dissatisfaction among focus group participants who had used counseling services at the university is important to investigate. We suspect that it may be a reflection of poor understanding or unrealistic expectations of mental health counseling. It should also be noted that others have reported a generation difference in the utilization of mental health services by Asian Americans (Miller et al, 2011).

Our findings indicate the need to develop culturally appropriate mental health services for Asian American college students. Universities can make psychological counseling seem more relevant to Asian American students, perhaps by integrating mental health interventions with career counseling services, which are perceived as more accessible. College officials could also explore the use of other sources of support, such as Asian American studies, which may enhance self understanding and provide a space for students' ethnic identity development. This approach may also be perceived as more accessible because of its academic orientation. Many students also reported that Asian American cultural groups, at school and in the community, enhance identity development, suggesting that they may benefit from opportunities to develop the leadership and interpersonal skills that may have been underemphasized or discouraged in their upbringing. Formal mentorship programs may also be useful, as they connect students with role models who serve as an alternative to the stereotypical images of Asian Americans in society. Finally, students can be recruited and trained to increase awareness of mental health related issues in the larger Asian American community, using techniques such as story-telling and social marketing.

The participatory action research model used in our study may be an effective means of empowering Asian American youth to promote mental well-being. Suyemoto et al. (2009) used a similar model with Asian students at an east coast college, and reported that it helped increase dialogue about the Asian American student experience on campus. We are also convinced that there is a need to investigate the levels of chronic stresses faced by Asian American youth and their long-term effects on physical health. Emerging research shows that chronic stress may increase risk for metabolic conditions such as diabetes and obesity (Gee, 2008), and that these conditions are occurring at younger ages than previously reported (Clark, 2009). Given the paucity of research on the physical health of Asian American youth, there is an urgency to promote interdisciplinary research among mental health and physical health researchers to better understand the effects of chronic stress in Asian American youth on overall health and well-being. Our data show that Asian American college students face various socio-emotional stresses that are largely eclipsed by their academic achievement. Universities need to take steps to ensure that counselors are aware of the various pressures Asian American college students face and offer culturally competent mental health services. Researchers and educators should take action to address the stress experienced by Asian American students with programs and services that are sensitive to students' needs.

References

Appel HB, Huang B, Ai AL, Lin CJ. 2011. Physical, Behavioral, and Mental Health Issues in Asian American Women: Results from the National Latino and Asian American Study. J Women's Health (Larchmt). Jul 21. [Epub ahead of print]

Arifuku, Isami. 2004. Issues confronting Asian and Pacific Islander Youth in San Francisco and Oakland. Oakland, CA: Asian Pacific Islander Youth Violence Prevention Center.

Bankston, Carl L., III and Min Zhou. 2002. "Being well vs. doing well: Self-esteem and school performance among immigrant and nonimmigrant racial and ethnic groups." *The International Migration Review* 36(2): 389–415.

Benton, Sherry, John Robertson, Wen-Chih Tseng, Fred Newton, Stephen Benton. 2003. "Changes in Counseling Center Client Problems Across 13 Years." *Professional Psychology: Research and Practice* 34(1): 66–72.

Castro, Jennifer R. and Kenneth G. Rice. 2003. "Perfectionism and ethnicity: Implications for depressive symptoms and self-reported academic achievement." *Cultural Diversity and Ethnic Minority Psychology* 9(1): 64–76.

Clark, Peter A. 2009. "Type 2 diabetes in youth." *J S C Med Assoc* 105: 51–4.

Eisenberg, Daniel PhD; Golberstein, Ezra BA; Gollust, Sarah E. BA. 2007. Help-Seeking and Access to Mental Health Care in a University Student Population. Medical Care, 45(7) : 594–601. doi: 10.1097/MLR.0b013e31803bb4c1

Eng, Sothy, Kirti Kanitkar, Harrington, H. Cleveland, Richard Herbert, Judith Fischer and Jacquelyn D. Wiersma. 2008. "School Achievement Differences among Chinese and Filipino American Students: Acculturation and the Family. " *Educational Psychology* 28(5): 535–550.

Gee, Gilbert C., Annie Ro, Amelia Gavin and David T. Takeuchi. 2008. "Disentangling the effects of racial and weight discrimination on body mass index and obesity among Asian Americans." *Am J Public Health* 98: 493–500.

Haas, A.P., Hendi, H., Mann, J.J. 2003. Suicide in college students. American Behavioral Scientist 46(9): 1224–1240.

Hwang, Kwang-Kuo. 1999. "Filial piety and loyalty: Two types of social identification in Confucianism." *Asian J Social Psychology* 2: 163–183.

Kiang L, Witkow MR, Baldelomar OA, Fuligni AJ. 2010. Change in ethnic identity across the high school years among adolescents with Latin American, Asian, and European backgrounds. J Youth Adolesc.;39(6):683–93.

Kim, Bryan S.K., Bradley R. Brenner, Christopher T.H. Liang, Penelope A. Asay. 2003. "A qualitative study of adaptation experiences of 1.5-generation Asian Americans." *Cultural Diversity and Ethnic Minority Psychology* 9(2): 156–170.

Kroger, Jane. 2007. *Identity development: Adolescence through adulthood.* Thousand Oaks: Sage Publications.

Kvale, Steinar. 1996. *InterViews.* London: Sage.

Lee, Richard M. 2003. "Do ethnic identity and other-group orientation protect against discrimination for Asian Americans?" *Journal of Counseling Psychology* 50: 133–141.

Lee, Sunmin, Hee-Soon Juon, Genevieve Martinez, Chiehwen E. Hsu, E. Stephanie Robinson, Julie Bawa, and Grace X. Ma. 2009. "Model minority at risk: expressed needs of mental health by Asian American young adults." *J Community Health* 34(2): 144–52.

Lew, Angela S., Rhianon Allen, Nicholas Papouchis, and Barry Ritzler. 1998. "Achievement orientation and fear of success in Asian American college students." *Journal of Clinical Psychology* 54(1): 97–108.

Liu, William, Elena S.H. Yu, Ching-Fu Chang, and Marilyn Fernandez. 1990. "The mental health of Asian American teenagers: A research challenge." pp. 92–112 in *Ethnic Issues in Adolescent Mental Health*, eds. Arlene Rubin Stiffman and Larry E. Davis. Newbury Park: Sage Publications.

Liu FF, Goto SG. 2007. Self-construal, mental distress, and family relations: a mediated moderation analysis with Asian American adolescents. *Cultur Divers Ethnic Minor Psychol.* 13(2):134–42.

McKewen, M. K., Corinne Maekawa Kodama, Alvin N. Alvarez, Sunny Lee, Christopher T.H. Liang, eds. 2002. Working with Asian American college students: New directions for student services. San Francisco: Jossey Bass.

McKinney, Kristen. 2005. "Mental health among UCLA undergraduates." Student Affairs Information and Research Office (SAIRO) <*http://www.sairo.ucla.edu/2005Reports/Mental%20Health%20Among%20UCLA%20 Undergraduates%20Oct%202005.pdf*> as of June 15, 2009.

Miller MJ, Yang M, Hui K, Choi NY, Lim RH. 2011. Acculturation, enculturation, and Asian American college students' mental health and attitudes toward seeking professional psychological help. J Couns Psychol. 58:346–57.

Museus, Samuel and Mitchell Chang. 2009. "Rising to the challenge of conducting research on Asian Americans in higher education." *New Directions for Institutional Research* 142: 95–106.

National Center for Health Statistics. 2000. *Health, United States, 2000.* Hyattsville: U.S. Public Health Service.

Okazaki, Sumie. 1997. "Sources of ethnic differences between Asian American and White American college students on measures of depression and social anxiety." *Journal of Abnormal Psychology* 106(1): 52–60.

Park, Mijung and Catherine Chesla. 2007. "Revisiting Confucianism as a conceptual framework for Asian family study." *J Fam Nurs.* 13(3):293–311.

Qin, Desiree Baolian. 2006. " 'Our child doesn't talk to us any more': Alienation in immigrant Chinese families." *Anthropology and Education Quarterly,* 37(2), 162–179.

Qin, Desiree Baolian. 2009. "Being 'good' or being 'popular': Gender and ethnic identity negotiations of immigrant Chinese adolescents." *Journal of Adolescent Research,* 24(1), 37–66.

Ramanjuan, Krishna. 2006. Health expert explains Asian and Asian-American students' unique pressures to succeed. Chronicle Online, *http://www.news.cornell.edu/stories/april06/chung.ksr.html*

Reeves, Terrence J. and Claudette E. Bennett. 2004. *We the people: Asians in the United States, Census 2000 special reports (CENSR-17).* Washington, D.C.: U.S. Department of Commerce, U.S. Census Bureau.

Schoen, Cathy, Karen Davis, Karen S. Collins, Linda Greenberg, Catherine Des Roches, and Melinda Abrams. 1997. *The Commonwealth Fund survey of the health of adolescent girls.* New York: Louis Harris and Associates, Inc.

Shuchman, M. 2007. Falling through the Cracks—Virginia Tech and the Restructuring of College Mental Health Services. N Engl J Med 357:105–110.

Shea, S and Yeh, CJ. 2008. Asian American Students' Cultural Values, Stigma, and Relational Self-construal: Correlates of Attitudes Toward Professional Help Seeking. J Mental Health Counseling 30(2): 157–172.

Smedley, Brian, Hector Meyers, and Shelly Harrel. 1993. "Minority-status stresses and college adjustment of ethnic minority freshmen." *Journal of Higher Education* 64(4): 434–452.

Sue, Derald Wing, Christina M. Capodilupo, Gina C. Torino, Jennifer M. Bucceri, Aisha M. B Holder, Kevin L. Nadal, Marta Esquilin. Racial microaggressions in everyday life: Implications for clinical practice. *American Psychologist,* Vol 62(4), May–Jun 2007, 271–286.

Sue, Stanley and Nolan W.S. Zane. 1985. "Academic achievement and socio-emotional adjustment among Chinese university students." *Journal of Counseling Psychology* 32(4): 570–579.

Suzuki, B. H. 2002. Revisiting the model minority stereotype: Implications for student affairs practice and higher education. In M. McEwen, C. Kodoma, A. Alvarez, & C. Liang (EDS.), *Working with Asian American college students* (pp. 21–32). San Francisco: Jossey-Bass.

Suyemoto, Karen, Grace Kim, Miwa Tanabe, John Tawa and Stephanie Day. 2009. "Challenging the model minority myth: Engaging Asian American students in research on Asian American college student experiences." *New Directions for Institutional Research* 142: 41–55.

Ting Julia Y. and Wei-Chin Hwang. 2009. "Cultural influences on help-seeking attitudes in Asian American students." *Am J Orthopsychiatry:* 79(1):125–32.

Toupin, Elizabeth S.W. Ahn and Linda Son. 1991. "Preliminary findings on Asian Americans: "The model minority" in a small private East Coast college." *Journal of Cross-Cultural Psychology* 22(3): 403–417.

Tsai, Jeanne L., Yu-Wen Ying, and Peter Allen Lee. 2001. "Cultural predictors of self-esteem: A study of Chinese American female and male young adults." *Cultural Diversity and Ethnic Minority Psychology* 7(3): 284–297.

Uba, Laura. 1994. *Asian Americans: Personality patterns, identity, and mental health.* New York, NY: Guilford.

U.S. Census. 2010. *Facts for features, Asian Pacific Heritage Month: May 2010, http://www.census.gov/newsroom/releases/archives/facts_for_features_special_editions/cb10-ff07.html,* March 2nd

USDHHS. 1999. *Mental Health: A Report of the Surgeon General.* Rockville: U.S. Department of Health and Human Services, Substance Abuse and Mental Health Services Administration, Center for Mental Health Services, National Institutes of Health, National Institute of Mental Health.

Willgerodt, Mayumi Anne. 2008. "Family and peer influences on adjustment among Chinese, Filipino, and White youth." *Nurs Res.* 57: 395–405.

Woo, Deborah. 2000. *Glass ceilings and Asian Americans: The new face of workplace barriers.* Walnut Creek, CA: AltaMira Press.

Wu, Jenai. 1992. "Masochism and fear of success in Asian women: Psychoanalytic mechanisms and problems in therapy." *The American Journal of Psychoanalysis* 52(1): 1–12.

Yang, Raymond K., Steven R. Byers, Linda M. Ahuna, and Kimberly S. Castro. 2002. "Asian-American students' use of a university student-affairs office." *College Student Journal* 36(3): 448–470.

Ying, Yu-Wen, Peter A. Lee, Jeanne L. Tsai, Yuan Hung, Melissa Lin, and Ching Tin Wan. 2001. "Asian American college students as model minorities: An examination of their overall competence." *Cultural Diversity and Ethnic Minority Psychology* 7(1): 59–74.

Ying, Yu-Wen, Peter A. Lee and Jeanne L. Tsai. 2004. "Inventory of college challenges for ethnic minority students: psychometric properties of a new instrument in Chinese Americans." *Cultural Diversity and Ethnic Minority Psychology* 10(4): 351–364.

Yoo, Hyung Chol and Richard M. Lee. 2005. "Ethnic identity and approach-type coping as moderators of the racial discrimination/well-being relation in Asian Americans." *Journal of Counseling Psychology* 52(4): 497–506.

Young CB, Fang DZ, Zisook S. 2010. Depression in Asian-American and Caucasian undergraduate students. *J Affect Disord.* 125(1–3):379–82. Epub 2010 Mar 19.

Zhang, Amy, Lonnie Snowden, and Stanley Sue. 1998. "Differences between Asian and White Americans' help seeking and utilization patterns in the Los Angeles area." *Journal of Community Psychology* 26(4): 317–326.

CHAPTER 18

"Splitting Things in Half Is So White!": Conceptions of Family Life and Friendship and the Formation of Ethnic Identity among Second Generation Vietnamese Americans

Hung C. Thai

The new second generation Americans, a term technically referring to the children of contemporary immigrants, has just recently been given attention by immigration scholars. Only a few studies have looked at the subjective experiences of children of these immigrants, particularly with regard to issues of identity and how youths negotiate between "new" and "old" worlds. The future demographics of the United States will include a large percentage of children of immigrants; among Asian American children, for example, it is estimated that over 90 percent live in a household with at least one immigrant parent. In fact, in some states such as California and Texas, children of immigrants will soon outnumber whites.[1]

This article examines the ways Vietnamese Americans form ethnic identity through cultural ideology. Given the need for a wider focus on the subjective experiences of children of contemporary immigrants, this article attempts to join existing discussions by exploring how second generation Vietnamese American college students and young working adults portray and interpret their experiences of growing up as children of immigrants, and for some, as immigrants themselves. Drawing on eighteen open-ended interviews, my data indicate that young adult

[1] Contemporary immigrants are those individuals who arrived in the U.S. after the Immigration Act of 1965. Since then, most immigrants have come from Asia or the Americas. See Min Zhou, "Growing Up American: The Challenge Confronting Immigrant Children and Children of Immigrants," *Annual Review of Sociology* 23 (1997): 63–95. For a brief discussion of the Immigration Act of 1965, see Alejandro Portes and Ruben G. Rumbaut, *Immigrant America: A Portrait*, 2nd ed. (Berkeley: University of California Press, 1996), 8–15. For recent studies focusing on children of *contemporary* immigrants, see Rumbaut, "The Crucible Within: Ethnic Identity, Self Esteem, and Segmented Assimilation among Children of Immigrants," *International Migration Review* 28:4 (1994), 748–794; Min Zhou and Carl L. Bankston III, "Social Capital and the Adaptation of the Second Generation: The Case of Vietnamese Youth in New Orleans," *International Migration Review* 28:4 (1994), 795–820; Nazli Kibria, "The Construction of 'Asian American': Reflections on Intermarriage and Ethnic Identity Among Second-Generation Chinese and Korean Americans," *Ethnic and Racial Studies* 20:2 (1997), 523–544; Portes and Rumbaut, 1996; and Zhou, 1997. Although there are distinctions, depending on the interpretation, the terms "second generation" and "children of immigrants" will be used interchangeably in this paper for ease of presentation. And, for an in-depth discussion of the "coming white minority" in California, see Dale Maharidge, *The Coming White Minority: California Eruptions and America's Future* (New York: New York Times Books, 1996).

second generation Vietnamese Americans experienced the classic "marginal man" situation in their childhood and adolescent years, but in early adulthood, they began to shift in their cultural self perceptions. Initially conceptualized by Park and later formalized by Stonequist,[2] the "marginal-man" situation is one in which "the individual who through migration, education, marriage, or some other influence leaves one social group or culture making a satisfactory adjustment to another finds himself on the margin of each but a member of neither."[3] My informants began to challenge traditional patterns of immigrant assimilation when they entered college and the workforce. Instead of continually identifying themselves with the host culture, they began to form a strong ethnic identity, drawing upon traditional Vietnamese cultural ideologies and practices in their everyday life with family and friends.

Research on contemporary immigrants has generally been structural in nature ignoring cultural ideology[4] and devoting more consideration to such dimensions as the labor market and educational attainment. Until recently, immigration scholars have focused almost exclusively on adult immigrants and the ways they cope with social and economic changes. Much of this research is organized around the straight line assimilation model, a classic theoretical perspective, which argues that immigrants eventually abandon their cultures and enter into the host society as a way of ensuring upward mobility and economic security.[5]

But, as Joane Nagel argues, the resurgence of ethnic nationalism in the United States and around the world has challenged the assimilation model.[6] Immigrant scholars examining the lives of children of immigrants have begun to explore how "new" ethnic minorities resist hegemonic notions of assimilation, often creating new identities and images of themselves.[7] In my exploration, I seek to understand ways in which second generation Vietnamese Americans experience bipolar marginality—the sense of being on the margins of two cultures[8]—and how as young adults, they utilize cultural ideologies to help them construct, create, and recreate ethnic identity. This study

---

[2] Robert E. Park and Ernest W. Burgess, *Introduction to the Science of Society,* 2nd Edition (Chicago: University of Chicago Press, 1924), 161–64, 280–87; and Everett Stonequist, *The Marginal Man* (New York: Charles Scribner's Sons Publications, 1961).

[3] Stonequist, *Marginal Man,* 3.

[4] I use the term "ideology" to refer to a set of beliefs and theories people construct to make sense of the world and guide their actions in it, as opposed to other considerations of what ideology mean, such as Mannheim's classic analysis of ideology as beliefs promoted by ruling elites in order to maintain positions of dominance. See Karl Mannheim, *Ideology and Utopia* (New York: Harcourt and Brace Press, 1985).

[5] Informed by classical theory of urbanism, the assimilation model began with the Chicago School sociologist Robert E. Park (1924). For a critique of the assimilation model and the limits of using structural analyses to discuss immigrant's lives, see Joane Nagel, "Constructing Ethnicity: Creating and Recreating Ethnic Identity and Culture," *Social Problems* 41:1 (1994), 152–176; Jean Bacon, *Life Line: Community, Family, and Assimilation Among Asian Indian Immigrants* (New York: Oxford Press, 1996); Karen Pyke, " 'The Normal American Family' as an Interpretive Structure of Family Life Among Children of Korean and Vietnamese Immigrants," Paper presented at the annual meeting of the American Sociological Association, San Francisco, 1998; Kibria, 1993, 1997; and Zhou.

[6] Nagel.

[7] For example, Pyke argues that second generation Vietnamese and Korean Americans reject mainstream cultural ideologies of self-sufficiency and individualism, thereby promoting ethnic continuity, in the realm of filial care by declaring that they intend to support their parents in the elderly years; Kibria, "The Construction of 'Asian American'," finds that second generation Chinese and Korean Americans' reflections on intermarriage show that a preference for same-ethnic or same-racial marriages shapes ethnic and racial identity.

[8] Stonequist, *Marginal Man;* and Zhou and Bankston III.

adds their voices to the discussion of the new second generation, putting a new dimension to research on contemporary immigrants for at least two reasons. First, it offers a glimpse into how a particular population group of contemporary children of immigrants perceive ethnic identification via relationships with family and friends and via the larger society. Second, the Vietnamese, either as refugees or as members of family reunification programs, are a unique set of immigrants because of the nature of their departures from their old world. Strictly speaking, many were not voluntary migrants and this provides an interesting angle into questions of their ethnic identification.

Second Generation Vietnamese Americans, Their Parents, and the Cultural Ideology of Collectivism

Post-1965 Vietnamese Immigrants

The Vietnamese are contemporary immigrants to the United States since few actually arrived before 1965. Along with Mexico, the Philippines, China/Taiwan, and South Korea, Vietnam has been one of the top countries to send immigrants since then.[9] However, unlike other contemporary immigrants, the Vietnamese were mostly forced out of their homeland because of political turmoil and the majority of Vietnamese immigrants arrived in the U.S. after South Vietnam lost the war to the North in the mid-1970s. As a result, regardless of their economic standing prior to migration, most experienced some level of poverty and were forced to depend on government assistance upon arrival in the U.S.[10] Vietnamese immigrants in the United States and elsewhere can be categorized into six different waves. The first exodus of Vietnamese immigrants who arrived as political refugees began shortly after April 30, 1975 after the South had lost the war in Vietnam.[11] The second wave, which included mostly ethnic Chinese, left in 1978 and 1979; the third wave included those who escaped by boat or overland between 1978 and 1982. The fourth and fifth waves occured between 1983–1989 and after 1989 respectively, most of whom were asylum seekers and those who sought resettlement from refugee camps in countries such as Thailand and the Philippines. Currently, those arriving in the U.S. come from refugee camps abroad or as participants in family reunification programs.[12]

---

[9] Zhou, 63.

[10] Darrel Montero, *Vietnamese Americans: Patterns of Resettlement and Socioeconomic Adaptation in the United States* (Boulder, Colorado: Westview Press, 1979); William O'Hare and Judy Felt, *Asian Americans: America's Fastest Growing Minority Group* (Washington, D.C.: Population Reference Bureau, Inc., 1991).

[11] Between April and December 1975, the United States admitted 130,400 Southeast Asian refugees, 125,000 of whom were Vietnamese. Annual arrivals of Southeast Asian refugees had increased exponentially: 20,4000 in 1978, 80,700 in 1979, and 166,700 in 1980. Refugees quickly earned "legal" statuses as immigrants, but tensions had arisen from the public and refugees themselves about resettlement programs, including unorganized mass resettlement. For a discussion of refugee law and policies on the Vietnamese American community, see Bill Hing, *Making and Remaking Asian America Through Immigration Policy* (Palo Alto: Stanford University Press, 1993), ch. 4.

[12] Prior to 1965, there were about 18,000 Vietnamese in the United States, mainly as university students or as war brides to U.S. servicemen. See James Freeman, *Changing Identities: Vietnamese Americans 1975–1995* (Boston: Allyn and Bacon, 1995), 30. For further discussion of Vietnamese immigration history to the U.S., see also Freeman, *Hearts of Sorrow: Vietnamese-American Lives* (Palo Alto: Stanford University Press, 1989); and Kibria, *Family Tightrope*.

Different waves of Vietnamese immigrants are closely associated with social class and whether one came from an urban or rural background. In general, the earlier waves came from more affluent, urban backgrounds. Since 1975, a short period of time relative to the broader picture of U.S. immigration history, over 900,000 Vietnamese have made the U.S. their new homeland.[13] Of this total, over 56 percent live in California and Texas, two states in which children of immigrants will soon outnumber whites.[14] Because the Vietnamese arrived in such a large number in a relatively short period of time, their visibility in the dominant culture and their reactions to adaptations have been extensively researched by social scientists.[15] Few, however, have focused on the second generation's subjective experiences as children of immigrants, as immigrants themselves, and as minorities.

Researchers studying children of Vietnamese immigrants have often separated them into various generations. Among the foreign born, for example, three groups are categorized by age on arrival: the "second generation," those arriving before their fifth birthdays; the "first generation," those arriving at adolescence;[16] and the 1.5 generation are those who arrived between the ages of five and twelve partly because they "straddle the old and new worlds but are fully part of neither."[17] For the purpose of this study, second generation Vietnamese Americans are classified as those who were either born in the United States or those who came here before they reached the age of twelve.[18]

Vietnamese Collectivist Ideology

The Vietnamese have drawn extensively on the Chinese Confucian ideology of family collectivism. The process of migration creates much uncertainty about life in their new world, with respect to both social and economic resources. In this transitional period, Vietnamese immigrants often merge resources from different relatives to support each other, including members of the extended kin group. Rooted in a belief system emphasizing family obligation and patchworking

---

[13] This number may exclude over 200,000 persons from Vietnam who identified themselves as Chinese for the U.S. census. See Kibria, *Family Tightrope*, ch. 1.

[14] See Maharidge, *The Coming White Minority*.

[15] For example, see Tricia Knoll, *Becoming Americans: Asian Sojourners, Immigrants, and Refugees in the Western United States* (Portland: Coast to Coast Publishers, 1982); William Liu, Maryanne Lamanna, and Alice Murata, *Transition to Nowhere: Vietnamese Refugees in America* (Nashville: Charter House Press, 1979); Rebecca Allen, "The Social Organization of Migration: An Analysis of the Uprooting and Flight of Vietnamese Refugees," *International Migration Review* 23:4 (1985), 439–452; Paul Strand and Woodrow Jones, *Indochinese Refugees in America: Problems of Adaptation and Assimilation* (Durham: Duke University Press, 1985); Paul Starr, "Attitudes Toward New Americans: Perceptions of Indo-Chinese in Nine Cities," *Research on Race and Ethnic Relations* 3 (1982), 165–186; Freeman; Kibria; and Zhou and Bankston III.

[16] Rumbaut, "The Agony of Exile: A Study of the Migration and Adaptation of Indochinese Refugee Adults and Children," in *Refugee Children: Theory, Research, and Services* Frederick Ahearn and Jean Athey, eds. (Baltimore: Johns Hopkins University Press, 1991).

[17] Zhou, 65.

[18] Researchers have used this age bracket to classify second generation children of immigrants. See Zhou and Bankston III; Zhou; Leif Jensen and Yoshimi Chitose, "Today's Second Generation: Evidence from the 1990 U.S. Census," *International Migration Review* 28:4 (1994), 714–735; Maria Patricia Fernandez-Kelly and Richard Schauffler, "Divided Fates: Immigrant Children in a Restructured U.S. Economy," *International Migration Review* 28:4 (1994), 662–689; and Kibria.

of resources,[19] the Vietnamese often reject the values of self-sufficiency, individualism, and egalitarianism that are generally prevalent in mainstream U.S. culture.[20] For the Vietnamese, the ideology of family collectivism is also practiced in the realm of friendship and as such, friends are often spoken of as family.[21]

The collectivist ideology around family carries with it several definitions. Traditional Confucian notions of collectivity prescribe a great emphasis on hierarchical relations in terms of both age and gender in the realm of family life. Children and younger siblings are expected to pay great respect to their elders and older siblings and women to show deference to their husbands, older brothers, parents, and parents-in-law. It has been pointed out that for some, this traditional ideology somewhat shifts as children of immigrants develop autonomy and parents lose authority in family life in their new world.[22] Despite new and often lessened patterns of hierarchical relations in the family as indicated by the younger generation's desire for autonomy and adults' lack of parental control—an empirical statement that has not been widely supported by the literature[23]—this study indicates that young adult second generation Vietnamese Americans continue to maintain a strong sense of family obligation and patchworking, which remain central to meanings of family collectivism.

For instance, adult children of Vietnamese immigrants often criticize their American peers' plans for filial care of elderly parents. In a study of adult children of Vietnamese and Korean immigrants, Karen Pyke found that many plan to help their parents financially prior to their elderly years by living with them once they got old, with the fifties commonly regarded as old. Those who wanted to maintain autonomy reported that they would live near their parents as neighbors to help in the care of their elderly years.[24] Because few Vietnamese arrived in the U.S. before 1965, the second generation's experience with biculturalism is a relatively new phenomenon and it is no surprise that experiences of new and old worlds with no frame of reference from earlier generations of Vietnamese immigrants often put them in situations of negotiating with their identities. I have found that the meanings and significance of family life and friendship patterns drawn from a collectivist ideology allow them to cast their own identity against and next to the dominant culture. Moreover, the manner in which they observe and keep the ideology of

---

[19] For a discussion of Vietnamese collectivist ideology, see Kibria, *Family Tightrope (77)*. In this study of Vietnamese immigrants living in Philadelphia, Kibria argues that "pooling" was an inadequate term to apply to show how Vietnamese immigrants support each other. She pointed out that social scientists often use this term to denote the sharing of income or finances. The dynamics of Vietnamese families, she maintained, are "more fully and powerfully suggested by *patchworking*, a term that presents an image of jagged pieces of assorted material stitched together in a sometimes haphazard and uncalculated fashion . . . the merging of many different kinds of resources (77)."

[20] For an extensive discussion of individualism in American culture, see Robert Bellah, Richard Madsen, William Sullivan, Ann Swidler, and Steven Tipton, *Habits of the Heart: Individualism and Commitment in American Life* (San Francisco: Harper and Row, 1985). For an analysis of how children of Vietnamese immigrants reject this cultural ideology, see Pyke.

[21] Hien Duc Do, "The New Outsiders: The Vietnamese Refugee Generation in Higher Education," Ph.D dissertation, University of California at Santa Barbara, 1995.

[22] See Kibria, *Family Tightrope*, ch. 6, for a discussion of the "generation gap" among recent Vietnamese immigrants and their children.

[23] For further discussion of the apparent "generation" gap amongst Vietnamese children and their parents, see Kibria, *Family Tightrope*, ch. 6; and Pyke.

[24] Pyke.

family collectivism may offer keen insights into how ethnic identity gets produced, and in many cases, boundaries constructed and maintained between them and the dominant culture.

Ethnicity and the Social Constructionist Perspective

The principal theoretical perspective that guides this study is the social construction of ethnicity. This model conceptualizes ethnicity as a fluid, situational, volitional, and dynamic phenomenon, one in which "ethnic boundaries, identities, and cultures, are negotiated, defined, and produced through social interaction inside and outside ethnic communities."[25] Through social interactions, individuals are able to define and express their identity as "ethnic actors."[26]

Two of the basic building blocks of ethnicity are identity and culture.[27] In everyday social arenas, we use culture to give meanings to our identity and we use identity to construct affiliations and boundaries with other individuals and groups. The complex interplay of identity and culture is a salient feature of the experiences of ethnicity for immigrants, especially when their marginality is highlighted by the host society. For example, in a discussion of Korean and Chinese Americans' reflections on intermarriage, Nazli Kibria observes that second generation Asian Americans often experience a sense of "not belonging."[28] Growing up as children of immigrants, for Kibria's respondents, problems of "not fitting in" were often easily recollected and act as constant reminders of their identity as ethnic individuals. Unlike the experiences of second generation European Americans, such as Italian Americans who eagerly invoke honorific experiences of growing up "American,"[29] Asian Americans more often than not identify themselves as being different and not fitting in with their peers, especially whites.

Thus, to a large extent, second generation Asian Americans are in the position of the "marginal man" while growing up, an experience similar to those of first generation immigrants when they are "pulled in the direction of the mainstream culture but drawn back by cultures of their own."[30] The experiences of second generation Asian Americans are often centered around the "immigrant story," a discourse that effectively positions them as both outsiders and insiders.[31] Experiences of marginality help them understand the different layers of their identity. As young adults, reflections on these experiences allow them to see how as children of immigrants, they were ethnic and at the same time, they were on pathways into being Americans. In many ways, these reflections help them process cultural ideologies and practices that are central to their ethnic self, which later help to produce a heightened sense of ethnic continuity.

---

[25] Nagel, 152.

[26] Stanford Lyman and William Douglas, "Ethnicity: Strategies of Collective and Individual Impression Management," *Social Research* 40:2 (1973), 344–365.

[27] Nagel, 152–153.

[28] Kibria, "The Construction of 'Asian American'," 535.

[29] See, for example, Herbert Gans, "Symbolic Ethnicity: The Future of Ethnic Groups and Cultures in America," *Journal of Ethnic and Racial Studies* 2:1 (1979), 1–20; and Richard Alba, *Italian Americans: Into the Twilight of Ethnicity* (Englewood Cliffs, New Jersey: Prentice-Hall Press, 1985).

[30] Zhou and Bankston III, 822.

[31] Bacon, *Life Line*; and Kibria, "The Construction of 'Asian American'."

In discussing ethnicity, it is useful to look at culture and how it helps to manufacture meanings of ethnicity. Culture is one of "the basic materials used to construct ethnic meaning," and the construction of culture is "a tale of human agency and internal group processes of cultural preservation, renewal, and innovation."[32] When individuals engage in constructing culture, they are also in the process of building ethnic boundaries which would determine who they are and what they are. For example, Pyke argues that in their young adulthood, children of immigrants identify "differences" between them and their American peers by defining their beliefs in maintaining certain cultural ideologies and practices.[33] She found that as children, Vietnamese and Korean second generations fantasized about having "American" parents; but, as young adults, they switched to an Asian ethnic framework when asked about their future plans for filial care.

In my exploration of the lives of children of Vietnamese immigrants, I found the metaphor of the *shopping cart* to be useful in understanding how culture operates as a vehicle to shape ethnic identity:

> We can think of ethnic boundary construction as determining the shape of the shopping cart size, number of wheels, composition, etc.); ethnic culture, then, is composed of the things we put into the cart—art, music, dress, religion, norms, beliefs, symbols, myths, customs. It is important that we discard the notion that culture is simply a historical legacy; culture is not a shopping cart that comes to us already loaded with a set of historical goods. Rather, we construct culture by picking and choosing items from the shelves of the *past and the present*.[34] (emphases added).

Norms and beliefs are mechanisms of culture which help to create our sense of ethnic identity. As we engage in relationships with others, those who are both close and distant to us, we might alter, negotiate, or revise our identity, including categories of ethnicity.[35] I suggest that for second generation Americans, intimate relationships with family and friends act as important arenas for merging both past and present experiences and ideologies, the "old" and "new" worlds. In this article, I illustrate how constructions of ethnic identity are processes that are interwoven in experiences of culture and identity for the new second generation, particularly Vietnamese Americans. By looking at the ways they describe their experiences of marginality as both children of immigrants and young adults, we can see how relationships with friends and family help shape processes of ethnic identity formation. In this process, we also see how they draw on and utilize cultural ideologies to help them construct and maintain boundaries from the larger society.

---

[32] Nagel, 161.

[33] For example, one of Pyke's informants explained, "With the *American* culture, it's . . . not much frowned upon to put your parents in a [nursing] home when they grow old. In *our* culture, it is a definite no-no (22)." (Italics added).

[34] Nagel, 162. Although I use the metaphor of the shopping court to illustrate that second generation Vietnamese Americans choose and pick from their past and present to shape their cultural beliefs, I also point out that the metaphor should also be viewed critically. Historically, the immigrant experience in the U.S. has shown that not all Asian Americans and ethnic groups have been able to "pick and choose" with regard to culture.

[35] Matti Simila, "Situation and Ethnic Identity," *International Migration Review* 26:4 (1988), 453–460.

Methods

The analysis presented here is drawn from eighteen open-ended interviews with young adult second generation Vietnamese Americans in the San Francisco Bay area, where the second highest concentration of Vietnamese resides in the United States.[36] The study was limited to young adults between the ages of eighteen and twenty-seven with an average of twenty-two. Eight were undergraduate students (although two were part-timers), two were professional/graduate students, seven were in the workforce, and one was an unemployed recent college graduate. There was an equal number of men and women. None of the informants were married nor had children. Three were born in the U.S., while the rest immigrated prior to the age of twelve with the average age of arrival being five-and-a-half years old. Informants were located through three organizations, a student club at two universities and a volunteer association.[37] I created a sample for my study based on principles of theoretical sampling, a strategy in which the sociologist "may begin the research with a partial framework of local concepts, designating a few principal or gross features of the structure and processes in the situations that he [or she] will study."[38]

I wanted to get a wide variety of waves of immigration, college majors, and age. I also wanted to get a balance of females and males and those in the working force. In general, the wide variety of year of arrival in the United States also reflects a range of social class, with those arriving earlier coming from urban, more affluent backgrounds. Although they come from homes which varied in economic standing, the sample consisted of college students or graduates—those headed toward middle and upper-middle class occupations. As such, we would expect the second generation in this sample to be more acculturated than individuals in the larger immigrant population.[39] Interviews were conducted between August 1997 and May 1998 and were done in English, although most shifted to Vietnamese (often slang terms) to express or clarify certain points to me.[40] The interviews took the form of a life history lasting one to four hours and were mostly unstructured. I asked questions about friendship and family life in the various spheres of their lives including experiences during childhood, adolescence, college, and work. I conducted second interviews with eleven of the eighteen informants to get further clarifications on important issues. These

---

[36] The site of this study—the San Francisco Bay area—has the second highest concentration of Vietnamese in the U.S. In addition, over 46 percent of all Vietnamese in the U.S. reside in California, according to the 1990 census. See Freeman, *Changing Identities*, 11.

[37] To get access, I became a member of all three organizations.

[38] Barney Glaser and Anselm Strauss, *The Discovery of Grounded Theory: Strategies for Qualitative Research* (Chicago: Aldine Press, 1967), 45.

[39] As Pyke notes in her study of Korean and Vietnamese second generations, "academic accomplishments are commonly used in the immigration literature to suggest successful adaptation." (7) Among my informants, there were differences in the levels of acculturation; but, compared to the larger second generation immigrant population, we would expect higher levels of acculturation because of their exposure *and* pressures from the educational system.

[40] Except for few exceptions, I translated the interviews when Vietnamese was used as I transcribed. There were times where my role as an "insider" researcher—that I am a second generation Vietnamese American who speaks Vietnamese—made it easier for my informants to reveal certain information to me. In studying the Jewish community, Samuel Heilman, also a Jew, asserts that there were times when he had methodological doubts about being an insider, but that, "indeed certain observations and the insights they provide seem possible precisely and only because I am informed as an insider." (105) See Samuel Heilman, "Jewish Sociologist: Native-as-Stranger," *The American Sociologist* 15 (1980), 100–108. Indeed, many of the questions and issues that arose, especially our conversations about the collectivist ideology, were possible because I shared the same cultural experiences, although I don't always shared the same practices, with my informants.

latter interviews usually lasted under one hour and most were about thirty minutes long. With their informed consent, I taped all the first interviews and I later transcribed them. Most of the second interviews, except for two, were recorded only as field notes.

I read and analyzed the interviews using the strategy of the "constant comparative method of analyses," a strategy of data analysis that calls for continual "making comparisons" and "asking questions."[41] I coded the interviews with phenomena labeled and sorted into emerging themes, which were then compared to each other for generalizablity. I noted categories which were exceptions, but relevant to the study, such as differences in gender. In general, as I was conducting the interviews, I probed about the possible significance of age, class, wave of immigration, and (in one case) sexual orientation, especially where I felt these factors might play a role in experiences. However, the coding of data revealed only subtle differences, and these dimensions became peripheral to my analysis of ethnic identity.

Marginality and the Formation of Ethnic Identity

My findings show that right before early adulthood, during the childhood and adolescent periods ranging from elementary to high school, my informants experienced the marginal-man situation, often having conflicting images of who they were and feeling a sense of "not belonging" to either their "old" or "new" social worlds. As children and adolescents, pressured by both outsiders and insiders to acculturate as fast and as much as possible, they attempted to blend into the dominant culture in various ways through their dress, language, and consumer patterns. In their accounts, they remembered often feeling uncomfortable, especially at "acting white," during these episodes. At the same time, they were often reminded by individuals of their own ethnicity to remain loyal to traditional cultural ideologies and practices. Many recalled being reprimanded by older relatives for being *my qua* (too Americanized), especially during adolescence when peer pressures were particularly strong.

However, when adulthood approached, my informants began to reassemble and reevaluate their own feelings about ethnicity and, at times, even nationality.[42] As they navigated through new institutional experiences such as college and work, they formed a heightened sense of ethnic identity, especially those who continued to experience marginality from the dominant culture. Thus, the sense of being on the margins of two cultures ended when they began to recreate their identity in early adulthood, a crucial stage resulting in a cognitive decision to selectively choose to maintain certain traditional cultural ideologies.[43] In their everyday life, my informants have challenged U.S. mainstream cultural beliefs of individualism, self-sufficiency, and egalitarianism and in their relationships with family and friends, specifically, they subscribe to a collectivist ideology. I argue that

---

[41] Glazer and Strauss, *Discovery of Grounded Theory*, 101; and Anselm Strauss and Juliet Corbin, *Basics of Qualitative Research: Grounded Theory Procedures and Techniques* (Newbury Park, California: Sage Publications, 1990).

[42] Although this topic is not a focus of this article, some informants referred to citizenship and nationality as salient issues for them in their identity formation. Many pointed to globalization and transnational relations with extended kin as opportunities to see themselves as "truly" Vietnamese rather than Americans or Vietnamese Americans.

[43] See Jonathan Okamura, "Situational Ethnicity," *Journal of Ethnic and Racial Studies* 4:4 (1981), 452–465. It is useful to draw upon the notion of "situational ethnicity," which social anthropologists have used to analyze immigrants and ethnic minorities in different societies. This perspective involves the structural and cognitive dimensions. The latter "pertains to the actor's subjective perception of the situation in which he finds himself and to the salience he attributes to ethnicity as a relevant factor in that situation." (454)

when they subscribe to a collectivist ideology in the various spheres of their lives, a formation of ethnic identity takes place and at times, these informants resign from being *my qua* (too Americanized).

Being the Marginal-Man

Most of my informants described their childhood and adolescent years as a time often characterized by ambiguity, tension, and uncertainty about who they were culturally. They spoke of schools and other public spheres as areas where they were pressured into being an "American kid" and homes and private spheres where parents and relatives insisted that they not "lose" their culture. Especially where older and traditional relatives lived in the same household,[44] constant encouragement, but often reprimands, were given to remind them not to be *my qua* (too Americanized). The sense of being on the margins of two cultures was perplexing to their identities. Mong-Cam,[45] a twenty-two year old teacher who came to the U.S. when she was five, described a representative experience of growing up in a position of marginality. Like most respondents, she gave an account of how at times this "marginal-man" situation created tension in family life. In Mong-Cam's case, identity and marginality were also flavored with gender issues:

> I think throughout my life, thinking back now, I've always battled with the two sides of me. Always at home, I was the Vietnamese daughter and sister; at school I was supposed to be like everyone else: I'm a student, I'm supposed to be independent and think for myself. But, when I'm at home, you are expected to act within the tradition, right. Do what your parents expect of you. I always had problems when these two values conflicted. And for a while, my father and I didn't get along because of that, especially when my father let my brother do something and not me. Back then, I didn't think it was because of the culture; I thought it was because we were very different and that my parents were old fashioned. I always said that the American kids at school get to do this and that. I thought it was a generation thing, and not a cultural thing. For me, saying that I am Vietnamese, especially now, is acknowledging the differences between my culture and the American culture . . .

In general, the women I interviewed did not recall a stronger sense of marginality, compared to the men, arising from gender hierarchy in their households. A few explained that during childhood, their parents restricted them from doing certain things, such as walking alone late at night; however, they noted these practices were just as likely if they were Americans. For some of the women informants like Mong-Cam, the double ambivalence about who they were culturally often resulted from the expectations of Vietnamese parents to be traditional and their own initial desire to acquire American values of independence and self sufficiency. Some explained that during childhood, particularly the teenage years, the expectations of parents and their own personal desires became the core of intergenerational conflicts. Hue, a twenty-two year old education senior who came to the U.S. when she was six, gave the following account:

> When I was in high school, my father was afraid that I would have a boyfriend, because in Vietnam, girls don't date, they're only given off to their husbands' families. I guess when my American friends started dating at the beginning of high school, I wanted a boyfriend, too. I wanted to do my own things, sort of being independent from my parent's, like my American friends.

---

[44] One-third of my informants reported that an extended relative, usually a grandparent, lived in the same household with them while they were growing up. This concurs with research which shows that Vietnamese American families have a diverse size and composition of households where extended kin often live together to share resources. See, for example, Kibria, *Family Tightrope*.

[45] All names have been changed in order to protect the anonymity of informants.

For one of my informants, sexuality was central to his identity, an identity marked by uncertainty, conflict, and often depression. Loi, a twenty-year-old gay male who immigrated when he was six, spoke of how difficult it was for him to initially acknowledge his sexuality to his friends and himself. He emphasized that the process was even more complex when he realized he had to explain it to his Vietnamese family:

> It's funny, but most Asian people I know consider that being gay is an American thing, a white thing. Asian people, especially Vietnamese, don't talk about gay issues because for some reason, they believe that only American people can be gay. When I was growing up and when I realize I was gay, I would never dare tell anyone in my family about my feelings and my frustrations. My mom always wanted me to have American friends when I was younger, but she always told me to not be too "Americanized"; so when I was growing up, to me, being gay was being too Americanized!

Both U.S. and foreign-born informants recalled often contradictory patterns of encouragement from their parents; for the foreign-born, these contradictions were especially apparent during the early years of settlement. On the one hand, they were encouraged to make American friends in order to learn the language and culture rapidly;[46] but on the other, making too many American friends meant that, in their parents' eyes, they were trying to lose their *nguon* (roots). As explained by Minh, a twenty-three year old computer sales agent who came here in 1975 right after the war, these double insistences often left him unsure of what his parents wanted him to be and as a result, produced identity conflicts:

> In middle school, I saw myself as the all-American kid when I was out in the neighborhood playing football and chasing people with our bicycles and doing your typical suburban American things. And my parents at first wanted me and my brothers to hang out with the white kids a lot. They always said *di choi voi may dua My di con* (go play with the American [white] kids, sons) When we were beginning to use English in the house more than Vietnamese, both my parents, especially my mom, I think, became scared and set aside special hours for us to learn Vietnamese. They also took us to these Vietnamese cultural centers almost every weekend at one point so that we could meet other Vietnamese kids and do Vietnamese things. So then I had weekend Vietnamese friends and weekday American friends. It was really weird 'cause I had to switch back and forth talking hickey and sometimes I thought I had lost that accent. [Why?] You try learning a country accent and leave it for the weekend and switch back for school.[47] It's hard!

Some informants asserted that marginality led to undesirable impressions of both cultures. They spoke of being different or "unequal" to peers in both cultures. Oanh, a twenty-two year old U.S. born law student, interpreted the constraints of her bicultural experiences:

---

[46] Among recent immigrant Vietnamese parents, as Fernandez-Kelley and Schaulffler discovered, encouraging their children to make American friends was a way to quickly learn the language and culture of their new country. My informants explained that this was true in the early years of settlement for them, but tensions often resulted if they acculturated too quickly.

[47] Minh's family first settled in the southern part of the U.S. He explained that hickey meant speaking in a "country way, a country accent," which, to him, are characteristics associated with individuals living in the south.

There were times when I just wanted to say I didn't belong to both and others where I wanted to see myself as equal to everyone (in both cultures). [What do you mean by equal?] The kids I hung out with at school were white, but I didn't have many of the things they had because my parents didn't know about it. You know, like the nice trendy clothes and everything. At home, when I met other Vietnamese kids who were FOBS I felt like I was such a foreigner to them.[48] I mean, you know, I didn't know how to behave like they did to the adults and the way I spoke was different. I hated feeling different. But, I knew I was like the Americans and the Vietnamese. I don't know about other Vietnamese people my age, but, I mean, you know, my parents didn't understand this. It was really, really confusing for me and it made me so not appealing to the Vietnamese and the Americans.

Acting and Being White

The second generation Vietnamese Americans I interviewed spoke of trying to "act" or "be" white during the early stages of their lives in the U.S. Embedded in their everyday life as children of immigrants was a belief that being "American" was equivalent to being white. As one of my informants, Nam, a twenty-four year old graduate psychology student, exclaimed, "I mean, all the prom kings and queens year after year were white. All the leaders in the school were white and so you knew that if you act or behave like one of them, you too could be those things or at least be one of their friends!"[49] Trung, a twenty-seven year old human resource manager, who came here at age eight, explained how before he moved to California to work, he saw himself as a white person. He noted later in the interview how working in California has made him much more "culturally aware," especially of his Vietnamese identity:[50]

---

[48] FOBs or "Fresh of the boat," as my informant clarified, is most commonly used by young Vietnamese Americans to refer to the more recent arriving immigrants.

[49] Scholars studying minority students in schools have discussed the ways minority students face the "burden of acting white" in order to succeed. See Signithia Fordham and John U. Ogbu, "Black Students' School Success: Coping with the Burden of Acting White," *The Urban Review* 18:3 (1986), 176–206; and Donna Y. Ford, John L. Harris, Karen S. Webb, and Deneese L. Jones, "Rejection or Confirmation of Racial Identity: A Dilemma for High-Achieving Blacks?" *The Journal of Educational Thought* 28:1 (1994), 7–33. Although Fordham and Ogbu and Ford focus on African American students, they point out that other minority groups, including immigrants, are also faced with similar problems. Ogbu and Matutue-Bianchi also explain how Mexican American students see themselves and their peer groups as doing the "Anglo thing" and those who resist say these "linear acculturation" mechanisms are detrimental to the integrity of their cultures and identity. See John U. Ogbu and Maria Eugenia Matute-Bianchi, "Understanding Sociocultural Factors in Education: Knowledge, Identity, and Adjustment," *Beyond Language: Sociocultural Factors in Schooling, Language, and Minority Students* (Los Angeles: California State Department of Education, 1986), 71–143.

[50] Although sixteen of the eighteen individuals I interviewed experienced secondary migration in the U.S., only three said they were raised in neighborhoods and went to elementary and secondary schools where the majority consisted of whites. Secondary migration refers to the process in which the Vietnamese moved from one state to another after being settled in arbitrary parts of the U.S. in the mid 1970s and throughout the 1980s. This pattern of settlement was because of a federal policy initiated by President Gerald Ford in 1975 to "disperse Vietnamese refugees as widely as possible in the U.S." (129) The policy was enacted to prevent the formation of ethnic enclaves similar to those of the Chinese and Japanese in earlier years. The result of the policy, known as the Interagency Task Force (IATF), led to "sloppy sponsorship arrangements, some of which broke down almost immediately, leaving many refugees alone and unaided. Others served employers looking for cheap labor or subservient workers and exploited refugees." (129) See Hing, *Making and Remaking Asian America.*

Before coming out here to work, I didn't have any Vietnamese friends, although at home, my mom made sure I didn't lose the language. Most of the friends I had in high school and college were white and so I always saw myself as one of them. Although I don't think I was like a token minority to those friends, not really, there were times where I clearly made a big effort to be white, you know, with my posture, the ways I talked, the clothes I wore and things like that. [What did being white mean to you?] I don't know, American I guess. I mean all the cool guys, the jocks, were white at my school, they were tall and they wore nice clothes . . . they were Americans.

Similarly, Huong, a twenty-five year old sales clerk who immigrated here at the age of three, explained how she saw herself as being white even though there were quite a large number of Asian students at her high school:

All the Asian girls in high school thought it was so cool to have a white boyfriend. It was so retarded of me, but I thought I was one of the white girls. I tried dying my hair blonde once and I put on makeup to look like one of them! (laughs) There was a period I would say that I felt very white and I guess at the time it was cool, because I got to be friends with the white kids and I did have a white boyfriend.

For some, the "acting and being white" stage lead to temporary negative images of the self and of their culture.[51] This painful process was intensified through conflicts caused by pressures from parents to be both Americanized and traditionally Vietnamese. Loi explained how he didn't like himself and, consequently, felt alone in high school because he constantly compared himself to his white peers:[52]

Before coming to college I was very afraid of people and I felt alone because I didn't have friends. [Why?] I really disliked myself, because I disliked my culture. I disliked my parents, I disliked all the things that happened to me, all the Vietnamese things. Now I see it in terms of me basically

---

[51] In a thoughtful collection of essays written by Asian American professionals, editors Pyong Gap Min and Rose Kim found that despite their strong ethnic identity, some adult children of contemporary immigrants felt more comfortable making friends with and dating whites, rather than co-ethnics or other Asians. See Min and Rose, "Living in Two Worlds: A Bicultural Identity," in *Struggle for Ethnic Identity: Narratives by Asian American Professionals* (Walnut Creek, California: Altamira Press, 1999), 111–140. While these children of immigrants were also likely to have experienced the acting white phenomenon, they did not feel that it was inhibiting to their ethnic identity formation. Two of the writers who identified strongly with their ethnicity ended up marrying white Americans. Min and Rose suggests that neither of these Asian Americans, who were Japanese and Bangladeshi, "were forced to relinquish their Asian and ethnic cultures as a precondition for marrying white partners. They married white men who accepted their Asian and ethnic backgrounds. This indicates that in contemporary America, intermarriage and multi-culturalism go together." (112) Although I am not arguing here that adult children of Vietnamese immigrants are unable or unwilling to have a strong ethnic identity while at the same time developing friendships and intimate ties with white Americans, I point out the "acting and being white" phenomenon, especially during childhood, did lead them to view" American-ness" as a monolithic cultural category—that of "whiteness." The crucial point is that as young adults, these reflections are evidence of a "bicultural dilemma" during childhood and adolescence. For second generation Vietnamese Americans, cultural ideology and practices during young adulthood *within* the realm of family life and friendship act as powerful articulators of ethnic identity.

[52] Although I found small variations in gender as it relates to ethnic identity, in a few cases, the Americanization and identity formation processes were flavored by gender and sexuality. For example, Loi explained to me how he saw being gay and gayness as such an "American thing" since it is often not spoken of in the Vietnamese and Asian community.

comparing myself, the distorted self image I got because I compared myself to a white person, a white standard. And I wanted to be white. That's why when I first came out as being gay, the only people I was attracted to were white men and I thought that Asians and Vietnamese were not attractive. But, that's why right now I'm so keen into the race issue—so keen on the Vietnamese identity, because I have realized that that was the crux of my problem and not just mine, but a lot of other (Vietnamese and Asian) people.

For my informants, the acting and being white phenomenon was a temporary period in their lives lasting from a few years after migration, usually once they were acclimated in elementary school, until they entered college or the workforce. Young adulthood provided new social arenas for which to understand and, perhaps, transform themselves. In these new social arenas, most of my informants underwent a typical process in which Loi called "deprogramming the self."[53]

Deprogramming the Self

All of my respondents described the entrance into college and to a lesser degree for some, the workforce, as periods of identity change, periods that were highly marked by critical observations of the ways their American peers subscribed to and practiced mainstream U.S. cultural values of individualism, self-sufficiency, and egalitarianism in the realms of friendship and family life. In many ways, the college campus was seen and understood as a site of ethnic recovery, and for some, ethnic discovery.[54] Toan, a twenty year old biology sophomore who immigrated here at age eleven, expressed, "I realized how much I loved being Vietnamese when in college the only people I could rely on without any hesitation were my Vietnamese friends. They help me and I never feel like I owe them anything. Americans help their friends too, I think, but you have to pay them back. You have to owe them something."

The processes of "deprogramming the self" and assessing mainstream cultural practices with their own cultural lens were largely interactional. In other words, while they gradually ceased from acting and being white, they began to draw upon traditional cultural ideologies to help them see differences and, more often than not, preferences for Vietnamese over American values. Loi explained this process for himself since entering college:

> Basically, I have been deprogramming myself for over two years now. Actually this self-deprogramming thing is not a very uncommon thing. I had comments from other Vietnamese people. One guy just said at the beginning of this year who came to me and said he wanted to be involved in this club I'm in with a lot of other Vietnamese people. He shook his head and said, "I'm so fucking whitewashed. I need to get exposed to my culture. I'm so whitewashed." So I got involved with the Vietnamese students at school [college] because I just wanted to be with Vietnamese people. I had a theory—I had a theory—that if I was exposed enough and if I saw enough

---

[53] Although only Loi coined his experiences as "deprogramming the self," most of my informants spoke of it in this way and the term powerfully described the processes they underwent to withdraw from "white culture."

[54] For example, in a collection of essays written by second generation college students, including Vietnamese Americans, many pointed out that college provided an opportunity for ethnic discovery and for others, rediscovery. See Thomas Dublin, ed., *Becoming American, Becoming Ethnic: College Students Explore Their Roots* (Philadelphia: Temple University Press, 1996).

faces, just as when I learned the piano or when I picked up classical music, because I was exposed I realized its subtlety and I realize the beauty and the differences in it.

Similarly, Hue gave the following account:

Near the end of high school, I began to see Vietnamese culture as cool. [How so?] I mean I liked it more than me trying to be American. When I started making really good friends . . . now that I look back, I had chosen to make good friends with the Vietnamese girls. [Why?] The ways we did things were different than the Americans [white]. [How so?] I mean, when we went out to eat, we didn't have to split the bills; someone just paid. Gosh, I think splitting things in half is so white! (laughs). I used to do that and I hated it and I'm trying to get away from that. When I began college, living in the dorm and stuff, I liked the ways Vietnamese folks do things, especially when it comes to helping your friends.

Why was college a physical and social space for deprogramming the self? The second generation Vietnamese Americans I interviewed maintained that college provided coursework where they could talk openly about issues of race and ethnicity; they noted that courses in such departments as Asian American Studies and Ethnic Studies were crucial in helping them see who they were relative to the larger dominant society.[55] College life presented possibilities for participation in issues such as politics and economic mobilization for Vietnamese minority communities. However, the most important and most often cited reason for deprogramming of the self and constructing a new identity were the formations of new friendships with other Vietnamese individuals; most informed me that they had chosen to participate in their college ethnic clubs to meet other Vietnamese people and many spoke of not "being conscious" of trying to act and be white until college. As MongCam recalled, "I mean I grew up thinking that I'll somehow be white one day! I think I was conscious of this since, probably since college, and since I've taken Asian American courses and ethnic studies courses. Before that I mean, you know this is a phenomenon where a lot of people go through where you know where you're conscious of the fact that you're different and that you are who you are except there's no name for it."[56]

Another informant, Theo, a twenty-three year old recent physics college graduate who immigrated from Vietnam when he was seven, affirmed his identity in the following statement:

Yeah, I had that white phase. I even picked a white name [Andy] for people to call me in high school, because I thought Americans [whites] would see me as someone like them. When I came here [college], I got rid of Andy, because I wanted people to see me as a Vietnamese person. Man, it was like coming out of the closet, like once being a closeted gay person or something. [Why did you want people to see you as a Vietnamese person?] I started meeting

---

[55] Loewen convincingly argues through a careful analysis of history textbooks that elementary and secondary schools in the U.S. do not teach students about race and class. As he notes, teachers expressed fear that exposure to these issues might leave students knowing about the "injustices and inadequacies of their economic and political institutions." (206) My informants claimed that until college, lack of knowledge about minorities in the U.S. often left them feeling inferior to their white peers. See James Loewen, *Lies My Teacher Told Me* (New York: Simon & Schuster Press, 1995).

[56] In addition to living in a highly diverse metro area, the two universities where some of my informants attend have large ethnic studies departments and a large Asian American population. Many of them referred to learning about "who they were" in these courses.

Vietnamese people in the community organization I'm in and the friendships we have are different from the ones I have with my American friends and so I didn't care about being white or even American or not.

Boundaries and Constructing Ethnic Identity

It is well known that the notion of boundaries is often used to study ethnic groups who undergo differentiation and identity formations.[57] Individuals and groups create boundaries as a way of differentiating themselves from the larger society and as a way of affirming their ethnic identity. Ethnic boundaries are situational and changeable, resulting from external and internal sources, that is how we see ourselves relative to the larger society and how the larger society positions us are both important factors in the shaping of ethnic identity. Through reviewing past and present relationships, my informants consistently assembled new ways of seeing themselves, resulting in new identity formations. After the elementary and adolescence school years of being the "marginal man" in which they bargain with meanings of biculturalism—who they were relative to whom—introduction into college and the workforce became important social territories for viewing mainstream U.S. culture in relation to their own.

When reviewing their current and past friendships, for instance, most of my informants pointed out that as they got older, they acquired and kept more Vietnamese friends than they used to and they perceived that it was not due to being rejected by non-Vietnamese individuals.[58] A few also stated that they gradually drifted away from their previous friendships with non-Vietnamese individuals, especially white Americans, and many maintain intimate friendships almost exclusively with other Vietnamese individuals. They attributed this transition, forming and maintenance of strong friendships with other Vietnamese, to different cultural ideologies about the rules and practices of friendship which became more salient once they emerged into their young adulthood. Likewise, as adults, all of my informants provided divergent and often negative feelings about the ways their non-Vietnamese peers approached family life, particularly with their emphasis on the values of self-sufficiency and egalitarianism. Most explained that during childhood, these feelings were often not troubling because they were taught to glorify all American values in the process of being "Americanized."

While most informants described their friends and family as people to whom they could turn for emotional support, they also saw friends and family as utilitarian interpersonal relationships embodied in a collectivist ideology. It was clear and unequivocal that friends and families are individuals they could turn to and depend on for practical assistance, including financial support; in turn, they said they were readily available for their friends and families. Most informants explained that they were frequently disturbed and appalled by the economic boundaries their American peers practiced with friends and family, such as the calculation and division

[57] See, for example, Fredrik Barth, *Ethnic Groups and Boundaries* (Boston: Little Brown Publishing, 1969); Sandra Wallman, "Ethnicity and the Boundary Process in Context," in *Theories of Race and Ethnic Relations* John Rex and David Mason, eds. (Cambridge: Cambridge University Press, 1986), 226–245; and Nagel.

[58] Given what my informants perceived to be the case, it is important to note research which has shown how college students congregate themselves in different racial groups in their leisure moments. See, for example, Stella Ting-Toomey, "Ethnic Identity and Close Friendship in Chinese-American College Students," *International Journal of Intercultural Relations* 5:4 (1981), 383–406; Bradley Fisher, "The Impact of Race on the Social Experience of College Students at a Predominantly White University," *Journal of Black Studies* 26:2 (1995), 117–133; and Katherine Tuan-MacLean, "The Interracial Friendships of White and Asian College Students," Ph.D dissertation, Northwestern University, 1996.

of financial expenses during their leisure moments.[59] My inquiry shows that for these second generation Vietnamese Americans, the contrast between a collectivist familial ideology and an "American" identity led them to reassert a Vietnamese ethnic identity.

Articulating Ethnic Identity through a Collectivist Familial Ideology

The ways my informants described their rules and practices in relationships with friends and family strongly suggest that a collectivist ideology acts as a tool for an expression of ethnic identity; as part of deprogramming the self, my informants began to recapture these earlier learned values during their young adulthood. Generally, this process occurred in two ways. By critically viewing mainstream U.S. cultural values of egalitarianism and self-sufficiency as pathological, my informants recognized differences between their American peers and themselves based on ethnic lines. And, by specifying certain rules and practices of collectivism as exclusively stemming from their Vietnamese origin, my informants defined themselves ethnically.[60] Toan typified this sort of account when he stated, "American individualism is a mentality that I'm my own person, that I can think for myself. I don't need you to tell me. In that way, I think Vietnamese people tend to think about other people's opinions. They tend to depend on other people and tend to cooperate with other people more. They help each other."

Most of my informants emphasized that their family, especially their parents, were the most crucial influence to the development of their self identity. What they wanted to be, what they might become, and how they relate to people in interpersonal relationships, were all directly affected by the connection they had to their family. Most also made clear that the central reason why they had high aspirations for a college education was because of their parents. Individual goals were also important, but they were of secondary significance; family, especially parents determined such things as what they would study and where they would go to school. In fact, those who were in graduate or professional schools asserted that if it weren't for their parents' desire, they probably would not have gone on to pursue an advanced degree. It was not uncommon for informants to say that they had future plans to live with or near their parents so that they could support them. For instance, those who had already begun working said they regularly send money home to their parents and younger siblings who were attending college. Viewed in these ways, relationships with family are in part utilitarian among second generation Vietnamese Americans. When they compared themselves to their "American" counterparts, those who they claim practice a culture of individualism and egalitarianism, my

---

[59] Unlike friendships in most Western cultures, where expressions of emotions and feelings are arguably the most important components of the intimacy in friendship patterns, friendships for my informants are very much utilitarian in nature in addition to the sharing of emotions and feelings. For a discussion of how friends in Western culture practice economic and social boundaries, see Lillian Rubin, *Just Friends: The Role of Friendship in Our Lives* (New York: Harper & Row Publishers, 1985).

[60] Some informants saw the collectivist ideology along racial lines, as an "Asian thing," which to a large extent, acts as an ethnic cue. In this way, they subscribe to a panethnic Asian American identity. By seeing themselves along racial lines, the Asian American identity helps to facilitate ethnic identity. For a discussion of how an Asian American identity acts an ethnic cue, see Yen Le Espiritu, *Asian American Panethnicity: Bridging Institutions and Identities* (Philadelphia: Temple University Press, 1992).

informants emphasized that a collectivist ideology helps them recapture a sense of ethnic identity. As Lam succinctly put it, "Vietnamese families have to help each other. There are some things we know we have to do for our parents and our brothers and sisters when we get older." Manh, a twenty-four year old chemistry technician who immigrated here by himself at age seven and later sponsored his parents and younger sister to the U.S.,[61] gave the following account:

> My little sister is a freshman in college now in the South and I know she's working hard in school and doesn't have a lot of money. I send her money each month and I tell her, "here's this and this amount of money, go and have some fun." My parents can't help us out because they don't make a lot of money. [Do you help your parents?] Yeah. [How so?] I mean they live with me so I pay for everything, the rent, food. They help me out when they can but I want them to enjoy. They are getting old, you know.

One might conjure up images of immigrant families who only pool resources in times of economic insecurity, as a reciprocal "moral economy,"[62] but this is not necessarily true as suggested by the descriptions of my informants. For example, Bach-Lan, a twenty year old engineering sophomore who was born in the U.S., said all four of her college-educated older siblings understand that if anyone needed money to buy a bigger house or invest in a business, the capital was readily available within the family. Likewise, she said she often received monetary gifts from siblings for leisure activities:

> When I went to Europe last summer, I could have lived off $800 dollars, but when I told my older sister how much I had, she was shocked (laughs). [Why?] She didn't think I would have enough money to spend. A week later, I received a check from all four of my brothers and sisters for the trip . . . this is one of the cool reasons to be the youngest in a Vietnamese family. (laughs)

My informants consistently spoke about family life as generated, as well as regulated by, the meanings of collectivism. In these accounts, they saw these meanings as ethnically defining. That is to say, most viewed obligation, non-egalitarianism, and pooling resources to the family unit as deriving from Vietnamese culture, and sharply contrasted with American values. Lien, a twenty-three

---

[61] Manh was put under the guardianship of one of his father's friend during the boat journey, although he was later left alone at a refugee camp in Thailand. A catholic church sponsored him to the U.S., where he was adopted by one of the church's member. Shortly after the first wave of immigration in 1975, some Vietnamese parents sent their sons as unaccompanied minors via the "boat refugee experience." Some have been lucky to settle in the U.S. with other extended relatives, but a large number are currently in refugee camps abroad in countries such as the Philippines and Thailand. For a discussion of accompanied minor refugees, see Freeman, *Changing Identities*, ch. one. According to Kibria in *Family Tightrope* (158) this group flowed out of Vietnam especially in the 1980s. Their status as sons and avoidance of the military draft were two important reasons why they left.

[62] According to the moral economy perspective, family members help each other as a natural response to the need and interests of the household. I suggest, rather, that second generation Vietnamese Americans pool resources together because of practices that are grounded on larger structural, cultural, and ideological contexts. For a discussion of the moral economy perspective, see Diane Wolf, "Daughter, Decisions, and Domination: An Empirical and Conceptual Critique of Household Strategies," *Development and Change* 21:1 (1990), 43–74; and Sherri Grasmuck and Patricia Pessar, *Between Two Islands: Dominican International Migration* (Berkeley: University of California Press, 1991). For a critique of the perspective, see Kibria, *Family Tightrope*, ch. 4.

year old senior education major who immigrated here at the age of three, explained how all her family members live together to support her polio-ridden brother:

> I have five siblings including me. My older brother, he has polio. He's like thirty-five or thirty-six, around there. All of my siblings live together to help him out, especially after my mom died. Two of them are married and so there's a lot of people in the house, but it's fun . . . It's sad how the Americans leave their handicapped family living by themselves. I mean the other day I saw a sign at school of someone looking for an attendant because he was quadriplegic. I mean, where is his family?!

Similarly, when Le-Thuy, a twenty-four year old sales clerk who immigrated here at age six, told me she considered herself more imbued with Vietnamese ideologies than American ones, she gave the following explanation:

> I like to *oi nha voi ong ngoai* (stay home with maternal grandfather) because he's eighty-nine years old and he needs someone to play with him. [Why do you think this is more Vietnamese than American culturally?] I don't think American people stay home with their grandparents. They usually put them in the old people's home anyways. None of my American friends live with their grandparents. I mean I don't see anything wrong with that, but I wouldn't do it [put grandparents in nursing homes]. I know Vietnamese people wouldn't do it.

Friends as Family

When I asked my informants about their friendship patterns, the overall picture that emerged was that friends are treated "just like family." Friendships, like family, are permeated by a sense of obligation, non-egalitarianism, and sharing of resources. When I asked my informants in what ways were they close to their best friends, most gave answers such as "they will help me when I need it" or "I can depend on them." Sharing feelings and common interests were important, although secondary to material help and support in their friendship development.

In fact, when I inquired about intimacy in friendship, such as what kinds of things they talk about and what emotions they share with their friends, most of my informants were uncertain about what I meant. Some were surprised that I asked such questions. Many saw their friends as people with whom they share similar activities, but "true" or "best" friends were people who shared material support with each other, including money and who provided for each other in non-calculating terms.[63] Mong-Cam, who said she didn't have Vietnamese friends until entering college, described how her new Vietnamese friends take care of each other, creating a sense of "familization" through friendships and at times, there might be conflicts where non-Vietnamese friends were part of the picture:

> They (Vietnamese friends) truly do it because that's who they are and that's how they were raised . . . to take care of one another. They'd cook for me, they'd clean. The guys and girls. The only way I can view it is that it was communal. Nothing's like "this is mine, this is yours." The weird thing with this American

---

[63] Classical sociologist Marcel Mauss argued that gift giving is a process involving a "return to the old and elemental" (67) and that the "gift morality" in modern life must depend upon "people and classes who uphold past customs." (63) In this way, my informants provide for friends and family by drawing upon traditional ideology of collectivism. See *The Gift* Ian Gunnison, Translator (London: Cohen and West Press, 1954).

friend of mine[64] . . . when she and two of my other Vietnamese friends were living together, we shared all the food, there was no question about it and cleaning up, we shared all of those deals; right now there's some problems. The first thing the American friend said was that "I'm not gonna share food." I had asked her and she said, "I want to keep it separate because I like to eat different things." And I was like, "all right." I mean that's so weird to me. I don't like the fact that some people are so damn stingy . . . I don't like counting everything—just being more free with things. I don't like people who count everything, who make you aware that "Oh, you owe me this, you owe me that." It's a give and take. For some people, they don't understand that you don't have to count every single thing. You shouldn't expect your friend to give something in return, just like your family. If you are truly sincere about it, it shouldn't matter. With American friends, they only do things if they owe you something.

Like their convictions about the rules and practices in family life, the ideology of collectivism in the realm of friendship was also regarded as a culturally bound affair. This was reflected in Le-Thuy's account:

Once I needed to pay my insurance, but I was short fifty bucks, a Vietnamese friend gave it to me. She offered me a hundred bucks so that I would have an extra fifty bucks in my account in addition to paying for the insurance. I told her I didn't need it—just fifty bucks. Money is just an object in Vietnamese friendships. Vietnamese when you *muon tien* (borrow money), they don't ask for it right away. Most of the times, they don't even ask for it. My (Americans), they want it right away. That's why it's so *co* (difficult) to borrow from them. If you borrow from them, even if it's only two dollars, they will ask for it. That's why I get very *ngay* (uncomfortable) with sharing with American friends.

Similarly, Loi, a psychology sophomore, distinguished what he sees as differences between Vietnamese and non-Vietnamese friends:

They (Vietnamese friends) take care of me. They see me as a little brother. And they do things like . . . they will call me and say when certain things happen. Like the other day when one of my friends was involved in a very socially complicated situation, and I was like, "do you want to talk about it." He said, "I don't want to talk about it. I don't want to distract you because you need to study. And I can't have these things distract you from your study." Very much like my mom would say, "go study." They'll be doing things like when they come for dinner, they say, "no, don't pay. We know you're as poor as shit. Let us pay for you." Kind of like that taking care, which I very much treasure in our culture. This is a Vietnamese thing. I identify it as a Vietnamese thing. My American friends don't do this. Americans are fifty-fifty even in their friendships, which is a problem with me. There's not that sense that the relationship between you should be boundless. That there should be no sense of strict give and take and that it should just happen naturally. You know it's kinda like if you think about your own experiences with being with your family, they would just give and they don't expect you to just give back.

Constructing and Maintaining Boundaries

The cultural ideology of collectivism acts as a tool for the second generation Vietnamese Americans I interviewed to see differences between them and their American peers. In recognizing these differences, I suggest boundaries are often put into place and are interwoven into the formation of ethnic identity. Most of my informants explained that at some point in their

---

[64] Because of the sensitivity of these conversations, I asked my informants not to refer to their friends' names.

lives, particularly once they reached college and into adulthood, they began critically to look at "American" lives with their own cultural lens.[65] While growing up as children of immigrants, they contended, they saw American ideals as glorifying and appealing, but the pathways into adulthood with new ways of viewing family life, friendship, and intimate relationships presented divergent feelings. These feelings often resulted in the construction and maintenance of boundaries. Lam, an American-born twenty-three year old computer programmer, discussed how he began to view American individuals as distant, cold, and often removed from intimate ties with family and friends:

> I think as we get older, we look at friends differently . . . I think we expect more out of people. American people are very *lan va mac cam tinh* (cold and lack feelings). [How so?] I don't know, I feel very *ngay* (uncomfortable) about asking *My* (Americans) for something, I always feel like I have to pay them back. You know, I can ask my Vietnamese friends for anything and I know I will get it. If they can't get it for me, they will ask other people. That's what *ban* (friends) are for, they *hie sinh* (sacrifice) for each other. That's why I prefer Vietnamese friends . . . I like them more.

Lien explained how she began to label herself as being a Vietnamese, and not Vietnamese-American:

> Just the other day, I was talking to some of my [Vietnamese] girl-friends and we were arguing about politics in the U.S. And, I ended up saying that I thought of myself as a Vietnamese and not Vietnamese American. And I was surprised that they all were thinking about the same things. I mean I just don't term myself Vietnamese American. I don't like that term. I am Vietnamese. Vietnamese to me is like believing in your culture. I hate it when Americans try to teach immigrants they should call themselves Americans. [Why?] I mean they shouldn't lose their *nguon* (roots). [When did you begin labeling yourself as Vietnamese?] When I got to college and I started to getting really close with Vietnamese people. It's hard to explain, but you know, just the way we do things. [Such as?] Like when we go out to eat, everyone would fight over to see who would pay for each other, but with Americans, we have to fight over how to divide the tab equally. That's being Vietnamese to me.

Similarly, Ngu, a twenty year old chemistry major who came here at the age of eight, explained how a difference on the ideology of family obligation created boundaries between her and an American friend:

> There was this girl (American) I knew in high school who had so many problems at home. We were becoming good friends and I remembered when her mom was abused by her father, the first thing she thought about was leaving home for college. I told her not to, I thought that was so selfish! [Why?] If that was me, you know like, I would try to get a job and stay home and get my mom the hell out of there. I mean if that's how she treated her own mom, what is a friend to her then? That's so a white thing to do, to want and just leave your family as soon as you turn eighteen. I hate that. We stopped hanging out with each other because she didn't like the advice I gave her. That's fine with me. I guess I'm just too Vietnamese for her.

---

[65] Nagel cautions that if we consider ethnic identity and boundaries as a personal choice, we run risks "of emphasizing agency at the expense of structure." (156) Although my informants mentioned such things as an as uninviting campus life as being inhibiting for them to form non-Vietnamese friends, overall, their friendships with Vietnamese individuals (and often exclusively), were motivated by personal tastes in cultural ideology and practices.

For a few of my informants, the construction of boundaries not only meant rejecting American ideologies and relationships with American individuals, but also rejecting broader American social structures, such as the criminal justice system and pop culture. As Toan indicated, "When I first came to the U.S., I wanted to be just like an American kid, you know with the accent and everything. But after growing up here, you know, I see a lot of wrong things about life in America that I don't like and I feel blessed to be Vietnamese. That's why sometimes I feel good to be a minority, have something to [be] proud of."

About one-fourth of my informants have recently been back to Vietnam and they claimed the trip "back home" made their critical observations of American ideologies in family life and friendships more pronounced. Some even noted how families and friends in Vietnam appeared to be more intimate than their own. Oanh exclaimed, "They help each other with everything over there! It's just amazing what friends do for each other. It's not uncommon to see children of friends living with your family." A few of my informants actually spoke of going back to Vietnam to live once diplomatic ties are solidly developed with the United States.[66] As Manh said, "I went back there, and when I came back to the U.S., I was so 'homesick;' I missed the warmth of the people, especially the friends and family who were willing to help each other, no matter how rich or poor they were. That is one thing that most Americans don't do. They sometimes help, but only when someone is suffering . . . I want to bring my kids there to live at least for some time."

This process of constructing and maintaining ethnic boundary is inextricably linked to Vietnamese Americans' understandings of family life and friendship. Beneath these meanings and feelings were the intense belief in and practice of the collectivist family ideology. As young adults, these boundaries may be set as continuous symbols of ethnic identity for second generation Vietnamese Americans—what they believe in and what they practice in social relationships determine who they are. If these ethnic boundaries are indeed dynamic and changeable, then we might argue that the lives of these Vietnamese Americans are characterized by certain conditions that are affected by a particular time and place and more specifically, conditions that are built around the new second generation experience.

Conclusion

By tracing second generation Vietnamese American descriptions of growing up as children of immigrants and their experiences as young adults, my findings suggest that the experiences of ethnicity involve the fluid and complex interplay of culture and identity. Working under the social constructionist perspective on ethnicity, which conceptualizes the formation of ethnic identity as a dynamic, situational, and changing process, I argue that the experiences of ethnicity for the children of Vietnamese immigrants are shaped largely by rules and practices in past and present relationships which they pick from their cultural shopping cart. These experiences are situated under a specific context. For second generation Vietnamese Americans, this context may be understood as a stage in the life cycle, a stage characterized by constant sifting and assembling of new identities and identities which have been put into place.

Growing up as children of immigrants, the second generation Vietnamese Americans I interviewed described their childhoods as often infused with ambiguity, uncertainty and tension

---

[66] Driven by the collectivist ideology, two of my informants who came here as accompanied minors spoke of going back to Vietnam to live with their parents. Others who maintain transnational relations with extended kin reported they would like to go back and live for a period of time.

about who they were. Given the opportunities and constraints presented to them from both their old and new worlds, they experienced the classic "marginal man" situation in which constant negotiations of identity took place. Under these conditions, they equated "American-ness" with "whiteness." As children and adolescents, like other "racialized" minority groups, they tried to "be" American by acting and being white in order to fit in with peer groups. Once they progressed into their adulthood, they undertook a process of "de-programming the self" as they challenged notions of American-ness.

As young adulthood introduced new possibilities for friendship patterns and as they began to reevaluate meanings they assign to family life, the collectivist familial ideology became a crucial mechanism for ethnic identification. This reevaluation was particularly active during the college years, a time when some adults first leave their family. In short, friendship and family life turned into social arenas where a collectivist ideology acts as an articulator of ethnic identity. Although my findings show that ethnic identity formation may contribute to lessen internalization of negative self-images during young adulthood relative to childhood experiences of marginality, it is important to recognize that in these processes, boundaries with a pejorative emphasis are often put into place.

While I only paint a picture of how second generation Vietnamese Americans use cultural ideology to form and recapture ethnic identity and to position themselves next to members of the host society, it might be argued that ethnogenesis, or "collective identity shift," occurs for the children of Vietnamese immigrants in this process. Kibria shows that ethnogenesis among second generation Korean and Chinese Asian Americans takes place through their reflections on intermarriage. She found that most Korean and Chinese second generations wanted to preserve "ethnic purity," even when they used an Asian American identity.[67] With similar insights, using friendships and family life as the center of analysis, I found that for second generation Vietnamese Americans, relationships act as powerful devices for maintaining ethnic values as indicated by the boundaries they construct.

Drawing on these eighteen interviews, this study interprets and illustrates how rather than continually bargaining with the "bicultural dilemma," second generation Vietnamese Americans draw upon the ideology of collectivism in their family life and friendships, especially during their young adulthood to turn more exclusively to their "original" ethnicity. I argue that ethnic identity gets assembled and produced, where it otherwise might not for children of immigrants under an "assimilation track" into adulthood. If they were to apply hegemonic values such as individualism, egalitarianism, and self-sufficiency that are embedded in everyday life in the U.S., they believe loss of ethnic identity will inevitably be the result.

As many have pointed out, research on immigrants in much of the past century has focused on the experiences of Europeans.[68] Much of this research applies the straight line assimilation model which holds that immigrants move on a continuum of change—contact, competition, conflict, accommodation, and assimilation—where they eventually lose their ethnic identity and locate themselves in mainstream U.S. culture once acculturation and assimilation have been achieved. In addition, most of this research maintains that change is often necessary for successful upward mobility. Rejecting this approach, I propose that ethnic continuity can help contribute to mobilize rather than inhibit the successful pathways into U.S. society.[69]

One of the clearest examples of how ethnic continuity helps to mobilize rather than inhibit minority groups is when children of Vietnamese immigrants challenge hegemonic American

---

[67] Kibria, "The Construction of 'Asian American'."

[68] For example, see Kibria's works; Zhou and Bankston III; Zhou; and Pyke.

[69] *Ibid.*

values of individualism, egalitarianism, and self-sufficiency to show that they intend to provide care for family members and friends who are in need. Given the diminishing care from the state and other public spheres in the past decade, care that comes from the family and the private sphere is increasingly important.[70] For immigrants, ethnic continuity may help facilitate and balance the necessary forms of care in private life.

The data presented here are preliminary, given the small and distinct nature of this sample—that they live in California in a highly populated Vietnamese and Asian metro area. Clearly, given the ways Vietnamese Americans have settled in the U.S. since the mid-1970s, the next step in this research should be to examine second generation Vietnamese Americans from different geographical areas. California is not a typical U.S. state and it is well known that social and political activism from the Asian American community originated here in the 1960s and has since remained alive.[71] Part of this activism has led to a resurgence of ethnic identity and the maintenance of boundaries.

The social forces built around the new second generation experience, especially for Asian Americans, provide a myriad of complex questions about immigrant lives. For example, how will second generation Vietnamese Americans choose where they live, in terms of neighborhoods and cities, given their social experiences as children of immigrants? Who will second generation Vietnamese Americans' children (the third generation) interact with in schools and neighborhoods? By looking at the subjective experiences of a specific group of the new second generation, we see how trajectories into young adulthood can often result in rigid constructions of boundaries, which seemingly and possibly can not be removed. The ways identity and culture grow in relationships for second generation Vietnamese Americans rely heavily on the influence of institutions such as schools, neighborhoods, and the workforce in the host society. Thus, proper and useful analysis of immigrant lives should explore the dynamics of relationships within these terrains to see how negotiations with, and often challenges to, mainstream cultural values take place. It is necessary, as many have done, to go beyond the assimilation model in order to explore both processes of ethnic identification and ethnic boundary constructions. To do otherwise would simply mean to ignore or minimize the experiences of members of the new second generation.

Notes

Many thanks to Arlene Kaplan Daniels, Jerome Karabel, Hien Le, Pyong Gap Min, Russell Leong, and Kyeyoung Park, for comments on earlier drafts; to Allison Pugh for suggestions; to Ajay Deshmukh, Sergey Ioffe, Chris King, Tram Le-Nguyen, Anil Reddy, Aman Sappal, Sheila Swaroop, and Alice Wong for discussions; and to Barrie Thorne for numerous discussions, comments, and guidance.

---

[70] For a thoughtful discussion of the decline of "public" or state care and the need for public and private care, see Arlie Hochschild, "The Culture of Care: Traditional, Postmodern, Cold-Modern, and Warm-Modern Ideals of Care," *Social Politics* (Fall 1995), 331–346.

[71] For a discussion of Asian American activism in California, see William Wei, *The Asian American Movement* (Philadelphia: Temple University Press, 1993).

College and Notions of "Asian American": Second-Generation Chinese and Korean Americans Negotiate Race and Identity

Nazli Kibria

The traditional college years, the late teens through the mid-twenties, are years of extraordinary maturation and growth. These are the years when many young people leave home, often for the first time, meet very different kinds of people (also often for the first time), come upon previously unheard ideas, and have the opportunity, and indeed the task, of defining for themselves and others who they are—what they think, the values they hold, their place in a world beyond the one in which they grew up.[1]

As evident to even perhaps the most casual observer, Asian American students respond in highly varied ways to the challenges and opportunities for self-exploration that are offered by the complex racial environments of contemporary U.S. college campuses. Drawing on materials from a qualitative study of post-college, second-generation Chinese and Korean Americans, in this article I explore negotiations of race and identity during the college years, focusing on the development of approaches to the "Asian American" concept, in particular its meaning and significance as a basis of affiliation and community. My analyses focus on those persons who had for the most part, not been involved in pan-Asian organizations and activities during college. While pan-Asian organizations are present on most college campuses today, many Asian American students do not participate or become affiliated with them.

While the institutional and political development of the Asian American concept has been extensively studied, we know far less about how the rank and file of those who are widely viewed as "Asian American" understand and respond to this notion. That is, the "public" dimensions of pan-Asian ethnicity have been more extensively studied than its "private" aspects.[2] This is particularly so when it comes to the large segment of Asian Americans who are generally detached or uninvolved in pan-Asian activity, networks or organizations. Yet an exploration

---

[1] Ruth Sidel, *Battling Bias: The Struggle for Identity and Community on College Campuses* (New York: Penguin Books, 1994), 12.

[2] For a discussion of the distinction between "public" and "private" ethnicity, see Philip Kasinitz, *Caribbean New York: Black Immigrants and the Politics of Race.* (Ithaca: Cornell University Press, 1992).

of the experiences of such persons can provide important insights into the opportunities and constraints that surround the development of pan-Asian coalition and community.

Race, Asian Americans, and the Post-Civil Rights Campus

The post-civil rights college campus is one in which issues of race have been prominent. The decades since the 1960s have seen a rise in the numbers of racial minority students attending college.[3] While this increase has not been uniform across types of institutions or affected minority groups equally, it is nonetheless one that has transformed the overall racial composition of the college population. Drawing on a 1991 report issued by the American Council on Education, Paul Loeb notes that "students of color presently number 1 out of 6 at four-year colleges and 1 out of 5 if you count two-year community colleges."[4] Asian American students have been an important part of this development. According to Hune and Chan, in 1994, Asian Pacific Americans constituted 4.8 percent of those obtaining bachelor's degrees.[5] Between 1984 and 1995, the numbers of Asian Pacific Americans enrolled in higher education institutions rose 104.5 percent, with comparable figures of 5.1 percent for whites, 37 percent for African Americans and 104.4 percent for Hispanics. Students of Asian origin have also been an important part of the growth in the foreign student population on U.S. college campuses.[6]

Reflecting this rise in minority student presence, the college campus has been an important arena for larger societal debates on questions of racial equity and integration. Issues of race, for example, have been at the core of controversies over curriculum and course content as well as faculty hiring and student admissions policies. These controversies appear as "hot buttons" in a campus environment that some describe as highly polarized along racial lines.[7] There are, for example, disturbing reports of widespread harassment and violence against minority students.[8] After describing the hostilities experienced by Black students following the acquittal of O.J. Simpson (a verdict that was viewed by Blacks and whites in sharply divergent ways), a 1995 *New York Times* article concludes: "The overall picture of racial relations on campus is one that seems to get more brittle as time goes by."[9] Racial polarization among students is also suggested by what has been described as "balkanization." That is, in ways that violate the expectations of integration,

---

[3] See Dana Y. Takagi, *The Retreat From Race: Asian-American Admissions and Racial Politics* (New Brunswick: Rutgers University Press, 1992) and Shirley Hune and Kenyon S. Chan, "Special Focus: Asian Pacific American Demographic and Educational Trends," in *Minorities in Higher Education,* edited by D. Carter and R. Wilson (Washington D.C.: American Council on Higher Education). Minority enrollment rose from 6.4 in 1960 to 13.8 percent in 1977. And in 1995, 11.7 percent of those obtaining bachelor's degrees were minority students, and 16.8 percent in 1994.

[4] Paul R. Loeb, *Generation at the Crossroads: Apathy and Action on the American Campus* (New Brunswick: Rutgers University Press, 1994), 190.

[5] According to Hune and Chan, 52, in 1995, 60 percent of Asian Pacific Americans attending college were enrolled at four-year institutions. 80 percent were in public institutions.

[6] See Sidel, 42. Asians have constituted about half of the foreign student population.

[7] See Diversity Project, "An Interim Report to the Chancellor" (Berkeley: Institute for the Study of Social Change, 1989), 22.

[8] Sidel, 7–8

[9] Peter Applebome, "Nation's Campuses Confront an Expanding Racial Divide," *The New York Times,* October 25, 1995

some observe that the current trend is for students to engage in social activities that are divided along racial lines. Whether it is in terms of the campus organizations that they join or those with whom they spend their spare time, students stick to their own racial groups:

> A quick glance at the local eateries on campus is more suggestive of segregation than integration. Blacks sit with blacks, whites sit with whites, Asians sit with Asians, each group clustered at separate tables.[10]

Asian Americans have been positioned within these currents of racial controversy in complex and at times seemingly contradictory ways. Particularly important here has been the image of Asians as a "model minority," a group that is culturally predisposed to socioeconomic achievements. In educational settings, this stereotype is tied to the assumption that Asians are good students, an idea that is supported by several general indicators of high academic performance among Asian American students.[11] As analyzed by Dana Takagi, the example of Asian Americans—as a minority group that is successful through merit—has thus often been used to support arguments in favor of ending affirmative action in college admissions. As a result of this perception, Asian Americans are less likely to experience the label of "undeserving" that is often applied to minority students. In other words, while Black and Latino students may be resented and even condemned for having reputedly been admitted due to preferential policies and not merit, the same charge is less likely to be made of Asian American students, given their reputation for academic excellence. Among the potential consequences of this positioning are tensions and feelings of distance between Asian American and other racial minority students, as well as their differing attitudes on such issues as affirmative action.[12] Related to this is the possibility of greater uncertainty among Asian American students in comparison to those of other minority groups about the prevalence of racism on college campuses.

However, the construction of Asian Americans as "meritorious" does not mean that they have been immune from racial hostility on college campuses. The reputation of Asians for academic achievement means that they are not only applauded but also feared and resented. In selective colleges and universities for example, the significant presence of Asian-origin students has elicited hostility, in ways that echo the hysterical fears of a "yellow invasion" that marked the environment in which laws to halt Asian immigration were enacted in the late nineteenth-early twentieth century. Anxieties about an "Asian takeover" are reflected in the appearance, in informal student cultures, of such phrases as "Made in Taiwan" to refer to MIT and "University of Caucasians living among Asians" to refer to UCLA. Asian students are also resented for generating competition in the struggle for grades. They are the "damned curve raisers," making the academic game more difficult for everyone else. In short then, racial hostility towards Asian-origin students often takes as an explicit focus the problems created for others by their academic achievements.

---

[10] Takagi, 145

[11] For example, Hune and Chan, 51, report better preparation and higher expectations of going to college for Asian Pacific Americans in comparison to other racial-ethnic groups.

[12] The 1991 Diversity Report from the University of California at Berkeley mentions several cases in which the assessment of Black and Chicano/Latino students as undeserving and having received admission through preferences, was made by Asian American students. The report also cites survey results showing sharp discrepancies between the support of affirmative action between Asian American and other minority students. Thus 12.1 percent of Asian American students surveyed said that they "definitely" agreed with the under-represented ethnic minority policy. This was in contrast to 61.5 percent of Blacks, 40.6 percent of Chicanos, 40.2 percent of Latinos, and 35.7 percent of Native Americans.

Besides these broad racial currents, there are also the racialized images of the "typical Asian student" that are part of contemporary campus life. For Asian American students, these images are an important part of the context within which negotiations of identity take place. While quite varied in certain respects, these images affirm an understanding of "Asianness" as embodying qualities or traits that are deeply contradictory to U.S. culture's emphasis on individuality. More generally, there is an affirmation of the "foreignness" of Asians, or their location outside of what is prototypically "American."

The reputation of Asians as academic achievers is tied to the popular image of Asian students as "nerdy"—extremely studious, serious, shy, mathematically inclined and lacking in social skills and outside interests. The "Asian nerd" embodies qualities that are fundamentally antithetical to individuality. There is a routine or machine-like quality to academic achievements here, as highlighted by the charge that Asian students are "good but not exceptional."[13] In other words, while competent in a routine sense, Asian students lack the edge of individual spark and creativity that could lead them into exceptional achievement. The idea of "foreignness" is also deeply embedded in this image. The deficient social skills, passivity and orientation towards math and technical subjects that are part of the image suggest a certain lack of comfort and familiarity with the norms and expectations of U.S. culture.

In recent years, there has developed another, seemingly contradictory Asian student image, one that while perhaps specifically associated with foreign students from Asia, affects Asian Americans as well. This is the image of the frivolous and well-to-do Asian student who is "cliquey" and focused on parties and conspicuous consumption. Folded into this image are other popular stereotypes of Asian cultural behavior. This includes the idea of Asians as group-oriented, driven by the dictates of conformity to group life. Thus the party-oriented Asian student is obsessed with the display of material goods (e.g., clothes, cars) that will gain him or her status within the clique. The particular markers that are part of this status game can be viewed as further affirmations of the foreign status and nature of Asian students. That is, in their character and substance, the markers (e.g., a particular style of clothing) are seen as off cue or not in sync with what is "culturally American." Also embedded in this image is the association of Asian culture with gender traditionalism. That is, the Asian cliques are marked by a culture of gender traditionalism that supports male dominance and enforces separate standards for men and women's behavior. In essence, these notions affirm "foreignness"—the Asian-origin student is an outsider to what is "American."

For many Asian Americans, college is a time when they first come to seriously consider the notion of "Asian American" and its relationship to themselves. Here it is important to bear in mind that college students have been critical to the history and development of the Asian American movement. The movement was organized on college campuses in the 1960s by young U.S.-born Asian American activists who were inspired by the civil rights struggles of the time.[14] The founders of the movement defined an ideology of pan-Asianism which has continued to provide a basic framework for the organization and activities of pan-Asian American groups. In essence, "Asian American" is defined here as a signifier of a strategic political community,

---

[13] Deborah Woo, "The 'Overrepresentation' of Asian Americans: Red Herrings and Yellow Perils," in *Race and Ethnic Conflict,* edited by Fred Pincus and Howard Ehrlich (Boulder: Westview Press, 1994):314–326.

[14] Yen Le Espiritu, *Asian American Panethnicity: Bridging Institutions and Identities* (Philadelphia: Temple University Press, 1992)

one that is driven by the shared racial interests of persons of Asian origin in the U.S. as well as a larger struggle against racism.[15]

Among the legacies of this history is the widespread presence on campuses of pan-Asian student associations that aim to bring together students of varied Asian ethnic origin for political and social events. Some colleges and universities have also developed courses and programs in Asian American Studies, and student centers devoted to Asian Americans. For Asian-origin students, such forums offer an opportunity to explore the concept of "Asian American" and become exposed to the ideology of pan-Asianism, often for the first time in their lives. For those students who choose to do so, perspectives on "Asian American" are likely to be shaped in important ways by this ideology.

The development of Asian American institutions and forums on college campuses has been supported by the rising numbers of Asian American students. It has also been encouraged more generally by the prominence of racial issues on campuses as described earlier. Asian American groups and organizations have been part of the discourse and debate that surrounds these issues. Ironically however, the potential for a strengthened pan-Asian campus presence has also coincided with increasing questions and concerns about the limited involvement of Asian American students in pan-Asian groups. Often cited here is the growing ethnic and generational heterogeneity of the Asian American population. In the 1960s, the Asian-origin college population was largely U.S.-born and of Japanese or Chinese origin. Reflecting the demographic shifts experienced by the Asian American population since the immigration reforms of 1965, today however it includes many first-generation persons as well as students from a wide range of Asian ethnic backgrounds. These developments can make the possibility of organizing along ethnic lines (e.g., Chinese American, Korean American) both more feasible and attractive than pan-Asian activity. This is particularly so for first-generation students, for whom ethnic loyalties and a sense of connection to the historically rooted conflicts and enmities between Asian societies are likely to be sharper than that among U.S.-born Asians.

Even however for those students who remain distant from formal pan-Asian activity, the college years are likely to be a time of encounters with the Asian American concept and reflection about what it means for identity and community. For one thing, regardless of whether or not one chooses to be involved, pan-Asian groups and organizations are a visible part of campus life. It is also the case that the notion of "Asian American" has become an established part of the discourse that surrounds racial issues in the contemporary US. Thus while an Asian-origin student may very well avoid pan-Asian activities on campus, she or he is nonetheless likely to confront the idea of "Asian American" in some fashion.

Methods

The materials presented here are drawn from sixty-four in-depth interviews with Chinese Americans and Korean Americans in the Los Angeles and Boston areas. The study was limited to 1.5 and second-generation Chinese and Korean Americans between the ages of twenty-one and forty. I define this group to include those who are the children of immigrants, and have been born and/or raised in the U.S. since the age of twelve or earlier. Interviewees were asked to talk about the role and meaning of their racial and ethnic affiliations in such life spheres as work, family

---

[15] Nazli Kibria, "The Construction of 'Asian American': Reflections on Intermarriage and Ethnic Identity among Second-Generation Chinese and Korean Americans," *Ethnic and Racial Studies* 20:4 (1997):77–86.

and neighborhood over the life course. The interviews, which lasted from one-and-a-half to four hours, were tape-recorded and later transcribed. Informants were initially located through the membership lists and referrals of a variety of churches, professional and social clubs, and college and university alumni associations. The sample was expanded through "snowballing" whereby informants were asked for referrals to others who fit the criteria for inclusion in the study.

In terms of family of origin, the social background of the sample was varied. Some, for example, had grown up in working-class or small business families while others were from professional upper-middle class homes. However, the majority of the sample was college-educated. Fifty-five of the sixty-four informants had Bachelor's degrees from four-year colleges or universities, and in some cases, graduate or professional degrees as well. Of these fifty-five persons, twenty-three had attended public institutions (i.e., state/city colleges or universities), while thirty-two had been to private ones. Two of the others interviewed had obtained two-year Associates degrees from community colleges. Of the remaining informants, two had never attended college and five had attended but had left before completing their undergraduate degrees. The sample included persons who had attended college in the period ranging from 1975 to 1995, with a large number clustered in the 1980s.

A wide range of specific colleges and universities was represented in the experiences of the sample. Although concentrated on the East and West Coasts, there was also diversity in the regional location of the institutions. These variations are important given the tremendous differences in racial environments across institutions. For example, institutions differ in the relative numbers of minority students, and more specifically of students of Chinese, Korean and other Asian origin. Related to this are the variations across institutions with respect to policy on issues of race and multiculturalism. Reflecting these variations, those of my informants who had attended college in the 1980s and 1990s and in California were most likely to have found themselves on campuses with a significant Asian American student presence as well as Asian American Studies programs and centers. As I have mentioned, my analyses here focus on the segment of informants who indicated a lack of involvement in pan-Asian organizations during their college years. This segment constituted a majority of forty-one out of the sample of sixty-four persons.

Identity Negotiations and Perspectives on "Asian American"

The second-generation Chinese and Korean Americans' accounts of their college years revealed several different perspectives on "Asian American." In what follows I explore these perspectives, focusing on the processes—the events, circumstances, decisions and negotiations that surrounded them. While the narratives tended to be dominated by one perspective over another, it was also the case that they often appeared in shifting and overlapping ways in the accounts of individuals.

The "Comfort" of Asian American Friendships

Among the accounts of social life during the college years were those that involved the development of a primary friendship network composed mainly of Asian Americans of varied ethnicities, usually of Japanese, Chinese and Korean origin. For some, this development was one that overlapped with participation in organized pan-Asian groups and events on campus. My focus here however is on the experiences of those who remained uninvolved in such activities, despite an Asian American social circle.

Few informants spoke of their Asian American social circle as the outcome of a highly conscious decision or choice. Instead, the immediate response most often offered was that it had "just happened." In their view, underlying this "natural" course of events were the special ties of Asians. These derived from the commonalities of race and culture among Asians, and the shared experiences and personal histories implied by them. That is, because Asians had a shared racial identity in the U.S., they had all experienced certain things—being racially labeled and lumped together as "Asian", and being stereotyped as "nerdy," "foreign," and so forth. Related to this, there was the shared experience of feeling the sting of racial rejection from others, particularly from whites. It was also felt that Asian Americans shared common experiences that derived from the values that had been part of their upbringing—an emphasis on education, family and work. In short, the conception of "Asian American" embedded in this account was that of a community of shared worldview or understanding, stemming from the commonalities of race and culture. Given all of this, it was not surprising that friendships with Asian Americans had "just happened."

Wai Han, a Chinese American, had attended a state college in California in the mid-1980s. In speaking of how her college friendship circle had been primarily Asian American, she refers at first to being extremely busy, with the pressures of both classes and jobs. Friendships with others required some active effort, in contrast to those with Asian Americans that developed in a natural, almost organic fashion. She felt that there was a greater sense of social ease and receptivity among Asian Americans:

> I was working, and didn't have a lot of time. I lived at home part of the time. My friends were from classes. They were all Asian. I mean not just Chinese, but Korean, Japanese. It wasn't planned, it just happened. I've noticed that Asians are more receptive to me in terms of friendships.

Rather than something that had "just happened," for George, a Korean American, a pan-Asian social circle had developed in active response to the college environment. George spoke of how he had found white students at the Ivy League University he had attended in the 1970s to be stand-offish and unreceptive to him. In contrast, relationships with Asian American students were easy and comfortable. He felt this was in part because of family backgrounds that had been marked by the common values of education and family:

> I found myself mainly with Asian American friends. In fact there were three of us who were really close and they used to call us the Three Musketeers. Interestingly, one guy was Chinese American, the other was Japanese American, and of course I was Korean American. Maybe it's because _____ University is such an old, conservative and white place. But we felt more comfortable with each other. I found a lot of the students snobbish, unfriendly. Asian Americans tend to have more in common, you know. They have similar views on education and family. Similar family experiences like pressure from parents to do well when you're growing up.

As suggested by George's words, the negotiation of Asian stereotypes was part of his involvement in an Asian American friendship network. For George, the "Asian nerd" stereotype was part of a general environment of hostility towards racial minorities, one that only strengthened the bonds of his Asian American friends. The stereotypes then, contributed to his understanding of "Asian American" as a community of solidarity against racism. But there were also other ways in which the stereotypes were negotiated and incorporated into notions of "Asian American." Several informants with pan-Asian friendship networks spoke of how the stereotypes of Asian students as "nerdy" and party-oriented were more applicable to the Chinese or Korean groups on campus. This was, they felt, because of the large numbers of first-generation as well as foreign student Chinese and Koreans that were part of these ethnically bounded groups. Creating a pan-Asian friendship network was a means to differentiate oneself from these groups and by extension, the stereotypes and connotations that were a part of them. This was because those who were part of pan-Asian friendship networks tended to be second or later-generation Asian Americans. Meg, for example, spoke of avoiding the Chinese crowds on campus even as she "hung out" with Asian Americans. A Chinese American, she had attended a private university in California in the early 1990s:

> I've thought about this before. I think it would have been good for me to have had a variety of friends. But psychologically . . . I didn't feel comfortable around Caucasians. I felt more in control of the situation when I was with other Asians. There's a common background there with Asians. The other day my friends and I were talking about how whenever we got together, we always asked each other about how our parents were, how the family was, that kind of thing. And how that just wouldn't be a normal topic of conversation for whites. Also, all our growing-up experiences were the same . . . you can't date until you're this age, or your parents disapprove of you dating this type, that type. We all understood that. My girlfriends especially. (What was the ethnic background of your friends? Were they Chinese, or . . .) Oh no. It was real mixed. There was like a Chinese student crowd, and there was the CSA (Chinese Students Association). I guess I could have been involved but I felt a lot more comfortable with Asians. A lot of the Chinese crowd was not very American-ized. They're very different from me. More into the group thing, the material thing. You know, parties and stuff. I wouldn't fit in.

Meg's words highlight the ways in which consciousness of generational divisions was often an important aspect of understandings of "Asian American" among these informants. But the variable of generation was asserted not simply to achieve distance from the Asian stereotypes. It was, more gen'erally, implicated in efforts to construct a more nuanced and selective understanding of the special ties of Asians. That is, discussion of the greater comfort and ease of relationships with Asians was punctuated with comments about how these were more likely to be felt with some Asians and not others. Sandra, for example, viewed the second-generation experience— that of growing up in the U.S. as a child of Asian immigrants—to be a vital aspect of the shared personal history and worldview of Asian Americans. A Korean American, Sandra had attended a private women's college in the mid-1980s. It is important to note that the working-class Asian immigrant history that she invokes is homogenizing of the realities of socioeconomic diversity among contemporary Asian immigrants:

> I would say the whole immigrant experience really brought us closer together. It's like they know what it's like to have parents who do not speak the language fluently, who are handicapped . . . culturally and verbally. And they know what it's like to see their parents working seven days a week and in these often dangerous settings or very kind of blue-collar work like dry cleaning. So I think that common experience ties us together.

Although in far more muted or less explicit ways, informants also recognized differences of Asian ethnic background in their discussion of the natural ties of Asian Americans. Due to similarities in physical characteristics as well as overlaps of history and culture, especially a tradition of Confucianism, this bond was far more pronounced among persons of East Asian descent. This point was made by George, a Korean American. As described earlier, George's closest friends in college had been Chinese American and Japanese American:

Of all the Asian groups, Koreans, Japanese and Chinese have the most in common. (In what way?) Everybody gets us mixed up; they can't tell us apart. (That doesn't happen with a Vietnamese or Filipino?) It can happen, but it's less likely, especially if you're talking about Asians looking at each other. It's much easier I think to tell a Korean from a Filipino person than Chinese. It's also that there are common roots for Koreans, Japanese and Chinese if you go way back. Like our writing is from the same family. And the cultures are based on Confuciansm.

What I have described above are accounts of the college years that are marked by a sense of identification with "Asian American" as an affiliation, despite non-involvement with organized pan-Asian activity. This lack of involvement was reflected in important ways in the understandings of "Asian American" articulated here. While race and racism were widely acknowledged as part of the special bond of Asians, these ideas did not always translate into recognition of the shared political interests of Asian Americans or a conception of Asian American as signifying a strategic, political community. Also differentiating these perspectives from the ideology of pan-Asianism is the idea of a pan-Asian culture, in particular the shared Asian values of family and education. Mindful of the realities of diversity among Asian Americans, the Asian American movement has been critical of efforts to construct "Asian American" as a cultural community.

There was an elasticity to the notion of pan-Asian community articulated here. That is, while informants spoke of these bonds as encompassing Asian Americans in general, they also at times made distinctions. As I have described, generational divisions, especially that between immigrant and second-generation persons, were a particularly prominent distinction. For the second-generation Chinese and Korean Americans," Asian American community" emerged out of a central experience and identification with the U.S., one that those who had not grown up elsewhere did not fundamentally share.

"Asian American" as an Artificial Construct

Some of the second-generation Chinese and Korean Americans spoke of their college social life with reference to a friendship circle that was primarily Chinese American or Korean American. Participation in Chinese or Korean organizations on campus could be part of these accounts, but not necessarily so. This pattern of ethnically oriented social involvements, somewhat more prevalent among the Korean Americans than Chinese Americans,[16] meant that perspectives on "Asian American" were forged here in contrast and often in opposition to understandings of Chinese or Korean American as a basis of identity and community. In essence, "Asian American" was understood here as a weak and relatively insignificant basis of identity and community—a construct that was artificial and externally imposed, masking the more natural ties and solidarity of specific ethnic groups, such as Chinese or Koreans. For some, the activities of pan-Asian organizations on campus only highlighted the contrived character of Asian American community. For a variety of reasons, they felt distant from the political agenda of these organizations, and did not see their interests and ideas to be represented by them.

While in some accounts, a pattern of friendships with fellow ethnics was continuous with social life before college, for others it was something new. In the latter case informants often spoke of how college had for them been a time of exploring and coming to terms with their Chinese or Korean identity. The presence on campus of significant numbers of Chinese and Korean Americans

---

[16] Possible explanations for this discrepancy include the greater heterogeneity of the Chinese American population in comparison to Korean Americans, in terms of nationality, class and generation.

both allowed and encouraged such explorations. Often mentioned here was the experience of encountering for the first time, fellow ethnics who were U.S.-born and/or raised and who thus contradicted the Asian stereotypes. That is, they were not "nerdy," "foreign" or "traditional" in their attitudes towards men and women. Thus as in the case of the earlier accounts, negotiations of identity were marked by the Asian stereotypes and the use of generation to achieve distance from them. We see this in the account of Susan, a Korean American who had attended a state college in California in the early 1980s:

> When I started going to _____ I was really anti-Korean because I thought all Korean men or boys were really chauvinistic and domineering like my dad. Or really wimpy and nerdy. And I didn't really have respect for Korean girls because my sense was they didn't have any ambition in life. They just wanted to marry right and to gossip about clothes, boys, that type of thing. They weren't conscious about other things that were going on. I don't know where I got this idea but I was really dissatisfied with Korean women. So I had this stereotype of Korean women and I used to tell myself: I'm not going to hang out with Koreans when I get to college because they're so narrow-minded and they only speak Korean and they don't assimilate. But then once I got there I met Koreans and they encouraged me to join their Korean student organizations and stuff. I realized that it was kind of a bonding that almost comes natural. I think I realized my identity and I also realized that not all the Korean kids fit the stereotype. There were Korean kids just like me who grew up in predominantly white neighborhoods, and had a lot of white friends. They weren't all nerdy or chauvinistic. We could relate to whites really well. (So your friends in college were mainly Korean American?) Yeah, I mean there were so many Korean Americans there that I didn't need to go beyond that. I mean I had a lot of friends. I did have some Chinese and Japanese friends I met through a pre-law Asian students group. But still, with Koreans it's different, I feel like there's a natural attraction.

In Susan's account, the meaning and significance of friendships across Asian groups is assessed in contradistinction to Korean ones. In this comparison, intra-Asian bonds come up short, appearing weak and insignificant. For Jeff, a Korean American who had attended a private university in the Northeast in the early 1990s, intra-Asian ties were not only weak in comparison to ethnic ones but also had an aura of falsity about them. For him, the transition to a primarily Korean American social circle had taken place during college. It had been triggered by a growing sense of discomfort and alienation from the predominantly white social groups around which he had initially organized his social life. Also important to note is that Jeff's perspective on racial issues had been deeply affected by the 1992 Los Angeles riots, during which his parents' small business had been seriously damaged:

> I would say that the first time that I started feeling a close bond with Koreans was in college. It's funny because when I started, in my freshman year, I joined a white fraternity and I was fairly active. I didn't really participate in any of the Korean functions, and I guess the Koreans called me whitewashed. Then I had a good friend who was part of that Korean clique. By my second year I kind of assimilated into the Korean crowd. (What happened with the fraternity?) I was less and less involved. I was one out of three Asians in a very large organization, and it felt strange. It was subtle, but I don't think I was accepted. So my friends were pretty much Korean in college and it's been that way since then. I find it's more comfortable. (Is that also the case with Asian Americans from other groups? Do you have other Asian friends?) No, not really. I mean I had acquaintances in college who were Chinese, that kind of thing. I can't say I had more in common with them than whites or blacks or whatever. It's a mistake to think there's any real bond going on there. We speak different languages, have different perspectives.

> I was in college during the riots. I remember reading right after the riots about how the Chinese and Japanese communities in L.A. were just ... unfazed. I mean it didn't concern them—it was a Korean problem. You know, I just don't see that there's too much in common going on there. Why do we have to go around pretending that Asian Americans are the same?

The resentment felt by Jeff about what was felt to be the pretense of Asian American unity was echoed by several informants. Some referred to encounters with pan-Asian groups and activities in which the fiction of Asian American community was made sharply visible to them. This was the case for Terry, a Chinese American who had attended a state college in California in the early 1980s. Unlike the accounts described so far, for Terry, a pattern of Chinese American friendships was not new, but something with which she had grown up, having been raised in the Chinatown areas of San Francisco and Los Angeles. Terry draws on her exposure to an Asian American student organization and its internal tensions as a point of contrast for highlighting the cultural and other similarities of Chinese in comparison to Asians in general. It is of note that she also qualifies this notion of a natural Chinese bond by recognizing generational divisions among Chinese, and demarcating her sense of ethnic affinity to American-born Chinese in particular:

> Most of my friends were Chinese, I felt more comfortable socially with Chinese. (How about Asian friends, I mean from other Asian groups?) I did have some Asian friends in college who were not Chinese. At first I went to the Asian students association. But it was very political. One group would say: we're not getting represented, we want a voice. I couldn't get into it, I couldn't see the point. I find it less stressful with Chinese; I'm talking mainly American-born Chinese. We have the same history, we grew up with the same superstitions, foods.

Several informants echoed the general sense of discomfort voiced by Terry about the pan-Asian organizations on campus. Some complained of the "radical" political agenda of the pan-Asian groups. Their own sense of dissonance and distance from the progressive politics of Asian American groups only confirmed the fake, contrived character of "Asian American" as a basis of identity and community. We see this in the words of Bill, a Chinese American who had attended a private university in California in the early 1980s. Bill had found the progressive political agenda of the pan-Asian groups on campus to be unconvincing and in fact distasteful. While he was not very interested in the Chinese student groups either, in the latter half of his college career he found himself with a "Chinese clique." Besides connoting a certain economic glamor, Chinese ties were natural and primordial—rooted in blood:

> In college I stayed away from Chinese for a long time. I mean I didn't go looking for Chinese. The Chinese Students Association was not very interesting to me. Neither were the Asian student groups. They were too crazy. Always spouting off about oppression. I really think this whole Asian thing is overplayed. In the last couple of years I got into a Chinese clique. It was a change—I'd spent all this time avoiding Chinese. And then it seemed kind of exciting. China is such a booming area economically. I felt kind of drawn to it. I think it's like they say, being Chinese is in your blood.

The pattern of ethnic social involvements described above was one that provided the social context for an understanding of "Asian American" as peripheral if not false or artificial as a basis of identity and community. It was a community of fellow Chinese or Korean Americans rather than a pan-Asian American one that provided the means for coping with the social challenges of college life. As was true of the understandings described in the previous section, here too, talk of the "natural" bond of Chinese and Koreans was constantly punctuated with qualifications, in particular that of the distinction between immigrant and second-generation persons.

"Asian American" as Stifling to Indivduality

The last accounts that I turn to are distinguished by a lack of connection to Asian, Chinese or Korean American communities on campus.[7] Some informants (especially those who went to college before the 1980s) explaineded this absence with reference to a lack of opportunity, or the presence of very small numbers of fellow ethnics or Asian Americans on campus. More often though, what was related was an active rejection of the available opportunities to make these connections. "Asian American" was understood here as a force that stood in opposition to individuality and the exercising of freedom and choice with respect to affiliation and identity. This was so in two ways. First, Asian American communities were seen to collectively embody qualities and traits that were antithetical to individualism. These included the stereotypical qualities of clannishness, group conformity and gender traditionalism. Second, individuality was challenged by the very fact of prescribed membership. That is, the fact that one was expected to belong to Asian American group(s), regardless of how one felt about it, was stifling. As we will see, informants experienced this expectation of belonging as emanating not just from non-Asians but also from within the Asian American communities on campus.

For Gordon, a Chinese American, the expectations of Asian friendship were particularly troubling. Students of Asian-origin on campus responded to his refusals to join them by labeling him as "banana"—someone striving to be white and denying his true heritage. The significance of this expectation as well as his discomfiture about it were only compounded by the reaction of his white friends who teased him about belonging to the "Asian crowd." Thus the dynamics of these expectations, along with his negative impressions (e.g., close-minded, serious) of the Asian student groups meant that the very idea of Asian American community made him feel claustrophobic:

> It was very strange at _____ University because that was the first time that I was surrounded by other Asian people. And it was kind of funny but I felt uncomfortable with it. (How did it make you feel uncomfortable?) I never really looked at myself as Asian. Well I never really looked at myself as anything, you know growing up in this white suburb. When I got there I was solicited to join the Korean Club and the Chinese Club and the Asian Club. But I had never grouped myself in Asian or Chinese or anything like that. And so it was just something new. I met a lot of them and it really turned me off. It's the close mindedness to the point where they kind of shun out other people. It's kind of mean to say, but I didn't enjoy being with them. They were—they were typically Asian. They were—they were not very fun. They were very serious.
>
> (Were these people mainly Asian immigrants? Or were they raised here?) Both, I didn't see a huge difference there. I would get a lot of flak, from both sides. The Asian group, they would give me a hard time . . . hey, why aren't you hanging out with us? Are you a "banana"? My friends [white] would kid around about it, and ask me why I wasn't hanging out with the Asians. They were joking, they knew I wouldn't fit in with the Asians.

As suggested by Gordon's response to my question about differences between immigrant and U.S.-born Asian students, distinctions among Asians did not figure heavily in his understandings of Asian American community. What becomes clear here is the quality of fluidity that surrounds the stereotypes, in particular their shifting ability to apply to both pan-Asian boundaries and the ones contained with it. We see this in the words of Ben, who like many others voiced a sense of repulsion to the "cliquey" and conformist character of Asian campus communities. He begins by speaking of his experience with Korean students, but then slips into talking about Asians in general. Ben had attended a private university in the Northeast for a year in the early 1990s, before dropping out and joining the armed services:

> These Korean guys came up to me and said, why aren't you hanging out with us? Why aren't you part of the gang, the Korean posse? I was thinking, are we still in high school? A Korean posse? Is this for real? It was too stifling, I didn't want to be part of some group. I think it's important for people to be themselves. You always see these Asian people in a group, everything's a group.

For women in particular, an aversion to "traditional," male-dominant gender roles often marked their accounts of why they had steered clear of the Asian, Chinese or Korean communities on campus. This was suggested by Katherine, a Korean American who had attended a private university in the Northeast in the early to mid-1980s. Katherine begins by speaking specifically of her experiences with the Korean Students Association, but then moves on to Asians in general. What she felt to be the male chauvinism of the Asian men, along with the general emphasis on group activity, led her to stay away from the Asian groups:

> I had a really broad group of friends. We had a rooming group of ten women and we looked like the United Nations. Puerto Rican, Japanese American, Jewish American, a woman from Seattle, two Black women from the South. I did find though that I couldn't hang out with Koreans who were in Korean groups; that wouldn't work for me. I went to the Korean Student Association meetings and I felt like they were pointless. The men pretty much led the meetings. Basically I really like Asian women and I don't really get along with Asian men. There are few Asian men who are willing to let down all preconceptions about women, I've even seen that with a lot of really liberal, well-educated Asian guys. And I seem to break a lot of the stereotypes about Asian women. In any case, the whole group thing drove me nuts.

While Katherine's concerns about gender traditionalism focused on the behavior of Asian men, for Jane they centered around impressions of the women who were part of the Chinese student groups on campus. According to her, not only were the women deferential to men but also frivolous in nature, focused on ostentatious material displays. As a student from a modest financial background, Jane was particularly offended by these displays. A Chinese American, she had attended a private university in California in the early 1980s:

> I was working and going to school at the same time. I had a scholarship and I felt a lot of pressure to do well. You know I had basically gone to an inner-city school, and I don't think the academic standards had been too high. I had to work really hard to get good grades. I was on scholarship, but financially it was still not easy. So socially I wasn't all that active, until about my third year. My close friends were people I met in class. Pretty much Caucasian. (Did you join any Asian or Chinese student groups?) No. I did have a Chinese friend who dragged me to a couple of meetings and a dance organized by a Chinese group. It was a real turn-off. I was almost offended in some ways. It was a big status thing, expensive clothes, cars. And I didn't like the whole male-female dynamic. It was too much like the delicate Asian flower waiting for the man to sweep her off her feet.

Men informants too, voiced complaints about an excessive "party focus," particularly in relation to the Chinese or Korean groups and organizations on campus. Thus Sung, a Korean

American, spoke of being turned off by the "drinking club" atmosphere of the Korean Students Association on campus. He also felt no sense of connection to the Asian American organizations on campus. He did not agree with the fundamental political agenda of the organizations, and felt a lack of space for dialogue within them. All of this only enhanced his association of the idea of Asian American affiliation with conformity and the restriction of free choice. Of note is his comment that his friends were a diverse group, a point often made by informants in the course of affirming through contrast the cliquish and conformist character of the Asian groups. Diversity in friendships thus becomes a kind of proof of individuality and the ability to make choices apart from groups:

> My friends in school were really just a motley crew, and that was something I really liked. I wasn't interested in the Korean Students Association, which was a social thing. I mean it was like a drinking club, a place to find a future wife, that kind of thing. It was like a fraternity. (How about Asian American groups?) I went to a couple of Asian American meetings my first year but the agenda that they had just didn't sit well with me. I mean I couldn't get all that interested in what they had to say. They were very much oriented towards trying to frame the Asian American experience using a language or way of describing things that is similar to civil rights. There was no room for disagreement, for dialogue. You know I thought it was kind of a stretch. African Americans have been screwed in this country for a long long time. Whereas the Asians have generally been treated better.

The accounts of the informants so far are dominated by negative impressions and reactions to Asian student groups on campus. A somewhat different perspective was provided by Connie, a Chinese American who had attended a state college in California in the late 1970s-early 1980s. Having grown up in a largely Chinese neighborhood, she saw college as an opportunity to meet people from other groups. She felt that her college experiences had taught her to feel comfortable with different kinds of people. Thus while for her, Asian American community did not have the kinds of negative connotations that it did for the other informants described here, it was nonetheless associated with limitations, a restriction on individual choice. Once again, a racially diverse friendship network is associated with free choice in contrast to the constraints of an Asian or Chinese social circle:

> As soon as I got there, I found myself in an Asian clique. These Asian persons that I didn't know came up and invited me to sit with them in the dining hall. And every night we'd eat together and there would be this long table of about twenty Asian Americans . . . Japanese, Chinese. And then I decided, what's going on here, I want to meet some other kinds of people. So after my first year I kind of expanded, joined some different groups and met other people. I had some white friends for the first time in my life, and I had Hispanic friends. (How did you feel with the other, the non-Asian friends that you made? Did you feel accepted?) Oh yes, absolutely. I think it was really important for me, because I started to feel more comfortable with other people

To summarize, the perspective described here is one in which "Asian American" is understood as stifling, claustrophobic and contradictory in an essential sense to individuality. Popular stereotypes of Asian culture clearly play an important role in shaping and giving form to such understandings. Also important was the sense of pressure felt by informants to belong to pan-Asian, Chinese or Korean communities on campus. Resisting these pressures was a means to affirm one's individuality.

Conclusions

This article highlights the diversity of social patterns and experiences among second-generation Chinese and Korean Americans during the college years. This diversity is not surprising, given the range of backgrounds, resources and specific college contexts involved. At the same time, my materials also suggest some ways in which experiences are shaped by a common racial context. These include racialized constructions of persons of Asian descent as "foreign," as captured by popular stereotypes of the "typical Asian student." These stereotypes entered into the identity negotiations of my informants in powerful yet varied ways, affirming different understandings of "Asian American." For some it provided the basis for an understanding of Asian American as a community of solidarity while for others it was an affiliation that violated identity choice. Moving across these variations was a common response—a tendency to deflect the stereotypes onto immigrant or foreign national Asians. My findings thus highlight the ways in which these stereotypes contribute to and play on immigrant versus later-generation fissures in Asian American communities.

Those who are the focus of this article were disengaged from pan-Asian student organizations and activities during their college years. Many specific explanations were offered for this absence of connection, ranging from a lack of time and energy to invest in extracurricular activities to disagreement with the progressive politics of the organizations. The lack of engagement was perhaps most striking among those who expressed a sense of pan-Asian connection and identification. As I have discussed, the understanding of Asian American community here was both less political (at least in an explicit sense) and more focused on issues of culture than that offered by the ideology of pan-Asianism. Some of these informants described themselves as "apolitical" while others did not find the political agenda of Asian American organizations to be of much relevance and interest. While quite tentative and diffuse in nature, a process of ethnicization of "Asian American" is suggested here. That is, there are hints of a transformation, one by which "Asian American" is seen by those who are encompassed by it as not simply an externally imposed category but a signifier of community, of shared culture and history. In invoking a pan-Asian culture, this process of ethnicization drew on ideas embedded in the model minority stereotype—in particular the presumed Asian emphasis on education and family. Also noteworthy were the ways in which distinctions of immigrant versus later-generation and East Asian versus "other Asian" were used to demarcate the boundaries of pan-Asian American community.

But while some of the second-generation Chinese and Korean Americans identified "Asian American" as a natural basis of community, most rejected it as a significant basis of affiliation and identity. For some it signified an effort to impose an artificial and fake social and political unity. Yet for others "Asian American" signified a restriction on individuality. These rejections capture the contradictions that are part of the notion of Asian American. That is, while "Asian American" has come on the one hand to signify a political strategy of empowerment, it also remains for persons of Asian descent, a homogenizing and externally imposed category.

Notes

Thanks to Linell Yugawa for helping me to think through my ideas about the college experiences of Asian Americans. Also thanks to Karen Pyke for her careful feedback.

PART VII Intermarriage, Multiracial Identity, and Sexuality

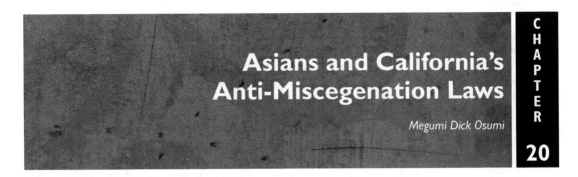

Asians and California's
Anti-Miscegenation Laws

Megumi Dick Osumi

C
H
A
P
T
E
R

20

Introduction

Until recently the Asian has been neglected in any study of American society. However, an increasing number of people have come to see the mis-treatment of Asian immigrants and their descendants not so much as an isolated, insignificant development, but rather as a crucial aspect of American racism and oppression. In the middle nineteenth century American business needed a cheap labor force. But if such a work force was to be taken from non-white people, considered to be inferior and subversive, methods would have to be found which "simultaneously permit the exploitation of them in a wide variety of settings" and yet keep them separate from and subordinate to the rest of society.[1]

In California, this approach has been clearly discernible. All Asian peoples—Chinese, Japanese, Korean, Pilipino, and East Indian—have entered this country as a cheap labor force for such dominant industries as rail-roads and agriculture. These immigrants encountered extreme hostility and endured numerous acts of violence from other Americans. Further, an unprecedented amount of discriminatory legislation was passed against Asian Americans. These laws were designed to oppress and control these Asian peoples, depriving them of their basic human rights and separating them from white society. Connie Yu Young made the following observation: "What is significant is that all of these varied Asian groups, each representing a separable country and unified culture, encountered a similar or identical pattern of racial oppression and economic exploitation."[2]

Between 1850 and 1950, there were passed approximately fifty laws specifically aimed to restrict and subordinate the Asian. They included the Foreign Miners Tax of 1850, the "Queue"

---

[1] Stanford Lyman, *The Asian in the West*, Social Science and Humanities Publication No. 4 (Reno: Western Studies Center, Desert Institute, University of Nevada, 1971), p. 8.

[2] Connie Yu Young, "The Chinese in American Courts," *Bulletin of Concerned Scholars*, Vol. 4, No. 3 (Fall, 1972), pp. 22–30.

and "Laundry" ordinances of 1873, the Chinese Exclusion Act of 1882, the Scott Act of 1888, the Alien Land Laws of 1913 and 1920, and the Exclusion Act of 1924.[3] Though not slaves, Asians were limited to certain exploitable types of employment, denied essential legal rights, including citizenship, and considered too unworthy and undesirable to become part of American society.

Anti-miscegenation laws were an integral part of this manipulative and exploitative treatment of Asians in California. However, they have generally been ignored or discussed briefly and inaccurately.[4] Originally, anti-miscegenation laws were an outgrowth of America's slavery. As early as 1661, Maryland passed the first anti-miscegenation law, directed at prohibiting white female and black male marriages. Thirty-eight States, at one time or another have passed legislation preventing interracial unions between blacks and whites.[5]

California's original miscegenation statute was enacted by the State Legislature in 1850. Later, Section 60 of the new Civil Code in 1872 replaced the older statute.[6] California's anti-miscegenation laws, like the laws of the other Western States, proved to be readily expandable to include Asians as they began to immigrate to the State. Thus, in 1880, amidst the severe anti-Chinese agitation of the times, Section 69 (an ancillary to Section 60) was amended to prohibit the issuance of a license authorizing the marriage of a white person with a "Negro, Mulatto, or Mongolian."[7] In 1905, resulting from strong anti-Japanese sentiments, Section 60 itself was changed, declaring marriages between whites and Mongolians "illegal and void."[8] Finally, in 1933, both statutes were amended again to include Pilipinos ("Malays") on the list of racial groups forbidden by law to intermarry with whites in California.[9]

These anti-miscegenation laws against Asians reveal the exploitative and oppressive use of American law. In this article we will attempt to show the close relationship between the passage of these laws against the Chinese, Japanese and Pilipinos, on the one hand, and the influential and strong anti-Asian movement in California, on the other. We especially will examine the role of these laws within the context of the subjugation of these Asian groups in California and the United States. Further, we will discuss the legal, legislative, and social effects of these laws against the above groups and their communities, concluding with an examination of *Perez v. Sharp* (1948), which ruled California's anti-miscegenation laws unconstitutional, and *Loving v. Virginia* (1967), which ruled such statutes in the United States unconstitutional.

---

[3] Lowell Chun-Hoon, "Teaching the Asian-American Experience: Alternative to the Neglect and Racism in Textbooks," *Amerasia Journal*, Vol. 3, No. 1 (1975), p. 47.

[4] Surprisingly, many scholars have been inaccurate in their discussion of these laws ranging from the giving of incorrect dates to the fabrication of non-existent legislation. For example, Frank Chuman in his recent *The Bamboo People: The Law and Japanese-Americans* (Del Mar, California: Publisher's Inc., 1976) discusses some anti-miscegenation laws erroneously. He states that the amendment of Section 60 applying this statute to Asians was first passed in 1945 and became law in 1946. As we will discuss later, this amendment was actually passed in 1905. The 1945 legislation he refers to in his discussion (page 111) did not even apply to Section 60 and was not an enactment of any anti-miscegenation law in California.

[5] Robert J. Sickels, *Race, Marriage and the Law* (Albuquerque: University of New Mexico Press, 1972), p. 64.

[6] *Cal. Stats.*, 1850, Ch. 140, p. 424.

[7] *Cal. Stats.*, 1880, Code Amendments, Ch. 41, Sec. 1, p. 3.

[8] *Cal. Stats.*, 1905, Ch. 481, Sec. 2, p. 554.

[9] *Cal. Stats.*, 1933, Ch. 104, 105, p. 561.

The Chinese

The first Asian group to be victimized by these laws was the Chinese. In this section, we will attempt to discuss this experience within the context of the anti-Chinese movement in this period.

In 1848, growing numbers of Chinese began to migrate to the Western United States. Most of these immigrants came from Kwangtung Province in Southeastern China, an area devastated by poverty, war (Taiping Rebellion, 1850–1864) and famine. The majority of them were laborers, young men from the poor villages of Toisan District in Kwangtung. Few Chinese women came to America during this period—the most common reasons given for this development were that the custom discouraged women from leaving their villages, and that very few Chinese men came here in that period with intentions to stay permanently. Most of these male "sojourners" left their poor and war-ravaged Province, drawn by the lure of the gold discovery in California, the relatively low cost of ship passage, the availability of employment, and the emerging Chinese communities of California. Thousands of these workers migrated during this period. According to the United States census, the number of Chinese in this country reached 34,933 by 1860, 63,199 by 1870, and 105,465 by 1880.[10]

The most constant driving force behind this great migration was the demand for cheap labor. California's rapid growth especially consumed all available cheap labor. Large business interests, like railroads, promoted and encouraged this migration of workers, often employing labor contractors to obtain more laborers from China especially in the 1860s. These interests benefited both from revenues made from the immigrants' boat fares and from the exploitation of their cheap labor. Chinese merchants also came to America, where they controlled community and business associations like the Chinese Consolidated Benevolent Association, commonly known as the Six Companies in San Francisco. These merchants dispersed jobs and business opportunities, arbitrated disputes, formed credit and employment agencies, and participated with the merchant fleet in the credit-ticket system by which many Chinese borrowed money to come to America. The merchant leaders of the district associations, or *hui kuan*, also acted as subcontractors for white labor recruiters.

Chinese workers first labored in the mining industry and later in rail-road construction in the 1860s. The Central Pacific Railway employed approximately 15,000 Chinese at the dangerous chore of "boring the Sierra tunnels and building the transcontinental line across Nevada and Utah."[11] Others irrigated and harvested the new crops for California's ranches and farms. By the 1870s, Chinese laborers formed one quarter of the State's work force. They especially dominated the service trades throughout California. By the 1870s, thousands of Chinese workers began to enter the growing manufacturing industries of cities like San Francisco.

Throughout this period, the Chinese received lower wages than white laborers for the same work. The Central Pacific bought "Chinese labor something like two-thirds the price of white."[12] In 1876, the president of the San Jose woolen mills acknowledged: "To Chinamen, on an average, we pay less . . . if the Chinamen were taken from us, we should close up tomorrow."[13] In the same

---

[10] U. S. Census Office, *Tenth Census of the United States, 1890* (Washington, D.C.: Government Printing Office, 1883), I:379, Table IV.

[11] Alexander Saxton, *The Indispensable Enemy: Labor and the Anti-Chinese Movement in California* (Berkeley and Los Angeles: University of California Press, 1971), p. 65.

[12] *Ibid.*, p. 63.

[13] Victor G. and Brett de Bary Nee, *Longtime Californ'* (New York: Pantheon Press, 1973), p. 43.

year, another owner of a San Francisco factory boasted that he paid "white male laborers $2.25 to $5.00 a day, white child laborers $1.00 a day, and young Chinamen $.90 a day."[14] Chinese labor, thus, offered many advantages to the entrepreneurs of the period.

With this exploitation, the Chinese immigrant endured extreme forms of racism and violence which later coalesced into a powerful anti-Chinese movement. Composed of "opposition by apparently competing economic groups, physical violence, highly publicized exploitation of racial and color prejudices by politicians, enactment of laws constitutional or otherwise by national legislation to deny admittance to the Chinese," this movement was not caused by one single factor. Support of the movement came from all classes of American society. Anti-Chinese sentiments became popular political stances on which hundreds of campaigns for public office were launched. Business interests viewed the Chinese as an exploitable labor force predicated upon prevention of their full citizenship or social and legal equality. Thus, "scorned by officials, patronized by missionaries, defamed by labor leaders, and battered by mobs, the Chinese suffered nearly the full panoply of injustice that a racist society could impose."[15]

Many scholars have attempted to examine and analyze this movement. Elmer Sandmeyer's view has been a prevalent one in recent years. He felt that while the movement's supporters were diverse, the fundamental motive was "racial antagonism reinforced by economic competition."[16] Sandmeyer viewed the movement as an essentially regional force using political leverage to gain national legislation. Two recent scholars, Stuart Miller and Alexander Saxton, have modified this view, linking anti-Chinese feelings and actions to the mainstream of American racism. Both have shown the national roots for what had been assured to be a basically far western movement. Miller's *The Unwelcome Immigrant* demonstrates that racist attitudes towards the Chinese existed in American thought long before they came, thus adding a new factor in understanding the success of the Sinophobic movement, and "the unfavorable image of the Chinese that preceded them to the United States."[17] Professor Saxton's *The Indispensable Enemy* focuses on the national and California labor movement, which all authorities agree was the leading source of "organizational opposition to the Chinese in the United States." His thesis was that the anti-Chinese sentiments provided the "indispensable cement to hold together the strong California labor movement."[18] In the last half of the nineteenth century, organized labor was very active in the anti-Chinese movement in California as well as the whole United States. It also joined with other groups in the influential "anti-Oriental crusade" to exclude other Asian immigrant workers from this country. Saxton attempts to analyze some of the complex reasons behind the role of the white workingman in this development:

> Each of white America's three great racial confrontations—with the Indian, the African slave, and the Oriental contract laborer—has involved economic exploitation of colored peoples by the dominant white society. In all these transactions, and especially in the two that began with systems of enforced labor, white workingmen have played the dual role of exploiters and exploited. On the

---

[14] *Ibid.*, p. 43.

[15] Elmer Sandmeyer, *The Anti-Chinese Movement in California* (Urbana: University of Illinois Press, 1973), p. 109.

[16] *Ibid.*, p. 110.

[17] Roger Daniels, "American Historians and East Asian Immigrants," in *The Asian American*, edited by Norris Hundley, Jr. (Santa Barbara: CLIO Press, Inc., 1976), p. 9; Stuart Miller, *The Unwelcome Immigrant: The American Image of the Chinese, 1785–1882* (Berkeley and Los Angeles: University of California Press, 1969), p. 201.

[18] Daniels, p. 9.

one hand, thrown into competition with racial minorities (whether slaves or "cheap labor"), they suffered economically; on the other hand, being white, they benefited by that very exploitation which was compelling the racial minorities to work for low wages, or for nothing. Ideologically they were pulled in opposite directions. In one direction they were drawn to advocate unity in defense of the interests of all workers (or *producers,* to use the earlier Jacksonian term) as a class. In the opposite direction, they were drawn to separate themselves from members of racial minorities in the labor force in order to seek special dispensations as members of the white society.[19]

In the 1870s, the anti-Chinese crusade grew to be a powerful factor in California and national politics. Depression and financial chaos ruled the decade. After the Civil War, there was a surplus of wage labor in the United States. The completion of the Transcontinental Railroad in 1869 and the panic of 1873 caused a new influx of workers from the East to California. With mining and railroad jobs declining and a generally undeveloped state economy, employment opportunities were scarce for the working class. After 1875, this dangerous situation worsened. Business failures increased during this period. Banks also began to close as the depression deteriorated. These events caused the withdrawal of capital from industry, a subsequent decrease in business activity, and yet more unemployment among workingmen.

Amidst the increasing competition for jobs, the white laborer's hostility against the Chinese, who worked generally for lower wages, became increasingly more violent and irrational. Looking for survival during the financial crisis, many white laborers focused their hatred on the Chinese: "However laboring men might disagree on other points, there was one cause to which they subscribed in common—' the Chinese must go!' "[20] Mobs began to destroy the homes and property of the Chinese, and attempted to drive them out of the community. With this increased violence, the passage of discriminatory and racist legislation against the Chinese also accelerated in this decade. Political opportunists and demagogues used the "Chinese Question" to win labor support.

In the summer of 1877, a series of railroad strikes hit the nation. A mass meeting called in San Francisco to support the railroad strikers was taken over by anti-Chinese agitators: "In spite of efforts by the chairman to prevent it, anti-coolie sentiment was injected into the meeting, while the hoodlum element rushed into Chinatown, burned several buildings, sacked fifteen washouts, and broke windows in the Methodist Chinese Mission."[21] A few months later in October, 1877, out of this violence and chaos, emerged the Workingmen's Party of California. Its president, Denis Kearney, an Irish immigrant himself, owned a draying business in San Francisco. He became a powerful figure in that city's trade-union forces. A demagogic speaker, Kearney gained much of his political support because of his inflammatory anti-Chinese speeches usually given on the street corners of San Francisco: "Treason is better than to labor beside a Chinese slave."[22] The manifesto of the new Party, written by Kearney and H.L. Knight, expressed emphatically its members' point of view:

> We have made no secret of our intentions. We make none. Before you and the world, we declare that the Chinamen must leave our shores. We declare that white men, and women, and boys, and girls, cannot live as the people of the great republic should and compete with the single Chinese coolies

[19] Alexander Saxton, "Race in the House of Labor," in *Race in the Mind of America*, edited by Gary Nash and Richard Weiss (New York: Holt, Rinehart and Winston, 1970), pp. 98–99.

[20] Carl B. Swisher, *Motivation and Political Technique in the California, 1878–79* (Claremont, California: Pomona College, 1930), p. 10.

[21] Sandmeyer, p. 64; *San Francisco Bulletin*, July 19, 20, 23–25, 1877.

[22] *San Francisco Chronicle*, October 16, 1877.

in the labor market. We declare that we cannot hope to drive the Chinaman away by working cheaper than he does. None but an enemy would expect it of us; none but an idiot could hope for success; none but a degraded coward and slave would make the effort. To an American, death is preferable to life on a par with the Chinaman.[23]

Although the Workingmen's Party disintegrated by the early 1880s, and its members returned rapidly to the two major political parties, its meteoric success furthered the development and influence of the anti-Chinese movement. Much of the new Party's strength came from its exploitation of the anti-Chinese issue. Kearneyism reigned especially in San Francisco. Kearney would ask crowds as large as 7,000 people, "Are you ready to march down to the wharf and stop the leprous Chinese from landing?"[24] The Workingmen's Party reached its zenith of influence in 1878, especially during the Constitutional Convention in September of that year. The convention's purpose was to draw up California's second constitution. The Kearney forces were able to elect fifty-one of the 152 delegates to the Convention.[25] Not surprisingly, the Workingmen took the lead in writing a series of anti-Chinese sections. Most famous were a definition of suffrage that "provided no native of China, no idiot, insane person, or person convicted of any infamous crime . . . shall ever exercise the privileges of an elector of this state," and Article XIX which forbade employment of "any Chinese or Mongolian (except in punishment of crime) on state or local public works or, directly or indirectly, by any corporation operating under the laws of California."[26]

The Workingmen were not alone in their anti-Chinese sentiments. Most delegates, including those from the Democratic and Republican Parties, agreed to the passage of anti-Chinese provisions. The majority of the California public also shared these attitudes. In the 1879 election, 150,000 people voted for the end of Chinese immigration; only 900 cast their votes in opposition.[27] Reflecting this negative view of the Chinese, in a Convention debate on Article XIX, John F. Miller, chairman of the Committee on the Chinese, claimed:

> Already two-fifths of the adult male population of California is (sic) Chinese, and despite the assertions of optimists, the number is constantly, steadily increasing. It is an unassimilative population and unfit for assimilation with people of our race . . . We are confronted on the other side of the Pacific with four hundred and fifty millions of the same type and variety as those already here, and these have disorganized our labor system, brought thousands of our people to wretchedness and want, degraded labor to the standard of brute energy, poisoned the blood of our youth, and filled our streets with the rot of their decaying civilization. There are millions yet ready to come, and millions more determined to come.[28]

Most delegates strongly shared a view of Chinese men as inferior, disease-ridden, immoral subhumans, and Chinese women as debased prostitutes "degrading to all around them." Like Kearney and Miller, they feared possible "commingling" or intermarriage between Chinese and white men or women. Chairman Miller warned, "Were the Chinese to amalgamate at all with

---

[23] *Ibid.*

[24] Hubert Howe Bancroft, *Popular Tribunals*, 11 (Vol. XXXVII, *Works*, San Francisco, 1887), p. 722, as quoted in Saxton, p. 118.

[25] *San Francisco Examiner*, July 5, 1878.

[26] *Debates and Proceedings of the Constitutional Convention of California, 1878–9* (Sacramento: State Office, 1880) E. B. Willis and P. K. Stockton, Official Stenographers, Vol. 11, 1511, 1518.

[27] Sandmeyer, pp. 62–63.

[28] *Debates, I*, p. 632.

our people, it would be the lowest, most vile and degraded of our race, and the result of that amalgamation would be a hybrid of the most despicable, a mongrel of the most detestable that has ever afflicted the earth."[29] Consequently, it was not surprising when John C. Stedman, a San Francisco delegate and a "prominent and trusted member of the Workingmen's Party," proposed on October 28, 1878, the following amendment to the Constitution:

> The intermarriage of white persons with Chinese, negroes, mulattoes, or persons of mixed blood, descended from a Chinaman or negro from the third generation, inclusive, or their living together as man and wife in this State, is hereby prohibited. The Legislature shall enforce this section by appropriate legislation.[30]

In the next session of the California Legislature, after the ratification of the Constitution by vote of the electorate in May, 1879, both the Assembly and the Senate approved Assembly Bill No. 36 which proposed to amend many sections of the Civil Code.[31] The bill became law effective April 6, 1880.[32] Part of this bill was an amendment of Section 69 of the Civil Code which dealt with the issuance of marriage licenses: "provided, that the said Clerk shall not issue a license authorizing the marriage of a white person with a negro, mulatto, or Mongolian."[33] Thus, Stedman's proposal for an anti-miscegenation law preventing Chinese-white marriages was implemented by the Section 69 amendment. Surprisingly, an attempt to amend California's other anti-miscegenation statute, Section 60, to include the Chinese, failed. On March 16, 1880, Assemblyman J. N. Young of Sacramento introduced a bill to amend it so as to prevent marriages of whites with "negroes and persons of other races (Mongolians)."[34] Perhaps the legislators were hesitant over the possible legal implications of voiding retroactively all previous Chinese-white marriages. Whatever the reasons, for the next twenty-five years, these two conflicting anti-miscegenation statutes in the California Civil Code stood.

Also Stedman's Convention proposal appears to support the interpretation that the term "Mongolian" as used in Section 69 meant "Chinese" to the legislators who passed the bill. The delegate referred specifically to the Chinese and did not use the more general term of Mongolian. A close scrutiny of the proceedings revealed ample evidence that when the delegates and politicians of the period employed the terms "Asiatics," "Coolies," and "Mongolians" they were referring to the Chinese. Indeed, Delegate Horace C. Rolfe of San Diego complained about this practice: "If we wish to put in a clause prohibiting their employment, why not say Chinese at once, instead of saying that no person of the Mongolian race shall be employed upon any of the public works, etc. We mean Chinese, and why not come out squarely and say so."[36]

Stuart Miller believes this fear of miscegenation, which helped to pass Section 69, was inflamed by the controversy over whether the "races of mankind had sprung from a single origin (monogenesis) or diverse seed (polygenesis)."[37] According to Samuel Norton, a leading advocate

---

[29] *Ibid.*

[30] *Ibid.*, p. 225.

[31] *The Journal of the Assembly*, 23rd Session, 1880, p. 600; *The Journal of the Senate*, 23rd Session, 1880, p. 702.

[32] *Cal. Stats.*, 1880, Code Amendments, Ch. 41, Sec. 1, p. 3.

[33] *Ibid.*

[34] *The Journal of the Assembly*, 23rd Session, 1880, p. 527.

[35] *Debates*, I, II, pp. 601–692.

[36] *Debates*, 11, p. 655.

[37] Miller, p. 154.

of polygenesis, the Chinese were inferior to and separate from the Caucasian race. As a distinct species, their presence in this country would present the threat of hybridity, "something to be strictly avoided in the view of the polygenesists." Further, the germ theory of culture which was popular among the social scientists and historians of the period contributed to the public's fear of miscegenation in reference to the Chinese "menace." The belief that American institutions were peculiarly racial products made the disciples of the new historical school "especially conscious of supposed racial differences between the old . . . and the new immigrants."[38] American institutions, they emphasized, were "designed by and for Teutonic people." Gerritt Lansing in *Popular Science Monthly* warned of the dire dangers of "commingling" between races, because "when two races exist side by side, acculturation takes place in favor of the largest established traits, not necessarily the superior ones."[39] Another factor supporting anti-miscegenation fears was the widely held belief that the Chinese were full of filth and disease and endangered the safety and welfare of the American people. Former President of the American Medical Association and permanent Secretary of the California Board of Health, Thomas M. Logan initiated investigations of "the evils likely to result from the combined intermixture of races and the introduction of habits and customs of a sensual and depraved people in our midst."[40]

Another popular attitude which contributed to the passage of the amendment was the prevailing belief that Chinese were sexually promiscuous and perverse. Miller believes that this racist stereotype derives ultimately from early nineteenth century anti-Chinese propaganda from Protestant missionaries. They wanted to exploit China as an example of the evils of paganism and the benefits of Christianity. Thus, their writings especially impressed on the minds of the American public this negative misconception of the Chinese as lascivious and immoral. Missionary Samuel Wells Williams declared that the Chinese were preoccupied with lechery and were "vile and polluted in a shocking degree."[41]

This observation and many other missionary castigations of alleged Chinese licentiousness and perversion prepared the way for later popular acceptance of this negative stereotype. As early as 1856, the *New York Tribune* accused the Chinese as "lustful and sensual in their dispositions; every female is a prostitute of the basest order."[42] In 1876, various papers stated that the Chinese men attended Sunday school in order to debauch their white, female teachers.[43] In the same year, a writer in *Scribner's Monthly* warned that "no matter how good a Chinaman may be, ladies never leave their children with them, especially little girls."[44] As we will see later, becoming an article of faith for most Americans, this stereotype was broadened to include other Asian groups.

The Constitutional Convention and the following state legislation formed the climax of Californians' efforts to solve the problems arising from the "Chinese Question" by local legislative measures. In 1879 and 1880, the courts ruled in two cases that most of the anti-Chinese legislation

---

[38] Edward Saveth, "Race and Nationalism in American Historiography: The Late Nineteenth Century," *Political Science Quarterly*, Vol. LIV (1936), p. 435.

[39] Gerritt Lansing, "Chinese Immigration: A Sociological Study," *Popular Science Monthly*, Vol. XX (1882), p. 735.

[40] Miller, p. 162.

[41] Samuel Wells Williams, *The Middle Kingdom* (New York: 1848), II, p. 96, as quoted in Miller, pp. 62–63.

[42] *New York Tribune*, Oct. 2, 1854, as cited in Miller, p. 169.

[43] *New York Herald*, April 3, 1876; *Scribner's Monthly*, Vol. XII (1876), p. 741.

[44] Sarah E. Henshaw, "Chinese Housekeepers and Chinese Servants," *Scribner's Monthly*, Vol. XII (1876), p. 736.

passed by the Constitution Convention was unconstitutional.[45] However, at the federal level, the nationwide anti-Chinese movement, inspired by fears and anxieties about the Chinese "menace," reached the climax of a long campaign for the passage of regulations or restrictive legislation. This Sinophobic agitation culminated in the Exclusion Act of 1882 which provided that no Chinese laborer or miner could enter the United States for ten years. In 1884, a federal court ruling interpreted the provisions of the 1882 Act as also excluding the wives of Chinese laborers from entering the United States. During the next twenty years, six other acts and two treaties were negotiated for the purpose of controlling and strengthening the exclusion of Chinese immigration to the country. Under pressure from anti-Chinese groups like American Federation of Labor, the Knights of Labor, and the Native Sons and Daughters of the Golden West, in 1903 and 1904, Congress passed legislation which extended indefinitely the exclusion of Chinese and the denial of their privilege of naturalization. By 1910, most of the Chinese in America were confined to urban ghettoes which provided an easily exploitable labor force.

As noted earlier, most of the first Chinese immigrants were "sojourners" who saved their hard-earned money and sent it back to their families in their native land. The discriminatory Exclusion Acts of 1882, 1884, and 1924 prevented the male Chinese immigrant from bringing his wife and family over to this country from China. Consequently, few Chinese women traveled to the United States. By 1890, only 3,868 Chinese women were in this country.[46] Not surprisingly, from 1860 to 1960, the ratio of Chinese males per 100 Chinese females was high: 1,858 in 1860, 1,887 in 1900, 695 in 1920, and even 135 in 1950.[47]

This unbalanced ratio has been one of the important factors shaping the Chinese people's personal, social, and community life in this country. When combined with anti-miscegenation laws, the establishment of a family in America for most of the Chinese "sojourners" was impossible. They were denied the basic right to marry and to raise families in this country. Thus, the majority of these men lived homeless and alone, attempting to satisfy their social and sexual needs through community organizations, prostitution, gambling, and other recreations.

While intermarriage would not have solved the problem of the shortage of Chinese women, its negative effects might have been mitigated if the Chinese "sojourners" had not been prohibited from marrying Americans. Thus, only a relatively few Chinese in this country had intermarried until recent times, especially in the nineteenth century. Contemporary newspapers reported the existence of only a handful of Chinese-white marriages. In 1883, the *San Francisco Call* mentioned three cases of this kind of intermarriage, and in 1903 the *San Francisco Chronicle* wrote that there were twenty white women married to Chinese in Chinatown.[48] The cultural differences, the segregation of the two races as practiced in California until 1948, and the extreme anti-Chinese sentiments combined to discourage intermarriages. Additionally, anti-miscegenation laws like the 1880 amendment to Section 69 made marriages between Chinese and Caucasians illegal in many States, thus employing law to implement this oppressive policy.

The anti-Chinese movement attempted desperately to prevent the procreation of a second generation of Chinese, thereby insuring that the "Chinese problem" would eventually disappear.

---

[45] *In Re Tiburcio Parrot*, 6 Sawyer 349 (1879); *In Re Ah Chong*, 6 Sawyer 451 (1880).

[46] U. S. Bureau of the Census, *Sixteenth Census of the United States, 1940: Population* (Washington, D.C.: Government Printing Office, 1943), 2:19, Table IV.

[47] *Ibid.*; U.S. Bureau of the Census, *Seventeenth Census of the United States, 1950: Special Reports*, "Non-White Population by Race," (Washington, D.C.: Government Printing Office, 1953), Vol. 4, Pt. 3, 3B-87, Table 29.

[48] Mary Coolidge, *Chinese Immigration* (New York: Henry Holt and Company, 1909), p. 441.

With other discriminatory and exclusionary legislation, the passage of the 1880 amendment in California was an integral part of this crusade: "Permitted neither to procreate nor to intermarry, the Chinese immigrant was told, in effect, to re-emigrate, die out—white America would not be touched by his presence."[49]

The exclusionists' actions did delay for nearly a hundred years the birth and maturation of a substantial second generation. In 1890, only 8.7 percent of the Chinese in this country was native-born.[50] Sixty years later, this figure was a scant fifty percent.[51] However, while the number of Chinese decreased to a low of 77,504 in 1940, changes in the exclusion laws and the increase of births among the American Chinese combined to augment the number to 117, 140 in 1950 and 237,084 in 1960.[52] The Chinese did not die out and vanish without a trace from America. In that sense, the anti-Chinese movement failed. However, its toll is still evident in the aging sojourners, their "paper sons," a relatively small number of second and third generation Chinese, an exploitable labor force, and the oppressive Chinese ghettoes themselves.

The Japanese

The Japanese were the next large group of Asian immigrants to draw the enmity of the anti-Asian forces in California. In 1884 Japan finally permitted the migration of Japanese laborers first to Hawaii and later to Canada, the United States, and South America. Mainly because of severe overpopulation in rural areas and the threat of military conscription, thousands of young, single male laborers emigrated from Southern Japan, especially from Hiroshima. The first immigrants went to Hawaii to work as low-paid contract laborers for the sugar industry.

By the 1890s, small-scale *Issei* labor contractors started bringing Japanese laborers to the continental United States to fill a need for cheap labor in the Western States created by the successful exclusion of Chinese laborers. The Japanese population in the United States jumped from 2,039 in 1890 to 24,326 in 1900.[53] During this time many Japanese workers moved from Hawaii to the mainland in order to escape the extremely low wages and oppressive conditions of the plantations. From 1900 to 1910, 132,706 Japanese workers joined the U.S. urban trades and agriculture,[54] although nearly half of them eventually went back to Japan. Before 1907, they settled generally in the areas around San Francisco, Sacramento, and Stockton. Later they moved to Fresno and Los Angeles. According to U.S. census figures, the number of Japanese reached 77,157 in the United States and 41,356 in California by 1910.[55]

---

[49] Lyman, p. 6.

[50] *Abstract of the Twelfth Census of the United States, 1900* (Washington, D.C.: Government Printing Office, 1943), p. 8, Table IV.

[51] U.S. Bureau of the Census, *Seventeenth Census of Population, 1950: Special Reports*, "Non-White Population by Race," (Washington, D.C.: Government Printing Office, 1953), Vol. 4, Pt. 3, 3B-87, Table 29.

[52] *Sixteenth Census of the United States, 1940*:2:21, Table 6; *Seventeenth Census of the United States, 1950*: Vol. IV, Pt. 3, 3B-19, Table 5.; U.S. Bureau of the Census, *Eighteenth Census of the United States, 1960: Subject Reports, Non-White Population by Race, Final Report*, PC(2)-IC (Washington, D.C.: Government Printing Office, 1963), p. 4, Table 4.

[53] *Sixteenth Census of the United States, 1940: Population* (Washington, D.C.: Government Printing Office, 1943), 2:19, Table IV.

[54] *Annual Report of the United States Commissioner-General of Immigration, 1928*, pp. 200–202.

[55] *Sixteenth Census of the United States, 1940: Population*, 2:19, Table IV; *A Demographic and Socioeconomic Perspective, California Fair Employment Practices Commission*, in *Racism in California: A Reader in the History of Oppression*, edited by Roger Daniels and Spencer C. Olin, Jr., (New York: The MacMillan Company, 1972), p. 69.

This Japanese immigration reawakened the anti-Asian movement which had successfully stopped Chinese immigration. These anti-Chinese forces had developed techniques to propagate the anti-Asian myths, stereotypes, and arguments which with minimal editing could be turned against the Japanese. They turned their attention and their attack against the Japanese, and worked for nearly fifty years to prevent the entry of Japanese immigrants to this country and to eliminate their presence from this society. Relying heavily on the support of all elements of the Republican Party, which controlled the State Government from 1898 to 1938, and the San Francisco trade unions, anti-Japanese forces promoted and exploited American fears of an unrelenting influx of "unassimilable, inferior Asiatics" who allegedly would take away jobs from white workers and would defile American racial purity and culture. Also during this half-century, the United States and Japan were fighting for domination of the Pacific area. This struggle increased the American public's fear of the "yellow peril" and their hostility towards Japanese Americans.

At the turn of the century, the "California-Japanese War," as Carey McWilliams calls it, began with the first substantial outburst of anti-Japanese sentiments.[56] Among other effects, this agitation led to the passage of the first anti-Japanese legislation in the State, including an amendment to the original California anti-miscegenation statute, Section 60 of the Civil Code. Although this amendment later was ruled unconstitutional because of a procedural defect, the history of its passage is important to relate, because it reveals the development of anti-Japanese activities and oppression.

This initial anti-Japanese campaign was started, directed, and financed by the strong San Francisco trade union movement. After the panic of 1893, a period of prosperity returned to California from the late 1890s to the early 1900s. With the subsequent increase in demand for labor, urban workers, determined to share in the returning prosperity, organized unions in all trades. By 1901, there were 125 unions in San Francisco, organized into two major labor federations, the Labor Council and the Building Trades Council.[57] With San Francisco virtually a closed-shop city, these two organizations exerted great influence and power over its government and citizens.

From the time of Kearney and the Workingmen's Party, the trade union movement and its leaders had used the anti-Asian issue to rally public and rank-and-file support for their political policies and programs. Incited by newspaper reports that Congress might not renew permanently the expiring Chinese Exclusion Act, the trade unionists again promoted anti-Chinese agitation in order to pressure the federal legislature to pass a permanent Exclusion Act. However, as a "tail to the anti-Chinese kite," some of the labor leadership decided to begin an additional anti-Japanese campaign, exploiting the increased public resentment over the 12,635 Japanese immigrants who, according to census figures, entered the U.S. in 1900.[58]

The two leaders of this campaign were Olaf Tveitmoe, Secretary of the Building Trades Council, and Patrick McCarthy, President of the Council and later Mayor of San Francisco on the Union Labor Party ticket. Both labor leaders became prominent participants in the anti-Japanese movement and helped to establish the influential Asiatic Exclusion League. Edited by Tveitmoe, the Council's newspaper *Organized Labor* launched a newspaper campaign against the Japanese. On March 17, 1900, in a front-page editorial, Tveitmoe wrote that the Japanese were replacing "white workmanship both in field and factory" and driving American girls "into the stifling beer joints"

---

[56] Carey McWilliams, *Prejudice, Japanese-Americans: Symbol of Racial Intolerance* (New York: Archon Books, 1971), p. 14.

[57] Ira B. Cross, *A History of the Labor Movement in California* (Berkeley and Los Angeles: University of California Press, 1935), p. 228.

[58] Yamato Ichihashi, *Japanese in the United States* (Palo Alto: Stanford University Press, 1932), p. 55.

and "into the bawdy-house and slums of the tenderloin district and the Barbary Coast."[59] He issued a series of articles urging the Japanese to be included with the Chinese Exclusion Law. Other labor papers like *The Seaman's Journal* and the *San Francisco Labor Clarion* also joined the campaign with editorials on the evils of Japanese competition and the need for restrictive legislation. A familiar tactic, the newspaper campaign fomented increased anti-Japanese sentiments among the public. Joining forces with labor, Mayor James Phelan, an anti-Asian spokesman throughout his long political career, capitalized on the public's increasing anti-Asian mood. Thus, in March, 1900, based on the death of a single Chinese with bubonic plague, Mayor Phelan quarantined the Chinese and Japanese sections of the city.[60] He did not quarantine other sections of the city. Furthermore, he ordered a mass innoculation of all Asians in San Francisco. The local Japanese protested the action as discrimination that was politically and economically motivated. To help protect their rights against this oppression, they founded the Japanese Association of America which became the leading organization in Japanese communities in the early 1900s.[61]

Phelan's action and the labor agitation led to the first mass meeting against the Japanese in California. On May 6, 1900, organized mainly by the Labor Council and the Building Trades Council, this rally was addressed to workers and held for the purpose of "seeking protection against Asiatic hordes."[62] Reflecting the close relationship between labor and the City Government on this issue, two of the speakers were Phelan and Patrick McCarthy. The meeting sanctioned a resolution urging the re-enactment of the Chinese Exclusion Act and its extension to include Japanese laborers. Phelan emphasized one of Kearney's arguments that the Japanese were unassimilable: " . . . they will not assimilate with us . . . let them keep at a respectful distance."[63] Another speaker, Professor Edward Ross of Stanford University, also joined Phelan in attacking the Japanese people's alleged biological unassimilability with the "superior Anglo-Saxon stock" of the white race.[64] The meeting's main importance was that it reinforced public support for the anti-Japanese campaign.

The San Francisco labor movement then exerted its considerable influence with the State Republican Administration, dominated by the political machine of the Southern Pacific Railroad Company, on the California Legislature in order to pass anti-Asian legislation. The Southern Pacific machine's choice for the office, Governor Henry T. Gage, had lost much public support because of his ineptness.[65] With anti-Gage clubs organizing throughout the State, he could not afford to antagonize the powerful San Francisco labor forces. Thus, on January 8, 1901, in an address to the legislature, Gage called for the exclusion of Chinese and Japanese workers in order to protect the jobs of American laborers.[66] With the support of both conservative Republican and labor forces, the anti-Asian movement generated enough strength to pass easily two items of legislation in the 1901 legislature. The first item was a joint resolution urging Congress to stop the immigration of both Chinese and Japanese workers.[67] Reflecting the anti-Asian movement's

---

[59] Floyd Matson, *The Anti-Japanese Movement in California, 1890–1942* (M. A. Thesis, University of California, 1953).

[60] *San Francisco Chronicle*, March 7, 1900.

[61] *Ibid.*, May 30, 1900.

[62] *San Francisco Chronicle*, May 8, 1900.

[63] *Ibid.*

[64] *Ibid.*

[65] Ralph J. Roske, *Everyman's Eden: A History of California* (New York: MacMillan Company, 1968), p. 449.

[66] *Appendix to the Journals of the Senate and Assembly of the State of California*, 34th Session, 1901, II, 6–7.

[67] *Journal of the Assembly of the State of California*, 34th Session, 1901, p. 101.

concern with the alleged Asiatic threat to white racial purity, the second was a bill dealing with the miscegenation issue. On February 8, 1901, Assemblyman E. F. Treadwell of San Francisco, Chairman of the Committee of Revision and Reform of Laws, introduced Bill No. 683, which would amend Section 60 of the Civil Code to prohibit the marriage of whites with "Negroes, Mongolians, and mulattoes."[68] The amendment became law on March 16, 1901.[69]

By 1902, the campaign against both Chinese and Japanese immigration had achieved some success. In late 1900, pressed by this agitation in California, the Japanese Government announced that it would no longer issue passports to Japanese contract laborers attempting to enter this country.[70] Consequently, the number of Japanese arrivals decreased from 12,626 in 1900 to 4,909 in 1901.[71] Furthermore, on April 29, 1902, Congress renewed the Chinese Exclusion Act.[72] Seemingly achieving both Chinese and Japanese exclusion, the anti-Asian movement lost much of its momentum. Thus, when the Section 60 amendment was declared unconstitutional, it was not immediately re-enacted by the legislature. For the next few years, even in San Francisco, not much was "heard about the Oriental menace."[73] However, in 1905, the anti-Japanese forces launched a more far-reaching and effective campaign against Japanese immigration. This agitation resulted in an international incident, which many feared might lead to war between Japan and the United States. Not surprisingly, this campaign, which put anti-Japanese agitation on a permanent basis in California, saw the reintroduction of the old amendment to Section 60.

Various factors contributed to the 1905 outbreak of extreme anti-Japanese sentiments and activities. Desiring a political organization to implement its programs and policies, various elements of the trade union movement in San Francisco combined to form the Union Labor Party in 1901. Reflecting labor's strength in that city, the new Party elected as mayor from 1901 to 1907 its candidate, Eugene Schmitz who was the president of the Musicians Union.[74] By 1905, the Party controlled all eighteen seats in the city's Board of Supervisors, and nearly all of San Francisco's twenty-four seats in the State Legislature.[75] Ostensibly a workingmen's party, the Union Labor Party was really controlled by Schmitz and especially by Abe Reuf, a well-born Republican lawyer, representing business interests.[76] An opportunist, who later went to prison for bribery, "Boss" Reuf maintained close ties with the big business interests, led by Southern Pacific, which controlled the Republican administrations and legislatures of this period. With a platform calling for Japanese exclusion and segregated schools for all Asian students, Reuf and the Party were blatantly anti-Asian.[77] Moreover, Reuf and his chief supporters in the Party, such as Schmitz and Supervisor James Gallagher, were members of other anti-Japanese organizations, like the Native Sons of the Golden West which had considerable political influence. The membership of this

---

[68] *Ibid.*, p. 416.

[69] *Cal. Stats.* 1901, Ch. 157, p. 336, Section 20.

[70] Statement of K. Uyeno, Japanese Consul-General, *San Francisco Chronicle*, April 5, 1905, as cited in Raymond Leslie Buell, "The Development of the Anti-Japanese Agitation in the United States," *Political Science Quarterly*, 37 (December, 1922), 609.

[71] *Annual Report of the United States Commissioner-General of Immigration, 1928*, pp. 200–202.

[72] Daniels, p. 24.

[73] *Ibid.*

[74] Walton Bean, *California: An Interpretative History* (New York: McGraw Book Company, 1968), p. 314.

[75] Walton Bean, *Boss Ruef's San Francisco* (Berkeley and Los Angeles: University of California Press, 1967), pp. 57–58, 64.

[76] Buell, pp. 611–612.

[77] Bean, p. 22.

fraternal organization, dedicated to keeping California white, included such prominent figures as Governor George C. Pardee and Attorney General U.S. Webb, who was an anti-Asian spokesman for all of his thirty-six years in office, as well as publishers like William Hearst and Valentine McClatchy.[78] Consequently, by the beginning of 1905, the anti-Japanese movement included many of the most powerful economic and political interests in California.

Rekindling of anti-Japanese sentiments during the period from late 1904 to early 1905 involved two other factors. The first factor concerned Japan's failure to fulfill its commitment to restricting the number of passports issued to immigrant laborers. Corruption in the passport administration allowed Japanese laborers to still enter the United States in considerable numbers. Following a temporary interruption of immigration flow in 1901, the number of Japanese immigrants entering the continental United States, Alaska, and Hawaii increased to 14,455 in 1902, 20,041 in 1903, and 14,382 in 1904.[79] Even more controversial was the increased remigration of laborers from Hawaii to the mainland, which reached 13,801 in 1904-5.[80] This failure to restrict Japanese immigration incited fears of Japanese laborers undercutting white workers' wages and taking their jobs. The second factor was the Russo-Japanese War, which started in February, 1904, and ended in June, 1905. While sympathizing in the beginning with the underdog, Japan, Americans observed uneasily Japanese successes in the war, and began to express fears of the new "yellow peril." The Chinese "yellow peril" stereotype was transferred to the Japanese, inspiring rumors that they were spies and soldiers in disguise, representing the first wave of a "peaceful invasion" which threatened to overrun the country and "Mongolize" it.

By the end of 1904, all these factors combined to revive an organized anti-Japanese movement. The Labor Council and the American and California Federations of Labor warned publicly in November, 1904, that the increase of Japanese laborers presented a "problem of race presentation . . . which can only be solved through a policy of exclusion."[81] The *San Francisco Chronicle* editorialized on October 24, 1904, that the Japanese were a "threat of the American way of life." Two days later, the *Sacramento Bee* also warned about the Japanese menace. Further contributing to this agitation was the public's increasing fear that, after the end of the Russo-Japanese War, there would be an "invasion" of large numbers of discharged Japanese soldiers, looking for employment in the United States.

In February, 1905, the newspaper campaign was intensified and coordinated to incite even greater public animosity against the Japanese "menace." On February 23, 1905, just before the Japanese siege of Mukden, the *Chronicle* capitalized on the increasing public apprehension about the "yellow peril" and printed a front-page article headlined, "The Japanese Invasion, the Problem of the Hour."[82] The article warned that "once the war with Russia is over, the brown stream of Japanese is likely to become an inundating torrent." Following this article, the *Chronicle*, owned by Michael de Young, a conservative Republican, printed a series of anti-Japanese articles for almost a year. These inflammatory articles aroused considerable public feeling against the Japanese in California and throughout the United States. McClatchy's *Sacramento Bee* and Hearst's *San*

---

[78] *Ibid.*, p. 62; McWilliams, p. 22; *Grizzly Bear*, Sept. 1907, p. 34; Peter Thomas Conmy, *The Origin and Purposes of the Native Sons and Native Daughters of the Golden West* (San Francisco: Dolores Press, 1956), pp. 20–22.

[79] *Annual Report of the United States Commissioner-General of Immigration, 1928*, pp. 200–202.

[80] *Third Report of Commission of Labor on Hawaii*, p. 378, cited in Buell, p. 614.

[81] *San Francisco Call*, November 16, 1904, p. 31; and November 19, 1904, p. 3/7.

[82] *San Francisco Chronicle*, February 22, 1905, p. 1/3.

Francisco Examiner were among the numerous newspapers that joined this newspaper campaign against the Japanese. Exploiting this renewed agitation, the San Francisco labor councils, and their newspapers, the *Labor Clarion* and the *Organized Labor*, campaigned during the first part of 1905 for the formation of an anti-Japanese exclusion league.[83] Led by San Francisco labor and political leaders like Tveitmoe, McCarthy, Schmitz, and Reuf, the two major labor councils and the Union Labor Party organized a mass meeting on May 7 with delegates from sixty-seven civic and labor organizations. The representatives formed the Asiatic Exclusion League, the first organization whose sole purpose was to work for the exclusion of Japanese immigrants from this country.[84] Until 1913, the League was the leading Japanese exclusion organization, using legislation, boycott, and propaganda to achieve its goal.

Throughout all its history, the anti-Japanese movement exploited the miscegenation issue. Most Californians of the early 1900s believed in the polygenetic concept of the superiority and purity of the white race. They were convinced that an "eternal law of nature is decreed that the white cannot assimilate the blood of another without corrupting the very springs of civilization."[85] Even Republican "progressive" reformers like Hiram Johnson and Chester Powell insisted that separate races could not mix, and that the "instinct of preservation of our race demands that its future members shall be members of our race."[86]

The public's fear of miscegenation expressed itself in two forms. One was Californians' belief in the familiar stereotype, first applied to the Chinese and then the Japanese, of an immoral, sexually aggressive Asiatic. This stereotype was especially exploited in anti-Japanese propaganda seeking school segregation. Denis Kearney warned that the Japanese students knew "no morals but vice, who sit beside our sons and daughters in our public schools that they may help to debauch, demoralize and teach them the vices which are the customs of the country whence they come."[87] Conservative Republican leader, Governor Johnson, stated before the California Assembly that he was appalled at the sight of white girls "sitting side by side in the schoolroom with matured Japs, with base minds, their lascivious thoughts. . . ."[88] The second manifestation of this fear was hostility against intermarriages between whites and Japanese. The anti-Japanese advocates exploited this sentiment with inflammatory propaganda. The *Grizzly Bear*, the official paper of the Native Sons, warned that Japanese were "casting furtive glances at our young women. They would like to marry them."[89] Rowell, editor of the *Fresno Republican*, wrote that intermarriage between a Japanese and a white would be "international adultery."[90] In its 1905 campaign, the *Chronicle* published an article entitled, "Japanese a Menace to American Women."[91]

---

[83] Buell, p. 617.

[84] The League was initially called the Japanese and Korean Exclusion League until 1907, when the name was changed to the Asiatic Exclusion League. *San Francisco Chronicle*, May 7, 1905.

[85] Daniels, p. 28.

[86] *Letter*, Rowell to Charles P. Huey, Sept. 1, 1915, quoted in Daniels, p. 49.

[87] *Sacramento Record Union*, July 7, 1892, p. 31.

[88] Franklin Hichborn, *The Story of the Session of the California Legislature of 1909* (San Francisco: James H. Barry Company, 1909), p. 207.

[89] *Grizzly Bear*, July, 1923, p. 27.

[90] *Letter*, Rowell to Charles P. Huey, Sept. 1, 1915.

[91] McWilliams, p. 19.

Consequently, it was not surprising that the State Legislature and Government passed two items of legislation in the legislative session of 1905, a resolution urging Congress to "limit and diminish" Japanese immigration,[92] and a bill amending Section 60 to prohibit Mongolian-white marriages. Introduced as Assembly Bill No. 264 on January 11, 1905, the amendment (identical in language to the 1901 version) was approved unanimously by both the Assembly and the Senate.[93] On March 21, 1905, it became law.[94] After a quarter of a century of inconsistency, Section 60 was reconciled with its ancillary provision, Section 69, in their prohibition of Mongolian-white marriages. In its influential 1911 report, the United States Immigration Commission commented that the 1905 amendment regarded Japanese as Mongolians and "meant to relate specifically to marriages between them and white persons."[95]

Appropriately, the sponsor of the bill was Assemblyman Alexander M. Drew from Fresno, Chairman of the Commission of Revision and Reform of Laws and later a strong member and supporter of the Asiatic Exclusion League.[96] A member of the "progressive" Lincoln-Roosevelt Republicans, Drew was actively anti-Japanese throughout his political career, introducing state legislation against the Japanese especially in the 1907 and 1910 legislative sessions, and working closely with the Asiatic Exclusion League.[97] In 1910, in a letter to the League endorsing its program, Drew wrote that he favored the passage of a stronger anti-miscegenation law prohibiting marriages between Japanese and whites.[98]

In the wake of the devastating earthquake of 1906, the anti-Japanese agitation continued to develop especially in San Francisco. On October 11, the Union Labor Party and the Asiatic Exclusion League pressured the San Francisco School Board to order the segregation of Japanese students from white students. The Japanese community of San Francisco and the Japanese Government protested the act of the School Board. They were joined in the protest by President Theodore Roosevelt and the United States Government. All the elements of the anti-Japanese movement combined to support the School Board. This school segregation issue became an international incident evoking rumors of war between Japan and the United States. However, the crisis was temporarily defused when, after meeting with Mayor Schmitz, President Roosevelt announced that the School Board agreed to withdraw the segregation order in return for the Government's promise to negotiate with Japan regarding the restriction of Japanese immigration to this country. After a year and a half of negotiation, Washington and Tokyo reached a "Gentlemen's Agreement," whereby the Japanese Government promised to restrict the issuance of passports for the continental United States only to residents returning from a visit to Japan, and the immediate family members of laborers already residing in this country.[99] This Agreement continued in force from 1908 to 1924.

Historian H. L. Millis wrote in 1913 that the issue of intermarriage, in his opinion, was not important in the Japanese community, and that there were only fifty instances in all the Western

---

[92] *Journal of the Assembly of the State of California*, 1905, 36th Session, pp. 1468–69, 1522.

[93] *Ibid.*, p. 103; *Ibid.*, p. 745; *Journal of the Senate of the State of California*, 36th Session, p. 744.

[94] *Cal. Stats.*, 1905, Ch. 215, Sec. 2, p. 554.

[95] *Immigration Commission Reports*, XXIII (Washington, D.C., 1911), p. 163.

[96] *Journal of the Assembly*, 1905, p. 103.

[97] Hichborn, pp. 204–206.

[98] *Correspondence from Candidates for Federal Offices and State Offices*, (Asiatic Exclusion League, 1910), p. 19.

[99] *Annual Report of the United States Commissioner-General of Immigration* (Washington, D.C.: Government Printing Office, 1908), pp. 221–222.

States where "Japanese men have married American women."[100] Another scholar has said that there would be many more Japanese-white marriages "if it were not for the artificial and unjust restrictions placed by law and usage."[101] However, while it is difficult to ascertain exactly the effects of the anti-miscegenation laws on Japanese Americans, the available facts implied that these laws were less crucial to the Japanese than they were to the Chinese and later to the Pilipinos. Yamato Ichihashi in *Japanese in the United States* stated that "in the case of Japanese immigrants, intermarriages have been few and will continue to be, for one thing, because of a rapid normalization of the sex-distribution among them."[102]

In this statement, Ichihashi was implicitly referring to the fact that while the early Japanese immigrants were mainly single men, unlike the Chinese, many of them were able later to bring wives to California, and thus were not forced to be sojourners living alone in a ghetto for the rest of their lives. Within two decades of their arrival, the Japanese had brought over enough women to guarantee that, although husbands might be quite older than their wives, a community with a family life would be established in America. Women constituted only 4 percent of the Japanese American population in 1900.[103] But, since women could enter the United States under the Gentlemen's Agreement of 1908, the number rapidly increased through 1920. Initially, Japanese immigrants were mainly agricultural workers seeking opportunities to earn money and planning to return to Japan with their hard-earned "riches." However, especially after 1907, as soon as many workers accumulated enough capital, they bought or leased land for farming. With the increasing migration of Japanese women to this country, the Japanese family and home became more common. The Japanese had decreasing needs for the brothels and gambling halls which marked Chinese and Pilipino communities. Instead, the Japanese community, centering around the family units with churches, schools, and small shops, began to appear in California.

By 1920, there were 38,216 women, of whom 22,193 were married, constituting 34.5 percent of the Japanese American population. Thus the number of American-born children of the *Issei* naturally increased, reaching 29,672 by 1920 and 68,357 by 1930.[104] This rapid growth of a second generation of Japanese rekindled anti-Japanese feelings among Californians. In 1920, Governor William Stephens warned, "The fecundity of the Japanese race far exceeds that of any other people."[105] The anti-Asian movement protested the coming of Japanese women because members were afraid of the creation of a Japanese community. Exclusion and anti-miscegenation laws were again used as tools by the anti-Japanese forces, so that the *Issei* would be left to die out.

During the years that the Gentlemen's Agreement was in force, 120,317 Japanese entered the United States.[106] It allowed the Japanese American community to grow with homes, families,

---

[100] Millis, pp. 273–274.

[101] Juichi Soyeda and Tadao Kamiya, *A Survey of the Japanese Question in California* (San Francisco, 1913), p. 9.

[102] Ichihashi, p. 219.

[103] U.S. Bureau of the Census, *Abstract of the Twelfth Census of the United States, 1900* (Washington, D.C.: General Printing Office, 1904), p. 8. Table V.

[104] *Sixteenth Census of the United States*, Vol. 2, Pt. 1, p. 19, Table IV and p. 21, Table VI; and U.S. Bureau of the Census, *Abstract of the Fourteenth Census of the United States* (Washington, D.C.: Government Printing Office, 1920), p. 217.

[105] California State Board of Control, *California and the Oriental* (Sacramento, 1922), p. 9.

[106] Ichihashi, p. 406.

children and business. According to the Japanese Association, Japanese farmers controlled through ownership, leasing, sharecropping and contract 281,687 acres in 1913 and 458,056 acres in 1920.[107] Most of them were growing fruits and vegetables as truck farmers on small farms around Los Angeles, and in the San Joaquin and Sacramento Valleys. This trend triggered a movement for discriminatory legislation like the Alien Land Laws. The Asiatic Exclusion League and Governor Hiram Johnson helped to pass the first Alien Land Law of 1913, sponsored by Attorney General Webb, which restricted Japanese land ownership and leasing.

After World War I, the anti-Japanese forces reorganized themselves under the leadership of Valentine S. McClatchy, former director of the Associated Press and retired publisher of the *Fresno Bee* and *Sacramento Bee*. The Japanophobic campaign also received support from four powerful pressure groups: the Native Sons of the Golden West, the California State Federation of Labor, the American Legion, and the California State Grange. Eliciting public and political support and propagating anti-Japanese sentiments, under the unifying direction of McClatchy and Hiram Johnson, this organized coalition was able to achieve the passage of the 1920 Alien Land Law, the exclusion of picture brides in the same year, and the passage of the Cable Act in 1922. The latter bill provided that any American woman would lose her citizenship if she married an alien ineligible for naturalization.[108] Its aim was to discourage *Nisei* women and women of other races from marrying *Issei* men. With these successes, the movement organized public and political backing for legislation excluding all Asian immigration to this country. In Congressional hearings, McClatchy testified that the Japanese were dangerous and unassimilable, and that they came here "specifically and professedly for the purpose of colonizing and establishing here permanently the proud *Yamato* race. . . . In pursuit of their intent they seek to secure land and to found large families. . . ."[109] Under extreme pressure from the anti-Japanese elements, Congress passed the Quota Immigration Law, commonly known as the Japanese Exclusion Act, which nearly halted Asian immigration to the United States from 1924 to 1952.[110]

The 1920 census showed that over 42 percent of all Japanese males over fifteen years old were still single.[111] Thus, combined with the anti-miscegenation laws, the above legislation made it very difficult for the large numbers of *Issei* bachelors to find women to marry, slowing the development of Japanese families in America. Instead, there developed a class of single Japanese sojourners who worked as migrant workers, and who lived in the Japanese-owned boardinghouses and hotels. However, unlike the Chinese and Pilipinos, the Japanese American community maintained its family orientation as a second generation grew. By 1930, the second generation comprised 50 percent of the Japanese population. Throughout the 1930s, the Japanese community continued to prosper and grow. Indeed, some of the *Nisei* women were becoming old enough to marry *Issei* bachelors, thereby decreasing the number of single men in the Japanese community. However, the "California-Japanese War" also persisted, culminating in the imprisonment of 110,000 Japanese Americans during World War II. In this infamous instance, American society dropped its policy of institutionalized racism for blatant oppression through total incarceration of a non-white people.

---

[107] *Ibid.*, p. 193.

[108] *42 Stat.*, 1021, Sept. 22, 1922.

[109] U.S. Congress, Senate, *Japanese Immigration Hearings*, 68th Congress, 1st Session (Washington, D.C., 1924), pp. 5–6, 34.

[110] *Congressional Record*, 68th Congress, 1st Session, May 8, 1924, p. 8711; *43 Stat.*, 53, May 26, 1924.

[111] *United States Census Report (Abstract), 1920*, p. 216.

The Pilipinos

After the 1924 Exclusion Act stopped Japanese immigration, American agricultural interests tried to meet the subsequent need for cheap labor by recruiting Pilipino laborers from both the Philippines and Hawaii. Thus, increasing numbers of Pilipino workers came to the West Coast in the 1920s and 1930s. Unlike the Chinese and Japanese, the Pilipinos were able to immigrate freely into the United States. Because the Philippines was part of the American territory, the Pilipinos were technically "nationals" of this country, neither citizens nor aliens. The Exclusion Act of 1924 expressly provided for no restriction on the immigration of Pilipinos to the mainland.

By 1930, there were 45,208 Pilipinos in the United States with 30,470 living in California.[112] After 1924, over 90 percent were young male laborers from the Ilocos Provinces of Luzon. They left their homes for Hawaii or the West Coast in order to assist their families financially, seldom planning to stay permanently in this country. Instead, they intended to return home eventually and to purchase land with their earnings. By 1930, 82 percent of the total Pilipino male population in the United States was engaged in agriculture.[113] In California, Pilipino farm workers formed much of the migrant labor force which farmers used to harvest their crops, especially in the asparagus industry around Stockton and in the lettuce fields of the Salinas Valley. Not surprisingly, the agricultural interests exploited the Pilipino workers. They were among the lowest paid agricultural workers during the 1920s and 1930s. The average Pilipino farm worker earned wages ranging from thirty to fifty cents per hour and $2.50 to $5.00 daily.[114] The agricultural capitalists were primarily interested in making profits by paying the Pilipino the lowest possible wages for which white workers were not willing to work. In order to survive, the Pilipino laborers had to work for such low wages, but during the Depression, they struggled against this exploitation through strikes and union organizing.

The influx of Pilipino workers aroused the enmity of the powerful and influential anti-Asian movement, composed of labor, patriotic organizations, newspapers, and state and federal office-holders, who had worked successfully for the passage of the Japanese Exclusion Act in 1924. After 1924, the California Joint Immigration Committee was created, headed by Valentine McClatchy who became its permanent secretary. Supported by the four major anti-Asian pressure groups, Native Sons of the Golden West, the American Legion, the California State Federation of Labor, and the State Grange, McClatchy and the Joint Committee became the advance guard of the anti-Pilipino movement, disseminating propaganda, giving speeches, and organizing support for the passage of appropriate legislation. McClatchy often mobilized the membership and resources of the sponsoring organizations behind various anti-Pilipino programs and policies. The Native Sons was especially influential among California politicians, having helped to elect "scores of legislators, judges, state officials, Congressmen, and Senators." An exclusion organization of the California-born, dedicated to preserving the State as "the White Man's Paradise," the Native Sons had among its members almost all the leading Republican politicians such as Governors Clement Young, James Rolph and Frank Merriam, and United States Senators Hiram Johnson and

---

[112] *U.S. Census, 1930*, Vol. III, Pt. 1, p. 120.

[113] Louis Bloch, *Facts About Filipino Immigration into California, California Department of Industrial Relations* (Washington D.C.: Government Printing Office, 1930), p. 13.

[114] H. Brett Melendy, "Filipinos in the United States," in *Counterpoint: Perspectives on Asian America*, edited by Emma Gee (Los Angeles: UCLA Asian American Studies Center, 1976), p. 427.

Samuel Shortridge.[115] This kind of political influence contributed to the movement's ability to pass anti-Pilipino legislation at both the state and federal levels.

Pilipino immigration evoked again these groups' racist fear of a new "Oriental invasion." These elements began to preach to a receptive audience of California citizens the old fear of economic competition, the Mongolization of California, the lowering of public morality, and the creation of a "hybrid race" through miscegenation. The anti-Pilipino movement, like the previous anti-Asian movements, also used its considerable influence among Californian legislators to gain their support of exclusionist programs and policies.[116]

In 1929, Pilipinos increasingly competed with white farm laborers in the agricultural areas. The worsening depression increased the intensity of this economic competition, and the anti-Pilipino propaganda spread by the exclusionist movement fanned the flames. As with the Chinese and Japanese, the agitation caused race riots in the West Coast States during the late 1920s and 1930s. These outbreaks focused national attention on the "Pilipino problem." Carey McWilliams stated that the "anti-Pilipino riots were part of the movement to exclude further Pilipino immigration; indeed it would be hard to say whether the riots stimulated this movement or the movement stimulated the riots."[117]

Supported by this mounting anti-Pilipino animosity, the exclusionist forces decided to try another approach. They now joined with "certain economic groups who desired to erect a tariff wall against Philippine commodity imports, in demanding independence for the islands, knowing that only in this way could Pilipinos and Philippine commodities be excluded."[118] Finally, in 1935, Pilipino exclusionists achieved their main goal. Providing for an annual quota of only fifty Pilipino immigrants to this country, the Tydings-McDuffie Independence Act was passed by Congress in 1934 and by the Philippine legislature the following year. This quota was the lowest provided for any nation. Obtaining virtual exclusion of Pilipino laborers, the anti-Pilipino movement worked for further measures that would eliminate them completely. In 1935, Congress also passed a repatriation act, which incited bitter Pilipino hostility: "They regard it as a trick, and not a clever trick, to get them out of this country."[119]

The anti-Pilipino movement's most successful tactic in exciting public sentiment was to appeal to Americans' fear of miscegenation and concern for racial purity. In 1929, one of the leading anti-Pilipino organizations, the Commonwealth Club, held forums and compiled a report on Pilipino immigration in order to warn the public of this new "Oriental invasion."[120] Including most of the leading Pilipino exclusionists in California, the various speakers particularly emphasized the Pilipinos' threat to American racial superiority.[121] Vaughan MacCoughey, editor of the *Sierra Educational News*, predicted that if this rising tide of immigration continued, it could have but "one end, namely miscegenation . . . a hybridizing at the bottom, often under the most wretched circumstances, of your lower racial stocks."[122]

---

[115] Conmy, pp. 20–22.

[116] *Journal of the Assembly*, 48th Session, 1929, pp. 2160, 2300, 2847; *Journal of the Senate*, 1929, p. 2690.

[117] Carey McWilliams, *Brothers Under the Skin* (Boston: Little, Brown and Company, 1964), p. 242.

[118] *Ibid.*

[119] Carey McWilliams, "Exit the Filipinos," *The Nation*, September 4, 1935, p. 265.

[120] Commonwealth Club of California, *Transactions*, XXIV (1929), p. 312.

[121] *Ibid.*, pp. 312–378.

[122] *Ibid.*, p. 341.

Again the racist stereotype of the lascivious, aggressive Asiatic who chased lustfully after white women reared its ugly head, while anti-Pilipino spokesmen and their groups exploited it publicly. In the 1930 Congressional hearings on immigration, Secretary McClatchy testified that "you can realize, with the declared preference of the Pilipino for white women and the willingness on the part of some white females to yield to that preference, the situation which arises."[123] Anti-Pilipino spokesman Judge D. H. Rohrock of North Monterey County engaged in the most reprehensible kind of racist stereotyping when he described the Pilipinos as "little brown men attired like 'Solomon in all his glory' strutting like peacocks and endeavoring to attract the eyes of young American and Mexican girls."[124]

This propaganda inflamed the public's hostility toward Pilipino-white "intermingling." Two of the worst California race riots, occurring at Exeter and Watsonville, were first incited by the anger of white men at the socializing of Pilipino men with white women. Sociologist Emory Bogardus, in his study of the 1930 Watsonville riot, pointed to the rioters' resentment of Pilipino-white interrelationships as one of the main causes of the violence: "But the idea of Pilipinos dancing with white girls (no matter who the latter were) incensed white young men of Watsonville, and they determined to break up the procedure. . . ."[125] Another manifestation of Californians' often uncontrollable fear of miscegenation was the drive for legal prohibition of Pilipino-white marriages during this period. Anti-Pilipino spokesmen wailed loudly and publicly about the evils of intermarriages between whites and Pilipinos. The Commonwealth Club's David Burrows, Vaughan MacCoughey, and C. M. Goethe, President of the Immigration Study Commission, warned of "race mingling" which would create a "new type of mulatto," an "American Mestizo."[126] Judge Ruhrock claimed hysterically that "if the present state of affairs continues, there will be 40,000 half-breeds in California before ten years have passed."[127]

This agitation fueled a long-existing controversy over whether Pilipino-white marriages were legal or not in California. Were Pilipinos racially classified as Mongolians? Did the Legislature intend to include Pilipinos when it amended Sections 60 and 69 by adding the word "Mongolian?" While there were attempts to answer definitively these questions, the controversy was not legally settled until 1933 when a California high court finally ruled on the above issues. Before this date, because of the legal confusion about the meaning of the statutes, county clerks in California made the decision whether or not to issue marriage licenses to Pilipino-white couples. On June 8, 1929, in an attempt to influence these county clerks not to issue licenses, California Attorney General U. S. Webb, who later spoke for Pilipino exclusion in the 1929 Commonwealth Club forums and the 1930 Congressional hearings, ruled that Pilipinos were Mongolians and thus were prohibited from marrying white persons under Sections 60 and 69.[128] Webb's opinion was

---

[123] Statement of Valentine Stuart McClatchy in *Hearings Before the Committee on Immigration and Naturalization*, H.R. 8708. 71st Congress., 2nds., 1930, Vol. 1, pp. 35–36.

[124] *Evening Pajaronian*, January 8, 1930, quoted in Manuel Buaken, *I have Lived with the American People* (Caldwell: Caxton Printers, Ltd., 1948), pp. 169–170.

[125] Emory S. Bogardus, *Anti-Filipino Race Riots* (San Diego: Ingram Institute, May 15, 1930), pp. 7–8.

[126] C. M. Goethe, "Filipino Immigration Viewed as a Peril," *Current History*, June, 1931, pp. 353–56; Commonwealth Club, *Transactions*, XXIV (1929), p. 341.

[127] *Evening Pajaronian*, January 10, 1930, p. 1, as quoted in Bogardus, pp. 7–8.

[128] Opinion No. 5641, Legal Department, rendered June 8, 1926, to the Hon. C. C. Kempley, District Attorney of San Diego County, as cited in Nellie Foster, "Legal Status of Filipino Intermarriages in California," *Sociology and Social Research*, 16 (November-December, 1931), p. 447.

not binding, and county clerks throughout California continued to make their own decisions on how to apply the statutes. For example, while the Santa Barbara County Clerk refused to do so, the County Clerk of Los Angeles, L. E. Lampton, did issue marriage licenses to Pilipino-white couples.[129] Lampton's decision to do so was based on a 1921 legal opinion given by the County Council of Los Angeles which declared that Pilipinos were not Mongolians and thus not included under the provisions of Section 69.

The Commonwealth Club's strongly anti-Pilipino section on immigration criticized the failure of various counties in California, especially Los Angeles, to cease issuing marriage licenses to Pilipino-white couples. In its 1929 report, the section complained that "in some of our southern counties, such marriages are performed notwithstanding the terms of the statute."[130] In order to correct this situation, the section vigorously recommended the amendment of Section 60, so that it expressly "prohibits marriages between Pilipinos and members of the white races."[131] All the principal anti-Pilipino organizations in California—the American Legion, the Native Sons of the Golden West, California State Federation of Labor, and the California Joint Immigration Committee—endorsed this recommendation and joined together with the Commonwealth Club to work for its implementation. The campaign to amend Section 60 especially continued in the courts and in the California Legislature until obtaining success in 1933. Attorney General Webb was especially active in this drive. Before his fellow members in the Commonwealth Club, he stated that biologically unassimilable races like the Pilipinos should no longer be allowed to mingle with "the dominant race in this country."[132]

The increased public agitation for the imposing of intermarriage restrictions affecting Pilipinos became especially strident in the County of Los Angeles, which issued marriage licenses to Pilipino-white couples and had the largest number of applications from Pilipinos in the State. As Nellie Foster shows in her article, "Legal Status of Pilipino Intermarriages in California," there was a great deal of discussion and legal activity concerning this issue in Los Angeles from 1930 to 1931.[133] In *Stella F. Robinson vs. L. E. Lampton (1930)*, Judge Smith of the Superior Court prohibited the county clerk from granting a marriage license to Tony Moreno, a Pilipino, and Ruby Robinson, a white.[134] This decision, influenced by Attorney General Webb's opinion, convinced the county clerk to reverse his previous position and to refuse all applications from Pilipinos for marriage licenses. The Pilipino community of Los Angeles, outraged by this decision, sought to change this policy through further litigation. Thus, in 1931, four more cases involving the question of Pilipino intermarriages were filed in the Superior Court of Los Angeles. In *Gavina C. Visco v. L. A. County, Estanislao P. Laddaran v. Emma P. Laddaran, Illona Murillo v. Tony Murillo, Jr.,* and *Salvador Roldan v. L. A. County,* the Superior Court ruled that Pilipino-white marriages did not violate the state laws because Pilipinos were not classified as Mongolians.[135] More importantly, the *Roldan* decision was to be reviewed by the California Court of Appeals.

---

[129] Bruno Lasker, *Filipino Immigration to Continental United States and to Hawaii* (Chicago: University of Chicago Press, 1931), pp. 213–216.

[130] Commonwealth Club of California, *Transactions*, XXIV (1929), p. 319.

[131] *Ibid.*, pp. 320, 375.

[132] *Ibid.*, p. 348.

[133] Foster, p. 448.

[134] *Stella Robinson v. L. E. Lampton, County Clerk of Los Angeles*, No. 2496504 (1930), Superior Court of L. A. County, cited in Foster, pp. 450–452.

[135] Foster, pp. 450–452.

To all parties, this action was welcome, since it finally meant that a higher court decision would be forthcoming on this controversial issue. Members of the Pilipino community in Los Angeles, as in previous cases, supported the respondent with contributions, so that the well-known lawyers, Gladys Towles Root and George B. Bush, could be hired to represent Roldan.[136] The anti-Pilipino forces rallied around the County's position, with Attorney General Webb presenting an argument as a friend of the court on behalf of the appellants.[137] On January 27, 1933, the Appellate Court ruled for Roldan in a disputed 3-3 decision, stating that Pilipino-white marriages were not prohibited.[138] Pilipino writer-worker Carlos Bulosan, who lived through this oppression, wrote how the *Roldan* case generated great resentment against the Pilipinos: "The sentiment against them was accelerated by the marriage of a Pilipino and a girl of the Caucasian race in Pasadena. The case was tried in court and many technicalities were brought in with it to degrade the lineage and character of the Pilipino people."[139]

In this case, Roldan, a Pilipino, and Marjorie Rogers, a white, were denied a marriage license by the County Clerk. The couple then petitioned the courts to order the County to issue the license to them. Affirming the Superior Court's decision, Judge Archibald's majority opinion dealt mainly with two questions: (1) What was the most common racial classification between 1850 and 1905?; and (2) Did the State Legislature in 1880 and 1905 mean to include Pilipinos in its use of the word "Mongolian"? The opinion discussed how the most popular dictionaries of the late nineteenth century classified the different races. Archibald determined that the most common classification was that of Blumenback who concluded that there were five: Caucasian (white), Mongolian (yellow), Ethiopian (black), American (red), and Malay (brown). He also discovered that other ethnologists and dictionaries of the period did include the Malays as among the "Mongoloid" group. However, Judge Archibald concluded that the "early classification of Blumenback left its impression on the writers from his day to 1905, at least, so that his classification is spoken of as the more commonly used."[140] Thus, he determined that the framers of the amendments of 1880 and 1905 probably followed the common classification of race as designated by Blumenback and did not intend the Malay race to be included as part of the Mongolian race.

Judge Archibald also attempted to discover what was the intention of the California Legislature when it framed and passed the 1880 amendment to Section 69 of the Civil Code. After reading many of the legislative reports and proceedings from 1878 to 1880, the Court came to the conclusion that the intention of the statute was to prevent the marriages among Chinese and whites. There was no intention by the legislature to apply the classification of Mongolian to a Malay: "From 1862 to 1885 the history of California is replete with legislation to curb the so-called 'Chinese invasion,' and as we read we are impressed with the fact that the terms 'Asiatics,' 'coolies' and 'Mongolians' meant 'Chinese' to the people who discussed and legislated on the problem. . . ."[141] Thus, the Court affirmed that Pilipinos were not prohibited by Sections 60 and 69 of the Civil Code from marrying whites in California. The judge emphasized that this was not "a social question before us, as that was decided by the legislature at the time the Code was amended." He further

---

[136] Foster, pp. 450–451.

[137] *Salvador Roldan v. L. A. County*, et al., 129 Cal. App., 267.

[138] *Ibid.*, p. 272.

[139] Carlos Bulosan, *America Is in the Heart* (New York: Harcourt Brace Jovanovich, Inc., 1946), p. 143.

[140] *Roldan*, pp. 268–269.

[141] *Ibid.*, p. 270.

added that "if the common thought of today is different from what it was at that time, the matter is one that addresses itself to the legislature and not to the courts."[142]

Archibald's suggestion had already been followed. During the long controversy over this issue, the anti-Pilipino forces continued to campaign for the legislative amendment of Sections 60 and 69 to expressly prohibit Pilipinos or "Malays" from marrying whites. Nine days before the issuing of the *Roldan* decision, State Senator Herbert C. Jones of Santa Clara, an exclusionist who voted for the passage of the 1929 Legislature Resolution urging Congress to exclude Pilipino immigration, introduced Senate Bills Nos. 175 and 176 amending, respectively, Sections 60 and 69.[143] On the same day, using a familiar tactic, Secretary McClatchy of the California Joint Immigration Committee requested its sponsoring organizations, the American Legion, the Native Sons and Daughters of the Golden West, and the California State Federation of Labor, to ask their members to urge representatives of the State Legislature to adopt the bills "forbidding the intermarriage of Caucasians and Filipinos."[144] On March 14, both bills passed the Senate unanimously.[145] The Assembly also passed the bills on April 5 by votes of 66-1 for Bill No. 175 and 63-0 for Bill No. 175 and 63-0 for Bill No. 176.[146] The only dissenting Assemblyman in the voting was Frederick Roberts from Los Angeles County, whose large Pilipino community had agitated against the passage of the bills. On April 20, Governor James Rolph, a prominent member of the Native Sons of the Golden West, signed the bills into law, effective four months later on August 21.[147] Retroactively voiding all previous Pilipino-white marriages, Section 60 now read that all marriages of Caucasians with "negroes, Mongolians, members of the Malay race, or mulattoes are illegal and void."[148] Section 69 was amended to state that no license could be issued authorizing the marriage of "a white person with a negro, mulatto, Mongolian, or member of the Malay race."[149]

After the passage of the amendments, there continued to be discussion about the application of Section 60. There were public complaints about "loopholes" in the law which reduced its effectiveness. Frederick Duhring, in the Commonwealth Club report on Pilipinos, pointed out the practice of Pilipino-white parties going to neighboring States to be lawfully married. Californians began to ask whether such marriages were valid when the married couples returned to California.[150] However, the case law in this area indicated that such marriages were indeed legal in that State.

To better understand the workings of Section 60, we should discuss certain aspects of the way it operated in practice. First, the courts had repeatedly determined that any attempted interracial marriage was wholly void and created no status.[151] However, while no marital status could be created by an attempted marriage of a white and a "colored" person within the jurisdiction of California, it was not clear whether such a marriage contracted in a jurisdiction where interracial marriages were allowed was valid in California. Civil Code Section 63 seemed to contain the

---

[142] *Ibid.*, pp. 270–273.

[143] *California Journal of the Senate*, 40th Session, 1933, p. 807.

[144] *Grizzly Bear*, LV (March, 1933), p. 4.

[145] *California Journal of the Senate*, p. 846.

[146] *California Journal of the Assembly*, pp. 1859–60.

[147] *Cal. Stats.*, 50th Session, 1933, Ch. 104, p. 561.

[148] *Ibid.*, pp. 561–562.

[149] *Ibid.*

[150] Commonwealth Club, *Transactions*, XXIV, p. 19.

[151] *Estate of Lee*, 200 Cal. 31 (1926).

answer which adopted the general conflicts of the law principle that: "All marriages contracted without this state, which would be valid by the laws of the country in which the same were contracted, are valid by the laws of this state." Applying this principle to interracial marriages was an 1875 California Supreme Court case, *Pearson v. Pearson*.[152] In this case, a white man married his black slave in Utah, where such a marriage was declared void by Section 60 of the Civil Code. In a suit filed after the death of the husband, it was claimed that the marriage was void. The Court ruled that the validity of a marriage was to be listed by the place where it was celebrated, with the exception of polygamous and incestuous marriages.[153]

The answer was not quite as clear in cases in which a couple were living in a State which prohibited interracial marriages, but left the State and went to one which permitted such marriages, then returned to reside in their original State. In many States, this type of marriage would not be valid.[154] However, in California, the language of the cases discussing this issue appeared to sanction such marriages. In *Estate of Wood* (1902), the California Supreme Court ruled that it was not material if a couple went to Nevada in order to evade the prohibition of California's divorce laws.[155] Justice Garouette stated that the Court did not have to consider the motive of the parties in its decision. Citing *Pearson* and Section 63 of the Civil Code, he ruled that if the marriage was valid in Nevada, then it is "valid in this state."[156] Similarly, in *McDonald v. McDonald* (1936), the parties who were minors at the time and did not have their parents' consent went to Nevada to be married with the avowed purpose of evading the prohibition of California law.[157] While not valid in California, according to Nevada law, the marriage was valid in that State. On the issue of whether the parties' intention had any influence on the validity of such marriages, Justice Langdon ruled that the motive of the parties would not change the operation of Section 63, and that a "marriage which is contrary to the policies of the laws of one state is yet valid therein if celebrated with and according to the laws of another state."[158] Finally, in 1936, the California Appellate Court ruled specifically on whether a Pilipino-white marriage that took place in another State where it was legal was also valid in California. In *People v. Godines*, the appellant, a white woman, had attempted to annul a marriage with a Pilipino on the ground that she had been induced to marry by the fraudulent representation that he was of Spanish descent.[159] Since a Pilipino-white marriage was not legal in California, the husband's mis-representation that he was a Spaniard was a fraud that touched a "vital spot in the marriage relation" and constituted a cause for annulment. On this issue, however, Justice Roberts stated that the marriage, taking place in New Mexico, where it was legal, was also valid in California. Thus, "hence of itself, the ethnological status of the parties was not a ground of annulment."[160]

There were no statistics on how many Pilipino-white marriages became legalized in California because of this "loophole" in Section 60 of the Civil Code. Iris Buaken, the white wife of

---

[152] *51 Cal.*, 120 (1875).

[153] *Ibid.*, p. 122.

[154] Irving Trager, "Statutory Prohibition against Interracial Marriage," *California Law Review*, Vol. 32 (1944): 279.

[155] *137 Cal.*, 129.

[156] *Ibid.*, p. 136.

[157] *6 Cal. (2d)*, 457.

[158] *Ibid.*, p. 459.

[159] *17 Cal. (2d)*, 721.

[160] *Ibid.*, p. 723.

Pilipino writer Manuel Buaken, wrote that only a few Pilipino-white couples, who knew of the legal rulings and who had enough money to do so, traveled to other States, got married and later returned to California. For many years, Mrs. Buaken herself was unable to marry her husband legally because of the 1933 amendment: " . . . we have no children. If we had, we would have made the desperate sacrifice required to get to a state where we could be 'married.' "[161] By 1938, Pilipino-white marriages were prohibited by law in five Western States: South Dakota (1913), Nevada (1919), Arizona (1931), Wyoming (1931), and California (1933).[162] New Mexico and Utah were the nearest States to California where a Pilipino and a white could be married legally. Because of anti-Pilipino agitation and inflammatory newspaper reports claiming that more than two hundred young white women residing in California had been taken to Utah by Pilipinos for the "purpose of marriage, thereby evading the California law," on March 11, 1938, Assemblyman Dilworth of Hemet introduced Joint Resolution No. 14.[163] It passed both the Assembly and the Senate by votes of 51–4 and 30–0, respectively.[164] Issued on March 16, it requested the Legislature of Utah to enact such law or laws as may be necessary to "aid the State of California" in preventing the flouting of its laws "prohibiting marriages between white persons and members of the Pilipino or Malay race."[165] Even though Utah did pass legislation prohibiting Pilipino-white marriages in 1939, the California Legislature was unable to halt this method of evading Sections 60 and 69.

In 1941, Senator Chris Jespersen introduced Senate Bill No. 48 which sought to amend Section 63 of the Civil Code by declaring void in the State of California, marriages of persons of different races who had been legally married in other States.[166] However, the bill failed to pass the Committee on Judiciary.[167]

While it is difficult to ascertain exactly to what extent anti-miscegenation laws did prevent Pilipino-white marriages in California, it is clear that the 1933 laws made it difficult for California Pilipinos to marry whites. After 1933, with some exceptions, the laws were enforced with some diligence in California. Moreover, it was expensive and arduous during the Great Depression to travel to neighboring States where Pilipino-white marriages were allowed, and to return to California. However, some authorities felt that these laws were not very effective in preventing interracial marriages.[168]

In contrast, most Pilipinos who lived through this difficult period believed strongly that the laws severely restricted Pilipino-white marriages. Carlos Bulosan describes the harsh animosity unleashed by the events of 1933: "It was now the year of the great hatred: the lives of the Pilipino were cheaper than those of dogs. . . . It was then a simple thing for the state legislature to pass a law forbidding marriage between members of the Malayan and Caucasian races."[169] The Buakens

---

[161] Iris B. Buaken, "You Can't Marry a Filipino," *The Commonwealth* (March 16, 1945), p. 534.

[162] "Anti-Miscegenation Laws and the Pilipino," *Letters in Exile: An Introductory Reader on the History of Pilipinos in America* (Los Angeles: UCLA Asian American Studies Center, 1976), p. 70; Pauli Murray, Comp., *States' Laws on Race and Color* (Cincinnati: Women's Division of Christian Services, the Methodist Church, 1950 and 1955 Supplements).

[163] *California Journal of the Assembly*, 1938, p. 162.

[164] *Ibid.; California Journal of the Senate*, 1938, p. 172.

[165] *Journal of the Senate*, p. 172.

[166] *Ibid.*

[167] *Ibid.*, pp. 265, 2833.

[168] Emory Bogardus, "Citizenship for Filipinos," *Sociology and Social Research*, XI (1933): 612.

[169] Bulosan, p. 143.

saw the anti-miscegenation laws as an integral part of the general discrimination and racism against Pilipinos in California: "Many thousands of Pilipinos of the United States . . . are denied the right to marry in the Pacific Coast, are still to patronize prostitution for the benefit of vice and disease, are still living under the regime of double-talk Christianity and racist exploitation."[170]

The anti-miscegenation laws exacerbated one of the most serious problems that faced Pilipinos in this country, i.e., the lack of single Pilipina women. According to the 1930 census, there were in the United States 40,904 Pilipinos fifteen years old and over, but only 1,640 Pilipinas in the same age bracket.[171] While more than 75 percent of the women were married, approximately 80 percent of the male immigrants were single and between the ages of sixteen and thirty.[172] The disproportionate sex ratio plagued the Pilipinos throughout their history in the United States. Even in 1940, there were seven Pilipino men for every Pilipina woman in this country.[173] By 1960, there were still almost two Pilipinos for every Pilipina.[174]

This lack of marriageable Pilipina women slowed greatly the normal development of a Pilipino community with homes, families, children, and small businesses. The *sacada* generally remained a single, migrant worker moving from job to job in the "factories in the fields" or fish canneries throughout the Pacific Coast. Pilipino communities in Stockton and Los Angeles were essentially transient, bachelor societies with hotels, boarding-houses, poolrooms, social clubs, and taxi dance halls. In California, with only 31,408 Pilipinos in 1940 and 40,424 in 1950, the small number of women within the childbearing ages appeared to retard the growth of this Asian group until the 1960s.[175]

Harassed by racism, exploitation, and discrimination, most of the first generation immigrants were denied a family and home life with strong social and community ties. Anti-miscegenation laws particularly made it difficult for the Pilipino to marry and to have children. Instead, the majority of these *sacadas* were left with such exploitative "recreations" as gambling and prostitution. Pilipinos literally had nowhere else to go. Bulosan wrote that the Pilipino was "the loneliest thing on earth."[176] Farm worker Sebastian Sahugan lashed out at the oppression that was the cause of this inhumanity and suffering: "On top of the worst kind of exploitation of our labor, we were not allowed to own our land or house, and not even permitted to marry or raise a family."[177]

The Constitutionality of Anti-Miscegenation Laws

Immediately after World War II and the internment of the Japanese in concentration camps, the anti-Asian sentiment in California still continued especially against the Japanese. They had difficulty in returning to their old communities and homes in California, and were the victims

---

[170] Buaken, p. 534.

[171] *Fifteenth Census of the United States, 1930*, Vol. 2, p. 845.

[172] *Ibid.*

[173] *Sixteenth Census of the United States, 1940: Population*, Vol. 2, Pt. 1, p. 21, Table VI.

[174] *A Study of Selected Socio-Economic Characteristics of Ethnic Minorities Based on the 1970 Census, Volume III: Asian Americans* (Washington, D.C.: Department of Health, Education, and Welfare, July, 1974) HEW Publication No. (05) 75–121, pp. XII-XVII.

[175] California Fair Employment Practices Commission, *Demographic and Socioeconomic Perspective*, in Daniels and Olin, p. 69.

[176] Bulosan, p. 143.

[177] "Letter From a Manong," *Ang Katipunan*, December 15, 1973, p. 4.

of many acts of violence during the 1945–46 period especially in the agricultural areas of the Salinas and San Joaquin Valleys. A national poll indicated that 89 percent of Americans favored denying alien Japanese equal opportunities.[178] Backed by the Hearst and McClatchy papers, Governor Earl Warren consistently acted in the anti-Asian tradition, supporting restrictive legislation and making anti-Japanese public statements.[179] Warren and Attorney General Robert Kenny, based on the Alien Land Law, started a program to remove Japanese farmers from the vicinity of important military installations. California voters indicated their support of this land-grabbing program through a 1946 ballot measure, while the State Legislature appropriated money and passed legislation to support the seizure of valuable Japanese-owned farm land.[180]

Through such organizations as the Japanese American Citizens League, the Japanese began in the courts to "defend their property rights in current land seizure proceedings by the State of California."[181] After a long and costly court struggle, the California Supreme Court in 1952 declared the unconstitutionality of the Alien Land Law, the product of "the anti-Japanese race baiting groups," in *Fujii v. State of California*.[182] Another legal victory occurred in the 1948 *Takahashi* case, in which the United States Supreme Court ruled unconstitutional two statutes denying aliens the right to obtain commercial fishing licenses.[183]

Applying this tactic of struggling for repeal of discriminatory legislation through the courts, rather than through the more hostile legislature, interested groups managed to get the State Supreme Court to review the constitutionality of the anti-miscegenation laws in 1948. The Asian groups—Chinese, Japanese, and Pilipinos—had never challenged the constitutionality of these statutes in the courts. The *Roldan* and *Godines* cases dealt with the meaning and application of the laws, not their constitutionality. However, ironically using some legal principles established by the 1944 "evacuation cases," especially *Korematsu* and *Hirabayashi*, the State Supreme Court ruled in *Perez v. Sharp* (1948) that the anti-miscegenation laws of California were unconstitutional.[184]

In this crucial case, Andrea Perez, a white woman, and Sylvester Davis, a Black, applied to the County Clerk of Los Angeles for a marriage license. The respondent refused, relying on Sections 60 and 69. In a mandamus proceeding, the couple sought to compel the County Clerk to issue them a license to marry, contending that these statutes were unconstitutional in that they prohibited the free exercise of their religion. Since both Davis and Perez were members of the Roman Catholic Church, they maintained that since the Church did not forbid marriages between Blacks and Caucasians, they had the right to receive the sacrament of matrimony.

Justice Roger Traynor's majority opinion argued that in violation of due process the statutes were too vague and uncertain to constitute a valid regulation, and that the statutes were denials of the equal protection of laws guaranteed by the Fourteenth Amendment. The Justice emphasized

---

[178] Audrie Girdner and Anne Loftis, *The Great Betrayal: The Evacuation of the Japanese-Americans during World War II* (New York: Macmillan, 1969), p. 404.

[179] Bill Hosokawa, *Nisei: The Quiet Americans* (New York: William Morrow, 1969), pp. 288–289.

[180] Girdner and Loftis, pp. 429–430.

[181] *Pacific Citizen*, December 1, 1945.

[182] *Sei Fujii vs. State of California*, 38 Cal. (2d), 718, April 17, 1952.

[183] *Takahashi vs. Fish and Game Commission*, 334 U.S. 410, June 7, 1948.

[184] *Korematsu vs. U.S.*, 323 U.S. 214 (1944); *Hirabayashi vs. U.S.*, 320 U.S. 81; *Perez vs. Sharp*, 32 A.C. 757 (1948), 198.

the latter argument. It dealt with two questions: (1) Is there discrimination?; and (2) If there is, is there sufficient justification for it?

Dealing with the first question, Traynor determined that if the right to marry, which included the right to choose one's mate, was one of the fundamental rights protected by the Fourteenth Amendment, and if such rights were given equally, then anti-miscegenation laws which necessarily denied this right to marry were discriminatory. There could be no equality when a person was denied the personal right to choose his marital partner irrespective of race.

Having determined that the statutes were discriminatory, the court had to decide if the discrimination complied with the requirements of the equal protection clause. The discriminatory statutes could be upheld only if the discrimination was based on a reasonable classification with a legitimate legislative end in view: "There can be no prohibition of marriage except for an important social objective and by reasonable means."[185]

Did Sections 60 and 69, which restricted the rights of individuals to marry and classified them according to race, meet this test? Traynor's majority opinion concluded that the statutes did not and thus violated the equal protection clause. Under the Fourteenth Amendment, he stated, the legislation could be sustained only (1) if there was a clear and present danger established, or alternatively, (2) if there was a reasonable classification by the legislature. The burden was placed upon the legislature to overcome a presumption that the laws were invalid since they involved a racial classification. The court ruled that statutes survived neither test and was, in addition, unconstitutionally vague. Justice Carter concurred, arguing that these statutes did not reflect a strong state policy since California recognized "carefree" marriage, whereby local residents went to another State to avoid the California statutes. These laws also imposed no criminal sanctions.

Traynor's opinion accepted the legal doctrine that "racial classifications amounting to discrimination are always specifically suspect in the courts, and are the subject of more rigid scrutiny than other kinds of classifications."[186] The Justice stated that the Fourteenth Amendment "expresses a definite national policy against discriminations because of race or color . . . Any state legislation discriminating against persons on the basis of race or color has to overcome the strong presumption inherent in this constitutional policy."[187] This "rigid scrutiny," supported by cases like *Korematsu v. United States* (1944) and *Oyama v. California* (1948), has become a crucial constitutional doctrine in equal protection issues. Using this test, Traynor ruled that in *Perez* there was no compelling justification for California's antimiscegenation laws, and thus such discrimination was not constitutional.

When the *Perez* decision came out in 1948, it was the first case to rule anti-miscegenation laws unconstitutional. However, legal authorities predicted that this case would set a trend, stimulating similar suits in other jurisdictions, including the issue eventually to be settled by the U.S. Supreme Court.[188] Others did not agree: "Social sanctions have always been many times more powerful than legal sanctions with respect to sex behavior and the institution of marriage; deep-rooted attitudes and prejudices are not to be done away with on the strength of a judical decision."[189]

---

[185] *Perez*, p. 714.

[186] "Constitutionality of Statutes Against Anti-Miscegenation Laws," *111.Law*, 43 (1948): 867.

[187] *Perez*, p. 719.

[188] "Anti-Miscegenation Law and Due Process and Equal Protection Clauses of U.S. Constitution," *University of P.A. Law Review*, 97 (1948), p. 48.

[189] "Constitutionality of Statutes," p. 867; *Ibid.*, p. 871.

Subsequent events proved the latter opinion more predictive. The California Legislature resisted the court decision. The unconstitutional statutes remained on the California Civil Code, though not enforceable, until 1959. There were four unsuccessful attempts in 1949, 1951 (twice), and 1955 to expunge the court-invalidated laws from the code.[190] California legislators refused to accept even the *pro forma* repeal of the court-invalidated statutes for eleven years.[191]

Other States also continued to enforce their anti-miscegenation statutes. There was no "sweeping invalidation" of these laws in the United States. However, there was growing legislative sentiment against these discriminatory laws. As of 1967, sixteen States still had anti-miscegenation laws, although fifteen States had repealed their counterparts since 1945.[192]

Finally, in *Loving v. Virginia* (1967), the U.S. Supreme Court took a step that many thought long overdue.[193] It ruled unanimously that the anti-miscegenation laws of the remaining States were unconstitutional. Representing the Japanese American Citizens League, William Marutani of Philadelphia appeared as a "friend of the court" and argued for the position of the Lovings.[194] Many egalitarians welcomed the decision as heralding the end of statutory racial discrimination in America. Furthermore, the ruling marked the end of the court's reluctance to decide on the hard question of the constitutionality of anti-miscegenation statutes.

In this case, Richard Loving, a white male, and Mildred Jeter, a Black woman, were legally married in the District of Columbia. Shortly after they returned to Virginia they were convicted of violating a state statute prohibiting interracial marriage. Both were sentenced to one year in jail, but their sentences were suspended on condition that they leave the State and not return together for a period of twenty-five years. The Supreme Court of Appeals of Virginia upheld the constitutionality of the statute and affirmed the convictions. On appeal, the U. S. Supreme Court reversed the decision.

Chief Justice Earl Warren's majority opinion relied greatly on two theories used previously in the decision of *Perez v. Sharp*. One theory asserts that marriage is a fundamental legal right and may be regulated only by a statute that is a legitimate exercise of the State's police power in pursuit of a valid objective. Advocates of this position contend that anti-miscegenation laws do not meet this test and therefore deny due process. Chief Justice Warren ruled that the right to marry is a fundamental freedom. He continued that the Fourteenth Amendment "requires that the freedom of choice to marry not be restricted by invidious racial discrimination."[195] This ruling made freedom of marriage one of the fundamental legal rights entitled to the protection of the due process clause.

The other major theory is based on the premise that these statutes impose invidious discrimination which violates the equal protection clause. Closely following Traynor's reasoning in *Perez*, the court rejected the respondent's argument that it defer to the wisdom of the state legislature in adopting its policy of prohibiting interracial marriages. Instead, Warren's opinion accepted Traynor's concept of a strong presumption of invalidity inherent in any racial classification and

---

[190] "Anti-Miscegenation Laws and the Pilipino," *Letters in Exile: An Introductory Reader on the History of Pilipinos in America* (Los Angeles: UCLA Asian American Studies Center, 1976), p. 70.

[191] *Ibid.*

[192] Sickels, p. 164.

[193] *Loving v. Virginia*, 388 U. S. 1 (1967).

[194] Girdner and Loftis, p. 441

[195] *Loving*, p. 12.

used, as in *Perez*, the "rigid scrutiny" test of *Korematsu*: "At the very least, the equal protection clause demands that racial classifications, especially suspect in criminal statutes, be subjected to the 'most rigid scrutiny.' "[196] Using this test, Chief Justice Warren concluded that "there is no legitimate overriding purpose independent of invidious racial discrimination which justifies this classification." Since Virginia banned only interracial marriages involving white persons, this fact demonstrated that the race classifications were "designed to maintain White Supremacy."[197] The Chief Justice ruled that restricting the freedom to marry solely because of racial classification violated the central meaning of the equal protection clause.

Like in the *Perez* case, the decision in *Loving* was not a popular one. Indeed, it ran counter to the attitudes of most Americans. Only a year after the decision, a Gallup Poll indicated that 72 percent of American adults disapproved of marriages between whites and nonwhites. Only 20 percent approved of interracial marriages.[198] Despite the legal advances of the civil rights movement, this poll indicated the deep-rootedness and prevalence of racist attitudes among the American public. Thus, a discussion of antimiscegenation laws still has relevance to the problems our society presently faces.

Conclusion

As we have noted earlier, laws prohibiting interracial marriages were first legislated in States which had legalized slavery. Such laws were aspects of the institutional slavery system. Since female slaves were not permitted to marry legally, the sexual abuse of them by the slaveholding class was not considered a crime. For example, the concept of raping a slave did not legally exist. One cannot rape one's own property. Thus, it was not surprising that these laws were not applied against white slaveholders' sexual abuse of female slaves. Instead, the slavocracy used these laws to oppress white women and to punish black men who entered into sexual relationships with them. Under these circumstances, white women were also deprived of equal rights and considered as another form of property. Indeed, the Slave States had these laws passed to restrict the sexual independence of white women and to maintain the legally sanctioned enslavement of Blacks.

Needing cheap and controllable labor, American society recruited Asian immigrants to work usually undesirable jobs at low wages and under poor working conditions. Previously, Americans exploited the labor of slaves or indentured servants. However, Asians did not work as slaves, for American industry now desired a more mobile but still controllable working force. Instead, through the use of social, political, and economic oppression, American society created a labor caste system based on racial origins, under which non-white workers were effectively excluded from meaningful participation in the mainstream of this country. In this new type of enslavement, Asians were limited to work at specific low-paying jobs (railroad, agriculture, and service work), and were segregated from the rest of society so that they could be exploited, subordinated, and manipulated more effectively and cheaply.

Anti-miscegenation laws were an integral part of this policy. On one level, the anti-miscegenation laws were enacted for a blatantly racist purpose, to prevent the intermingling of whites with an allegedly inferior and debased race. On another level, because most Asian immigrants were male, the laws

---

[196] *Ibid.*, p. 11.

[197] *Ibid.*

[198] George Horace Gallup, *The Gallup Poll, 1935–1971*, Vol. 3 (New York: Random House, 1972), p. 2168.

were sexist, chiefly aimed at restricting the sexual independence and freedom of white women. Also, these laws contributed to the attempt to control the number of Asians and to treat them as economic and sexual threats. If they could not marry, they would find it difficult to have families and political power of their own in this country. Furthermore, when the economic need for their labor diminished, American society embarked on a policy of excluding Asians from this country, driving those already here out of the country, or forcing them to die childless without a trace. These anti-miscegenation laws were part of the attempt to reduce Asian communities to impotent and dying ones, easily exploited by business interests. Subjecting Asians to a form of forced extinction, this approach eventually failed, but it did succeed for a period of time especially in the cases of the Chinese and Pilipino communities in this country.

This organized exploitation has followed a similar pattern. Asians, like all oppressed minorities, were excluded from equal rights, and were either expelled from American society or segregated economically, socially, and politically into exploitable ghettoes and enclaves. Even though these antimiscegenation laws no longer exist, they should not be considered as obscure relics of the past. The relatively recent overturning of these laws is just one indication that the racism and oppression which created these restrictions are deeply-rooted phenomena, and that the struggle to eliminate them is a crucial process.

Glimpses Into the Future: Interracial and Interethnic Marriage

C. N. Le

The final outcome of assimilation among Asian Americans that I will examine is marital assimilation, represented in this chapter by having an endogamous (same ethnicity), pan-Asian (spouse of a different Asian ethnicity), or White spouse. Previous chapters have moved from structural-level forms of assimilation (socioeconomic attainment) into more individual-level outcomes (self-employment and residential integration) and as such, this chapter concludes the analysis of assimilation by analyzing marriage as a form of social assimilation. While there is debate over whether intermarriage represents cultural assimilation on the individual or the structural level, there is little doubt that it symbolizes a powerful component of social integration for racial/ethnic minorities and immigrants.

Of course, there are other measures of behavioral and cultural assimilation. One is naturalization or the degree to which immigrants become naturalized U.S. citizens. However, as we discussed in Chapter Two, because of their unique refugee experiences of escaping communist domination, Vietnamese Americans were predisposed to having high rates of naturalization as they relinquished their political affiliation and loyalty to the new government of Viet Nam in favor of their new adopted homeland of America. As a result, their naturalization process is unique and cannot be accurately compared to that of other Asian American groups who do not have refugee backgrounds. Similarly, linguistic assimilation (becoming fluent in English or conversely retaining one's native language through subsequent generations) has also been used as a measure of behavioral assimilation but because census data cannot determine whether English fluency occurred before or after immigration, it is not used here as an accurate measure of cultural assimilation.

Therefore, for our purposes, marrying outside one's own ethnic group is perhaps the most tangible and most visible form of cultural assimilation. In fact, several sociologists note that intermarriage (also known as outmarriage) is perhaps the ultimate and final breakdown of social distance and completion of assimilation (see Alba 1990; Bogardus 1967; Gordon 1964; Waters 1990) and in recent years, addition, demographers, social scientists, and community activists are keenly observing recent intermarriage trends in an effort to predict the political, demographic, and cultural consequences for the Asian American population (Lee and Edmondson 2005). Within this context, the measure of cultural/behavioral assimilation that concerns us is marriage patterns of the five Asian American ethnic groups in question. The three specific outcomes we will examine are rates and factors associated with having an endogamous, pan-Asian (an Asian of a different ethnicity), or White spouse. The goal is to analyze the effect that structural and ecological measures may have on the cultural environment that frames such an individual-level choice as race/ethnicity of one's spouse.

The History of Asian American Intermarriage

As historians point out, early immigrants from Asia, and in particular China, were frequently characterized as evil, filthy, and completely incompatible with American society (Tchen 2001). As Kitano and Daniels (2000) detail, historians such Hubert Howe Bancroft, the first important English-language historian of California, is an ideal example of this era of hostility and contempt directed against Asian immigrants, as he insisted that the Chinese were "alien in every sense" and derided the "color of their skins, the repulsiveness of their features, their undersize of figure, their incomprehensible language, strange customs and heathen religion." (Kitano and Daniels 2000). As another example before becoming president, Woodrow Wilson wrote that "Caucasian laborers could not compete with the Chinese . . . who, with their yellow skin and debasing habits of life, seemed to them hardly fellow men at all, but evil spirits rather" (Kitano and Daniels, 2000).

At the height of this anti-Chinese and anti-Asian "yellow peril" movement and on the heels of other restrictive legislation, antimiscegenation laws were enacted that prohibited "Mongolian" races from intermarrying with Whites (Chan 1991; Fong 1998; Takaki 1998). While there have been interracial marriages since before the U.S. was founded as an independent nation (Pagnini and Morgan 1990), strict anti-miscegenation laws restricted marriage between Whites and racial/ethnic minorities from becoming commonplace (Kalmijn 1993; Moran 2001). In fact, not until 1967 did the U.S. Supreme Court rule that such laws were unconstitutional. While these anti-miscegenation laws affected virtually all immigrants from Asia, they seemed to have the most negative impact on the emerging Filipino community in that Filipinos had developed the reputation of being the most inclined toward socializing with White women and history shows that they encountered much hostility because of this real or perceived tendency (Chan 1991). Filipinos fought these anti-miscegenation laws by arguing that they were of "Malay" origin, rather than "Mongolian" but were ultimately unsuccessful in escaping these restrictions.

The primary effect of such laws was to severely restrict marriages between Asian Americans and Whites and to cripple incorporation into American society, despite wishes and sincere attempts on the part of many Asian Americans to do so. At the same time, many scholars argue that such restrictions facilitated the development of Asian ethnic enclaves as a reaction to the exclusion and discrimination they received at the hands of American society. Retreating into their own immigrant enclaves as a matter of economic and physical survival, many of these isolated Asian communities eventually became largely self-sufficient and ultimately played a vital role in the slow social-psychological and cultural incorporation of Asian immigrants and successive Asian American generations into mainstream society (Hing 1993; Okihiro 2001; Zia 2000).

However, when anti-miscegenation laws were repealed in the late 1960s, the demographic structure of intergroup contact began to assert itself. Asian Americans, because of their small population size, were much more likely to have interpersonal contact with Whites, as the overwhelmingly largest population, than with other racial/ethnic groups (Blalock 1967; Blau and Duncan 1977). Combined with the rapidly growing nature of the Asian American population, this structural phenomenon played a key role in the expansion of intermarriage between Whites and Asian Americans.

Contemporary Dynamics of Asian Intermarriage

Class and Status Mobility

Sociologists offer some hypotheses on why Asians (or any other racial/ethnic minority group) may want to intermarry with Whites. For example, Gordon's (1964) theory suggests that marrying a White person is the ultimate form of assimilation and signifies full acceptance by White society. Therefore, an Asian American may marry a White person because s/he (consciously or unconsciously) wants to be fully accepted in White society. Merton's (1941) exchange thesis posits that racial/ethnic minorities could attain high income and occupational success to offset their perceived lower racial/ethnic status in order to intermarry with Whites (Jacobs and Labov 2002). The exchange thesis has been used to explain the predominance of Blacks men intermarrying with White women at a much higher rate than Black women intermarrying with White men. However, its applicability to Asian Americans (and to a lesser extent Hispanic Americans) has been challenged (Fu 2001; Jacobs and Labov 2002; Zai and Ito 2001).

Following from this notion, the theory of hypergamy argues that Asian Americans (and other racial/ethnic minorities) marry Whites to increase their social status, since Whites generally occupy the highest socio-cultural position in the U.S.'s racial hierarchy (Hwang, Saenz and Aguirre 1997; Kitano et al. 1984; Root 2001). In other words, even if a working-class Asian American marries another working-class White, her social status will still improve, compared a marriage to someone else in her ethnic group or even another Asian. In this sense, intermarriage can also be seen as a strategy to augment socioeconomic attainment or as a corollary development as the racial/ethnic minority achieves income and occupational mobility and becomes more structurally assimilated into mainstream American society.

Another hypothesis points out that a racial/ethnic minority who marries a White may be motivated to abandon his ancestral identity, possibly to escape perceived societal stigmas associated with that identity in favor of identifying with the majority group (Kalmijn 1993; Pagnini and Morgan 1990). The case of Japanese Americans after their internment during World War II illustrates this notion. Takezawa (2000) explains that many Japanese Americans ceased to identify themselves as Japanese in the aftermath of their internment experiences, as they associated being Japanese with shame and embarrassment, and that only through the subsequent events surrounding the redress movement did they "rediscover" their Japanese identity and feel comfortable identifying as such again. In their study of Asian American intermarriages in New York City, Zai and Ito (2001) also find that Asian American women were more likely than their male counterparts to exhibit linguistic and behavioral patterns that suggested attenuation of their cultural/ethnic attachment after marrying Whites.

Many scholars also point out that beyond cultural factors, structural-level conditions can have important influence in the marriage process. Specifically, geographic location is one factor that can significantly impact available marriage pools (Blau, Blum and Schwartz 1982; Kalmijn 1998). Simply put, in areas where there is a large concentration of a given racial/ethnic group, there will be more chances to marry endogamously compared to areas in which a given racial/ethnic group is more dispersed (Edmondson and Passel 1999). In this context, the research generally finds that intermarriage is more common inside metropolitan and urban areas (Lee and Yamanaka 1990). The effects of group size and marriage market size on intermarriage have been the subject of debate among sociologists and many strategies have been used to account for geographic and locational variability (Schoen 1986). For example, Harris and Ono (2005) caution that collapsing local marriage markets into one large national statistical agglomeration lead to overestimates of intermarriage between Whites and Asian Americans and Latinos. Lee and Fernandez (1998) prefer to account for group size by calculating the Index of Intermarriage Distance to illustrate relative levels of social distance between two groups, and which has controls for group size built into the equation.

Gender Differentials

The extant research also consistently shows that Asian American women are much more likely to intermarry with Whites than are Asian American men, even after controlling for socioeconomic characteristics (Jacobs and Labov 2002; Lee and Fernandez 1998; Zai and Ito 2001). Many scholars argue that historically, it was very common for Asian women to be portrayed as docile, subservient, exotic, and/or mysteriously seductive and that these distorted images lead White males to "fetishize" Asian American women (Fong 1998; Lee 1999; Yu 2000). These images can be traced back to Chinese prostitutes who were "imported" into the U.S. back in the 1800s and continue to be perpetuated in many contemporary television shows and movies. These biased perceptions can also lead to the stereotype of Asian women of being more accepting of traditional patriarchal forms of marriage and gender roles (Kalmijn 1998). Further, the presence of U.S. military personnel in Asian countries such as Japan, Korea, the Philippines, and Viet Nam after World War II led to the phenomenon of "war brides" (Asian women marrying U.S. military servicemen) that further contributes to the gender imbalances in regard to intermarriage among Asians (although the presence of war brides obviously does not exist in regard to Asian American women born or raised in the U.S.)

These critics of Asian American intermarriage point out that in most areas of popular American culture, rarely does one see the opposite happening—Asian males being the subjects of infatuation or sexual desire by White women. Such critics also note that Asian males have been and continue to be popularly portrayed as non-sexual martial arts experts, nerds and geeks, or evil villains and that this portrayal serves to eliminate Asian males as potential rivals to White males for the affection of Asian women (Fong 1998; Lee 1999; Yu 2000). This ongoing debate on the motivations for White intermarriage, particularly among Asian women, directs us to look at how both Asian American men and women can become the targets of objectification and how this reinforces and perpetuates ethnic stereotypes against both. At the same time, there are several barriers that can impede Asian intermarriage with Whites and other non-Asian racial/ethnic groups. For example, the legacy of anti-Asian sentiment in America has led to persistent cultural stereotypes about Asian Americans, including but not limited to Asians being all the same, Asians as perpetual foreigners who are not interested in assimilating into American society, and perceptions of Asians (particularly men) as "nerdy," strange, evil and or at least devious (Lee 1999; Lowe 1996; Yu 2000).

On the "supply" side, cultural traditions that have historically restricted intermarriage include many families' strict adherence to ethnic traditions and attitudes on marriage and the family. These norms and behaviors often prescribe that Asian American children concentrate on their academic performance and professional preparation rather than their social activities and that they give deference to their parents' authority and wishes on how the children's lives should develop. In addition, cultural norms about Asian children and adults having to take care of their parents as they grow older and more frail often preclude intermarriage proclivities (Ferguson 2000; Lee and Yamanaka 1990). Many times, particularly for young Asian immigrant women, they are forced into marrying within their own ethnic group by family members and cultural traditions (Fong and Yung 2000). These critiques may also gloss over how patriarchy and sexism can still exist within many elements of traditional Asian culture and that many Asian women conclude that these beliefs are rather restrictive and clash with contemporary notions of gender equality in American society.

Asian Intermarriage with non-Whites

While most forms of Asian American intermarriage involve partnering with White spouses, we cannot neglect that there are sizeable instances in which Asian Americans intermarry with other Asians of a different ethnicity (a "pan-Asian" marriage), or with Blacks, Hispanics, or Native Americans (although examples of marriages with last group are exceedingly rare). In fact, many scholars have noted that the prevalence of pan-Asian marriages seems to be increasing among Asian Americans (Lee and Fernandez 1998; Shinagawa and Pang 1996). Such pan-Asian marriages were quite scarce a few decades ago, mainly because the relatively small size of the Asian American population mitigated a large marriage pool of potential pan-Asian spouses. However, with the unprecedented influx of Asian immigrants starting in the late 1960s, the Asian American population and resultant marriage pool as increased substantially.

Along with that, the development of a pan-Asian racial identity has also facilitated more inter-ethnic Asian contact and interaction. While scholars such as Espiritu (1992) note that there are numerous historical and contemporary political and cultural barriers that potentially attenuate a strengthening of the pan-Asian racial identity (i.e., no common language, histories of military conflict between Asian countries, etc.), others observe that there may be a cultural and political connection between more pan-Asian marriages and the development of a pan-Asian racial identity, especially among the U.S.-born generations (Rosenfeld 2001; Shinagawa and Pang 1996). The question becomes, what exactly is the relationship between greater pan-Asian racial identity and more pan-Asian marriages, how likely are both phenomena to increase in the near future, and what implications does this connection have for the larger assimilation picture of Asian Americans?

In contrast, the prevalence of Asian American intermarriages with Black and Latino spouses are generally much lower than pan-Asian intermarriages. There are very few studies on these forms of Asian American intermarriage, mainly because the prevalence of such unions remains low, although there are individual exceptions with particular Asian groups to be described. In reading the occasional personal narrative, we find that in many cases, there seems to be a strong cultural taboo within Asian communities against unions with Blacks and to a slightly lesser extent, Latinos (Root 2001). One reason for this is the perceived racial hierarchy of the U.S. with Whites at the top and Blacks and Latinos at the bottom. Many Asian immigrants may be heavily influenced by stereotypical images of Blacks and Latinos in the American media and many Asian small business owners find themselves located in inner city urban areas where most of their customers are poor and working class Blacks and Latinos. In these situations, biased perceptions by Asian immigrants can be more readily reinforced against Blacks and Latinos.

Because Asian-Black and Asian-Latino marriages are still relatively rare[1], this chapter will focus on describing the general patterns of marriage among the five Asian American ethnic groups in question in terms of endogamous marriage, pan-Asian intermarriage (marrying an Asian of a

---

[1] Although not characteristic of just Asians, the traditional Asian pursuit of status within the community and the larger society frequently leads to a rigid prohibition against interpersonal relationships with groups that are perceived to be of "lower" social standing than themselves, in this case Blacks and Hispanics/Latinos. This bias can also be further fueled by persistent stereotypes, exaggerated negative media portrayals, or strained owner-customer relations in Asian small businesses (Abelmann and Lie 1995; Cheng and Espiritu 1989; Jo 1992; Waldinger 1995). In this context, it is not surprising that many Asian families, being foreign-born and not yet fully integrated in the particulars of American history and race relations, translate these images and beliefs into strong opposition against intermarrying with Blacks and Hispanics/Latinos. The question will be to what extent younger and presumably, more assimilated Asian Americans refute these prohibitions and marry Blacks and Hispanics/Latinos.

different ethnicity), and intermarriage with Whites. In addition, following the lead of Hwang, Saenz, and Aguirre (1997), the analysis will focus on those Asian Americans who were either born in the U.S. or came to the U.S. as children (the 1.5 generation), since the goal is to determine which factors affect marriage decisions in the context of their lives as Asian Americans. In doing so, we avoid confounding the results by including Asians who were already married once they arrived in the U.S. These patterns will be further analyzed along selected characteristics including gender, nativity, and U.S. birth. The purposes of these analyses are (1) compare intermarriage rates between Vietnamese Americans and other Asian American ethnic groups and (2) identify and interpret the role that the cultural environment have in the role of such a personal and individual choice such as decisions about marriage partners.

Data and Methodology

To measure and analyze how various demographic, structural, and individual-level factors influence rates of endogamous Asian marriage, pan-Asian intermarriage, and intermarriage with Whites for Vietnamese, Chinese, Filipino, Asian Indian, and Koreans of both genders, data comes from the 2000 Census 5% PUMS national sample. The research is limited to adults who are at least 18 years of age and who are married with spouse present. Japanese Americans are not included in this analysis because in terms of demographic characteristics, contrary to the five other Asian groups included herein, they are largely third and fourth generation (Census Bureau 2001), thereby making meaningful comparisons among the other Asian ethnic groups difficult. Also, in order to focus on factors of Asian American life that influence marriage decisions, the analysis is limited to the U.S. raised—those who are either U.S.-born or who immigrated to the U.S. before age 13 (the 1.5 generation). Excluding respondents that got married prior to immigration avoids the potential of confounding the results, as this group tends to inflate in-group marriage rates (see Hwang, Saenz and Aguirre 1997).

Logistic regression models will be used, with three separate dependent variables analyzed: having an endogamous (intraethnic), pan-Asian (another Asian from a different ethnic group), or White spouse. Models that have an endogamous spouse as the dependent variable will be analyzed using ordinary logistic regression while the two remaining dependent variables (having a pan-Asian or White spouse) will be analyzed using multinomial logistic regression—one set with the endogamous spouse model used as the comparison model and a final set for pan-Asian spouse using White spouse as the comparison model. Using multinomial logistic regression allows us to more accurately compare the effects of independent variables between the pan-Asian and White spouse models, since these two outcomes best represent greater marital assimilation vis-à-vis having an endogamous spouse.

In these logistic regression models, independent variables will include three categories of factors. First are factors relating to human capital including having a college degree or higher versus less than high school completion, being a homeowner, having a high skill occupation, working in a professional services industry, working in an "enclave-associated" industry (see the Methodology section of the Introduction chapter), not being proficient in English, and logged income. Also used are "social capital" variables that include being self-employed, U.S.-born (to differentiate the second generation from the 1.5), living in either the Los Angeles/Orange County, and New York/Northeastern New Jersey, or San Francisco/San Jose CMSA (an rough proxy of social capital in the form of a greater likelihood of living near or participating in an Asian American ethnic community or enclave).

The third set of factors that will be used in logistic regression models is ethnic group identity—Chinese, Filipino, Korean, and Vietnamese (with Asian Indian excluded as the reference category).

These variables allow us to determine if being a member of that particular Asian ethnic group, by itself and net of independent factors, is directly associated with the likelihood of being married to Whites, Blacks, Hispanics, or Other Asian Americans. With the inherent limitations of Census data, this is the best approximation available to measure ethnic culture characteristics that may impact the intermarriage decision. Further, interaction variables involving Vietnamese and college degree attainment, high skill occupation, and living in the LA/OC, NYC, or SF/SJ areas are also included to measure how these variables influence intermarriage outcomes for Vietnamese specifically. We also note that another limitation regarding Census data (and cross sectional data in general) is the ambiguity surrounding causality. That is, while using Census data, we cannot be completely certain that independent factors (college attainment, occupation, being self-employed, homeownership, etc.) occurred before the dependent variable (becoming married). As such, we must exercise caution in interpreting regression analyses with an eye toward considering alternative explanations and uncertainty regarding causality.

Results

Descriptive Patterns

Table 21.1 presents descriptive statistics on the proportion of marriages by Asian ethnicity of husbands and wives and the race/ethnicity of their spouses. It also disaggregates these statistics by total U.S.-raised and by U.S.-born only. In looking at the rates across all five all U.S.-raised Asian American groups, it becomes clear that there is a notable gender difference when it comes to the choice of spouse among U.S-born and 1.5 generation Asian Americans. Specifically, for all five Asian ethnic groups, women are more likely to outmarry than men. Also, in each of the five Asian groups, women are more likely to be married to Whites and Blacks than are men. On the other hand, in all instances, Asian men are more likely to have a pan-Asian spouse than are women. Looking at the rates for each of the Asian groups separately, the results reveal that Vietnamese American husbands have the highest rates of endogamous marriage among all Asian husbands listed while Vietnamese wives have the highest inmarriage rates among Asian American women, along with Chinese and Asian Indians.

The results also show that Chinese and Vietnamese men and women have the highest rates of having a pan-Asian spouse. Further, Korean, Filipino, and Asian Indian men have the highest rates of having a White spouse while for women, Koreans have the highest White intermarriage rates by far (the only Asian group to be over 50%). The results in Table 21.1 also indicate that Chinese and Vietnamese husbands have rates of being in an endogamous marriage that are more than twice that for a marriage to a White spouse. Among the women however, only Asian Indian, Chinese, and Vietnamese wives have endogamous rates that higher than that for White intermarriage and in fact, Filipino and Korean wives are significantly more likely to be married to a White spouse than to an endogamous one. In short, there are significant gender differences in U.S.-raised Asian American marriage patterns, with women much more likely to outmarry than men. In addition, these gender differences roughly correspond to ethnic differences as well, as Filipinos and Koreans of both genders are more likely to outmarry than Asian Indians, Chinese, and Vietnamese.

The proportions of each marriage outcome for U.S.-born Asian American husbands and wives do not differ much at all from the total proportions and generally confirm the overall findings. In fact, there are only a few instances in which there are statistically significant differences between proportions for the total U.S.-raised and U.S.-born. Nonetheless, these few instances of difference

TABLE 21.1   Rates (Percents) of Marriage by Spouse's Race/Ethnicity, Gender, and Nativity Status, 2000

Asian Indians

	Total		U.S.-Born	
	Husbands (632)	Wives (708)	Husbands (309)	Wives (352)
Asian Indian	51.7	46.2	52.4	47.2
Pan-Asian	3.2	2.0	2.9	2.0
White	35.3	40.5	34.0	36.6
Black	2.8	5.4	3.9	7.4
Hispanic	5.5	3.1	4.9	3.7

Chinese

	Total		U.S.-Born	
	Husbands (2,781)	Wives (3,319)	Husbands (2,052)	Wives (2,400)
Chinese	55.4	46.4	53.2	44.9
Pan-Asian	12.9	10.7	14.4	11.4
White	25.5	36.5	25.6	37.3
Black	0.3	0.8	0.3	0.8
Hispanic	3.2	3.1	3.3	2.8

Filipino

	Total		U.S.-Born	
	Husbands (2,251)	Wives (2,940)	Husbands (1,436)	Wives (1,753)
Filipino	36.6	28.0	32.9**	27.0
Pan-Asian	10.2	7.1	12.0*	8.2
White	36.1	46.3	37.5	44.8
Black	0.7	4.3	0.8	4.1
Hispanic	9.4	8.2	8.6	8.1

Korean

	Total		U.S.-Born	
	Husbands (631)	Wives (1,153)	Husbands (247)	Wives (373)
Korean	46.6	25.5	39.3*	25.5
Pan-Asian	10.6	7.7	16.2*	12.3**
White	37.1	60.7	36.0	55.2*
Black	0.3	1.9	0.4	1.3
Hispanic	3.3	2.6	4.5	2.9

Vietnamese

	Total		U.S.-Born	
	Husbands (514)	Wives (651)	Husbands (85)	Wives (130)
Vietnamese	62.3	49.2	75.3*	53.8
Pan-Asian	11.3	8.6	3.5*	3.1*
White	19.5	36.7	11.8*	36.2
Black	0.8	1.2	1.2	1.5
Hispanic	3.7	2.9	5.9	3.1

Differences between Total U.S.-Raised and U.S.-Born significant at the *p≤.05 and **p≤.01 levels.

[a] Sample sizes for husbands and wives in parentheses.

[b] Universe: At least 18 years of age and U.S.-Raised.

[c] "Other Asian American": Asian Indian, Chinese, Filipino, Japanese, Korean, or Vietnamese (excluding the reference group).

[d] Percentages for each group do not add up to 100 because spouses may be of a difference race/ethnicity than those listed.

are particularly noteworthy. Specifically, U.S.-born Filipino and Korean men are less likely to have an endogamous wife and are more likely to have a pan-Asian spouse than their 1.5 generation counterparts. In addition, U.S.-born Korean women are less likely than their 1.5 generation counterparts to have a White husband but more likely to have a pan-Asian husband (although the final rate of having a White spouse still overshadow that for having a pan-Asian spouse). These aforementioned instances may suggest that pan-Asian marriages are increasingly common among U.S.-born Filipino and Korean men and Korean women, which tend to be viewed as an indicator of greater assimilation compared to being in an endogamous marriage.

However, the situation for U.S.-born Vietnamese seems to represent the opposite finding. That is, U.S.-born Vietnamese men are more likely to have an endogamous spouse and less likely to have either a pan-Asian or White spouse than their 1.5 generation counterparts. In addition, U.S.-born Vietnamese women are less likely to have a pan-Asian spouse than their 1.5 generation counterparts. Although the sample sizes for U.S.-born Vietnamese men and women are still relatively low, these findings may suggest that in contrast to other Asian groups for whom being U.S.-born is increasingly associated with greater marital assimilation, being U.S.-born for Vietnamese may be associated with more endogamous marriage and therefore, less marital assimilation.

Logistic Regression Results

Now that we have a basic statistical description of marriage patterns among U.S.-raised Asian Americans, the question becomes, what factors are associated with which marriage outcome? To examine this question, we turn our attention to factors that affect the likelihood of having a co-ethnic, pan-Asian, or White spouse. Tables 21.2 and 21.3 present results of logistic regression analysis on these dependent variables, with all five Asian American ethnic groups combined into a single sample, for husbands and wives respectively. According to conventional research on assimilation, we would expect endogamous marriages to be associated with lower levels of structural assimilation. On the other side of the spectrum, conventional assimilation models would predict that marriages to Whites should be associated with higher levels of structural assimilation.

Therefore, being U.S.-born, college degree, logged income, high skill occupation, and professional services industry should have negative effects on the likelihood of endogamous marriage but positive effects on White intermarriage. Conversely, lack of English proficiency, less than high school education, being self-employed, and living in the LA/OC, NYC, or SF/SJ metropolitan area should have positive effects on endogamous marriage and negative effects on White intermarriage. We might consider pan-Asian marriages to occupy a middle ground along this continuum, from a cultural standpoint. Therefore, making assumptions about how different factors may affect this particular marriage outcome is bound to involve much uncertainty so for now, we will refrain from doing so and will just observe what the actual results tell us.

Looking at Table 21.2 for Asian American men, the results for the first marriage outcomes, endogamous Asian American marriages, reveal that for the most part, the conventional assumptions hold true. That is, lack of English proficiency, less than a high school education, and LA/OC, NYC, or SF/SJ metro area all have positive effects on the likelihood of being in an endogamous marriage while logged income has a negative effect. However, results regarding other variables did not conform to these conventional assumptions. Specifically, college degree and high skill occupation both had positive effects on endogamous marriage, contrary to usual sociological expectations. The results for endogamous marriage in Table 21.2 also point out that each Asian ethnic group in the model had a negative effect relative to Vietnamese as the reference group and that none of the Vietnamese interaction variables had any effect. Therefore, it appears that while there is still support for conventional assimilationist assumptions, there are enough irregularities in the results to suggest that the support is less than complete.

The factors that affect the likelihood of having a pan-Asian spouse, the results from Table 21.2 (calculated using multinomial logistic regression, along with the White spouse model) suggest that the conventional assumptions once again generally hold true. That is, lack of English proficiency, less than high school education, and living in LA/OC, NY/NJ, or SF/SJ areas had negative effects on the likelihood of having a White spouse, while being U.S.-born had a positive effect. These results are in line with what we would expect according to conventional assimilation models and as previously mentioned, they are stand in contrast to the results for factors affecting being in an endogamous marriage. That is, there are no instances in which the effects for the independent variables are the same between the endogamous and pan-Asian model. Rather, the multinomial logistic regression coefficients tell us that in relation to having an endogamous spouse as the base comparison model, those Asian men who have a pan-Asian wife are much

TABLE 21.2 Factors Affecting the Race/Ethnicity of Spouse among Asian American Men, 2000

	Race/Ethnicity of Wife			
	Endogamous (Ordinary Logistic)	Pan-Asian (Multinomial, Endog. Base)	White (Multinomial Endog. Base)	Pan-Asian (Multinomial, White Base)
Intercept	.31	−1.53	−.99	−.54**
Age	.01**		−.02**	.02**
U.S.-born	−.33**	.55**	.25**	.30**
Not English proficient	1.24**	−1.25**	−1.75**	
Less than high school	.59**	−.66**	−.88**	
College degree	.19**			
Logged personal income	−.08*		.10**	
Homeowner	.19**			
Self-employed				
High skill occupation	.16*		−.17**	
Professional services ind.				
Enclave industry				
LA, NY, or SF CMSA	1.00**	−.62**	−1.30**	.69**
Asian Indian	.27*	−1.43**	.63**	−2.06**
Chinese	−.33**		.53**	−.57**
Filipino	−.88**		1.07**	−1.00**
Korean	−.57**		.88**	−.83**
χ^2	665		782	
−2 Log Likelihood	8,514		10,603	

Note: Endogamous model coefficients calculated using ordinary logistic regression; Pan-Asian and White models calculated using multinomial logistic regression with endogamous spouse as the base comparison; Final Pan-Asian model calculated using multinomial logistic regression with White spouse as the base comparison.

[a] *p≤.05; **p≤.01.

[b] Universe: Married, at least 18 years of age, and U.S.-raised.

[c] Omitted category: Vietnamese.

more likely to be U.S.-born and proficient in English and less likely to live in the LA/OC, NY/NJ, or SF/SJ metropolitan areas.

In fact, the bulk of the results are more similar to the White intermarriage model. The results for factors that affect the likelihood of having a White spouse reveal that similar to the pan-Asian model being U.S.-born has a positive effect while lack of English proficiency less than high school education, and living in LA/OC, NY/NJ, or SF/SJ areas all had negative effects. The White spouse model also adds age and high skill occupation (interestingly) as negative factors and logged income as a positive factor. Because the White spouse model was analyzed using multinomial logistic regression along with the pan-Asian model, we are able to compare the magnitude of effects between these two models.

Looking at the last column in Table 21.2 that shows multinomial logistic regression coefficients for having a pan-Asian spouse vis-à-vis a White spouse as the base comparison, we see that being U.S.-born has a positive effect. This funding seems to suggest that either U.S.-born Asian Americans, controlling for other factors, are more likely to have a pan-Asian rather than a White spouse, or that among Asian American men in a pan-Asian marriage, they are overwhelming U.S.-born. Another interesting comparison is that living inside the LA/OC, NY/NJ, or SF/SJ metropolitan areas also has a positive effect for having a pan-Asian spouse, a clear indication that Asians who live outside areas with large numbers of Asian Americans are much more likely to have a White versus a pan-Asian spouse. At the same time, the results from this column in Table 21.2 show that age has a positive effect for having a pan-Asian spouse, meaning that younger Asians are more likely to be married to Whites than to other Asians, a finding that appears to contradict the notion that the most recent cohort of Asian Americans tends to be very likely to have a pan-Asian spouse. If anything, these conflicting findings illustrate that the entire landscape of marital assimilation among Asian Americans is quite complex and requires more detailed examination to completely understand the multidimensional dynamics of this process Nonetheless, these comparisons between the pan-Asian and White spouse models do support the notion that pan-Asian marriage might represent a middle ground between endogamous and White marriages.

Looking at the same analyses for U.S.-raised Asian American women in Table 21.3, the results are generally comparable. Similar to the results for their male counterparts, the data show that in the endogamous model, age, lack of English proficiency, less than a high school education, and living in LA/OC, NY/NJ, or SF/SJ areas all had positive effects. At the same time, being U.S.-born and logged income all had negative effects, similar to their male counterparts. At the same time and again similar to Asian American men, there are some exceptions including a positive effect for professional services industry (compared to no effect for men) and negative effects for college degree (positive for men) and self-employment (no effect for men). Further, there was no effect on being a homeowner or high skill occupation for women, compared to the positive effects for men. In addition, the results for the endogamous model show that Filipinos and Koreans had negative effects relative to Vietnamese as the reference category while Chinese had a positive effect, whereas all four Asian groups had negative effects for men. Once again, the conventional assimilation assumptions are generally confirmed in the results for endogamous marriage for women.

Also similar to their male counterparts, the results for U.S.-raised Asian American women in the pan-Asian marriage model (again calculated using multinomial logistic regression, along with the White spouse model) suggests that the traditional assimilationist assumptions are once again confirmed. For instance, using endogamous marriages as the base comparison model, being U.S.-born and logged income have strong positive effects on pan-Asian marriage. In addition, age and living in the LA/OC, NY/NJ, or SF/SJ areas have negative effects on pan-Asian marriage, compared to positive ones for endogamous marriage. These results for factors associated with having a pan-Asian spouse for Asian American women are also rather similar to those for having a White spouse. That is, for both models, age, lack of English proficiency, less than high school completion, and living in the LA/OC, NY/NJ, or SF/SJ areas all have negative effects while being U.S.-born, college degree attainment, logged income, and being self-employed all have positive effects. All these factors confirm traditional assimilationist assumptions, with the possible exception of the

TABLE 21.3 Factors Affecting the Race/Ethnicity of Spouse among Asian American Women

	Race/Ethnicity of Husband			
	Endogamous (Ordinary Logistic)	Pan-Asian (Multinomial, Endog. Base)	White (Multinomial, Endog. Base)	Pan-Asian (Multinomial, White Base)
Intercept	−.28	−2.29	−.15	−2.15**
Age	.02**	−.01**	−.02**	.01**
U.S.-born	−.23**	.49**	.17**	.32**
Not English proficient	1.12**	−1.39**	−1.2**	
Less than high school	.47**	−.69**	−.63**	
College degree	−.14*		.26**	
Logged personal income	−.07**	.11*	.08**	
Homeowner				
Self-employed	−.36**	.38*	.43**	
High skill occupation				
Professional services ind.	.12*			
Enclave industry				
LA, NY, or SF CMSA	.81**	−.57**	−.97**	.41**
Asian Indian		−1.65**		−1.87**
Chinese	.22*			
Filipino	−.87**		.81**	−.67**
Korean	−1.11**	.48*	1.27**	−.80**
χ^2	671		806	
−2 Log Likelihood	9,068		11,549	

Note: Endogamous model coefficients calculated using ordinary logistic regression; Pan-Asian and White models calculated using multinomial logistic regression with endogamous spouse as the base comparison; Final Pan-Asian model calculated using multinomial logistic regression with White spouse as the base comparison.

[a] *p≤05; **p≤.01.

[b] Universe: Married, at least 18 years of age, and U.S.-raised.

[c] Omitted category: Vietnamese.

positive effect for being self-employed, since conventional hypotheses hold that self-employment is associated with lower levels of structural assimilation (although her self-employment in some cases may be in a high skill occupation as a doctor or lawyer, for example).

However, using multinomial logistic regression allows us to more directly compare the effects between the pan-Asian and White spouse models. In doing so by examining the last column in

Table 21.3, we observe that similar to males, being U.S.-born again has a positive effect in the pan-Asian model. This may suggest that either U.S.-born Asian Americans are much more likely to marry a pan-Asian spouse than a White spouse (net of independent factors) or that a predominant number of those who have pan-Asian spouses possess these characteristics of being U.S.-born. However, once again similar to their male counterparts, age has a positive effect which means that young Asian American women are more likely to marry Whites than a pan-Asian husband. Therefore, we must proceed with caution in hypothesizing that while pan-Asian marriages are still relatively rare compared to White intermarriages, there are indications that the emerging U.S.-born group of Asian Americans (men and women) may be more likely to choose pan-Asian marriages over White ones (also as suggested in Table 21.1 for U.S.-born Filipino and Korean men and Korean women).

Now that we have a better idea about factors that affect marriage outcomes for Asian Americans as a combined group, we turn our attention to analyses that compare these factors among the five Asian ethnic groups, as presented in Table 21.4. (The models for each Asian group include both men and women, with a control variable for male.) The same expectations on which factors are likely to affect which marriage outcomes still hold true here. With that in mind, the results

TABLE 21.4 Factors Affecting Spouses' Race/Ethnicity by Asian American Ethnic Group

	Asian Indian	Chinese	Filipino	Korean	Vietnamese
Endogamous Spouse					
Intercept	.73**	−1.11**	−.32**	−2.61**	−.64**
Age		.03**		.02**	
Male	.48**	.40**	.49**	1.05**	.51**
U.S.-born		−.44**	−.30**		.41*
Not English proficient		1.25**	.74**	1.79**	1.44**
Less than high school		.98**	.46**	.62†	.52*
College degree		.12**	−.28**	.91**	−.33*
Logged income	−.13*	−.09**	−.08*		
Self-employed		−.16†	−.28†	−.42†	
Homeowner		.41**	.15*	−.20†	
High skill occupation		.11†			.58**
Professional services ind.					
Enclave industry		−.18†		.32†	.28†
LA, NY, or SF CMSA	.66**	1.03**	.65**	1.43**	.77**
χ^2	46.7	656	180	295	90.5
−2 Log Likelihood	1,548	7,104	5,741	1,645	1,320

	Asian Indian	Chinese	Filipino	Korean	Vietnamese
Pan-Asian Spouse (Multinomial Endog. Base)					
Intercept	−4.57	−.90	−2.95	−2.35	−.70
Age		−.03**	.02**		−.07**
Male				−.55**	
U.S.-born		.62**	.61**	.61**	−.97†
Not English proficient		−1.19*	−1.20†		−1.15†
Less than high school		−.98*	−.73*	−1.07†	
College degree			.29*	−.58*	
Logged income					
Self-employed					
Homeowner	−.93*	−.35**			
High skill occupation					
Professional services ind.					
Enclave industry		.29†			
LA, NY, or SF CMSA		−.74**	−.68**	.54*	.32†
χ^2	72.3	717	300	403	169
−2 Log Likelihood	1,578	9,348	7,035	2,259	1,592
White Spouse (Multinomial Endog. Base)					
Intercept	−1.91	.73	−.29	2.97	−.59
Age		−.03**		−.03**	
Male	−.52**	−.58**	−.52**	−1.25**	−.90**
U.S.-born		.37**	.26**		−.54*
Not English proficient		−1.56**	−1.15**	−1.80**	−1.51**
Less than high school	−.56†	−1.12**	−.64**	−.79*	−1.13**
College degree			.46**	−.91**	.35†
Logged income	.14*	.10*	.10*		
Self-employed		.18	.39*	.54*	
Homeowner		−.37**			−.27†
High skill occupation					−.63**

(Continued)

TABLE 21.4   Factors Affecting Spouses' Race/Ethnicity by Asian American Ethnic Group (*Continued*)

	Asian Indian	Chinese	Filipino	Korean	Vietnamese
Professional services ind.					
Enclave industry				−.40†	
LA, NY, or SF CMSA	−.82**	−1.21**	−.75**	−1.78**	−1.43**
χ^2	72.3	717	300	403	169
−2 Log Likelihood	1,578	9,348	7,035	2,259	1,592
Pan-Asian Spouse (Multinomial White Base)					
Intercept	−3.37	−1.62	−2.67	−5.33	.46
Age		.01**	.02**	.04**	−.08**
Male		.54**	.49**	.70**	.94**
U.S.-born		.25*	.35**	.61**	
Not English proficient	1.95†				
Less than high school					1.25*
College degree				.34†	
Logged income					
Self-employed					
Homeowner	−1.08**				
High skill occupation					
Professional services ind.					
Enclave industry			.35*		
LA, NY, or SF CMSA	1.04*	.48**			
χ^2	72.3	717	300	403	169
−2 Log Likelihood	1,578	9,348	7,035	2,259	1,592
N	1,153	5,598	4,729	1,544	1,023

Note: Endogamous model coefficients calculated using ordinary logistic regression; Pan-Asian and White models calculated using multinomial logistic regression with endogamous spouse as the base comparison; Final Pan-Asian model calculated using multinomial logistic regression with White spouse as the base.
[a] †p≤.15; *p≤.05; **p≤.01.
[b] Universe: Married, at least 18 years of age, and U.S.-raised.

across the endogamous spouse model generally show that for most Asian groups, the conventional assimilationist hypotheses are confirmed. For example, in instances where there is an effect, lack of English proficiency, less than high school education, and living in the LA/OC, NY/NJ, or SF/SJ metropolitan areas all have positive effects (with logged income having a negative effect) on being in an endogamous marriage.

At the same time, there are some inconsistencies that preclude full support of the traditional assimilationist model. Specifically, U.S.-born has a negative effect for Chinese and Filipinos but a positive one for Vietnamese, which is particularly interesting and suggests that even U.S.-born Vietnamese may still exhibit less marital assimilation (in the conventional sense) compared to other Asian groups. In addition, college degree has a positive effect for Koreans but a negative one for Filipinos and Vietnamese. Finally, although their effects are only statistically significant at the 0.15 level and therefore not valid here, the negative effects for self-employment among Chinese, Filipinos, and Koreans tentatively stand in contrast to conventional expectations. The results for the Vietnamese seem to show some contradictory findings. For instance, being U.S.-born and high skill occupation have positive effects on endogamous marriage (contrary to our expectations) but lack of English proficiency, less a high school degree and enclave-associated industry also have positive effects (in line with our expectations). In general, the results for endogamous marriages in Table 21.4 tend to confirm the findings from Tables 21.2 and 21.3 in that in most cases, the conventional assimilationist expectations are confirmed in regard to factors associated with having an endogamous spouse. However, the results from Table 21.4 once again highlight that there are notable differences among the separate Asian groups and interesting exceptions to the conventional assimilationist expectations, particularly among the Vietnamese.

The results for the pan-Asian marriage model are decidedly much more mixed and represent a more eclectic combination of factors that mimic both the endogamous and White marriage models. Although the incidences of such pan-Asian marriages are still relatively small, they are abundant enough to warrant our attention and plentiful enough to produce significant results. Looking at the multinomial logistic regression coefficients (using the endogamous model as the base comparison), age has positive effects for Filipinos but a negative one for Chinese and Vietnamese. Interestingly, being U.S.-born has positive effects for Chinese, Filipinos, and Koreans but a negative one for Vietnamese. Lack of English proficiency and less than high school completion generally have negative effects (which would indicate that pan-Asian marriage represents higher levels of structural assimilation) as we would expect. Finally, living in the LA/OC, NY/NJ, or SF/SJ metropolitan areas has positive effects for Koreans but negative ones for Chinese and Filipinos.

On the other side of the assimilation spectrum, the results for factors affecting the likelihood of having a White spouse generally show that once again, most of the assumptions according to the traditional assimilation perspective are fulfilled. Again, using multinomial logistic regression for the White spouse model (using the endogamous model as the base comparison), age, lack of English proficiency, less than high school completion, and living in the LA/OC, NY/NJ, or SF/SJ metropolitan areas have negative effects in almost all cases, as we would normally expect. Similarly, being U.S.-born, logged income and college degree attainment both have positive effects. But once again, there are some notable anomalies—college degree has a negative effect for Koreans but more importantly, being U.S.-born has a negative effect for Vietnamese. Therefore, although the results for the White intermarriage model generally correspond to conventional expectations, the results for Vietnamese once again suggest that they stand as notable exceptions to these general patterns of marital assimilation among Asian Americans.

As we compare the multinomial logistic regression results for the likelihood of having a pan-Asian spouse (with having a White spouse as the base comparison), we note one interesting observation. That is, once again being U.S.-born has a positive effect vis-à-vis having a White spouse for Chinese, Filipinos, and Koreans. For these three Asian groups, it once again lends support to the notion that the second, third, and later generation of Asian Americans may be increasingly likely to marry a pan-Asian spouse, although it is likely to take some time before the numbers of pan-Asian marriages equals that for White marriages among U.S.-born Asian Americans. At the same time, we again acknowledge that for Chinese, Filipinos, and Koreans, age has a positive effect and that this finding tempers the hypothesis that contemporary Asian Americans are more likely to have a pan-Asian spouse than ever before. Interestingly however, this last model shows that age has a negative effect for Vietnamese, meaning that younger Vietnamese are more likely to have a pan-Asian spouse than a White one, controlling for other factors.

All in all, the results from Table 21.4 illustrate three main points. First, similar to the findings in Tables 21.2 and 21.3, the data generally support the conventional expectations contained within the traditional assimilationist perspective about which factors are likely to be associated with endogamous versus White intermarriages. Of course, there are the occasional exceptions but for the most part, these expectations hold true. Second, there is a lot of diversity between the five Asian ethnic groups when it comes to specific factors that affect their marriage outcomes. For U.S.-raised Vietnamese specifically, the results across each of the three marital assimilation outcomes suggest some interesting patterns that seem to contradict the traditional assimilation expectations.

For instance, Vietnamese are the only group in which being U.S.-born has a positive effect when it comes to endogamous marriage but a negative effect for both pan-Asian and White marriage models. Vietnamese are also distinctive in exhibiting a positive effect on high skill occupation in the endogamous model combined with a negative effect for the White marriage model. While there are other instances in which the results for Vietnamese conform to the traditional assimilationist model, there are enough notable exceptions to suggest that even those Vietnamese who seem to have high levels of structural assimilation may be less assimilated in terms of exogamy, a finding that is supported by their overall marriage patterns as described in Table 21.1.

Third, the multinomial comparisons between the pan-Asian and White spouse models again support the notion that while still representing a fraction of all outmarriages among Asian Americans, pan-Asian marriages seem to be increasingly prominent within the Asian American population. This trend seems to be especially conspicuous for the latest cohorts of Asian Americans—the U.S.-born, as the results consistently indicate that those who are in pan-Asian marriages are overwhelmingly U.S.-born Asian Americans, or even perhaps that U.S.-born Asian Americans may be increasingly likely to choose a pan-Asian spouse over a White one, controlling for other factors.

Discussion and Analysis

In this discussion of marital assimilation, the data on marriage outcomes among U.S.-raised Asian Americans reveal some interesting comparisons. The results across both genders and Asian American ethnic groups tend to show that in most cases, the traditional assimilationist expectations hold true when it comes to hypothesizing how various independent factors are associated with having either an endogamous, pan-Asian, or White spouse. That is, in regard to endogamous marriages, the data suggests that Asians with endogamous spouses tend to have less human capital and are more likely to live within one of the three metropolitan areas that contain the largest Asian American populations. Conversely, the factors that influence White intermarriage seem to reflect an almost opposite mirror image—Asians with a White spouse tend to be have much higher levels of human capital and are much more likely to live outside of either the either the LA/OC, NY/NJ, or SF/SJ CMSAs.

The finding that Asian Americans living in one of these three CMSAs are much more likely to have an endogamous (and to a lesser extent a pan-Asian) spouse rather than a White one is not surprising. This may suggest that Asian ethnic communities and enclaves may play a significant role in influencing the very personal, individual-level decision of choosing marriage partners. As scholars such as Zhou and Bankston (Bankston and Zhou 1995; Zhou and Bankston 1998) have demonstrated using Vietnamese Americans as an example, the ethnic solidarity within certain Asian communities can be powerful enough to overcome external assimilation pressures in influencing the behaviors of the second and 1.5 generation.

Alternatively, and considering the lack of clarity regarding causality, it may be a demographic-driven phenomenon in which the increasing size of the Asian American population has led to more abundant opportunities for different types of marriage partners. Further, it is certainly possible that this finding may reflect how many endogamous couples tend to gravitate toward Asian-heavy metropolitan areas. Similarly, the finding that human capital variables tend to favor marriages with pan-Asian or White spouses is not surprising either since, as previous chapters have shown, socioeconomic attainment is generally associated with greater structural and cultural assimilation. In the case of marriage decisions, Asians who are more highly skilled, educated, and affluent are more likely to have interpersonal contact with a larger range of racial/ethnic groups, thereby increasing their range of marriage choices.

Ultimately, the comparison of factors affecting the likelihood of having a pan-Asian versus a White spouse seems to tell the most interesting story. In many respects, the regression results in Tables 21.2 and 21.3 indicate that U.S.-raised Asian American men and women who have high levels of human capital and socioeconomic attainment are most likely to have a White spouse, as conventional assimilationist hypotheses predict. At the same time, there are several instances where the same characteristics are also significantly associated with having a pan-Asian spouse. Perhaps the most notable of these findings is in regard to being U.S.-born. That is, for Asian American men and women and two of the Asian ethnic groups, being U.S.-born apparently has stronger associations with having an pan-Asian spouse than with having a White spouse. However, we temper this hypothesis based on the finding that age has a positive effect for pan-Asian marriage, contrary to the pattern suggested by the U.S.-born finding.

On the one hand, this result for being U.S.-born may simply reflect that the overwhelming majority of those in pan-Asian marriages are U.S.-born, much more so than those with White spouses. On the other hand, it may represent a more meaningful pattern whereby U.S.-born Asians who outmarry are exercising a greater range of choices in regard to their marriage partners. While pan-Asian marriages are still relatively rare, the results suggest that as a larger proportion of the Asian American population are composed of the second and later generations, its incidence among and cultural significance for the Asian American population is likely to increase, although it is more difficult to predict just how common the practice actually becomes.

Of course, there is still a considerable amount of socioeconomic diversity and cultural differences among Asian Americans. As some scholars have noted, pan-Asianism as a united voting bloc on the political front still remains an elusive goal (Espiritu 1992), whether or not it is tied to marriage patterns. Nonetheless, the increasing prominence of pan-Asian marriages is certainly plausible for many reasons. For instance, Shinagawa and Pang (1996) hypothesize that there may be several possible reasons for the apparent increase in pan-Asian marriages in recent years. They include the growing size and urban concentration of Asian Americans and the resultant growth of social networks, increased similarity in socioeconomic attainment among Asians, greater acculturation, and a greater degree of a shared group identity based on heightened racial consciousness. Although we cannot say that this trend automatically translates into a broader acceptance and support of a pan-Asian American identity in the cultural or political sense and while rates of pan-Asian marriages will probably have to increase substantially before they significantly impact the dynamics of American race relations, this demographic and sociological phenomenon certainly deserves more attention in years to come.

How does this affect the assimilation patterns of Vietnamese Americans? As previously mentioned, one of the most interesting findings is that in among Asian American men and women and for most Asian ethnic groups, being U.S.-born is strongly associated with having a pan-Asian or White spouse. However, one of those exceptions is Vietnamese Americans for whom being U.S.-born has a strong negative association with having a pan-Asian or Whites spouse and conversely, a positive association for having an endogamous spouse. Combined with the descriptive statistics in Table 21.1 that show Vietnamese already having the highest endogamous (and therefore the lowest exogamous) marriage rates, these results clearly support the notion that when it comes to marital assimilation, Vietnamese are the least socially integrated of the Asian ethnic groups in this research. Perhaps this is due to the relatively recent refugee experiences of many Vietnamese. That is, although U.S.-born Vietnamese Americans have no personal experiences with being refugees from Viet Nam, their parents are likely to have been direct participants in that episode and may still have sentiments and/or family situations that continue to exert a strong influence over the lives of their children, even as their children becomes adults and enter marriage.

While it would be a safe assumption to categorize foreign-raised Vietnamese as the least assimilated of all the major Asian groups due to their refugee status, applying the same categorization to U.S.-raised Vietnamese might be somewhat surprising. At the same time, this finding is not entirely inconsistent with previous chapters that showed that those Vietnamese who have lower levels of human capital and socioeconomic attainment, whether they are foreign- or U.S.-raised, tend to exhibit lower levels of structural assimilation. As such, the marital assimilation patterns of Vietnamese Americans are likely to have lasting repercussions on the racial/ethnic composition of the Vietnamese American population for years and decades to come.

Conclusion

This chapter used 2000 Census data to compare assimilation outcomes between Vietnamese Americans and other Asian American ethnic groups and found that when it comes to choice of spouse (either endogamous, pan-Asian, or Whites), a prominent marker of social assimilation (Alba 1990; Bogardus 1967; Gordon 1964; Lee and Yamanaka 1990; Pagnini and Morgan 1990; Waters 1990). While there are definite indications that pan-Asian and White intermarriages are on the increase among most U.S.-raised Asian Americans, Vietnamese (especially the U.S.-born generation) exhibit characteristics that may call into question the traditional assimilationist expectation that second and later generations are almost instinctively inclined to outmarry.

At the least, the finding among Vietnamese that being U.S.-born is strongly associated with having an endogamous spouse stands in direct contrast to other Asian ethnic groups and lend support to the notion that Vietnamese Americans continue to be the least assimilated of the major Asian ethnic groups in the analysis. Nonetheless, as the incidence of marrying outside one's ethnic group becomes more common, whether the spouse is pan-Asian or White, the sociological dimensions of this phenomenon deserve close scrutiny as a new generation of multiracial, multiethnic, and pan-Asian individuals (Vietnamese and otherwise) will undoubtedly challenge fundamental notions about the meaning of racial/ethnic identity.

Greater than the Sum of Its Parts: The Private & Public Identity of Multiracial/Multiethnic People

Teresa Williams-Leon

Multiracial/multiethnic people (or people who identify as having multiple racial and ethnic backgrounds), are one of the fastest growing socially and politically recognized racial/ethnic groups today. With the election of President Barack Obama in 2008 and the high profile images of "multiracial/multiethnic individuals" in politics, journalism, media, sports, and popular culture such as "first sister," Maya Soetoro-Ng, interim White House Chief of Staff, also known as the "101st Senator, Peter Rouse, Ann Curry of the *Today Show,* Olympic gold medalist, Apolo Ohno, fashion icon Kimora Lee Simmons, professional golfer Tiger Woods, NFL player Hines Ward, and actor Dwayne "the Rock" Johnson, "being mixed with Asian ancestry" has become an integral part of the mainstream racial discourse in the United States. Furthermore, being "part" or "mixed" Asian-Pacific Islander has been placed front and center within and across Asian Pacific American (APA) communities with the proliferation of identity descriptions such **as "hapa," "Amerasian," "mestizo," "biracial," "mixed" and even "quapa."**

Previous debates within Asian American Studies tended to revolve around "the coming of age of multiracially-identified Asian Pacific Islanders," "Where do multiracials belong?," or "Will APA communities disappear with high rates of intermarriage?" (Root, 1992; Root, 1995; Houston & Williams, 1997; Zack, 1997, Williams-Leon & Nakashima, 2001). No longer are multiracial people treated as detrimental, threatening, inconvenient, problematic, or marginal in relationship to APA community status and identity. Increasingly, there has been a recognition of how the growing number of Asian-descent multiracial/multiethnic people has transformed and contributed to the diversity and complexity of how we have come to conceptualize, understand, and appreciate APA identity and community in the 21st century. University courses explore and examine multiracial/multiethnic subjects, conferences incorporate research projects on these topics, students groups have formed, disbanded, and re-formed around multiple racial/ethnic identities, multiracial/multiethnic television personalities and film characters grace magazine covers and headline media programs, news articles and segments commonly feature partial/mixed Asian-descent identity issues.

On one hand, the "What are you?" and "How do you fit in?" questions of personal and social identity seem not as prevalent or urgent for Asian Pacific Islander communities as they once were in the 1980s and 1990s. On the other hand, as the racial and ethnic landscape of the U.S. continues to change dynamically, "race" continues to be articulated and represented in the mainstream as "Black and Brown versus White," "minority versus majority," "legal versus illegal," and "foreign versus American." Within this socio-political backdrop, multiracial/multiethnic people—particularly those of partial/mixed Asian descent—within the context of Asian Pacific

Contributed by Teresa Williams-Leon, Ph.D., Professor in Asian American Studies Department at California State University, Northridge.

Islander communities and Asian American studies, continue to represent how "race" (its so-called positives and negatives) continues to form and transform as it affects and informs the public discourse and every lives of people in the U.S. Multiracial/multiethnic people also continue to create their own spaces of identity expression, to negotiate their private and public identities and to assert the complex, contradictory, and paradoxical characteristics associated with the social processes, organizational realities, and identity formations of "race/ethnicity" and "multiraciality/multiethnicity." This chapter highlights some recurring themes in understanding personal, social and political identity issues as multiracial/multiethnic individuals continue to cultivate a complex understanding of the sociohistorical locations and boundaries of the racial/ethnic groups to which they belong and their interrelationships as they manage, manipulate and present the private and public aspects of their multiple racial and ethnic identities within the U.S. context.

The Growing Presence of Multiracial/ Multiethnic Realities

In 2010, 97% of the total population in the U.S. indicated it identified with only "one race." Those who self-reported as "White" were among the largest "single race" identifying group at 231 million. However, the Black-White multiracial population grew by an astounding 134% from 2000 to 2010. After much debate among various interest groups, the 2000 Census became the first to allow respondents to check "two or more races" (Williams-Leon, 2003; DaCosta, 2007). A New York Times article from March 24, 2011, reported that the number of people in the U.S. who identified with being of "two or more races" in the 2010 Census grew to about 9 million (nearly 3% of the total population in the U.S.). The number of children who identified as multiracial totaled over 4 million and had increased by 50% making it the fastest growing "youth group." (Saulny, March 24, 2011). Between 2008 and 2009, the Pew Research Center also found that one in seven new marriages was between partners of different races and ethnicities (Passel, Wang and Taylor, 2010). Among all newly married couples, 9% of Whites, 16% of African Americans, 26% of Latinos, and 31% Asians married a person of a different race or ethnicity. Among Asians, 40% of women and 20% of men married outside of their race or ethnicity. While the rates of outmarriage doubled for both Whites and Blacks since the 1980s, Asian American and Latino intermarriage rates remained about the same since 1980. (Passel, Wang and Taylor, 2010).

James P. Allen and Eugene Turner in their research on the "Fractional assignment of multiracial populations," had identified in the 1990 and 2000 Census Data that "part White" multiracial populations were among the largest groups to identify with "two or more races." (Allen and Turner). In the 2010 Census, among the majority of those who reported having "more than one race" "part-White" multiracials were again among the most numerous: 1) African American-White (1.8 million), 2) "Some other race" and White (1.7 million); 3) Asian-White (1.6 million); and 4) American Indian or Alaska Native-White (1.4 million). http://2010.census.gov/news/releases/operations/cb 11 cnl25.html

The Asian-White multiracial population stands out as "over-represented" in proportion to the overall size of the APA population in the U.S. Asian-White multiracials are the third largest multiracially-identified group, trailing closely behind Black-White multiracials and Some Other Race-White multiracials. Considering the relatively small,—though the most rapidly growing single-race-identified group,—the Asian American population went from being 10.2 million in 2000 to 14.7 million people in 2010. Native Hawaiians and other Pacific Islanders have been identified as about half a million or 0.2% of the total U.S. population in 2010. When multiracial populations without European ancestry are combined to the overall Asian-descent multiracial/ multiethnic totals, this adds to the multiracial/multiethnic make-up of all communities, but most especially the Asian Pacific Islander communities in which significant demographic shifts seemed to be taking place from immigration, intermarriage, and other structural changes.

No other racial reality than that of examining multiracial/multiethnic identity illuminates the idea that race is a socially constructed and politically maintained invention originally defined on the basis of so-called "shared genetics," and "gene frequencies" (Williams, 1995; Williams-Leon & Nakashima, 2001). Therefore, the concepts of "biracial," "multiracial," and "multiethnic," are also historically constructed, socially maintained, and politically contested markers (Omi and Winant, 1994). For example, while census data provide opportunities to investigate trends and patterns, the data are based upon the "identity choices" expressed by the respondents within the preset categories offered by a government agency, not based on an objective measure of one's genetics (and sense of group identification) articulated as "race." All people are racially mixed with at least two or more "races" and multiple ethnic influences that make up their humanity. Many people often do not know beyond a few generations or so what twists and turns their genealogical paths have taken in order for them to arrive at their fixed understanding of who they are monoracially and monoethnically. I have often been struck by the racial irony when I meet someone of Mexican ancestry and national origin, for example, who will freely talk about being a blend of Spaniard, French, Indian, and African ancestries and in the next sentence describe him or herself as "puro Mexicano!" (pure Mexican). As Williams and Thornton have written in their article, "Social Construction of Ethnicity Versus Personal Experience: The Case of Afroasians ," from *Journal of Comparative Family Studies* (1998), "Perhaps no experience better exposes the contradictions regarding how we view race in America than that of racially mixed individuals . . ." (Williams and Thornton, 1998, p. 255).

The Miscegenated History of Asian Pacific America

While "multiracial people" and "interracial families" have been treated as post-1967 social phenomena and reality, particularly for those of Asian descent, the historical origins of multiraciality among Asian Pacific Islanders date back to the first contact and migration/immigration beginnings in the 1700s. (Williams and Nakashima, 2001). Despite informal and formal mechanisms that discouraged and even prevented the intermingling of Asian Pacific Islanders with non-Asian Pacific Islanders, particularly those of Euro-American descent, multiracial and multiethnic peoples of partial and mixed Asian/Pacific Islander ancestry continued to be born (e.g. the Native Hawaiian-British "hapa ha'ole," the Chinese-Hawaiians and the Portugese-Hawaiians in Hawai'i, the Punjabi-Mexicans in Central California, the Black-Chinese in Mississippi, and Filipino Cajuns/Creoles in Louisiana, etc.). From Filipinos in Louisiana, to Native Hawaiians in Hawai'i, to male Chinese, Filipino, and South Asian Indian laborers and to individuals like Eng and Cheng Bunker (the "Siamese Twins") or Lalu Nathoy (Polly Bemis from the novel, *Thousand Pieces of Gold*), intermarriage and/or the birth of multiracial people of Asian descent have been part of the Asian Pacific American (APA) social landscape.

Anti-Asian immigration exclusion (e.g. Chinese Exclusion Act of 1882, Immigration Act of 1924), anti-Asian naturalization laws and cases (1912 Albert Henry. Young case, 1922 Takeo Ozawa Case, 1923 Bhagat Singh Thind Case), anti-Asian land laws (1913, 1920) and anti-miscegenation laws (Roldan v. Los Angeles County, 1933) and other anti-Asian social and labor movements all served to prevent interpersonal interactions between Asians and non-Asians as equals and therefore curtailed the birth and growth of Asian-descent multiracial and multiethnic peoples.

While structural barriers played a role in keeping "intermarriage rates" and the number of multi-racial people of Asian descent low, it did not prevent them altogether. The history of Asian Pacific America continued to be one that was "miscegenated."

During World War II, those who were 1/8 or more of Japanese ancestry were subject to intern-ment under Executive Order 9066—in essence a "one-drop rule" for the Japanese that cast the widest ancestry net possible to insure that anyone with any amount of Japanese ancestry was subject to this policy. And in the 1940s, when American servicemen were keeping company with women from Japan during the U.S. Occupation and eventually from China, Korea, and Philip-pines, many were not able to marry and bring them to the United States until the War Brides Acts were passed in the mid-1940s. In 1948, California repealed its anti-miscegenation law that had prevented, Indians, Mongolians, Mulattos, Negros and eventually Malays (to include Filipinos) from marrying Whites. And in 1967, the Supreme Court ruled that anti-miscegenation laws were unconstitutional. In 1982 (the Amerasian Immigration Act) and in 1987, the Amerasian Home-coming Act were passed to permit mixed-race American and Southeast Asian children left behind in Southeast Asia to immigrate and "return" to the United States.

The invisibility and "foreign-ness" construction of Asian Americans and Pacific Islanders in the American racial discourse, the proliferation of the one-drop rule and the either-or binary con-struction of race in which a person belonged to "one race only" have all contributed to the further invisibility of multiracial and multiethnic people of Asian-descent. Yet, when re-examining the history of Asian Pacific Islanders as part of the United States, one can see how intermarriage and multiracial/multiethnic peoples have always been an essential part of APA communities and histories. The current state of high APA outmarriage rates and the visibility of Asian-descent mul-tiracials are consistent with the miscegenated history of Asian Pacific America. Williams-Leon & Nakashima have written (2001):

> While Asian American history has been periodized as "pre-1965 and post-1965 migration/immi-gration," it is perhaps more useful to characterize Asian American history as having three periods: (I) pre WWII, a period of antimiscegenation laws as well as interracial cohabitation, marriage, and families; 2) WWII to 1967; and 3) post-1965 immigration and the post-1967 biracial baby boom. Furthermore, U.S. government and military involvement in Asia throughout the twentieth century has produced a continuous flow of multiracial Asian American births, which comprises the largest portion of the multiracial Asian American population.
>
> The removal of legal barriers and ideological shifts around racial constructions and locations have provided the context for growth in legal interracial marriages and multiracial families post-civil rights era. Indeed, for Asian Americans, social integration and open-door immigration policies have contributed to an increase in intermarriage that Joel Crohn (1995) has terms a 'quiet revolu-tion'. It has also let to the exponential growth of the multiracial population or what Maria P.P. Root (1992a) has called 'the biracial baby boom.'" (Williams-Leon & Nakashima, 2001, p. 4–5)

In addition to these continuing trends within and across Asian Pacific America, the interracial mail-order bride families, U.S. families of international and transracial adoptees, and Lesbian/Gay/Bisexual/Transgendered families[1] are becoming part of the discussion in Asian American studies regarding the growing diversity and complexity in the blended constitution of Asian Pacific America.

---

[1] Thomas Beatie, a transgendered Filipino and European American man became one of the first "biological" men to give birth. Beatie made headlines when he crossed gender boundaries and challenged the male-female/mother-father dichot-omy when he gave birth to his children as a man, but it's also interesting to note that Beatie, is multiracial and multiethnic of Filipino and European American ancestries (White mother and Filipino father).

Multi-Raciality/Multiethnicity: Identity Markers & Context

"Race" and "multiraciality' as well as "ethnicity and "multiethnicity" are the primary markers of identity discussed in this chapter. "Multiraciality" is used to indicate "multiple" or more than one "race" and "multiethnicity" for more than one ethnicity. When using the concept, "race," and "multiraciality," I am referencing shared genetics and gene frequencies, in which ancestry, phenotypical descriptions, identity and the history of racialization are embedded. When I use the concept, "ethnicity," and "multiethnicity," I am referring to shared cultural characteristics in ideas, beliefs practices, customs and socialization as well as identity—a sense of one's cultural group self—based on a combination of blurred racial and cultural affiliations as Williams and Thornton have identified in their study of Afroasians,

> There are two significant contributors to ethnicity or racial group identity: a thread of historical experience that is shared by each member of the collectivity, and a sense of potency/strength inherent in the group (see Phinney, 1990). In social science research, racial identity, ostensibly feelings toward the group, is rarely examined with explicitly measures of group feelings. Usually, a racial label is correlated to psychosocial development of group members. In this regard, racial group membership—and not actual experience is normally featured. Thus, race is often used as a proxy for experience and attitudes, a practice embedded in premises of social science literature. (Wilkinson, 1984) (Williams and Thornton, 1998)

It is useful to consider sociologist W.I. Thomas' notion that even though the biological reality of race is void, the sociological consequences of race remain salient, significant and arguably determinant in the everyday reality of multiracial/multiethnic people in the U.S.

It is important to distinguish and note the use of the two multiracial/multiethnic descriptions and their identity implications and emphasis to illustrate the socially constructed nature of these identifications: 1) "Multiracial/multiethnic Asian American" and 2) "Asian-descent Multiracial/Multiethnic." By using, "Multiracial/multiethnic Asian Pacific American" (other variants of this would be, for example, "Interracial/ interethnic Chinese American" and "biracial/biethnic Thai American"), that is to locate "his or her multiracial identity within an Asian American or Asian ·context. (Williams Leon & Nakashima, 2001, p. 10). The central identity in this marker is "Asian American" and the adjectives "interracial/interethnic," "multiracial/multiethnic," and "biracial/biethnic" would describe "what kind of Asian American." Employing the multiracial/multiethnic indicators, "hapa haole" or "mestizo Filipino" or "Amerasian" would be to historically contextualize those mixed-race/mixed-ethnicity experiences within the amalgamated experiences of Native Hawaiians, the Spanish colonial experience of the Philippines, or the U.S. military experience of Asian women and American servicemen. These labels of "mixed-race/mixed-ethnicity" experiences situate these populations within Asian Pacific ethnic-specific and/or historically and geographically-specific identities. Although "hapa" has been appropriated by multiracial/multiethnic people of Asian descent, the origins of the term is ethnically and geographically specific to the "half Native Hawaiian" experience, just as to refer to "mestizo Filipinos" locates "being mixed" within the Spanish colonial, Filipino identity that acknowledges blending. The term, "Amerasian" coined by novelist Pearl S. Buck, also originates from the transnational, U.S. military involvement in Asia, and the children who were born from the unions between Asian women and U.S. servicemen. Though "American" and "Asian" are seemingly equal in importance in the usage of the term, "Amerasian" (and one might even argue that the "American" part is privileged over the "Asian,"), Amerasians have been represented as "mixed-race Asian;" they are a kind of Asian refugee or Asian immigrant. Like Asian war brides, who were not American (or part-American) it took an act of Congress (Amerasian Homecoming Act 1987 for example) to allow Amerasians to "come home" to America. However, the identification, "Asian-descent multiracial/multiethnic," centers and privileges one's racialized, ethnic identity within his or her overall "mixed-ness" or "multiraciality/multiethnicity," while acknowledging that at least one of his or her ancestries is "of Asian descent." When employing the marker, "Asian-descent multiracial/multiethnic" it is not describing a "kind of Asian," "a mixed Asian," or hyphenated Asian American (i.e. an Indonesian American, a Japanese American, and a multiracial Asian American are all "Asian Americans") but rather a multiracial person who is mixed with Asian ancestry (i.e. African-descent multiracial, European-descent multiracial, and an Asian-descent multiracial). The distinction between being a "multiracial Asian" and "Asian-descent multiracial" reflects where one locates, centers, and anchors one's identity—in multiraciality first or in a specific ethnic/racial identity first. This discussion was reflected in the 2000 Census debate when some advocated for a separate "multiracial" box and others argued for a "check more than one" option.

Public versus Private Identity

One of the things that people often want to know definitively once they find out that I have conducted qualitative research on multiracial populations is "How do mixed people identify?" or "Whom do they marry?" People are often disappointed when the answer isn't as simple as "If a man has a Sri Lankan father and a Latina mother, he will grow up to identify as Sri Lankan and marry a Latina woman." Those like Maria P.P. Root, Christine Iijima Hall, and Michael Thornton have written about the "identity" models in which gender, family structure, specific ethnic ancestry, socioeconomic class, socialization, social ecological influences, phenotype, generation, environment and so on influence and inform the ethnic identity choices and interpersonal relationships (Hall, 1992; Root, 1992; Thornton, 1992; Hall, 1992; Root, 1995; Williams, 1995; Houston and Williams, 1997; Root, 1997; Williams and Thornton, 1998; Spickard, 2001; Root, 2001; Tashiro, 2001; Williams-Leon and Nakashima, 2001). However, a combination of interactive factors play a role in influencing and informing individual identity choices. It is important to differentiate between a publicly articulated identity and intuitive or experiential identity. (Williams,1997; Zack, 1997). One's articulated identity is what one class oneself publicly (this may shift based on context or audience). One's public identity is often a political statement. It may or may not be in concert with one's intuitive or experiential identity. A multiracial person who looks "European American" (or who may be able to pass for "European American") may identify publicly by articulating her or himself as a "person of color" because of her/his understanding of American racial history and her/his social locality in the U.S. However, because of his/her cultural upbringing, primary relationships with European American family members, and ambiguous phenotype that may allow her/him to pass for white in some contexts, this multiracial person also intuitively and experientially understands that her/his European American ancestry is an integral part of his/her personal and social identities. Identity is necessarily both personal and political. That is to say, identity—how we see ourselves in relationship to others—is articulated, intuitive and experiential. (Williams, 1997).

If we examine the private/informal and public/formal identity expressions and articulations of the 44th President of the United States, Barack Hussein Obama, depending upon who is describing him, he is considered "the first Black president," "the first Asian American president," (Yang, 2008), "the first multiracial president," "the first global president," (Sharma, 2011) or "the

Aloha Zen president" (Haas, 2011). In the so-called, "race" speech that was touted as "historic,"' Senator Barack Obama, candidate for president, described his own international, multiracial/multiethnic family heritage as one that spans many continents around the globe,

> I am the son of a black man from Kenya and a white woman from Kansas. I was raised with the help of a white grandfather who survived a Depression to serve in Patton's Army during World War II and a white grandmother who worked on a bomber assembly line at Fort Leavenworth while he was overseas. I've gone to some of the best schools in America and lived in one of the world's poorest nations. I am married to a black American who carries within her the blood of slaves and slaveowners—an inheritance we pass on to our two precious daughters. I have brothers, sisters, nieces, nephews, uncles and cousins, of every race and every hue, scattered across three continents, and for as long as I live, I will never forget that in no other country on Earth is my story even possible.
>
> It's a story that hasn't made me the most conventional candidate. But it is a story that has seared into my genetic makeup the idea that this nation is more than the sum of its parts—that out of many, we are truly one. (*A More Perfect Union*, March 28, 2008)

On November 7, 2008 during his first press conference only days after winning the election in 2008, when President-Elect Obama was discussing a lighter subject matter—about getting the "first dog" for his daughters in the White House—, he gave the criteria for what his family was looking for in a pet and then stated somewhat jokingly, "Our preference is to get a shelter dog but a lot of shelter dogs are mutts like me," articulating himself as "mixed."

In his inaugural speech on January 20, 2009 in which the world watched and listened with great anticipation for this young, vibrant, articulate "African American President" who would lead the world into a new era, being inaugurated, the new president made a poignant point about his father who was Kenyan, a black African man, who would not have been served in a restaurant locally in Washington D.C. just 60 years ago where he would now make his residence as President. On this very world stage at that historic moment, he did not make any reference to his European American ancestry or family.

In contrast, on the television talk show, *The View*, on July 29, 2010, President Obama was asked by Barbara Walters about how he identified racially, "Why don't you say, 'I'm not a black person. I'm biracial'?" He responded,

> "... Part of what I realized was that if the world saw me as African American then that wasn't something I didn't need to run away from. That was something I could embrace. The interesting thing about the African American experience in this country is that we are sort of a mongrel people. We're all kind of mixed up. That's actually true for White America as well but we just know more about it. And so, I'm less interested in how we label ourselves. I'm more interested in how we treat each other. And if we're treating each other right, then I can be African American. I can be multiracial. I can be you name it. What matters is am I showing people respect? Am I caring for other people?"

Although in a more informal talk show setting, President Obama emphasized the importance of how he treats people rather than how he labels himself, according to a White House spokesman, President Obama, "the son of a black father from Kenya and a white mother from Kansas, officially checked African American on the 2010 census questionnaire." (Roberts and Baker, April 2, 2010). The same *New York Times* article went on to describe this official racial designation selection by the President,

> "The president, who was born in Hawaii and raised there and in Indonesia, had more than a dozen options in responding to Question 9, about race. He chose 'Black, African Am., or Negro."

(The anachronistic 'Negro' was retained on the 2010 form because the Census Bureau believes that some older blacks still refer to themselves that way.) Mr. Obama could have checked white, checked both black and white or checked the last category on the form, some other race," which he would then have been asked to identify in writing. There is no category specifically for mixed race or biracial."(Roberts and Baker, April2, 2010)

And yet, his wife, the first lady, Michelle Obama, has said of him, "You can't really understand Barack until you understand Hawaii." He too has said of himself, "What's best in me, and what's best in my message, is consistent with the tradition of Hawaii."—Hawai'i, a state in the 2010 Census, that unsurprisingly claimed the most "multiracially- identified" populations than anywhere else in the U.S. In many of his speeches, President Obama discusses his "White" heritage and his "Black Kenyan" heritage. In a speech he made in Kansas on December 6, 2011, he humorously put forth, "I'm sure you're all familiar with the Obamas from Osawatomie." (Southall, December 6, 2011). Ashley Southall elaborated in her article titled, "In Kansas, Obama Relishes His 'Deep' Roots," (2011)

> In fact, it was his mother's family, the Dunhams, that lived in Kansas until 1955. Mr. Obama has never lived in Kansas, but he told the crowd that his mother, Stanley Ann Dunham, was born in Wichita to parents from the outlying suburbs: a mother from Augusta and a father from El Dorado. ' So my Kansas roots run deep,' he said. . . By emphasizing his family's history on the United States mainland, which is less familiar to the public than his Kenyan ancestry and his childhood in Hawaii and Indonesia, Mr. Obama tried to tie his background to that of the mainstream middle class . . . Making an oblique reference to his father's absence, Mr. Obama said, 'I got my name from my father, but I got my accent and my values from my mother.' "

President Obama's half-sister, Maya Soetoro-Ng, describes herself as "half White, half Asian . . . a hybrid." Author Ellen Goodman from the article, "transcending race and identity," from *The Boston Globe*, described Soetoro-Ng as "a Buddhist, married to a Chinese-Canadian, the mother of a 2-year-old and a woman who is so routinely identified as a Latina that she learned Spanish." (Goodman, 2008). When asked what she thought about her brother as "Black," Soetoro-Ng replied that "that is how he has named himself. Each of us has the right to name ourselves as we will." Goodman contextualizes the personal and political, the private and public aspects of both President Obama and his sister, Maya Soetoro-Ng, who share a personal family history and affinity in part as "half- siblings" and yet have come to articulate their public identities differently:

> "How often are children of multiracial families asked, 'What are you?' Stanford's Shelby Steele, himself the son of a white mother and black father, writes that what people really want to know 'is what it is like to have no race to go home to at night. We commonly think of race as a kind of home, a place where they have to take you in; and it seems the very stuff of alienation to live with-out solid footing in such a home.' But for a growing number of Americans, especially children, home is not one race or ethnicity, if it ever was. Home is where—and who—your family is. The children of what we label 'mixed marriages'—ethnic, religious, or racial are often assumed to be torn by divided loyalties and identities. Yet the children that I have known may also—more so—be natural mediators, translators, connective tissue between multiple worlds. Obama once described the tension African American politicians feel between 'speaking in universal terms and speaking in race-specific terms.' In this campaign we see that tension between his 'name' and his 'home.' And as this play out on the national stage, we are also witnessing the challenge for an increasing number of multicultural families who try to build identities that are not contained by someone's view of 'what we are.' Maya Soetoro-Ng described her mother as someone who 'thought of life as sort of this beautiful tapestry full of possibilities.' Whatever this campaign brings, her children are living a

reality out loud that is far more like that tapestry than it is like the neat boxes on the Census Bureau forms.'" (Goodman, 2008)

Examining their own descriptions of who they are and how they identify contextually in private and in public, President Obama and his sister, Maya Soetoro-Ng, give insight into the complexity of each of their gendered and racialized, (multi-)ethnic, international identities. Depending upon context (public or private, formal or informal), President Obama, in particular, seems to emphasize different aspects of his multiracial/multiethnic background and upbringing, drawing upon his many personal, social, and political resources. On one hand, there is a private identity, how one sees oneself and practices one's cultural ways of being and values with family, friends, and primary circles. Perhaps, describing himself as a "mutt" at his first news conference after winning the election in 2008 or explaining to Barbara Walters on a day time talk show that "how he lives and treats people, not how he labels himself" are what matter, give rare glimpses into the "multiracial/multiethnic" reality of this President, on one hand. After writing a book about his quest and search for his identity and seemingly finding an inner peace and understanding of his own personal, genealogical history of a part of him that may have been missing, President Obama has stated in the preface of his book, *Dreams from My Father*, "I think sometimes that had I known she would not survive her illness, I might have written a different book—less a meditation on the absent parent, more a celebration of the one who was the single constant in my life."[2]

The first impression in public spaces, even before one's face is known and Phenotype coded racially is one's name. In school on the first day of class, the teacher reads the class roster or at a job interview, the name of the application is read before meeting the applicant in-person. President Obama who went by "Barry" as a child came to embrace the African name he was given after a "foreign" father who was absent from his life. He often describes himself as "a skinny kid with a funny name." Names are also racially coded. Daniel A. Nakashima has explained,

> "In a diverse society, we read names as signifiers not only of one's individual identity and membership in a particular family, but of one's membership in a particular racial, ethnic, and/or cultural group. Very often when reading the name of a multiracial/multiethnic person for racial and ethnic clues, challenges arise both for the 'reader' and for the multiracial/multiethnic person being read.' The reader might be confused by a name that does not 'match' with the person's physical appearance or mannerisms whereas the multiracial/multiethnic person might feel that his or her name is not an accurate reflection of his/her race, ethnicity, and identity." (2001)

One's name is part of one's public identity, as much as one's cultural practices, mannerisms, and the "raw" eyeball-interaction of "race."

In addition, when the role of parenting and socialization is examined, women have most often taken on the role of primary childrearer in most cultures and societies which means that the mothers' conscious and unconscious cultural ways of being play an important role in one's internal socialization and cultural acquisition and the surname passed on by the father in American society provides an external "ethnic" recognition. While two biracial individuals may share overarching experiences, there may be some cultural/ethnic differences that could be identified based on the parents' gender, class, generational status, and cultural backgrounds. For example, a biracial Chinese-Black individual whose mother is immigrant Chinese and father is African

---

[2] In his book *Dreams from my Father*, Barack Obama describes a "black man" named "Ray" who becomes a close high school friend and mentors Obama. Ray's real name is Keith Kakugawa. He is Japanese-African American.

American named "Ronald Smith" and another biracial Chinese-Black individual whose father is second generation Chinese American and mother is African American named, "David Chen," may have different cultural references, emphases, and practices (among other idiosyncratic differences among individuals) as well as a different public identity. Likewise, a Black White biracial individual whose mother is White and father is Black American and a biracial individual whose mother is White and father is Japanese American may find they have similar cultural ways of being, though people may not recognize this because they are fixated on the so-called "racial differences" of someone who is part-Black and someone who is "part-White."

Cultural transmission, development of psyche, manipulation of mannerisms, language acquisition, and world view are all powerful, often unspoken gifts passed on by one's caregivers. A biracial Japanese-Black son who is being raised by a Japanese immigrant mother in the United States speaking Japanese at home, for example, may not realize until he is much older that his mother had been passing on a more "feminized form of Japanese" because she was speaking appropriately to him as a mother would to her child. His African American father who speaks little or no Japanese with no other Japanese-speaking male adults around may not understand the complexity of how gendered the Japanese language is, not to mention the hierarchical nature and the intricate levels of formality and informality of the Japanese language (Root, 1992; Williams, 1992; Root, 1995; Houston and Williams,1997; Williams and Thornton,1998).

President Obama has stated in his December, 2011 Kansas speech that he received his name from his father (public, formal identity) and his accent and values (private, personal identity) from his mother. In his 2008 inaugural speech, President Obama referenced his father's racial background and its historical hindrances, affirming to the world the idea that he can legitimately claim being "the first Black president" and had broken a major barrier in American political life by elected President of the United States. Furthermore, President Obama made his "race" official when he marked off "Black," in the 2010 Census, in essence, publicly and politically declaring his African American identity. However, he has also openly articulated in various political contexts and less formal interviews his multiracial, multiethnic background by drawing upon both his African and European American heritages, as well as his Indonesian and multicultural upbringing from Hawai'i, even at times referring to himself as a "mutt." Christine Iijima Hall has illustrated in her early study of Black-Japanese Americans that when they were asked about cultural practices and values beyond what racial label her respondents used to describe themselves, a more complex ethnic identity was often revealed by Black-Japanese American multiracial/multiethnic individuals (Hall, 1980; Hall, 1992). Williams and Thornton (1998) in examining the personal and social identities of "Afroasians" have argued that racially mixed people but especially those of African ancestry best exposes the contradictions of how race is viewed and represented. Perhaps, an indicator that many individuals, especially multiracial/multiethnic individuals have personal and private identities beyond what they publicly articulate and acknowledge. When Maya Soetoro-Ng was asked to comment on her famous brother whose presidency has sparked a discussion on "a post-racial society," as "Black," she referred to it as "how he has named himself," rather than describing it as his essential being or primordial identity. Soetoro-Ng's characterization of President Obama calling himself "Black" as "naming," coupled with what President Obama told the ladies of *The View* that it's more important how he treats people than how he labels himself, might be one of the many ways in which the complexity of his private identity has been negotiated and expressed publicly. Multiracial/multiethnic people, regardless of how they may name themselves or racially/ethnically emphasize themselves in various contexts must often learn to navigate, manipulate, access, conceal, shift, and anchor between their private selves and public identities.

Quapas: The Next Generation?

As first-generation multiracial/multiethnic people of partial and mixed Asian descent (that is to say, those who are products of one parent who identifies as one "race" and another parent who identifies as a different race from the other parent) form partnerships and/or have children of their own, what will become of their second generation/multigenerational multiracial offspring's public "race," and lived (multi-)ethnic experiences, as well as their private identity? At Cafe-press.com, a website in which people can purchase customized clothing, buttons, bumperstickers, mugs, pins, among a whole host of personalized items, "Quapa" products are for sale. One t-shirt reads, "Quapa (quarter hapa)" and another reads, "Quapa Love" with a drawing of a heart below in which with three-quarters of the heart is filled in with the color red. In Japan, where the term, "haafu"「ハーフ」is still used (the Japanized version of the word, "half"), it is not so uncommon to hear the description, "kuwootaa"「クオーター」(or "quarter") to refer to the children of "haafu." Of course, the term, "quarter" assumes that the biracial individual who is "half Asian" (or "only half Asian") had offspring with someone who is "full," "unmixed" or "monoracial." So for instance, a first-generation biracial Filipino-white individual who procreates with a "one full white" individual then has a "one-quarter Asian quapa" child. On the other hand, if a first generation biracial African American-Korean American individual has children with someone who is "full Korean" their offspring would be three-quarters Asian and one-quarter African American "inverse quapa." Of course, the actual mixtures, intimate interpersonal relationships, and procreative practices of Asian descent multiracial/multiethnic peoples are far more complex than these assumptions of the racialized categorizations of Asian-descent multiracial/multiethnic people and their relationship partners and do not always take the course of marrying "back into" (or simply producing offspring with) one or the other of his or her parent groups. Nevertheless, the next generation (the multi generational blending) of Asian-descent multiracial/multiethnic people in which the racial quantification of people in a highly racialized, race-conscious society such as the United States has also come to have a tentative name ("quapa")- different from but slightly reminiscent of African Americans under slavery with quadroons and octoroons or the colonial vestiges of the "mestizaje" with mestizos, mulatos, and zambos and were part of the sociolinguistic realities. It is different, because much of the naming and constructing of identity now comes from the people who call themselves as "hapa" and "quapa" on one hand, in which some of the structural gaps in racial inequality have been lessened (e.g. heterosexual people of different "races" are now allowed to marry legally as "equals"). As Maya Soetoro-Ng has put forth, "Each of us has the right to name ourselves as we will." However, it is also reminiscent in that the racialization process of identity remains relevant and hierarchically problematic (e.g. we still refer to these marriages as "interracial").

Some of the questions that plagued first generation Asian-descent multiracials and multiethnics in relationship to Asian Pacific Islander communities may still remain: "Will they assimilate into the dominant society?", or "Will Asian American communities be diluted and eventually disappear?" "Will these mixed people and their children even identify as Asian Pacific Islander?" However, when one closely and critically examines the histories, the social realities, and the pan-ethnic diversity within and across Asian Pacific America, one can not help but to notice since the first contact, arrival, and settlement of APAs in Hawai'i and in the continental United States and beyond, racial and ethnic blending has been a vital and vibrant part of Asian Pacific Islander communities and identities. And the recognition that people with multiple racial and ethnic ancestries may identify in a variety of ways, throughout the course of their lives, negotiating their personal, social and political identities in private and public spaces, informally and formally but still be acknowledged and celebrated as contributing members and integral parts of APA communities.

Bibliography

Allen, James P. and Eugene Turner.

Cafepress.com

http://www.cafepress.com/+quapa baby doll tshirt.l1940628

http://www.cafepress.com/+guapa quarter hapa womens plus size vneck tsh. 486907809

DaCosta, Kimberly McClain. *Making Multiracials: State. Family and Market in the Redrawing of the Colorline.* Stanford, CA: Stanford University Press. 2007.

Goodman, Ellen. "Transcending race and identity," *The Boston Globe,* January 25, 2008.

Obama, Barack. *Dreams from My Father.* Crown Publishing Group. 2004.

Haas, Michael (editor), *Barack Obama. The Aloha Zen President: How a Son of the 50th State May Revitalize America Based on 12 Multicultural Principles.* Praeger, 2011.

Hall, Christine Iijima. The ethnic identity of racially mixed people: A study of *Black- Japanese.*" Unpublished doctoral dissertation , University of California, Los Angeles, 1980.

Hall, Christine Iijima. "Please Choose One: Ethnic Identity Choices for Biracial Individuals" in Maria P.P. Root (ed.) *Racially Mixed People in America.* Thousand Oaks, CA: Sage Publications, 1992.

Houston, Velina and Teresa Kay Williams. "No Passing Zone" *Amerasia Journal.* Vol. 23, No. 1, 1997.

Ifekwunigwe, Jayne. *'Mixed Race' Studies: A Reader.* New York: Routledge, 2004.

Omi, Michael and Howard Winant. *Racial Formation in the United States.* New York: Routledge, 1994.

Passel, JeffreyS., Wendy Wang, and Paul Taylor. *"Marrying Out." Social and Demographic Trends.* Pew Research Center Publications. June 4, 2010.

Root, Maria P.P. *Racially Mixed People in America.* Thousand Oaks, CA: Sage Publications, 1992.

Root, Maria P.P. *The Multiracial Experience: Racial Borders as the New Frontier.* Thousand Oaks, CA: Sage Publications, 1995.

Saulny, Susan. "Census Data Presents Rise in Multiracial Population of Youths," *The New York Times.* March 24, 2011.

Sharma, Dinesh. *Barack Obama in Hawai'i and Indonesia: The Making of a Global President.* Praeger Publishers Inc. 2010.

Southall, Ashley. "In Kansas, Obama Relishes His 'Deep' Roots," *New York Times,* December 6, 2011.

Williams, Teresa Kay and Michael C. Thornton. "Social Construction of Ethnicity Versus Personal Experience: The Case of Afroasians ," *Journal of Comparative Family Studies,* vol. XXIX, No.2, 1998.

Williams, Teresa Kay. "Prism Lives: Identity of Binational Amerasians" in Maria P.P. Root (ed.) *Racially Mixed People in the America.* Thousand Oaks, CA: Sage Publications, 1992.

Williams-Leon, Teresa. "Census, Consensus? APAs and Multiracial Identity," in Eric Lai and Dennis Arguelles (ed.) *The New Face of Asian Pacific America: Numbers, Diversity and Change in the 21st Century.* 2003.

Williams-Leon, Teresa. "Check All That Apply: Trends and Prospectives Among Asian-Descent Multiracials." 2003. pp. 158–175.

Winters, Loretta I. and Herman L. DeBose. *New Faces in a Changing America: Multiracial Identity in the 21st Century.* Thousand Oaks, CA: Sage Publications, 2003.

Yang, Jeff, "Asian Pop/Could Obama be the first Asian American president?" SFGate.com July 30, 2008.

Zack, Naomi (ed.) *American Mixed Race: The Culture of Microdiversity.* Lanham, Maryland: Rowman & Littlefield Publishers Inc. 1995.

Queering Tết

Gina Masequesmay

C H A P T E R

23

This chapter is a reflection of my work in raising awareness about the struggles of lesbian, bisexual, transgender, intersexual, queer, and questioning (LGBTIQQ)[1] people in the Vietnamese American community. I use a Tết[2] parade controversy in Little Saigon to illustrate some of the thinking of Vietnamese Americans about LGBTIQQ people. Highlighting these different attitudes, I dispel some of these misperceptions that create struggles for LGBTIQQ Vietnamese Americans, and reiterate the need of queering[3] Tết and Vietnamese America.

On February 13, 2010, the Lunar New Year's eve morning of the Year of the Tiger in Little Saigon began with a parade march in the City of Westminster by Vietnamese Americans to celebrate our cultural heritage as a Vietnamese people living outside of Việt Nam. The event signified not only a continuation of tradition by a diasporic people but also a reclamation of a negotiated identity vis-à-vis assimilative pressure of an American political economy. Marchers included cultural, religious, veteran groups, Việt Nam-oriented political groups, businesses and politicians. New this time in Little Saigon's parade was the participation of the Partnership of Việt Lesbian, Gay, Bisexual and Transgender (LGBT) Organizations from Northern and Southern California. While this Vietnamese American LGBT coalition had marched in the past years in San Jose, this was first

Contributed by Gina Masequesmay, Ph.D., Professor in Asian American Studies Department at California State University, Northridge.

---

[1] I use "LGBTIQQ" as an inclusive term for people who do not abide to the normative sex, gender and sexual structure, or people who identify themselves as lesbian, gay, bisexual, transgender, intersexual, queer and questioning people. Sometimes, the "IQQ" may drop out to become just "LGBT" to refer to names or specific groups of lesbian, gay, bisexual and transgender people. The term "queer" refers to those who do not identify as straight, lesbian, gay, bisexual, transgender, or intersexual. While "questioning" may be more descriptive than an identity, some prefer this label to LGBTIQ. Note that I do my best to use LGBTIQQ or LGBT as an adjective rather than a noun because identity is slippery and contextual and because sexuality and gender are social constructs and not absolute biological facts.

[2] Tết is Vietnamese lunar New Year, a mark of Spring and a time of renewal. The eve of New Year is a time for family gathering where food preparation and house cleaning have been done prior to welcoming the new year. Family and friends visit each other to wish prosperity, health, peace and luck, and children greeting adults will receive lucky money in a red envelope. The eve and first three days of the New Year are official holidays although some carry out the celebration for 15 days.

[3] I use "queer" or "queering" as a verb to suggest the process of destabilizing the norm. To problematize what is taken-for-granted as normal by inserting in the experiences of LGBTIQQ people helps to question the everyday actions that normalize some groups while deviantize other groups. By disrupting the normative process, we re-imagine a more inclusive universe of human beings deserving of equal treatment.

time that the group marched in the capital of Vietnamese America, where an estimated 150,000[4] people of Vietnamese-descent live within a ten mile radius and where one-third of Westminster City's population is Vietnamese (Census 2000).

A few days after the press release of the coalition's intention to march, the coalition faced oppositions from a few Vietnamese American politicians and the Vietnamese Interfaith Council of America, a religious group claiming to be leaders of the various Vietnamese American, religious groups (Lutheran, Catholic, Cao Đài, Buddhist) in Little Saigon. The interfaith council held a press conference and called for a boycott of the parade because of the LGBT coalition's presence. For the interfaith council members, LGBTIQQ people are a shame, illness, or problem in the Vietnamese community and should not be celebrated and paraded at a traditional cultural holiday where children would see us. The Vietnamese American press had a field day with this controversy as readers wrote in and casted their heterosexist, homophobic, and/or misinformed "scientific" judgments.

Westminster Councilman Andy Quách, who was chairman of the Tết parade committee, voiced his opposition to our participation in the Vietnamese press and expressed: "Personally, I oppose the participation of this group in a traditionally joyous cultural celebration of the Vietnamese people . . . However, as an elected official of the City of Westminster, I cannot discriminate any group or individual for political, religious, sexual orientation, or personal reasons. These are limitations in the law that all of us must accept" (Prevatt, 2010). Hùng Nguyên, one of the parade organizers and member of the Vietnamese Cultural and Heritage Foundation, had a different legal stance and offered, "I think our community recognizes that they are human beings too." He thus "welcome[s] anyone to celebrate with us—as long as they are not terrorists or communists" (Bharath, 9 Feb. 2010).

Councilman Andy Quách forewarned that if we were to "display any extreme or outrageous material not suited for children" then the city would have discretion to exclude us (Bharath, 11 Feb. 2010). Ironically, on the Tết parade day, Councilman Quách joined the parade in his low-rider convertible with a painting on the trunk of scantily clad women provocatively pole dancing (Bolsavik, 13 Feb. 2010).

Reverend Sỹ Nguyễn, director of the Vietnamese Catholic Center and member of the interfaith council, said that although he appreciated "the freedom of individuals to express themselves . . . Tết is a cultural event for Vietnamese whether in Vietnam or anywhere in the world" and "[p]arading members of Vietnamese gays, lesbians and transgender groups as part of Tết celebration is not only irrelevant to the meaning of Tết, but is perceived at best as a complete lack of sensitivity to the Vietnamese traditions, and at worst a cultural attack on the Vietnamese community here in Orange County" (Bharath, 11 Feb. 2010).

Similar to the stance of the Catholic Priest Nguyễn, Pastor Vân Trần of the Reformation Lutheran Church in Westminster and a member of the interfaith council said, "Gays and lesbians are not accepted by The Holy Bible" and that "homosexuality is also not accepted in 1,000 years of Vietnamese culture" (Ibid.).

By far the greatest opposition came from religious stances that condemned homosexuality. Hence, Garden Grove Councilwoman Dina Nguyễn publicly announced that she didn't believe in homosexuality (Vu, 13 Feb. 2010) as if it was a religion or some leap of faith. Other sources of anti-LGBT stances were traditional views of gender roles and incorrect citation of scientific studies to claim that LGBTIQQ people are abnormal or mentally ill.

---

[4] This is my estimate from the Census 2000 Fact Sheet. *www.census.gov*. 3 January 2011.

The days after the press conference by the interfaith council, many LGBTIQQ members had second thoughts about marching in fear of possible violence. For some of us who had witnessed bomb threats, death threats and vicious boycotts and protests by our community members against people alleged as communist-friendly or communist, the boycott and protest by our religious elders did make us question our safety. Along with our own experiences of **homophobia** (fear or hatred of homosexuals[5]) and **heterosexism** (the belief that heterosexuality is the only normal sexual orientation and the assumption that everyone is straight) in mainstream community, we were not sure what to expect in Orange County, a conservative stronghold. We decided that love would be our guiding force despite being thrown unkind words and/or objects. We would not retaliate with violence and that we would only do our best to avoid harm and danger. We rallied our allies to march with us because our anticipated participants had decreased. We also asked our allies to bring cameras and be our witnesses if violence broke out.

Our last minute call for help was answered with great generosity from our friends and allies. Two reverends from St. Anselm of Canterbury Episcopal Church and Orange Coast Unitarian Universalist Church came to march with our brides and grooms. Friends and allies from API Equality, Asian Queer Women Activists, the Asian Pacific AIDS Intervention Team, and other Asian Pacific queer organizations drove from Los Angeles to march with us. The Orange County LGBT Center, Parents and Friends of Lesbians and Gays (PFLAG), LGBT groups in Orange County came out in large numbers to offer help and to march with us. We ended up with more people wanting to march than we had registered. Right before the march, the police came by and told us that they would be marching along with us to ensure our safety. They had heard of possible tomato throwing and assured us that they would go after the perpetrators should that occur.

Taking in deep breaths and remembering the festive atmosphere of Tết, we exhaled and marched forward with a banner addressing parents to love all their children and a banner reminding people that whether gay, straight, bisexual or transgender, we are all part of the larger family of Vietnamese people. Signs advocating equality for all, same-sex marriage, and tolerance were also visible. In addition, signs of well wishes for the new year were also prevalent. The messages were in English and Vietnamese. Assessing everyone's experience, we concluded that there were four boo's in the audience with two signs opposing us. Otherwise, the march was smooth with loud cheers from the audience. A few veteran groups even gave us a salute. Some elders smiled and waved at us. Most endearing was an old couple passing by us at the end of the parade and offering, "We love you. We love all of you." It was a historic and triumphant moment for many of us who marched. The news reported that only the Knights of Columbus and the Vietnamese Martyrs Council, joined the interfaith council to boycott the parade (Bharath 11 Feb. 2010).

There was an opinion piece after the parade that used individual freedom of expression argument to criticize the strategy of the interfaith council. The author, Nguyễn Phương Hùng, was a KBC Board Administrator, a Vietnamese veteran organization. He saw the interfaith council's boycott call as a reckless act that sabotaged the many objectives of other groups' marching in the parade, specifically political groups that try to raise human rights issues in Việt Nam. Although he was not gay-friendly, he did give positive feedback about us as "cheerful and respectful folks" (Nguyễn, Feb. 2010).

Reflecting on the different reactions we received, I address the wrong perceptions about LGBTIQQ people by our co-ethnics as well as how our Vietnamese American rhetoric on freedom and individual rights tempered these negative sentiments. Referencing my 2010 pilot study of

---

[5] The often-used definition obfuscates the term phobia, which suggests fear and paranoia but not hatred.

Vietnamese American attitudes toward LGBT issues, I discuss the survey results and the harm endured by LGBITQQ Vietnamese folks, and suggest recommendations for remedies.

Misinformed Scientific Facts

Many opinion pieces that were published in the newspapers before and after the parade suggested that the authors were misinformed about scientific studies on homosexuality, bisexuality, transgenderism and intersexuality. Firstly, most opinions did not distinguish between homosexuality, bisexuality and transgenderism. For them, the three were interchangeable. They did not see that **homosexuality** was about same-sex attraction and **bisexuality** as about attraction toward both men and women and that **transgenderism** was about gender identity and not about **sexual orientation**, which was an enduring emotional, romantic, sexual, or affectional attraction toward others (American Psychological Association). Intersexuality was a mystery to many and only when the word "hermaphrodite" was used that people make some connection. However, many did not know that **intersexuality** includednot only people with ambiguous genitalia but also people with other than XX or XY chromosomes.

For many heterosexists, heterosexuality was the only normal and preferred sexuality. Often times, the link to reproduction for species continuation was used to assert the naturalness of heterosexuality. This logic, however, would also exclude infertile, heterosexual couples and heterosexual couples who had sex for recreation rather than procreation. Insisting on species survival, proponents of the unnaturalness of homosexuality and transgenderism omitted to see the problem with overpopulation of humans on the planet and how our species' longer life and technology had created an unsustainable Earth for future generations. An alternative argument could be made that we needed more gays and lesbians to slow down human population for the sustainability of the planet. The type of mandatory reproduction argument also failed to see that gays and lesbians do have children. In short, biology was often used to assert people's assumed agenda instead as evidence from which to infer about human nature. Thus, the short assertion of naturalness of heterosexuality did not necessarily render homosexuality, bisexuality and transgenderism as unnatural.

In contrast, from reviewing decades of scientific studies, scientist Milton Diamond (2011) has concluded, "Nature loves variety. Unfortunately, society hates it." Homosexual behaviors exist in Nature, but unlike humans, animals do not proclaim a sexual identity. The American Medical Association has stated that sexual orientation is not a choice but rather a natural part of a human being (Trevor Project). In human species, longitudinal studies show that while some individuals may vary greatly in sex-partners, some individuals do not change much (Diamond, 2008). The American Psychiatric Association asserted how harmful it is to one's psychological and physical well-being to try and "control" sexual orientation (Trevor Project). From the American Psychological Association, sexual orientation exists along a continuum that ranges from exclusive heterosexuality to exclusive homosexuality and includes various forms of bisexuality. Researchers who have looked at both human and animal sexual behaviors have concluded that homosexuality and bisexuality are results of both nurture and nature, or environment and biology (Milton 1995; Diamond 1993). In studies on identical twins, the data seem to indicate some genetic component in sexual orientation (Diamond 1982; Diamond 1993; Whitam, Diamond, & Martin 1993). Comparing across selected nations, we also see male same-sex behaviors as occurring from 2 to 9% of the population (Diamond, 1993).

In Nature, intersexuality is seen in hamlet reef fish that can copulate and reproduce as both male and female simultaneously (Ross, Losey & Diamond 1983). In human species, the estimate of intersexual people is about 1.89%.[6] If one were think more deeply about intersexuality, one will note that the intersexual baby is born naturally so. But, because a particular human culture constructs a binary sex category, anything that does not fall in the ideal categories is considered a deviation to the "normal." "Normal" here is no longer about what's in nature but what is in human perception of nature. Thus, although born naturally as intersexual, these babies often have to undergo surgeries to be "corrected" into our limited categories of male and female. With this understanding in mind about human limited construction of sex, we can then see why that normalizing view would render transgender people as abnormal or unnatural. Yet, studies on gender and sex conclude that there could be at least five categories of sex[7] (Fausto-Sterling 2002).

Transgenderism also exists in nature as we witness the sex transformation of some species of reef fish (Ross, Losey & Diamond 1983). For humans, the transgender estimate is about 0.2% to 1% who seek sex-reassignment surgeries (Human Rights Campaign). This is an undercount given that there are those who cannot afford to obtain sex-reassignment surgeries. In U.S. popular culture, however, transgenderism is seen as a mental illness of someone hating his or her body. In other cultures and in different time periods, there are third gender categories as seen in the Hijras of India, the Mahus of Hawaii, and the two-spirited people of some Native American tribes.

Given these accumulated scientific studies, it is regretful that people still misuse science to assert that homosexuality, bisexuality, transgenderism and intersexuality are abnormal.

Religious Based Bigotry

Probably the most influential source of negative feelings toward LGBTIQQ people is Christianity. Quoting the Bible, religious extremists assert that homosexuality is an abomination to the Lord and deserves death. Yet, there are many interpretations of the Bible.[8] Passages used to cite God's condemnation are debated to be about temple prostitution (Leviticus), unkind treatment and raping of strangers (Sodom and Gomorrah) and not about homosexuality per se. The selectiveness of what to follow and what not to follow (eating shelled seafood and pork, cutting one's hair, etc.) also makes this type of argument weak. That is, if one were to claim that the King James' version of the Bible to be the words of God rather than an interpretation and that we must follow strictly every word of the Lord, then all prohibitions such as those aforementioned should be condemned equally. Selective condemnation indicates biases. Furthermore, one cannot cite Jesus to have said anything against homosexuality. As a matter of fact, one can cite other parts of the Bible to stress Jesus' teaching on love and inclusiveness.

The Buddha also said nothing condemning about homosexuality. Indeed, if one were to consider the major religions in the world, the basic teaching is the golden rule of treating others as you want to be treated. So, the logic of condemning homosexuality is really based on faith of one's religious leader's interpretation.

Considering the history of how the Bible has been used in this country to condemn blacks, women and interracial couples, The Faith in America Report suggests that a person of faith may

---

[6] This is my calculation from the webpage "How common is intersex?" of the Intersex Society of North America site. http://www.isna.org/faq/frequency

[7] Fausto-Sterling identifies five categories: male, female, true hermaphrodites or herms, male pseudohermaphrodites or merms, and female pseudohermaphrodites or ferms. Herms possess one testis and one ovary; merms have testes and some aspects of female genitalia but no ovaries; and ferms have ovaries and some aspects of the male genitalia but lack testes.

[8] The following about Christianity is borrowed from Frank Jernigan's work.

want to consider the harm that has been done in the name of religion. Understanding that religion can be a cohesive force for our society that bonds us to one another and to help us imagine a common good, perhaps it makes more sense to work toward that goal of love and inclusiveness. Considering that LGBT youth are up to four times more likely to attempt suicide (Trevor Project) than their heterosexual peers and one third of LGBT youth report having made a suicide attempt due to internalized homophobia, people of faith should work toward promoting understanding and compassion instead of prejudice and discrimination.

Unfortunately, this consideration was not taken by the members of the Vietnamese Interfaith Council of America. Using their religious influence, they denounced us and called for a boycott. Fortunately, their religious-based bigotry was tempered by American laws on liberty and freedom.

Buffered by Individual Freedom and Rights

Having fled one's country to find liberty in terms of political, religious and individual freedom, Vietnamese Americans deeply appreciate what they have in the States compared to what they went through in Việt Nam or what they went through in refugee camps. Rhetorics about freedom and liberty as ideals of America are juxtaposed in contrast to repression and oppression in Communist Việt Nam. The right of LGBTIQQ individuals to march in the parade, thus, buffered us from the opposition. We saw this in Hùng Nguyễn's statement that he would welcome us as long as we were not communist or terrorist and in Andy Quách's regret that he could not discriminate us when had registered properly to march.

Understanding religious persecution and repression in Vietnam, it would be hypocritical for Vietnamese Americans to use religion to condemn a minority group within the community. In this legal discourse, however, the appreciation for the First Amendment of separating religion and the state and for the Fourteenth Amendment of equal protection under the law were not often articulated. Rather, the notion of individual freedom of expression from the First Amendment seemed to have created an inalienable pass for LGBTIQQ people to march in the parade. However, this pass was stopped at the ethnic cultural door of a Tết celebration. The next section discusses the cultural issues that LGBTIQQ people challenge to Vietnamese traditions.

Challenges of Cultural Tradition

Who Defines What Vietnamese Culture and Tradition Are?

What is Vietnamese culture and tradition? Do we go with matriarchal values before Chinese domination and Western Christianity? Do we apply some values of Western colonialism and imperialism? Who gets to decide what is and is not Vietnamese culture is a question that has played on in Vietnamese American families and communities.

According to Dr. Steven Paul Chamberlain (2005), culture is "the values, norms, and traditions that affect how individuals of a particular group perceive, think, interact, behave and make judgments about their world." Another notion of culture to consider is that it changes over time. Cultural change is inevitable because of changes in society, especially technological changes. Yet, we often mistake culture to be static. Another source of cultural change is when there is contact with another culture. The process of acculturation occurs where there are interchanges of cultures. Depending on the power dynamics of the two societies, one culture may overpower the other.

When we consider this issue of cultural change for Vietnamese Americans, we note how traditional gender roles have been re-negotiated to survive in a fast-paced, capitalist America. America's notion of traditional middle-class family values, in itself, has changed as the sexual revolution of the 1960s and the restructuring of the economy in the 1970s have challenged the notion of a middle-class two-parent family where the husband/father is the breadwinner and the wife/mother is a homemaker. Similarly, Vietnamese immigrants and refugees reaching American shore in the 1970s faced economic reality that challenged traditional gender roles as a woman's duty is not just to be married and stay at home to take care of the children and a man's duty cannot just be to marry a woman, father children and be the sole breadwinner. In addition to the changing gender roles, to move from a collective orientation to a more individualist orientation created profound conflict between parents' and children's expectations for Vietnamese Americans. The old days of filial piety where saving face and sacrificing individual needs for one's family are of utmost importance are challenged by American individualism.

In Việt Nam, individual needs are usurped by family needs. The social structure of Vietnamese society didn't allow a lot of room for individual expressions. Everyone has a role from birth to death. A child learns obedience to be a dutiful daughter or son. Then he/she grows up to marry the opposite sex and becomes a wife or husband. Then he or she becomes a parent and provider for the family emotionally or materially. Then he or she becomes a parent-in-law and then a grandparent before he or she dies.

What does this mean for individuals who do not want to marry and start their own family? Few choices are available. If one is not married, usually one remains in the house to take care of one's parents. Or, one can become a monastic to leave the family. In both paths, one's sexuality is curbed and regulated by one's close-knit family or by the monastic lifestyle. In few instances, one with privileged class background can leave the family to go to school or work. The excuses for not getting married yet would be that one is too busy with school or work and having to establish a career or taking care of one's parents that left no room for marriage. In the chaotic time of war, less privileged men became soldiers, servants, or peddlers and less privileged women became prostitutes, concubines, servants, or peddlers.

Given the few choices of livelihood, it is no wonder that there is a near invisibility of LGB-TIQQ lives then. There were limited avenues for visibility except underground and in the entertainment industry. Unlike some assertions that there were no LGBTIQQ Vietnamese people, we did exist. Otherwise, there would be no slang terms to refer to LGBTIQQ people as "Bê Đê", "La De", "Ô-môi", etc.

The issue of LGBT "non-existence" in Việt Nam is because strict gender and filial roles made it impossible to live out one's life openly. It is no wonder that some Vietnamese elders assert that too much freedom in America is what made their children LGBT.

Despite the near invisibility of LGBTIQQ people in Vietnam, we have anecdotes of men getting married but still have their gay fling on the side and fewer stories of women with lesbian lovers on the side. Whether they identify as homosexual or not is a different matter. Homosexual behaviors do not necessarily have to be linked to a homosexual or bisexual identity. As long as one fulfills one's role of a dutiful child, spouse and parent, one's occasional homosexual encounters if kept secret can be of no consequences to one's role and identity in the family.

In the U.S., an individual has a little bit more leeway to not marry, especially if one can gain economic independence, although the pervasive pressure still leads many to marry and then divorce or stay in unfulfilling marriages. Some people do not marry because they don't want to marry. Some do not want to have children because they do not want to have children. None of these people have to be LGBTIQQ. Given the changes in Vietnamese Americans deviating from the traditional gender roles, LGBTIQQ people coming out and wanting same-sex marriage is just part of the many changes in Vietnamese American culture. Given the continuous changes in Vietnamese diasporic culture, to claim an authentic Vietnamese culture is problematic. It is a person's fantasy of what was Vietnamese culture and this nostalgia excludes all of the exceptions to the rule of only straight Vietnamese existence.

If we examine closer the argument about culture, it is often conflated with the issue of nature. The next subsection traces this convergence.

The Yin and Yang of the Universe

Much of Vietnamese culture is influenced by Taoism, Confucianism and Buddhism. Taoism discusses the universe as operating on two opposite and complementary energies that constantly flow to balance each other: the yin and the yang. One interpretation is that yin is the feminine energy and yang is the masculine energy. Basing on this interpretation, a man naturally needs a woman and vice-versa. However, from this logic, one can also theorize that a lesbian is a woman with more yang and would need to find another yin or woman to balance her life. From this logic, one can also theorize that a bisexual person sometimes has more yin and sometimes more yang and would need his/her complimentary energy at different points in time. From this logic, one can also argue that an intersexual person is the most balanced, having both feminine and masculine energy. In short, these logics can be twisted to one's agenda.

Nonetheless, I suspect this notion of yin and yang is the undercurrent of thoughts about culture and nature. People opposing to LGBTIQQ people often say that LGBTIQQ people are not natural and goes against tradition and culture. The presupposition behind this statement is that culture flows from the natural order of yin and yang. That idea of culture as reflecting the yin and yang dynamics of Nature stems from Taoist and Confucian philosophies. The connection to Nature is the influence of Taoism and the social order and patriarchy stem from Confucianism. Together, these different strains become an interpretation of the order of the universe at the level of metaphysics and Nature (Taoism) and of society (Confucianism). Confucianism's patriarchy requires a man to fulfill his role of continuing the family lineage and his wife to support his duty. For gays and lesbians who do not marry, they are interrupting that social order. In sum, a role of a man and a woman is then strictly defined by the order of not just social rules and duties but Nature's law and universal law. So, when one goes against culture and tradition, one is also going against nature and the universe itself.

These sources for oppositions against LGBTIQQ people reflect an older paradigm and we see how they manifest in the attitudes of older versus younger generations.

Current Vietnamese American Attitudes on LBTIQQs

In a pilot survey based on a snowball-sampling of 233 respondents from students' networks of friends and family in mostly Los Angeles area, I found that about 70% Asian Americans I surveyed were open and accepting of LGBTIQQ people. This was due to the fact that we had a younger population of respondents and many were second generation Asian Americans. We found that Buddhists and agnostics and atheists were most open and accepting (80 to 90%) and Protestant Christians were least accepting followed by Catholics. These results parallel mainstream surveys that found religiosity, age and political affiliation to affect attitudes toward LGBT issues (Egan & Sherrill 2009; Kosmin & Keysar 2008; The Pew Forum on Religion & Public Life 2003). That is, older, religiously observant Christian of conservative political views were more likely to have an anti-LGBT stance. For Asian Americans, the Gallup poll of our political beliefs showed that we were more left leaning (Jones 2010) and that Christianity was not the dominant religious affiliation. Hence, we expect a variegated result for Asian Americans. Similarly, the result of the Vietnamese Americans whom I surveyed was a mixed bag. The Buddhist tended to be more open than the Catholics and Protestants but age and generation factored into their responses on same-sex marriage, perception of (ab)normality of LGBTIQQ people, and rights of LGBTIQQ people. Another interesting finding was that those who were open also reported knowing of other LGBT people in their lives. Exposure to LGBTIQQ people reduced their prejudice. This exposure tended to also correlate with age and generation. The younger folks and those, who were 2nd generation or beyond, expressed more openness, especially if they were not devout Protestants or Catholics. The older folks who abided by traditional gender roles had a harder time accepting LGBTIQQ people as normal whether or not they were religious.

From student interviews, I learned that people of Protestant or Catholic faith had attitudes that often coincided with their priest's or pastor's attitudes. This was consistent with the Faith in America Report that emphasized religious-based bigotry as the main source of hatred and intolerance that were expressed upon LGBTIQQ people or internalized by LGBTIQQ people.

In sum, my survey results of Vietnamese American attitudes toward LGBT reflected the mixed reaction we received in Little Saigon Tết parade. The older and first generation Vietnamese Americans who were religious saw us as upsetting tradition and culture. The younger and second-generation Vietnamese Americans were more open unless they were religious Christians or observant of traditional gender roles.

"Why We Have to Come Out"

While some Vietnamese may not have biases against LGBTIQQ people, they often ask why is it that we have to come out and display ourselves in public when this is a private matter. They do not object to our being LGBTIQQ but they do object to our public announcement and politicizing of a personal matter. The lesson from the recent spate of teen suicides in Fall 2010 (McKinley 2010) should have us understand that the personal and private does not live in a vacuum. The personal has been pressured by peers, condemned by churches, stereotyped by entertainment media, and disenfranchised by the general public. Dishearteningly, the accumulation of these types of oppression—internalized, interpersonal, discursive, social policy (Yep 2002)—takes a toll on our most impressionable and vulnerable youth. Thus, we must speak out publicly and stand up to raise awareness about the struggles of the marginalized and to offer alternative views of love and acceptance.

Furthering the invisibility of LGBTIQQ Vietnamese is the practice of "Don't ask. Don't tell" by many Vietnamese families with LGBTIQQ family members. Given the heterosexist assumptions, the practice of harmony by not raising sensitive issues further marginalizes the existence of LGBTIQQ people and this contributes to the larger environment of **heteronormativity** where society organizes social institutions to normalize and serve heterosexuals as it simultaneously deviantizes and excludes non-heterosexuals. Embedded in this heteronormative thinking and structuring of society is **cisgenderism**, the assumption that there are two fixed discrete sex categories of male and female in human beings and that they correspond to two unchanging gender identities of boy/man/masculine and girl/woman/feminine, respectively. In other words, the heteronormative and cisgenderist structuring of our current society have marginalized and excluded homosexual, bisexual, transgender, intersexual, queer and questioning individuals who do not fit neatly into the current sex-gender-sexuality regime of heteronormativity and cisgenderism. Offering visibility and a language that normalizes our experiences is an ongoing challenge that Vietnamese American LGBT advocates and allies must do against such a hetero-patriarchal and cisgenderist Vietnamese American environment that narrowly defines and affirms our Vietnamese-ness.

Another Vision of Vietnamese American Community

For Vietnamese LGBTIQQ people who have always celebrated Tết with family and community, we are continuing tradition by celebrating Tết except that we now do it openly. While heterosexism of Vietnamese traditions may be a virtue that some want to uphold, some of us would like to envision a more open Vietnamese America that is less heterosexist just as some of us have envisioned and worked toward a less sexist, less racist, and less classist Vietnamese America. The reasoning behind the prejudices is not based on scientific evidence but prejudiced assumptions and selective cultural citations.

When Reverend Sỹ Nguyễn said that our participation in Tết parade was "irrelevant to the meaning of Tết," he was coming from a position of ignorance or denial of our existence as family members and community members of the Vietnamese diaspora. He also said that our participation showed a complete lack of sensitivity to Vietnamese traditions, but rhetorical questions to his statement would be, "Which authentic tradition of Vietnamese culture would you like to uphold? Heterosexist patriarchy or matriarchy? Would questioning of traditions that exclude and abuse women be a "cultural attack on the Vietnamese community?" Possibly he had never thought of LGBTIQQ as part of his community. Perhaps it was because he had never met one, or that he had stereotypes about us that colored his judgment about us. People like him are the reason why we need to be out in the public to dispel stereotypes and to assert that we are a part of Vietnamese America.

The reception of our first Tết march in Little Saigon gave us hope about the future of Vietnamese America. Despite the strong opposition from some religious and political leaders in our community, we also received a lot of love and openness from the rest of our community. We have talked to many since then who supported us but would not publicly proclaim their support in fear of being condemned or out of respect for not contradicting our so-called leaders. For Vietnamese American LGBTIQQ people, we will continue to march in Little Saigon and other Vietnamese American communities to create more understanding and acceptance. We have all experienced the multiple levels of oppression due to racism, sexism, classism, etc., and know that we need our Vietnamese American community to shelter us from American xenophobia, immigrant-bashing, and white supremacy. To be able to be a part of our community but living in the closet or having bifurcated lives would not be ideal for growth of community when not all of its members have full "citizenship." It has been said that a society is judged by how it treats its most vulnerable. Applying this idea to the visioning of a Vietnamese American community, then doing our part in creating a more supportive Vietnamese America is another progressive process of community formation and development. That is, to queer Tết is to create a more inclusive Vietnamese America for LGBTIQQ Vietnamese Americans to come out and come home.

Works Cited

American Psychological Association. "Sexual Orientation Homosexuality." http://www.apa.org/helpcenter/sexual-orientation.aspx Web. 26 January 2011.

Bharath, Deepa. "Vietnamese Gays to March in Tet Parade." *OC Register* 11 Feb. 2010. http://articles.ocregister.com/2010-02-09/cities/24650186_1_vietnamese-community-vietnamese-cultural-gay-marriage-issue Web. 26 January 2011.

_____. "Religious Groups Don't Want Gays in Tet Parade." *OC Register* 11 Feb. 2010. http://articles.ocregister.com/2010-02-11/politics/24641718_1_religious-groups-gay-groups-lesbian-groups Web. 26 January 2011.

Bolsavik. "Andy Quach Has Best Car of Tet Parade." *Bolsavik.com* 13 Feb. 2010. http://bolsavik.com/2010/02/andy-quach-has-best-car-of-tet-parade/ Blog. 26 January 2011.

Census 2000. "Fact Sheet for a Race, Ethnicity, or Ancestry Group." http://factfinder.census.gov/servlet/SAFFIteratedFacts?_event=&geo_id=05000US06059&_geoContext=01000US | 04000US06 | 05000US06059&_street=&_county=orange+county&_cityTown=orange+county&_state=04000US06&_zip=&_lang=en&_sse=on&ActiveGeoDiv=geoSelect&_useEV=&pctxt=fph&pgsl=050&_submenuId=factsheet_2&ds_name=DEC_2000_SAFF&_ci_nbr=048&qr_name=DEC_2000_SAFF_R1050&reg=DEC_2000_SAFF_R1050%3A048&_keyword=&_industry= Web. 27 January 2011.

Chamberlain, Steven Paul. "Recognizing and Responding to Cultural Differences in the Education of Culturally and Linguistically Diverse Learners. *Intervention in School and Clinic* 40.4(2005), 195–211. Web. 26 January 2011.

Diamond, Lisa. "Female Bisexuality from Adolescence to Adulthood: Results from a 10-Year Longitudinal Study." *Developmental Psychology* 44.1(2008): 5–14. Web. 26 January 2011.

Diamond, Milton. "Pacific Center for Sex and Society Home Page." Web. 3 January 2011.

_____. "Biological Aspects of Sexual Orientation and Identity." *The Psychology of Sexual Orientation, Behavior and Identity: A Handbook*. Eds. Louis Diamant and Richard McAnulty. Westport: Greenwood, 1995. 45–80. Web. 26 January 2011.

_____. "Some Genetic Considerations in the Development of Sexual Orientation." *The Development of Sex Differences and Similarities in Behavior*. Eds. Marc Haug, Richard E. Whalen, Claude Aron, & Kathie L. Olsen. 73(1993): 291–309. Web. 26 January 2011.

_____. "Sexual Identity, Monozygotic Twins Reared in Discordant Sex Roles and a BBC Follow-Up." Archives of Sexual Behavior, 11.2(1982), 181–185. Web. 27 January 2011.

Egan, Patrick J. and Kenneth Sherrill. "California's Proposition 8: What Happened, and What Does the Future Hold?" Report commissioned by Evelyn & Walter Haas, Jr. Fund. National Gay and Lesbian Task Force Policy Institute, January 2009.

Faith in America. "Addressing Religious Arguments in Achieving LGBT Equality." http://www.faithinamerica.org/report/ Web. 27 January 2011.

Fausto-Sterling, Anne. "The Five Sexes: Why Male and Female Are Not Enough." *Sexuality and Gender*. Eds. Christine L. Williams and Arlene Stein. Malden: Blackwell, 2002. Web. 26 January 2011.

Gust A. Yep. "From Homophobia and Heterosexism to Heteronormativity: Toward the Development of a Model of Queer Interventions in the University Classroom." *Journal of Lesbian Studies* 6.3/4(2002): 163–176. Print.

Human Rights Campaign. "Transgender Population and Number of Transgender Employees." http://www.hrc.org/issues/9598.htm Web. 25 January 2011.

Intersex Society of North America. "How Common Is Intersex?" http://www.isna.org/faq/frequency Web. 25 January, 2011.

Jernigan, Frank. "What Does the Christian Bible Say?" Source from GLBSB Newsletter (August/September 1992). Downloaded from CSUN Positive Space Program's Ally Project "Notes on Religion" Page. http://www.csun.edu/~psp/handouts/Notes%20on%20Religion.pdf Web. 27 January 2011.

Jones, Jeffrey M. "Asian-Americans Lean Left Politically: Asian-Americans More Liberal Than Other Racial /Ethnic Groups." *The Gallup Daily* February 3, 2010. http://www.gallup.com/poll/125579/asian-americans-lean-left-politically.aspx Web. 12 March 2010.

Kosmin, Barry A. and Ariela Keysar. American Religious Identification Survey: Summary Report. Hartford, CT: Trinity College, 2008. http://commons.trincoll.edu/aris/publications/aris-2008-summary-report/. Web. 12 February 2010.

McKinley, Jesse. "Suicides Put Light on Pressures of Gay Teenagers." *New York Times,* New York Edition, October 4, 2010, A9.

Nguyễn Phương Hùng. "Thiên Hạ Sự" 18 Feb. 2010. Translated from Vietnamese into English by VietLGBT. org and posted at http://lgbtiqtet.blogspot.com/ Web. 3 March 2010.

The Pew Forum on Religion & Public Life. "Republicans Unified, Democrats Split on Gay Marriage: Religious Beliefs Underpin Opposition to Homosexuality." The Pew Research Center for the People and the Press, November 18, 2003. http://pewforum.org/uploadedfiles/Topics/Issues/Gay_Marriage_and_Homosexuality /religion-homosexuality.pdf Web. February 13, 2010.

Prevatt, Chris. "Andy Quach Uses Anti-LGBT Rhetoric to Regain Support in Vietnamese Community." *Liberal OC,* February 12, 2010. http://www.theliberaloc.com/2010/02/12/andy-quach-uses-anti-lgbt-rhetoric-to-regain-support-in-vietnamese-community/. Web. January 14, 2012.

Ross, Robert M., George S. Losey, and Milton Diamond. "Sex Change in a Coral-Reef Fish: Dependence of Stimulation and Inhibition on Relative Size." *Science,* 221(1983), 574–575. Web. 27 January 2011.

Trevor Project. "Suicidal Signs and Facts". http://www.thetrevorproject.org/suicide-resources/suicidal-signs Web. 26 January 2011.

Vũ, Hào Nhiên. "Viet Religious Say: Don't Be Gay on Tet in Little Saigon." *New American Media* 13 Feb. 2010. Posted by Andrew Lam. http://blogs.newamericamedia.org/nam-round-table/1897/viet-religious-say-dont-be-gay-on-tet-in-little-saigon. 26 January 2011.

Whitam, Frederick, Milton Diamond, and James Martin. "Homosexual Orientation in Twins: A Report on 61 Pairs and Three Triplet Sets." *Archives of Sexual Behavior* 22.3(1993): 187–206. Web. 27 January 2011.

PART VIII   Intergroup Relations and Anti-Asian Violence

Los Angeles "Riots" and the Korean-American Community[1]

Edward T. Chang

C
H
A
P
T
E
R

24

After the verdict in the King trial, a Korean merchant was notified by a "regular customer" that if he wanted to be alive he should leave as soon as possible. He immediately closed the store and went home. On the way home, he tuned in to the Korean radio station and heard of the violent mayhem in his business area. His store at Normandie and Florence was being looted and set on fire. Never in their lives did they feel so much rage and injustice in the American system. They had no way to protect their businesses from fire and the looters. Korean American businesses suffered major damages, accounting for almost 50 percent of the city's total property damage.[2] The initial estimate for the property damage in the city was around $750 million. According to the Radio Korea report based on self-reporting by the Korean American victims, 2,300 Korean businesses suffered total or partial loss, and the total damages suffered by Korean Americans are estimated to be around $400 million.

Korean Americans were outraged and saddened by the loss of life and property damages suffered during the "riots." The hopes and dreams that each Korean immigrant yearned to attain were suddenly shattered. I heard many stories that "it is very difficult to describe how I feel towards the riots in Los Angeles, but if I had to choose one word to express how I feel, it would be betrayal." To these Korean American "victims," "America . . . the land of opportunities," was nothing more than just a gimmick to lure vulnerable immigrants.

The issue of racism, in the "amalgamation" or "melting pot" of America, was beginning to erupt. All of a sudden, we were forced to confront the myths of Los Angeles as a model of the multiethnic and multicultural city. Los Angeles has been promoting itself as a "world city," and

---

[1] Although I am using the term "riots," the choice of the term depends on one's perspective. Some prefer "upheaval," "rebellion," or "uprising." Since the most popular term is riot, I will use the term in this paper with quotation marks.

[2] The initial estimate for the property damage was around $750 million. According to the Radio Korea report based on self-reporting by the Korean American victims, 2,300 Korean businesses suffered total or partial loss, and the total damages suffered by Korean Americans are estimated to be around $400 million. It is also important to note that 48% of victims of the "riots" were not insured, according to the Department of California Insurance survey (*Korea Times,* July 4, 1992).

a shining example of multiculturalism. In retrospect, the myth of multiculturalism disguised the sad reality of a "separate and unequal" Los Angeles. Ong and others (1989) in the landmark study of widening inequality in Los Angeles documented that "to achieve full integration, over three-quarters of all Blacks and over half of all Chicanos would have to move into Anglo neighborhoods."[3]

During the "riots," I was forced to wear three different hats: a scholar who is engaged in "objective" research, a community advocate for the Korean victims, and a member of the Black Korean Alliance trying to bridge the gap between the two communities. I soon realized that wearing three hats was an impossible task. I had to choose between doing "objective" scholarly research and assuming a partisan role and serving as a spokesperson for the Korean American community.

Reporters kept my phone busy 15 hours a day for almost two weeks after the "riots." They wanted to know if Korean-African American tensions contributed to the "riots." They also wanted to hear Korean American reactions to the "riots." One of the most common complaints of the reporters was that they could not find Korean American spokespersons who could articulate their feelings in the English language. I had to play the role of voicing the anger, rage, betrayal, resentment, and abandonment of Korean American victims who lost everything they owned.

There are too many unanswered questions about the April 29 Los Angeles "Riots." What happened? Was it a righteous uprising or an anarchistic riot? Where did Los Angeles go wrong? Where were the police? Who was responsible for the failure to protect the lives and properties of innocent citizens? What can we do to prevent this from happening again? It is too premature to answer all of these very important questions. More importantly, answers probably depend upon one's political perspective.

No doubt, the social, economic, and political conditions of South Central Los Angeles, and the ideological shift to the right were the main causes of the Los Angeles "riots" of 1992. The "riots" are telling us that we have ignored these problems for too long. The purpose of this paper is two-fold. First, I will try to analyze the "riots" from a multi-ethnic perspective by tracing its causes. To what extent did racial and class inequality contribute to the explosion of the city? Second, I will attempt to document the voices of Korean American victims who suffered major property and psychological damage. What does it now mean to be Korean American in Los Angeles?

Beyond Black and White

The Kerner Commission Report concluded that America was divided into two separate and unequal nations - one black, the other white. This is how race relations experts used to describe race relations in America. In the past, the race problem meant "black" problem. However, the demographic composition of urban cities has undergone rapid changes during the past twenty years, and it has profoundly altered our way of life. Race relations can no longer be defined as a white-black issue. Indeed, the Los Angeles "riots" of 1992 were America's first multi-ethnic "riots."[4]

---

[3] Paul Ong et al. *The Widening Divide: Income Inequality and Poverty in Los Angeles.* Los Angeles: UCLA Urban Planning Department, 1989.

[4] According to the arrest record of the Los Angeles County Sheriff's Department reported by the *Los Angeles Times* (May 21, 1992), 12,545 arrests were made between the 6:00 p.m. April 29 and 5:00 a.m. May 5 period of civil disorder. The racial breakdown of those who were arrested during the "riots" is as follows: Latinos 45.2 percent, blacks 41 percent, and whites 11.5 percent.

However, race relations theories still focus primarily on the relationship between the white "majority" and the black "minority."[5] Thus, existing theories are no longer viable and relevant since they are without explanatory power. There is an urgent need to develop new theories that can adequately reflect the rapidly changing demography of the United States.

In Los Angeles, whites constituted less than half of the city's population as of 1980 (40%). The demographic shift of South Central Los Angeles has been even more dramatic during the past two and a half decades. Indeed, the face of South Central Los Angeles changed as the "black flight" to suburbs accelerated during the 1980s. The African American population in South Central Los Angeles declined 20 percent from 369,504 to 295,312 between 1980 and 1990. At the same time, the African American population in nearby Inland Empire of Riverside and San Bernardino County increased 99 percent and 134 percent during the same period.[6] In 1965, South Central Los Angeles was largely known as a "black area" with 81 percent African American residents. Now, 48 percent of the population is Latino, which reflects the dramatic demographic change of South Central Los Angeles.

Demographic shifts have increased tensions and polarization among different ethnic and racial groups in the United States. The tensions have reached a potentially explosive point. African Americans feel that they are being squeezed by the increasing numbers of immigrants from Latin America and Asia. Latin American immigrants often compete with African American residents for affordable housing, jobs, education, health and social welfare programs. Highly publicized Latino-African American confrontations at South Central Los Angeles construction sites have occurred shortly after the "riots." Danny Bakewell and the Brotherhood Crusade chased away Latino workers after the Los Angeles "riots," and they proclaimed that "if black people can't work, nobody works."

African Americans are also worried that they are losing political and economic "gains" they have made during the 1960s' civil rights struggle. As South Central Los Angeles has been transformed into a multi-ethnic community, African Americans are concerned that they are losing influence and control in what used to be their "exclusive" domain. They are understandably suspicious of the rapidly growing Latino immigrants and Korean shopowners in "their neighborhoods." In fact, rights already have occurred between the Latino and African American communities over the issues of redistricting for the city council, employment opportunities, and economic justice in Los Angeles. Latinos are demanding proportional representation to reflect population changes, while African Americans argue that they are entitled to retain their share of gains to compensate for past injustices.

In the meantime, Asian Americans are beginning to participate in the political process. For example, the Korean American Victims Association staged daily protests at City Hall for a month to demand compensation of Koreans who lost their businesses during the riots.

If this "politics of race" continues to dominate city politics, Los Angeles will suffer from polarization along racial boundaries, pitting one minority group against another. Obviously the system has failed to provide "justice" for all. Where did it go wrong?

---

[5] See Edward T. Change. "New Urban Crisis: Intra-Third World Conflict" in Shirley Hune et al. eds. *Asian Americans: Comparative and Global Perspectives*. Pullman: Washington State University Press, 1991: 169–178.

[6] According to the 1980 and 1990 Census, the African American population increased from 30,088 to 59,966 in Riverside County, and from 46,615 to 109,162 in San Bernardino County between 1980 and 1990. Source: *Los Angeles Times*, August 13, 1992.

Los Angeles Riots: 1965 and 1992

Is there a difference between the Watts riots and the Los Angeles riots of 1992? What took place in Los Angeles for a few days in April 1992 showed a remarkable resemblance to the Watts riots in 1965. The following description of the Watts riots can easily be mistaken for the Los Angeles "riots" of 1992. They looted stores, set fires, beat up white passersby whom they hauled from stopped cars, many of which were turned upside down and burned, exchanged shots with law enforcement officers, and stoned and shot at firemen. The rioters seemed to have been caught up in an insensate rage of destruction.[7] Also, gun sales tripled as citizens armed to protect themselves during and shortly after the Los Angeles "riots." During the Watts riots of 1965, we witnessed a similar reaction, "some pawn shops and gun stores have been robbed of firearms and gun sales reportedly have tripled since the riots." (Kerner Commission Report, p. 153).

Was there a conspiracy to riot before the Rodney King verdict? Many believed that a civil unrest was organized and planned by gang members. However, both the Kerner Commission report and the FBI investigation of the Los Angeles "riots" could not find any concrete evidence to support these suspicions. Charles J. Parsons, head of the FBI Special Agent in Charge, said, "I am not ruling out the possibility that there was pre-rioting plan, but we don't have any hard evidence of that." (*Los Angeles Times*, July 25, 1992.)

However, the similarities end here. There are several important differences between the Watts riots of 1965 and the Los Angeles "riots" of 1992. As I discussed earlier, the 1992 Los Angeles "riots" involved a multi-ethnic uprising, whereas the Watts riot was primarily and African American revolt against injustice and racism. The Watts riot was confined to geographical areas largely known as South Central Los Angeles, whereas the "riots" of 1992 spread north of South Central Los Angeles into Koreatown, Hollywood, Pico-Union, and other middle class neighborhoods.

In the 1960s, the civil rights movement had gained momentum, and many Americans, including whites, were sympathetic to the minority (i.e., black) issues of poverty, racism, unemployment, and injustice. Whites were willing to pay for and provide assistance to improve the quality of life for African Americans and other disadvantaged minorities. However, as I will discuss later, white Americans are no longer willing to "pay for" social and economic programs to aid the underprivileged with the rise of the neoconservative movement during the late 1970s and 1980s.

In the 1960s, many African Americans were optimistic; they had hope of improving their lives by actively participating in the electoral process. African Americans believed the "American Dream" was attainable as they integrated into mainstream American society. However, despair, hopelessness, and a sense of abandonment are widespread in the African American community in the 1990s. The gap between haves and have-nots widened, and many African American lost their "American Dream" as they dropped out of the labor market.[8] In addition, the rise of neoconservative ideology in the middle 1970s let to a massive assault on social and public policy programs designed to aid minority groups in the United States. In the 1960s, racial disorder was about rising expectations, but today it is about diminishing expectations.[9]

---

[7] A Report by the Governor's Commission on the Los Angeles Riots *Violence in the City—An End of a Beginning?* December 2, 1965.

[8] According to the 1990 census, 41.8 percent of residents of South Central Los Angeles dropped out of the labor force.

[9] Kevin Phillips. *Politics of Rich and Poor.* Random House; 1991.

Deindustrialization and South Central Los Angeles

In the United States, the restructuring of the economy in the form of plant shut-downs, runaway shops, and foreign investments has deepened racial and class inequality in the city. Deindustrialization, the structural realignment of the American economy during the 1970s and 1980s, was a strategy U.S. corporations used in response to the economic crisis created by increasing global competition. "Runaway shops" and overseas investment were an aggressive tactic by capitalists to regain competitiveness and increase profits. "By the beginning of the 1980s, every newscast seemed to contain a story about a plant shutting down, another thousand jobs disappearing from a community, or the frustrations of workers unable to find full-time jobs utilizing their skills and providing enough income to support their families." (Bluestone and Harrison, 1982:4.) Although some politicians blamed the increase of imports from Asia for the loss of American jobs, it was apparent that the structural realignment (deindustrialization) of the American economy caused the closure of plants and factories. In fact, at least 32 million jobs were probably eliminated in the United States as a direct result of private disinvestment in plants and equipment during the decade of the 1970s. (*Ibid*, p. 35.)

Suddenly, unemployment was no longer a problem of the poor. Many companies simply decided to pick up and move to other areas where wages were lower, unions weaker, and the business climates better. The traditional manufacturing sectors such as steel, rubber, and auto were the hardest hit as middle class workers experienced permanent displacement with no prospect of finding equivalent employment. "The lower-middle and middle rungs of the American occupational structure are at risk: the top and the bottom grow." (Harrington: p. 166.)[10] In other words, the deindustrialization has polarized class inequality in the United States—there was a growth of high-tech industries and low-paying unskilled jobs, and a decline of the traditional middle class jobs. For example, New York City lost 400,000 jobs, but there was a 17 percent increase in white collar industries between 1970 and 1980. Simultaneously, there was a growth of sweatshops in the lower depths of the New York economy.[11] Indeed, disinvestment has had a profound social and economic impact, as the gap between haves and have-nots has increased.

Deindustrialization has had a disproportionate impact on South Central Los Angeles. General Motors, Goodyear, Firestone and Bethlehem Steel used to provide jobs and economic security to the residents of South Central Los Angeles. By the 1980s, they had vanished. In a study of racial inequality in Los Angeles, Paul Ong et. al. (1988: 203) found that "in the late seventies and early eighties alone, Los Angeles lost over 50,000 industrial jobs to plant closures in the auto, tire, steel, and nondefense aircraft industries. Since 1971, South Central Los Angeles, the core of the African American community, itself lost 321 firms."

South Central Los Angeles has suffered from chronic poverty, high unemployment, inferior schooling, and soaring rates of high school drop outs. Studies found that "one in four black men in their 20s is in jail or otherwise involved in the criminal justice system. Black men in poor neighborhoods are less likely to live to age 65 than men in Bangladesh. A majority of black babies are born in single-parent households."[12] Despite the warning of the Watts riot of 1965, the socio-economic conditions of South Central Los Angeles continued to deteriorate during the past twenty years.

---

[10] Michael Harrington. *The New American Poverty.* New Jersey: Princeton University Press, 1981.

[11] Saskia Sassen-Koob, "Recomposition and Peripheralization at the Core" in *New Nomads.* S.F. Synthesis Publication, 1982.

[12] *Los Angeles Times,* August 1, 1992: 1

In fact, 1990 census data shows that the status of African Americans has deteriorated since the 1960s. The poverty rate of 1990 was 30.3 percent, which is higher than it was at the time of the Watts riot (27 percent). Per capita income of South Central Los Angeles in 1990 was a mere $7,023, compared with $16,149 for Los Angeles County. More importantly, half of those 16 years and older were unemployed and not looking for a job. These statistics clearly show the failure of the "trickle-down" theory; the economic recovery and boom of the 1980s did not help to improve socio-economic conditions of residents of South Central Los Angeles. Instead, African Americans who live in the inner city often had to endure the burden of the "black tax" - higher insurance rates, mortgage interest rates, abusive police patrols, and lower quality of education.

The future prospects are even more gloomy, since African Americans are grossly underrepresented in high-tech related industries. Park (1992) argues that high technology managers have used race and ethnicity to mitigate a class-based consciousness. With the increasing globalization of the economy, high-tech industries have made a conscious decision not to hire a "traditional industrial labor force" (i.e. white and black). In order to compete in the international market, high-tech managers prefer Asian immigrant workers over African Americans because Asian immigrants are perceived as being docile, diligent, and easily exploitable.[13]

1980s: Era of Neoconservatism

The Los Angeles "riots" of 1992 exposed the failure of the neoconservative policies of the 1980s. Since the passage of the Civil Rights Act of 1965, the Republican Party has captured and dominated the presidency of the United States with strong support from white middle-class voters. The only exception came when former President Nixon was forced to resign from the presidency because of the "Watergate" scandal. Beginning with the landmark Bakke decision (1975), the attitudes of white Americans began to shift from progressive (willing to support social and economic programs to aid minorities) to conservative views (emphasis on morality, strong family values, law and order, and lowering taxes).[14]

The resurgence of neo-conservatism has had a detrimental impact on minority groups during the 1980s through the domestic cutting of social programs for inner cities. White Americans were willing to spend more tax dollars for a military build-up than to address so-called "black problems." Most white Americans now believe that "blacks have been given more than a fair chance to succeed" with the passage of the Civil Rights Act and the implementation of the affirmative action programs.[15] In fact, many whites believe that liberals and Democrats "gave-in" too much to the demands of black Americans at the expense of whites. As I discussed earlier, the economic boom of the 1980s primarily benefitted white Americans and increased the gap between the haves and the have-nots. Simply put, the poor got poorer and the rich got richer. At the same time, the neoconservative attack on social programs left thousands of inner city residents in a state of despair, hopelessness, and alienation during the prosperity of the 1980s' economic boom.

---

[13] Edward Park, "Asian Immigrants and the High Technology Industry in Silicon Valley," Ph.D. dissertation in Ethnic Studies at the University of California, Berkeley, 1992.

[14] For more information on the Allen Bakke case, see Nathan Glazer, *Affirmative Discrimination: Ethnic Inequality and Public Policy*. Basic Books, 1975.

[15] See Andrew Hacker, *Two Nations: Black and White. Separate. Hostile. Unequal*. New York: Charles Scribners's Sons, 1992.

The resurgence of neoconservatism helped the election of conservative presidential candidate Ronald Reagan in 1980 and his landslide election in 1984. The election of George Bush in 1988 solidified the neoconservative movement. Neoconservatism continues to play a major role in the 1992 elections as candidates have focused on "middle class" issues, while failing to address the pervasive issues of poverty, unemployment, school dropouts, and racism.

Republican administrations have implemented a "politics of race" by blaming victims and scapegoating immigrants and minorities for societal problems. Although there is no concrete proof to suggest that the state has promoted or justified the recent waves of anti-Asian activities, there seems to be a correlation between the Republican Party's policies of scapegoating and the increase of anti-Asian violence. As a result, we have witnessed the sudden increase of inter-minority conflicts such as Korean-African American and Latino-African American tensions and the rise of anti-minority violence during the 1980s. It is consistent with the historical development of the majority-minority relationship that the power structure has a way of blaming the victims for social and economic problems in this country.

Police Brutality and the Justice System

The demand for justice was heard loud and clear during the "riots." Police brutality is nothing new to African Americans living in the inner city. The Los Angeles Police Department (LAPD) has had a reputation for brutalizing African American suspects. In fact, the Watts riot of 1965 was triggered by the mistreatment of an African American suspect by a LAPD officer. Los Angeles has learned very little from its history. Little has changed. Although the King videotape came as a shock to most Americans, it was nothing more than confirmation of the reality that African Americans face on a daily basis. Young African American men are often stopped just because they fit a "description" or are in the wrong neighborhood. African Americans are often treated as "guilty" until proven innocent although the constitution of the United States guarantees otherwise.

Many African Americans argue that whites would probably feel sympathy and compassion for King after watching the Rodney King beating video tape. In contrast, African Americans would feel threatened and alarmed that "it could have been me." White Americans cannot even begin to grasp what it is like to be harassed by police or denied a job just because of the color of their skin. It is important to note that many Asian Americans also were shocked and expressed dismay over the brutal beating of Rodney King.

The Latasha Harlins and Rodney King verdicts added to the perception that the justice system does not serve the interests of African Americans. A Korean immigrant grocer, Soon Ja Du, shot and killed a 15 year old African American girl, Latasha Harlins, on March 18, 1991. Mrs. Du was found guilty of voluntary manslaughter. However, she was give a sentence of five years of probation. The lenient sentencing of this Korean grocer exacerbated tension between Korean American and African American communities. The verdicts indicated that the justice system operates on a double standard: one for whites and another for blacks.

It is against this background that Los Angeles County Supervisorial candidate Diane Watson distributed campaign literature stating "Remember Latasha Harlins: The LIFE of a CHILD MUST be WORTH more than a $1.79 bottle of orange juice," to exploit the anger, rage, and frustration of African Americans toward Korean Americans and the judicial system. African Americans had patiently waited for more than a year hoping that justice will prevail in both the Latasha Harlins and Rodney King trials. However, they were dismayed and shocked by the not guilty verdict that reinforced belief that America is still a racist country. Many African Americans still fear that racist white America has the power to control this country.

Inter-Ethnic Relations: Korean-African American Tensions

The media has continued to portray the Los Angeles "riots" of 1992 as an extension of the ongoing conflict between Korean merchants and African American residents, despite the fact that more than half of the looters arrested were Latino.[16] Indeed, Korean-African American conflict has surfaced as one of the most explosive issues facing many cities in the United States since the early 1980s.[17] Despite many efforts to alleviate tensions, the situation has gotten worse in the 1990s.

In January 1990, the Red Apple boycott, which lasted a year and a half in the Flatbush section of Brooklyn, New York, focused national attention on increasing tensions between African Americans and Korean Americans. The relationship between the two communities turned for the worse when two African American customers were shot and killed by Korean American merchants in Los Angeles within a three-month period, March to June 1991. The Latasha Harlins case intensified this volatile situation and ignited boycotts of Korean-owned stores, led by Danny Bakewell of the Brotherhood Crusade. During the boycotts, Bakewell was seen on television almost daily making highly charged remarks against Korean Americans. This certainly heightened the tensions and contributed to the polarization of the two communities.

Inter-ethnic tensions in African American neighborhoods have historical roots. Jewish merchants and African Americans clashed during the 1960s. During the Watts riots, many Jewish-owned stores were looted and burned down, accounting for 80 percent of furniture stores, 60 percent of food markets, and 54 percent of liquor stores destroyed.[18] Korean immigrants are also perceived as part of "a long line of outsiders who came into African American neighborhoods to exploit the community." It was whites, Jews, Chinese, Japanese, and now Koreans who dominated the business interests in the African American community. It does not matter whether you are green, red, yellow, brown. You are simply perceived as an "outsider." It is not, therefore, a racial issue, but a class issue involving small business and residents.

African Americans complain that Korean merchants behave rudely and fail to contribute economically to the community. African Americans also complain that Korean merchants do not hire African American workers, overcharge for inferior products, and do not contribute profits back to the community.

One of the most common complaints focuses on "rudeness." Some merchants are indeed rude, although the majority are kind and courteous to their customers. Korean Americans are exceptionally family-oriented, and that affects their attitudes in dealing with people they don't know. It is also a common complaint by Korean Americans that they too, have experienced "rudeness" from fellow Korean merchants. In general, Korean Americans are centered around their families, so they are nice to people they know but are "rude" to strangers. Part of this "rudeness" is prejudice, but part is misunderstanding. Therefore, it is wrong for Korean Americans to deny they are prejudice, but it is also wrong for African Americans to accuse all Korean merchants of being "rude."

It is also important to understand the notion of "relative deprivation." In the eyes of the underclass who has nothing to lose, the merchant class represents wealth. On the other hand, Korean Americans perceive themselves as simply trying to "make a living." Korean Americans often complain that life in the United States is a life of making "payments." Although Korean merchants are

---

[16] According to the study by Rand Corporation, *Los Angeles Times*.

[17] For more detail on Korean-African American relations, see Edward T. Chang, "New Urban Crisis: Korean-Black Conflicts in Los Angeles." University of California, Berkeley, Ph.D. dissertation in Ethnic Studies, 1990.

[18] Sholmo Katz, ed. *Negro and Jew: An Encounter in America*. London: The MacMillan Company, 1966: 76.

able to make some profits from their stores, many are barely able to keep up with their monthly payments, such as mortgage, car, utility, or merchandise payments. These different perceptions of the status of Korean merchants has exacerbated the tensions and polarized the two communities.

In any colonial situation, it is inevitable that the middleman is perceived as a target of oppressed people. For example, Korean independence fighters saw Koreans who collaborated with the Japanese colonial government as enemies of the Korean people. Japanese collaborators were protecting the interests of the colonial government in Korean. Therefore, Japanese collaborators had to be eliminated in order to achieve independence for Korea. That's how some African Americans are perceiving Korean Americans, as a "layer" that protects the interests of white America and preserves the status quo. Korean Americans have become a "symbol of oppression."

Do Korean Americans function as a "layer" between haves and have-nots? As Korean immigrants are struggling to adjust in the American mosaic, they are wondering where they fit into American society. If Korean Americans occupy this middle "layer," they will be used to benefit someone else's agenda. Korean Americans feel that they are boxed in. Korean Americans must find an answer to this fundamental question.

Korean American Perspectives: A Turning Point

The Los Angeles "riots" of 1992 will be remembered as a turning point in Korean American history similar to the internment experience for Japanese Americans. The "riots" opened the eyes of the Korean immigrants to the problems of institutional racism, social and economic injustice, and the shortcomings of the "American Dream."

In the Korean American community, the Los Angeles "riots" are called "4–29 riots" (*Sa-I Gu Pokdong*). It rhymes with "4–19 student uprising" (*Sa-Il Gu Hak Saeng Undong*) of 1960 which overthrew the dictatorial government in South Korean. The student uprising of 1960 was the first student protest movement that successfully ousted a dictator from the power. C.W. Mills (1959) mentioned the significance of this student uprising in his introduction to *Yankee Go Home* on the Cuban revolution.

Not many people are aware that the global student movement of the 1960s began in South Korea. Today, student movements in South Korea are still very active. If *Sa-Il Gu* (4–19) was a turning point of modern Korean history, *Sa-I Gu* (4–29) will be remembered as a turning point of Korean American history. I strongly believe that the events represent the transformation from "Koreans in America" to "Korean Americans."

As usual, the media focused on superficial and biased images of the "riots," and Korean Americans were again victimized. Korean Americans were outraged by the live coverage of Korean American merchants who were shooting at a drive-by shooter on KABC-TV (channel 7). What KABC-TV failed to show was that the individuals were trying to loot the stores and had shot at the merchants first. The Korean store owners were simply trying to protect and defend themselves against the drive-by shooters. The "Eyewitness News" (KABC-TV) team stigmatized the Koreans as gun-toting vigilantes.

During the crisis, Korean Americans had to rely upon "nationalism" or "ethnic solidarity" to survive the crisis.[19] What is the relationship between this nationalism and racism? "Nationalism" often is very dangerous for Korean Americans because it is exclusive and closes off any possibility

---

[19] I thank Elaine Kim for raising this question in my earlier talk on this topic at the Association for Asian American Studies meeting in San Jose, May 1992.

of open dialogue and discussion with others. At the same time, it is an essential part of the Korean American community psyche for survival. Thus, during the crisis, I heard Korean immigrants exclaim: "We don't have anything except the nationalism." This mentality grew out of thousands of years of oppression and suffering. It was the immigrants' only way to survive, given the historical background of countless foreign invasions and aggressions.

In the Korean American community, one burning question is whether Korean-owned stores were targeted by African American protestors. There is indirect evidence that Korean-owned stores were targeted. Why did this happen? Korean immigrant merchants are viewed as a "layer" of white racist structure that protects the system. In order to attack the basic problem, you have to get rid of the "layer" that protects the core. That is how some groups explain their selective targeting of Korean stores.

Will Korean merchants go back to South Central Los Angeles? According to the informal survey of 194 Korean Grocery Victims Association members, 65 percent (127) would not go back in to South Central Los Angeles if they received full compensation for their losses. Only 33 percent (64) responded that they would go back.[20] Although it is highly unlikely, some are considering a return to Korea. One merchant expressed his anger, "it is hopeless here, and we must go back to Korea." Actually, most Korean Americans cannot go back due to financial and sociopolitical reasons.

For second generation Korean Americans, the Los Angeles "riots" provided an opportunity to understand their ethnic identity. What does it mean to be a second generation Korean American in the aftermath of the "riots?" A former student of mine confessed her feelings:

I used to just consider myself an American, usually neglecting to express my ethnic background. I was embarrassed and ashamed because many Koreans had established a negative image among the media and the African Americans and the fact that I had accommodated with the American lifestyle so much, that I had no interest in the Korean culture. Because of this incident, I have found so much respect for the Korean race because they are standing up for their rights and creating a positive name for themselves.

Indeed, many second generation Korean Americans found a new sense of belonging and self-awareness. For many the "riots" were a turning point from being "banana Americans" to becoming "Korean Americans." As a result, the "riots" brought immigrants and the second generation closer. One second-generation Korean American student summed up her feeling that "I was especially proud of my people when they had the peace march to demonstrate that Koreans aren't just the passive and silent immigrants. Rather, we re the new voice of America, and we will speak out against any more actions targeted against us."

In the aftermath of the Los Angeles "riots," many problems in the Korean American community have been exposed. These problems include the generational split, conservative ideology, and lack of leadership. However, I intend to focus on two major structural problems. First, the "riots" showed that Korean Americans suffer from "dual oppression." The immigrant community is still controlled and dominated by the homeland government.[21] The fact that the Republic of Korea Consulate in Los Angeles organized and led community meetings in the aftermath

---

[20] *Joongang Ilbo*, July 18, 1992. It is important to note that this sentiment may not reflect the general attitudes of Korean merchants since 95 percent of the respondents suffered from the total loss of their businesses. For Korean business owners who suffered a partial loss or looting, they would be more likely to reopen their stores in South Central Los Angeles.

[21] For more information see Edward T. Chang. "Korean Community Politics in Los Angeles: The Impact of the Kwangju Uprising" in *Amerasia Journal* vol. 14:1 (1988), 51–67.

illustrates this problem. In addition, Korean Americans learned the painful lesson that they have no friends in Sacramento or Washington, D.C. after the "riots." In short, the Korean American community lacks self-determination. The community must develop political power to over-come home-land intervention in community affairs and develop strategies to strengthen political power in America as well.

Second, the Korean American community has not worked sufficiently with other communities of color. Although the Black Korean Alliance (BKA) has been actively involved in mediating conflicts between Korean merchants and African American residents since 1986, it has not been effective because of the lack of grassroots support, financial resources, and commitment by politi-cal leaders of Los Angeles. The Korean American community must seek ways to reach out to Latino, Jewish, Native American, African American, and white communities.

As the Korean American community tries to recover from the "riots," one of the most pressing problems is a new ordinance passed by the city council shortly after the "riots." The city council hastily passed an ordinance that liquor stores, swapmeet stores, and pawnshops/gunshops must obtain a conditional permit to reopen in South Central Los Angeles.[22] The city council never con-sidered the potential social and economic implications of this ordinance to victims of the "riots." There were no public hearings on this issue. Korean Americans without effective political clout, believe they have been victimized again by politicians.

African American activists have complained about the proliferation of liquor stores in their neighborhoods for many years. These activists saw the current situation as an oppor-tunity to reduce the concentration of liquor stores in their neighborhoods, and mounted a campaign. The real challenge for Korean Americans is to confront and overcome the misplaced aggression of rioters, neglect of law enforcement agencies, and political decisions by selfish politicians.

Conclusion

The Los Angeles "riots" of 1992 was a turning point in Los Angeles history. It has provided us with a unique opportunity to reexamine our ways of life and ideas. It awakened us to the new American reality. What is the new reality? It is the end of the white-black era and the beginning of a multiethnic and multiracial community. Race relations can no longer be narrowly defined in terms of white-black, merchant-customer, or Korean-black conflicts. We have to be more "inclusive" of all racial and ethnic groups in Los Angeles.

Peaceful coexistence for different racial, ethnic, and national groups cannot be accomplished without much more educational, social, and political efforts. How can we promote understanding, harmony, and trust between different racial, ethnic, and religious groups? Multicultural education in the United States has many insights and theories needed to strengthen and lead radical challenges to racism. Through a multicultural education curriculum, we must not only learn to appreciate our differences but also to teach our children to challenge the roots of racism in America. The aftermath of the "riots" teaches us to play an active role in creating a truly inclusive multi-racial and multi-ethnic society.

---

[22] It is important to note that the issue of liquor licenses in African American neighborhoods is not necessarily racially motivated anti-Korean activities by African American activists. The African American community has been complaining about the higher per capita distribution of liquor stores in their neighborhoods than other areas. See Lindsay Chaney "The Bottom Line: Liquor Licenses—A Race Issue?" *Los Angeles Herald Examiner*, November 22, 1977.

Hate Violence as Border Patrol: An Asian American Theory of Hate Violence

Terri Yuh-lin Chen

CHAPTER 25

Lexisnexis Summary:

. . . Violence has been an integral part of the histories and experiences of Asian Americans in the United States from our arrival in this nation to the present. . . . Furthermore, there is widespread underreporting of hate crimes against Asian Americans because of linguistic barriers between victims and police and the lack of bilingual law enforcement personnel, a lack of knowledge on the part of Asian Americans regarding hate crime laws and civil rights protections, a mistrust of the police and thus a reluctance to report hate crimes, and finally, shame or embarrassment of being a victim. . . . The alien land laws diminished the ability of Chinese, Japanese, Korean, and South Asian immigrants to earn a living in agriculture. . . . Although the deaths of Vincent Chin and Navroze Mody are widely known examples of anti-Asian hate crimes, there are countless others who have suffered the same type of hate violence as border patrol. . . . Victor Hwang, in his experience with the Race Relations: Hate Violence Project at the Asian Law Caucus, finds that law enforcement generally does not take hate crimes seriously. . . . Even if law enforcement did take hate crimes against Asian Americans more seriously, the issue still remains with legalized hate violence in the form of border patrol. . . . This paper has attempted to place hate violence against Asian Americans as part of a larger context of increased border patrol. . . .

Highlight:

Chico, California 1877

Arsonists of the Order of Caucasians, a white supremacist group that blamed Chinese immigrants for all the economic sufferings of white workers, tried to burn down the Chinatown in Chico and murdered four Chinese men by tying them up, dousing them with kerosene, and setting them on fire.

Rock Springs, Wyoming 1885

A mob of white miners massacred twenty-eight Chinese laborers, wounded fifteen, and chased several hundred out of town. The white miners opened fire at a crowd of unarmed Chinese, burned their huts to the ground, and threw the bodies of the dead Chinese as well as the wounded Chinese who were still alive into the flames. A grand jury did not indict a single person.

Detroit, Michigan 1982

Vincent Chin was a Chinese American male beaten to death a few days before his wedding with a baseball bat by two white laid-off autoworkers who screamed during the killing that the "Japs" were taking all the jobs. The killers were fined less than $ 4000 each and sentenced to three years of probation.

Denver, Colorado 1984

Helen Fukui, a fifty-two year old woman, disappeared in Denver on December 7, 1984. Her decomposed body was found weeks later. The fact that she disappeared on Pearl Harbor Day when anti-Asian speech and incidents heightened racial tensions was considered significant in the Asian American community, but the case was not investigated as a hate crime. No suspects were ever arrested.

New York City, New York 1985

Ly Yung Cheung, a nineteen year old seamstress in New York's Chinatown, was waiting for a subway train when she was pushed into the path of a train by a man claiming to have a psychotic "phobia about Asians." Cheung was decapitated by the oncoming train. She was seven months pregnant at the time.

Jersey City, New Jersey 1987

A Jersey City gang who called themselves the "Dotbusters" (a reference to the red bindi that some South Asian women wear as a sign of marital fidelity) published a letter in the paper stating that they would take any means necessary to drive the Indians out of Jersey City. Numerous racial incidents from vandalism to assault followed. Later that month, the Dotbusters used bricks to bludgeon and beat Navroze Mody, a South Asian male, into a coma. No bias charges were brought against the killers.

Stockton, California, January 1989

A gunman dressed in military clothes entered the schoolyard of Cleveland Elementary School in Stockton and opened fire with an AK47 assault rifle. He killed one Vietnamese and four Cambodian children: Raphanar Or, age 9; Ram Chun, age 8; Thuy Tran, age 6; Sokhim An, age 6; and Ocun Lim, age 8. The killings were driven by the gunman's hatred of Southeast Asians because of the Vietnam War.

Houston, Texas, August 1990

Hung Truong, a fifteen-year old Vietnamese American teenager, was walking down the street with three friends when they were accosted by persons in two cars that stopped alongside them. Two men stepped out of one car with a club and began to chase Truong, who was separated from his friends. While shouting "white power," the two men kicked and beat Truong. Truong begged them to stop and said "God forgive me for coming to this country. I'm so sorry." After they left him bleeding on the ground, Truong's friends called the paramedics who claimed that Truong seemed well enough to go home. Truong died the next morning.

Alpine Township, Michigan, June 1995

Thanh Mai, a 23-year old Vietnamese American, visited a teen nightclub with two of his friends in Alpine Township, Michigan on June 18, 1995. Mai was sitting alone and was accosted by three young white males who taunted Mai with racial slurs, including "What the f—k are you looking at, gook?" Mai tried to walk away from the situation, but when his attention was diverted, one of the white men surprised Mai by hitting him in the face. Mai fell to the concrete ground with such force that his skull split open, sending him into convulsions. Mai died five days later from major head trauma.

Southern California, August 1999

Joseph Ileto, a Filipino postal worker was gunned down by a white supremacist on a shooting rampage in Southern California, which included opening fire in a Jewish community center. The killer shot Ileto nine times in the chest and later confessed that he killed Ileto because he looked Asian or Latino. The media initially invisibilized the murder of Joseph Ileto and characterized the rampage as a solely anti-semitic one.[1]

Text:

[*71] Introduction

Violence has been an integral part of the histories and experiences of Asian Americans in the United States from our arrival in this nation to the present. Anti-Asian violence can occur at any given moment, but it is especially prevalent during periods of anti-immigrant sentiment.[2] Most hate crimes committed against Asian Americans draw upon notions of Asian Americans as perpetual foreigners who do not belong in this society.[3] Indeed, Victor Hwang notes how violence based on notions of foreignness has been an integral theme in Asian American history when he writes:

> The Asian American community is based on an understanding and appreciation for the fact that we have struggled for nearly two centuries against this violence and exclusion in the plantations, in the courts, and on the battlefields. . . . It is in our struggle against this pattern of violence and its underlying message of physical, political, and historical exclusion that we find ourselves as Asian Pacific Americans.[4]

---

[1] There are so many more victims of anti-Asian violence, many of whom we do not even know. The lost lives recounted here are not intended to be a complete representation.

[2] I use the term "anti-Asian violence" to include hate violence against both Asians and Asian Americans.

[3] *See* Telephone interview with Victor Hwang, Staff Attorney at Asian Law Caucus and Director of Hate Crimes Project (Nov. 20, 1998) [hereinafter Hwang Interview]; Jerry Kang, *Racial Violence Against Asian Americans*, 106 HARV. L. REV. 1926 (June 1993); National Asian Pacific American Legal Consortium, Audit of Violence Against Asian Pacific Americans: Anti-Asian Violence, A National Problem, First Annual Report (1993) [hereinafter NAPALC Audit I]; National Asian Pacific American Legal Consortium, Audit of Violence Against Asian Pacific Americans: Anti-Asian Violence, A National Problem, Second Annual Report (1994) [hereinafter NAPALC AUDIT II]; National Asian Pacific American Legal Consortium, Audit of Violence Against Asian Pacific Americans: The Consequences of Intolerance in America, Third Annual Report (1995) [hereinafter NAPALC AUDIT III]; National Asian Pacific American Legal Consortium, Audit of Violence Against Asian Pacific Americans: The Violent Impact on a Growing Community, Fourth Annual Report (1996) [hereinafter NAPALC Audit IV]; National Asian Pacific American Legal Consortium, Audit of Violence Against Asian Pacific Americans: Continuing the Campaign Against Hate Crimes, Fifth Annual Report (1997)[hereinafter NAPALC Audit V]. The National Asian Pacific American Legal Consortium is affiliated with the Asian American Legal Defense and Education Fund in New York, the Asian Pacific American Legal Center of Southern California in Los Angeles, and the Asian Law Caucus in San Francisco.

[4] Victor Hwang, The Interrelationship Between Anti-Asian Violence and Asian America, 22 CHICANO-LATINO L. REV. 18, 19 (2000).

In the United States, wherever there is foreignness, there is also a negative reaction to foreignness. This negative reaction includes setting up borders and expelling foreigners. Robert S. Chang and Keith Aoki note, "in the same way that the cell wall or membrane serves a screening function, the border operates to exclude that which is dangerous, unwanted, [*72] undesirable."[5] The United States guards its borders seriously and marks foreigners within its physical borders according to race. Not all foreigners are treated the same by the United States. Angelo Ancheta uses the term "outsider racialization" to describe the construction of Asian Americans and other non-whites as foreigners. Outsider racialization operates on two different levels:

First, Asian Americans, Latinos, and Arab Americans are racially categorized as foreign-born outsiders, regardless of actual citizenship status. Racialization operates on multiple levels: through psychological cognition and learning, social and political discourse, and institutional structures. Second, ostensibly race-neutral categories such as "immigrant" and "foreigner" are racialized through the same social processes. Just as Asian Americans, Latinos, and Arab Americans are presumed to be foreigners and immigrants, foreigners and immigrants are presumed to be Asian, Latino, or Arab.[6]

Thus, some immigrants are able to cross the border into the United States and gain immediate acceptance as un-foreign because of their white appearance. Racialized others may physically enter the country, but not without foreignness stamped on their faces through their racial uniforms. Accordingly, hate crimes against Asian Americans take on the unique dimension of operating as a form of border patrol and protection of the nation against the foreign "alien." An analysis of anti-Asian hate violence must recognize the social context of foreignness in which the violence manifests as well as the reactions that foreignness triggers from the state and from private actors.[7]

Part I of this paper briefly examines violence as a form of systemic oppression against people of color throughout history and its prevalence in particular against the Asian American community. Part II addresses how perceptions of Asian Americans have always been and continue to be informed by stereotypes grounded in foreignness and focuses on the treatment of Asian Americans by the state. Part III explores white American national identity in the context of immigration, white American anxiety over cultural security and over maintaining borders as a way to deal with the resulting identity crisis. This section also focuses on popular and cultural perceptions of Asian Americans as foreigners. Part IV builds upon the notion of Asian Americans as perpetual foreigners and analyzes how perceptions of foreignness cause Asian Americans to be subject to both official state and unofficial private forms of border patrol. Hate violence is examined as constituting a form of border patrol by both state and private actors. Finally, this section considers how the construction of [*73] individual hate crimes as the sole problem ignores the border patrol function of hate violence and the role of the state in perpetrating hate violence.

---

[5] Robert S. Chang and Keith Aoki, *Policy, Politics and Praxis: Centering the Immigrant in the Inter/National Imagination*, 85 CAL.L.REV. 1395, 1411 (1997).

[6] ANGELO N. ANCHETA, RACE, RIGHTS, AND THE ASIAN AMERICAN EXPERIENCE 64 (1998).

[7] This paper will focus on the nativist violence against Asian Americans although other groups of color such as Latina/os and Arab Americans certainly also face such nativist violence. Because this paper focuses on nativist violence and racism, I do not discuss hate violence within the Asian American community (which includes domestic violence and sexual assault against many Asian American women) and between communities of color (particularly between the Asian American, Latina/o, and African American communities). I do not intend to imply that these forms of violence do not exist.

I. Violence: The American Way

I believe in revolution
because everywhere the crosses are burning,
sharp-shooting goose-steppers round every corner,
there are snipers in the schools . . .
(I know you don't believe this.
You think this is nothing
but faddish exaggeration. But they
are not shooting at you.)[8]

A. The Face of Oppression: Violence

Group-based violence has been a means of maintaining dominant power relationships throughout the history of the United States. Violence played a major role in the initial colonization of North America and genocide of Native Americans, the subjugation of African Americans into slavery, the conquest and annexation of Mexico and its people, and the exclusion of Asian Americans. It has been used strategically to circumvent any protective laws and to suppress any rebellion from the subordinated. One representation of such violence is evident during the reign of terror when the Ku Klux Klan commanded during Reconstruction to prevent the Thirteenth, Fourteenth, and Fifteenth Amendments from being effectively implemented. Physical violence and the psychological terror that accompanies it have been some of the most effective tools of the state to oppress people of color, and they are tools that the private citizenry has utilized fully. Violence by private individuals and by organized white supremacist groups like the Ku Klux Klan has a long history and continues today as a major threat to targeted groups, especially with new media such as the Internet available to spread its message of terror.[9]

While oppression occurs in many different forms, violence is one of its oldest and most pervasive forms. Iris Young explains:

> What makes violence a face of oppression is less the particular acts themselves, though these are often utterly horrible, than the social context surrounding them, which makes them possible and even acceptable. What makes violence a phenomenon of social injustice, and not merely an individual moral wrong, is its systemic character, its existence as a social practice.[10]

[*74] Thus, the violence that people of color experience is not simply a random, individual act, but a widespread and systematic act of domination with all institutions of society in complicit support of the violence. Young further describes:

---

[8] Lorna Dee Cervantes, *Poem for the Young White Man Who Asked Me How I, an Intelligent, Well-Read Person, Could Believe In the War Between Races, in* UNSETTLING AMERICA, AN ANTHOLOGY OF CONTEMPORARY MULTICULTURAL POETRY 248, 248–49 (Maria Mazziotti Gillan and Jennifer Gillan eds., 1994).

[9] *See* NAPALC Audit II, *supra* note 3, at 13. *See also* ANTI-DEFAMATION LEAGUE, HIGH-TECH HATE: EXTREMIST USE OF THE INTERNET (1997).

[10] IRIS YOUNG, JUSTICE AND THE POLITICS OF DIFFERENCE 61–62 (1990).

> Violence is systemic because it is directed at members of a group simply because they are members of that group. . . . The oppression of violence consists not only in direct victimization, but in the daily knowledge shared by all members of oppressed groups that they are *liable* to violation, solely on account of their group identity. Just living under such a threat of attack on oneself or family or friends deprives the oppressed of freedom and dignity, and needlessly expends their energy.[11]

Consequently, people of color understand that violence is a part of racial oppression which must be struggled against in the quest for liberation.

Violence is a tool of the state as well as a tool of individuals over oppressed groups. The two forms of manifested violence are interrelated: violence by the state is approved and supported by the private citizenry, and violence by private actors is tolerated and encouraged by the state. Thus, violence by police officers, border patrollers, and the military are all state forms of violence supported by the citizenry, and the state's condoning and ignoring violence by private actors by failing to prosecute such behavior is a form of state complicity with private acts of violence.

B. Pervasiveness of Hate Violence Against Asian Americans

For this paper, I define hate violence according to how it is defined by the National Asian Pacific American Law Consortium (NAPALC).[12] Under this approach, hate violence includes:

> any verbal or physical act that intimidates, threatens, or injures a person or person's property because of membership in a targeted group. That membership can be based on actual or perceived race, ethnicity, national origin, immigration status, religion, gender, sexual orientation, or age. Such acts may include verbal or written threats, harassment, graffiti, property damage, and physical assaults, some of which result in serious injury or death.[13]

This definition is broader than the legal definition of a hate-motivated crime used by the Federal Bureau of Investigation (FBI) in collecting its statistics. Under the FBI's approach, hate crimes only consist of criminal offenses motivated by a person's race, religion, ethnicity, or sexual orientation.[14] In addition, the FBI requires more than the mere utterance of racial epithets as evidence of bias motivation in order to consider an incident as a hate crime.[15] NAPALC's broader definition "recognizes the role of racist language in dehumanizing, humiliating, and ultimately [*75] creating an atmosphere that both fosters and condones violence against racial minorities."[16] The more inclusive definition also reflects the common occurrence of racial slurs that escalate into physical violence.[17] The effects of hate violence reach far beyond the physical consequences, as the

---

[11] *Id.* at 62. 62 (1990).

[12] NAPALC is a collaboration of major civil rights organizations in Asian American communities across the country and is specifically affiliated with the Asian American Legal Defense and Education Fund in New York, the Asian Pacific American Legal Center of Southern California in Los Angeles, and the Asian Law Caucus in San Francisco.

[13] NAPALC Audit III, *supra* note 3, at 7.

[14] *See id.*

[15] *See* NAPALC Audit II, *supra* note 3, at 7.

[16] NAPALC Audit III, *supra* note 3, at 7.

[17] *See id.*

psychological, sociological, and political costs of hate violence reverberate throughout the larger Asian American community as well as other oppressed communities of color.[18]

Hate crimes are committed against all subordinated groups in the United States, but they exist as particular forms of control over people of color who are perceived as foreign.[19] Victor Hwang, staff attorney at the Asian Law Caucus in San Francisco and head of its Race Relations: Hate Violence Project, states that most hate crimes against the Asian American community reflect the notion of Asians as foreigners who need to be expelled from the country.[20] Asian Americans are the fourth most likely group to be hate crime victims, yet are only 3% of the U.S. population.[21] In fact, hate violence against Asians has increased at a faster rate than for any other ethnic group.[22]

The Asian American civil rights community recognizes the prevalence of violence as a major civil rights issue for Asian Americans. In 1993, the National Asian Pacific American Legal Consortium began to track hate incidents and published its first annual report on anti-Asian violence. It was the first comprehensive, nationwide, non-governmental attempt to collect and assess data on anti-Asian violence.[23] However, it is critical to note that severe underreporting problems exist for a variety of reasons. Not all law enforcement agencies collect data on hate crimes, and although the federal Hate Crimes Statistics Act, enacted in 1990, sought to develop a uniform system of data collection, reporting is only voluntary for law enforcement agencies. Furthermore, there is widespread underreporting of hate crimes against Asian Americans because of linguistic barriers between victims and police and the lack of bilingual law enforcement personnel, a lack of knowledge on the part of Asian Americans regarding hate crime [*76] laws and civil rights protections, a mistrust of the police and thus a reluctance to report hate crimes, and finally, shame or embarrassment of being a victim. Even when racially motivated incidents are reported to the police, law enforcement may still fail to classify the incident as a hate crime, sometimes deliberately to avoid further investigation and additional paperwork.[24] Even with severe underreporting, the statistics are alarming because they reveal that Asian Americans are twice as likely to be assaulted than harassed and thus more likely to be physically injured during a hate crime.[25]

---

[18] *See* Richard Delgado, *Words that Wound: A Tort Action for Racial Insults, Epithets, and Name Calling*, 17 HARV. C.R.-C.L. L. REV. 133 (1982).

[19] On some level, all people of color are perceived as the "other" and thus, foreign and not belonging to this nation which claims white as its color. Because this paper concentrates on anti-Asian violence, the focus is on Asian Americans and foreignness. There are unique ways in which the Asian American, Latino, and Arab-American communities have been constructed as foreign which differs from the African American and Native American experiences. See Robert Chang, *Dreaming in Black and White: Racial-Sexual Policing in The Birth of a Nation, The Cheat, and Who Killed Vincent Chin?*, 5 ASIAN L.J. 51 (1998), for a description of how Blacks suffered racism as the "real" racial Other while Asians suffered nativistic racism as the "real" foreign Other.

[20] *See* Hwang Interview, *supra* note 3.

[21] *See* Jerry Kang, *Racial Violence Against Asian Americans*, 106 HARV. L. REV. 1926 (1993) (citing ORGANIZATION FOR CHINESE AMERICANS, IN PURSUIT OF JUSTICE 2 (1992)). *See generally* U.S. Comm'n on Civil Rights, Civil Rights Issues Facing Asian Americans in the 1990s 45–48 (1992) [hereinafter Civil Rights Issues]; U.S. Comm'n on Civil Rights, Recent Activities Against Citizens and Residents of Asian Descent 40–57 (1986) [hereinafter RECENT ACTIVITES].

[22] *See* Kang, *supra* note 21 (citing Brief of the National Asian Pacific American Legal Consortium, Amici Curiae at 3, Wisconsin v. Mitchell, (U.S. 1993) (No. 92–515)).

[23] *See* NAPALC AUDIT II, *supra* note 3.

[24] *See* CIVIL RIGHTS, *supra* note 21, at 46; NAPALC AUDIT I, *supra* note 3, at 6.; NAPALC AUDIT II, *supra* note 3, at 9.

[25] *See* NAPALC AUDIT I, *supra* note 3, at 6; NAPALC AUDIT II, *supra* note 3, at 8.

II. The Perpetual Foreigners: State Treatment of Asian Americans As Foreigners

"Mrs. Hammerick . . . Boiling Spring Elementary School . . . I was scared of her like no dark corners could ever scare me. You have to know that all the while she was teaching us history . . . she was telling all the boys in our class that I was Pearl and my last name was Harbor. They understood her like she was speaking French and their names were all Claude and Pierre. I felt it in the lower half of my stomach, and it throbbed and throbbed until I thought even you sitting three rows away could hear it . . . It would be so many years . . . I would understand that Pearl Harbor was not just in 1941 but in 1975."[26]

The state has historically classified Asian Americans as foreigners and has treated Asian Americans as threats to U.S. solidarity and security. In this section, I will explore three specific examples of how Asian Americans were perceived as foreign by the state and the impact of such perceptions.

A. Chinese Exclusion

The fear of non-white immigration can be seen in the Chinese Exclusion laws of the 1880s and 1890s. In fact, U.S. immigration law is fundamentally based on the exclusion of Chinese immigrants.[27] In 1882, 1884, 1888, and 1892, Congress passed the Chinese Exclusion laws, which were the first set of federal immigration laws to be challenged in the judicial system.[28] In the Chinese Exclusion Case, *Chae Chan Ping v. United States*, 130 U.S. 581 (1889), the Court worried about the refusal of Chinese immigrants to assimilate and feared that Chinese immigrants presented a "great danger" because "at no distant day that portion of our country would be overrun by them [Chinese], unless prompt action was taken to restrict their immigration."[29] Justice Field, writing for a [*77] unanimous Court, stated that "it seemed impossible for them [Chinese] to assimilate with our people, or to make any change in their habits or modes of living."[30] He also referred to Chinese immigrants as an "Oriental invasion" and as a "menace to our civilization."[31]

In *Chae Chan Ping*, the Supreme Court sought to answer for the first time the question of which branch of government had the authority to set immigration policy and invented the plenary power doctrine. The Constitution does not grant authority to Congress to regulate immigration.[32] Despite the idea that the United States is a government of enumerated powers, the Supreme Court declared that the power of the United States to regulate immigration and control its borders was so basic that it was inherent in the sovereign power of the state.[33] This plenary power doctrine defies the constitutional structure of delegated powers and allows the power to exclude foreigners

---

[26] Monique Thuy-Dung Truong, *Kelly, in* ASIAN AMERICAN LITERATURE: A BRIEF INTRODUCTION AND ANTHOLOGY 288, 289 (Shawn Wong ed., 1996).

[27] *See* Chae Chan Ping V. United States, 130 U.S. 581 (1889).

[28] *See* THOMAS ALEXANDER ALEINIKOFF ET AL., IMMIGRATION AND CITIZENSHIP: PROCESS AND POLICY 179 (4th ed. 1998).

[29] Chae Chan Ping, *supra* note 27, at 595 (1889).

[30] *Id.*

[31] *Id.*

[32] *See* ALEINIKOFF, *supra* note 28, at 178.

[33] *See* Chae Chan Ping, *supra* note 27, at 609 (1889).

to remain unchecked by the Constitution. The doctrine of plenary power has continued to domi-nate immigration law and virtually exempts it from judicial review.[34] Consequently, judges are very reluctant to intervene and usually defer to the legislative branch instead. Although Chinese Exclusion was later modified by legislation, *Chae Chan Ping* is not merely an ugly remnant of the past. In fact, *Chae Chan Ping* is valid precedent as the case has never been modified or reversed and continues to be cited by modern courts to support the plenary power doctrine.[35]

The states have also sought to exclude Chinese immigrants from entering its borders. Cali-fornia's State Constitution, for example, included an entire section devoted to how Chinese must be excluded from sectors such as corporations and public works. As declared in the constitu-tion: "No corporation now existing or hereafter formed under the laws of this state shall, after the adoption of this constitution, employ, directly or indirectly, in any capacity, any Chinese or Mongolian. The legislature shall pass such laws as may be necessary to enforce this provision."[36] The next section stated, "no Chinese shall be employed on any state, county, municipal, or other public work, except in punishment for crime."[37] In referring to Chinese immigrants, the state con-stitution also stated, "the presence of foreigners ineligible to become citizens of the United States is declared to be dangerous to the well-being of the state, and the legislature shall discourage their immigration by all the means within its power."[38]

[*78] B. Alien Land Laws

Even for the Asian Americans exempted from the Chinese Exclusion laws, the alien land laws ensured their subordinate position in society by denying them the right to own land. The Califor-nia legislature began to discuss proposals to prohibit land ownership by Japanese immigrants in 1907 and introduced such bills within the next few sessions.[39] In 1913, the California legislature passed the first Alien Land Law, which restricted land ownership to U.S. citizens. It stated that only "aliens eligible to citizenship may acquire, possess, enjoy, transmit, and inherit real property or any interest therein."[40] Since the federal 1790 Naturalization Act prohibited non-whites from becoming naturalized citizens, only white immigrants could satisfy the phrase 'aliens eligible to citizenship,' thus effectively precluding Asians from owning land.[41] The proponents of the legislation openly acknowledged the racially discriminatory intent of the law and claimed that it was necessary to combat the Japanese threat. State Attorney General Ulysses Webb maintained

---

[34] *See* ALEINIKOFF, *supra* note 28, at 217–18 (citing Henkin, *The Constitution and United States Sovereignty: A Century of Chinese Exclusion and its Progeny*, 100 HARV. L. REV. 853, 862–63 (1987)).

[35] *See* ANCHETA, *supra* note 6, at 88.

[36] CAL. CONST. of 1879, art. XIX, § 2.

[37] CAL. CONST. of 1879, art. XIX, § 3.

[38] CAL. CONST. of 1879, art. XIX, § 4.

[39] *See* RONALD TAKAKI, STRANGERS FROM A DIFFERENT SHORE: A HISTORY OF ASIAN AMERICANS 203 (1989).

[40] BILL ONG HING, MAKING AND REMAKING ASIAN AMERICA THROUGH IMMIGRATION POLICY 1850–1990 30 (1993).

[41] *See* TAKAKI, *supra* note 39, at 82. Although the 1870 post-Civil War Naturalization Act extended citizenship to African Americans and the question of whether to extend citizenship to Chinese Americans was debated, Congress ultimately refused to extend citizenship to Chinese Americans. *See* SUCHENG CHAN, ASIAN AMERICANS: AN INTERPRETIVE HISTORY 47 (1991). It is important to point out that even though the 1870 reform did technically extend citizenship to persons of African ancestry, this was in name only as Blacks were still effectively disenfranchised.

that the concern of "race undesirability" prompted the bill since Japanese individuals would probably not immigrate and remain in the United States if they could not acquire land and settle here.[42]

Other states were quick to follow California's lead and soon a multitude of alien land laws spread rapidly in the early 1900s.[43] Arizona passed one in 1917, Washington and Louisiana in 1921, New Mexico in 1922, Idaho, Montana, and Oregon in 1923, and Kansas in 1925.[44] These laws were facially neutral and survived constitutional challenge but were targeted towards Asian immigrants as a group because the racial bar on naturalization made them ineligible for citizenship. The alien land laws diminished the ability of Chinese, Japanese, Korean, and South Asian immigrants to earn a living in agriculture. Although California's 1913 Alien Land Law was not enforced by prosecutors much during World War I due to the need for food production, once the war was over Californians passed a ballot initiative in 1920 to eliminate the ability of Asian non-citizens to lease farm land completely. In 1923, an amendment made sharecropping agreements between landowners and Asian non-citizen farmers illegal even though technically no legal interest in the land itself was conferred.[45]

[*79] While the Chinese community focused on the legal challenges to the exclusion laws, the Japanese community challenged the validity of the alien land laws.[46] Four landmark cases were heard by the U.S. Supreme Court in 1923, all of which eliminated any rights the Japanese farmers may have previously exercised. The Court upheld Washington's and California's alien land laws in *Terrace v. Thompson* and *Porterfield v. Webb*.[47] In *Webb v. O'Brien*, the Court held that sharecropping agreements were illegal, and in *Frick v. Webb*, the Court upheld laws prohibiting non-citizens from owning stocks in corporations formed for the purpose of farming.[48] It was not until *Oyama v. California* in 1947 that California's alien land law was finally struck down.[49]

C. Japanese American Internment

The construction of Japanese Americans as foreigners began long before the Pearl Harbor bombing, as evidenced by the alien land laws and the anti-japanese hysteria that shrieked for the removal of Japanese Americans. The Los Angeles Times editorialized, "[a] viper is nonetheless a viper wherever the egg is hatched—so a Japanese American, born of Japanese parents—grows up to be a Japanese, not an American."[50] Henry McLemore, a prominent syndicated columnist for the Hearst papers, called for the internment of Japanese Americans:

I am for immediate removal of every Japanese on the West Coast to a point deep in the interior. I don't mean a nice part of the interior either. Herd 'em up, pack 'em off and give 'em the

---

[42] *See* TAKAKI, *supra* note 39, at 204.

[43] *See* CHAN, *supra* note 41, at 47.

[44] *See id.*

[45] *See id.*

[46] *See id.* at 49.

[47] *See* IAN F. HANEY LOPEZ, WHITE BY LAW: THE LEGAL CONSTRUCTION OF RACE 129 (1996). *See also* Terrace v. Thompson, 263 U.S. 197 (1923); Porterfield v. Webb, 263 U.S. 225 (1923).

[48] *See* CHAN, *supra* note 41, at 95–96; *see also* Webb v. O'Brien, 263 U.S. 313(1923); Frick v. Webb, 263 U.S. 326 (1923).

[49] *See* HANEY LOPEZ, *supra* note 47, at 129; *see also* Oyama v. California, 332 U.S. 633 (1947).

[50] TAKAKI, *supra* note 39, at 388. (1989).

inside room in the badlands. Let 'em be pinched, hurt, hungry and dead up against it . . . . Personally, I hate the Japanese. And that goes for all of them."[51]

This anti-Japanese rhetoric was also present in governmental documents. General DeWitt, military commander for the western states, stated in his formal recommendation for removal, "In the war in which we are now engaged racial affinities are not severed by migration. The Japanese race is an enemy race and while many second and third generation Japanese born on United States soil, possessed of United States citizenship, have become 'Americanized,' the racial strains are undiluted."[52]

Japanese American Internment exemplified the fear of the "alien" within our borders and the need to expel the foreigner. Neil Gotanda writes, "It is within this dynamic—the evolution of the treatment of Other non-whites—that the concentration camp cases are best understood. . . .[*80] these cases were crucial steps in the development of the complex links of the social and legal categories of race and alienage. Most important in this development has been the persistence of the view that even American-born non-Whites were somehow 'foreign.'"[53] In *Korematsu v. United States*, the Court upheld the internment of Japanese Americans even under its own strict scrutiny test because internment supposedly constituted a military necessity.[54] The Court insisted that it was not merely looking at race but the issue of military necessity and "national security": "To cast this case into outlines of racial prejudice, without reference to the real military dangers which were presented, merely confuses the issue. Korematsu was not excluded from the Military Area because of hostility to him or his race. He *was* excluded because we are at war with the Japanese Empire."[55] However, white immigrants like German and Italian Americans were not interned like the Japanese Americans because they did not seem foreign in the same way; unlike the foreign and "otherized" Japanese Americans, German and Italian Americans did not threaten the existence of a white national identity or its security.

III. The Perpetual Foreigners: Identity and Border Crises

> *"excuse me, ameriKa,*
> *I'm confused.*
> *You tell me to lighten up,*
> *but what you really mean is whiten up.*
> *You wish to wash me out,*
> *melt me into your cauldron.*
> *Excuse me, if I tip your melting pot,*
> *spill the shades onto your streets."*[56]

---

[51] ANCHETA, *supra* note 6, at 69. (citing COMM'N ON WARTIME RELOCATION AND INTERNMENT OF CIVILIANS, PERSONAL JUSTICE DENIED 71–72 (1982)).

[52] TAKAKI, *supra* note 39, at 391 (citing DANIELS, CONCENTRATION CAMPS USA 65 (1972); COMM'N ON WARTIME RELOCATION, PERSONAL JUSTICE DENIED 66 (1982)).

[53] *See* Neil Gotanda, *Other Non-Whites in American Legal History: A Review of Justice at War*, 85 COLUM. L. REV. 1186 (1985).

[54] *See* Korematsu v. United States, 323 U.S. 214 (1944).

[55] *Id.* at 223.

[56] ANIDA ROUQUIYAH YOEU ESGUERRA *of* I WAS BORN WITH TWO TONGUES, *excuse me, ameriKa, on* BROKEN SPEAK (Fist of Sound Records 1999)(transcribed by the author).

A. White American National Identity and Immigration

In order to fully understand the dynamics occurring in anti-Asian hate violence, we must examine the role that race and foreignness play in the construction of white American identity.[57] American national identity is defined as a white one, and thus, anyone not white is "otherized." The status of being the "Other" implies being "other than" or different from the assumed norm of white national identity.[58] Because America sees color as [*81] fundamental to its very core identity and existence, it needs to label and drive out the "Other" to preserve this color of white. This dynamic is reflected in American immigration history.

After over a century of Asian exclusion, the Immigration and Nationality Act of 1952 (McCarran-Walter Act) nullified the 1790 Naturalization Act restricting naturalization to whites, finally allowing Asian Americans to naturalize, and technically ended exclusion by allowing a small number of immigrants from South and East Asia.[59] However, it was post-1965 immigration that really changed the landscape for Asian immigration. The 1965 Immigration Act was framed as an amendment to the McCarran-Walter Act of 1952, but it substantially changed the immigration system by reforming the "national origins quotas" as the basis for immigration.[60] The 1965 Act provided for an annual admission number from the eastern and western hemispheres and enacted a new preference system for immediate family members and skilled laborers.[61]

The 1965 Act changed immigration patterns and demographics more dramatically than the proponents of the legislation could have imagined. Although the original supporters of the Act had predicted that European immigration would continue to predominate, in actuality, Asian immigration has dominated, behind only Mexico. The proponents appeased nativist groups opposing the legislation by arguing that Asian immigration could only increase slightly because the number of Asian citizens in the United States was too small to really take advantage of the family preference system for reunification of immediate family members.[62] However, because of the 1965 reforms, Asian immigration has increased steadily. The Philippines, Korea, China, and Vietnam rank as the second through fifth largest sending countries of immigrants to the United States, behind only Mexico which sends the highest number of immigrants.[63] Prior to 1965, immigration had been predominately European and from the western hemisphere.

Differential racialization of immigrants is obvious when examining the treatment and acceptance of white immigrants as compared to immigrants from Africa, Asia, the Caribbean, and Latin

---

[57] The capitalization of terms in this Comment is done purposefully, with the names for people of color capitalized and the term "white" left in the lower case. Gotanda explains, "As a term describing racial domination, 'white' is better left in lower case, rather than privileged with a capital letter. 'Black,' on the other hand, has deep political and social meaning as a liberating term and, therefore, deserves capitalization." For a more complete discussion, see Neil Gotanda, *A Critique of Our Constitution Is Color-Blind*, 44 STAN. L. REV. 4, n. 12 (1991).

[58] For a discussion of othering, see Patricia Hill Collins, *Learning from the Outsider Within: the Sociological Significance of Black Feminist Thought*, 33.6 SOC. PROBS., S14, S18 (1986).

[59] See TAKAKI, *supra* note 39, at 413–417. (1989).

[60] See CHAN, *supra* note 43, at 145–146. (1991).

[61] See *id.* at 145.

[62] See *id.*

[63] See *id.*

America. Chang and Aoki explain, "Fear of immigration, often discussed in generalized terms, is colored so that only certain immigrant bodies excite fear. . . . The 'problem' of legal and illegal immigration is colored in the national imagination: fear over immigration is not articulated solely around foreignness per se; it includes a strong racial dimension."[64] The ability to label a group of people as foreigners enables white America to define itself in opposition to the foreigners, because white Americans are not [*82] foreign. Different non-white groups experience being the "Other" as a foreigner outside of white American national identity in different ways. Obviously no group of color fits the definition of white American national identity, but the specific ways in which foreignness may be constructed and experienced varies across different communities of color. For Asian Americans, the image of the perpetual foreigner is a pervasive stereotype, which informs our experience as the "Other."[65]

The process of "othering" necessarily involves a relational system of defining identity in a social and historical context of domination and subordination. Thus, "othering" involves the categorization of people in terms of their difference from one another so that one derives its meaning only in relation to the other. Patricia Collins explains, "for example, the terms in dichotomies such as black/white, male/female, reason/emotion, fact/opinion, and subject/object gain their meaning only in *relation* to their difference from their oppositional counterparts."[66] In this relational system, American national identity is inextricably tied to non-American (foreign) identity. The positive, superior American national identity is white, good, patriotic, and belonging; the negative, inferior non-American identity (foreign) is non-white, bad, treacherous, and invasive.

Edward Said's work on "Orientalism" examines how the western colonial gaze constructed "the Orient" in opposition to itself, "the Occident" so that its self-identity relied on a negation: what we are, they are not; what they are, we are not.[67] Keith Aoki elaborates on Said's notion of "Orientalism" by analyzing a particular strand of "American Orientalism" which explains the process of "othering" for Asian Americans in the context of foreignness:

> the national identity of the United States has been constructed in opposition to racialized 'Others' like Asian immigrants and Asian Americans. 'American Orientalism' also carries a significant additional component: the idea of 'foreignness,' which refers to the construction of the American nation-state that involves categorization of persons as 'citizens' or 'foreigners.' . . . In a complex fashion, the American 'Orientalist' gaze deeply inscribes 'otherness' on Asian Americans and Asian immigrants as simultaneously 'racialized' as 'non-white' and 'foreign and unassimilable.'[68]

Thus, Asian Americans are "otherized" as non-whites, but are also "otherized" as foreign.

---

[64] Chang and Aoki, *supra* note 58, at 520.

[65] *See* note 19.

[66] Collins, *supra* note 58, at S20.

[67] *See* EDWARD W. SAID, ORIENTALISM (1978).

[68] Keith Aoki, *"Foreign-ness" and Asian American Identities: Yellowface, World War II Propaganda, and Bifurcated Racial Stereotypes*, 4 UCLA ASIAN PAC. AM. L.J. 1, 6–9 (1996).

[*83] B. White American National Identity Crisis and Cultural Insecurity

The desire to protect white national identity has often been framed in terms of "national security."[69] However, this term must be distinguished from cultural insecurity on the part of anxious whites. Often, "national security" points to cultural insecurity and the preservation of a white, Eurocentric national identity. This is exemplified by Pat Buchanan's statement, "if we had to take a million immigrants in, say, Zulus, next year or Englishmen and put them in Virginia, what group would be easier to assimilate and would cause less problems for the people of Virginia? There is nothing wrong with us sitting down and arguing that issue, that we are a European country."[70] Multiculturalism and people of color are perceived as threats to this illusory notion of a cohesive white cultural security. Consequently, it does not take a large number of Asians to trigger the perceived threat to cultural security. The mere presence of Asians in America and their impact on the national culture, in terms of, for instance, languages other than English being spoken, is enough. Immigration policy has historically reflected such fears. Enid Trucios-Haynes explains, "The current immigration debate fully illustrates that U.S. society will accept only a multiracial population that is subordinate and nonthreatening to the dominant Western European culture."[71] Fears that Chinese immigrants would be unable to assimilate and would challenge the cultural/"national security" were certainly reflected in the Chinese Exclusion legislation. The Court in *Chae Chan Ping* articulated concern over the unassimilability of the Chinese, but it was really trying to protect American cultural/"national security" from an "Oriental invasion."[72] Ruben J. Garcia notes, "Assimilationism is also proxy for the fear of shifting demographics which [*84] will make whites the minority in some areas of the country."[73]

---

[69] The concept of "national security" must be deconstructed to its many different meanings, none of which are racially neutral for those who are racialized as foreigners. When the rhetoric of "national security" is employed, we should remember the ways in which it can and has been used against Asian Americans. For instance, "national security" can be a territorial idea of protecting United States soil and physical land. This concern for "national security" is reflected by Chinese Exclusion which warned against invasion, the alien land laws which protected U.S. soil from "foreigners" by not allowing them to own it, and "protection" of the U.S. from Japan by interning the Japanese Americans. "National security" can be a militaristic secret intelligence notion of protecting the American people. This concern results in racial profiling in the Department of Defense where Dr. Wen Ho Lee was admittedly targeted because of his race. Although the targeted investigation lasted over two years, no evidence was found of espionage on his part. He was held in jail without bail for security violations of which other people in the department are also admittedly guilty. "National security" can also be a financial type of security depending on how healthy the U.S. market economy is. This is reminiscent of the anti-Japan bashing which occurred in the 1980s when Japanese cars gained popularity and Japan was doing well in trade, culminating in the murder of Vincent Chin by two laid-off automobile workers in Detroit who beat Chin to death with a baseball bat while yelling that "Japs" had taken all the jobs. "National security" can also be a cultural security which is at stake, as reflected in the fear of multiculturalism and the fear of multiple languages, as seen in "English-Only" laws.

[70] Bill Ong Hing, *Beyond the Rhetoric of Assimilation and Cultural Pluralism: Addressing the Tension of Separatism and Conflict in an Immigration Driven Multiracial Society*, 81 CAL. L. REV. 863, 863–64 (1993) (citing Patrick Buchanan on *This Week With David Brinkley*, ABC News television broadcast, Dec. 8, 1991).

[71] Enid Trucios-Haynes, Symposium, *Citizenship and Its Discontents: Centering the Immigrant in the Inter/National Imagination (Part I): Section One: Race, Citizenship, and Political Community Within the Nation-State: Article: The Legacy of Racially Restrictive Immigration Laws and Policies and the Construction of the American National Identity*, 76 OR. L. REV. 369, 377–78 (1997).

[72] Chae Chan Ping, *supra* note 27, at 595.

[73] Ruben J. Garcia, *Critical Race Theory and Proposition 187: the Racial Politics of Immigration Law*, 17 CHICANO-LATINO L. REV. 138 (1995).

Indeed, efforts to either expel or assimilate Asians in this country have always had roots in white cultural insecurity.

C. Nativistic Racism and Figurative Borders

The interplay of racialized foreignness results in what Chang and Aoki term "figurative borders":

> Foreignness is inscribed upon our bodies in such a way that Asian Americans and Latinas/os carry a figurative border with us. This figurative border, in addition to confirming the belonging-ness of the 'real' Americans, marks Asian Americans and Latinas/os as targets of nativistic racism. It renders us suspect, subject to the violence of heightened scrutiny at the border, in the workplace, in hospitals, and elsewhere.[74]

Asian Americans and Latinas/os are threatening to whites as we have crossed the physical border and have "penetrated" into the interior. Despite being physically inside the border, we can still be marked with figurative borders.

These figurative borders have serious consequences because "violence operates to regulate boundaries."[75] Borders have historically been places of violence, and those marked as foreign are likely to experience violence.[76] Chang and Aoki explain:

> This violence is spurred on by certain narratives of America which permit and perhaps encourage the pathological impulse toward nativistic racism. This violence is not confined to the geo-political periphery; it may explode anywhere that there is a border (and remember: the border is everywhere). This has serious consequences for those who carry a figurative border on our bodies. Asian Americans and Latina/os, as perpetual internal foreigners, allow "real" Americans to reassure themselves that the national community begins and ends with themselves, ensuring, at least momentarily, a stable notion of the national community and the fiction of a homogeneous American identity.[77]

This ability to mark non-whites with figurative borders allows white Americans to believe in cultural security and temporarily stabilizes the white American national identity crisis.

D. Stereotypes of Asian Americans: Threats to Cultural Security

Stereotypes of foreignness abound in the popular imagination, mostly with Asian Americans and Latinas/os as the epitome of foreignness. Stereotypical portrayals of Asian Americans are very much informed by [*85] foreignness. Both the "model minority" and the "yellow peril" stereotypes have elements of foreignness embedded in them. Gary Okihiro describes, "the yellow peril

---

[74] Chang and Aoki, *supra* note 5, at 1396, 1414 (1997).

[75] *Id.* at 1416.

[76] For a discussion of border violence, see Michael J. Nunez, Note, *Violence At Our Border: Rights And Status Of Immigrant Victims Of Hate Crimes And Violence Along The Border Between The United States And Mexico*, 43 HASTINGS L.J. 1573 (1992) and Jesus A. Trevino, Comment, *Border Violence Against Illegal Immigrants and the Need to Change the Border Patrol's Current Complaint Review Process*, 21 HOUS. J. INT'L L. 85 (1998).

[77] Chang and Aoki, *supra* note 5, at 1396, 1416.

and the model minority are not poles, denoting opposite representations along a single line, but in fact form a circular relationship that moves in either direction."[78]

The characterization of foreignness of Asian Americans is what allows dominant society to move freely between these two seemingly contradictory stereotypes.[79] The underlying constant of foreignness provides the continuity needed to transform from positive to negative to positive. Natsu Taylor Saito notes the slipperiness and interconnectedness of the traits: "The positive versions of these stereotypes include images of Asian Americans as hardworking, industrious, thrifty, family-oriented, and even mysterious or exotic. It is striking that the negative images almost invariably involve the same traits. Hardworking and industrious become unfairly competitive; family-oriented becomes clannish; mysterious becomes dangerously inscrutable."[80]

These stereotypes of Asian Americans as foreigners and the enemy are reinforced through the media, educational, and political institutions of dominant society. An almost infinite number of examples exist which perpetuate Asian Americans as foreigners and as the enemy. Anti-immigrant scapegoating is often triggered by current events, which portray Asian Americans as negative foreigners. In June of 1993, a freighter (the *Golden Venture*) carrying 300 Chinese indentured servants ran aground in Queens, New York. The resulting media coverage perpetuated negative stereotypes of Asians as foreign illegal smugglers (specifically, Chinese as undocumented immigrants) and fueled anti-immigrant sentiment across the nation.[81] In reality, Italians were the largest group of undocumented immigrants in the state of New York in 1993.[82] Next on the list were undocumented immigrants from Ecuador and Poland. In fact, illegal Chinese did not even make the top ten list of groups of undocumented immigrants in the state of New York.[83] The *Golden Venture* incident ignited serious backlash, which had ramifications for the Asian American community, including unwarranted detention of Asian Americans at international airports, searches for undocumented immigrants at Asian American homes, and a flood of hate mail to Asian Americans.[84] One letter sent in East Brunswick, New Jersey in July 1993 was signed by the "Ping Pong Exterminators." The letter stated:

> Enough is Enough. It is now time to send these illegals and slave traders to where they come from. We will get rid of Chinese from the Garden State beginning one month from July 4th. They are criminals hiding [*86] behind their BMW's, Benz and use their laundry, restaurant and massage parlors to cheat this country. They are infiltrating into safe communities of the Garden State and bringing big city criminal gangs with them. Look what happened in Teaneck. We will start with Edison and East Brunswick, two of the safest communities these Chinese gangs have picked to infiltrate. If you think what is happening in Germany is violent, you ain't seen nothing yet. There will be Chinese blood and bones all over if they don't quit voluntarily by August 5th. God save and bless America. God bless the Ping Pong Exterminators.[85]

---

[78] GARY Y. OKIHIRO, MARGINS AND MAINSTREAMS: ASIANS IN AMERICAN HISTORY AND CULTURE 142 (1994).

[79] *See* Natsu Taylor Saito, *Model Minority, Yellow Peril: Functions of "Foreignness" in the Construction of Asian American Legal Identity*, 4 ASIAN L.J. 71, 76 (1997).

[80] *Id.* at 72.

[81] *See* NAPALC AUDIT I, *supra* note 3, at 19.

[82] *See* Jeff Yang and Karen Lam, *Could It Happen Here?*, VILLAGE VOICE, Dec. 6, 1994, at 14.

[83] *See* Deborah Sontag, *Study Sees Illegal Aliens in New Light*, N.Y. TIMES, Sept. 2, 1993, at B1.

[84] *See* NAPALC AUDIT I, supra note 3, at 19.

[85] *Id.*

The backlash also resulted in increased efforts to pass restrictive immigration laws and to dismantle political asylum.[86] The National Asian Pacific American Legal Consortium notes, "Anti-immigrant sentiment has become legitimized in that it is permissible to openly discriminate against people who look different, speak a language other than English, have a non-Anglo name or appear otherwise 'foreign.'"[87]

Other recent examples of Asian Americans as the perpetual foreigner include the portrayal of the Chinese boat people in *Lethal Weapon 4* (which was the top-grossing film the first week it was released), the MSNBC headline reporting on Tara Lipinski winning the gold medal over Michelle Kwan's silver as "American Beats Kwan," and the Democratic political donations scandal portraying Asians taking over the American government with dirty money.[88] Being the perpetual foreigner has serious ramifications for Asian Americans in the context of anti-Asian hate violence.

IV. Hate Crimes as Border Patrol

La Migra

I.

Let's play La Migra *I'll be the Border Patrol. You be the Mexican maid. I get the badge and sunglasses. You can hide and run, but you can't get away because I have a jeep. I can take you wherever I want, but don't ask questions because I don't speak Spanish. [*87] I can touch you wherever I want but don't complain too much because I've got boots and kick—if I have to and I have handcuffs. Oh, and a gun. Get ready, get set, run.*

II.

Let's play La Migra *You be the Border Patrol. I'll be the Mexican woman. Your jeep has a flat, and you have been spotted by the sun. All you have is heavy: hat, glasses, badge, shoes, gun. I know this desert, where to rest, where to drink. Oh, I am not alone. You hear us singing and laughing with the wind,* Agua dulce brota aqui, aqui, aqui, *but since you can't speak Spanish, you do not understand. Get ready.*[89]

excuse you, ameriKa

*excuse you, ameriKa, While I scratch your name with 3 'K's, mark 'X' for your xenophobic tendencies, scrape the violence off your skulls, and ask you why. Why are you so angry, ameriKa? You whip out wisecracks, attack the defenseless, flashing the superior color of your badge. You beat us down, blameless as victims, who remain nameless. Bashing the heads of all our Vincent Chins, you serve violence, a beating for culture's sake, [*88] fist fights that finish a Denny's meal. You dig graves for forgotten faces, steal lives for petty skin crimes, bury our dead with bullet wounds, slay the living with foreign stares. Why don't you stop hating me? Why don't you stop killing me?*[90]

---

[86] *See id.*

[87] *See* NAPALC AUDIT II, *supra* note 3, at 12–13.

[88] *See "Lethal" Unleashes Firepower at Box Office*, USA TODAY, July 13, 1998, at 1D; Eric Sorensen, *Asian Groups Attack MSNBC Headline Referring to Kwan—News Web Site Apologizes for Controversial Wording*, SEATTLE TIMES, Mar. 3, 1998, at A15; *No Medals for an American Gaffe*, S.F. CHRON., Mar. 4, 1998, at A18; Joann Lee, *Mistaken Headline Underscores Racial Presumptions*, EDITOR & PUBLISHER MAG., Apr. 25, 1998, at 64; NAPALC AUDIT V, *supra* note 3.

[89] Pat Mora, *La Migra, supra* note 8, at 366–68 (*La migra:* term along the border for Border Patrol agents, *Agua dulce brota aqui, aqui, aqui:* sweet water gushes here, here, here).

[90] YOEU ESGUERRA, *supra* note 56.

Those who are marked as foreign are forever subject to border checks, both officially and unofficially. Border patrols occur all the time, everywhere, and in all different forms by both state and private actors. Hate violence is one such form of border patrol and can also be executed by either state or private actors.

A. State Forms of Border Patrol

Officially, the state controls the border carefully through a complex web of institutions and legal restrictions on non-citizens.[91] The enforcement function of the Immigration and Naturalization Service (INS) consists of four different programs, which include Inspections, Investigation, Detention and Deportation, and Border Patrol.[92] The mission of the Border Patrol is to police the border and stop illegal immigration into the United States.[93] However, border patrol does not exist just on the border. For instance, the INS border checkpoint on Interstate 5 is located approximately halfway between San Diego and Los Angeles, many miles away from the literal United States-Mexico border.[94]

The anxiety of whites has led to an intense anti-immigrant hysteria and has spurred a renewed policing of the border with Asians and Latinas/os as the special targets of the INS and Border Patrol. Both the Asian American and the Latina/o communities are perceived to be perpetual foreigners to the United States. The similarities between these two groups have increased even more as an anti-immigrant climate has led to both communities being seen as illegal immigrants. At the same time, the INS has stepped up efforts against these two groups. For Asians, the focus now is on accusing Asian immigrants of being smuggled through the Mexico-United States border.[95] The INS has described the problem as one of multilingual smugglers in a global network who are bringing in an influx of Chinese into the United States.[96] The concern of the INS has prompted [*89] President Clinton to announce the creation of a multi-agency federal offensive against the trafficking of immigrants.[97]

Such border patrol targeted against Asians has also intensified along the U.S.-Mexico border along the Rio Grande.[98] In 1993, the Border Patrol launched "Operation Hold the Line" (originally named "Operation Blockade") in El Paso, Texas, which stationed 450 agents (three times the normal number) on an around-the-clock watch along the twenty miles of the Rio Grande River separating El Paso, Texas from Ciudad Juarez in Mexico.[99] This new strategy was to saturate the

---

[91] Although the legal and widely-used term for non-citizens is "aliens" (legal/illegal), I choose not to use that term here because I find it to be very degrading to a group already so dehumanized and exploited. The term reveals just how differently non-citizens are treated in the United States which is, ironically, a nation of immigrants.

[92] See <http://www.ins.usdoj.gov/graphics/workfor/overview/working.htm> (last visited 1998).

[93] See Trevino, *supra* note 76, at 88–89.

[94] See Chang and Aoki, *supra* note 5, at 1397 n.4.

[95] See Sam Dillon, *Asian Aliens Now Smuggled From Mexico*, N.Y. TIMES, May 30, 1996, at A9.

[96] See Sebastian Rotella and Lee Romney, *Smugglers Use Mexico as Gateway for Chinese Immigration: the Increasing Influx of Illegal Immigrants is Largely Because of an Alliance Between Latin American and Asian Crime Syndicates, INS Authorities Say*, L. A. TIMES, June 21, 1993, at A3.

[97] See id.

[98] See Dillon, *supra* note 95.

[99] See ALEINIKOFF, *supra* note 28, at 623.

border with agents instead of the old strategy of allowing movement across the border and then apprehending illegal immigrants once they were on United States soil. [100]

Following the implementation of "Operation Hold the Line" in Texas, the Border Patrol instituted "Operation Gatekeeper" in Southern California and "Operation Safeguard" near Nogales, Arizona in 1994. These operations also saturated the border with agents and erected new fences and lights. [101] However, even before "Operation Gatekeeper," the INS had already replaced the traditional chain-link fencing with "solid metal fencing, fashioned from obsolete military landing mats used for temporary runways." In 1994, the INS also added new computerized fingerprinting technology, which would identify repeat illegal crossers. [102] Doris Meissner, commissioner of the INS, attributes the increased smuggling of Asians through Mexico to the heightened crackdown on maritime smuggling that followed the 1993 *Golden Venture* incident.[103] Thus, with respect to Asians, the Border Patrol now focuses on the United States-Mexico land border in addition to maritime and airport patrol. Asian Americans are increasingly being targeted as part of a crackdown on smuggling rings involving Asian and Latina/o members. This demonstrates how Asians and Latinas/os are being linked together in Border Patrol raids and operations. In November 1998, federal officials were involved in a yearlong investigation called "Operation Seek and Keep" to catch smuggling cartels of Asian immigrants who attempted to illegally enter the U.S. through Russia, Cuba, and Latin America. [104] "Operation Seek and Keep" was the first investigation authorized to use new wiretap technology in illegal immigrant smuggling cases that was approved by Congress in 1996.[105]

The state takes its duties of border control seriously and supports this with the necessary funding. Border Patrol funding increased from 374 million dollars in 1994 to 631 million dollars in 1997. In addition, Congress has authorized increased funds for additional Border Patrol employees. In November 1999, the INS Border Patrol website contained a [*90] recruitment list of 2000 open INS agent positions. [106] Over 90% of Border Patrol agents are concentrated on the Southwest border where the number of border agents has jumped from 3,300 in 1994 to 6,200 in 1997. Furthermore, the number of prosecutions brought by U.S. attorneys in the Southwest for immigration-related violations has increased threefold between 1994 and 1997.[107]

The last decade's intensification of immigration control has been accompanied by a climate of anti-immigrant hysteria. This hysteria has further encouraged law enforcement and private actors to discriminate against foreigners. Because so much of their job is based on discretionary judgments, Border Patrol agents possess a very powerful tool against anyone they perceive to be foreign. Border Patrol agents can subjectively determine whether reasonable suspicion exists that someone entered the U.S. illegally and have the right to stop and question a person solely to discern if the person has the right to be in the United States.[108] Such discretion allows Border

---

[100] *See id.*

[101] *See id.*

[102] *See id.*

[103] *See* Dillon, *supra* note 95.

[104] *See* Frank Davies, *Agents Crack Three Crime Cartels That Traded in Asian Immigrants,* THE BUFFALO NEWS, Nov. 21, 1998, at 6A.

[105] *See id.*

[106] *See* <http://www.ins.usdoj.gov/graphics/lawenfor/bpatrol/bpcareer/index.htm> (visited Nov. 18, 1999).

[107] *See* ALEINIKOFF, *supra* note 28, at 625.

[108] *See* Trevino, *supra* note 76 (citing 8 U.S.C. § 1357(c) and 8 U.S.C. § 1357(a)(1) (1994)).

Patrol agents to target Asian Americans driving across the border or arriving on international flights and to question them more aggressively.

While such harassment by INS agents may simply lead to inconvenience, it can also result in more tragic consequences. The Hwang case is one example of such tragedy. Stephen Hwang contends that "some immigration officers are overly aggressive when they question immigrants, Asians in particular, seeking re-entry into the United States." [109] Unfortunately, Stephen Hwang knows this from personal experience. His sixty-six year-old mother, Chen Seu-Ing Hwang, collapsed on the floor in customs at Los Angeles International Airport while being harassed by an immigration inspector. She suffered a stroke, which left her partially paralyzed, and died a few weeks later. Stephen Hwang filed suit against the INS and inspector Craig Porter.

The suit charges that the stroke Chen Seu-Ing Hwang suffered was the result of undue harassment by Porter, who had been aggressively questioning her in customs. An airline employee who was translating for Mrs. Hwang in customs said that Porter had tried to get Mrs. Hwang to admit that she had been out of the country for longer than 12 months, in violation of her permanent residency status. In fact, Mrs. Hwang had originally traveled to Taiwan to meet her husband who was undergoing eye surgery. However, he suffered chest pains after the surgery and died after a heart bypass operation. Mrs. Hwang stayed in Taiwan to take care of her late husband's affairs, which led her to be absent from the United States longer than anticipated.[110] Stephen Hwang believes that Porter did not give [*91] Mrs. Hwang a chance to explain her circumstances and instead, harassed her and tried to bully her into admitting she had done something wrong.[111]

Linda Wong, an immigration attorney formerly with the Mexican American Legal Defense and Education Fund, has said that many non-white permanent residents have had problems with airport immigration inspectors. Wong has encountered numerous complaints of agents targeting permanent residents at the airport and at the U.S.-Mexico border. Agents ask more aggressive questions, and even try to entrap non-white immigrants into saying that they have been out of the country for so long that they have abandoned their residency.[112]

B. Legal Restrictions for Non-citizens

Legally, non-citizens, or permanent residents, are an incredibly vulnerable class because they have limited rights and increasingly fewer constitutional protections.[113] Since non-citizens are disenfranchised, they cannot participate in the political process and have no political clout. Even though "immigrant rights [groups] and some ethnic groups lobby aggressively for immigrants, their pull with politicians naturally is restricted by the electoral powerlessness of their constituency."[114] Hence, it is easy for politicians to trample on them since their voices cannot be

---

[109] David Reyes, *Son Says Intent in Suing INS Is to Give Value to Mother's Death*, L.A. TIMES, Sept. 19, 1989, at Metro 3.

[110] *See id.*

[111] *See id.*

[112] *See id.*

[113] Based on an equality principle, non-citizens should not be treated as a lower or less-respected group than citizens. Non-citizens participate in and contribute to society and should not be treated as inferior. *See* ANCHETA, *supra* note 6, at 100.

[114] Kevin R. Johnson, *Symposium on Immigration Policy: An Essay on Immigration Politics, Popular Democracy, and California's Proposition 187: The Political Relevance and Legal Irrelevance of Race*, 70 WASH. L. REV. 636 (1995).

heard at the election booth. Permanent residents' lack of input in the political process is exacerbated by the plenary power doctrine. The doctrine compels the judiciary to defer to the other political branches when reviewing immigration policies.[115] Thus, the political branches which immigrants have little influence over are given significant freedom by the judiciary in immigration matters.

Although permanent residents are obliged to pay taxes and serve in the United States military if called upon, they do not have the right to vote or to serve on juries.[116] Permanent residents are now ineligible for most benefits, especially since the passage of the 1996 Welfare Reform Act, which made permanent residents ineligible for Social Security Insurance (SSI) and food stamps.[117] The plenary power doctrine gives the legislature broad latitude to restrict federal public benefits for permanent residents.[118] [*92] For example, a challenge to the 1996 Welfare Act brought in New York district court was struck down in *Abreu v. Callahan*.[119] The court in that case upheld the Welfare Act denying SSI benefits to lawful permanent residents who would have been eligible before the 1996 Act. The court found the government's interests legitimate and rationally related to the statute.[120]

In the employment arena, all sorts of restrictions exist which make an already vulnerable class even more susceptible to exploitation. The 1986 Immigration Reform and Control Act permits discrimination based on one's citizenship status if required by state or local governmental authority.[121] For instance, states can make citizenship mandatory as a job requirement in certain professions such as state troopers, public school teachers, and deputy probation officers.[122] In addition, employers may give preference to a citizen over a legal permanent resident if the two are "equally qualified."[123] The rights and privileges of citizenship are not fixed. The plenary power doctrine allows the executive and legislative branches to determine which rights to attach based on citizenship.[124] For example, during the nineteenth century, some states granted non-citizens the right to vote, partly to increase the number of white male voters.[125] Some cities have also permitted non-citizen parents to vote in school board elections.[126] However, the overwhelming trend is to deny rights to non-citizens, not to extend them.

---

[115] *See id.* at 637.

[116] *See* ANCHETA, *supra* note 6, at 99.

[117] *See* ALEINIKOFF, *supra* note 28, at 551.

[118] *See* Mathews v. Diaz, 426 U.S. 67 (1976)(holding that it is constitutional for Congress to condition a non-citizen's eligibility for participation in a federal medical insurance program on continuous residence in the U.S. for a five year period and admission for permanent residence). The Court went on to state that, "for reasons long recognized as valid, the responsibility for regulating the relationship between the United States and our alien visitors has been committed to the political branches of the Federal Government." *Id.* at 81.

[119] 971 F.Supp. 799, 826 (1997).

[120] *See id.* at 820.

[121] *See* ALEINIKOFF, *supra* note 28, at 628.

[122] *See, e.g.,* Foley v. Connelie, 435 U.S. 291 (1978), Ambach v. Norwick, 441 U.S. 68 (1979), Cabell v. Chavez-Salido, 454 U.S. 432 (1982).

[123] *See* ALEINIKOFF, *supra* note 28, at 628.

[124] *See* ANCHETA, *supra* note 6, at 99–100.

[125] *See id.* at 100.

[126] *See id.*

C. Private Forms of Border Patrol

The state engages in various forms of border patrol, but it does not end with the state, for the citizenry also performs border patrol in its own way. Every time people who are marked as foreign are asked how long they have been here or where they are from with the assumption that they must not be from the U.S., how they learned to speak English so well, or told to go back to another country, that is a type of unofficial border check. By relying on popular notions of foreignness, individuals participate in border patrol when they mark others as foreign and ask questions or make comments implying that the others must be foreigners. As signals of foreignness, accent discrimination and racial discrimination are forms of unofficial border patrol.[127] Because the American national identity is defined by whiteness, border patrol is practiced within the physical borders [*93] of the United States. Those individuals inscribed with figurative borders will be subject to internal policing mechanisms of foreignness.

A group in San Diego called "Light Up the Border" exemplifies private individuals taking border patrol into their own hands and performing their own border checks. In 1989, a group of private residents started a campaign where more than 1,000 volunteers parked their cars along the U.S.-Mexico border and shined their headlights toward Tijuana. Critics claim that "Light Up the Border" has heightened racial tensions and fueled anti-immigrant and anti-Latino sentiments. Since the group began its vigilante campaign, the U.S. Border Patrol has placed lights on the U.S.-Mexico border and the California National Guard has begun to improve the dirt roads that the Border Patrol drives on in its patrols.[128] The "Light Up the Border" group highlights private actors attempting to informally participate in border patrol.

In addition to the annoying questions regarding birthplace, shining lights on the border, and accent and racial discrimination, those inscribed with figurative borders must also worry about a more dangerous form of private border patrol. Hate violence has become a way of protecting cultural security and a form of border patrol over people marked as foreign which the private citizenry has taken upon itself to perform. Hate crimes are a manifestation of this border control on a much more physical and extreme level. Most hate crimes against Asian Americans involve anti-immigrant, nativistic racism and place Asian Americans in the context of foreignness.[129] One of the most well-known hate crimes against Asian Americans occurred in 1982 when Vincent Chin, a Chinese American, was killed in Detroit, Michigan by two white laid-off autoworkers who yelled "you Japs are taking all our jobs" while beating Chin with a baseball bat.[130] During the early 1980s, anti-Asian sentiment in the United States was intensely heightened, especially against Japan. Paula Johnson describes this sentiment as "particularly acute in Detroit, Michigan, where the heart of the American auto industry was economically depressed and Japanese auto imports

---

[127] It is important to note that only accents of certain groups are considered to be foreign in this negative way. For instance, while a French or British accent may appear to be intellectual, an Asian or Spanish accent is perceived to be an indicator of foreignness and/or ignorance. For an excellent discussion of accent discrimination, see Mari Matsuda, *Voices of America: Accent, Antidiscrimination Law, and a Jurisprudence for the Last Reconstruction*, 100 YALE L.J. 1329 (1991).

[128] *See* Ernesto Portillo Jr., *Protests At Border Turn 1 Year Old But Participation In 'Light Up' Declines On Anniversary*, SAN DIEGO UNION-TRIB., Nov. 16, 1990, at B-3.

[129] *See* NAPALC AUDIT II, *supra* note 3. (1994).

[130] *See* Paula C. Johnson, *The Social Construction of Identity in Criminal Cases: Cinema Verite and the Pedagogy of Vincent Chin*, 1 MICH. J. RACE & L. 347 (1996) for a detailed analysis of the legal case.

gained in sales and popularity in this country."[131] Bumper stickers saying "Unemployment-Made in Japan" and "Toyota-Datsun-Honda-and-Pearl Harbor" were popular in Detroit and other areas of the country.[132] Johnson explains, "It was within this social climate and other social contexts that the killing of Vincent Chin occurred, bringing national and international attention to the issue of racially motivated violence against Asian Americans in the United States." [133]

The Vincent Chin murder must be seen in this context of foreignness and border patrol. Although this case involved two private individuals, they were supported and implicitly condoned by a legal system, which did [*94] not bring any justice to Vincent Chin. Neither killer served any time in prison for the murder. They each instead received small fines and only three years of probation.[134] Robert Chang recognizes the context of the murder of Vincent Chin in terms of borders when he writes, "The border and the color line are inscribed on his body, marking him as a foreign and racial other, a legitimate target for nativistic racism. Through his construction as a foreigner, he and others who look like him, help define America."[135]

Nativistic racism also manifested itself in the tragic death of Navroze Mody in Hoboken, near Jersey City, and is another incident of hate violence as a form of border patrol by private actors. On September 27, 1987, Mody, a 30-year old South Asian, was "bludgeoned with bricks, punched, and kicked into a coma" by a gang of eleven youths who shouted "Hindu! Hindu!" during the attack.[136] Mody's white friend who was walking with him that night was not harmed. No bias charges were brought, and the jury convicted four of the attackers on assault charges. No one was found guilty of murder or even manslaughter.[137] This case must also be placed in its social and historical context to fully understand what occurred.

In the weeks before Mody's death, racial tensions and anti-South Asian sentiment were heightened after a racist group called the "Dotbusters" (referring to the red bindi worn by South Asian women on their foreheads as a sign of marital fidelity) published a letter in the *Jersey Journal* stating that their mission was to drive all South Asians out of Jersey City.[138] A campaign of racial harassment, vandalism, and assault was launched against the South Asian community. Three days after Mody's attack, another South Asian man, Dr. Kaushal Sharan, was severely beaten while walking home.[139] For at least a year after Mody's violent death, anti-South Asian Incidents continued to occur in the Jersey City area.[140] In this case, private actors banded together to form their own border patrol gang, the "Dotbusters," to expel South Asians through the use of hate violence. The police failed to protect the South Asian community, and the legal system failed to render justice to Mody's life. Mody's family later brought a civil rights action against the city of Hoboken for racial discrimination in failing to protect the South Asian community and in failing

---

[131] *Id.* at 399.

[132] *See* TAKAKI, *supra* note 39, at 483.

[133] Johnson, *supra* note 131, at 399-400.

[134] *See id.* at 400.

[135] Chang, *supra* note 19, at 61.

[136] *See* CIVIL RIGHTS ISSUES, *supra* note 21, at 28–29; *see also* Corey Takahashi, *Killed In Action*, A. Magazine 32 (1997).

[137] *See* Takahashi, *supra* note 136.

[138] *See id.* 28–29.

[139] *See* NAPALC AUDIT I, *supra* note 3, at 9–10.

[140] *See* CIVIL RIGHTS ISSUES, *supra* note 21.

to prosecute Mody's attackers in earlier assaults on other South Asians.[141] However, a federal judge dismissed the suit, claiming that there [*95] was no evidence of racial bias and at worst, there was only negligence on the part of the police.[142]

These attacks involve more than just the message of hatred but also include the message of hatred based on xenophobia, immigrant scapegoating for economic woes, and a sense of border control. Although the deaths of Vincent Chin and Navroze Mody are widely known examples of anti-Asian hate crimes, there are countless others who have suffered the same type of hate violence as border patrol.

Hate violence by private actors has escaiated along with the increase in immigration from Asian and Latin American countries. Demographic changes between 1970 and 1990 have certainly fueled the perception that there has been an influx of Asians who are taking over the country. Between 1970 and 1990, the United States population experienced a total growth of 22.4%. The African American population increased by 33% and comprised 12.1% of the total population. The Native American population grew from 0.4% of the population to 0.8%. However, it is the Asian American and Latina/o populations, which have increased the most dramatically. The Asian American population grew by 384.9% to reach 2.9% of the population while the Latina/o population grew by 141% to reach 9% of the population.[143] During the period from 1970 to 1990, approximately nine million immigrants entered the United States from Asian and Latin American countries. [144]

One popular perception is that the country is being overrun with immigrants of color, and studies have revealed that most whites believe that the United States is being taken over by people of color and that whites are the new minority in the United States. For instance, a recent *New York Times* poll showed that whites believed that African Americans comprised 23.8% of the population, Asian Americans 10.8%, Latinas/os 14.7%, and whites only 49.9% when in reality, African Americans are 11.8% of the population, Asian Americans 3.1%, Latinas/os 9.5%, and whites 74%. [145] The dramatic gap between reality and perception reflects the anxiety of whites that the "invasion" has begun.

On a state level, by 2001, the state of California will be officially majority non-white.[146] This demographic has frightened many whites into action, spawning an onslaught of conservative ballot initiatives in the 1990s attacking immigration, affirmative action, and bilingual education. These initiatives were supported by the majority of white California voters.[147]

---

[141] *See* Robert Rudolph, *Civil Rights Suit In Death of Indian Is Dismissed*, STAR-LEDGER NEWARK, Apr. 25, 1991.

[142] *See id.*

[143] *See* Bill Ong Hing, *Beyond the Rhetoric of Assimilation and Cultural Pluralism: Addressing the Tension of Separatism and Conflict in an Immigration Driven Multiracial Society*, 81 CAL. L. REV. 863, 865 (1993).

[144] *See id.*, 81 Cal. L. Rev. 863, 865 (1993).

[145] *See* Priscilla Labovitz, *Immigration-Just the Facts*, N.Y. TIMES, Mar. 25, 1996, at A15. For a study of college students who estimated the university to be over 70% people of color when in fact the university was 70% white, see also Charles A. Gallagher, *White Reconstruction in the University*, 24 SOCIALIST REV. 165, 172 (1995).

[146] *See* Brad Edmondson, *The Minority Majority in 2001*, AM. DEMOGRAPHICS, Oct. 1996, at 16.

[147] *See* Proposition 187 (anti-immigrant), Proposition 209 (anti-affirmative action), and Proposition 227 (anti-bilingual education) have passed with the majority of white voters in 1994, 1996, and 1998, respectively; *see also* Garcia, *supra* note 73, at 130.

[*96] D. Blurring Of State and Private Border Patrol: Proposition 187

Proposition 187, passed by California voters in November 1994, collapsed the distinction between state and private border patrol by effectively transforming private citizens into state agents.[148] Proposition 187 restricted undocumented immigrants from public benefits, public education, and non-emergency health care and created serious criminal penalties for the sale or use of false citizenship papers.[149] Proposition 187 also requires employees in social services, health care, and education to report any persons who are "reasonably suspect" of being undocumented to the State Director of Social Services, the Attorney General of California and the United States, and the Immigration and Naturalization Service. [150] Thus, private actors are basically made to assume the duties of an INS agent. Proposition 187 creates a police state mentality by forcing public officials to report anyone who they "suspect" of being illegal. Proposition 187, however, does not define what constitutes proper suspicion, thereby increasing the probability of discrimination occurring. Linda Bosniak notes different bases for suspicion: "Will the suspicion be based on the way you speak? The sound of your last name? The color of your skin?" [151] As Chang and Aoki describe Proposition 187, "Foreign-ness then becomes a proxy for questionable immigration status. Foreign-ness triggers further scrutiny."[152] This police state would regulate the borders with the participation of the state and its citizens. Racist literature supporting Proposition 187 stuffed into mailboxes in Los Angeles demonstrates citizen border patrol occurring: "WE NEED A *REAL* BORDER, FIRST WE GET THE SPICS, THEN THE GOOKS, AND AT LAST WE GET THE NIG-GERS. *DEPORTATION* THEY'RE ALL GOING HOME."[153]

The Proposition 187 campaign was premised on the idea of immigrants as "aliens" who needed to be taught a lesson. Proposition 187 represented a new chapter in the history of nativism in California and the nation. Proponents of Proposition 187 staunchly maintained that the issue was not race but immigration and saving America, but the immigration problem was definitely framed in racialized terms. There was no mention of the Immigration Act of 1990, which had just increased dramatically the number of immigrants from Northern Europe, particularly Ireland. Instead, the focus was on portraying illegal "aliens" as Mexicans running across the border and of Chinese boat people.[154] Stop Immigration Now founder Ruth [*97] Coffey could only explain her position on the immigration issue in a racial manner when she said, "I have no intention of being the object of 'conquest', peaceful or otherwise, by Latinos, Asians, Blacks, Arabs or any other group of individuals who have claimed my country."[155]

---

[148] Even though parts of Proposition 187 have been enjoined, the negative repercussions of the proposition have already inflicted their damage.

[149] *See* ALEINIKOFF, *supra* note 28, at 663.

[150] *See* Proposition 187 §§ 5(c)(3), 6(c)(3), 7(e), (November 8, 1994).

[151] Linda S. Bosniak, *Opposing Proposition 187: Undocumented Immigrants and the National Imagination* 28 CONN. L. REV. 555, 561 n.9 (1996).

[152] Chang and Aoki, *supra* note 5, at 1414.

[153] NAPALC AUDIT II, *supra* note 3, at 4.

[154] *See* Nancy Cervantes, Sasha Khokha, and Bobbie Murray, *Hate Unleashed: Los Angeles in the Aftermath of Proposition 187,* 17 CHICANO-LATINO L. REV. 1, 5 (1995); Chang and Aoki, *supra* note 5, at 1400.

[155] Cervantes, Khokha, and Murray, *supra* note 155, at 3.

Especially after Proposition 187 passed, those individuals inscribed with figurative borders and marked as foreigners regardless of citizenship status or length of residence in the United States experienced intensified discrimination and increased hate violence. The rhetoric permeating the debate over Proposition 187 created an environment that encouraged discrimination and intolerance for anyone who was marked with figurative borders. Both the Latina/o and the Asian American communities suffered increased discrimination in places of business, increased hate crimes and hate speech, and increased police brutality.[156] Anti-Asian hate violence more than doubled in Northern California and increased by 40% in Southern California in 1994 from the previous year. The dramatic rise in anti-Asian violence in California was attributed to anti-immigrant sentiment supporting Proposition 187.[157] The Coalition for Humane Immigrant Rights of Los Angeles (CHIRLA) set up a hotline after the passage of Proposition 187 to document the rise in incidents against the Latina/o community. Hundreds of phone calls poured in on the first day of the hotline describing people not being allowed to cash a check unless they showed passports, police demanding documents while beating those who they called "aliens," and Latina/o households being burned by arsonists who spray painted "white power" and "Mexico" with an "X" through it.[158] Essentially, Proposition 187 gave citizens a license to carry out their own border checks against anyone who looked foreign. The National Asian Pacific American Legal Consortium reported that in the months leading up to the passage of Proposition 187, there was a significant increase in incidents which included references to "go home" and get out of America.[159] There was an unprecedented number of hate fliers stuffed into grocery bags, home mailboxes, and student lockers. The fliers referred to the 'invasion' of the 'Gooks' and demanded that they 'had to go.' Most references in the fliers were to 'genocide' and to taking back America.[160] The result is that anti-immigrant sentiment has become legitimized and legalized so that it is acceptable to openly discriminate against people who are marked as foreign.[161] This includes border checks from questions regarding citizenship status to hate speech and hate crimes manifesting this anti-immigrant sentiment in a more physical manner. Proposition 187 [*98] authorized private actors to perform border patrol and gave them the legitimacy and power of the state to do so.

A group in San Diego formed after the passage of Proposition 187 demonstrates just how much authority civilians believe they possess to conduct border patrol. In 1996, Win Housley and 200 other private citizens formed a band of vigilantes into the "Airport Posse" and began to patrol the San Diego International Airport to find undocumented immigrants.[162] The group roams the airport in blue shirts that read "U.S. Citizen Patrol," imitating government uniforms with the belief that the government has failed in its duty to end illegal immigration. Jose Luis Perez Canchola of Mexico's National Commission on Human Rights reported an incident in which the posse had confronted a group of 22 individuals and demanded proof of citizenship. He said,

---

[156] See id.; NAPALC AUDIT II, *supra* note 3.

[157] See NAPALC AUDIT II, *supra* note 3, at 12–13; *see also* Kenneth B. Noble, *Attacks Against Asian Americans on the Rise, Especially in California*, N.Y. TIMES, Dec. 13, 1995, at B16.

[158] See Cervantes, Khokha, and Murray, *supra* note 155, at 14–15; *see also* Tanya Broder; Clara Luz Navarro, *A Street Without An Exit: Excerpts From The Lives Of Latinas In Post-187 California*, 7 HASTINGS WOMEN'S L.J. 275 (1995).

[159] See NAPALC AUDIT II, *supra* note 3, at 12–13; *see also* Kenneth B. Noble, *supra* note 157, at B16.

[160] See NAPALC AUDIT II, *supra* note 3, at 12.

[161] See generally NAPALC AUDIT II, *supra* note 3.

[162] See Dana Calvo, *Vigilante-Type Posse On Patrol At Airport For Illegal Immigrants*, SEATTLE TIMES, May 16, 1996.

"They are civilians assuming the role of an immigration officer." In response to criticism that it is difficult to identify illegal immigrants, "Airport Posse" leader Housley insists that they are easy to spot. He explains, "They're nervous. They're in out-of-style clothing. When they talk to one another, it's always in Spanish. They're all, as I said, real nervous."[163] Obviously the "Airport Posse" is relying on their notions of foreignness as proper suspicion and targeting those with inscribed figurative borders.

E. Blurring Continued: State Engages in Hate Violence

Border patrol is clearly performed by both the state and non-state actors as the divisions have become blurred. As a form of border patrol, hate violence necessarily involves both state and private actors. However, hate violence has been constructed as a private problem of individual perpetrators. So construed, hate violence seems easily controlled under the traditional view advocated by law enforcement, the media, and mainstream society: that the law will protect subordinated groups if they would just let the system work. The problems with this approach are numerous, including what happens when law enforcement does not react to a hate crime or when law enforcement is the perpetrator of a hate crime. Victor Hwang, in his experience with the Race Relations: Hate Violence Project at the Asian Law Caucus, finds that law enforcement generally does not take hate crimes seriously.[164] This is confirmed by the fact that although almost 9000 hate crimes were reported to the FBI in 1996 (with reporting by law enforcement agencies covering only 84% of the U.S. population), only 38 of these resulted in prosecution by the Department of Justice.[165] Thus, the state implicitly sends a message condoning hate violence by failing to prosecute hate crimes. The recent failure to pass the federal Hate Crimes Prevention Act (HCPA) also demonstrates an unwillingness on the part of [*99] the state to recognize the need for protection from hate crimes and the need to send an unequivocal message that hate violence will not be tolerated. The HCPA would have given the federal government a strong, uniform statute on which to prosecute hate crimes and would have closed the gaps in existing federal hate crime laws. The HCPA would have authorized the Department of Justice to prosecute hate crimes based on sexual orientation, gender, and disability, which are currently not covered by federal hate crime laws. [166] Furthermore, under current law, federal prosecutors may only file hate crime charges if the victim was exercising a federally protected right such as voting or attending school when attacked, leaving a loophole for a situation where a victim is killed in her/his home. The new statute would have allowed the Department of Justice to prosecute hate crimes involving bodily injury or death regardless of whether the victim was exercising a federally protected right.[167]

The violent death of Kuanchung Kao exemplifies the participation of the state in hate violence and in policing the perceived foreign enemy who can and will attack with his martial arts skills. Kuanchung Kao, a 33-year old father of three, was shot to death by Rohnert Park police

---

[163] *Id.*

[164] *See* Hwang Interview, supra note 3.

[165] *See* Rebecca Leung, *Hate Crimes In America: Texas Killing Spotlights Nation's Racial Divide*, ABCNEWS.COM (June 17, 1998) available at <http://www.abcnews.go.com/sections/us/DailyNews/hatecrimes980611.html>; *see also* <http://www.fbi.gov/ucr.htm>.

[166] *See* Dianne Feinstein, *Feds Need More Tools to Fight Hate*, S.F. EXAMINER, May 19, 1999, at A19.

[167] *See id.*

on April 29, 1997.[168] Earlier that evening, Kao had been drinking after being racially harassed in a separate incident. He returned home and began crying and screaming for help in front of his house. Officer Jack Shields and Officer Mike Lynch responded to a disturbing-the-peace call at the Kao residence. Within 34 seconds of their arrival, the officers shot Kao in the chest from at least 7 feet away, killing him. [169] Officer Shields claimed that Kao was waving a stick he was holding in a threatening and "martial arts" like manner and that he had to shoot because he did not know where Mr. Kao was from and feared him to be an expert in martial arts. Certainly the fact that Mr. Kao was Asian American informed the officers in their fear and judgment that Mr. Kao must know martial arts and their quick decision to shoot and kill him. Mr. Kao died on the front lawn and police would not allow Mrs. Kao, a registered nurse, to attend to her husband or to call for help.[170] The District Attorney cleared the officers of any wrongdoing, mainly because one of the officers claimed self-defense. This was the same officer who had been demoted by his own police department after being convicted of falsifying records the year before. The U.S. Department of Justice also refused to file federal civil rights charges in this case.[171] Thus, the state is just as capable of committing hate violence based upon racial stereotypes of the foreigner as individual citizens are in the private sphere.

In fact, the National Asian Pacific American Legal Consortium's 1994 audit of anti-Asian violence found that the main perpetrator of racially motivated violence against Asian Americans in New York City was the [*100] police.[172] The data reveals that the New York City police committed 50% of the total number of anti-Asian violent incidents in 1994. In over half of these incidents involving police brutality, racial slurs such as "Go back to China," "F—ing Orientals," "Go back to Pakistan," and "This is not f—ing Pakistan" were uttered.[173] Many of these incidents involved South Asian American taxi drivers whose police encounters ranged from racial slurs to assaults. The police also issued false traffic violations in retaliation for civilian complaints the South Asian American taxi drivers have filed against the police officers for their discriminatory treatment.[174] Two years later, the 1996 National Asian Pacific American Legal Consortium report on anti-Asian violence again noted that police brutality continued to be a problem in New York City.[175]

F. A Community Response to Hate Violence

With the collapsing of state and non-state forms of border patrol into the same capacity, we must realize the potential for hate violence by anyone in the private or public sector. The narrow construction of hate crimes focuses on the individual actor who perpetrates hate crimes and obscures the legalized aspects of border patrol, which are also drawing on the same notions of foreignness and result in anti-Asian violence. However, by focusing only on the individual aspect, we ignore the state's role in border patrol as well as the historical context behind the systematic oppression

---

[168] *See* NAPALC Audit V, *supra* note 3, at 19.

[169] *See id.*

[170] *See id.*

[171] *See id.*

[172] *See* NAPALC AUDIT II, *supra* note 3, at 12.

[173] *Id.*

[174] *See id.*

[175] *See* NAPALC AUDIT IV, *supra* note 3, at 10–11.

of people of color through violence. Violence occurs in our social and historical system of domination and subordination and not in a vacuum. Even if law enforcement did take hate crimes against Asian Americans more seriously, the issue still remains with legalized hate violence in the form of border patrol. As previously discussed, border patrol exists officially and unofficially with the blurring of the two by laws such as Proposition 187 so that individual hate violence perpetrators are working in compliance with the state to protect white American national identity and cultural security.

Because anti-Asian violence may come from both state and private actors, solutions to anti-Asian violence must be pursued on multiple fronts. We must turn inwards for strength, community education, and empowerment and not rely on the state and law enforcement agencies to meet our needs. Victor Hwang explains that because hate crimes are social-political crimes, Asian Americans should look beyond the strictly legal aspect and concentrate on political and community pressure in order to be taken more seriously by law enforcement.[176] Thus, we must turn to the community for solutions and not solely rely on the state to protect us.[177]

[*101] Conclusion

This paper has attempted to place hate violence against Asian Americans as part of a larger context of increased border patrol. Asian Americans are marked with figurative borders, which has serious consequences, especially in the present anti-immigrant climate. Hate violence has become another way to patrol the borders of the nation which both state and private actors can participate in to preserve a white national identity and cultural security. As a community, we must turn inwards for strength rather than depend on the State to protect us. Anti-Asian violence has been a part of the Asian American community from the moment we arrived in this country and will unfortunately, continue into the future. It is through our collective struggle against violence and exclusion that we ensure our survival.

Legal Topics:

For related research and practice materials, see the following legal topics:
    Civil Rights LawSection 1983 ActionsLaw Enforcement OfficialsGeneral OverviewCopyright LawForeign & Internationa-l ProtectionsGeneral OverviewImmigration LawAdmissionSelection SystemGeneral Overview

---

[176] *See* Hwang Interview, *supra* note 3.

[177] Solutions are always difficult for we face complex problems, and a complete discussion of solutions is beyond the scope of this comment. However, it is clear that because we cannot completely rely on the state to protect us, community activism should be a part of the struggle. Through community work, Asian Americans can struggle against hate violence whether perpetrated by the state or non-state actors.

Homeland Security and Racism

Peter Chua

In 2002, the U.S. government reorganized its Immigration and Naturalization Services agency to be part of the new Department of Homeland Security (DHS) to manage and coordinate more effectively antiterrorism, national security, and immigration activities. This reorganization formally ushered in racism in homeland security. This novel form of institutional racism has negatively and disproportionably targeted particular racial and ethnic heritage groups for social exclusion, harassment, and violence, thereby maintaining white racial supremacy. These groups include U.S. Asians such as Pakistanis, Filipinos, Cambodians, and Chinese, in addition to Middle Easterners, Latinos, and Africans who have been typically known to be targets of government monitoring and civil liberties curtailment.

Background and Contexts

The September 11, 2001, events in New York City and other U.S. areas brought destruction, social misery, and the national crystallization of homeland security racist policies. Months after these events, mass media depicted images of government agents searching, interrogating, and detaining individuals as possible so-called foreign terrorists and undesired residents. Those affected ranged from Pakistanis and other Asian individuals with Muslim or Middle Eastern—sounding surnames, and Filipinos working as checkpoint agents and baggage handlers at airports to Chinese immigrant scientists working at national defense laboratories.

The logic and apparatus of homeland security racism draws from earlier anti-nativist practices that consider certain racial and ethnic groups as national outsiders.[1] For example, the U.S. government enacted the Chinese Exclusion Act, criminalized particular "Asian" cultural practices, interned people of Japanese background, and deported U.S. Filipino labor organizers as suspected communists. These antinativist and Eurocentric practices asserted the inadmissibility of cultural group traits common to certain Asian and other groups and the impossibility of assimilation based on these cultural traits.

---

[1] See Mae M. Ngai, *Impossible Subjects: Illegal Aliens and the Making of Modern America*. (Princeton, NJ: Princeton University Press, 2004), 1–14.

While earlier legal gains in the Asian American immigrant movement gave the pretense of national openness and societal inclusion of Asians in the United States, restrictive and racist state policies have reemerged since the 1990s. In particular, the 1996 Illegal Immigration Reform and Immigrant Responsibility Act (IIRAIRA), implemented by President Clinton, dramatically derailed immigrant rights by seeking to curtail unauthorized residence in the United States and removing undesirables, including those with legal permanent U.S. residence status.[2]

With the September 11, 2001, events and the 2002 enactment of the Uniting and Strengthening America by Providing Appropriate Tools Required to Intercept and Obstruct Terrorism (USA PATRIOT) Act, the Homeland Security Act, and other similar legislation, President George W. Bush sought to subsume immigration into national security under the pretext of capturing suspected al-Qaeda—linked terrorists. This newer legislation provided the mechanisms and procedures to implement IIRAIRA on a broad national scale under the new DHS. The policy underlying these legislations assumes undesired "foreigners," such as those from Asian Muslim communities, are terrorist suspects and that a broad entrapment net is the optimal approach to safeguard the nation.

Proliferation

Institutional racism results from DHS policies, procedures, and programs that systemically and selectively target particular racial-ethnic communities for harassment, detention, and mass removal.[3] These policies, procedures, and programs have not been enforced uniformly, without regard to racial-ethnicity, cultural heritage, and national origins. Instead, DHS and other government agencies monitor personal cues drawn from physical bodily appearances (such as clothing), markers of group identification (such as birth place, first name, and last name), and racial-ethnic and national-cultural practices (such as food preferences on air travel) to profile and determine the possible conduct of political activities to destabilize governmental institutions. Based on such personal cues, the U.S. government targets individuals and communities for harassment, mass detention, and mass removal.

U.S. Asian communities have been severely affected. The full scope of homeland security racism on these communities has not been fully determined because of the secretive aspects of homeland security activities. Mass media accounts and the release of limited government records demonstrate the extensive network of selected surveillance with the intent to harass, detain, and remove particular racial-ethnic groups.

For example, the government has contracted private air carriers to transport possible terrorists, criminals, and undesirables from national security "immigration" detention centers to their countries of origin or ancestry. These contracts were arranged prior to the capturing of the "criminals." Furthermore, formal agreements with receiving countries have allowed these private carriers to transport the individuals and their families, to land, and to grant those removed some form of legal status of residence in the receiving countries. Cambodian young men who entered the United States as refugees and who had legal resident status provide a notable example of this. These men—many of whom spent their lives in the United States, are not fluent in the Cambodian

---

[2] See Edward W. Park and John W. Park. *Probationary Americans: Contemporary Immigration Policies and the Shaping of Asian American Communities*. (New York: Routledge. 2005), 45–62.

[3] See Critical Filipina and Filipino Studies Collective, *Resisting Homeland Security: Organizing Against Unjust Removal of U.S. Filipinos* (San Jose, CA: Critical Filipina and Filipino Studies Collective and the National Alliance for Filipino Concerns, 2004).

language, and have no relatives in Cambodia—were deported for suspected gang activities. They were transported to Cambodia via private air carriers, and placed indefinitely in Cambodian prisons for suspected criminal activities in the United States. In this way, the Cambodian government becomes a strong ally of the United States in its war against global terror and, as a result, garners favorable economic and humanitarian benefits from the United States.

Removal is one of the severe examples of racism in homeland security. Formally, DHS considered inadmissibility and deportation as two forms of removal. Inadmissibility usually occurs at the port of entry when DHS officers do not allow tourists, U.S. legal residents, or U.S. citizens to enter or return to the U.S. because of violation of federal laws, certain "inadmissible" convictions, or suspected security, criminal and health reasons. These officers rely on government electronic databases—which bring together demographic characteristics, corporate information (involving credit cards, banks, air travel, and so on), and governmental details (from DHS, the Internal Revenue Service, Social Security, public schools, employment records, public library, and so on)—to flag people who would be inadmissible. Once inadmissible, an individual has to initiate the challenge of database errors from outside the United States.

Regardless of legal resident status, individuals can be deported because of certain criminal convictions, procedural violations, or deemed security risks. The USA PATRIOT Act expands grounds for deportation and detention to include U.S. citizens. Detention during the processes of inadmissibility and deportation can be short-term, extended, or indefinite.

The post—September 11, 2001, effect of homeland security racism can be seen in the analysis of DHS removal data from 2001 to 2003. Filipinos and Pakistanis residing in the United States were systematically targeted for deportation. Filipinos were ranked seventh for "noncriminals" removed, with one hundred people removed in 2001 and increases of more than fifty each year in the following two years; Pakistanis were ranked ninth. The others at the top of the list include those with Lebanese, Egyptian, Jordanian, and Moroccan heritage. In the case of U.S. Filipinos, there was a 65 percent increase of removal. In contrast, for all groups combined, there was only a 5 percent increase. This is significant because it shows that the U.S. Filipinos are removed at a greater rate than the overall removal rate. A significant number of U.S. Filipinos who were removed were permanent residents. More than 42 percent had legal documents, and they were removed because of felony convictions. DHS stopped making public these figures after 2003. In total in 2003, DHS expected to remove 85,000 Filipinos.

The experiential impacts of racism in homeland security have been far-reaching. Many who have been targeted for mass removal face greater uncertainty. They have been caught by surprise with immediate deportation, inadmissibility, and detention, without a sense of their human rights and without economic resources to respond adequately. Since the implementation of these, they have lacked adequate understanding, capable legal counsel, and adequate due process.

Individuals and families have faced greater economic and social hardships. Some, if not all, family members have lost jobs, homes, and economic security. Their careers and schooling are interrupted. They have lacked support from friends and neighbors because of racial, religious, and political stigmas. While isolated, they have lacked family and community networks, forcing spouses and children to rebuild their lives alone. Some have sought greater support and services from public assistance and underfunded local agencies.

As a result, racism in homeland security has made it difficult for Asians living in the United States, regardless of citizenship status. They have been unduly targeted for unjust mass detention and removals and placed under detrimental legal uncertainties. They have faced greater family hardships and have been living through legislatively generated fear and harassment.

Amardeep Singh, left, legal director of the Sikh Coalition, discusses a new policy by the Metropolitan Transit Authority (MTA) that requires Sikh employees to wear MTA logos on their turbans, during a news conference in 2005 in New York. Five Sikh station agents announced their intention to file discrimination charges against the MTA. The Sikh workers charge that a post-9/11 policy requiring them to brand their turbans with an MTA logo amounts to religious discrimination, and to put an MTA logo on their turban would be equivalent to asking a Christian to put the logo on the cross. (AP Photo/Julie Jacobson)

While racism in homeland security remains invisible to many, some grass-roots community organizations have been transforming themselves from simply focusing on immigrant rights and citizenship advocacy to more broadly addressing homeland security criminalization, incarceration, and racism. Instead of simply demanding comprehensive immigration reform, the organizations have been considering the need to demand for the dismantling of DHS and termination of racist practices. They have been forging a broader struggle against the increasing suspension of civil liberties by the U.S. government and organizing for social justice and their human rights and security.

Further Reading

Bâli, Ash Ü. "Scapegoating the Vulnerable: Preventive Detention of Immigrants in America's 'War or Terror.'" In Austin Sarat, ed, *Studies in Law, Politics, and Society*, 38, Greenwich, CT: JAI Press, 2006: 25–69.

Criminal and Deportation Defense. The National Immigration Project. http://www.ationalimmigration project.org/CrimPage/CrimPage.html.

Hing, Bill Ong. *Defining America through Immigration Policy*. Philadelphia: Temple University Press, 2004.

Puar, Jasbir K. and Amit Rai. "Monster, Terrorist, Fag: The War on Terrorism and the Production of Docile Patriots." *Social Text* 72 (2002): 117–148.

PART IX   Politics and Social Activism

From Vincent Chin to Kuan Chung Kao: Restoring Dignity to Their Lives

Eric Mar

CHAPTER 27

Introduction

The Granada Hills, California, killing of Filipino immigrant Joseph Ileto on August 10, 1999, was déjà vu to many of us who have been fighting racial violence and hate crimes since the national movement Justice for Vincent Chin began in the early eighties. The quick upsurge of nationwide community actions organized with the leadership of groups like Filipino Civil Rights Advocates (FILCRA), Asian Pacific American Labor Alliance (APALA), and others following Ileto's killing was a reflection of the level of awareness within our communities that had been built over the last two decades, especially within California.

The National Asian Pacific American Legal Consortium (NAPALC) reports that Joseph Ileto was the fifth Asian American killed as a result of anti-Asian violence in 1999. Although the other killings occurred in Indiana, Maryland, and Illinois, the Ileto case is significant because of California's growing Asian and Pacific Islander and immigrant populations. It is no coincidence that many of the attacks on Asian Americans have coincided with the rising wave of anti-immigrant initiatives such as the "English Only" Proposition 63 passed by California voters in 1986, the anti–undocumented immigrant Proposition 187 in 1994, and the anti–bilingual education Proposition 227 in 1998. It is no surprise to many of us in the immigrant-rights movement that the immigrant status of Vincent Chin, Joseph Ileto, and others—or the fact that they "looked foreign"—was an important factor in their killings.

California has undergone a dramatic demographic shift since the passage of the 1965 Immigration Act, which ended a long era of racist exclusion laws against Asians and other people of color. Immigrants, especially from Mexico, Latin America, and Asia, are fueling much of the growth of this new California. Census bureau reports from 1996 show that nearly one in ten people in the United States is foreign born. But in California, over one in five residents is foreign born. The California Research Bureau reports that Asian immigrants make up about one quarter of the state's immigrants, while Latinos make up about half. From 1960 to 1980, the Asian and Pacific Islander population in the state more than quadrupled from less than a third of a million to 1.3 million. The Population Reference Bureau (PRB) estimates that Asians and Pacific Islanders now make up over 3.5 million people in California and are expected to increase to over 6.5 million people by the year 2015. According to the PRB, Latinos will outnumber Whites in California 16.4 million to 15.8 million by that year.

But Paul Ong, Yen Le Espiritu, and other ethnic-studies scholars have also noted that in the decades following the 1965 immigration law, Asian American communities have become more "class polarized," with a growing "professional and managerial class" in addition to the large sectors of our communities locked into low-wage industries or dependent on public assistance. They point out that California's demographic shifts are also occurring in the context of capitalist restructuring on a global scale. The growing disparity between rich and poor, the increasing elimination of U.S. manufacturing-sector jobs, and the expansion of part-time, temporary, and contingent work are all domestic consequences of this process of "corporate globalization," according to anti-WTO (World Trade Organization) labor, environmental, and social-justice activists who organized the massive protests in early 2000 to disrupt the Seattle meeting of the WTO. The impact of this restructuring is increasing California residents' feelings of economic insecurity even in an era of supposed nationwide prosperity—an issue at the heart of the growing resurgence of anti-Asian violence and anti-immigrant scapegoating.

California is experiencing a growing number of "hate crimes" against not just people of color, but also other groups like Jews and lesbian/gay/bisexual and transgender people. Of the two thousand hate crimes reported in California in 1996, only 7.4 percent were committed against Asian Americans. While NAPALC reported an overall decrease in anti-Asian incidents in their nationwide report in 1997, they noted significant increased reports in California and New Jersey, both states with dramatically changing demographics. Similarly, in multicultural Los Angeles, the Asian Pacific American Legal Center of Southern California found in 1995 that one quarter of the nation's reported anti-Asian incidents occurred in Southern California alone. Karen Umemoto of the University of Hawaii has also noted in her research that hate crimes in Hawaii have been concentrated in areas undergoing demographic changes that typically displace one ethnic or racial group with another.

The San Francisco/Oakland Bay Area, considered one of the most tolerant and "progressive" regions of the country, has been the site of many incidents of anti-Asian and racial violence, especially during the 1980s. During this period, organizations such as Davis Asians for Racial Equality (DARE), Sacramento's Coalition of Asians for Equal Rights (CAER), and the Bay Area's Asian Network for Equality and Justice (ANEJ) formed in direct response to numerous incidents of racial violence against Asians and other people of color in the area. Another, more advocacy-oriented group called Break the Silence Coalition against Anti-Asian Violence (BTS) formed as well after a successful May 1986 conference. At the time, ANEJ and others importantly connected the individual acts of racial violence with a much larger system of institutionalized racism in the United States that serves to "degrade, dehumanize, and reinforce the unequal status" of Asian Americans and other people of color. Some of the leaders also sought to link the fight against anti-Asian violence with a much larger struggle against White supremacy and capitalism in the United States, which they saw as the basic root causes of oppression of Asian and Pacific Islander peoples. While none of these organizations exist today, with the exception of DARE, many of their leaders and members have continued their work through other social-justice community campaigns and organizations.

My personal reflection begins where these activists left off. It chronicles my initial involvement in the Justice for Vincent Chin movement and traces the impact that the April 1997 killing of Chinese immigrant Kuan Chung Kao had on my personal and political lives.

Awakening

The funeral of George Lee was an awakening for me. I had never wept publicly before. But my own very powerful feelings, my fifteen years of activism and work against racism and economic injustice, the pride of my community's history of resistance to oppression—all flowed out of me the minute I saw his body lying there motionless in the casket. Partly embarrassed and somewhat relieved about being human after all, I walked by George Lee's body with tears streaming down my face and gave him a symbolic yellow-power salute.

In February 1998, the eighty-five-year-old Mr. Lee died a hero in Chinatown and in the broader tenants'-justice and social-justice movements in San Francisco. He had come to the United States at a very early age and spent most of his adult life working two to three jobs a day to support his family. He and his wife, Chang Jok Lee, had been leaders for decades in the movement for tenant rights and dignity for public-housing residents. With the Ping Yuen Residents Improvement Association (PYRIA) in 1978, Mr. Lee led what has become known as the first "public housing project" rent strike in San Francisco history after the brutal rape and killing of a woman at the Ping Yuen development in Chinatown. PYRIA and its supporters were successful in organizing a bold and courageous four-month strike and in winning many of their twelve demands for improved living conditions and gaining real decision-making power for the Ping Yuen residents and others throughout the city.

In the early seventies, Mr. and Mrs. Lee and others of their generation joined with younger Asian American activists to found the Chinese Progressive Association (CPA), a mass-based people's organization in San Francisco's Chinatown. I have been active in this grassroots organization since 1984. Recently, CPA honored Mr. and Mrs. Lee to loud cheers of respect and love from hundreds of people representing generations of activism in our community. Unfortunately, Mr. Lee had died, of natural causes, the week before he was to receive this honor. But his life will be remembered as one of struggle. He fought the good fight for the building of a better society and for the dignity of all people. The many community people and activists like me that he influenced and touched will never be the same.

I was so profoundly moved by Mr. Lee's death because I knew that he died with dignity and with the respect of his family and community. Kuan Chung Kao had no dignity when he was shot in front of his wife and children by a White police officer in Sonoma County, California, in 1999 and then allowed to die with his hands cuffed behind him, lying face down in the quiet suburban street where he lived.

The Sonoma County Police Killing of Kuan Chung Kao

On April 29, 1997, police officer Jack Shields shot and killed thirty-three-year-old engineer Kuan Chung Kao, a Taiwanese immigrant and father of three in the predominantly White middle-class suburb of Rohnert Park, California (about fifty miles north of San Francisco). The sheriff's department and district attorney's offices both found the killing justifiable because Kao had been "brandishing the [broom] stick in a threatening martial-arts fashion." The killing and the blatant racism within the law enforcement agencies and the local media spurred communities throughout northern California to organize for justice for the Kao family, and to call for greater police accountability and an end to racist violence.

The racial stereotypes of Asian people adopted by officials in this case and the attempted justifications for the Kao killing verge on the absurd. The other officer on the scene claimed that Kao was spinning the broomstick like a "ninja fighter." The D.A.'s report included other outrageous comments from neighbors, describing Kao as taking a "Samurai warrior–type stance" before he was killed. Witnesses reported that Shields shot Kao from a distance of about ten to twelve feet. According to Ayling Wu, Kao's widow, he had never studied martial arts. Following the shooting, the police searched the Kao residence in vain for evidence of Mr. Kao's alleged martial-arts expertise.

Reports by police and by the Asian Law Caucus confirm that Kao had been drinking heavily for some seven hours and had a blood alcohol level of 0.23, almost three times the legal limit. Neighbors called 911 after hearing the shirtless and drunk Kao yelling and asking for help. Shields, the second officer to arrive at the scene, shot and killed Kao within seconds of his arrival. As Kao lay dying in his driveway, his wife, a registered nurse, was prevented from administering any emergency medical care for her husband and was threatened with arrest. According to reports, Kao was handcuffed and left face down unattended for eight or nine minutes before the other officer on the scene began any medical treatment. When the ambulance arrived about a minute later, it was too late to save Kao's life.

On June 19, 1997, exactly fifteen years to the day after Vincent Chin was killed in Detroit by being beaten to death with a baseball bat,[1] the Sonoma County district attorney cleared the officers of any criminal charges for Kao's death. The result of the district attorney's investigation is not surprising given that Kao's death was the fourth police-related death in Sonoma County in 1997 and the ninth in two years. In all cases, the district attorney cleared the police of any wrongdoing. Mainstream media reports and local officials were largely influenced from the beginning by the report of the sheriff's investigation, which asserted that Kao assaulted the officer with a "deadly weapon" (the broomstick). The report also failed to acknowledge any of the racism in the incident. In February 1998 the U.S. Department of Justice announced upon completion of its investigation that it would not seek federal civil-rights charges against the police officer because of what it called "a lack of evidence."

Out of Oppression Arises Resistance

My first reaction when I heard of Kao's death through one of my many e-mail lists in early May 1997 was not one of immediate outrage, but instead just a passing thought—" another dead Chinaman." You see, I had become somewhat numbed by the huge string of killings, beatings, and assaults on Asian Americans since Vincent Chin's death in 1982. On June 22, 1997, after reflecting on the Kao case a little more, I cranked out a typical e-mail message to the Asian American and progressive e-mail lists I often "spam" with my rambling thoughts:

> On the fifteenth anniversary of Vincent Chin's death: Given the recent "justified" homicide ruling in the Rohnert Park, CA, police killing of Kuan Chung Kao, the racial violence against Southeast Asians in San Francisco public-housing projects, and other increasing incidents across the country, you'd think President Clinton, in his April 14, 1997, speech at UC San Diego on his Initiative on Race, would have mentioned or acknowledged the rise in anti-Asian sentiment and anti-Asian violence.

---

[1] Vincent Chin was a twenty-seven-year-old Chinese immigrant draftsman and waiter who was killed a week before his wedding by two White, laid-off Chrysler autoworkers who thought Chin was Japanese and blamed him for the decline in the U.S. auto industry. Nine months later, in March 1983, the killers pleaded guilty; they received three years of probation and were fined $3,780.

Instead, Clinton's only mention of Asian Americans was to characterize all of us as "grocers" and to play up "our" tensions with "Black and Latino customers." Don't get me wrong, I think the initiative is important (but so was the Kerner Commission thirty years ago :->). And the appointment of progressive Korean American attorney Angela Oh from Los Angeles to the seven-person task force is a great move. But the last time I remember hearing (a simple) acknowledgement at the national level of anti-Asian violence was during Jesse Jackson's talk about Vincent Chin's killing at the 1984 Democratic National Convention in San Francisco!

Interesting to note that police officer Jack Shields, who killed the thirty-three-year-old Mr. Kao, said that the victim had "brandished a [broom]stick in a threatening martial arts fashion." So he had to shoot him in the chest. And the cops had to prevent Mr. Kao's wife, a nurse, from administering any first aid. And Mr. Kao had to die lying in his own driveway while his wife looked on. The *San Francisco Examiner* reported today that there have been at least five other shooting deaths in Sonoma County (one hour north of SF) since April 1995. . . . Oh, and all of these killings were ruled "justifiable" as well.

Mr. Kao's killing also occurred on the fifth anniversary of the Rodney King uprising. Weird historical parallels. . . . The SF and Sonoma County community groups coming together around the Kao killing are keeping the pressure on. A SF coalition formed last week was pulled together by the Asian Law Caucus. . . . We are planning fundraising, media, and legal support for the family of Mr. Kao and a number of other events. We'll see whether federal civil-rights charges are filed.

Along with a number of other community activists and advocates, I spoke at a June 20, 1997, Justice for Kao press conference held in San Francisco's city hall. My talk emphasized the importance of the grassroots organizing done during the 1980s by my group, the Chinese Progressive Association, and many other, progressive groups in the Justice for Vincent Chin movement. I also repeated a point that Helen Zia, an anti-Asian-violence activist, had made in the Justice for Vincent Chin movement: that no civil rights case is ever brought to prosecution without community mobilization and organizing.

On August 7, 1997, the newly formed Coalition for Justice for the Kao Family organized a candlelight vigil at Portsmouth Square in San Francisco's Chinatown to commemorate the hundredth day after Kao's killing. The hundreds of people in attendance remembered Kao by lighting candles to commemorate his death. They also witnessed visual images of his life through a montage of photos of Kao and his family. The vigil proved important by renewing the cry for justice in the case. Prior to the event, mainstream forces in the coalition actually had opposed the vigil. It took the foresight and organizing of two of the younger activists in the coalition—Debbie Ng, an intern at the Chinese Progressive Association and a student at UC Santa Cruz, and Michael Chang, an Asian Law Caucus intern and Ph.D. student at UC Berkeley—to make the vigil happen.

The diverse coalition initiators included leadership from the Asian Law Caucus, Chinese for Affirmative Action, American Civil Liberties Union, Organization of Chinese Americans, Chinese Progressive Association, Japanese American Citizens League, Redwood Empire Chinese Association of Sonoma County, Bay Area Police Watch, and other groups. From the beginning, many of the grassroots activists, including me, were wary of getting involved in yet another "united front" effort that was clearly dominated by lawyers, politicians, and "experts," and that limited opportunities for more mass involvement and progressive action. But we nonetheless helped build the coalition, always promoting the importance of the victim's family's wishes and their leadership role.

Our second public event was also tremendously successful and helped build more mass participation in the campaign. Some one thousand people turned out at the Rally for Justice for the Kao Family on August 16 in San Francisco's Union Square. The rally was intended to keep public pressure on government authorities for an independent investigation into Mr. Kao's shooting and the subsequent clearing of those involved by the Sonoma County D.A.'s office. The call for justice issued at the rally by Kao's widow, Ms. Wu, for her husband was reminiscent of the courage and strength displayed by Vincent Chin's mother, Mrs. Lily Chin, in the campaign for justice for her son fifteen years earlier. Despite the petty bickering that occurred backstage between local politicians, most of the rally speakers—like young African American activist Van Jones of Bay Area Police Watch—stressed the need for building a "rainbow coalition" against police brutality and for community control of police.

The Union Square rally, notably, included a broader spectrum of groups beyond the usual collection of "professional" activists. The Northern American Guangzhou High School Alumni Association turned out in the hundreds, carrying flowing red-ribbon banners to dramatize the blood shed by victims of racist police violence.

Individual members of the coalition supported other actions. At a rally on October 22 in support of the National Day of Protest against Police Brutality and the Criminalization of a Generation, alongside family members of victims of police violence, I spoke in front of the Stolen Lives Project's huge mock gravestones. The gravestones are engraved with the names and faces of hundreds of victims like Kao. I stressed that Kao's killing must be connected with broader occurrences of legislative and political attacks on immigrants, people of color, and the poor, such as increased INS and border-patrol violence and sweeps, and the devastating impact of welfare "reform" on our communities.

Our work to vindicate Kao's killing seemed to take a positive turn when we learned that the U.S. Commission on Civil Rights was planning formal hearings on the case in northern California. As part of the effort of the Coalition for Justice for the Kao Family, on February 20, 1998, I drove one of several vans full of Chinatown activists and tenant leaders to the hearings called by the U.S. Commission on Civil Rights. Many of the elderly community folks whom we mobilized for the ninety-minute trip to Santa Rosa had worked with the late George Lee on public-housing and social-justice reforms in San Francisco. The Kao coalition was required to provide its own translation equipment and translators for the hearing. Ms. Wu, Kao's widow, was visibly shaken when we arrived to find an intimidating crowd of police officers and their families all wearing yellow ribbons and taking up most of the seats in the tiny auditorium. We were forced, seniors and all, to stand outside the auditorium for hours, and many of us never even made it into the hearing room to witness the bureaucratic drama inside.

The hearings were intended to assist the commission in its investigation of the numerous recent police killings in Sonoma County. The pressure brought to bear by the Kao coalition through community mobilization was a major factor in forcing the commission to come to the Bay Area. Unfortunately, the commission bowed to local police and conservative community pressure and "toned down" its original plans. At the last minute it was decided that instead of a joint forum convened equally by the federal commission and its state advisory committee, all sixteen members of the state advisory committee would actually preside over the meeting, with the federal commission taking a much diminished role. In addition, the commission abruptly reversed its decision to subpoena witnesses after objections from law enforcement officials led to a letter of protest from the Santa Rosa police chief.

Late in the evening, after returning from the hearings and dropping off the last activist, I found myself questioning why I work fifteen-hour days, driving in the pouring rain, trying to speak or give voice to the voiceless, when no one in power seems to be even willing to listen. Were we fooling ourselves to think that by using the methods we had adopted we could stop anti-Asian violence and all hate crimes?

Personal Journey

As a past director of the Northern California Coalition for Immigrant Rights, a nonprofit advocacy group based in San Francisco, I have worked for years to address the day-to-day needs of immigrants and poor and working people. But my other political work outside of my nine to five job often pulls me closer to the kind of real impact I want to make in this world.

My family roots start in Guangzhou, China, and wind through Hawaii and the California Central Valley. My dad is an immigrant from China who settled in the Sacramento Delta area with his family around 1920 when he was a baby. My mom's father was born in Hawaii and settled in Sacramento to raise his family. Mom was born and raised in Sacramento during the Depression. I think her experiences with poverty and racism have given her a special fighting spirit and a unique resourcefulness and practicality that only folks of her generation seem to share. Both of my parents, along with many of my aunts and uncles and cousins, worked for the state of California almost their whole lives. Although my father joined the U.S. Army and fought in World War II, neither he nor my mother had the luxury of a college education. They placed much of their hope for success in me and my brothers and sisters.

Besides my twin brother, Gordon, a longtime activist in the Asian American and environmental-justice movements and executive director of the Chinese Progressive Association, I have four other siblings. One of my sisters was active in the Asian American Political Alliance at UC Berkeley in the late 1960s. My mother and other relatives have historically been active in Asian American community organizations in Sacramento. I am fortunate to have grown up in an environment where community service was so highly regarded. But my family and cloistered surroundings in Sacramento also sheltered me from the blatant racism and exploitation around me.

It wasn't until the early 1980s, after Vincent Chin's killing, that my racial and class identity really hit me. In the midst of the so-called Ronald Reagan revolution, the 1982 Chin killing sparked a nationwide campaign for justice that drew connections between racial violence and the era's pro-corporate, trickle-down economic policies and fanatical anticommunism. Importantly, the community organizing and mobilizing that came out of the movement greatly influenced a new generation of community activists like me.

The classes in Asian American studies and ethnic studies I took as a student at UC Davis formed the beginning of my "political life." About a year after Vincent Chin's death, Davis High School student Thong Huynh was stabbed to death by a group of White youth that had been taunting him with racial slurs. During classroom discussions of Huynh's killing in my first Asian American studies class, in the fall of 1983, I was able for the first time to talk collectively with other Asian Americans about issues of concern to our community. I later joined Davis Asians for Racial Equality (DARE), a community group that was formed to address the growing anti-Asian sentiment in the area. Angela Oh, one of the members of President Clinton's Initiative on Race, was a founder of DARE, along with other law students, undergraduates (like me), and community members.

I later became active in many other struggles—covering issues from Asian American student and educational rights to fighting anti-immigrant laws and policies and the "English Only" movement. I also developed internationalist politics through my work in the antiapartheid and Central American solidarity movements and in my stint as the editor of *Third World*, a student newspaper on campus.

In my studies I grew fascinated with our country's racist history of immigration and exclusion laws targeted at Asian peoples and with the interconnections between labor and foreign policies. My two mentors at UC Davis, Professors George Kagiwada and Isao Fujimoto, helped me make the link between academic study and my role in the Asian American community and the broader society. They taught me to understand through integration of theory and practice the importance of grassroots community empowerment in any effort to address anti-Asian violence or racial oppression in general. Through their teaching I was ingrained with the principle, now popularized by UCLA scholar/activist Glenn Omatsu, that "knowledge is too important to stay in the classroom."

Today, more than fifteen years later, both Kagiwada and Fujimoto have retired. And I have been teaching at the predominantly working-class San Francisco State University since 1992. My students in the evening courses I teach in Asian American studies and ethnic studies give me hope for the future. We dialogue about the meaning of the 1992 Rodney King uprisings in connection to the 1965 Watts rebellion. We compare the president's Initiative on Race today with the Kerner Commission Report in 1968. We discuss anti-Asian violence in the broader context of our country's history of racial oppression and its class exploitation of Third World peoples.

When we collectively view Christine Choy and Renee Tajima's classic documentary *Who Killed Vincent Chin?*, it is the students who connect Kuan Chung Kao's killing to the unprecedented domestic and worldwide economic changes caused by corporate globalization—including the elimination of our society's safety net, the ongoing downsizing of our workforce, and the constant pitting of workers and communities against each other to fight over crumbs thrown out by the transnational corporations.

Importantly, my students also see right through the shallow "liberal" approaches to eliminating hate crimes promoted by many of our politicians and self-proclaimed community leaders. My students' proposed solutions are decidedly more radical. They emphasize the importance of addressing root causes of racial violence and of promoting strategies like grassroots community organizing and building multiracial coalitions with other people of color and progressive movements. They talk about the "long-term struggle" and are very skeptical of strategies for community "empowerment" that focus solely on electoral and individual economic advancement, because they understand the inherent inequality and deep corruption of our existing political system.

I have tried to give my students at San Francisco State the same opportunity that my teachers gave me: to learn in a supportive environment through practical work about their key role in our community's progress and development. But ultimately, I benefit from our interactions as well, for their hopefulness and idealism help inspire me and keep me going in this difficult political period for immigrants, people of color, and the poor and working classes.

Toward Lives of Dignity

A few months after I learned of Kuan Chung Kao's killing, I saw a picture of the twin baby boys and the six-year-old daughter he left behind. I wondered what their mother, Ayling Wu, would say to her children as they grew up to help them understand the meaning of the racist killing of their father. Would she raise them as my mother has raised my twin brother and me: to stand up for what is right and just? Would she turn the death of her husband into the birth of hope and struggle in her twins and daughter?

Few of us are fortunate to live a life of dignity like that led by Chinatown housing-movement leader George Lee. That is why I am moved to tears by the incredible moments, such as his funeral, when our heroes pass their legacy to those of us willing to carry on their struggles, their dreams of a better world. George Lee passed his torch to many of us who remember his life. I have hope that we can turn Kuan Chung Kao's and Vincent Chin's lives from tragedies into lives of dignity, like George Lee's, through our work to organize, educate, and empower our communities.

Playing the Racial Trump Card: Asian Americans In Contemporary U.S. Politics

Claire Jean Kim

As we [Asian Americans] work for our own empowerment, we must ask ourselves a series of questions. Will we fight only for ourselves, or will we embrace the concerns of all oppressed peoples? Will we overcome our own oppression and help to create a new society, or will we become a new exploiter group in the present American hierarchy of inequality? Will we define our goal of empowerment solely in terms of individual advancement for a few, or as the collective liberation for all peoples?

—Glenn Omatsu

Since the Asian American movement of the 1960s, Asian American scholars, activists, and advocates have urged Asian Americans to resist the lure of the model minority myth, which represents them as exemplars for other, culturally challenged minorities, especially Blacks. Indeed, an entire generation of Asian Americanists has engaged in a sustained critique of the myth, challenging its empirical claims and exposing its ideological functions. Today, with the myth still thriving, scholars, activists, and advocates continue to exhort Asian Americans to refuse the status of a "racial bourgeoisie" or "buffer zone" between Blacks and Whites.[1] Asian Americans, they argue, must forcefully distance themselves from the White exercise of domination over Blacks. They must declare in no uncertain terms: "We will not be used."[2] This spirited resistance to being used as a pawn in the White project of domination has been one of the hallmarks of Asian American politics in the post-1965 period.

In this article, I argue that a certain trend in contemporary Asian American scholarship and politics may actually facilitate the White project of using Asian Americans against Blacks, thus contravening this tradition of resistance. Here I am talking about the tendency among racial advocacy groups and, to some degree, scholars and activists, to represent Asian Americans as a *bona fide* minority group equivalent in status to all other minority groups and deserving of the same attention from the neutral arbiter state. This representation, I explain

---

[1] See Mari Matsuda, "We Will Not Be Used," *UCLA Asian American Pacific Islands Law Journal* 1 (1993), 79–84 and Elaine Kim, "Korean Americans in U.S. Race Relations: Some Considerations," *Amerasia Journal* 23:2 (1997), 69–78. My focus in this article is on liberal and progressive scholars, activists, and advocates. I briefly touch upon conservative Asian American advocates in the discussion of the *Ho* lawsuit below.

[2] Matsuda, "We Will Not Be Used."

below, can be all too easily appropriated by White elites determined to silence Black claims and grievances. To the extent that this facilitation of the White project of using Asian Americans against Blacks occurs, it is clearly unintended and unforeseen. Because Asian American empowerment rhetoric and practices are embedded in the American racial order in ways that have not been fully thought through, they can and sometimes do have implications for White-on-Black domination that contradict the explicit intentions of Asian American actors. My primary aim in this article is to draw attention to some of these implications.[3] Ultimately, my argument raises important normative questions about whether or not Asian Americans are responsible for the effects that their struggle has upon other racially subordinated groups. My sense is that such responsibility does exist, and that to meet it, Asian Americans must go beyond the principle of "do no harm" and embrace a more proactive commitment to achieving racial justice for all communities of color. I will return to these issues in the final section of the article.

How does it happen that Asian American scholars, activists, and advocates who share a commitment not to be used sometimes end up facilitating this very outcome? This outcome may occur through the conjunction of two factors: the dynamics of the American racial order and Asian American narrative choices.[4] First, consider the American racial order. In an earlier article, I argued that American society is best characterized not as a racially level playing field but as a complex, hierarchical order in which racially designated groups enjoy differential status, privilege, and power in relation to one another.[5] Since the present article builds upon this earlier work, I will very briefly review it here.

My contention is that White opinionmakers have discursively constructed, since their first encounters with "others" in the New World, a "field of racial positions" within which they have categorized, defined, and located different groups relative to one another—with Whites situated on top, Blacks on the bottom, and other groups somewhere in between. This field of racial positions consists not of a single-scale hierarchy—A over B over C—but of a plane defined by two major axes: that of superior/inferior and that of insider/foreigner. It is a shared cognitive map that has served as a blueprint for the distribution of status, opportunities, and privilege in American society, generating and mapping onto a concrete American racial order.[6] Since their first arrival in the mid-1800s, people of Asian descent have been "racially triangulated" between Whites and Blacks in the field of racial positions by means of two types of simultaneously operating White discursive practices: practices of "relative valorization" (by which Whites explicitly valorize

---

[3] In making this argument, I am joining a conversation about interminority hierarchy, conflict, and justice that progressive race scholars associated with Asian American Studies have initiated in earnest over the past decade. See Eric Yamamoto, *Interracial Justice: Conflict and Reconciliation in Post-Civil Rights America* (New York: New York University Press, 1999); Elaine Kim, "Korean Americans in U.S. Race Relations"; and Glenn Omatsu, "The 'Four Prisons' and the Movements of Liberation: Asian American Activism from the 1960s to the 1990s," *The State of Asian America: Activism and Resistance in the 1990s*, edited by Karin Aguilar-San Juan (Boston: South End Press, 1994), 19–69.

[4] By "narrative choices," I mean the ways in which public spokes-people such as scholars, activists, and advocates choose to represent Asian Americans to the general public and the state through position papers, policy pronouncements, speeches, writing, etc.

[5] Claire Jean Kim, "The Racial Triangulation of Asian Americans," *Politics & Society* 27: 1 (March 1999), 105–138.

[6] I distinguish here between the "field of racial positions" as a shared cognitive map and the "racial order" as patterned material inequalities; the former is the blueprint, the latter the resulting structure. Although I confine my analysis to the White-Black-Asian American triad in both the earlier article and this one, this is more a decision of economy than of principle. My sense is that some of what I have to say about Asian Americans as a "triangulated" group applies to Latinos as well.

Asian Americans relative to Blacks, placing them between Black and White on the superior/inferior scale) and practices of "civic ostracism" (by which Whites construct Asian Americans as immutably foreign and unassimilable with Whites, placing them on the foreigner end of the insider/foreigner scale).[7] This pattern of racial triangulation, which first took hold with regard to Chinese immigrants in the mid-1800s and was then applied, with important exceptions and variations, to subsequent streams of Asian immigration from Japan, Korea, and elsewhere, has stubbornly persisted for over a century and a half into the contemporary era. As a result, Asian Americans are, on the whole, persistently less advantaged than Whites and more advantaged than Blacks in the American racial order.[8]

The second factor concerns Asian Americans' "narrative of self-representation"—or how some Asian American scholars, activists, and advocates have chosen to define "Asian Americans," their relation to other groups of color and the nation, and the nature of their struggle in the contemporary period.[9] On this point, I argue the following. First, the original Asian American narrative of self-representation, which first emerged during the Asian American movement of the late 1960s and early 1970s, was linked from the start to what I call a Third World frame, or a notion of united Third World struggle against White/Western racism and imperialism.[10] Second, from the mid-1970s forward, many Asian American scholars, activists, and advocates have responded to the incentives and constraints of the newly institutionalized civil rights regime by revising the original narrative of self-representation and adopting what I call an antidiscrimination frame. According to this frame, Asian Americans are a *bona fide* minority group equivalent in status with all other minority groups, including Blacks, and deserving of equivalent attention from the goods-dispensing state. Let me emphasize that I am talking about a general trend toward the adoption of this frame; there are many dissenting voices contesting this move, some of which I will discuss in the final section. In the main part of this article, however, I am interested in this overall trend and its implications.

It is the playing out of this Asian American antidiscrimination frame in the context of the American racial order—or the assertion of formal interminority equivalences in the face of persistent interminority differentials in status, privilege, and power—that facilitates the White project of using Asian Americans against Blacks. When Asian American scholars, activists, and advocates argue that Asian Americans are minorities, too, deserving of equal consideration with Blacks, they abstract from history and decline to explore the ways in which Asian Americans are, on the whole, persistently advantaged relative to Blacks. These narrative choices then enable conservative Whites (and, occasionally, conservative Asian Americans) to essentialize and thereby denounce certain Black protests/acts of rebellion that impinge or appear to impinge on Asian

---

[7] Both types of practices are grounded upon an essentialized reading of Asian/Asian American "culture" that elides distinctions both between Asians and Asian Americans and among Asian American subgroups.

[8] As a "triangulated" group, Asian Americans are vulnerable to ostracizing practices on the part of Whites and Blacks alike. To say that Asian Americans are relatively advantaged compared with Blacks is not to say that they are immune to racism or nativism by the latter. On the other hand, it is not enough to say that all groups exhibit prejudice toward one another; we must pay attention to their positionality as well.

[9] The phrase "narrative of self-representation" is taken from Ruth Hsu, " 'Will the Model Minority Please Identify Itself?' American Ethnic Identity and Its Discontents," *Diaspora* 5:1 (1996), 37–63.

[10] Here I borrow David Snow and Robert Benford's notion of a "collective action frame," a schema which establishes a collective identity, diagnoses a social problem, and mandates what is to be done about it. See "Master Frames and Cycles of Protest," *Frontiers in Social Movement Theory*, edited by Aldon Morris and Carol McClurg Mueller (New Haven: Yale University Press, 1992), 133–155.

Americans as "reverse discrimination" against the latter. After all, if we view all minorities as formal equivalents, it seems presumptively unfair that one minority group should burden another in its efforts to advance. I refer to this phenomenon of automatically overriding the claims of one minority group (Blacks) through reference to the moral authority of the claims of another minority group (Asian Americans) as *playing the racial trump card*. Conservative Whites (and Asian Americans) play Asian Americans as a racial trump card when they invoke the Asian American story of victimization for the purpose of presumptively nullifying certain Black claims and grievances. It is by furnishing an Asian American narrative of self-representation that is easily appropriated as a weapon against racial redress, therefore, that some Asian American scholars, activists, and advocates unwittingly lend themselves to being used.

In the first and second parts of this article, respectively, I discuss the emergence of the original Asian American narrative of self-representation during the 1960s and its revision from the mid-1970s onwards. In the third part of the article, I look at how Asian Americans get played as a racial trump card around two issues: Black-Korean conflict and race-conscious remedies in education. In the final part of the article, I consider what is to be done if what I am arguing is right.

The Original Asian American Narrative: Yellow Power and Third World Solidarity

As Lisa Lowe observes, "The grouping 'Asian American' is not a natural or static category; it is a socially constructed unity, a situationally specific position, assumed for political reasons."[11] Prior to the 1960s, the prevailing pattern among Asian-descent groups in the U.S. was one of mutual disidentification.[12] The Asian American movement, which emerged on college campuses and in communities during the late 1960s, gave rise to an Asian American collective subjectivity for the first time. As a strategic response to being lumped together and racialized as "Mongolian" or "Oriental," those of Chinese, Japanese, Filipino, Korean and other Asian descent developed an "Asian American" identity and consciousness—just as African Americans embraced Blackness as a response to being racialized as "Negro" or "colored." In this way, Asian American activists turned a subordinative racial category on its head and transformed it into a framework for group solidarity and empowerment.

For students of Asian descent, initiating the Asian American movement and taking up the banner of Yellow Power was a way of finally naming their own oppression. Inspired by the various movements of the time—especially the Black Power movement, with its call for racial solidarity and pride—Asian American students felt the need for their own distinct movement. The Vietnam War powerfully reinforced this sentiment. The racism expressed by the U.S. anti-war movement alienated Asian American students, who gradually came to identify not with the American G.I.s but with the Vietnamese people as victims of White/Western aggression. While the mainstream antiwar movement used slogans such as "Give Peace A Chance" and "Bring the G.I.s Home," Asian American antiwar activists promoted slogans such as "Stop Killing Our Asian Brothers and Sisters" and "We Don't Want Your Racist War," dramatically redrawing the boundaries of "we" and "them."[13] From the start, Asian American collective subjectivity was defined

[11] Lisa Lowe, *Immigrant Acts: On Asian American Cultural Politics* (Durham: Duke University Press, 1996).

[12] Yen Le Espiritu, *Asian American Panethnicity: Bridging Institutions and Identities* (Philadelphia: Temple University Press, 1992).

[13] Paul Wong, "The Emergence of the Asian-American Movement," *Bridge* 2:1 (1972), 33–39, 35–36.

in opposition to the "nation" as the agent of White/Western racism and imperialism.[14] Like their Black Power counter-parts, Asian American activists believed that racism was deeply embedded in the very fabric of American society and that nothing except fundamental (and perhaps revolutionary) change could extirpate it. The American government was, in the view of Asian American activists, not a neutral arbiter to whom they could appeal for redress but the major agent of racial and economic oppression around the globe.

If Asian Americans believed that they were distinct from other nonWhite groups, they also believed that they were inextricably connected to them. Yellow Power was articulated in clear connection with a Third World frame.[15] Asian American activists saw themselves as united with Third World communities at home and abroad in the global struggle against White/Western domination—again embracing a transnational framework of identification over that of the American "nation." According to the Third World frame, communities of color within the U.S. (Black ghettos, Chicano and Puerto Rican barrios, Chinatowns, etc.) were internal colonies comparable in important ways to the former European colonies in Africa, Asia, and Latin America. Activist Franklin Odo and colleagues commented during the movement: "Peoples of color in the U.S. have responded to the . . . Third World concept and growing numbers insist on a world view which places them in positions related to their brothers overseas."[16] Thus all Third World communities were thought to share the same struggle against a common enemy, and their fates were seen as profoundly linked. The idea that one could be liberated while the others remained oppressed was as absurd as that of socialism occuring in one country alone.

Just as Asian American activists began to mount a challenge to the political and economic status quo, the mainstream media began to disseminate the model minority myth—almost as if White opinionmakers hoped to placate Asian Americans through praise. In the mid to late 1960s, commentators marveled about Asian American "success"—which they all attributed to an essentialized "Asian" culture—and pointedly asked why Blacks couldn't follow suit. Asian American activists responded by exhorting Asian Americans to repudiate the exaggerated story of Asian American "success," to reject the status of being honorary Whites, and to embrace a Third World framework of struggle. Activist Amy Uyematsu declared: "Frightened 'yellows' allow the white public to use the 'silent Oriental' stereotype against the black protest . . . The yellow power movement envisages a new role for Asian Americans."[17] Just as Stokely Carmichael said "Every Negro is a potential Black man," so did Asian American activists see every Oriental as a potential Asian American. From the start, becoming an Asian American signified not only resistance to being used but also a declaration of solidarity with other oppressed groups.

---

[14] It is worth noting that the antidiscrimination regime was in place at this point, and that Asian American activists had the option of embracing a more traditional civil rights approach to group empowerment. Some did, but the Third World frame held the center of gravity during the movement.

[15] Through the late 1960s and early 1970s, Asian Americans demonstrated their commitment to the Third World frame through various campus and community activities. Significantly, the first "Asian American" student organization—the Asian American Political Alliance (AAPA)—made its public debut as part of the Third World United Liberation Front responsible for organizing the Third World strikes at San Francisco State College and University of California, Berkeley from 1968 to 1969.

[16] Franklin Odo et al., "The U.S. in Asia and Asians in the U.S.," *Roots: An Asian American Reader*, edited by Amy Tachiki et al. (Los Angeles: UCLA Asian American Studies Center, 1971), 223–244, 225.

[17] Amy Uyematsu, "The Emergence of Yellow Power in America," *Roots*, 9–13, 11.

The rhetoric, program, and vision of the Asian American movement were nebulous in places, as was the Third World concept itself. But these ideas were no less powerful politically for being ambiguous. During the movement, for the first time, Americans of Asian descent came together and constructed a racial or panethnic self, defining their collective subjectivity, their relations with other groups of color and the nation, and their struggle according to the Third World frame. In doing so, they declared their solidarity with Blacks and other groups of color and joined these groups in condemning the state as an agent of racism and imperialism and calling for a fundamental redistribution of power in American society. Although the Third World frame did not direct attention to interminority differentials, the notion of a transnational united front of color allied against the White "nation" did not leave room for competitive victimization claims and racial trumping in the way that the antidiscrimination frame would.

The Revised Asian American Narrative: Racial Advocacy and the Antidiscrimination Regime

The regime of antidiscrimination laws, policies, and norms put in place in the mid-1960s has come to be seen by many progressive race scholars as a framework for containing, disciplining, and co-opting racial activism and forestalling major change. Mainstream conventional wisdom holds that the race-based movements of the 1960s gave way, in teleological fashion, to the inclusive mainstream politics of the contemporary period. By this account, the federal government gradually responded to minority demands by instituting an antidiscrimination regime of laws, policies, and norms—anchored by the Civil Rights Act of 1964 and the Voting Rights Act of 1965—all of which resulted in meaningful minority political "incorporation." Since the mid-1980s, critical race theorists and other progressive race scholars have criticized this account for exaggerating both the system's responsiveness to grievances and the meaningfulness of the reforms achieved.[18] They have shown that the antidiscrimination regime served, from the start, as a bulwark against more fundamental reform, since the federal government established it in order to maintain legitimacy in the face of escalating civil rights demonstrations and to forestall more radical challenges emanating from emergent race-based movements such as the Black Power movement.

In addition, these scholars have persuasively argued that the antidiscrimination regime's very conceptions of race and racism hinder meaningful movement toward racial justice. Antidiscrimination law sees race as a formal category with no social/historical substance and defines racism as overt individual acts of discrimination, aberrations from a normal baseline of colorblindness that can be corrected by aggressively enforced civil rights laws and/or carefully tailored race-conscious remedies. Progressive race scholars, on the other hand, see race as a concept that was historically and socially constructed for the purpose of domination and view racism as pervasive in American society and largely beyond the reach of antidiscrimination remedies. According to Neil Gotanda, the U.S. Supreme Court's increasing reliance upon what he calls the "formal-race"

---

[18] Despite their critique of the antidiscrimination regime, most critical race theorists do not want to "trash" it altogether. While they argue that civil rights laws are ideological constructs designed to serve power, they also believe that rights rhetoric has provided subordinated racial groups with one of their only weapons to counteract domination. It is all well and good to talk about resisting cooptation, but people have to worry about their basic survival, and rights have proven helpful in this regard. See Kimberlé Crenshaw, "Race, Reform, and Retrenchment: Transformation and Legitimation in Antidiscrimination Law," *Critical Race Theory*, edited by Kimberlé Crenshaw et al. (New York: The New Press, 1995), 103–122.

concept of race—which defines race as a formal category entirely abstracted from social reality and history and thus renders "Black" and "White" equivalent categories—is tantamount to the denial of Black-White inequalities and the assertion of a racially level playing field.[19] Using the formal-race concept of race, the Supreme Court has found certain racial classifications designed to redress historical discrimination to be indistinguishable from those designed to enact discrimination and therefore subject to the same (often fatal) strict scrutiny level of judicial review.[20]

To the extent that the antidiscrimination regime does recognize historically defined groups in its remedial allocation of certain political and economic goods along racial lines, it tends to see only two main categories: that of the fault-bearing majority and that of the minority deserving remedial aid. In this way, the distinct histories, circumstances, and needs of different minorities or groups of color are elided. Gary Peller writes:

> The fact that relations between Anglos and African-Americans, Asians, and Hispanics are all per-
> ceived as presenting the issues of "discrimination against racial minorities" in legal and political
> discourse reflects the same structure of abstraction. From this structure, it begins to appear that the
> social subordination of various groups does not have a complex, particular, and historical context,
> but rather is a formal, numeric problem of the relations of majorities to minorities, unified under
> the concept "discrimination."[21]

The antidiscrimination regime's majority/minority binary clearly obscures interminority differentials in status, privilege, and opportunities, thus making it difficult to address the unique severity of the Black experience of racial domination. With the bottom group firmly in place, the American racial order is stabilized.

How have Asian American scholars, activists, and advocates responded to the establishment of the antidiscrimination regime? From the mid-1970s forward, they have, like their counterparts in other groups of color, responded to the constraints and incentives of the antidiscrimination regime by revising the Asian American narrative of self-representation in accordance with it—or redefining their collective subjectivity, their relations to other groups and the nation, and their struggle for empowerment. They now represent Asian Americans as a *bona fide* minority group that is formally equivalent to other minority groups and deserving of the same attention from the state. At the same time, they engage in conventional political tactics to secure more resources, better protection, and more equitable treatment for their racially defined constituents. In other words, they are playing by the rules rather than challenging the entire game. I describe this shift as moving from the Third World frame to the antidiscrimination frame, or from Third World activism to "the politics of racial advocacy."[22] Given the persistence of the model minority myth, which effectively denies Asian Americans minority status by declaring them a "success story,"

---

[19] Neil Gotanda, "A Critique of 'Our Constitution is Color-Blind,' " *Stanford Law Review* 44:1 (1991), 1–68.

[20] Some of the key cases reflecting this trend include: City of Richmond *v.* J.A. Croson Co. (1989), Shaw *v.* Reno (1993), and Adarand Constructors, Inc. *v.* Pena (1995). To withstand strict scrutiny, racial classifications must serve a compelling governmental interest and be narrowly tailored to their specific purpose.

[21] Gary Peller, "Race-Consciousness," *Critical Race Theory*, 127–158, 130.

[22] This shift has given rise to revisionist histories that depict the Asian American movement as part of the teleological story of minority incorporation by neglecting or mischaracterizing the movement's radical and/or militant elements and foregrounding its moderate, middle-class, and reformist elements. For example, see William Wei, *The Asian American Movement* (Philadelphia: Temple University Press, 1993).

this drive to declare that "Asian Americans are minorities, too" is understandable, although its full implications, once again, remain unexplored.

Once again, I am not suggesting that all scholars, activists, and advocates have embraced the antidiscrimination frame. There are many activists (e.g., Grace Lee Boggs and Yuri Kochiyama), activist/scholars (e.g., Glenn Omatsu, Sumi Cho, Elaine Kim, Eric Yamamoto, Neil Gotanda, and Mari Matsuda), and advocates (e.g., Henry Der) who continue to embrace aspects of Third World thinking and/or express vigorous criticism of the antidiscrimination frame. In this sense, the contemporary Asian American narrative of self-representation is still contested and still, to some extent, up for grabs. However, there has been a general trend toward the adoption of an antidiscrimination frame in advocacy publications and some scholarship in Asian American Studies, and it is this trend that I seek to identify and analyze here.[23]

Clearly, the antidiscrimination regime's practice of allocating certain political and economic goods (e.g., political representation via redistricting, jobs and higher education through affirmative action, and social service funding) along racial lines discourages united front multiracial activism and invites the politics of racial advocacy. In other words, racial allocations by the state encourage solidarity within racial groups and competition among them.[24] The bigger and better organized the racial group, the more attention and resources it is likely to elicit from the state. This is why the Japanese American Citizens League (JACL), which was founded in 1930 as an exclusively Japanese American group, went racial or panethnic in the 1980s and started "cultivating relationships with other Asian communities in order to build political clout as an 'Asian Pacific American' voice."[25] Today many Asian American advocacy groups attempt to negotiate a dyadic relationship between Asian Americans as a constituency and the state-as-allocator, while defining Asian American collective subjectivity, at least in part, through a competitive distancing from other groups of color.[26]

Scholars in Asian American Studies have constructed an Asian American history of victimization which racial advocates frequently cite in their efforts to prove that Asian Americans are a *bona fide* minority group deserving remedial aid.[27] The building of this history has entailed recovering Asian American voices and experiences long marginalized by both Eurocentric thinking and the

---

[23] The Japanese American Citizens League, Leadership Education for Asian Pacifics, Organization of Chinese Americans, Asian Pacific American Legal Center of Southern California, National Asian Pacific American Legal Consortium, Asian American Legal Defense and Education Fund, and Asian Law Caucus are some of the leading Asian American advocacy organizations. Each group has its own distinct history and agenda, although I focus in this article on what they say and do in common.

[24] Espiritu, *Asian American Panethnicity*.

[25] Cited in Espiritu, *Asian American Panethnicity*, 66.

[26] Strikingly, the shift from the Third World frame to the antidiscrimination frame is reflected in the way that Asian American Studies programs are developing nationwide. Although Asian American Studies was originally conceived of as an element of Third World Studies during the campus strikes of 1968–1969, there are more and more Asian American Studies programs growing up today on their own, apart from a broader "ethnic studies" rubric.

[27] For examples of this kind of narrative construction, see Angelo Ancheta, *Race, Rights, and the Asian American Experience* (New Brunswick: Rutgers University Press, 1998), chapter 1; Kenyon Chan and Shirley Hune, "Racialization and Panethnicity: From Asians in America to Asian Americans," *Toward A Common Destiny: Improving Race and Ethnic Relations in America*, edited by Willis Hawley and Anthony Jackson (San Francisco: Jossey-Bass Publishers, 1995), 205–233; and Gary Okihiro, "The Victimization of Asians in America," *The World & I* (April 1993), 397–413. I should note that these authors do treat interminority issues in other aspects of their work. For instance, Okihiro's *Margins and Mainstreams: Asians in American History and Culture* (Seattle: University of Washington Press, 1994) is one of the most nuanced and insightful accounts of Asian-Black relations I have seen.

nearly exclusive preoccupation with Black-White dynamics. Like the Black and Chicano stories of victimization, the Asian American one is punctuated by certain landmark events: in this case, the exclusion of Chinese immigrants in 1882, the internment of Japanese Americans during World War II, the killing of Vincent Chin in 1982, and, most recently, *Sa-I-Gu* (or April 29, referring to the Los Angeles unrest of 1992). While most scholarship in Asian American Studies emphasizes what is distinctive about the Asian American experience—what makes it different from that of other racially subordinated groups, defiant of the Black-White framework of analysis, and deserving of attention in its own right—few works do more than mention in passing that Asian Americans are, on the whole, relatively advantaged compared with Blacks. Nor do they seriously explore the difference that this can or should make when it comes to Asian American political strategizing and narrative choices. As such, it is at least arguable that scholarship that decontextualizes Asian American oppression from the larger racial order and glosses over interminority differentials contributes, to some degree, to the strength and viability of the antidiscrimination frame.

Let's look at one prominent example of the antidiscrimination frame at work. The volume entitled, *State of Asian Pacific America: Policy Issues to the Year 2020* (1993), was published by the UCLA Asian American Studies Center in conjunction with Leadership Education for Asian Pacifics (LEAP), a nonprofit, nonpartisan racial advocacy group founded in 1982 with the aim of "achiev[ing] full participation and equality for all Asian Pacific Americans (APAs) through leadership, empowerment, and policy."[28] In it, leading scholars and advocates articulate the revised Asian American narrative of self representation. The volume's overall message is that Asian Americans are indeed a *bona fide* minority that has faced and continues to face distinctive forms of discrimination (e.g., quotas in higher education, the "glass ceiling," etc.), that they therefore have special policy needs, and that they should be seen as having equal standing with other minority groups.

The volume's discussions of the "glass ceiling"—by any measure, one of the highest-ranking items on the Asian American empowerment agenda—exemplify the narrowly dyadic focus of this kind of racial advocacy. Asian American professionals, the authors remark, are rarely promoted to top management; hence they are consigned to looking up through a "glass ceiling" at White vice presidents and supervisors. What is striking about these discussions is that they do not comment on where Blacks and other disadvantaged groups are standing in this scenario. Are they on the same floor with Asian Americans? Or, more likely, are they standing one story below, looking up through another "glass ceiling" at Asian Americans?[29] Although the volume's authors express hope for multiracial coalitions and the achievement of a "truly multicultural" and "pluralistic society," their comments on this topic strongly imply that all minorities are in equivalent situations, that their experiences are fungible, and that a rising tide will lift all boats. Yet the reality is that minority groups sometimes do engage in a zero-sum struggle over scarce goods.

The antidiscrimination regime thus seeks to discipline Asian Americans, to constrict their collective vision, and to transform them from Third World transnational warriors into "ethnic group" supplicants at the state altar. During the 1960s, activists talked about Yellow Power, embraced a Third World transnational framework in opposition to the "nation," viewed the state as the chief agent of racism and imperialism, and saw their own struggle as liberatory and even

---

[28] *In Support of Civil Rights: Taking on the Initiative* (Los Angeles: Leadership Education for Asian Pacifics Asian Pacific American Public Policy Institute, 1996), 2.

[29] The image of the "glass ceiling" as a physical/spatial barrier to group advancement fits nicely, it is worth noting, with the antidiscrimination regime's view of racism as aberrational rather than embedded in the social fabric: barriers are superficial, external obstacles that can be eliminated without rearranging basic social and political arrangements.

revolutionary. Today, many scholars, activists, and advocates talk about Asian Americans as a *bona fide* minority group that has its own distinctive history of victimization and therefore deserves formally equivalent status with other minority groups in the eyes of the goods-dispensing state. In the late 1960s, empowerment meant liberation from racial oppression for all groups of color, a fundamental redistribution of power and resources, perhaps even revolution. A decade later, it meant helping one's own group to overcome barriers, gain access, and secure a piece of the pie. If the antidiscrimination regime's majority/minority binary tends to obscure interminority differentials, the revised Asian American narrative of self-representation does little to illuminate them; in fact, it participates in this covering up. In this sense, it helps to set the stage for racial trumping.

Playing the Racial Trump Card

Conservative Whites play Asian Americans as a racial trump card when they appropriate the latter's revised narrative of self representation for the purpose of delegitimating specific Black claims or empowerment practices. Invoking the Asian American history of victimization, they say to Blacks: "What you are doing or saying to empower yourselves is illegitimate because it discriminates against another *bona fide* minority group." Occasionally, conservative Asian Americans play Asian Americans as a racial trump card as well, saying to Blacks: "We have been discriminated against, too, so it is unfair for you to burden us in any way in your effort to get ahead." Both scenarios depend upon a scrupulous neglect of interminority differentials in status, opportunities, and privilege. After all, if these differentials were acknowledged and explored, it would open up discussion over whether Black efforts that impinge on (or appear to impinge on) Asian Americans are nevertheless justified by the greater severity of Black oppression. The automatic, unreflective trumping of Black claims with the story of Asian American victimization depends upon neglect of these differentials. I will briefly talk here about the two most salient issues around which racial trumping arises—Black-Korean conflict and race-conscious remedies in education.

Black-Korean Conflict: The Trumping of Black Protest

Once we turn to concrete examples, it becomes clear that we need to deconstruct the category "Asian American"—at least in a preliminary way—in order to make sense of what is going on. On the ground, Asian American collective subjectivity continues to be tenuous and incomplete; it is always in the process of being simultaneously contested, challenged, undermined, and reproduced. This is reflected in the fact that groups such as liberal and progressive scholars, activists, and advocates; leaders of single national origin communities; and conservative advocates often diverge in their views and aims. Generally speaking, the first group aims to build and reproduce a racial or panethnic sensibility among both the native-born and immigrants; the second group seeks to promote and protect the interests of their respective communities, availing themselves of a racial or panethnic framework when and only when it serves this purpose; the third group seeks to combine racial pride with neoconservative ideas about individual merit and equal opportunity.[30] Asian America looks more and more complicated the closer to the ground one

---

[30] For more on Asian American conservatives, see Omatsu, "The 'Four Prisons.' "

gets. Nevertheless, White opinionmakers continue to appropriate the unidimensional, uniform representation of Asian Americans as a *bona fide* minority for their own purposes.

Consider the phenomenon of Black-Korean conflict in New York City and Los Angeles. Many first generation Korean Americans in both cities have interpreted Black protests/acts of rebellion as scapegoating or discrimination against Koreans as a distinct racial-transnational group. Closing ranks as Koreans, they have invoked a *Korean* rather than Asian American story of victimization with which to trump Black grievances about racial oppression in the U.S. For example, one Korean American leader who led opposition to the Flatbush Boycott of 1990—a boycott and picketing campaign led by Black nationalist and Haitian activists against two Korean-owned produce stores in Flatbush, Brooklyn—compared himself to the leader of the legendary March First Movement of 1919, in which Koreans mounted resistance to japanese rule.[31] Note that this move likened Black protesters to powerful, racist Japanese colonizers, eclipsing the fact that Blacks, too, are victims of racial oppression. Borrowing the symbols, rhetoric, and songs of the American civil rights movement, Korean American leaders have essentialized Black protests/acts of rebellion as discriminatory and anti-Korean, thus trumping the Black story of victimization with the Korean one. It is worth noting that some Korean Americans (especially 1.5 and second generation people) in both cities have dissented from this approach, urging their community to reach out to and find common ground with Blacks. In New York City, for instance, activist Christie Huh and Reverend Paul Kim formed an organization to challenge the Korean Association of New York's handling of the Flatbush Boycott. Similarly, some Korean Americans in Los Angeles sponsored a Peace Rally on May 11, 1992 where they held placards that read: "Justice for Rodney King," "Justice for All People of Color," and "More Jobs for the Inner-City."[32]

Liberal and progressive Asian American scholars, activists, and advocates have taken a different tack. They have tried to promote a racial or panethnic consciousness among Korean Americans by situating Black-Korean conflict within the ongoing story of *Asian American* victimization.[33] Speaking at a University of Southern California conference on *Sa-I-Gu*, Angelo Ancheta, a staff attorney with the Asian Pacific Legal Center of Southern California, exhorted Korean Americans to seize the opportunity to recognize their common bonds with other Asian Pacific Americans. Because of their political sensibilities, most liberal and progressive Asian Americans have also stopped short of directly trumping Black claims. Thus they have invoked the Asian American story of victimization as a way of raising concerns about Black actions rather than directly condemning them. The Asian American Federation in New York City, for instance, stayed out of the Flatbush Boycott

---

[31] Author's personal interview with Byun Chun Soo, New York City, December 2, 1992. Much of this discussion of the Flatbush Boycott is drawn from Claire Jean Kim, *Bitter Fruit: The Politics of Black-Korean Conflict in New York City* (New Haven: Yale University Press, 2000).

[32] Edward Park, "Competing Visions: Political Formation of Korean Americans in Los Angeles, 1992–1997," *Amerasia Journal* 24:1 (1998), 41–57, 48.

[33] Korean Americans have had mixed reactions to this move. In an interview conducted by Elaine Kim, Korean American community activist Bong Kim chastised Asian American advocacy groups for commenting on the Los Angeles "riots" without first consulting Korean American community leaders. During the same interview, however, Bong Kim compared the "riots" to the exclusion of Chinese immigrants and the wartime internment of Japanese Americans, thus situating the former event within the Asian American story of victimization. That Korean Americans alternately compare *Sa-I-Gu* to the Japanese colonization of Korea and the Japanese American internment experience suggests the complex way in which they interweave a Korean racial-transnational consciousness with an incipient Asian American one. See Elaine Kim, "Between Black and White: An Interview with Bong Hwan Kim," *The State of Asian America*, 71–100.

conflict until a violent incident prompted them to express concerns about anti-Asian violence.[34] While most Asian American activists have refrained from directly condemning Black empowerment efforts, they have also missed these important opportunities to go beyond the strictures of conventional racial advocacy and initiate a serious discussion about interminority differentials.

For their part, White opinionmakers have enthusiastically played Asian Americans as a racial trump card against Blacks during instances of Black-Korean conflict. Journalists, pundits, and many politicians interpreted the Flatbush Boycott of 1990 not as part of the Black struggle for community control and economic empowerment but rather as *essentially* anti-Korean or anti-Asian—as the Black "underclass" scapegoating the Asian American "model minority."[35] An editorial in *The New York Post*, entitled, "New York Wakes Up To a Civil-Rights Emergency," demonstrates this tack:

> While the conventions of journalism require reporters to convey both sides of a story, there can be no doubt where justice and decency lie in this dispute . . . Sometimes, one side is right and the other side is wrong—one party is the aggressor and the other party is the victim. When the Ku Klux Klan terrorized blacks in the Deep South, the KKK was guilty of criminal racism. At this point, the episode [the Flatbush Boycott] demands attention from the criminal-justice system. (May 9, 1990)

Comparisons between the Black boycotters, on the one hand, and Japanese colonizers and the KKK, on the other, reconstructed Korean/Asian Americans as innocent, powerless victims and Blacks as both racist and powerful. In this way, the history and reality of Black victimization was surpressed: Blacks could not be both the KKK and the victims of the KKK at the same time. As this example clearly shows, racial trumping creates good guys and bad guys. The revised Asian American narrative of self-representation helped White opinionmakers to construct Korean/Asian Americans as a beleaguered minority while providing no critical tools with which interminority differentials or the clashing narratives of Asian American and Black victimization could be evaluated. Largely as a result of the delegitimating effect of racial trumping, the Flatbush Boycott was shut down, the challenge that it posed to the status quo supressed, and the racial order once again reproduced.

Racial Classifications in Secondary Education: The Trumping of Black Remedies

Let's turn now to the issue of race-conscious remedies in education. Since the 1980s, White and Asian American conservatives have invoked Asian Americans repeatedly as the symbol of all that is unfair about race-conscious remedies in education.[36] In one journalist's memorable phrasing, Asian Americans "stuck a bamboo pole into the affirmative-action machinery" by proving that a

---

[34] The beating of Cao Tuan, a Vietnamese American man, by a group of Black youths near the boycott scene raised the specter of the Vincent Chin killing. As it turns out, the incident had nothing to do with the boycott or with mistaking certain Asians for others.

[35] That quintessential document of the antidiscrimination regime—the U.S. Commission on Civil Rights report, "Civil Rights Issues Facing Asian Americans in the 1990s" (1992)—included the Flatbush Boycott in a chapter entitled, "Bigotry and Violence Against Asian Americans," the same chapter that covers several notorious racially motivated killings of Asian Americans.

[36] During the 1980s, when a controversy arose over whether several selective universities were using quotas to depress Asian American admissions rates, conservatives hijacked the issue for their own anti-affirmative action purposes. They transformed the real issue of whether universities were capping Asian American admissions to preserve the Whiteness of their student bodies into the false issue of whether affirmative action for Blacks and Latinos was depressing Asian American admissions. See Dana Takagi, *The Retreat From Race: Asian American Admissions and Racial Politics* (New Brunswick: Rutgers University Press, 1992).

minority group can overcome discrimination and make it on its own.[37] In addition, Asian Americans are often inaccurately portrayed as the frontline victims of such remedies. When the Regents of the University of California voted in 1995 to end affirmative action in undergraduate admissions, they portrayed their decision as a boon for Asian Americans.

In the face of this conservative publicity campaign, liberal and progressive Asian American scholars, activists, and advocates have struggled to persuade Asian Americans that affirmative action in fact serves their self-interest. Their argument goes something like this: because Asian Americans, like other minorities, suffer from historical and ongoing discrimination, they both need and benefit from affirmative action in education and other areas; the notion that Asian Americans are burdened by affirmative action is simply a myth. As a *bona fide* minority group, they contend, Asian Americans deserve the same remedial consideration from the neutral arbiter state as other racially disadvantaged groups do. Two publications put out by Leadership Education for Asian Pacifics (LEAP)—*Common Ground: Perspectives on Affirmative Action . . . and Its Impact on Asian Pacific Americans* (1995) and *In Support of Civil Rights: Taking on the Initiative* (1996)—clearly reflect this antidiscrimination rationale for affirmative action.[38] The articles in *Common Ground*, written by leaders of prominent racial advocacy groups such as the National Asian Pacific American Legal Consortium, Coalition of Asian Pacific Americans, Asian Pacific American Legal Center of Southern California, and Asian Pacific Labor Alliance, all invoke the Asian American history of victimization to persuade Asian Americans that affirmative action programs constitute deserved remedial help rather than underserved preferential treatment. *In Support of Civil Rights*, a position paper opposing Proposition 209 (The "California Civil Rights Initiative"), cites numerous statistics as proof of ongoing discrimination against Asian Americans and other minorities.[39] Once again, Asian Americans have responded to conservative distortions of their reality by proclaiming "Asian Americans are minorities, too."

The problem with this argument from self-interest is that it again presents all minorities as formal equivalents, glossing over interminority differentials in status, privilege, and opportunities.[40]

---

[37] James Walsh, "The Perils of Success," *Time*, Special Issue (Fall 1993), 55–56, 56.

[38] Similarly, the Japanese American Citizens League flyer entitled, "Why Asian Americans Should Oppose Proposition 209, the Deceptively Named 'California Civil Rights Initiative'," argues that Asian Americans need affirmative action to break through the "glass ceiling" and gain meaningful equal opportunity. The antidiscrimination rationale for affirmative action is thrown into relief by the few pro-affirmative action appeals made on other grounds. See, for example, "An Open Letter to Our Fellow Asian Brothers and Sisters: JOIN THE FIGHT TO DEFEND AND EXPAND AFFIRMATIVE ACTION," *Hitting Critical Mass* 3:2 (Spring 1996), 135–140. The authors of this article, veterans of the campus strikes of 1968–1969, write: "[O]ur fight is not to side with the system against other minorities to reach the rung below the glass ceiling, just so a few of us are not on the bottom rung of society" (p. 137).

[39] Proposition 209, a state constitutional amendment approved by California voters (54% to 46%) in 1996, eliminated affirmative action programs in public employment, public education, and public contracting. For discussion of how Proposition 209 advocates wooed Asian Americans, see Kenneth Lee, "Angry Yellow Men," *The New Republic* (September 9, 1996), 11.

[40] A few Asian American scholars and advocates who write about affirmative action do acknowledge Asian-Black differentials, but they tend to do so in passing. See Theodore Wang and Frank Wu, "Beyond the Model Minority Myth," *The Affirmative Action Debate*, edited by George Curry (Reading, Massachusetts: Addison-Wesley, 1996), 191–207 and Henry Der, "The Asian American Factor: Victim or Shortsighted Beneficiary of Race-Conscious Remedies?" *Common Ground*, 13–18. Paul Ong's recent article does consider some of the ways in which Asian Americans are advantaged and disadvantaged compared to other groups: "The Affirmative Action Divide," *The State of Asian Pacific America: Transforming Race Relations*, edited by Paul Ong (Los Angeles: LEAP Asian Pacific American Public Policy Institute and UCLA Asian American Studies Center, 2000), 313–361.

Both of the above publications valorize notions such as "social justice," "multiracial coalitions," and "multiracial democracy," yet they appear to presume that all minority group experiences are fungible and that a rising tide will lift all boats. Are some minority groups worse off than others? Do these groups need or warrant a higher priority than others in affirmative action programs? These questions go unasked, with serious ramifications. One of these is that Asian Americans who support affirmative action in the name of self-interest rather than racial justice broadly conceived are almost certain to oppose affirmative action when it appears to burden them for the sake of other minority groups. In a recent interview, Glenn Omatsu said: "Don [Nakanishi] now says that Asian Americans focused the [college quotas] issue too narrowly around self-interest. So when the later struggle came up around affirmative action, not all Asian Americans understood why it was important to support affirmative action."[41] After all, if Asian Americans are themselves victims of discrimination deserving of remedial help, why should they be expected to bear any burden on behalf of another minority group?

This was precisely the question posed by the plaintiffs in the recent lawsuit, Brian Ho v. SFUSD (San Francisco Unified School District), first filed in District Court in California in July 1994. Plaintiffs in this highly publicized class-action case were Chinese American students seeking to challenge the desegregation consent decree that had governed the SFUSD since 1983, pursuant to a discrimination lawsuit brought against the city by the NAACP.[42] According to the consent decree, each public school had to have students from at least four of nine specified racial/ethnic groups in its student body, and it could not allow any single group to exceed 40 percent of the total (for magnet or alternative schools, the single group cap was set at 45 percent).[43] The Ho lawsuit concerned Lowell High School, one of the city's handful of alternative schools and widely considered the most prestigious public school in San Francisco. Unlike the other alternative schools, which used a lottery system to fulfill the consent decree's guidelines, Lowell High School applied differential admissions scores (based upon GPA, test scores, and other factors) to students of different racial/ethnic backgrounds to achieve this purpose. At the time of the lawsuit, Chinese American students were the single largest student group in the SFUSD, making up approximately one-third of all enrolled high school students. In order to keep the number of Chinese American students below the 45 percent cap, Lowell officials had repeatedly raised the group's admission score over the years.[44] Despite this differential score system, Blacks and Latinos were persistently underrepresented at Lowell.[45]

---

[41] "Amerasia Dialogue: Glenn Omatsu Interviewed by Russell Leong," Amerasia Journal 25:2 (1999), vii–xiv, viii.

[42] Given San Francisco's uniquely multiracial composition and its long history of segregating all students of color from White students, it is not surprising that a case about clashing minority imperatives arose here. For discussion of San Francisco's history of educational segregation, see Charles McClain, In Search of Equality: The Chinese Struggle Against Discrimination in Nineteenth Century America (Berkeley: University of California, 1994).

[43] The nine groups were: Spanish, White, Black, Chinese, Japanese, Korean, Filipino, American Indian, and "other nonwhite."

[44] As of 1992–1993, Chinese American students had to have a score of 66 to be accepted into Lowell; Japanese Americans, Korean Americans, Filipino Americans, American Indians, and "other nonwhites" had to have a score of 59; and Blacks and Spanish students had to have a score of 56. Selena Dong, "Too Many Asians': The Challenge of Fighting Discrimination Against Asian-Americans and Preserving Affirmative Action," Stanford Law Review 47 (May 1995), 1027–1057, 1033.

[45] Just before the lawsuit was filed, Blacks constituted 18.4% of the district's enrollment and only 4.5% of Lowell's student body; Latinos constituted 20% of the district's enrollment and only 9.3% of Lowell's student body. Peter Schmidt, "Cursed By Success," Education Week on the Web (April 5, 1995), http://www.teachermagazine.org/ew/vol14/28lowell.h14.

The San Francisco-based Chinese American Democratic Club (CADC), the driving force behind the *Ho* lawsuit, located the plaintiffs and persuaded them to challenge the consent decree. Both Roland Quan and Anthony Chow, two of the CADC's leading figures, joined the group after personally experiencing what they viewed as anti-Asian discrimination. The CADC embraced the argument from self-interest advanced by Asian American scholars, activists, and advocates: it supported affirmative action programs if and only if they countered anti-Asian discrimination or clearly benefited Asian Americans. Thus the group endorsed affirmative action in employment and contracting (areas where they thought Asian Americans would benefit from such programs), while opposing the SFUSD consent decree as discriminatory against Chinese Americans. Although the CADC represented a single Asian origin group rather than Asian Americans as a whole—the consent decree specified several different Asian origin groups, of which only Chinese Americans had hit the 45% single group cap—it named its new fundraising organization the Asian American Legal Foundation in a transparent effort to don the racial or panethnic mantle for the purpose of trumping Black remedies.

Counsel for the *Ho* plaintiffs used two complementary strategies to battle the consent decree. First, they made a legal argument from the perspective of protecting the plaintiffs' individual rights. That is, they argued that the consent decree's race-based formula "violate[d] their right to the equal protection of the laws guaranteed by the Fourteenth Amendment to the United States Constitution," and that it should therefore be subjected to the strict scrutiny level of judicial review, which it would not survive.[46] In support of their strict scrutiny claim, they cited numerous U.S. Supreme Court cases hostile to race-conscious remedies, such as City of Richmond *v.* J.A. Croson Co. (1989), Shaw *v.* Reno (1993), and Adarand Constructors, Inc. *v.* Pena (1995). Second, counsel for the plaintiffs trumped the consent decree, invoking the Chinese American story of victimization as a material fact that rendered the consent decree's discriminatory effects especially reprehensible: "This is not the first time that San Francisco residents of Chinese ancestry have had to turn to the courts to obtain equal protection of the laws . . . San Francisco has a long history of official discrimination against persons of Chinese ancestry."[47] Although this racial trumping strategy was clearly secondary in terms of the plaintiffs' legal argument, it dominated their public relations message. In their coverage of the lawsuit, the mainstream media suggested that the case pitted Blacks (and Latinos) against Chinese/Asian Americans.

It became clear during the course of the *Ho* lawsuit (July 1994 to February 1999) that Asian American advocates were deeply divided on the matter. Once again, community leaders from the single Asian origin group involved parted company, on the whole, with racial or panethnic advocates. The national headquarters of the leading Chinese American advocacy group, the Organization of Chinese Americans (OCA), remained neutral—which was noteworthy given the organization's ordinarily strong pro-affirmative action stance—and the San Francisco chapter of OCA supported the lawsuit. Many local Chinese American community leaders and laypeople endorsed the lawsuit.[48] On the other hand, another prominent advocacy group, Chinese for Affirmative Action (CAA)—which is a racial or panethnic group despite its name—forcefully opposed the lawsuit every step

[46] Brief of Plaintiffs-Appellants, August 5, 1997, 5.

[47] Brief of Plaintiffs-Appellants, August 5, 1997, 6, footnote 2. This long footnote cites numerous equal protection cases from Chinese American history, as well as the works of several noted scholars of the Chinese American experience.

[48] According to a 1998 Chinese American Voter Education Committee Survey of Chinese surname voters in San Francisco, 45% of respondents thought Lowell High School admissions quotas were a "bad idea," while 32% thought they were a "good idea," and 23% had no opinion. See Ong, "The Affirmative Action Divide," 339–340.

of the way.[49] Henry Der, the former executive director of CAA, provided expert testimony against the plaintiffs' claims and spoke out publicly against the lawsuit.[50] Der saw the lawsuit as a "tactical mistake" that would backfire upon Chinese Americans by contributing to the wholesale dismantling of race-conscious remedies. Some progressive Asian American scholars also opposed the lawsuit on similar grounds. Selena Dong urged the plaintiffs to challenge the single group cap but not the consent decree's use of racial classifications *per se*.[51] Eric Yamamoto criticized the plaintiffs for "invoking a civil rights paradigm that understands racial conflict narrowly in white-on-black, perpetrator-and-victim terms and fails to account for the unique dimensions of interracial group grievances."[52] Yet none of the lawsuit's critics asked the following crucial question: did the *Ho* plaintiffs simply take the politics of Asian American racial advocacy to its logical conclusion?

In February 1999, the parties to the *Ho* lawsuit reached a settlement which nullified the consent decree, eliminated the use of racial classifications in assigning students to different schools, and mandated that the SFUSD design a new enrollment plan to take effect in the fall of 2000.[53] Despite the school district's current efforts to maintain diversity by giving preferences to students from low-income families, there are already clear signs that the under-representation of Black and Latino students is increasing in the absence of the consent decree.[54] In addition, opponents of affirmative action have repeatedly invoked the Lowell High School controversy both on the state level (during the pro-Proposition 209 campaign) and on the national level (during Senate Judiciary Committee hearings on affirmative action held in June 1997 and during meetings related to President Clinton's Initiative on Race). What is the outcome of racial trumping here? Black claims are once again denied; the legitimacy of race-conscious remedies which challenge White privilege is diminished; and one Asian origin group has advanced its immediate material interests—but only at the expense of other Asian origin groups as well as Blacks and Latinos. The contours of the racial order remain intact. To what degree are Asian American narrative choices implicated in this outcome? This is a question that deserves serious consideration. It seems to me that Asian American scholars, activists, and advocates who persist in positing minority equivalences and ignoring interminority differentials will continue to have difficulty controlling the uses to which their narrative choices are put.

---

[49] San Francisco-based Chinese for Affirmative Action (CAA) is one of the most prominent Asian American advocacy groups in the nation. According to Diane Chin, its current executive director, the tacit division of labor among liberal/progressive Asian American advocacy groups in San Francisco led other groups to look to CAA for leadership in response to the *Ho* lawsuit, since the case concerned race-conscious remedies. Although most of these other advocacy groups did not take public stands against the lawsuit, they implicitly supported CAA's oppositional stance (Author's phone interview with Diane Chin, April 12, 1999). See note 53 below.

[50] Der argued that the plaintiffs' claim that they were denied access to their school of choice and thus subjected to unconstitutional harm was simply untrue. Although they were denied admission at Lowell High School, all of the Chinese American plaintiffs were accepted into other prestigious alternative schools that same year. See Der, "The Asian American Factor" and Jeff Chang, "On The Wrong Side: Chinese Americans Win Anti-Diversity Settlement—and Lose in the End," *Colorlines* (Summer 1999), 12–14.

[51] Dong, " 'Too Many Asians.' "

[52] Eric Yamamoto, "Critical Race Praxis: Race Theory and Political Lawyering Practice in Post-Civil Rights America," *Michigan Law Review* 95 (February 1997), 821–900, 828.

[53] Together with the Chinese Progressive Association, the Chinatown Youth Center, and individual Chinese American community leaders, Chinese for Affirmative Action has filed opposition papers challenging this settlement.

[54] Julian Guthrie, "Minority Admissions Plummet at San Francisco School," *San Francisco Examiner* (March 16, 1999): http://www.latinolink.com./news/news99.

What Is To Be Done?

I have argued that the revised Asian American narrative of self-representation facilitates racial trumping, or the invocation of the Asian American history of victimization for the purposes of overriding Black claims. It is by generating and reproducing this narrative in the absence of a critical interrogation of interminority differentials that scholars, activists, and advocates sometimes unwittingly lend themselves to being used. Simply by acceding to the constraints of the antidiscrimination regime and seeking to protect Asian American interests, they can become unwilling participants in the shoring up of the American racial order. This suggests to me that the time-honored Asian American political principle of doing no harm to other oppressed groups is not and has never been realistic. The embeddedness of Asian American political agency in the American racial order means that the choices of scholars, activists, and advocates will continue to play out in ways that they can neither foresee nor control. The common assumptions that one group trajectories are mutually independent and that one group can get ahead without impacting another are dubious indeed: in a racial order characterized by group positionality, one group's gain may well mean another's loss.

This raises the following questions: Are Asian Americans responsible for the effects of their struggle upon other racially subordinated groups? If so, what is to be done? Do Asian Americans face a choice between getting ahead at the expense of others and sacrificing their own advancement for the sake of others? Or is there still another option? Is there a viable alternative to the revised Asian American narrative under the current antidiscrimination regime? If so, what would it look like? Is it enough for Asian Americans to have a bigger room if the master's house is still standing? I hope that these questions—which echo those raised by Glenn Omatsu, Eric Yamamoto, Elaine Kim, Sumi Cho, Mari Matsuda, and others in recent years—will become the subject of a vigorous, even unruly debate among politically concerned Asian Americans. I do not know where the debate will lead, but I will, in closing, offer some of my ideas about alternative directions for the future, drawing upon the work of those who continue to contest current Asian American narrative choices. Although the antidiscrimination regime is powerfully constraining, no one would deny that Asian Americans exercise agency within this regime. And where there is agency, there is the possibility of changing course.

My sense is that Asian Americans do bear responsibility for their impact upon other oppressed groups. This responsibility arises from the accrual and enjoyment of benefits and privileges: to the extent that Asian Americans gain advantages from their current narrative and political choices, they are responsible for the latter's effects, in the same way that we think of Whites today as benefiting from and therefore sharing responsibility for the effects of slavery. I do not think this claim is a radical one—in fact, it seems to me a natural extension of the spirited resistance to being used that has been a hallmark of Asian American collective subjectivity from the start. The principle has always been: Asian Americans should do what is necessary so as not to oppress others. What I am arguing is that fulfilling this principle requires going beyond the refusal to be used; it requires a *proactive* commitment to addressing the responsibility that Asian Americans bear regarding other oppressed groups. I think that there are three interrelated ways in which Asian American scholars, activists, and advocates can begin to address this responsibility.[55] Together, they constitute what I think of as a responsible Asian American politics that may one day render itself obsolete.

---

[55] The three projects I outline below will be most effective if other groups of color undertake them simultaneously. It is a measure of the absence of interminority debate and conversation that Asian Americans scholars, activists, and advocates are presumed to have to direct their exhortations at Asian Americans; African Americans at African Americans, etc.

First, Asian American scholars, activists, and advocates can commit themselves to an ongoing, critical interrogation of interminority differentials. Rather than glossing over such differentials or presuming that a rising tide will lift all boats, they can confront head on the ways in which Asian Americans are, on the whole, persistently more advantaged than Blacks (and the ways they are not) and think through how this complicates both prospects for multiracial coalition-building and visions of racial justice. In my view, this project is compatible with—and in fact a logical extension of—the drive to explore class, national origin, cultural, and other differences among Asian Americans.[56] Clearly, this kind of critical interrogation entails contesting the revised Asian American narrative of self-representation and the reductionist majority/minority binary around which it is built. Far from taking the heat off of White practices of domination, this will, I think, yield a more nuanced understanding of how White domination works and how it seeks to coopt triangulated groups into its game. With regard to the "glass ceiling," for instance, scholars, activists, and advocates can move beyond a narrowly dyadic analysis to an examination of the ways in which different groups of color get slotted into the hierarchy of employment, how this occurs, and how such patterns might be challenged. Ideally, they will undertake this work in conjunction with scholars, activists, and advocates from other communities of color. The kind of critical intellectual work I have in mind is oppositional in spirit and will unfold within oppositional spaces away from the panoptic regulation of the state.[57] It will not prevent the kinds of interminority conflict invited by the American racial order but it will provide Asian American (and other) scholars, activists, and advocates with a considered theoretical perspective from which to respond to and work through such conflict.

Second, Asian American scholars, activists, and advocates can commit themselves to building anti-racist coalitions with other groups of color and engaging in political actions that pointedly benefit other groups of color as well as Asian Americans. Rather than responding to the competitive incentives of the antidiscrimination regime and going it alone, Asian Americans can take the initiative in organizing such coalitions wherever and whenever possible. The call to multiracial coalition-building is now trite, but I am suggesting that Asian Americans view it as a positive moral responsibility rather than just one good idea among many. I am also suggesting that the interrogation of interminority differentials lays a crucial foundation for coalition-building insofar as it enables Asian Americans to evaluate where different groups of color are coming from. As Eric Yamamoto suggests in his recent book *Interracial Justice*, recognizing the deeply felt grievances of other groups is a necessary first step in the forging of new relational bonds and the movement toward interracial justice and reconciliation. It may seem counterintuitive that attention to difference would facilitate coalition-building, but it is only by truly recognizing difference that coalitions can hope to work and survive.

---

[56] Although I have treated Asian Americans as a homogeneous category for the purposes of my argument here, I am mindful of the staggering internal diversity of this group. I am open to the idea, for instance, that some Asian American subgroups are faring better than others and thus bear more responsibility for the impact of the Asian American struggle upon other oppressed groups. It may be that the categorical statement that Asian Americans are more advantaged than Blacks will have to be strongly qualified. All of these complexities remain to be worked out in the kind of critical intellectual work I have in mind.

[57] In *The State of Asian Pacific America: Transforming Race Relations*, President Clinton's Initiative on Race is mentioned in the introductory and closing essays. I am doubtful that a state-sponsored dialogue can serve as a vehicle for progressive racial change. For a critique of the race initiative, see Claire Jean Kim, "Clinton's Race Initiative: Recasting the American Dilemma," forthcoming in *Polity* (Winter 2000).

Given the partially zero-sum nature of the current racial order, coalition-building will not eradicate interminority conflict altogether, but it may mitigate it in some instances. And Asian Americans and other groups of color share many common concerns around which coalitions can be and are being built. Anti-Asian violence, for instance, is a subset of the larger phenomenon of racially motivated violence affecting all groups of color; immigration-related problems are shared by many Latino and Black immigrants; media stereotyping is a problem for all groups of color, etc. Nor is there any reason why this coalition-building should be confined by national borders. The growth of transnational social movements and the continued development of the institutional framework for international human rights are promising trends that offer points of leverage against both the disciplinary thrust of the antidiscrimination regime and the power of increasingly transnationalized capital.

Real-life examples of Asian Americans acting on behalf of other groups and building coalitions with other groups give us some sense of what can be accomplished. In 1968, a group of Nisei formed the National Ad Hoc Committee for Repeal of the Emergency Detention Act and launched a four-year campaign to repeal Title II (known as the Emergency Detention Act) of the Internal Security Act of 1950.[58] Since Title II called for the maintenance of detention camps for the purpose of holding those "probably" engaged in espionage or sabotage in disregard of their rights to due process, Black leaders such as Malcolm X, Stokely Carmichael, and Martin Luther King, Jr. expressed concern during the 1960s that Black youths arrested in urban rebellions would end up in these camps. Activist Raymond Okamura and his colleagues recount: "[We] felt that it was imperative for Japanese Americans to assume the leadership in order to promote Third World unity. Japanese Americans had been the passive beneficiaries of the Black civil rights movement, and this campaign was the perfect issue by which Japanese Americans could make a contribution to the overall struggle for justice in the United States."[59] The repeal campaign developed from a grassroots effort to a high-level lobbying game and achieved success in 1971.

More recently, the work of Korean Immigrant Workers Advocates (KIWA) has demonstrated the power of groups of color working together.[60] In 1991, when the South Korean Koreana corporation purchased the Wilshire Hyatt Hotel in Los Angeles, it abrogated the hotel's contract with its mostly Latino unionized employees and hired workers willing to work for less. The mostly Latino Hotel Employees and Restaurant Employees Union (HERE) Local 11, which represented the former employees, called upon labor groups in other communities of color for help. KIWA and the Asian Pacific American Labor Alliance worked with HERE to organize civil disobedience and other measures that finally pressured Koreana into negotiating with Local 11 and rehiring union members. Again, in 1994, when the South Korean corporation Hanjin International took over the management of Los Angeles Hilton and Towers and terminated the hotel's contract with HERE members, KIWA joined Local 11 as a full partner in the organizing campaign. KIWA used as influence among Korean Americans and South Korean labor groups to pressure Hanjin International into settling with Local 11 the following year. In both cases, KIWA found class-based common ground with workers from another oppressed group and supported the principle of a living wage for all working people. In New

---

[58] See Raymond Okamura et al., "Campaign to Repeal the Emergency Detention Act," *Amerasia Journal* 2:2 (1974), 71–94.

[59] *Ibid.*, 76–77.

[60] This information about KIWA is drawn from Omatsu, "The 'Four Prisons'" and Leland Saito and Edward Park, "Multiracial Collaborations and Coalitions," *The State of Asian Pacific America. Transforming Race Relations*, 435–474.

York City, the work that Coalition Against Anti-Asian Violence (CAAAV) has done in building multiracial coalitions against racial violence and police brutality is similarly inspiring.

Third, and finally, Asian American scholars, activists, and advocates can commit themselves to a long-range vision of a society without racial categories. Because race is an intrinsically hierarchical concept, it inescapably implies that some groups have greater worth than others. In this sense, racial equality is a paradox: true equality is only possible once "races" are no longer recognized as such. The long-term interests of Asian Americans, Blacks, Latinos, and other racialized groups thus lie in the eventual obsolescence of race as a meaningful category of life. Although Asian Americans have shifted their position in the racial order over time—from "near black" to "near white," as Gary Okihiro puts it—they will never enjoy the full benefits of social and civic membership as long as they are designated a racial "other."[61] Let me be perfectly clear: I am not espousing the current notion of colorblindness which proposes that we overcome racism by pretending that it does not exist. To the contrary, I am advocating vigorous anti-racist struggle that takes place across racial lines and that aims for the eventual dissolution of racial categories. It is only by dismantling the master's house once and for all that the master/house slave/field slave relationship can be brought to an end. In a society without race, there will no longer be an Asian American politics, responsible or otherwise. In achieving its purpose, it will have rendered itself obsolete.

Notes

I dedicate this article to the memory of my friend, author Joe Wood. I am grateful to the following for their comments on an earlier draft of this paper: Elaine Kim, Eric Yamamoto, Rogers Smith, Edna Bonacich, Joe Feagin, Joan Scott, the anonymous reviewer at *Amerasia Journal*, and participants in the faculty seminars at the Center for the Study of Race, Politics, and Inequality at Yale University and the School of Social Science at the Institute for Advanced Study. Special thanks to Russell Leong for his thoughtful comments and advice.

---

[61] Okihiro, *Margins and Mainstreams.*

A New Gateway: Asian American Political Power in the 21ˢᵗ Century

James S. Lai

Don T. Nakanishi's prescient 1985. *Amerasia Journal* essay, "Asian American Politics: An Agenda for Research" argued for an interdisciplinary approach to gain a better understanding of Asian American politics. His essay provided an integrated micro/macro and a domestic/transnational approach that was well ahead of its time.[1] Nakanishi's timely essay would prove influential in defining future research parameters of the political behavior of Asian Americans. At the time of the essay's publication, Asians, compared to African Americans and Latinos, were not found in the extant political science literature. Nearly twenty-five years later, however, Nakanishi's interdisciplinary approach has become even more useful for studying Asian American politics. What follows is my incorporation and application of Nakanishi's earlier ideas to looking at Asian American political power today.

What does such an interdisciplinary approach entail? It would first take a historical and geographical approach to understanding patterns of community formation. Due to globalization and a restructuring of the U.S. economy, contemporary Asian American immigrants represent a wide range of socio-economic groups that include white collar professionals, middle and lower class small business entrepreneurs, H-1B visa high tech workers, and refugees. Many of them are now voluntarily moving directly into the emerging twenty-first century gateway—the small and medium size Asian influenced suburb throughout the continental United States.

Shifting Political Terrains: Twentieth and Twenty-First Century Gateways

Location does matter in understanding the trajectories of Asian American political behavior and incorporation. Large urban gateway cities will always remain central for studying Asian American politics. However, a significant percentage of Asian American immigrants are circumventing

---

[1] Don T. Nakanishi, "Asian American Politics: An Agenda for Research," Amerasia Journal 12:2 (1985): 1–27.

large urban cities for small to medium size suburbs.[2] For example, during 2004–05, forty percent of arriving Asian immigrants moved directly into the suburbs.[3]

The suburbanization of Asian American politics during the last twenty years parallels the rise of Asian American majority cities. The 2000 U.S. Census identified six Asian American majority cities in California.[4] In comparison, in 1980, only one Asian American majority city (the suburb of Monterey Park in Los Angeles County) existed in the continental United States. All of these Asian American majority cities are small to medium size suburbs with populations ranging from 25,000 to 110,000 and have gone through demographic and political transformations. Asian Americans choose to live in these cities because of their strong public schools, established ethnic networks, growing economic opportunities, and gravitational migration based on existing ethnic networks. As a result, it is within the context of small to medium size suburbs where the pathways to political incorporation are moving faster than in large metropolitan cities. Asian Americans, many of them immigrants, are rapidly winning seats in their local governments by building bi-racial political coalitions with whites and Asians. Class issues are less likely to emerge in the context of these small to medium size suburbs than in larger metropolitan cities because cross-racial and ethnic alliances can be built around common suburban interests around such issues as public schools and economic development.

An interdisciplinary focus would not only shift the focus of Asian American political mobilization and incorporation from large cities to the small to medium size suburbs, but it would also provide a more comprehensive and nuanced understanding of both the traditional and non-traditional forms of Asian American political participation that are part and parcel of these immigrant suburbs. While Asian American political muscle continues to be flexed in the form of campaign contributions, non-traditional political loci are rapidly emerging in these suburbs such as pan-ethnic public non-profit organizations and the ethnic media that cater to the interests of its large immigrant populations.[5] For instance, the understudied ethnic media in the political science literature can play an important role during group political mobilization by providing Asian American candidates with a cost-effective strategy for voter outreach that incorporates both old and new Asian Americans into the electoral process and for outreaching to potential Asian American contributors beyond local district boundaries.[6] Another recent study found successful Vietnamese American candidates in Westminster and San Jose, California "toggle" their campaign messages in nuanced and varied ways when going from the mainstream, English

---

[2] Wei Li and Emily Skop, "Enclaves, Ethnoburbs, and New Patterns of Settlement among Asian Immigrants." In Min Zhou and James V. Gatewood, eds., Contemporary Asian America: Multidisciplinary Reader, second edition (New York, NY: NYU Press, 2008), 222–236.

[3] Sam Roberts, "In Shift, 40% of Immigrants Move Directly to Suburbs." New York Times (October 17, 2007), http://www.nytimes.com/2007/10/17/us/17census.html.

[4] These six Asian American majority cities in California are the following: Daly City (50.8 percent Asian American), Cerritos (58.4 percent), Milpitas (51.8 percent), Monterey Park (61.8 percent), Rowland Heights (50.3 percent), and Walnut (55.8 percent).

[5] Chi-kan Richard Hung, "Growth and Diversity of Asian American Non-profit Organizations," in Paul M. Ong (ed.), The State of Asian America: Trajectory of Civic and Political Engagement, Volume V (Los Angeles, CA: LEAP Asian Pacific American Public Policy Institute, 2008), 181–206.

[6] James S. Lai and Kim Geron, "When Asian Americans Run: The Suburban and Urban Dimensions of Asian American Candidates in California Local Politics," California Politics & Policy 10:1 (Los Angeles, CA: California State Los Angeles, Pat Brown Institute of Public Affairs, June 2006), 62–88.

speaking constituency to their Vietnamese speaking constituency.[7] This trend is also in line with other Asian American ethnic groups containing a large immigrant population where the ethnic media is entrenched. These findings shed light on how newly emerging forms of Asian American political behaviors are taking shape in the suburban context.

Suburbs as "Political Incubators": Create an Asian American Pipeline of Local and State Representatives

Asian American influenced suburbs represent "political incubators" that have allowed communities to develop formal pipelines of candidates running for local elected offices eventually leading to higher levels including the state and federal legislatures. Within such incubator suburbs, Asian American political organizations, the ethnic media, and other important political loci are influential during group political mobilization around Asian American candidate campaigns. The result has been unprecedented Asian American political gains in American politics. In some California suburbs, such as Westminster and Monterey Park, Asian Americans have become the majority of their respective city councils with other suburbs rapidly following.

Scholars who exclusively study immigrant political incorporation in large cities have witnessed the opposite—a dearth of successful local Asian American candidates and no formal candidate pipeline. In the two cities, Los Angeles and New York City, with the largest aggregate Asian American populations, only one Asian American has been elected to each city's respective city councils—former Los Angeles city councilmember Michael Woo (District 13) in 1985 and current New York City Councilmember John Liu (District 20) in 2001. In Los Angeles, no serious Asian American candidate has emerged since Woo in any of its fifteen council districts. The complex reasons why Asian Americans have not attained descriptive representation even comparable to their population numbers in such large urban cities include the following factors: district elections in large cities that have harmed more than helped Asian American candidates due to the residential dispersion of Asian Americans; ethnic competition and the lack of common ideological interests that have limited political mobilization efforts; entrenched political interests that have made it harder for emergent immigrant groups like Asian Americans to attain descriptive representation; and the lack of a formal pipeline that has allowed for a systematic approach to building political power bases that other racial groups have achieved.

Asian American candidates in these suburbs are winning, sustaining, and building on Asian American elected representation in their respective local governments, an important measuring stick of political power. The emerging Asian American influenced suburb has provided a critical mass that has fueled local political mobilization efforts resulting in unprecedented numbers of descriptive representatives in local government. For the first time on the continental United States, like African Americans and Latinos, Asian Americans in California have established political power bases in the following areas. Santa Clara County and Orange County. In the former area, a pan-ethnic coalition among the distinct Asian American communities is forming along with incorporation into the local and state Democratic Party infrastructure that has contributed to it containing the largest number of Asian American elected officials for any county on the continental U.S. The latter area is fueled by the maturation of the Vietnamese American community in the key suburbs of Westminster and Garden Grove that comprise "Little Saigon" by the largest

---

[7] Christian Collet, "Minority Candidates, Alternative Media, and MultiethnicAmerica: Deracialization or Toggling?" Perspectives on Politics 6:4 (December 2008): 707–728.

number of Vietnamese Americans for any county in the continental U.S., and by incorporation into the local and state Republican Party infrastructure.

While California leads the charge in the suburbanization of Asian American politics, it is certainly not alone. In small to medium size suburbs throughout the continental United States, such as Bellevue, WA (outside of Seattle), Sugar Land, TX (outside of Houston), the suburbs of Montgomery County, MD, and Eau Claire, WI, Asian American immigrants and refugees are attaining elected representation in their respective local and state governments. In the case of Eau Claire, WI, Hmong Americans, a neglected and understudied Asian American ethnic group, are defying the belief that low socio-economic status determines low political participation. This Asian American refugee community has elected four different Hmong Americans to its city council over the past decade while larger Hmong American populated cities like St. Paul and Minneapolis still have not elected any Hmong American to their respective city councils.

The suburban phenomenon in Asian American politics in the continental United States has also for the first time in American politics created a formal Asian American candidate pipeline from the local to the state level. In California, after the June 2008 state primary elections, an historic eleven Asian American state representatives will serve in the State Legislature in comparison to the period of 1980 to 1993 when no Asian American was elected. Many of these Asian American state representatives are emerging in electoral districts of suburban cities that include significant Asian American populations. California Assemblyman Michael Eng's D-49th Assembly District contains large portions of suburbs like Monterey Park, Rosemead, San Marino, and Alhambra. California Assemblyman Paul Fong's D-22nd Assembly District contains large portions of suburbs like Cupertino, Sunnyvale, Milpitas, and Santa Clara. All are examples of state level Asian Americans who rely heavily on their suburban bases to win elections in the recent five years.

Future Trajectory

A nuanced understanding of the emerging modes of Asian American political behavior and power, both present and future, can be best attained through an inter-disciplinary approach. Such an approach would clarify the following political picture: for the first time in American politics on the continental U.S., Asian Americans are attaining unprecedented levels of political incorporation outside of the traditional 20th century gateway of the large metropolitan city in the context of the new 21st century gateway—small to medium size suburbs—by forming political pipelines, developing community political loci ranging from community-based organizations to the trans-national ethnic media that politically mobilize their respective large Asian American communities around Asian candidates in both traditional and non-traditional ways. This suburban dimension reflects the future trajectory of where Asian American political incorporation is most rapidly taking shape with its unique challenges and potential opportunities.

BIBLIOGRAPHY

1. Nash, Philip Tajitsu (1985), Inter-Change: Asian American Primer No. 2: Why Not 'Oriental'? No. 3: The Rise of Asian American No. 4: Asian/Pacific American . . . And Beyond, *NY Nichibei*, 5/30/85, 6/6/85, 6/13/85.

2. Spickard, Paul (2001), "Who is Asian? Who is a Pacific Islander? Monoracialism, Multiracial People, and Asian American Communities" in Teresa Williams-Leon and Cynthia L. Nakashima (eds.), *The Sum of Our Parts: Mixed Heritage Asian Americans*, Philadelphia: Temple University Press. pp. 13–24.

3. Fong, Timothy (2000), "The History of Asians in America" in Timothy P. Fong & Larry Shinagawa, *Asian Americans: Experiences and Perspectives*, Upper Saddle River, NJ: Prentice Hall. pp. 13–30.

4. Purkayastha, Bandana and Ranita Ray (2010), "South Asian Americans," in Edith Wen-Chu Chen and Grace Yoo (eds.), *Encyclopedia of Asian American Issues Today*, Santa Barbara, CA: Greenwood Press. pp. 51–63.

5. Trask, Haunani-Kay (1993), "From a Native Daughter" in Haunani-Kay Trask, *From a Native Daughter: Colonialism and Sovereignty in Hawai'i*, Monroe, ME: ommon Courage Press.

6. Li, Wei and Emily Skop (2007), "Enclaves, Ethnoburbs, and New Patterns of Settlement among Asian Immigrants," in Min Zhou and James V. Gatewood (eds.), *Contemporary Asian America: A Multidisciplinary Reader*, New York: New York University Press. pp. 222–239.

7. Chen, Edith Wen-Chu and Dennis Arguelles (2012), "Bamboo Ceilings, the Working Poor, and the Unemployed: The Mixed Economic Realities of Asian Americans and Pacific Islanders."

8. Lee, Jennifer (2007), "Striving for the American Dream: Struggle, Success, and Intergroup Conflict among Korean Immigrant Entrepreneurs," in Min Zhou and James V. Gatewood (eds.), *Contemporary Asian America: A Multidisciplinary Reader*, New York: New York University Press. pp. 243–258.

9. Su, Julie A. and Chanchanit Martorell (2001), "Exploitation and Abuse in the Garment Industry: the Case of the Thai Slave-Labor Compound in El Monte," in Marta Lopez-Garza and David R. Diaz (eds.), *Asian and Latino Immigrants in a Restructuring Economy: The Metamorphosis of South California*, Stanford, CA: Stanford University Press. pp. 21–45.

10. Shrake, Eunai and C. Alan Shrake (2012), "Emergence of a New Entrepreneurship: The Asian American Food Truck Phenomenon."

11. Murase, Mike (1976), "Ethnic Studies and Higher Education for Asian Americans," in Emma Gee et al., *Counterpoint: Perspectives on Asian America*, Los Angeles: UCLA Asian American Studies Center.

12. Hune, Shirley and Julie Park (2010), "Educational Trends and Issues," in Edith Wen-Chu Chen and Grace Yoo (eds.), *Encyclopedia of Asian American Issues Today*, Santa Barbara, CA: Greenwood Press. pp. 169–179.

13. Au, Wayne and Benji Chang (2008), "You're Asian, How Could You Fail Math?" *Rethinking Schools*, 22(2). Rethinkingschools.org.

14. Sue, Stanley and Sumie Okazaki. (1995), "Asian American Educational Achievements: A Phenomenon in Search of an Explanation." In Don Nakanishi and Tina. Nishida (eds.), *The Asian American Educational Experience*, New York: Routledge. pp. 133–145.

15. Fong, Timothy, Valerie Soe and Allan Aquino (2010), "Portrayals in Film and Television," in Edith Wen-Chu Chen and Grace Yoo (eds.), *Encyclopedia of Asian American Issues Today*, Santa Barbara, CA: Greenwood Press. pp. 635– 650.

16. Niwa, Paul (2012), "Taking Control of the News."

17. Murphy-Shigematsu, Stephen. Sein, Karen. Wakimoto, Patricia. and May Wang (2012). "Asian American Student Stress: The Other Side of Achievement."

18. Thai, Hung C. (1999). "Splitting Things in Half is So White!: Conceptions of Family Life and the Formation of Ethnic Identity among Second Generation Vietnamese Americans," *Amerasia Journal,* 25(1): 53–88.

19. Kibria, Nazli. (1999). "College and Notions of 'Asian American': Second-Generation Chinese and Korean Americans Negotiate Race and Identity," *Amerasia Journal* 25(1): 29–51.

20. Osumi, Megumi Dick (1982), "Asians and California's Anti-Miscegenation Laws," in John Tsuchida et al., *Asian and Pacific American Experiences: Women's Perspectives,* Minneapolis: Asian/Pacific American Learning Resource Center, University of Minnesota.

21. Le, C. N. (2007), "Glimpses into the Future: Interracial and Interethnic Marriage," in C. N. Le, *Asian American Assimiation: Ethnicity, Immigration, and Socioeconomic Attainment,* New York: LFB Scholarly Publishing. pp. 169–199.

22. Williams-Leon, Teresa (2012), "Greater than the Sum of Its Parts: The Private and Public Identity of Multiracial/Multiethnic People."

23. Masequesmay, Gina (2012), "Queering Tết."

24. Chang, Edward T. (1994), "Los Angeles Riots and the Korean American Community," in Ho-Youn Kwon (ed.), *Korean Americans: Conflict and Harmony,* Chicago: Covenant Publications. pp. 159–176.

25. Chen, Terri Yuh-lin (2000), "Hate Violence as Border Patrol: An Asian American Theory of Hate Violence," *Asian Law Journal* 69. Berkeley, CA: Boalt Hall School of Law, University of California–Berkeley.

26. Chua, Peter (2010), "Homeland Security and Racism," in Edith Wen-Chu Chen and Grace Yoo (eds.), *Encyclopedia of Asian American Issues Today,* Santa Barbara, CA: Greenwood Press. pp. 597–601.

27. Mar, Eric (2001), "From Vincent Chin to Kuan Chung Kao: Restoring Dignity to Their Lives," in Patricia Wong Hall and Victor M. Hwang (eds.), *Anti-Asian Violence in North American: Asian American and Asian Canadian Reflections on Hate, Healing, and Resistance,* Walnut Creek, CA: AltaMira Press. pp. 77–90.

28. Kim, Claire Jean (2001), "Playing the Racial Trump Card: Asian Americans in Contemporary U.S. Politics," *Amerasia Journal,* 26(3): 35–65.

29. Lai, James S. (2009), "A New Gateway: Asian American Political Power in the 21ˢᵗ Century," *Amerasia Journal,* 35(3): 133–138.

CPSIA information can be obtained
at www.ICGtesting.com
Printed in the USA
FSHW020815080119
54882FS